COLLECTED WORKS OF A.M. KLEIN

LITERARY ESSAYS AND REVIEWS

EDITED BY USHER CAPLAN and M.W. STEINBERG

The passionately held views of A.M. Klein are focused in these essays on literature and the arts. Ranging from the formally theoretical to the intensely personal, they reflect the enthusiasm and the conviction characteristic of all Klein's writing.

Among the subjects that come under the critic's unblinking eye are various genres of Jewish literature, illuminating not only on their own terms but also for what they reveal about Klein's Jewish poems. There are also essays on Canadian, American, English, and European literature as general subjects, and others on specific works and individual writers, including the acclaimed articles on James Joyce.

Throughout this collection is heard a critical voice sharpened with erudition and enriched with emotion. The essays are framed with an introduction, which presents a thematic analysis, and a biographical chronology, which places the essays in the context of Klein's life and work as teacher, poet, novelist, and critic.

USHER CAPLAN is an editor at the National Gallery of Canada.
M.W. STEINBERG is retired from the Department of English at the University of British Columbia.

A.M. KLEIN

Literary Essays
and Reviews

EDITED BY
USHER CAPLAN AND M.W. STEINBERG

UNIVERSITY OF TORONTO PRESS
Toronto   Buffalo   London

© University of Toronto Press 1987
Toronto Buffalo London
Printed in Canada

ISBN 0-8020-5686-5 (cloth)
ISBN 0-8020-6607-0 (paper)

Printed on acid-free paper

Canadian Cataloguing in Publication Data
Klein, A.M. (Abraham Moses), 1909–1972
  Literary essays and reviews
  (Collected works of A.M. Klein)
  Includes bibliographical references and index.
  ISBN 0-8020-5686-5 (bound). – ISBN 0-8020-6607-0 (pbk.)
  I. Steinberg, M.W. (Moses Wolfe), 1918–
  II. Caplan, Usher, 1947– . III. Title.
  IV. Series: Klein, A.M. (Abraham Moses), 1909–1972.
  Collected works.
  PS8521.L45A159 1987   C814'.52   C86-094643-6
  PR9199.3.K588A15 1987

FRONTISPIECE: Klein in the late 1920s.
Courtesy Colman and Sandor Klein

This book has been published with the help of grants from the
Canadian Federation for the Humanities, using funds provided by
the Social Sciences and Humanities Research Council of Canada,
and by the Samuel and Saidye Bronfman Family Foundation.

Contents

INTRODUCTION xi

ACKNOWLEDGMENTS xxv

BIOGRAPHICAL CHRONOLOGY xxvii

1 JEWISH LITERATURE AND CULTURE

Koheleth (1929) 3
    Review of *Koheleth: The Man and the Book* by Judah L.
    Zlotnik
Baal Shem in Modern Dress (1930) 6
    Review of *Lyric* by J.I. Segal
White Magic (1932) 10
    Review of *The Zohar in Moslem and Christian Spain* by Ariel
    Bension
Chaim Nachman Bialik (1937) 13
Music Hath Charm (1940) 19
    Review of *Jewish Music and Other Essays on Musical Topics* by
    Israel Rabinovitch
The Art of the Passover Haggadah (1942) 23
The Last of the *Badchanim* – Shloime Shmulevitz (1942) 26
Saadyah Gaon (1942) 29
Bialik Thou Shouldst Be Living at This Hour (1942) 32
Saul Tchernichovsky (1943) 36
The Thirteenth Apostle? (1944) 37
Palestine Moving-Pictures (1945) 40
Had Not Thy Torah Been My Delight ... (1945) 41
    Review of *From the Nazi Vale of Tears* by Pinchos Hirshprung
Some Praise the Lord – Some Pass the Ammunition (1945) 42
    Review of the *Sabbath Prayer Book* published by the Jewish
    Reconstructionist Foundation

The Snows of Yesteryear (1945) 46
    Review of *My Lexicon* by Melech Ravitch
The Poetry Which Is Prayer (1945) 49
    Review of *Lider un Loiben* by J.I. Segal
An Encyclopedic Work (1945) 52
    Review of *The Mishna* with translation and commentary by
    Symcha Petrushka
'Apples of Gold in Pictures of Silver' (1946) 54
    Review of *Milon Dikduki* ('Lexicon of Hebrew Homonyms') by
    Solomon Klonitzki-Kline
The Snows of Yesteryear (1946) 57
    Review of *Burning Lights* by Bella Chagall
Look on This Picture and on This ... (1947) 60
    Review of *A Palestine Picture Book* by Jacob Rosner and Alfred
    Bernheim and *Polish Jews: A Pictorial Record* by Roman
    Vishniac
Only Half the Language of Faith (1947) 63
    Review of *The Language of Faith: Selected Jewish Prayers*
    edited by Nahum N. Glatzer
Baedeker: Kasrilevke (1948) 67
    Review of *Inside Kasrilevke* by Sholom Aleichem, translated by
    Isidore Goldstick
The Dybbuk (1948) 70
    Text of a Trans-Canada Radio Talk
A Chassidic Anthology (1948) 74
    Review of *Tales of the Hasidim: The Later Masters* by Martin
    Buber
Melech Grafstein's Sholom Aleichem (1949) 77
    Review of *A Sholom Aleichem Panorama* edited by Melech
    Grafstein
Poet of a World Passed By (1950) 79
    Review of *Sefer Yiddish* by J.I. Segal
The Art of Hertz Grosbard (1952) 81
Poems of Yehoash (1952) 83
    Review of *Poems of Yehoash* selected and translated by Isidore
    Goldstick
Of Hebrew Calligraphy (1953) 85
    Review of *The Israel Art Haggadah* hand-lettered and
    ornamented by Jacob Zim
In Memoriam: J.I. Segal (1954) 87

2 JEWISH FOLK CULTURE

Jewish Folk-Songs (1932) 93
Of Hebrew Humor (1935) 99
On Translating the Yiddish Folk-Song (1946) 109
The Yiddish Proverb (1952–3) 112

3 THE BIBLE

The Bible as Literature (1941) 125
The Gesture of the Bible (1948) 131
The Bible Manuscripts (1951) 133
The Bible's Archetypical Poet (1953) 143

4 LITERATURE AND THE ARTS

From The McGill Daily (1927) 151
Proletarian Poetry (1932) 161
National Anthems (1943) 163
Queen Mab and Mickey Mouse (1946) 166
Annotation on Shapiro's Essay on Rime (1946) 169
A Definition of Poetry? (1946) 177
        A Reply to a Request
Sha! Sha! Shostakovitch! (1948) 181
Marginalia (1948–9) 182
Book Reviewing, in Seven Easy Lessons (1948) 193
The Usurper (1949) 195
In Memoriam: Alexander Bercovitch (1951) 198
The Case of Jascha Heifetz (1953) 199

5 CANADIAN LITERATURE

Mortal Coils (1934) 203
        Review of The Shrouding by Leo Kennedy
'The Decencies Had Perished with the Stukas' (1941) 205
        Review of Dunkirk by E.J. Pratt
The Poetry of A.J.M. Smith (1944) 209
        Review of News of the Phoenix by A.J.M. Smith
New Writers Series, No.1 (1945) 212
        Review of Here and Now by Irving Layton

Writing in Canada (1946) 216
　　A Reply to a Questionnaire

6 AMERICAN, EUROPEAN, AND ENGLISH LITERATURE

A Curse on Columbus (1930) 225
　　Review of *Jews Without Money* by Michael Gold
The Jew in English Poetry (1932) 226
Robinson Jeffers – Poet-Fascist? (1942) 232
　　Review of *Be Angry at the Sun* by Robinson Jeffers
Is This the Jew the Authors Drew? (1942) 235
The Heart of Europe (1944) 238
　　Review of *Heart of Europe* edited by Klaus Mann and Hermann
　　Kesten
Maimonides in Hollywood (1944) 241
　　Review of *A Guide for the Bedevilled* by Ben Hecht
Grand Invective (1944) 244
　　Review of *The Tempering of Russia* by Ilya Ehrenburg
Those Who Should Have Been Ours (1945) 246
Rilke and His Translators (1946) 251
　　Review of *Thirty-one Poems by Rainer Maria Rilke* translated
　　by Ludwig Lewisohn
Departure and Arrival (1946) 255
　　Review of *Thieves in the Night* by Arthur Koestler
Knut Hamsun (1947) 258
Isaak Babel (1948) 259
　　Review of *Benya Krik, the Gangster, and Other Stories* by Isaak
　　Babel
That Rank Picture (1948) 262
Cantabile (1948) 264
　　Review of *The Cantos of Ezra Pound*
Of Jewish Existentialism (1948) 266
　　Review of *Antisemite and Jew* by Jean-Paul Sartre
T.S. Eliot and the Nobel Prize (1948) 268
Hemlock and Marijuana (1948) 275
　　Review of *In the Penal Colony: Stories and Short Pieces* by
　　Franz Kafka
Old Ez and His Blankets (1949) 278
The Masked Yeats (1950) 282
　　Review of *Yeats: The Man and the Masks* by Richard Ellmann,
　　The Golden Nightingale by Donald Stauffer, and *The*

ix   Contents

Permanence of Yeats edited by James Hall and Martin
Steinmann
Homage to Ludwig Lewisohn (1952) 284

7 JAMES JOYCE'S *ULYSSES*

The Oxen of the Sun (1949) 289
The Black Panther (1950) 326
A Shout in the Street (1951) 342

TEXTUAL NOTES AND EMENDATIONS 367
NOTES 377
INDEX 415

Introduction

This selection of A.M. Klein's published writings on literary and cultural topics was conceived by the editors as a companion volume to *Beyond Sambation*, our previously published selection of Klein's newspaper editorials and essays on social and political topics.[1] Nearly all of the pieces in *Beyond Sambation*, as well as the majority in this book, were culled from the pages of *The Canadian Jewish Chronicle*, the weekly that Klein edited in Montreal from 1938 to 1955. It is worth bearing in mind, then, that much of what we might call Klein's literary criticism was essentially journalism – usually written in haste, rarely polished, and often consciously ephemeral. Yet despite the resulting unevenness in quality, the pieces gathered here form a rich body of material, sparkling with insight and wit and of immeasurable value to anyone seeking a deeper understanding of Klein's own aims as a creative writer.

Beyond Sambation was arranged in simple chronological order – no other arrangement was possible, for it is basically a collection of comments on passing events of the day, and indeed constitutes a skeleton history of the period. This volume, on the other hand, has been divided into sections dealing with several general areas of subject-matter, and then organized chronologically within those sections. In this way, it is hoped, the reader who so wishes will more easily be able to focus on areas of particular interest.

Section 1 includes Klein's writings on Jewish literature and literary culture, defined somewhat strictly to contain only subjects close to the mainstream of Judaism, such as Hebrew and Yiddish literature, Jewish religion, and Jewish history. Section 2 brings together a sampling of essays on Jewish folk culture, an area that greatly interested Klein all his life. The focal point of Section 3 is the Bible. Miscellaneous pieces on literature and the arts in general, many of them reflecting Klein's theoretical or aesthetic leanings, are presented in Section 4. Canadian literature is the subject of a small Section 5. Klein's writings on American, European, and English literature find their place in Section 6, with the exception of his three articles on James Joyce's *Ulysses*, which make up Section 7.

Jewish concerns dominate this volume. Even when Klein is ostensibly dealing with a broader subject, his discussion usually reveals a primary interest in some Jewish aspect of it. This is in part a reflection of his own interests, and equally explainable by the fact that the *Chronicle* was, of course, aimed at a specific audience.[2] Not that Klein ever regarded his Jewishness as a limiting factor in his relationship to other cultures; on the contrary, it was often his point of entry into foreign realms, his passport as a citizen of the Diaspora.

Many of the specifically Jewish works reviewed or discussed in this collection were written in Hebrew or Yiddish, and unfortunately few of these are available in English translation. Klein read a fair amount of modern Hebrew literature during the 1920s and 1930s, when he was active as a journalist and educator in the Zionist Organization of Canada. Chief among the Hebrew authors he admired was Chaim Nachman Bialik, whom he regarded as a model of the Jewish national poet. He began translating many of Bialik's poems after the latter's death in 1934, and hoped eventually to complete all of them. In 1943 he applied for a Guggenheim fellowship to see him through the rest of the work, but was unsuccessful in his application and abandoned the project.

Later in the 1940s Klein sampled the writings of the younger generation of Hebrew poets, but found himself out of touch with their style and ethos. In *The Second Scroll* he spoke critically of the new breed of 'Canaanite' writers 'who cultivated a hard intransigence, scoffed at all delusions intellectual, adored only the soil and the gun. They hated the ghetto and its melting, paralysing self-pity ... It was an exciting kind of poetry, large-gestured, primitive, tribal, but its insularity repelled me ... It did not belong to the essential thoughtways of our people.'[3]

Klein was particularly sensitive to the differences between the new Hebraic spirit – epitomized in the modern 'hard, clipped, guttural' Sephardic pronunciation of the language – and the 'soft, caressing' quality of Yiddish.[4] Culturally and temperamentally, he was more attuned to contemporary Yiddish literature than to the new Hebrew literature coming out of the land of Israel. Through journals and newspapers he kept up with all the latest currents of the Yiddish literary world. Two of its leading figures, Melech Ravitch and J.I. Segal, were among his friends in Montreal. The latter's importance to Klein is especially well documented in this collection. Segal's wistful nostalgia for tradition and the innocence of childhood, his sympathy for and identification with the downtrodden, his Chassidic background, his linguistic virtuosity – all of these qualities naturally appealed to Klein and are reflected in his own work.

Though Hebrew and Yiddish were undoubtedly the primary Jewish languages for Klein, he also believed that a genuine Jewish literature could exist in English, and hoped to see its flowering in North America. It was not a narrow chauvinism that he advocated; indeed, few things irritated him more than being labelled parochial. What he cultivated in himself and sought in others was a synthesis of English literacy and Jewish learning; his goal, in a sense, was to effect a modern 'translation' of Judaism into English. The very premise upon which this ambition rested – that one could unite the culture of one race with the language of another – was forcefully called into question by the Yiddish critic Shmuel Niger when he read Klein's first collection of poems, *Hath Not a Jew ...*, in 1940. Niger wondered whether the proper audience for such writing even existed: Jewish readers with a limited knowledge of English, like himself, would need a dictionary by their side, while for non-Jewish readers even a Jewish encyclopedia would not suffice unless they had already 'breathed the air' of Jewish life and lore. Niger's remarks evoked a thoughtful response from Klein:

> Today English is my daily tongue ... Naturally, therefore, if I had to write poetry – and the compulsion thereto I shall not now discuss – it had to be in English. What does, what should, a poet write about? Only about what he feels and what he knows. Borrowed emotions will not do. Unassimilated knowledge will not do. Rilke once made a very pertinent and indeed profound remark when he said that all poetry is an attempt to recapture one's youth and even one's childhood. For me that means recapturing the nostalgia and the beauty of my childhood, which was a Yiddish-speaking and Hebrew-thinking one, Mithnagid from my teachers, Chassidic from my father. The theology, I may say, has vanished but the tradition has remained.
>
> English being the language, it is its technique which is applied to the Hebrew theme. This is not any stranger than Yehuda Halevi writing Hebrew poetry in Arabic metres or Immanuel of Rome borrowing the sonnet form from Dante ... As for the difficulty of the English, believe me I did not make it so on purpose. One of the chief factors in the creation of poetry is language; my mind is full of linguistic echoes from Chaucer and Shakespeare, even as it is of the thought-forms of the prophets ...
>
> You are right when you say that my book presupposes on the part of the reader a knowledge of the Hebrew tradition. Apart from being written because I wished to write it, the book is addressed precisely to those who have that knowledge or those who may acquire it. In English literature reference to a so-called alien culture is not a novelty. Milton's 'Paradise Lost' presupposes great biblical knowledge. A better example, – large tracts of English poetry assume on the part of the reader an intimate knowledge of Greek mythology and the close relationship between the various gods and goddesses of Greek lore. To amalgamate factors, therefore, of two cultures does not to me appear to be an impossibility ... Joyce's 'Ulysses,' where every chapter has its counterpart in a similar chapter of Homer's 'Odyssey,' is to my mind a completely successful literary merger of the values of two cultures.

> Nor are examples lacking in our own literature. The Talmud, than which there is nothing more typical of the Jewish spirit, is a compilation in Aramaic! Maimonides' 'Guide to the Perplexed' was originally written in Arabic ...
>
> In Yiddish literature – is not the writing of Mani Leib a perfect example of the Slavic dressed up in Hebrew script? Moishe Leib Halpern, to my mind, was not a particularly Yiddish poet; he was essentially European and twentieth-century. Yehoash attempted – although I do not think with much success – the treatment of Oriental themes in Yiddish.
>
> My friend the poet Segal tells me that Bialik's *Hamathmid* – of all things! – is but the circumcision of a Russian theme!
>
> Certainly in a world where one culture impinges upon another, and where time and space have been considerably constricted, it is not surprising that the synthesis should be attempted.[5]

Klein believed, then, that the fusion of divergent languages and cultures, far from being an aesthetic liability, could constitute a positive virtue. The fact that so few talented writers were as interested as he was in the creation of a truly Jewish literature in English was a source of considerable disappointment to him. He was scornful of the many well-known Jewish-American writers of his era who were ignorant or ashamed of their heritage. Those of the older generation were, he noted, 'irrevocably committed to the thesis that the less Jewish they appear, the more American they will be. They are, to vary a notorious formula of the last century, Americans by Jewish dissuasion.' Klein was convinced that it was this very betrayal of their heritage that doomed them to secondary roles in American literature, as anthologists, reviewers, editors, and teachers. Having 'nothing original to contribute' they merely write but 'they do not create. One cannot create with another's genitals.'[6]

For a while in the 1940s, he thought that the younger generation of American Jewish writers might be different. He was encouraged by the example of Delmore Schwartz, a poet who though limited in his knowledge of Judaism was at least prepared to state publicly that he considered his Jewishness to be a 'fruitful and inexhaustible inheritance.' Klein would have liked to discover a similar measure of Jewish pride in Karl Shapiro, another young writer whose work he greatly admired. Instead he detected the all too familiar signs of negativism and ignorance.

> There is not any indication anywhere that the poet is aware of the rich cultural heritage which should have been his ... nothing worthy of reference in a culture which has spanned the centuries and covered the continents ... Let us not be misunderstood; it is not the function of the creative artist to be a public relations counsel for his people, though it is no disgrace if he is. But surely Shapiro's poetry is in no way enhanced, his Americanism in no way made more authentic, by this studied – and unalleviated – denigration of his own.[7]

Klein was not without his own ambivalence in these matters. On the one hand was his immense national pride and sense of duty to his race. Yet there was also a countervailing force in his character, an impulse towards privacy and individualism, and a chafing at the burden of having to be the hero and spokesman of the folk. Joyce's hero Stephen Dedalus epitomized the modern artist's refusal to 'merge his life in the common tide of other lives.'[8] Home, fatherland, and church were the treacherous nets that Dedalus had to fly past in order to attain the higher realms of freedom and art. Klein struggled all his life in an effort to come to terms with this basic dogma of modernism.

The truly Jewish artist, in his view, had necessarily to sacrifice a portion of his individualism. To be a poet of the people was to suffer a kind of anonymity and a frequent suppression of the private lyrical accent in favour of the public rhetorical voice. The Jewish writer is the Everyman of his people, a spokesman of the entire folk. Hence the aptness, Klein thought, of the nom de plume of the great Yiddish storyteller Sholom Aleichem – 'the Jew's hello; the individual writer in his very signature announces the approach of the total heritage: Sholom Aleichem – here come all of us!'[9] It was in this spirit that Klein sometimes described the folk song as the quintessentially Jewish genre. A folk singer is 'no poet seeking esoteric themes and an abstruse vocabulary to express the uniqueness of his personality ... a folk singer does not choose his subjects; his subjects are chosen for him by the folk.'[10]

Klein's writings on Canadian literature make up the smallest section of this book. As a field of academic study and research, Canadian literature barely existed in Klein's day, and insofar as it did exist it held almost no interest for him. What did matter, however, was the poetry being written by his own contemporaries. Leo Kennedy, E.J. Pratt, A.J.M. Smith, and Irving Layton, the Canadian poets whose works Klein reviewed, were all among his friends, and all expressed as much admiration for his poetry as he had for theirs. Klein's praise of *Dunkirk* as a great war poem was answered in Pratt's enthusiastic review of *The Hitleriad*. Smith, in 1943, introduced Klein in his *Book of Canadian Poetry* as 'the greatest poet living today in Canada.'

Klein's friendship or even mere acquaintance with certain writers seems to have inhibited his ability to dispense frank criticism. On one occasion, for example, he declined to review a book by the poet Earle Birney for fear that he might not find anything favourable to say – 'it is not I who would want to hurt his feelings.'[11] Even the Canadian Authors' Association, a favourite target of the younger generation of poets in Klein's day, was unfair game to him, as Louis Dudek once recalled. 'When asked to join a campaign of war on Canadian sentimental poetry (on the c.a.a.), he smiled shyly and retreated: he had "no desire to hurt kind old ladies".'[12]

Some of Klein's less guarded remarks on Canadian poetry may be found in a 1943 letter to Smith, in which he conveys his impressions on reading through *The Book of Canadian Poetry*. Of the earlier poets, he was most impressed by Charles Heavysege, and especially by his sonnets. He chided Smith for overrating Charles Sangster, one poet he seems to have disliked more than others. The late-nineteenth-century poets, including Archibald Lampman, Charles G.D. Roberts, and Duncan Campbell Scott, were hardly worthy of comment according to Klein: 'They have upon me a narcotic effect ... a total suspension of all my reacting faculties.' Coming to the modern period, he agreed with Smith's high praise of Pratt, but claimed he could still not appreciate W.W.E. Ross or – among the younger poets – Ronald Hambleton. Of Birney he now noted: 'I was wrong in our last conversation in underestimating Birney. "David" is a fine thing; I got a great deal of pleasure out of the reading of "Anglo-Saxon Street".'13

Despite his warm relations with a number of Canadian poets, Klein kept closer to the fringes than to the centre of the literary community. In his first year at college, he was introduced to the group of older students who had founded *The McGill Fortnightly Review*. Though he later came to be identified with this group, Klein in fact never appeared in the pages of the *Fortnightly*. In the spring of 1927, while the very last issue was being prepared, he submitted a sonnet. As Leon Edel, who witnessed the scene, later recounted, the editors (Smith and F.R. Scott), 'surveying this Semitic and most raw youth, admitted that it was a good sonnet, but asked him to change a word in the last line. Klein wavered, and was tempted, and reflected and hesitated: to appear in the sacred columns of the radical *Fortnightly* (and he a freshman!) was extremely tempting. But with a final gesture he withdrew his manuscript – he would not – damn it! – alter a comma.'14

In the early forties he was drawn into the *Preview* and *First Statement* circles of Montreal poets. He was formally connected with the older and more established poets of *Preview*, a group that revolved around F.R. Scott and Patrick Anderson, but his strongest association at the time was probably with Irving Layton, of *First Statement*. Poets in both groups sensed a certain shyness and reserve in Klein. Anderson recalled an edginess, 'a kind of anticipation of possible difference or difficulty.'15 Layton felt Klein was too buttoned-up – 'for all his exuberance and seeming extroversion, he never dwelt on anything personal.'16

There was also in Klein a certain degree of cultural aloofness towards Canada. He no doubt saw himself essentially as an English writer of Jewish background addressing a world-wide audience. In his 1946 reply to a questionnaire from the Toronto poet Raymond Souster, he wrote: 'Should the Canadian writer write about the Canadian scene? ... Of course, if he feels so impelled to write. But it is what he writes which will interest us in him as a writer, and not the emergent fact of his Canadian citizenship. Nor need he be any the less Canadian because his short story fails to mention Yonge Street, or his poem the Laurentians ... The proper study of mankind is Man – not paysage.' A 'factitiously nationalist' literature would 'inevitably end up by being parochial,' Klein argued. 'How, then, does a national character emerge in a literature? Mainly, I think, through the force of character, the personality of its writers; and for this emergence, it is necessary only that they possess talent.'[17]

Klein's work on James Joyce's *Ulysses* constitutes a separate and intriguing chapter in his life. The three articles on *Ulysses* that he published between 1949 and 1951 made him, for a number of years, more famous as a Joycean than as a poet. The articles were but a small part of what he actually intended to accomplish, and in a sense merely by-products of his original objective: an exhaustive, page-by-page commentary on the entire novel.

Klein had read *Ulysses* for the first time in the late 1920s, as an undergraduate at McGill, and had discussed it often with his college friend Leon Edel. The book immediately exerted a powerful hold on his imagination. Through the 1930s and early 1940s he reread it about every two years and made new annotations in his copy on each reading. When he returned to McGill in 1945 to spend three years there as Visiting Lecturer in Poetry, his original interest in Joyce was rekindled and he began devoting a great deal of his time to the study of *Ulysses*. (He probably would also have taught a course on Joyce were it not for the fact that *Ulysses* was still banned in Canada.) Harold Files, who was head of the English Department towards the end of Klein's stay, later recalled what it was that apparently attracted Klein to Joyce:

> Joyce fascinated him as artist and as person. He saw analogies between them despite the obvious differences. Both had been schooled in the tradition of a dogmatic culture, based on centuries of historic process and growth, with prolonged insistence on a system of logical and orthodox thinking about necessary moral, theological and social commitments; and both had broken through those nets, and taken a self-reliant stance, even while saturated with the thoughts that had dominated their forebears and their race. Both were artists highly sensitive to their natural medium, language ... I suspect there was more of natural piety and social loyalty in Klein, an inveterate sense of duty which led him in fact to some degree of political activism. Nevertheless ... he found a certain correspondence between Joyce's mental and moral training at the hands of Jesuits, and his own under rabbinical orthodoxy ...[18]

Files's speculations were very likely based on conversations he had with Klein in the late forties, but Klein himself never wrote about such matters and never seemed interested in exploring his own affinities to Joyce. He professed a purely intellectual fascination with the craftsmanship and complexity of *Ulysses*. In January 1948 he outlined the progress of his research to Edel:

> What I am engaged on is a line-by-line, or rather page by page, commentary on Ulysses, tracking down all the allusions, indicating in the abstruser stream-of-consciousness paragraphs the mental associations and sequence, explicating text, and relating the parts to the whole, etc. etc. ... Already I have completed the general spade work ... and now I am ready for the task. Commentary on the first hundred pages has taken exactly – one hundred pages ... I have, moreover, been fortunate – and this is the thing which keeps up my interest in something which, after all, is mere hobby – in stumbling upon some apocalyptic discoveries. I am having a good time.[19]

In the spring of 1948 Klein left McGill and returned full-time to his law practice, where, he thought, 'the duties are less onerous and the rewards – when they come – more generous.'[20] He hoped to obtain a grant to finance the completion of his research over a period of two years, but when his application to the Guggenheim Foundation in New York was turned down, he continued working on the commentary slowly in his spare time. The first draft of his first article was written in June 1948, in the form of a forty-four-page letter to the American Joyce scholar Ellsworth Mason. The published article, which appeared in January 1949, was virtually a duplicate of that letter, both in its contents and in its urgent short-hand manner of presentation.

Klein completed his second article, an analysis of the 'Telemachus' chapter, early in 1949, and it appeared in *Accent* the following spring. The third and final article, 'A Shout in the Street,' was a study of the 'Nestor' chapter. Klein first read it to the Joyce Society in New York on 2 February 1951. The audience was spellbound; it was, in a sense, the high point of his career as a Joycean. Edel, who was present, remembered it as one of the most brilliant lectures he had ever heard. 'The audience was asked by him to bring copies of *Ulysses* and we were treated as if we were a classroom ... He made us turn to certain pages and certain paragraphs and he explicated them with great humour and ingenuity.'[21] The article was subsequently published by James Laughlin in the *New Directions* annual for 1951.

In August of that year, Klein informed Laughlin that he was pushing on to the next chapter, 'Proteus': 'I am hard at work on the third chapter of Ulysses. And what do you think – everything that is in the sea, beneath, upon, above, the waters – but everything! is included, in Protean shape and shapelessness, in these thirteen fabulous pages! The explication, *mot à mot*, will run to over a hundred.'[22] A few weeks later he was completely distracted by the publication of his novel, *The Second Scroll*, and postponed further work on Joyce. In May 1952 he still referred to it as one of his works in progress.[23]

But then in October he wrote to Edel, tersely and with a note of finality: 'I must tell you now ... that because of other plans I am putting my Joyce work aside.'[24] He seems to have abandoned it completely by the mid-fifties, and only a tiny part of his voluminous notes survive among his papers.

In retrospect it appeared to Edel that Klein must have 'tuned in to the mad side of Joyce,' creating a kind of *folie à deux*.[25] Mason, who had been his most helpful critic, felt from the outset that Klein's exegesis was 'forced' and that he was paying too much attention to a part of Joyce's artistry that was ultimately of minor significance. As he candidly wrote to Klein: 'After the reader gets past the initial awe caused by Joyce's incredible ability to juggle five patterns at once, this aspect of the book should recede in importance because it is more or less mechanical ... While you certainly have passed this neophyte stage, you often seem to have passed on to it again on a new level ... You seem, at points, to be so awed by Joyce's ingenuity (this, to some extent, because it reminds you of your own) that you are carried away, and consequently overvalue, if I am right, what you see as Joyce's patterning ability.'[26]

Klein evidently so idolized Joyce that he came to treat *Ulysses* as holy writ. The interpretive method that he adopted was to a large degree inspired by the classical Jewish commentaries on the Bible, in which every single word must be explained and accounted for. Often the aim of such a commentary is not to provide the simple meaning of a word or phrase, but to uncover subtle and complex hidden meanings. Klein, it is true, had set out with the intention of providing a fairly basic glossary of terms and allusions; in the end, however, what interested him most was the analysis of abstract and buried patterns, perceived within a framework of elaborate and rigidly determined schemes.

The ingenuity and over-ripe imagination that this exercise required of him are manifest not only in his work on Joyce but are characteristic of much of his writing in the late forties and early fifties. It seems, too, that with the onset of mental illness Klein's thinking and behaviour in general came to display the same excesses that he had brought to his reading of Joyce. The symbolic import of even the simplest tale or event could become grotesquely distorted in his mind; like a cabbalist he would ponder the secrets hidden in random signs and ordinary remarks. Whether his work on *Ulysses* was a contributing cause or merely another symptom of this condition will probably always remain a mystery.

In his novel *The Second Scroll*, Klein has someone say of Uncle Melech – in many respects his own alter ego – that 'he greatly loves the right word, but he loves righteousness more.'[27] Writing as he usually did from a Jewish perspective, Klein had to strike a balance between his love of poetry for its own sake and his very deeply ingrained, almost prophetic, moral sense. Much as he admired, for example, the literary achievements of Pound and Eliot, he could not refrain from objecting when prizes were awarded to them shortly after the Second World War. He saw in Eliot a typical English anti-Semite, a man who 'despite his constant preaching of the Christian virtues, remains, in his attitudes as revealed in his work, a prig and a snob.'[28] He claimed that if Pound deserved the Bollingen prize, then 'Goebbels posthumously should be awarded the Pulitzer.'[29] In his attack several years earlier against the American poet Robinson Jeffers, whom he regarded as a Fascist sympathizer, he commented: 'We regret having to judge a poet's work for the opinions which it expresses. The fact remains that Robinson Jeffers still remains master of a peerless utterance, still, from a technical viewpoint, an incomparable poet. Our remarks are prompted only by a recollection of something we had read somewhere to the effect that a poet must possess a sense of common humanity ...'[30]

Klein hardly ever deviated from this very European sense of the writer as the conscience of his society. The relatively amoral, aestheticist strain in Anglo-American modernism was something he could not fully accept. Yet at the same time he was obviously influenced by that aspect of the modernist movement. Even within the context of Jewish literature, he followed closely the shift towards aestheticism among certain Yiddish and Hebrew writers in the early part of the twentieth century. In an editorial on the death of one such figure, Reuben Brainin, he noted that up to his time 'Hebrew literature, it was thought, had to be, above all things, didactic. To this puritan and almost pragmatic evaluation, Brainin contributed the aesthetic standard. Hebrew, he felt, ought not only to be piously written; it ought, above all things, to be well written. The theory of writing for the sake of beauty and style, a theory hitherto eschewed in Hebrew scripture, he made part and parcel of modern literature.'[31]

Klein's reluctance to view poetry as a mere instrument of social concerns happened to be reinforced by his lifelong abhorrence of communism. Though he himself experimented briefly with being a poet of the proletariat, he mocked the notion that 'literature is not literature unless it ends with a revolutionary moral,' and was quite wary of the corrupting influence of politics on literature. 'Although it must be admitted,' he wrote in 1932, 'that one of the functions of art, though certainly not the only one, is to rouse the reader to a realization of existing injustice and current oppression, it still is to be doubted whether this need be achieved only through the perversion of letters into a series of political phrases and economic clichés.' What offended him personally was not merely the reduction of art to ideology, but the frightening prospect of the poet becoming the servant of the politician. Stalin is wiser than Plato, he noted sarcastically, for 'Plato banished poets from his republic; but Stalin uses them.'[32] In fact Klein never could decide who was the more pitiable: the poet neglected or the poet used.

On one of the rare occasions when he was invited to state explicitly his own basic 'credo' as a poet (by A.J.M. Smith, for use in *The Book of Canadian Poetry*), Klein tried to evade the question, and replied rather enigmatically:

I do not ... intend to give you 'a brief statement of my attitude towards my art, etc.' I am surprised that you ask it. You know that such questions elicit only the sheerest of arrogant balderdash. What shall I say in reply: 'I sing because I must!' – How phoney! Or that I wish to improve the world with my rhyme! – How ridiculous! Or that I seek to express the standards of my age, etc. Me, I will have none of that cant. Simply expressed, I write poetry only to reveal my civilization, my sensitivities, my craftsmanship. This, however, is not to be quoted.[33]

Klein's most penetrating, and most self-revealing, comments on the poetic vocation occur in one of his last essays, 'The Bible's Archetypical Poet.' It is a disturbing piece, tinged with genuine paranoia. Following the same midrashic methods that he had applied to Joyce, he read into the biblical tale of Joseph and his brothers an allegory on the life and fate of all poets in every generation. His own personal identification with the character of Joseph probably began early in life and ran very deep. Like Joseph, he was the favourite child, the son of his parents' old age. Joseph's coat of many colours he took to be a symbol of the poetic imagination. Joseph is a poet in that he is a dreamer and interpreter of dreams. Seemingly arrogant and out of touch with things and with people, he is in reality the greatest lover of his brethren. This love, however, is met with envy and malice. The poet Joseph is stripped of his coat, flung into a pit, and sold into slavery. The entire story, according to Klein's reading, reveals the classic design of the relationship between the poet and his fellow men. 'It is a design which repeats itself down through the ages,' he writes, 'a design which, beginning with misunderstanding and envy, moves on towards conspiracy, suggests, at first, a mere humiliating of its victim, then, feeding upon its own thoughts, soon clamours for revenge, and thus, by its own clamorous blood encompassed, broods on the ultimate: murder. From that ultimate it recoils; it cannot bring itself to strike the killing blow, but by this time, the distinction is purely technical ...'[34]

Klein's own growing sense of undeserved neglect and anonymity was here transmuted into a frightening vision in which all true artists are persecuted and martyred by those closest to them. His hope, however, for the ultimate reconciliation between the poet and his brethren was symbolized in the blessing bestowed on Joseph by his dying father Jacob: 'Joseph is a fruitful bough by a well; whose branches run over the wall.'

Not isolated, not alone, not altogether self-sustained does the poet live; he lives hard by a refreshing and ever-renewed source of water; he lives and labours within a tradition ... Thus Jacob, addressing Joseph, conceals his unspoken reproach within the very heart of his blessing, and by indirection enjoins his favorite son from sundering himself from his brothers, themselves, in their way, the makers of a tradition. The bough is fruitful only near the well; removed therefrom, it thirsts, is parched, one withers away.

But to rest within a tradition, to remain content thereby, and not to seek to bring to it originality and innovation – this, too, would be a denial of the poet's devotion ... The true poet is he who, nourished upon the ancestral heritage, yet – if only in the slightest – deviates therefrom. Rooted in the common soil, he turns his eyes to new directions. He is, indeed, a fruitful bough; he springs from the earth fed secretly by a well, but his branches run over the wall. Thus are the ideas of convention and revolt, of tradition and innovation, conjured up in the single image of Jacob's benediction.[35]

Here as in many of his last writings, Klein's view of reality is dialectical. The 'true poet' is neither simply a moralist nor simply an aesthete, neither a traditionalist nor a revolutionary, neither completely bound to his people nor altogether sundered from them; rather is he poised – and perhaps sometimes torn – between these extremes. Within this creative tension, A.M. Klein, a true poet, lived and wrote.

UC

Notes

1 University of Toronto Press 1982. The introduction, by M.W. Steinberg, serves as background to some of the writings in this volume as well.

2 On Klein's relationship to the *Chronicle* and its readers, see also Usher Caplan, *Like One That Dreamed: A Portrait of A.M. Klein* (Toronto: McGraw-Hill Ryerson 1982) 79–81.

3 *The Second Scroll* (Toronto: New Canadian Library 1961) 79–80

4 'The Yiddish Proverb,' *The Canadian Jewish Chronicle* [*CJC*], 28 November 1952

5 YIVO Archives (New York), Shmuel Niger Papers, letter from Klein to Niger, 21 January 1941

6 'Those Who Should Have Been Ours,' *New Palestine*, 16 November 1945

7 Ibid.

8 James Joyce, *A Portrait of the Artist as a Young Man* (section IV)

9 'Baedeker: Kasrilevke,' *CJC*, 16 April 1948

10 'A Sculptor, a Singer, and a Statistician,' *CJC*, 8 January 1943

11 University of Chicago Library, *Poetry* Papers, letter from Klein to Peter De Vries, 20 November 1942

12 Louis Dudek, 'A.M. Klein,' *The Canadian Forum* xxx (April 1950) 10

13 Public Archives of Canada, A.M. Klein Papers, copy of letter from Klein to Smith, 5 November 1943
14 Leon Edel, 'Abraham M. Klein,' *The Canadian Forum* XII (May 1932) 300
15 Seymour Mayne, 'A Conversation with Patrick Anderson,' *Inscape* XI, 3 (Fall 1974) 56
16 Recorded interview by David Kaufman, Toronto, 1973
17 'Writing in Canada,' *CJC*, 22 February 1946
18 Letter from Files to Usher Caplan, 13 July 1973
19 Letter from Klein to Edel, 22 January 1948
20 Letter from Klein to Shonie Levi, 22 January 1948
21 Letter from Edel to Caplan, 12 March 1975
22 Letter from Klein to Laughlin, 2 August 1951
23 Humanities Research Center, University of Texas (Austin), Knopf Papers, letter from Klein to Herbert Weinstock, 30 May 1952
24 Letter from Klein to Edel, 15 October 1952
25 Letter from Edel to Caplan, 28 August 1974
26 Public Archives of Canada, Ellsworth Mason Papers, copy of letter from Mason to Klein, 21 July 1949
27 New Canadian Library edition, 42
28 'T.S. Eliot and the Nobel Prize,' *CJC*, 26 November 1948
29 'Old Ez and His Blankets,' *CJC*, 4 March 1949
30 'Robinson Jeffers – Poet-Fascist?' *CJC*, 6 February 1942
31 'The Late Reuben Brainin,' *CJC*, 8 December 1939
32 'Proletarian Poetry,' *CJC*, 5 August 1932
33 University of Toronto Library, A.J.M. Smith Papers, letter from Klein to Smith, 21 January 1943
34 'The Bible's Archetypical Poet,' *CJC*, 6–20 March 1953
35 Ibid.

Acknowledgments

The editors are grateful for the valuable help and advice of their fellow members, past and present, of the A.M. Klein Research and Publication Committee: Mark Finkelstein, Dr Gretl Fischer, Professor Noreen Golfman, Professor Tom Marshall, Professor Seymour Mayne, Professor Zailig Pollock, Dr R.J. Taylor, and Klein's sons, Colman and Sandor Klein. We are particularly grateful to Professor Pollock, the current chairman of the Committee, for his active role in the last stages of work on this volume and for his many contributions to the Notes. Important assistance of various kinds was also provided by Rabbi M. Feuerstein, Brad Sabin Hill, Professor Gordon Johnston, Susan Knutson, Linda Rozmovits, and Esther Steinberg.

The Public Archives of Canada was most helpful in making available its A.M. Klein Collection and in providing special use of its facilities. Other institutions whose research collections were used during preparation of the manuscript included the Jewish Public Library of Montreal, the Rare Book Department of McGill University's MacLennan Library, the New York Public Library, the University of British Columbia Library (Vancouver), the University of Western Washington Library (Bellingham), Jews' College Library (London, England), and the Hebrew University Library (Jerusalem).

The financial assistance provided to the A.M. Klein Research and Publication Committee by the Social Sciences and Humanities Research Council of Canada was invaluable in furthering the work of the Committee and the making of this book, and is very much appreciated.

Portions of the introduction to this book originally appeared in Usher Caplan's *Like One That Dreamed: A Portrait of A.M. Klein* (Toronto: McGraw-Hill Ryerson 1982).

Biographical Chronology

1909
born to Kalman and Yetta Klein, orthodox Jews, in Ratno, a small town in
the Ukraine, and brought to Montreal with his family probably the following
year (officially claimed to have been born in Montreal, 14 February 1909).
1915–22
attended Mt Royal School. Received Jewish education from private tutors and
at Talmud Torah.
1922–6
attended Baron Byng High School.
1926–30
attended McGill University, majoring in classics and political science and economics. Active in Debating Society with close friend David Lewis. Founded
literary magazine, *The McGilliad*, with Lewis in 1930. Associated with 'Montreal Group' of poets and writers, including A.J.M. Smith, F.R. Scott, Leo
Kennedy, and Leon Edel. Began publishing poems in *The Menorah Journal*,
The Canadian Forum, *Poetry* (Chicago), and elsewhere.
1928–32
served as educational director of Canadian Young Judaea, a Zionist youth
organization, and edited its monthly magazine, *The Judaean*, in which many
of his early poems and stories appeared.
1930–3
studied law at the Université de Montréal.
1934
established law firm in partnership with Max Garmaise, and struggled to earn
a living during the Depression. Served as national president of Canadian Young
Judaea.
1935
married Bessie Kozlov, his high school sweetheart.
1936
active in publicity and educational work, and on speaking tours, for the Zionist
Organization of Canada, and editor of its monthly, *The Canadian Zionist*.

1937
moved to Rouyn, a small mining town in northern Quebec, to join Garmaise in law practice there.

1938
returned to Montreal, and re-established law practice in association with Samuel Chait. Assumed editorship of *The Canadian Jewish Chronicle*, to which he contributed numerous editorials, essays, book reviews, poems, and stories.

1939
began his long association with Samuel Bronfman, noted distiller and philanthropist and president of the Canadian Jewish Congress, working as a speechwriter and public relations consultant.

1940
first volume of poems, *Hath Not a Jew ...* , published by Behrman's in New York.

1942–7
associated with the *Preview* group of poets – F.R. Scott, Patrick Anderson, P.K. Page, and others – and with the *First Statement* group, in particular Irving Layton.

1944
The Hitleriad published by New Directions in New York. *Poems* published by the Jewish Publication Society in Philadelphia. Nominated as CCF candidate in federal riding of Montreal-Cartier, but withdrew before the election of 1945.

1945–8
visiting lecturer in poetry at McGill University.

1946–7
wrote his first novel, an unpublished spy thriller, 'Comes the Revolution' (later retitled 'That Walks Like a Man'), based on the Igor Gouzenko affair.

1948
The Rocking Chair and Other Poems published by Ryerson in Toronto.

1949
published the first of several articles on James Joyce's *Ulysses*. Ran unsuccessfully as CCF candidate in the federal election of June 1949. Awarded the Governor-General's Medal for *The Rocking Chair*. Journeyed to Israel, Europe, and North Africa in July and August, sponsored by the Canadian Jewish Congress, and published his 'Notebook of a Journey' in *The Canadian Jewish Chronicle*.

1949–52
travelled widely in Canada and the United States, addressing Jewish audiences, principally concerning the State of Israel.

1951
The Second Scroll published by Knopf in New York.

1952–4
increasing signs of mental illness. Hospitalized for several weeks in the summer of 1954 after a thwarted suicide attempt.

1955
resigned from editorship of *The Canadian Jewish Chronicle*. Ceased writing and began to withdraw from public life.

1956
resigned from law practice and became increasingly reclusive. Awarded the Lorne Pierce Medal by the Royal Society of Canada.

1971
death of Bessie Klein, 26 February.

1972
died in his sleep, 20 August.

1 / JEWISH LITERATURE AND CULTURE

Koheleth

Review of *Koheleth: The Man and the Book* [in Yiddish] by Judah L.
Zlotnik   May 1929

The philosophies which have issued from the Orient, attired in the gorgeous
raiment of Eastern metaphor, may be divided, by the mathematically-minded,
into two colourful categories. In the first place there is the philosophy of
hedonism, which has found frenzied votaries in those lands whose sensuous
luxuriance has fostered such a conduct of life. The ideal of unrestrained pleasure, of an epicureanism spiced with poetry, the ideal of the refinement of
the five senses and the development of others, has found its reflection in the
mirroring pool of Eastern literature. The writings of the Abbasides, the work
of Li-Tai-Po, and the quatrains of Omar Khayyam, rendered so admirably
into a northern tongue by Fitzgerald, illustrate very obviously this pervasive
spirit.

As a reaction to this philosophy of the sated palate, came the metaphysics
of the broken heart, the philosophy of disillusionment verging on the cynical.
It is inevitable that after a thorough satisfaction of all desires indulged in with
the exuberance of the Orient, that the counterblast should come in a cynicism
which declares all things worthless, and as the chaff driven by the wind.
Whereas the former creed is shouted boisterously from the banqueting-boards
set with vaporous viands and flowing wines, the latter is the speculation
muttered after the goblets are empty and the plates strewn with clean bones.
It is nihilism born of despair and bred in anguish; to use the vernacular, it is
the philosophy of the morning after the night before.

This last philosophy is manifest in the hokkus of the Japanese, in the
religious poetry of the Hindus preaching a self-effacing nirvana, but most
emphatically in the verse of Ecclesiastes. It is here, in the twelve brief chapters,
that the King (according to Rabbi Zlotnik's erudite and to me convincing proof,
King Solomon) in the disillusionment of his old age, regarding his life in
retrospect, meditating on the cabals and the intrigues of his counsellors, hear-
kening amidst such excessive luxury as his age saw unto the groans of an
oppressed people, and viewing his righteous ambitions frustrated, that he
bursts, like an ancient Hamlet, into a bitter tirade on life. Disillusionment,
futility, and boredom are the three themes which repeat themselves with the
inevitableness of the varied versions of a dying man's groans. The monarch
has quaffed cups; he has quaffed philosophies; he has known the meaning in
the twittering of birds; he has read sermons in stones; he has probed the
secrets of the universe, and – he finds them all vanity and a pursuit after

wind. What has been, that again will be; and the inexorable circle reduces all things to a monotonous repetition. Out of the bitterness of his heart, therefore, and out of the anguish of his spirit, comes again and again the cry of the ultimate vacuum: Vanity of vanities, all is vanity ... Of such words is the refrain which the worms sing, as they ply their subterranean work ...

To translate this melancholia into Yiddish has been the undertaking of Rabbi Zlotnik. It is a difficult one. He has succeeded, admirably.

To appreciate the difficulty of such a translation one must distinguish between the essence of the Hebraic spirit and that of the Jewish. The Hebrew of the Solomonic age, endowed with what Matthew Arnold called the high seriousness – the puritan, rigid and actively religious – is hardly recognizable in the Jew of the Middle Ages, whose religion is passive resignation, and whose strong and self-asserting Judaism has been beaten into a pulpy impersonality. It is, therefore, clear that to translate from the Hebrew into that idiomatic Yiddish which Rabbi Zlotnik uses, is like translating not only from one language to another, but also from one spirit to another. The difficulty is minimized, however, by the fact that the philosophy of Koheleth, defeatist as it is, occasionally finds its echo in the philosophy of the latter-day Jew.

To realize fully the value of the translation, the achievement of each nuance, the insinuation of every subtlety, an analysis, perhaps a too pedantic and pedagogical one – and, for the columns of *The Judaean*, pedagogy is not to be shunned – would be in place. It is only by this method that it is possible to appreciate the technique which makes Rabbi Zlotnik's translation not merely a translation, but a poem *per se*.

In the first place the Yiddish is in vers libre, a form that is peculiarly appropriate for translations from the Oriental, and the vigour of which Arthur Waley and Amy Lowell have shown with reference to Chinese poetry. Rabbi Zlotnik manipulates the medium with perfect mastery, a mastery which proves that vers libre is not merely minced prose. The position of the word צופיל in Chapter 7, Verse 29, indicates the amount of suggestion which can be obtained by the free verse form.

It is true that rhyme occasionally inserts itself unconsciously, as in the Yiddish jingle-proverb, קײן קינד, קײן רינד . Or, if consciously, with such art, and 'ars artem celare est,' that it appears quite natural and unforced, thus:–

ענדליך —

ענדליך האָב איך דערוואכט,

זיך אַרומגעקוקט און באַטראַכט

און אַלץ וואָס איך האָב אָנגעהאָוועט —

הבל הבלים —

אַ פוסטער חלום !

נאַריש און נישטיק

דײן לעבן און שטרעבן,

מענטש, אונטער דער זון !

The whole translation brims with originality. Rabbi Zlotnik has managed, with great subtlety, to achieve a coherence between one verse and the
other by means of interpolations and parentheses, a coherence which is not
quite obvious in the original text. In other words, the translation is not only
translation, but also commentary. Thus Rabbi Zlotnik allows himself, in one
of his bracketed additions, to pun on the word עולם:

עולם וועלט — עולם אייביק

– a process sanctioned by King Solomon himself, who punned on the words
שמן and שם, and one which enhances the implications of the verse that follows.

A contrast between the King James version of the Old Testament, 1611,
familiar, no doubt, to most of our readers, and the work of Rabbi Zlotnik will
indicate the new poetical and definitely folk-idiomatic ingredient in this translation. Thus the 1611 version: 'I sought in my heart to give myself unto wine,
yet acquainting mine heart with wisdom.' What vividness is added by the use
of apostrophe:

דאן האָב איך געוואָלט דאָס לעבן אויספרובירן:
— דו פלייש, נא דיר ווײַן,
און דו הארץ — פילאָזאָפיר!

A typically Jewish gesture!

The definitely Yiddish influence is seen in the use of proverbial Yiddish
idioms for the translation of ordinary concepts; that is to say, the translation
is not literal, – it is literary; thus the King James version, and the Hebrew
original is no more metaphorical: 'Yet to a man who hath not laboured therein'
becomes in the translation:

איינעם וואָס האָט די האַנט ניט אריינגעלייגט
אין קיין קאַלט וואַסער ארײַן.

Or the verse: 'A man hath no preeminence above the beast' becomes

טאָ מיט וואָס איז דער מענטש
מער יחסן פון דער בהמה?

Or the verse: 'Him that ruleth among fools' becomes

דער... וואָס פירט ארום בײַם נאָז די נארן.

Or the verse: 'And the mourners go about the streets' becomes

און עס נייען זיך בײַטלען די הספד־מאַכער.

Further quotations are unnecessary.

The affinity between the philosophy of Koheleth and that of the diaspora-Jew is evidenced by the fact that many of the verses of Ecclesiastes have been translated wholesale as part and parcel of the Yiddish language. Rabbi Zlotnik makes use of this fact in his work. The use of delicate aposiopesis (the cutting short of a sentence for rhetorical effect) is also in the true *goluth* tradition, thus:

אונזער געלעכטער

איז געמישט מיט טרערן

און אונזער שמחה —

מ'שטיינס געזאָגט...

There may be some, as there have been, who would object to such words as כאַליאַסטרע and סאדזשעװוקעס as being archaic; the fact is, however, that if they are archaic they are that only in America; and again, even if they were archaic in Europe, a good poem is made better by the introduction of old words, even as a good banquet by old wines.

The discussion of the authorship of Koheleth is very intriguing and erudite; all we can say is that if Koheleth is not King Solomon, he ought to have been.

Rabbi Zlotnik's work ought to be read at least twice; once with the original at one's side to appreciate it as a translation, and once *per se* to appreciate it as a poem. We would like to see further work of a like character. We would suggest the Book of Job.

In conclusion, we may say that in this translation Rabbi Zlotnik has brought to the work of a philosopher the precision of a scholar and the appreciation of a poet.

Baal Shem in Modern Dress

Review of *Lyric* [in Yiddish] by J.I. Segal   14 November 1930

There has just appeared, still odorous of printer's ink and redolent of fresh paper, a volume of poems by J.I. Segal, entitled *Lyric*. The title, it must be admitted, is somewhat oracular; it suggests, but it does not explain. A name like that could cover a multitude of sins ... Within the black binding of this book there is none of that lyric, as the word is commonly understood, which lilts to facile rhythms, and which in every hop, step and jump of its frolicking metre, declares to an attentive universe that this is the best of all possible worlds. On the contrary, these lyrics do not sing themselves in the bright sunshine of common day; far better suited are they for the melodiously nasal humming in which God's worthy Jews indulge during the twilit moments of Sabbath afternoons. A hushed resignation pervades these pages, and throughout there is a wistful longing, not for Villon's fair ladies of yesteryear, but for the naive freshness of the Baal Shem and the Bratslaver, a wistfulness for this loveliness of the past, and in the face of its absence a resignation.

The book, we said, is still odorous of printer's ink. But it is a fleeting aroma. Overcoming the unpleasant smell introduced by Gutenberg's diabolic invention, there rises the fragrance of dead leaves rotting in autumnal pools. There is an old odour of things beautifully antiquated: ancient and musty parchments; phylacteries giving a nostalgic perfume of sanctified leather; samovars of fresh Sabbath tea; citrons redolent in cotton; oriental *besomim*-boxes reminiscent of myrrh and galbanum; heirloom prayer-shawls about which the odour of sanctity still floats; the familiar fragrance of worn and cherished things.

At first one obtains the impression that the author is an antiquarian. He seems to be collecting all the monuments of a faded Judaica. As one continues one perceives that it is not the hollow ceremonialism, not the picturesqueness of religious hocus-pocus that has won his soul; it is most obviously the spirit of innocence and faith and trustfulness that accompanied these ritual manifestations. At a time when innocence is unfashionable, and faith a cant word, and trustfulness a virtue only when supported by legal contract, it is refreshing to read these lines in praise of the simple. Where, cries the poet, is Levi Yitschok, of Berditchev, he who in his unaffected impudence did on a time summon the Almighty Himself to a law suit? He answers, and we translate his Yiddish reply:

> Such the retort they threw him from above,
> Such the black answer that the heavens threw,
> He has been silent in his chamber since;
> No more does he come forth ...
> O grant again the marvel of the prime;
> Festivity then shone from every eye,
> And in a quiet twilit hour came
> Our holy days ... O grant that it may be
> As once it was.

Greatly he desires to return to Beauty 'like Levites to the sacred temple,' 'like hermits stumbling into the desert.' He ekes out a small consolation from the fact that

> In homely houses of the world,
> Upon the tables of the lowly,
> The bridegrooms still count dowries, and
> The greybeards read the psalms, still holy ...

It is not surprising to find that he spits gall when he considers the modern substitute for the vanished halidom. We find that

> Our young men have long arms for blond-haired girls,
> And our virgins – woe is us –
> Stretch out their white immaculate thighs
> To heathens, flaxen haired ...
> Is it decorous, then, that our young men
> Should be enamored of odes to cathedral-crosses ...
> They love the gold upon their spires,
> Even as that gold on the gentile heads.
> And we,
> Scorned, rejected, and condemned,
> How shall we hail them before the Sanhedrin? ...

Why, then, has he come from these regions where these half-remembered beauties still prevail to a land of push-carts and skyscrapers? Even poets are governed by economic laws.

> Only that crust of bread of yours,
> To which I stretch my muzzle, lures
> Me forth, a mouse that leaves its hole,
> Lowly, in every nook to cower,
> Cramming its belly full from your sack of flour ...

Nonetheless, in spite of the sack of flour, he discusses poverty with a wealth of description ... He propounds economic problems with a rhyme, and in a world where the principle of private property is firmly established, he is all gratitude that at least verse is free ... The Yiddish language, as many philologists and paupers have long ago established, has at least a dozen synonyms for poverty; Segal's poems exhaust the list, and add a few nuances of their own.

Some of these descriptions of the sorrows of penury are rendered in such fine rhythms and felicitous phrases that one forgets for a moment that an empty pocket is a tragedy, and not an idyll. In one of his languorous odes Keats confesses that he has 'been half in love with easeful Death, called him soft names in many a mused rhyme.' Segal has flattered poverty with similar words, and like a poetic Nahum-Ish-Gamsu, has derived out of its barren picturesqueness a satisfaction and a perfect line. Nonetheless, the bile escapes, after the poet has almost achieved the accents of composure, and in a last line he indicates with acid insinuation and bitter innuendo, that the situation is blacker than he has painted it.

And yet the poems do not end on a didactic note, exhorting the reader to become class-conscious and hail the social revolution. Our carmine comrades, votaries of proletarian literature, may look askance at such taciturnity, – they would prefer to see his poem end with propaganda writ in red italics, they would feel pleased, if it not only adorned a penurious tale, but also if it pointed a Marxian moral. To draw a picture, and let its suggestiveness do the rest; there may be a whole revolution lurking in the three pregnant dots after one of these poetic and yet realistic descriptions of pennilessness.

Thus Segal's poems read like liturgies; whereas the one is as a devotional supplication, 'R'tsai, Adonai,' the other is as that invocation uttered on Passover nights, 'Spill out thy wrath, O Lord.' Yet one must not gather that the poems have in them the personality of a *shul*-president, a *gabbai*, a *maggid*, or of any other holy vessel. The author is neither a pillar of the orthodox church, nor an architrave of organized religion. His piety is a purely individual one, and his relations with God are strictly private. He and God are cronies. They meet very informally, and talk things over. Blake once wrote in his diary very naively and very simply: To-day I took a walk with an angel. That same simplicity runs through Segal's work.

> My child has just begun to walk.
> I watch her every little step.
> I hold her by her left hand,
> And God by her right.

Or in another poem:

> God – you are a Don Quixote,
> And I
> Your Sancho Panza.

Such sentiments express themselves most adequately in simple language. In the main Segal's vocabulary is of the vernacular; it is full of robust colloquialisms, and has the tang of folk-language. Howbeit, in poems of a more modern spirit he introduces original neologisms, coins a fine phrase. He speaks of 'deaf hats,' of 'the rust of silence,' of 'a green star playing with a whetted spear'; he permits himself the luxury of a title reminiscent of the Rebbe Alemelech – *Arim Melech*. He indulges in irony:

> There appear in town a group of actors,
> Singers, ar–tistes,
> They play; they sing; they act cute.
> I have seen my best friends,
> And clever men at that,
> Weep at their tomfooleries ...

But the main characteristic of the book is its elemental simplicity, its primitive naiveté. It is poetry unadulterated by literariness. Had no poet ever written before him, Segal could have still produced these lyrics. It is a naiveté that sometimes runs to child-like guilelessness. Often when the poet wishes to declare that in something there is the ineffable tertium quid, he uses the rubber-stamp '*Aza*,' – 'Such a light,' 'Such a comfort.' Within a few pages the word is used a dozen times. It is the expression of expressionlessness; it is the poetic outburst of one who has felt that which can be expressed only by a gesture.

Because of this we would naturally expect that his sympathy for children should express itself in the flower of his work. And it does. Segal has written some little masterpieces for children. But the book that we are discussing is for adults; those who still have in them, despite the onslaughts of sophistication, a grain of Chassidic simplicity, who can appreciate the Baal Shem and his commerce with babes and sucklings, his sympathy for the lowly, will find in these pages an echo of that still small voice. The book is an autobiography, a document, and an indictment.

White Magic

Review of *The Zohar in Moslem and Christian Spain* by Ariel
Bension   7 October 1932

It is with a supercilious lift of an all-too-logical eyebrow that the rationalist is wont to regard the revelation of mysticism. Creator of natural laws and inventor of scientific hypotheses, he knows no exceptions; all mysticisms are mystifying; they do not sit on syllogisms and are therefore foundationless all. Immune to parable and impervious to metaphor, he condemns every philosophy which he can not understand as being either the forgery of a fakir or the document of a lunatic. Attributing insanity to works mystical, he forgets that 'true genius is to madness close allied,' and imputing base motives to the poets of the esoteric, he commits the unpardonable offense of mistaking the Veil of the Shechina for the Mask of Mephistopheles ...

Most certainly there have been imposters and mountebanks, who, uttering the abracadabra of mysticism, have deluded millions with their polished abstruosities and their manufactured inspirations. Too true is it that mysticism is very frequently no more than complexes garbed in ritual, incoherency puffing with artificial afflatus, unintelligibility wearing a halo ... When one considers the thousands who have been duped by the theosophies of imposters, one justly hesitates before losing oneself in the labyrinths of any proffered mysticism. But there are exceptions.

One of these is the Zohar. Condemned as the forgery of Moses de Leon of the thirteenth century, the debate as to its authenticity has waxed furious for ages. Did Simeon ben Yochai really write it, as the orthodox Cabbalists would have us believe, or is it the product of a later day, as Leon de Modena and Jacob Emden argue? The point is not important. Dr. Bension, regretting this theological altercation, presents a compromise whereby, in an extremely interesting and scholarly chapter, he seeks to prove that 'the Zohar was revealed and developed in the garden of Spanish mysticism in the Middle Ages,' in fine that the Zohar is an anthology between whose pages are pressed the still-fragrant flowers, culled from the gardens of three continents: Africa and its Sinaitic decalogue, Asia and its Babylonian Talmud, Europe and its mediaeval mysticism. The remarkable comparisons between the work of the Spanish mystics and the Zohar, which he offers in catalogued and convincing form, lend colour to his contention.

To the writer of these lines, however, the controversy seems as futile as the Shakespeare-Bacon puz- [...] is important only because he presents in analytical and exemplary form the contents of the Zohar. It is a work which shines forth from the gloom of the Dark Ages with an effulgence all its own, accentuating the fact that while most practitioners of mysticism of that era prided themselves on being Masters of Black Magic, the Zohar springs forth as a Book of White Splendour ...

Indeed, in an age where the whirr of machines drowns out the still small voice, it is gratifying to behold this worthy descendant of Ben Chasdai of Barcelona, trafficking in things spiritual. It is with poetic ceremony, as becomes a Spanish-Jewish grandee, that he ushers us into the goodly company of Simeon ben Yochai, and to his talk of angels and heavenly ministers, and to his juggling of planets and his music of the spheres. When he loosens the shutter from the groove of the Window of the Righteous, there is flung open to our gaze those

> Magic casements, opening on the foam
> Of perilous seas, in faery lands forlorn ...

The largess of such lips is ample reward for the telepathic travel, enforced upon us by the writer, over seven centuries and into hundreds of new worlds.

In a typical passage in James Joyce's *Ulysses*, the hero, Stephen Dedalus, considering that all humanity is bound together in a net of allied and related navel-cords, is driven by the stream of consciousness to think of telegraph wires, at which reflection he mentally makes note of a telephone number: *Edenville, nought, nought, one. Adam Kadmon.* It is precisely this kind of telephonic connection that Dr. Bension, as mediator between the sublunar and the supernatural, achieves ... He is the dragoman of Reb Simeon ben Yochai, the Vergil guiding wandering Dantes through his Inferno, the cicerone of heaven ...

It is as a literary work that the Zohar can hope to live to-day. Couched in the language of mysticism, it is subject, as experience has shown, to myriad interpretations; it is a Torah with seventy faces. It has spoken in parables, and has been answered by sects. To-day, however, it is not primarily as a book of faith removing mountains that the Zohar is to be considered, but as an inspired collection of poetic flowers, impregnated with the pollen of truth. If, as some stylist once defined it, poetry is thought in blossom, then the Zohar is thought on the burning bush ... Inasmuch as it is poetry, it is prophecy ...

For one must indeed search long and zealously in world literature before one can find so naive, so simple and yet so inspired a character as Bar Yochai, who because of his convictions lived for thirteen years in a cave, his body buried up to the neck in sand; who said to the Heavenly One, 'If there be only two noble souls in the world, they are mine and my son's'; and 'who was the mill that ground the manna for mankind to gather every day.' ... One would have to delve seriously and long before discovering in the writings of men, such poetic utterances as: 'I know I am about to die, for my soul leaves me every night ... Yesterday, when saying my prayers, I glanced at the wall and saw that my shadow was no longer there ...' 'It is the hour when the Holy One remembers his children and their woe, and two tears drop from his eyes into the sea. But while they are falling, the tears are transformed into a column of fire from the woe that is in them ...' 'My habitation is a tower that flies in the air.' 'Rab Hamanouna, running and displacing mountains on his way to the Messiah.' 'At midnight, when the cock crows, the wind which blows from the north is suddenly stopped by the flow of grace which comes from the south ...' 'Israel, fleeing from the tigers of the world ...' 'The stars are the letters with which God has created the heavens and the earth.'

In English literature, only William Blake can be compared to the hero of the Zohar. Blake, who seriously wrote in his diary, 'To-day I walked with angels on the heath.' Blake, who had Yochai's sympathy for God's little creatures:

> A Robin Redbreast in a cage
> Puts all heaven in a rage,

and Blake, who like the Great Holy Assembly, could

> Hold infinity in the palm of the hand
> And eternity in an hour ...

Dr. Bension has rendered a great service to literature with his translation and analysis of the Zohar. It is an addendum to knowledge. Written with a high seriousness, it is not merely another appendix to the numerous brochures which are issuing from the printing presses of the world as Jewish literature; it is an actual contribution to Judaica. Considering the admirable description of the Seven Palaces, the author's intimacy with the cherubim and seraphim, his command of the Sphiroth, and how, with the eyes of Bar Yochai, he looks, as through a knot-hole into that Paradise (PRDS) made up of *Pshat, Remez, Drash* and *Sod*, Dr. Bension could aptly use Shakespeare's words:

> I come
> To answer thy best pleasure, be't to fly,
> To swim, to dive into the fire, to ride
> On the curled clouds; to thy strong bidding, task
> Ariel and all his quality ...

Chaim Nachman Bialik   June 1937

It is, alas, the usual fate of the works of those whom Mr. Rascoe is pleased to call the titans of literature, that for about a century they are read as best-sellers, and then for eternity they are placed on the shelves – classics unread. It has been, doubly alas, the fate of Chaim Nachman Bialik, to have become a classic on the American continent without having to go through the preliminary stage of best-seller. Indeed so overwhelming is ignorance on this subject that a complete anecdotage has arisen about the poet laureate and the groundlings who knew him not. It is told that when on an occasion, Bialik accompanied by a friend, appeared on a New York platform, the ever-courteous master of ceremonies forthwith declared his happiness 'at having with us tonight both Mr. Chaim Nachman and Mr. Bialik!' Dr. Coralnik, too, contributes his chairman to the valhalla of culture, his chairman who charmingly introduced Bialik with this shofar-blast of oratory: I do not know who this gentleman Bialik is; I never read his poetry (pronounced poultry) but our cantor made music for one of his songs, so I suppose he must be alright ...

Bialik must be alright. Following in the tradition of David, sweet singer in Israel, and Solomon, lyre of love, and Yehuda Halevi, nightingale of the middle ages, Bialik *must* be alright. This is, we are inclined to believe, if the chairman will pardon us, an understatement. For Bialik was no less than the personification of the Hebrew Renaissance, the accumulated silence of centuries miraculously become articulate. What W.B. Yeats was to the Celtic Revival, that Bialik was to the Semitic one, – a lord of language, a master of noble and prophetic thought. If poetry is, as Wordsworth said, emotion recorded in tranquility, then what finer manifestation thereof was there than the volcanic wrath which was poured forth by the incarnated dignity of his people, immediately after the massacre in the tragically immortal 'City of Slaughter.' If poetry, as Keats would have it, should surprise by a fine excess, what more picturesque example of such 'fine excess' than Bialik's presentation of the cat, in the hour of its boredom, plucking out her own whiskers? If poetry, as J.L. Lowes insists, is characterized chiefly by its technique of suggestion, what more magic casements opening on the Home are there than the national poems of Bialik? If it is poetry which is thought in blossom that you seek, go, then, to the efflorescent cerebrality of Bialik on Achad Ha-am. And if the function of poetry is to define the undefinable in terms of the unforgettable, open your volume of Bialik, and behold the definition exemplified!

By whatever measuring rod he is measured, he still appears a giant, by a head taller than any of his contemporaries. As such, his generation recognized him. It is moreover difficult to declare that Jews as a people are fond of poetry. 'The prophet is a fool, the man of the spirit is mad,' was a judgment in the mouth of Israel not only in the days of Hosea, the son of Beeri. The folk proverb, too, announced that the best of poetry is falsehood, and the ethics of Jewry were very emphatic about the virtue of truth. Of course, there was a distinction between secular rhymes and religious ones; the latter were dignified with the appelation *piyyut*, the former gestured away as *gram-shmam*. This being so, one is not surprised to read that the poems of Immanuel of Rome, non-liturgical and humorous to boot, were sniffed at by the rabbis.

But not so Bialik. He was probably the only poet in the history of both Parnassus and Hermon, who, when he ceased to write his verses, heard all about him the cries of Hebrew-speaking Jews, repeating the one hundred and thirty-seventh psalm: 'Sing us one of the songs of Zion.' Write us a poem about *chalutzim*; fashion an epic about Jewish navigation; a lyric about the Hebrew University, verses for all occasions. Such was the universal demand for encores. Wasn't he the national poet? For at the directly opposite pole of the chairmen who knew not Chaim Nachman, were all those who watched the horizon for the rays of Bialik's poetry breaking through the Hebraic twilight.

For he was of the people; he knew their agonies, their longings, their hopes. Born in the province of Volhynia in 1873, removed to Zhitomir at the age of six, bereft of his father, he knew poverty and the bitterness of poverty. 'Do you wish to know,' he wrote, 'the master of my song? It was the cricket, poet of poverty,' he answers. In the same poem, he goes on to describe, again with a fine excess, how his mother kneaded the dough for bread and wept thereon, and how when she gave the warm morning crust to her children,

> From the bread of her tears, and tragedy
> There entered my very bones, her sigh ...

His education was typical of the studious young Jew of that generation. He early assimilated the lore and learning of the Kabala, Maimonides' *Guide to the Perplexed*, the *Kuzari*, and spent some time at that great academy, the Hebrew Oxford of the nineteenth century, the Yeshiva of Volozhin. Even while he was conning the first letters of the alphabet his poetic imagination was aflame. Indeed, when he wrote notes for an autobiography, he remarked, how to his childish eye, the *Aleph* appeared to him like a gallant drummer-boy, with drum before him, and knapsack behind, leading a host of *Gimels* marching, as surely enough they do, with the goose-step ... His love of learning, his passion for books, remained with him to the end of his days; time and time again his attachment to the written word forms the subject of his poetic pen.

> Accept my greeting, ancient manuscripts
> Receive my kiss, ye dreamers in the dust ...

So, standing 'Before the Bookshelves,' does he hail those good companions of his days and nights. Hence, his boast, not a mere empty vaunting but a true and authentic self-characterization of the poet who wrote like a prophet:

> I did not teach my hand to clench the fist;
> With wine and women, did not spend my strength:
> To sing God's song to the world, I do exist.

In 1891, his first poem, 'To the Bird,' flew into the pages of Ravnitsky's

Pardess, and like Byron, he woke up and found himself famous. From that time, he continued to write, occupying himself with writing as an avocation, and lumbering as a profession. One of the most human qualities of Bialik was that he consistently refused to be regarded as of the Bohemian breed of anaemic poets, sighing themselves into spectredom, permitting their hair to become metamorphosed into hanging gardens of Babylon, the while they exhale the refined aestheticism of 'art for art's sake.' Thus, when on his fiftieth birthday his fellow-Jews desired to overwhelm him with banquets and celebrations, there issued the retort courteous from the pen of Bialik:

> Beneath the burden of your love
> Bowed down, I cannot lift me up!
> Ah, woe is me! I am become
> A penny shaken in your cup!
>
> Why do you so besiege my hearth?
> What evil have I done? What good?
> I am no prophet, no, nor bard, –
> I am a simple hewer of wood.

Later, however, he settled in Odessa as teacher and head of a modern Hebrew school, collaborating with Achad Ha-am on the paper of which the latter was editor. In 1905, together with Ravnitsky, his Boswell, he established the publishing house Moriah. After the revolution, however, he left Russia, and remained in Berlin 1921–24, in which year the poet who thirty years before sought greetings of Erez Israel from the *zippor,* settled in the country of his longing, where he became almost a legendary figure, a tradition of the new country, an institution in himself. What with the *Oneg Shabbos* organized in Tel Aviv by Bialik, and his activities with the Dvir publishing company, and his advice and counsel in the affairs of the Hebrew University, it would be no exaggeration to declare that Palestine culture rotated about his personality.

Though no votary of that art which contents itself merely with form, and is oblivious to content, Bialik is a master of *le mot juste,* a sculptor of the memorable phrase. His sources sunk deep in the Bible and Talmud, he did not, as poetasters before him, content himself with macaronics composed of concealed quotation from Holy Writ. He wrote poetry which was not merely *melitza.* He gave the Hebrew language a freshness and spontaneity, remarkable in a tongue which had rusted on its hinges for centuries … Thus in his poem, 'God grant my part and portion be,' the Gray's Elegy of the Hebrew language, eloquent tribute to mute and inglorious Herzls, he apostrophizes:

> Ye keepers of God's image upon earth!

Or this bold fancy:

> And the forged signature of God inscribed upon the flag
> Did pierce the eyes of the sun.

And that same sun, so transformed in the crucible of Bialik's imagination:

> The sun changed to a stain of your clear blood:
> The sign of Cain upon the forehead of the world!

Or this picture:

> A flock of tender clouds, the thoughts of heaven ...

And this ultra-modern picture of the scoffers of the book of Psalms:

> The cigarette between their teeth,
> The crafty smile that lies in ambush underneath mustache,
> The snare that lies in waiting in their eyes ...

And finally, this example of poetic observation:

> You will forget the memory of grass
> And the smell of fresh grass after rain ...

Bialik, too, is a poet of varied styles and form. Author of masterly prose, and writer of perfect poetry, he occasionally permits his elevated style to enter even into pedestrian unrhymed sentences. We have not read in Hebrew a more charming folk-tale in versified prose, than his story of 'Lord Onion and Sir Garlic.' There is about his lines, reminiscent though they be of the lofty epical speech of the prophets, something perfectly twentieth-century. In his poem 'Zohar,' he enumerates a number of phenomena on which he dotes: the flying bird, a tree and its shadow, the modest moon, the darkness of a cellar, the screech of a turning gate, light mingled with darkness, all of which may well be, by inspiration and certainly not by plagiarism, a Hebrew version of Rupert Brooke:

> These I have loved:
> White plates, and cups, clean-gleaming,
> Ringed with blue lines; and feathery faery dust;

Wet roofs beneath the lamp-light; the strong crust
Of friendly bread; and many-tasting food;
Rainbows; and the blue bitter smoke of wood;
The cool kindliness of sheets that soon
Smooth away trouble; and the rough male kiss
Of blankets ...

Or when he says:

דמעת לילי ראש אנחתי
הלמות לבי נשמת אפי
גם האחרון בחלומותי —
אלה יהיו קרבנותי
לך אקריבה עד בא יומי.

it is the Semitic tongue achieving as poignant and as modern an utterance as
W.S. Landor's 'Rose Aylmer':

Ah, what avails the sceptred race,
Ah, what the form divine?
What every virtue, every grace
Rose Aylmer, all were thine.

Rose Aylmer, whom these wakeful eyes
May weep, but never see,
A night of memories and of sighs
I consecrate to thee!

Above all, Bialik is powerful in his national poems; here his voice is a
very trumpet-blast. It was he who, when Jews displayed during the massacres
of Kishineff a cowardice unworthy of the descendants of the Maccabees, poured
forth the vials of his wrath upon these creatures from whom the ghetto had
stolen their manliness. In that poem – 'The City of Slaughter' – the macabre
vies with the satiric, Poe interrupts Isaiah. Thus:

For God called up the slaughter and the spring together:
The slayer slew, the blossom burst, and it was sunny weather ...

For the assimilated Jew, he was full of scorn and pity:

The chastisement of God is this His curse:
That you shall your own very hearts deny

To cast your hallowed tears on foreign waters,
Your tears on luminous false threads to thread
To breathe your breath in marble alien
And in the heathen stone to sink your soul.

Apart from his poetic works, Bialik acted as editor of numerous Hebrew classics. *Kinnus* – the gathering of the masterpieces of Hebrew literature, was one of the motivating influences of his life. He was the Matthew Arnold of Hebrew letters.

None can doubt the position which he will occupy in the Temple of the Bards. In the pessimistic poem 'The Lord Has Not Revealed to Me,' Bialik imagines the various fates that may befall him in after-days. He fears, for example, – with the same fear which beset Quintus Horatius Flaccus – that he may become a mere textbook for school children!

O, they will bind my soul in winding sheets of writing paper,
Inter me in the coffin of a book-case.
Upon my own grave I shall place my foot
And with my own mouth utter my own Kaddish.

But in that same poem, he also mentions, by way of casual possibility and merely for the purpose of dismissal, this contingency:

Perhaps, a pearl of an eternal glow
With my last tear, my life shall also fall
Trembling,
And after many generations shine
For eyes that never did behold mine.

The poet spoke prophecy that is being daily fulfilled.

Music Hath Charm

Review of *Jewish Music and Other Essays on Musical Topics* [in Yiddish] by Israel Rabinovitch   11 October 1940

The appearance of a book on music – and on Jewish music at that! – at the present time might strike the casual observer as essentially an anachronism. Certainly one might be entitled to doubt as to whether 'harmonious numbers' could possibly be heard to-day above the din of cannonade. For the symphony of the times seems to be an orchestration of various instruments hitherto unrecognized in the musical canon – the boom of bomb, the whirr of plane, the burst of shrapnel, and the ominous and recurrent refrain of the siren. Only the most courageous spirit could possibly hope that amidst this hurly-burly there should be heard the subdued devotional tones of the liturgy, the conversational accents of antiphonic music, or the nostalgic melody of a folk-song.

Such a spirit, however, is Mr. I. Rabinovitch's, whose book on Jewish music is now some time off the press. Mr. Rabinovitch is the editor of the *Montreal Jewish Daily Eagle*, and the author of its daily column '*Gut Morgen.*' For over a decade now Rabinovitch has through the medium of this column commented in witty and charming style upon the current news of the day. In writing his footnotes to the daily headlines, the company he has had to keep has not been of the best – his concentration upon Arcand long before Arcand was concentrated, his journalistic washing of all the dirty political shirts of Europe, his contacts, even at a distance, with that Hitlerism which he daily dissected, no doubt deepened his conceptions of realpolitik, and all those other manifestations of man 'that nasty brutish animal,' but, one imagined, were hardly conducive to the mood in which music, and the evolution of music, is appreciated.

With those who love music, however, the miracle which occurred to David repeats itself. 'A harp was hung' – we quote from Rabinovitch's citation of the Gemara *Berachoth* – 'over King David's bed; upon the stroke of midnight, the north wind rose, and blew upon it, and of itself, it played.' It was after he was through with his daily polemics, the eternal logomachy of the Jew against unreasoning prejudice, that Rabinovitch left his syllogisms and his barbed dilemmas for the pleasant atmosphere of music, which like the heart 'a des raisons, que la raison n'a pas.' The essays wrote themselves.

The book is not a book on music, as such; it is, as the author describes it, a collection of essays on musical topics. They range in time from the discussion of the music which accompanied the service in the Temple, to regretful notices upon the havoc which American jazz has wreaked upon the fine art of the now déclassé *klesmer*; they range in manner from the expositional analysis of the *Al-hagittith* – mysterious word! – of the Psalms, to merciless polemic with Saminsky and his snobbish Hebraism; they range in style from the charming essay on the metamorphosis of a melody to the erudite treatises on ancient music; they travel in space from a discussion of the Persian version of *Kol Nidre* to a detection of *Chad Gadya* echoes in a French-Canadian folk-song. But through all of them there runs a high seriousness, almost a reverence for the subject, and certainly that natural piety of which Wordsworth spoke:

And I could wish my days to be
Bound each to each by natural piety.

For one of Rabinovitch's principal objectives is to show the coherent and sequential development of Jewish music; he is averse to that compartmentalizing of music current in certain quarters. Certainly he lays to rest that popular misconception that all minor modes are typically Semitic, and all Jewish music is in a minor key. The theory he proves as falsetto as the music in whose name it speaks. In various instances he does bind together a note from old Bokhara and a melody of the Vistula – the days are truly bound each to each by natural piety.

This reverence for the written word and the word sung is evident nowhere as much as in Rabinovitch's references to Abraham Zvi Idelsohn, to whose memory the book is dedicated. With that modesty which is one of the author's chief characteristics, he arrogates to himself no new discoveries; he is merely, he says, a faithful follower of the immortal Idelsohn.

But whereas Idelsohn wrote in a fashion – Hebrew and English – which is not always fascinating to the layreader, Rabinovitch's book is one, not only for musicians, but for music-lovers, and all votaries of things Jewish. We must admit that we are not a note-reader; the quavers set us a-quiver, and the minims minimize us. The number of cuts and notationed transcriptions, therefore, somewhat abashed us; we feared they might be 'a burst of music down an unlistening street.' But the reading of the book, both because of the mine of information it contains, and the engaging manner in which it is relayed to the reader, holds him entranced.

For is it not worth much to discover that the traditional melody of the Song of Songs is a musical reproduction of the sound of the cuckoo, harbinger of spring and summer? A people which interpreted that great love-lyric as an antiphony between God and Israel, but was still natural enough to sing it – like birds! It explained to us also that oldest of Anglo-Saxon lyrics:

Summer is i-cumen in
Lhude sing cuccu;
Groweth sede and bloweth mede
And springeth the wood nu.
Sing cuccu, cuccu.

Only the Canticum said: 'Lo, the winter is past, the rain is over and gone, the flowers appear on the earth, the time of singing of birds is come.' And both tributes to the reviving year evoke the cuckoo!

The book is full of interesting facts – that revolutionaries in 1905 employed typical melodies from the Jewish thesaurus to pour out their melancholy emotions; that there is a parallel between 'cantorial recitative' and 'free verse'; that there is a difference – and a big one! – in music, as in literature, between sentiment, and sentimentality; that it is written 'in a book published in Mantua,' that the *tzilzail* of the Psalms was a 'trombone'; and more and more – as kernel'd as a pomegranate.

It was remarked above that the casual reader might see in this book an untimeliness; but only casually. A book of eclectic essays on a little-discussed subject is, of course, timely always; but upon this subject it is the timelier now. For it is of eternal verities in a universal language, it is of the spring of Jewish spirit, so hard beset these perilous times.

Mr. Rabinovitch quotes a very pertinent, albeit mystical estimate of music, attributed to Rabbi Shnayur Zalman of Lyadi with reference to one of his own compositions, composed while he was incarcerated in the prison at Petersburg, 1799. Its first stage aims at 'a pouring out of the soul,' it rises then to 'spiritual awakening,' it mounts to 'enthusiasm,' it soars to 'communion,' and it finally reaches 'ecstasy.' If this terminology, as to the wider implications of the musical effect, is too cabbalistic for the modern reader, let Paul Elmer More describe it in contemporary language: 'Music is a psychological storm, agitating the fathomless depths of the mystery of the past within us. Or we might say that it is a prodigious incantation. There are tones that call up all ghosts of youth and joy and tenderness; there are tones that evoke all phantoms of perished passion; there are tones that revive all dead sensations of majesty and might and glory, all expired exultations – all forgotten magnanimities.'

It is precisely 'the agitation of the fathomless depth of the mystery of the past within us' which has been Rabinovitch's objective. It is regrettable that as yet the book appears only in Yiddish; an English translation would be a consummation greatly to be desired. For it is a book which ought to be read by all those who have music in them, of one kind or another; as for those who haven't –

> The man who hath no music in himself
> Nor is not moved with concord of sweet sound
> Is fit for treason, stratagems, and spoils.
> Let no such man be trusted.

The Art of the Passover Haggadah   1 April 1942

Almost every year there comes off the presses a new edition of that most fascinating of Hebrew ritual books – the Passover Haggadah. Until recently no one has presumed to tamper with its text; century after century, the Haggadah included the same prayers, the same excerpts from Midrash and Talmud, the same maledictions upon the heathen, the same quotations from the Psalms and the same nursery-rhymes grandiloquently inflated into a theologico-national significance. Last year the Reconstructionists – Rabbi Mordecai M. Kaplan et al. – issued a new version which purported to modernize the Haggadah, and render it palatable to twentieth-century Americans. Of the merits or demerits of that edition we do not propose here to speak; we are naturally conservative when it comes to laying corrective hands upon scriptures sanctioned by long usage, and made sacrosanct by the loveliest associations and memories of our youth. In the first place, we deem the Passover service, like the Passover wine, intended only for Jewish eyes – otherwise it becomes *yain nesach* – and in the second place, it is the very quaintness, it is precisely the old-fashioned and quasi-mediaeval flavor of the Haggadah which endows it with all its charm and beauty.

The illustrations of the Haggadah are a case in point. We have thumbed numerous editions thereof, published during the last two decades, and showing all the refinements of the contemporary art of printing, and have invariably put the books down unsatisfied. 'Tis not the thing; not thus can we recapture the nostalgic poetry of the days when we asked our father the four questions, and spent the Seder evening – somewhat drowsy after the third cup – examining the mediaeval woodcuts, and the grotesque illustrations which adorned our Haggadah.

For although the contemporary Haggadahs may display a more realistic illustrativeness, it is their very realism which is objectionable. We can derive no artistic thrill, no poetic enjoyment, out of a picture showing a clean-shaved father, sitting with his sons, all dressed in Hart and Schaffner suits, and engaged, presumably, in telling them, in English pure and undefiled, the tales of the flight from Egypt and the reason for the 'hemstitched biscuits.' An old text requires old illustrations. Otherwise, the same degree of artistic absurdity would be reached, as would be reached, for example, and *l'havdil*, if Leonardo da Vinci's *Last Supper* were modernized to show the Twelve Apostles sitting in the twentieth story of the Empire State Building, leaning on a board of directors' table.

And thereby hangs a tale! The old Haggadah represents one of the rare examples of truly primitive Jewish art. We use the word primitive in its technical sense, much as the word is applied to the Italian primitives. Indeed, the first edition of this book constitutes the beginnings of specific Jewish drawing. Until the invention of printing, Jewish art was seriously handicapped by the prohibition of the Decalogue against the fashioning of any images, be they on land, sea, or in the air. While it is true that certain ethnologists have sought to prove that the ancient Hebrews had no artistic aptitudes whatsoever, it is safer and more logical to assume that whatever aptitudes there may have been, latent and undeveloped, were stifled and destroyed by theologic taboo. Gradually, however, the strictness of the law was relaxed; in the first place, the art of the calligraphist – so much akin to the ampler arts – was always cherished by Jewry; and secondly, the prohibition against painting and sculpturing seems to have been modified insofar as it was applied to sacred purposes. Of these arts, as evidenced in the synagogues of Eastern Europe, one may read in that most excellent of intellectual travel-books – Marvin Lowenthal's *Worlds Passed By*. And finally, with Gutenberg's invention, illustrations by way of woodcuts and copperplates began to appear in books. It is to be noted that it was the Haggadah which was the first Hebrew text to be so illustrated; the ancient scriptures still remained a Holy of Holies, not to be polluted by images, graven or etched.

The first printed Haggadah appeared in the 16th century, and it is estimated that there are more than 2,000 editions of such works. Prior to that the Haggadahs were illuminated, such manuscripts dating back to the 13th century. It is these illustrated Haggadahs, with their strange marginal devices, their clumsy but charming pictures, which have inspired, in their illustrations, the Haggadahs which we knew in our youth, and which we still find, in extremely cheap editions, in the book-stores. It was in 1904 that Mrs. Philip Cowen, in New York, brought out a Haggadah, many times reprinted, with reproductions from the old prints.

Take for example, the usual illustration of 'the four sons.' The picture to which we had been accustomed – and we shall never think of the four sons in any other way – is that originally appearing in Vienna in 1823. The wise son is shown wearing a *shtreimel* and a long robe, and his right arm is lifted as if expounding some text of the law. Beside him is the *rasha*, the wicked son; he wears a buckler on his right arm, a spear in his left, and he is mailed and plumed. He is seen in the act of running. The *tam*, the simpleton, is represented in short skirt, sandalled feet, and staff in hand – apparently a shepherd. The fourth son – 'who knows not how to ask' – is drawn half-scale, a little homunculus; arms lifted in uncomprehending bewilderment. Beneath the four characters, are Hebrew letters, identifying them – another touch of artistic naiveté. The drawing is not very good; the bodies are disproportionate and the heads seem to be attached in a purely formal and non-anatomical way.

But it is precisely these characteristics which endear the picture. The Haggadah is essentially a naive, a simple, a primitive text – almost a children's text. The four questions which are never answered except indirectly and in extenso, the pointing at the *matzoh*, the elementary calculations of the plagues, the giving of mnemonics, the *afikomen*, the four cups, Elijah's visit – all have the unforgettable quality of a good affair arranged for little children. To that spirit, the early prints, the primitive illuminations provide a perfect harmony. By way of contrast, take the four sons drawing of Siegmund Forst for Abraham Regelson's modern translation of the Haggadah. The *chacham* is shown at a desk, bearded, hand on brow, a hirsute imitation of Rodin's Thinker. The picture protests too much; it seeks in every line to assure you that profound reflection goes on behind that *yarmulka'd* dome. The *rasha* is only a modern version of the Vienna print: a man kneels before a globe of the world, putting it to the torch. The militarist is apparently unpopular in both centuries. It is the *tam*, however, who reaches the heights of illustrative didacticism: he is shown sitting on an hour-glass, strumming away at a mandolin. We are at a loss to understand how the concept put forward by this drawing can be made to harmonize with the Jewish ancient and mediaeval atmosphere of the Haggadah, unless it is supposed to conjure up memories of Nero's fiddling. But then Nero was no *tam*; he was a *rasha*! Finally, the half-wit who never asks questions is represented as a little boy, apparently naughty.

The old prints, simple though they may be in their workmanship, are yet full of the most revealing implications. Rabbi Zlotnik once referred to an old Haggadah which illustrated a Jew lying on a couch, his face turned to a wall, while his wife sat at a table. It was only after much pondering that one was able to understand why the anonymous artist had turned the face of his sitter to the wall. The man was purposely removing his gaze from his wife, remembering, as he was bound, that every Jewish male child was to be flung into the Nile!

On the other hand, another Haggadah – 15th-century – shows a different domestic relationship. A father is demonstrating the bitter herbs and is seen pointing simultaneously to his wife. The reference is obviously to Ecclesiastes 7:26 – 'And I find more bitter than death, the woman, whose heart is a snare.'

The old prints of the ten plagues are equally fascinating. Again, the drawing is very poor, primitive, content merely with conveying a meaning, and not interested in fine draftsmanship. In all of them the backgrounds are mediaeval, although realistically they should be Egyptian. One looks in vain for a pyramid, or at least an obelisk. One sees only the castles so typical of mediaeval Europe, and the rooms so reminiscent of Dutch interiors. The plague of blood is interestingly shown. A river flows under an arched bridge – unknown in Egypt; at its banks a woman stands shawled, weeping; men with mattocks appear to be digging the river banks. The mise-en-scène is laid. To show that the river has turned to blood, the artist has indicated fish on the *surface* of the river! The plague of lice is also shown in the same primitive, almost caricaturing style. Six persons, in various attitudes, appear on a hill fronting a castle – and each is scratching a different part of his anatomy! At first blush one would be inclined to condemn the illustration as a piece of vulgarity; but its unashamed simplicity, its unconscious pathos, redeem it.

As for the plague of darkness, providing in its theme so great an opportunity for *chiaroscuro*, it is not rembrandtesque, but it is cute! Three quarters of the illustration is shaded, and through the shaded lines one distinguishes buildings and figures. The rest of the picture is white space, broken by a couple of lines showing persons. The intention of the artist is clear: 'There was thick darkness in all the land of Egypt three days, but all the children of Israel had light in their dwellings.'

We think that these Hebrew primitives have by no means received their just estimate in our art. It is true that some of them are imitations; one has even been able to show how some of the old prints were copied from the works of Holbein. But by and large, they have a freshness, an unsophisticated viewpoint which it is well to cherish and preserve. And if new editions of the Haggadah have to be published, we think that the illustrators could do worse – and they have! – than to seek their inspiration in these works of artists who were nearer in spirit to the text than the contemporaries will ever be.

The Last of the *Badchanim* – Shloime Shmulevitz

15 May 1942

Not many of our readers, we imagine, have ever seen, in the flesh, and not as portrayed in an I.J. Singer play, a member of the great and honorable profession of *badchanim*. To this calling there took, in an age and day now past, many of the talented of our people, who failing the educational possibilities which would have converted them into bad poets, contented themselves by improvising, for the joy and delectation of their fellow-Jews, verses which recommended themselves to the listener, if not by their polished style, at least by their untarnished sincerity. Sometimes the *badchan* would serve the melancholy of a single individual, as in the case of Hershel of Ostropol who, for a while, acted as court-jester to Reb Baruch'l of Tulchin; but oftener, the badchanal services would be democratically dispensed, to all and sundry. In

another era, a wedding was no wedding unless the *badchan* would sentimen-
talize the bride in touching couplets, and satirize the wedding-guests in couplets which sought to make a touch.

Alas, this honorable institution is vanishing out of Israel. One of the
last bearers of the tradition of this sodality – a goodly company which once
comprised not only jesters, but folk-singers – is Shloime Shmulevitz, by
himself anglicized into Solomon Small, to-day seventy-five years of age, and
presently sojourning in Montreal. Of course, Mr. Shmulevitz is no longer a
badchan; that he was only in his apprentice-days; to-day, he is the somewhat
substantial personification of the literary taste and spirit of the Jewish masses.
For six decades, he has served as the minnesinger of Israel, the wandering
troubador of Jewry; for six decades, his simple pieces – both words and music
– have expressed the poignant sentimentality of his race, until to-day, many
a humble Jew hums his tunes or quotes his words without knowing that it is
to Shmulevitz that he is indebted. Greater immortality there is for no one
than to have his personal works attributed to folk-creativeness!

Do not my readers remember that piece of music that used to lean against
every Jewish piano, waiting for the daughter of the house to play it, whilst
the gathered relatives would sit in the stuffed upholstery, sighing with pleasure, glowing with pride? Are not the approving *oi-oi*'s recalled? That piece
was 'A Brivele der Mamen' – sure-fire tear-jerker, guaranteed to bring a sob
out of the bosom of any Jewish mother, certified to elicit from an otherwise
unimpressed Jewish father, some wise saw or modern instance. Well, the
'Mame's Brivele' is of the opera of Shloime Shmulevitz!

It would be difficult to explain the vogue and popularity of this verse
by ordinary literary standards. Mr. Shmulevitz will forgive us if we venture
the opinion that he is no Homer. His language and ideas are in verse what
were the language and ideas of Shomer – the housemaids' novelist – in prose.
We assume that the cantorial upbringing of Mr. Shmulevitz stood him in
good stead when he devised for his words, melodies which would catch the
Jewish imagination. They certainly did. Their sobbing, their tremolos, their
saccharine poignancy were just the proper ingredients for an orgy of self-pity.

One must not forget, too, that 'A Brivele der Mamen' – if we may be
permitted to write like a Marxian critic – aptly expressed the need of thousands.
This was the period of great emigration, when many East-European Jewish
families were broken up by the great westward trek of the nineties. A letter
from the adventuresome son in the New World to his waiting mother in the
Old was, indeed, solatium. 'A Brivele der Mamen' wasn't literature; it was
life.

We shall not stop to ask, therefore, touching the poem: Is it Art? It
didn't have to be; and examination of it shows that it wasn't. The Yiddish is
archaic, almost phoney; the ideas are trite and commonplace; but the senti-

ments are real, authentic. It is interesting in this connection to note that Shmulevitz himself was brought up by a step-mother. The feeling for Jewish maternal sentimentality, however, appears to be a national asset. In fact, we believe that the really difficult task is to write a poem about mother which will not be popular. Aye, let someone indite touching verses to one's mother-in-law and we will unhesitatingly proclaim him a poet!

It will be seen from the foregoing that Shmulevitz's forte is sentiment. We know of no man who has a surer finger in plucking at the Jewish heart-strings. A specialist in emotionalism, he has let pass no literary opportunity which might serve to dish up a facile melancholy, an easy pride, an acceptable piety. 'A Brivele der Mamen' proving such a huge success – eight million Jewesses can't be wrong! – he wrote 'A Brivele dem Taten.' As was to be expected, the father-poem was not as successful as mother's. He has written songs about 'Dos Talis'l' and 'Dos Tillem'l' – two symbols of Jewish national identification, made even dearer with diminutives. When Shmulevitz addresses poetic injunction to the Jew, he calls him 'Yid'ele.' In a word, all the para-phernalia of diminutives, nostalgic themes, current philosophy, are utilized to win popularity.

In a poem called 'The Jewish Woman' the opening sentiment announces: 'The Jewish woman is the model of chasteness and of loyalty.' In a poem called 'The Jewish Heart' he declares that 'Not in earlocks, not in beard, is my people shown, but rather in its heart.' We put it to an impartial Jewish jury: Will anyone deny these truisms?

As a true and typical folk-singer, Shmulevitz has also published that most fascinating of the folk-genre – the riddle. These have didactic implica-tions, and both point a moral and, as in his fables, adorn a tale. He has also written many vaudeville skits and playlets. For the masses at large, he has, indeed, served as general literary factotum.

All in all, his work bears the usual characteristics of literature made by the people for the people. It is only the sophisticated who require ingenious tragedies to touch them; the simple are moved by anything that is sad. Where the cultured poet will not begin to sigh in numbers, until he has developed a philosophy concerning his weltschmerz, people's bards, like Shmulevitz, sing of sorrow simply because it is sorrowful. Sometimes, of course, his choice of subject-matter verges on the melodramatic, but when it does, it is in response to something which is definitely melodramatic in the popular consciousness. Thus, for example, Shmulevitz, the dealer in the poignant, would not fail to write of 'The Orphan,' or of that most dreaded of all calamities – the for-lornness of old age. With genial cunning, he uses as theme for his song on this subject, that quotation from the liturgy which prays 'not to be forsaken in one's old age, not to be abandoned at the ebbing of one's strength.'

It is interesting here to compare Shmulevitz with Itzik Manger. Of course, Manger is incomparably the better poet. Shmulevitz, we feel, makes no pretensions to laureateship. But both are greatly influenced by the style of the folk-song, Manger consciously, out of reading, Shmulevitz, unconsciously, because he thinks and sings and writes like an average man. Let us not despise that which has been so aptly called The Divine Average.

The dilettante and aesthete may perhaps scoff at the quality of Shmulevitz's art. Let it be stated here that if it has not the adornments and frills of literary artificiality, it is authentic, real, sincere. It does not soar to any great heights, but on its own level, it walks sure and unfaltering. Upon that level, moreover, it expresses the emotions, the longings, the thoughts, not of salon critics, not of parlor litterateurs, but of the hoi polloi, the people, the masses. Let the nightingale sing for the chosen; the sparrow twitters for all.

Saadyah Gaon   22 May 1942

It is often stated that time is the great destroyer of reputations. It cannot be gainsaid, indeed, that many who in their somatic existence have enjoyed illustrious renown, have subsequently fallen victim to the oblivion which the clock measures out, second after second. To these can be applied the biting epigram which Heinrich Heine once levelled against his enemy Platen: 'He will be immortal – as long as he lives!'

Others there are, however, whose reputations are enhanced by the passing of the centuries. Shakespeare was one of those, Shakespeare who throughout his lifetime was only a very capable theatre-manager, and who after his death, inherited the renown which was justly his. It is ironical that the same phenomenon of 'long-distance appreciation' takes place also with regard to the illustrious in Jewry; only in Jewry it is not a gradually increasing reputation that we witness, but rather a suddenly articulate one, manifesting itself on commemorative occasions.

Thus, several years ago, readers of the Anglo-Jewish press were suddenly made aware that once upon a time – to wit, eight hundred years earlier – there had lived and wrought the great Maimonides. The octocentennial literary celebration had all the ear-marks of a re-discovery. Forgotten was the fact that the influence of Maimonides was exercised day in, day out, throughout those eight centuries. Everybody acted as if they had unearthed a *genizah*.

A similar occurrence is happening to-day with the commemoration of the thousandth anniversary of the death of Saadyah Gaon. How great is the dearth of Jewish knowledge amongst the reading public is evidenced by the fact that all of the authors of the literary paeans and millenial obituaries find themselves compelled to give biographical data concerning their subject. Saadyah Gaon, alas, is not a household word. At best, he is to-day a subject for essays which appear scholarly only because their theme is so esoteric; he is a name, at once outlandish and honorific, but his name, regrettably, does not conjure up any precise concepts.

And yet, no other man has exerted so fundamental an influence upon the course of Jewish philosophic and theological thought as the distinguished *Gaon* of the Academy of Sura. When it is remembered that Jewish life was not always as formless as it is to-day, when it is recalled that up to the French Revolution, and prior to the advent of assimilationism, Jewish culture was something definite and recognizable, and when it is realized that to the thought-processes of this culture Saadyah Gaon had made a vital contribution, the haze about the man is somewhat removed, the outline of his full stature is seen the more clearly.

It is customary to call anyone who introduces radical changes in art or science or philosophy, the 'father of such-and-such a movement.' Saadyah Gaon was a father, in this sense, several times over. He it was who laid the first foundation stones of Hebrew grammar, who compiled a text-book which pioneered through the desert of the Semitic noun, across the triple-peaked mountains of the Hebrew verb. Generations of grammarians were later indebted to him; the *tinnok shel bais rabbon* who conjugates a verb does it the more easily because of Saadyah Gaon.

Born in Egypt, imbued with Mohammedan culture, a master of tongues, Saadyah Gaon could not resist the charms of philology. He compiled a Hebrew dictionary, and – true mark of the scholar – he wrote a treatise on the hapaxlegomena in the Bible – words which appear in the Bible only once, or infrequently, and which Saadyah interpreted by means of Talmudic and Midrashic parallels, calling in, now and again, the aid of Arabic homonyms. At a time when comparative philology was a rarity, this was a most radical, albeit scientific, method.

Nor did Saadyah confine himself to the pedestrian rule of grammar and philology; he was not only scientist, he was also poet. Compiling a *Siddur* – prayer-book – the *Gaon* of Sura could not resist the temptation of including some of his own poetical litanies, written in a style which alternated between the simplicity of biblical utterance, and the complicated turgidity of the *paytanim*.

It is, however, as a man of action, a leader of Jewry, that Saadyah is most accurately estimated. His scholarship was, of course, his mightiest weapon, but it was his position and his character which endowed him with historic importance. The academy of Sura, where once the *Amoraim* uttered the first fine careless raptures of rabbinic Judaism, was in decline. For a while, indeed, it was planned by the Exilarch – *Resh Galutha* – the Prince of Israel, recognized by the Babylonian Government, to remove the scholars of Sura to the twin-seat of Pumbeditha. Fortunately, this was avoided; and the Exilarch, looking about him for a fit occupant of the Gaonate of Sura, had to turn to Egypt thence to invite Saadyah.

The choice was strange only in that appointments to the Gaonate were seldom based on the merits of the respective candidates. By this time, however, Saadyah had won himself an international reputation as a most vigorous opponent of the schism – Karaism – which threatened the integrity of Israel. Against the followers of Anan who would repudiate the whole tradition of Talmudic Judaism, who would destroy in one fell swoop that great edifice built up with so much zeal and care by the *Tannaim* and the *Amoraim*, Saadyah had loosed the full power of his polemic. No one better than he could diagnose the vulnerable spots in the Karaite thesis which sought to live by a literal interpretation of the Torah, and the Torah only. Had it not been for Saadyah, and his followers, Karaism might have assumed the dimensions of a Protestant movement in Israel; as it is, it has, after all these centuries, a following of no more than about 12,000 in Russia. No doubt that number has since been considerably diminished by the Marxian (Karlaite) thesis. It was in connection with his attack upon Karaism that Saadyah wrote his treatise on the Jewish calendar, adding yet another notch to his versatility.

As *Gaon* of Sura, he enhanced the reputation of that academy until that of Pumbeditha appeared, by comparison, a minor lyceum. It was in this office that he demonstrated the true strength of his character. Resisting the Exilarch who sought his co-operation in the passing of an iniquitous judgment, Saadyah was removed from office, and excommunicated. His enforced leave of absence he utilized as but another occasion to develop his philosophy of Judaism.

For Saadyah is the father of rationalism in Jewish theology. The problem which faced him has faced sincere men of all religions in all the ages. 'The world,' as an Arab contemporary of Saadyah said, 'is divided into two classes, those that have intelligence but no belief, those that believe but have no understanding.' It was to show the rational foundation of religion that Saadyah completed in 934 his *Emunoth ve'Deoth*. Here he sought to prove logically the existence of God, the truth of the Torah, the immortality of the soul. We shall not enter here into the nature of these proofs; suffice it to say, that generations of scholars after him lived by the syllogisms of the *Gaon*. Again there was established the dictum of Sir Francis Bacon: 'A little philosophy turneth a man's heart away from religion, but depth of philosophy bringeth him back again!'

Nor have we exhausted the achievements of the man whose life was over at fifty. Three great translations of the Bible there are – the Septuagint into Greek, the translation of Moses Mendelssohn into German, and – the translation of Saadyah into Arabic. No doubt the *Gaon* was motivated in making the translation by the desire to fashion yet another weapon against Karaism – a translation which would at once translate and Talmudize the Torah; the translation has survived its ephemeral design.

This, then, is the type of man whose memory Jewry is to-day delighting to honour. He is conjured up before us as a giant whose strength wrought mightily for us, long after he was gathered to his fathers, a titan of Hebrew thought, a veritable pillar of the *Kneseth Hagdola*. If in praising the memory of Maimonides it has been said that from Moses unto Moses none rose like Moses, in praising the last of the great *Gaonim* of Sura, let it be said: Of Saadyahs there was only one!

Bialik Thou Shouldst Be Living at This Hour

10 July 1942

Eight years ago, there passed from the Jewish scene the poet of the Hebrew national renascence, Chaim Nachman Bialik. For over forty years – the period of his creative life – he had been the tribune of his people. All the pent-up longing for national self-determination which inhered in the Jewish masses for over twenty centuries found expression in his poems; every important crisis in contemporary events evoked from him the sage word, the inspiring counsel. Now, as the whole world stands teetering upon a precipice, now, as the work for which he and his generation strove stands in grave peril, his thundering voice is missed more than ever. 'Bialik, thou shouldst be living at this hour.'

It is true, of course, that during the last decade of his life, Bialik but rarely put poetic pen to paper. Concerned with the diurnal problems of the Yishuv, dedicated to the routine enterprise of Hebrew scholarship, the bard was all too infrequently moved to the larger utterance, the jewelled word upon the forefinger of time. In fact, there was frequently marked in his attitude a certain impatience with his people who demanded of him, at the slightest provocation, 'a poem for the occasion,' as if he was a fashioner of birthday greeting-cards, or a writer of rhymed obituaries. There are, indeed, among his letters several polite little masterpieces refusing requests that he, Bialik, indite for the petitioner some appropriate gravestone inscriptions. One can well imagine the feelings which such epistles evoked in the man whose forte was eternity, not time, and certainly not the incidental.

To-day, however, history has given to the incidental the implications of eternity. A battle won or lost furnishes not only a headline for the day; it supplies also the groundwork for the future. How great, therefore, would be the boon to his people were the mighty organ-voice of Bialik heard above the din of battle! Bialik, thou shouldst be living at this hour!

For ours is not the attitude of Carlyle: 'As to songs so-called, we will talk of that a couple of centuries hence when things are calmer again. Homer shall be thrice welcome, when Troy is taken; alas, while the siege lasts and battle's fury rages, what can I do with Homer?' This is an approach to poesy which is of the essence of effete aestheticism. It implies that the poet is above and beyond the battle, a sort of inspired chronicler who records, but does not participate in the deeds of his fellow-men. Not such is the function of him who bears the name of a poet – the maker. He too is part of the fighting forces, as much so, indeed, as is the trumpeter, marching into the fray.

Hebrew literature has no war poet. Yiddish literature – created in exile – can not be expected to have a war poet. Perhaps some of the psalms of David, to which the old Ironsides of Oliver Cromwell marched into battle, might qualify for that epithet. But certainly none of the bards of the Middle Ages, neither Yehuda Halevi, nor all the nightingales of golden Spain, were adept at the iron ringing words of battle-hymns. Only the virile strength of Bialik showed the potentialities, unexercised, for this genre of writing.

And even the manifestation of this potentiality came with great effort. Sang Bialik in his poem 'Upon the Threshold of the *Beth Ha-Midrash*':

Not fist fights did I teach my arm,
With wine and women did not spend my strength.
To sing the Lord's song, was I born!

From the man who made immortal the sedentary *Mathmid*, no other attitude could be expected. Yet the truth is that the Lord's song may frequently be a battle-hymn, seeing that the Lord is Lord of Hosts.

It was in 'The City of Slaughter,' written after the pogrom in Kishineff, 1905, a pogrom at once characterized by the savagery of its perpetrators and the cowardice of its victims, that Bialik called up all the fighting spirit of his ancestors. The bitter condemnation which he levelled against those who passively submitted to the attackers constitutes one of the noblest pieces of invective in our literature, and reveals in Bialik the warrior spirit for so many centuries disguised in ghetto-rags.

Note also, do not fail to note –
In that dark corner, and behind that cask
Crouched husbands, bridegrooms, brothers, peering from the cracks,
Watching the sacred bodies struggling underneath
The bestial breath,

Stifled in filth, and swallowing their blood!
Watching – these heroes –
The ignominious rabble tasting flesh,
Morsels for Neros.

...

It was the flight of mice they fled,
The scurrying of roaches was their flight;
They died like dogs, and they were dead!
And on the next morn, after the terrible night
The son who was not murdered found
The spurned cadaver of his father on the ground.

The influence of this single poem, written by Bialik both in Hebrew and in Yiddish, cannot be overestimated. It transformed a people in a single generation. Never again thereafter did there occur in Jewish life that 'passive non-cooperation' which disgraced it at Kishineff. The Haganah was formed, and a nation which once trembled in its ghettoes was converted into a proud people, ready to defend the right! This was true of Jewry in Eastern Europe, but truer still of the Yishuv in Eretz Israel which atoned for the Kishineff of the exile by the Tel-Chai's of the Holy Land.

In another of his poems, 'The Song of Israel,' Bialik compares his lot with that of the warrior, much to the credit of the latter. For Bialik was no bespectacled academician, concerned merely with the polishing and re-polishing of words. No one realized better than he that all his creative work would be *vox et praeterea nihil*, if it were not supported by action, if it did not exist within the living fabric of a people fashioning its destiny in its own Homeland. Let the woodman romanticize the lot of the poet; he romanticized the lot of the woodman.

Why do you so besiege my hearth?
What evil have I done, what good?
I am no prophet, no, nor bard.
I am a simple hewer of wood.

At the same time Bialik was vitally concerned with maintaining morale on the home-front. Greater than the ravages of pogroms were the ravages of suicidal assimilation. Against the assimilators – the Vichyards of Jewry, the collaborationists of Israel – he poured out all the phials of his wrath. They constituted the danger from within; and as such were particularly dangerous.

The chastisement of God is this his curse
That you shall your own very hearts deny,

To cast your hallowed tears on foreign waters,
Your tears on luminous false threads to thread,
To breathe your breath in marble alien
And in the heathen stone to sink your soul.

The teeth of the gluttons of your flesh drip blood –
But you shall feed them also your own souls!

So shall you one by one the noblest spurn
And so shall you at last remain bereaved.
Your tent laid waste, and glory fled from your hearth,
Calamity and terror shall be yours.

The hope against these betrayers of their people lies not with the captains and the kings, but with the humble folk. In one of the most masterly of his writings – the Gray's Elegy of Hebrew Literature – Bialik pays tribute to those who, unknown, unsung, preserve the treasures of their race. They it is who, modest and unassuming, are the 'true keepers of God's image upon earth.'

Yea skilled in silence, voiceless, without speech,
Utters your mouth no arrogance, your hand
Fashions no masterpieces, works of pride.
Lonely and echoless your footstep dies.
Howbeit your life, the simple days of your life –
Behold the vision superb, the work of art,
Ye keepers of God's image upon earth!

What Bialik was capable of in moments of crisis may be gleaned from his poem 'La-Mithnadvim Ba'Am.' It is a call to battle, and a call even to those who are weaponless, and loaded with defeats. How timely it is now, as our cause is the victim of so many reverses. It was an Irishman – between the Hebrew Renascence and the Celtic Revival there are many parallels – who wrote the great lines of hope for the defeated.

Their wreaths are willows, and their tribute, tears.
Their names are old sad stories in men's ears.
Yet will they scatter the red hordes of Hell
Who went to battle forth and always fell!

The complement to this spirit is that of Chaim Nachman Bialik.

And we, much enfeebled, and ground in the dust,

Let us beat on the hearts of our sons with our clamor!
Let the word of our God be our hope and our trust,
And our God be our thundering hammer!
Not yet have we squandered all strength in the fight;
The Lord is our might!

Saul Tchernichovsky   20 October 1943

With the passing, at the age of sixty-eight, of Saul Tchernichovsky, Hebrew literature loses yet another of the giants of its renaissance. Always considered together with the late Chaim Nachman Bialik, as of the twin-titans of Hebrew letters, he complemented in his writings the great national achievement of Bialik. While the latter spoke in tones definitely Hebraic and of themes indubitably semitic, Tchernichovsky's muse was much more native to Parnassus and to the secular subject; Tchernichovsky opened for Hebrew literature a window onto Europe. He did this, not only by translating into the Holy Tongue the *Odyssey* of Homer, the *Odes* of Anacreon, the writings of the European classics, and the Finnish epic *Kalevala*; he introduced into his own verse a spirit hitherto unfelt – and indeed taboo – in Hebrew writing, the pagan call, the love of beauty for mere beauty's sake, the heritage of old Hellas.

Thus his nature poems were real and authentic; they were not, as were those of his predecessors, vicarious appreciations of beauty, the longings of a *Yeshiva-bochur* seeking the occasion to utter a benediction. His love poems were in the great tradition, love poems unparalleled since the days when Yehuda Halevi permitted himself to be unrabbinical. More important than any of these innovations, however, was the heroic spirit which was the almost constant object of his praise. Handicapped by no ghetto-memories, cosmopolite in his travels, and completely at home in the literatures of the world, he rebelled against the melancholy, self-pitying, almost masochistic accents of Hebrew threnody. He sang, not of victims, but of heroes. He sang of Bar Kochba; and where Bialik wrote the self-flagellating 'City of Slaughter,' he wrote of the Rabbi of Mayence and of his defiance. Not specifically patriotic in his verse – he did not write national anthems – his love for the Yishuv expressed itself in the most cherished of his creations. He was, in fact, a completed figure, a Jew, a man, and a poet! It will be long before we shall look upon his like again.

The Thirteenth Apostle?   18 February 1944

From the excited and excitable comments and editorials which have recently made hectic the Yiddish dailies, it would seem, to the naive observer, as if all of Jewry were going mad with surmising the mysterious meaning of the interview which Sholem Asch some time ago accorded the editor of *The Christian Herald*. Most of the commentators, it is only fair to say, admit not having read the actual report of Asch's presumably papal audience; they do, however, manage to work up a dangerously high blood pressure at some of the second-hand quotations gleaned here and there from that unfortunate report. When it is realized, moreover, that the original interview which was given without the advantage of Maurice Samuel's usual translation must itself have been somewhat of a second-hand affair, one can understand the universal bewilderment at the garbled and cryptic excerpts. No doubt, too, Asch's oracular manner – is he not a sort of retroactive John the Baptist? – added to the general confusion.

Out of this chaos, one was able to gather only that Sholem Asch had given a statement to *The Christian Herald*; that therein he had stated that ever since he remembered he was attracted by the personality of Jesus, that even his earlier works were a kind of preparation to his awed approach to *The Nazarene*, and that one of the objects he had in view in writing his testamentary novels was to breach the gap between Judaism and Christianity. He also stated that no other religious leader – and he named them, but did not name Moses except by general inclusion – was as significant as Jesus was to the world of to-day. At first, moreover, it was reported that Asch had indicated an admiration of Christ, both as the Son of God, and as the son of man. In a subsequent letter addressed to *The Christian Herald*, Asch declared that he was misunderstood and quoted himself as saying: 'Regardless of our attitude toward Jesus as the Son of God, if we only regard him as the son of man he still has exerted the most vital influence on mankind. I never mentioned the words "Son of God" ... Every other of my expressions in the interview on the role of Jesus and his importance still stands.'

Hinc illae lachrymae – hence this weeping and wailing in the Yiddish press, this donning of sackcloth over the supposedly imminent sprinkling of Asch. Frankly, the entire affair seems to us to be no more than a tempest in a baptismal font. In the first place, we find it difficult to understand the motivation of these men so suddenly become defenders of the faith, men who for the most part are self-confessing agnostics and non-observers. In the second place, we fail to see any intimations of apostasy in the pronouncements of Sholem Asch. And in the third place, who's worried about it?

Of what grave concern is it to anybody if Sholem Asch indulges in a bit of poeticising about a religion some aspects of which seem to please him? We can regret, it is true, the fact that Asch who took so much pains to study up on all the orgiastic practices of pagan Asia Minor, did not take the trouble to discover that all of the fine ethical teachings of Christianity are already adumbrated in the Talmud and in the Sayings of the Fathers. But there is no great calamity there; the world is full of uninstructed people. We can regret, too, that Asch did not find it necessary to say a word about how Christians observe their own Christianity especially in their relationship with Jews; but after all, Asch could not say everything. Besides, one must not forget that the interview was intended for a publication which heralds Christianity, and not one which specifically analyzes some of the practices of its votaries.

We believe that the real motive for the hue and cry against our novelist was the fact that he, a Jew, gave himself over to the writing of books which in certain quarters are considered as proselytizing. We do not think that this accusation will stand; not even Asch has enough talent for that. Insofar as we are concerned, the story which he tells in *The Nazarene* and *The Apostle* has already been much better told by the authors of his sources, the authors of the New Testament. In the writing of Asch, one will look in vain for those creative insights which characterize the biblic works of Thomas Mann. One finds merely a detailed scenario of incidents already revealed in the gospels, the whole ornamented with picturesque props erected in the best Hollywood manner. We read it, and do wonder at the motivation of a Yiddish author whose books first see the light of day in English translation; but we do not tremble at the possibility that the Jewish circulation is going to make a dash toward conversion.

Nor is there any likelihood that the Jewish soul of Asch himself was at any time in spiritual jeopardy. After all, Asch is just a writer trying to get along ... To treat of the personality of Jesus has always been a guaranteed assurance of rising to the best-seller class. The original has been a best seller for generations. Ernest Renan, Giovanni Papini, Emil Ludwig, all have approached this sacred subject and have not lost by it. So why begrudge Asch his share of the royalties? It seems that Jews just can't tolerate another Jew his hard-earned *parnassah*.

Accordingly, we do not think that, even for the future, Asch is in any danger of forsaking his Judaism, such as it is. A shrewd man, he no doubt realizes that one of the most attractive features of his latter-day gospels, at least to his royalty-providing non-Jewish readers, is the fact that they are written by a Jew. Let him become a Christian; and the wonder, together with the circulation, ceases. Is it likely that he will willingly allow himself to become also materially bankrupt? After all, there are still eleven apostles to write about. And what are post-war plans for, anyway?

It is, of course, true that Sholem Asch has not deigned to answer categorically the questions put to him by the Yiddish press. One still does not know, even at this late hour, exactly where he stands. In his telegram to Dr. Polling of *The Christian Herald*, he says, 'Christianity can no more be analyzed than Judaism. As a matter of fact, no faith can be analyzed.' In the light of this statement one is left wondering as to what the two hefty volumes, *The Nazarene* and *The Apostle*, really were about. But no matter; we know he did not write them for spiritual analysis, but for material synthesis. 'You either accept a faith or you reject it. I will not let either side provoke me into something I do not believe. If I would feel like making a profession I would choose my own time and definition.'

So, what is he? One can hardly blame Asch's co-religionists, co-religionists at least at this time and by present definition, for being totally at a loss before these sphinx-like utterances. This kind of answer is surely not according to the teachings of Christ who bade all his admirers answer either yea or nay, and not do as the Pharisees do. If, therefore, some injustice has been done to Asch by the querulous scribes of the Yiddish press, he has only himself to blame.

As for the scribes themselves, we do think that they manifest a deplorable inferiority complex in getting so troubled about Asch's semi-pseudo-quasi-defection. This is a free country, and a man can worship whatever gods he pleases. Should Asch do that which he is suspected of wanting to do, the loss is his, not ours. Nor would it even be a gain to those who won him over. In this connection we cannot forget the report of the Jerusalem Missionary Society which announced to its supporters that it cost approximately one thousand dollars to win over one convert – and even then you can't trust him.

Our writers, we believe, would be well advised, for the sake of their own dignity and for the general interest, to record these ephemeral incidents, not in their headlines, but in their agony columns. The spiritual meanderings of Sholem Asch are a purely personal affair, and certainly have neither historic nor religious significance. And if Asch's utterances and interviews are iniquitous, why, we all knew Asch when he had a God of Vengeance, and where he kept Him.

Palestine Moving-Pictures   9 February 1945

It is a far cry from the usual idyllic associations of Eretz Israel to the evocations which are conjured up by the moving-picture industry; nonetheless, it is with exultation that we herald the establishment of the first cinema company in Palestine, with headquarters at Nathania – Hollywood in Holy Land.

It is a rejoicing which is born of many factors. In the first place, the creation of any new industry in Palestine is an occasion for satisfaction. When it is further remembered that Palestine is located upon the crossroads between the East and the West, and when it is further realized that the moving-picture industry is one of the most powerful instruments of education yet developed, the Nathania enterprise certainly appears as a consummation greatly to be desired.

And there is yet another cause for rejoicing. The Jew as is depicted in the contemporary film, is hardly the creature whose image we would like to set up as typical exemplar. Despite the fact that Hollywood is reportedly under the control of Jewish tycoons, the Jew whom these worthies cast upon the scene is hardly a personage of heroic proportions. Invariably the Jew is pictured as an object of commiseration. It is quite true that the motive behind this kind of casting is an honorable one; the intention is to supply, through the medium of a single emotion – pity – a counteragent to current antisemitism. But our people is ill served if it is to be shown forever in this wretched light. There are also positive things in our history, as in our biographies, which deserve the narrative treatment of this film. Cinema entirely devoted to apologetics – even an Aristotelian apologetics which presumably purges with pity and with terror – becomes, at last, embarrassing even to those whom it is defending.

Certainly the air of Palestine would elicit a different concept of the Jew. Our heroes and our saints remain yet to be flashed upon the screen. The virile glories of our past, our warriors and our poets – in place of our victims and our scapegoats – will give the world totally a different impression of our qualities and our achievement. We are thankful that the MGM lion occasionally yawns over Israel's plight; but the lion of Judah, in Nathania laired, would, we believe, really roar.

Had Not Thy Torah Been My Delight ...

Review of *From the Nazi Vale of Tears* [in Yiddish] by Pinchos
Hirshprung   22 June 1945

One has only to look through the table of contents of Leo Schwarz's *Memoirs
of My People* to see how often during the troubled annals of our people, Jews
who under ordinary circumstances would either have scorned or been fearful
of the literary art, were prompted by the compulsion of contemporary event
to set down in writing the record of their suffering. Some commemorated the
trouble they had seen in memoirs; others in Responsa; others again in poems
destined to enter our liturgy. And this tradition, like the suffering which is
its cause, has not ceased. The latest to observe it is Rabbi Pinchos Hirshprung,
presently of Montreal, a scholar of so proverbial an erudition that there is no
doubt but that he would have preferred to devote his energies to writing
treatises Talmudic, a man of so sensitive a nature that he could not pass by
unrecorded the historic convulsions which he beheld and of which he himself
was victim.

   We are grateful that he did so; without literary frills or aesthetic ges-
turings, Rabbi Hirshprung tells simply and with not an inconsiderable power
the story of the Nazi occupation of Poland, that is to say, of his own home-
town, Ducla, of his flight from the German murderers, of his wanderings
upon the face of the earth, of his refuge in Japan, and of his final sanctuary
in Canada. In the details of the narrative, of course, the unhappy saga is no
different from that which can be told by thousands of our uprooted brethren;
it is the manner of the telling, however, which is as distinguished as it is
engrossing. For here a cultured and learned mind is focussed upon events of
the deepest significance, and here, above all, is a mood, an attitude, a piety
and faith that has not been found in Jewish secular writing for over a century.
While Rabbi Hirshprung describes with great effectiveness, because without
hysteria or hyperbole, the might and menace of the Nazi war-machine, he
continually makes it clear, by direct statement, by implication, by tone, that
he is not utterly abashed, that the people which has survived other persecution
will survive also this. The book, although replete with biblic verse and Talmudic parable, is not intended as a religious book; we doubt, however, whether
the religious attitude could be better illustrated than by the undeviating faith
which shines from its pages, by the holy piety which glows even from the
filth and agony of a Nazi forced-labour camp.

   Indeed, the writer brings us in contact with an atmosphere – once part of our tradition – which these many years has been singularly absent from the American-Jewish scene. It does not take much shrewdness to see why German Jewry crumbled – in a spiritual sense – so miserably before the onslaught of the Nazis, and why Polish Jewry – even to the last mortal quiver – knew itself superior to its taskmasters. Polish Jewry had intellectual and spiritual resources to fall back upon. Thus, Rabbi Hirshprung, when he describes the manner in which the Nazi ruffians shaved off the beards of Jews – half a beard off one, a mustache off another – does not write as if he beheld the end of the world. He recalls that Haman, too, was a barber, and that such tonsorial activities are to be expected from the seed of Amalek. Indeed, in none of his trials and tribulations is he unaccompanied by the faith and strength with which his heritage endows him. Leaders of Jewry in other ages, too, he remembers, were wont to meditate the Law even in the very act of flight.

This spirit of piety, re-enforced by a Yiddish vocabulary which has passed from contemporary writing but which can still be found in Yiddish prayers and in Chassidic tales, pervades the entire volume. Certainly subsequent event has justified it. Certainly the autobiographical excursion of Rabbi Hirshprung is in full harmony with the quotation from the Psalms with which he heads one of his chapters: *Had not Thy Torah been my delight, I should have perished in mine affliction.*

We have no doubt but that this volume will constitute source material for the future historian. Its reading, however, should not be postponed until such use; it should be read now, read for its masterful simplicity, its authentic unassuming honesty, its spirit of trust and devotion which shines like a Sabbath candle upon a naughty world.

Some Praise the Lord – Some Pass the Ammunition

Review of the *Sabbath Prayer Book* published by the Jewish
Reconstructionist Foundation   6 July 1945

We are really at a loss as to what standards to apply in reviewing a prayerbook. Shall the work be judged by purely aesthetic criteria? A prayerbook is certainly not a mere exercise in art for art's sake. Here, as nowhere else, handsome is as handsome does. Shall it be judged, then, for efficacy? Surely that is only for the Addressee to determine. Whether a prayer is to find favor in the sight of the Lord can be established only empirically. For ourselves, we refuse to surmise the reactions of Divinity.

Reviewing the prayerbook, edited by Rabbi Mordecai M. Kaplan and

Eugene Kohn, who were assisted by Rabbi Ira Eisenstein and Milton Steinberg, is further complicated by the recent history of the book. *Habent sua fata libelli.* Meeting in macabre conclave at the Hotel McAlpin, the Union of Orthodox Rabbis, using full horrific paraphernalia, pronounced against this volume and its editors, their dire anathema and excommunication. A young zealot, moreover, put the prayerbook to the fire – a burnt offering, no doubt. Amidst such smoke and brimstone, the work has been too much confused with its uncalled-for aftermath.

To us, it would seem, that this prayerbook should be judged – the standard is one which all books of piety attribute to God Himself and recommend for human emulation – should be judged by the intentions of the editors. Of their intentions, the editors were not at all reticent. They wanted to publish a prayerbook for modern use. In Hebrew and in English, it was to be based on the traditional exemplars of Saadyah and Amram, but, in order 'to retain the continuity of Judaism and at the same time satisfy the spiritual demands of our day, it was necessary to make changes in its contents.' Some of these changes consist of additions; David Frishman, Bialik, Hillel Zeitlin, and even Tagore (because Rabbin Dranath?) thus enter the liturgic canon. Also there are the controversial omissions; from the traditional prayers there are deleted all references to what the editors call 'the doctrine of the Chosen People,' 'the doctrine of the personal Messiah,' 'the doctrine of retribution,' and 'the doctrine of resurrection.' Against the Thirteen Principles of Maimonides, therefore, much havoc; that orthodox rabbis would not approve of this prayerbook was a foregone conclusion.

Accepting for the purposes of this review the premises upon which the Editors have based their compilation, their amendments, it seems to us, were in many instances unwarranted, the result of underestimating the average worshipper's appreciation of metaphoric language, and in many instances not thorough and consistent. On page 39, for example, the Editors, despite their repudiation of the doctrine of the Chosen People, still preserve in the accepted rendition of *Emes v'Emunah*: 'He is the Lord our God and none beside Him, and we Israel are His people.' The unity of God and the uniqueness of Israel are thus admitted as a parallel concept. Again on page 48, the Lord is praised for 'restoring His presence to Zion,' with the clear implication that that is His *chef-lieu*. Further, in the supplement, on pages 446 *et seq.*, the Editors compile a little anthology of rabbinic literature which emphasizes, again and again, at least the corollaries of the Chosen People doctrine. To us, moreover, the assertion that the Jews were the first to choose the Torah does not seem as reprehensible as the Editors would make it appear; we have yet to see a Jew, at least of those living in the Diaspora, misled by it into a spirit of arrogance and vainglory.

The Editors' treatment of the doctrine of resurrection also appears to have been subject to latent and unconscious inhibitions. From the Eighteen Benedictions they omit the *m'chayeh maisim*; why, then, do they preserve *u'mkayim emunosoi leeshainae ofor*: 'Thou keepest faith with those who sleep in the dust'? What faith, if not that of the resurrection? The concept of immortality, the Editors are careful to state in their introduction, is not denied; it must, however, be understood in a modern sense. Why cannot the same saving grace be argued for that of resurrection?

As for the quarrel with the belief in a personal Messiah, that leads the Editors to some drastic and, to our mind, heavy-handed revision. Even the *L'Chu N'ran'nah* does not emerge unscathed; both poetic allusions to the House of David are ruthlessly deleted. To this end, too, *Uva l'Zion* is gallantly mistranslated to read, in the English version, as saying that God will come as a redeemer.

With reference to the doctrine of retribution, in its various forms, the Editors, we feel, were much too finicky. There does not seem to us, again admitting the book's premises, any good reason for ejecting from the prayers (p. 40) *hamshalaim gmul l'chol oivai nafshainu*, a request that our enemies be rewarded for their hate. That the expectoration in *Aleinu* is out, together with the pertinent or impertinent verses, is all to the good; but that has been done before. At the same time it is beyond our comprehension why so honest and forthright a litany as *Elohai, n'tzor l'shoini* should be banished from the *Amidah*. Indeed, after all of these deletions and amendments, we wonder how Zangwill's translation of *Yigdal* (p. 68) still came to be included:

> The Law God gave He never will amend,
> Nor ever by another Law replace.

The true failing of the book, we think, lies in the fact that its Editors approached their work with metaphysics instead of with imagination. Many of the prayers read like pedestrian editorials; poems intended to raise the soul to religious ecstasy are full of a drab jargon where words such as 'proper perspective,' 'latent,' 'energy' compete for precision and flatness. O for a spate of Isaiah, a flight of Jeremy Taylor! The wonderful and picturesque *Maariv* benediction is 'interpreted' by a paragraph in which the following sentence is typical: 'The day with its light calls to activity and exertion.' Such language cannot exalt, and there is no worship without exaltation.

No doubt this characteristic arises out of the exaggerated fear entertained by the Editors lest the classic prayers be understood too literally. In this the Editors wrong not only their contemporaries but also their ancestors who first made poetry out of the simile and morals out of the parable. Indeed there is altogether too much insistence in the motif of this prayerbook upon a scientific literalness; the color and fancy of ordinary ritual language is everywhere reduced to a dry and prosaic equation. Yet a prayerbook without a *mystique* is a contradiction in terms. The truth, indeed, is that litanies are made by poets, not logicians; all compilers of *siddurim*, including the present ones, have felt this to be so; hence the preponderance of psalms in their books of synagogal service.

The Editors have also underestimated, we feel, the proleptic value of tradition. This is all the more surprising when one recalls that these men, the leaders of the Reconstructionist Movement, have more than others labored valiantly for the preservation of all that is good, true, and beautiful in that tradition. Now, the doctrines they discard are traditional; we believe this to be an error, for traditions, we think, though scientifically untenable can still be retained as evidences of that continuity of which the Editors speak in their introduction. Indeed, though they may lose, with the passage of time, a great deal of their validity, with the passage of time they indubitably take on new meanings and a richer color. Such, indeed, is the Protean potency of tradition, which, after all, is the first premise of organized worship. For communion with God can be had privately and *b'lachash*; its organization is a tribute to accepted custom. That the Editors sensed this necessity to make their obeisance to tradition is evident from the inclusion of prayers (p. 188) 'In Remembrance of Ancient Temple Service' and of concepts 'As Conceived by the Ancients.' Yet are not all the debated doctrines concepts 'As Conceived by the Ancients'?

Having said all this it is still necessary to repudiate as mediaeval and unworthy the act of the frenzied fanatics who organized a special Jewish 'burning of the book.' The fact is that no other group in American Jewry has, during the last two decades, evidenced a greater concern for the future of Judaism than have the Reconstructionists. No others have given so much sincere thought to the survival of 'our way of life.' Under the direct inspiration of Rabbi Kaplan, a great Jew and a noble man, an entire generation of communal leaders and rabbis (not of the arsonical type) has been brought up. Where others have made of Torah a crown for ornamental or an axe for pragmatic uses, here service has truly been *lishmo*. The prayerbook is an honest effort; it is motivated clearly by a desire 'to retain the continuity of Judaism and at the same time, to satisfy the spiritual needs of our day'; would that others would take for their own these lofty standards! Not content to stand by and see the condition of inertia and vacuity which prevails in American Jewish life, these Editors thought to devise something which would speak to hearts hitherto untouched. We do not think they have succeeded, but, at least, like the muezzin, they declared prayer better than sleep ...

Most of Jewry, we believe, has been deeply pained by the goings-on at the McAlpin. When one recalls that touching the order of the prayers, or even their content, there is nothing sacrosanct – Rabbi Judah boasted that he recited prayers only once in thirty days – and when one realizes that the burned book was all of psalms and Torah compact – the deletions, after all, could not be burned – the proceedings of the *sanhedrin* would-be *katlonith*, are shocking in the extreme. Not thus should honest intention and true labor in the vineyard of Israel be rewarded.

> He prayeth best who loveth best
> All things both great and small,
> For the dear God who loveth us
> He made and loveth all.

And if the credo of Coleridge is too universal or too foreign to be authority to the excommunicating ones, there is always the lore of the Baal Shem Tov who said that it was immaterial to the Lord whether the Hebrew of His worshippers was syntactically or even phonetically correct; for the Lord sat above, and caught the ascending letters of the alphabet and Himself arranged them according to the desire of the heart whence they issued.

The Snows of Yesteryear

Review of *My Lexicon* [in Yiddish] by Melech Ravitch

5 October 1945

The title of this book is somewhat deceiving; it is not, as might be suspected from its name alone, a dictionary; it is – and Mr. Ravitch has precedents in Yiddish literature for this use of the word 'lexicon,' as for example 'Reisin's Lexicon' – a series of personal sketches describing the ambitions, achievements, and eccentricities of the 'Jewish writers, novelists, poets, and dramatists' who flourished (*sic*) in Poland during the quarter of a century between the two wars. Because Mr. Ravitch is not writing a formal Dictionary of National Biography but only a number of intimate *esquisses* – indeed each item is half biography and half autobiography – he calls his work *My* Lexicon. It is this adjective, at once possessive and descriptive, which sets the tone to the volume.

For the volume is, above all things, a personal one, and no one, it must be said, is better fitted to act as the unofficial biographer, herald, critic, raconteur, and anecdote-purveyor of this period in Jewish literature than Melech Ravitch, who throughout his writing lifetime has ever been in contact with all those who take to the pen, for mortality or immortality's sake. Indeed of Ravitch's relation to Yiddish letters it may be said that whenever he is not fulfilling a creative task, he is at least performing an administrative function, and often, in truth, both simultaneously. It was inevitable, therefore, that his sketches of his contemporaries should be characterized not only by the narrative third-person but also by the spectatorial first; for of many movements in Yiddish writing Ravitch can with justice say: *Magna pars fui.*

It is a most interesting, and oft-times, pathetic collection of worthies that Ravitch gathers together in his own 'Lives of the Poets.' As the subjects pass, 'like sheep beneath the shepherd's staff,' one gets a triple impression of the kind of life led by the writers of this inter-bellum period, a life characterized for the most part, by a crushing poverty, by a universal desire for immortality, and by the not unentertaining incidents of literary rivalry. Ravitch himself well indicates the prevailing mood of these days of hectic high seriousness; the atmosphere was one, he says, 'of cigarette smoke, kettle-vapours, gossip, peeling walls, and vanity.' Thus we meet with the poet who takes poison because of an unfavorable review, or the Job-like writer, Beinish Silberstein, 'to whom every thing happens,' or the character who never forgave Ravitch for daring to say that Tolstoy was his superior. The great economic stress under which writers living in Warsaw labored is manifest almost on every page, manifest both in the description of the miserable habitats in which poets wrote about life, love, and the eternal verities, and in the almost pervasive envy and denigration which another's financial success evoked.

And yet the penury was characterized by a kind of inexpensive bohemianism. Almost every one of the writers mentioned by Ravitch felt certain that he cherished in his bosom the masterpiece which would storm the world, and many of them were men of undoubted talent and genius. In such an atmosphere where each participant took himself very seriously indeed, and yet beheld himself cabin'd and confined by extrinsic limitations, eccentricity must flourish. It is upon these eccentricities that Mr. Ravitch dwells, at great length; it could not be otherwise; the author makes clear that he is not writing either literary criticism or formal biography, but *caractères* of the men as he knew them. Travelling with Ravitch, therefore, we meet with the author who reads poetry to a *Gemara*-intonation, with the writer who grandly orders a cab and orders the cabman to travel 'in the direction of the wind,' and with the meticulous scribe who in speaking enunciates even the commas and semi-colons of his sentences. They are all very amusing; one leafs the pages of Ravitch's book with a sense of being entertained by a strange company of wits, poets, and eccentrics.

And then, suddenly, one shudders. Ravitch, one realizes, has been writing these sketches over a number of years, he publishes them in the last year of the war, and so many of the biographical notes end with the curt remark: *Killed in the Warsaw Ghetto*, or *Present Whereabouts Unknown*. And here they are in the pages of the book, cracking their jokes, planning their plans for fame and immortality! It is as if one were looking at a photograph of an airman, as one has so often looked, smiling, zestful, his youth and his happiness shining from his eyes, and then one reads the caption: *Killed in Action*, or *Reported Missing*. When it is realized that these missing persons in Ravitch's book constituted the literary elite of a generation, and that there are so many, so many of them, and we see them under Ravitch's photography, smiling and zestful, the effect is macabre. The tragedy of Polish Jewry, like something deranged, laughs and weeps at the same time.

It is a long *Ubi Sunt* which Mr. Ravitch has compiled, the PEN club secretary calling across ocean and a continent for his membership, for his lost brotherhood. How poignant are the amusing memories in the light of the bitter present! A generation full of hope and promise, of talent and creative will, – frustrated by the Polish economy, and by the German murder-machine, dispersed or liquidated! The snows of yesteryear are melted, only the mud of Maidanek shows ...

At the risk of incurring the wrath of Chaim Lieberman, who it appears, objects, like a prophet, to any discussion of the Jewish tragedy which concerns itself also with literary standards – that, says Lieberman, constitutes getting pleasure out of the tragedy – we add a note about Mr. Ravitch's biographical style. It is a style admirably suited to its purpose, the style of causerie; informal, urbane, at times almost gossipy, Ravitch moves from portrait to portrait. Sometimes he makes a background for an oil, sometimes, as in the case of the writer who looked like Gandhi, he does a cartoon. His informed style, indeed, sometimes drives him to do things which we are sure he would not otherwise do, such as punning on the names of the subjects he discusses (pp. 35, 74, 87, etc.). It is the same mood which persuades Ravitch to recount facts which have just that grain of malice necessary for good gossip, e.g., the anecdote on p. 170, the birth-calculations on p. 139, the wife 'who is much older than her husband,' on p. 176, and the writer who failed to acknowledge the receipt of his (Ravitch's) complimentary volume. As Ravitch says in his third-person biography of himself, he is not naif, far from naif. It must be admitted, however, that every time Ravitch does anything like that, he apologizes in the preceding paragraph.

The sketches, in addition to intimate revelations of fact provided by the curriculum vitae of the subject, also contain illuminating touches provided by the literary skill of the biographer. Thus Ravitch referring to a fastidious craftsman, declares that he polished his work so often 'that it broke, so thin did it become through polishing.' 'To emigrate a second time,' says Ravitch elsewhere, 'is like going on a second honeymoon with a first wife.' Of Oletski – 'his brows wrinkled, like water just before freezing.' And of the cemetery – 'the only garden in the Warsaw ghetto.'

We unqualifiedly recommend this book not only to those who are interested in the history of Yiddish literature – to which it constitutes a notable contribution – but also to those who would view a slice of Polish-Jewish life during the Pilsudski-Beck period. For Ravitch's *Lexicon* is at once a dictionary of biography, a literary *tour de force*, and a social document.

The Poetry Which Is Prayer

Review of *Lider un Loiben* [in Yiddish] by J.I. Segal

2 November 1945

It will not take the reader long to realize that this new volume of Segal's – five hundred pages chockful of piety – Segal is no compiler of slim volumes – is really a continuously personal and consistently lyrical *Siddur*. Its very title, if one has regard to etymologies, may be rendered as *Songs and Psalms*, and its contents fully justify the designation. The piety, it must be stated forthwith, is not of the orthodox or ceremonial kind; Segal's relationship to his God is much more intimate and much less formal. In this, he is the true heir, both lineal and intellectual, of a beloved tradition of our people, the tradition of the Berditchever, who dared to bring a law-suit against Divinity, the tradition of that host of rabbis, stemming from the Baal Shem Tov, who considered themselves as always on talking-terms, indeed, on theeing and thouing terms, with God.

Much of the pathos of Segal's volume arises out of his awareness that that tradition, as a reality, is a thing of the past. If the epithet did not have intrusive connotations, we would be inclined to call Segal the last of the Mohicans; as it is, he is both by birth and function, the last of the Cohens, the latest of the Chosen Ones – a latter-day son of the Aaronides still serving at the altar. And it is out of the comparison between the glory that was Koretz and the drabness that is the contemporary scene that there arises that nostalgia that palpitates on every page. Indeed, in a poem (p. 14) called 'Yoirdim – those who have fallen on evil days,' he cannot resist a personal utterance of his reaction to this contrast. Addressing his brothers, he says that it is only their shadows today that do give them the respectful nod of yore.

But it is not for the prerogatives of his heritage that he longs. It is that beautiful way of life represented by the Chassidic milieu – a beauty intrinsically involved with the beautiful associations of childhood, which, seeing that it is gone, and its values discarded, gives his heart its pain. When it is realized, as his poems amply realize, that that way of life is vanished, not only by the ravages of time, but by the horrific destruction of the evil which usurped the world for a decade, that pain reaches the degrees of agony.

Yet, singularly enough, this book of Segal's is pervaded by a sense of resignation. Unlike Job, he never blasphemes the Lord; at worst, he merely taunts Him. And even the taunting is of the tradition, a sort of *broigez*-dance, of which everybody knows the conclusion. Even the doves on page 46 coo the necessity of faith. He accepts; and continues his quiet murmuring about the world's woe, and the woe of Thy people Israel.

For the truth is that these poems establish between Segal and the Lord whom he professes to take to task so intimate and involved a relationship, that *volens-nolens*, Segal becomes the protagonist of the Lord's standards. If a *Lamed Vovnik* were, by definition, endowed with talent and not only with saintliness, he would write as Segal writes. For Segal is the praiser of all helpless things; he identifies himself with the poor, and even with the un-instructed; the old Jewesses who go to market are his kith and kin, spiritually as well as genealogically; and the sucklings of the kindergarten, learning the first difficulties of the *aleph-bais*, are his special wards. With the downtrodden, the persecuted, the cheated and the crippled, Segal makes common cause; he offers prayers for them, for them he argues at the Heavenly Throne; he brings them consolation.

A comparison with Francis Jammes, as a poet, or with Francis of Assisi, as a lover of the spurned and rejected, would be tempting, were it not so unnecessary to go outside of the Jewish tradition to find the mainsprings of the categorical imperatives which Segal translates into poetry of the subtlest and most touching kind. In the first place, to Segal the Bible is no mere text to be used in a theological seminary; it is a daily *vade mecum*, important not so much for its definite doctrine, but as a family *pinkos*, a diary kept by grandfathers, and discovered in a later day. That diary Segal lives; in speaking of his old home, Segal actually biblicizes the Ukraine. And even the streets of Montreal, under his description, emerge as alleys that run to the *Me'oras Hamachpelah*. And of course, continuous and ubiquitous in his poetry is the heritage of the Chassidic milieu for whose simple and sincere mores he en-tertains an ineradicable nostalgia.

Both in his theme, and in his handling of it, Segal is unique in Yiddish literature. No other contemporary poet has developed so authentically Yiddish a muse – it is not the muse of Mani Leib, which is essentially Slavic, nor that of the late Moishe Leib Halpern, which was much worldlier, nor of the Russian Yiddish poets, who show perhaps a wider scope, but certainly a thinner in-tensity. It is rather the poetry which might have been that of the Bratzlaver, if the Bratzlaver had spoken verse instead of prose.

An Anglo-Jewish periodical is hardly the place for an excursus upon Segal's use of the Yiddish language, but so great and masterly is this poet's control over his idiom that one cannot resist the invitation which the subject seems so insistently to extend. It will be noted forthwith, that Segal's Yiddish is by no means a 'literary' one; rather is it of the vernacular of our speech, which under Segal's touch becomes perfectly adaptable to his theme. Here are words taken out of the prayerbooks of the daughters of Israel, yet are they not maudlin, but pious and chaste, like white doves resting on the eaves of synagogues as falls the Friday dusk. Here are words drawn from the Hebrew liturgy – yet consider the miracle that has transpired – the Hebrew words do not Hebraize the text, the Hebrew words are themselves Yiddishized! The result is that the Hebrew has lost nothing of its original sacred connotations; the garments of the High Priest are still apparent, but it is now of a high priest who mingles with the folk. A 'Shir Ha-shirim which doth belong to Yiddish' is the title of one of Segal's poems, and it is a key to his approach to our oldest bilingualism. Thus it is that Segal can speak of the 'bnai farnem,' a composite which shows what a wonderful matchmaker of linguistic shid-duchim Segal is; and thus it is that Segal sees nothing incongruous, indeed, sees something specially effective in rhyming the good Talmudic word traklin with Brooklyn!

We are informed, as we write these lines, that the poet J.I. Segal has just been awarded the Louis Lamed Prize. This is an award which is given annually to the year's most distinguished works in Hebrew and in Yiddish. In a sense, Segal's volume Lider un Loiben was therefore entitled to the award on two counts. Segal is entitled to this distinction, moreover, not only for the present volume, but for the general corpus of his work, which has been consistently characterized by both the mood and the sincerity of the present one.

We are conscious of the fact that we have quoted but little of Segal's text. It is easier to quote from a volume of fifty pages than from one of five hundred. Perhaps the following lines, typical of both the themes and mood of Segal's poems, may convey in rough translation, some notion of the spirit of Lider un Loiben:

Speak to your people, therefore, in this wise:
To bear your burden, and to share your grief;
Make parables in your twilit synagogues;
Weave there your legends of most pure belief.

To ignore your tatters – the shoes polished –
Intent only upon your brilliancies;
In your humblest see Akiva, and in
Your loneliest a saint to recognize;

To reconcile myself to your low estate;
To follow your footsteps, seek your alley-ways,

And there to rent myself, a teacher of children,
And teach your children the sung *aleph-bais*;

To leave to the lofty brows their pompous tomes,
Research to the proud, the birth-proud smug patrician;
To be preserved from silken wealth; to go
In humble raiment on a humble mission.

A simple follower of the Baal Shem Tov,
Mere murmurer of the verses of his Psalms
And for the sake of his great love of a Jew
To bring to the faint and hurt, their salves and balms.

An Encyclopedic Work

Review of *The Mishna* with translation and commentary [in Yiddish]
by Symcha Petrushka   16 November 1945

After a decade of murder and chaos, in which the great European reservoir
of our population was systematically exsanguinated, and in which the renowned and century-old fortresses of our tradition and learning were ruthlessly laid low, it is somewhat consoling that upon this continent and at this
latter day there should appear definite signs that that tradition still moves,
and that the continuity of Israel, in our enemies' despite, is not broken. Not
the least important of the guardians of this tradition are those refugees, who,
with the advent of Nazism, fled the European gehenna, and brought to this
continent not only their own rescued persons, but also the remembered and
cherished intellectual heritage of our people; and not the least of these custodians of our culture is Mr. Symcha Petrushka, distinguished scholar and
Talmudist, formerly of Warsaw, and now a resident of our city.

The translation of the Mishna which we are here considering is not the
first work with which Mr. Petrushka has honored the city of his sanctuary.
Several years ago this scholar undertook and by himself completed the writing
of the first Yiddish encyclopedia, a work as simple as it was erudite, and as
popular as it was necessary. Under ordinary circumstances, such an undertaking should have been the labor of an academy; it speaks both for the dire
plight in which we find ourselves, and for the devotion which Mr. Petrushka
brought to his task, that in an era when the academies were destroyed or
dispersed, an individual, a solitary toiler should alone undertake what the
many – for they were no more – could not accomplish.

It is, indeed, not without significance that Mr. Petrushka's approach to the translation of the Mishna should also be an encyclopedic one. For this scholar has not contented himself merely with a literal or interlinear rendition of the Mishnaic Hebrew into the vernacular; his translation is a skillful and forthright amalgam, not only of the various *m'farshim* (interpretations) which in other editions surround the bold text of the Mishna like a series of printed phalanxes, but also a composite of sociological comment, biblical exegesis, and philological explanation. It is a variorum made into a running commentary, the effect of a technique hitherto unattempted in our literature.

The results, moreover, are worthy of the effort. The natural consequence of this method of joint translation and commentary is that Petrushka's text appears at once forthright and erudite. Lucid and unallusive, it is comprehensible to all who can read; thorough and painstaking, it omits none of the knowledge which might otherwise have still remained the special prerogative of the pedant. When it is realized that the subject matter of this first volume, the *Seder Zraim*, is such as belongs to the customs of long ago, is concerned with tithes, and heave-offerings, and the 'doubtful' (*Dmai*) and the gleanings, and the jubilee year, and divers other items which cannot be understood without a knowledge of contemporary social conditions, when it is realized that this volume also includes all of the relevant references, one can begin to surmise the gigantic nature of the work which Mr. Petrushka has undertaken, and now one-sixth accomplished.

The double phenomenon of simplicity and scholarship is well illustrated by two techniques which do not usually concur in volumes of this kind. In the first place, Mr. Petrushka has taken the trouble to *punctuate* the text of the Mishna, with colons, semicolons, periods, and commas. This is a revolutionary innovation; with the exception of a similar attempt made by Rabbi Israel Lipshitz, no edition of the Mishna, from the earliest published in Naples in 1492, to the latest, has ever boasted this rhetorical convenience. Nor does it require much imagination on the part of the reader to realize that the insertion in the vast ocean of uncharted print of the necessary islands of punctuation is a task both difficult and useful. Only a pilot who knows the depths and shoals of those waters could hope to make these addenda without coming to grief. The result is, that under Petrushka's latter-day proof-reading, a text which otherwise might read either like a puzzle or like breathlessness itself, becomes, at least for its syntax, simple and straightforward. At the same time – such is the translator's universality of approach – Mr. Petrushka exercises a choice between various versions of the Mishna as they appear in different editions, and thus adds to his labors the final index of scholarship – textual criticism.

Truly, this is an encyclopedic work. In scope it can be compared only to the labors of those scholars who, in France, took all knowledge for their province and are accurately described as the Encyclopedists; and in significance it may be compared, particularly because it is published at this time, to the labors of the Renaissance scholars who, also in their day, salvaged from the barbarian, the treasures of a threatened and glorious culture.

There may be some – we are embarrassed for our people's sake to have to mention this – there may be some who may question the relevance of a translation of the Mishna to contemporary life. Such a question, of course, would indicate a complete obtuseness both as to the nature of cultural development and as to the part which the code of the Mishna played and still plays in our life. We are not a mushroom people, sprung up over night after a rain; we are a people with a great past, a spiritual continuity, the possessors of a long and golden chain of tradition, lengthening out from link to treasured link. Not the least of these links is the Mishna, which formed the thoughtways, and indeed was formed by the thoughtways of our people for generations. If any single piece of literature can represent a *Weltanschauung*, the Mishna, for its time, and in many respects for later time, does represent ours. One has only to think of what our Judaism would be without it to realize that its subtraction or oblivion would create a suffocating vacuum in our spiritual life.

Mr. Petrushka, we are informed, is presently engaged upon the translation into Yiddish of the other five 'orders' of the Mishna. (We wish someone would undertake an English rendition in the same spirit.) He plans to publish two of these a year – about one thousand pages of organized intelligence and packed scholarship per annum. Mr. Petrushka, we understand, further, is his own proof-reader, editor, author, and in large measure, publisher. Really, this is an encyclopedism which goes too far; at least some of the responsibilities should be lifted from this scholar so as to permit him to devote himself to those tasks for which he, and he alone, is best suited. There is really no earthly reason why one who bestows this undertaking of largess upon our people, an undertaking which among other people would be financed by societies, organizations, patrons, and state departments, should be called upon to punctuate his punctuations with book-keeping. Such a phenomenon is in itself a commentary upon the commentary.

'Apples of Gold in Pictures of Silver'

Review of *Milon Dikduki* ('Lexicon of Hebrew Homonyms') by
Solomon Klonitzki-Kline   19 July 1946

It is not often that we undertake to review a dictionary – how *does* one review a dictionary? Does one accord so much for content, and so much for form? –

but the volume which presently lies before us is of such a nature and so full of insights into the myriad transformations of language that one cannot but succumb to the temptation of making it a *point de départ* for some general semantic comments. Rabbi Kline's is not, speaking precisely, a dictionary of homonyms; homonyms include words which though differently spelled are similarly sounded; Rabbi Kline, however, confines himself only to those words which possessing the same orthography and the same pronunciation have different connotations or are differently derived – in a word, pure homonyms. It is in this sense that the Hebrew title of the volume, *Milon Dikduki*, a grammatical dictionary, is much more exact; it is, indeed, by the touchstone of Hebrew grammar, and a very sensitive touchstone it is, that Rabbi Kline writes his little cryptic essays, full of laconic abbreviations and scholarly al- lusion, upon the ambidextrous vocabulary which in alphabetic order marches through the approximately three hundred pages of his text.

The method which Rabbi Kline adopts, at once thorough, erudite, and yet easy to understand, runs somewhat as follows: he takes the given word, and first of all identifies its grammatical construction – noun, verb, adjective or adverb; person and number; if verb, transitive or intransitive, and he then gives some parallel tri-literal verbs to facilitate the conjugation of the one under discussion. He proceeds, then, to indicate the varied meanings which the word may have, each meaning illustrated by quotation from the Bible or later authors. Very often, and this constitutes one of the special talents of our etymologist, he will demonstrate how that which is taken for a noun is also a verb, and vice versa. Such a recognition of the versatility of the language, as the author points out in his introduction, is an absolute prerequisite for the understanding of much of mediaeval Hebrew poetry, whose *paytanim* showed a remarkable, and, in their art a very fruitful, inclination to verbalize their nouns and nominalize their verbs.

We do not intend to dwell upon Rabbi Kline's treatment of individual words, each of which is fascinating both for its originality and palpable au- thenticity – but rather upon some general phenomena of language which are illustrated practically upon every page. As one browses through these pages – only a proofreader, we imagine, would read a dictionary holus-bolus, galley after galley – one is immediately struck by the great vitality, the startling liveliness of the Hebrew language. We are far and away from that inertness which one usually associates with a dead tongue. It is true that this dictionary is concerned with classical, not particularly modern Hebrew; nonetheless, as Rabbi Kline goes through the athletic conjugations, and as each verb flexes its muscles, one cannot but be impressed by that resourcefulness which when need urged it, changed verb into noun or noun into verb.

The second impression is one which is especially true of conjugated and declined languages – and that is, of how so much meaning may be due to so few letters. It is true, of course, that the tendencies in speech, as is so blatantly illustrated in the example of basic English, are towards a greater simplicity, and away from the declensions, the conjugations, the suffix possessives, and the internal vowel-changes, but nothing illustrates the advantages of the old dispensation better than the rules of this ancient tongue, where upon the triangle of the three-lettered Hebrew verb such a variety of meaningful architecture may be erected.

It is a dictionary of homonyms, moreover, which can best serve as an X-ray into what, for want of a better term, we may call the foetal development of a language. Thus, in a given word we will see how a noun derives, perhaps, its first meaning from a verb; how, in the course of time it changes its original meaning to acquire a secondary one, how the secondary one becomes endowed with tertiary implications – the whole paralleled by the biological history of the embryo. When, in a latter-day dictionary, we discover all of these meanings of the same word existing side by side, we do, indeed, get a linguistic exemplification of the rule touching ontogeny and ontology.

And, of course, as in all languages, one is struck again by the protean genius of words to change themselves from one aspect to another. It is the great achievement of Rabbi Kline to demonstrate how these metamorphoses are accomplished, not by any haphazard and arbitrary decisions of either the folk or of accredited authors, but by and according to the strict rules of Hebrew grammar – the *open sesame* of all of these magical linguistic transmutations.

Certainly Rabbi Kline has produced a singular, useful, and outstanding book. It is one of its kind; although the field of Hebrew grammar is probably one of the best tilled in that literature, nothing like this work has yet been undertaken, much less achieved. Nor is it merely a *tour de force*, designed to accentuate Rabbi Kline's indubitable scholarship. It has uses which go beyond the mere satisfaction of etymological curiosity; it gives a clear, an illuminating view of the nature of Hebrew syntax; it casts light upon scriptural expressions which can not otherwise be clearly understood; it serves as an invaluable key to the treasures of Hebrew poetry in the Middle Ages; and it is of extraordinary pedagogical potentialities.

Already scholars have hailed this book, both in America and Palestine, with an enthusiasm not usually extended to either grammars or dictionaries; and this is both. One of the leading pedagogues in Palestine, indeed, was completely unequivocal in his statement that this was the book the Hebrew teacher was looking for; that it was, through a volume such as this, that the Hebrew child might be led through the labyrinth of Hebrew grammar, and yet not feel that he was in durance vile, and to torture subject. For to study words via homonyms, and to have these explained as parts of speech, is to pursue a game, a game of puns and calembours, out of which the student must emerge painlessly, indeed, delightfully instructed.

All in all, this volume is an invaluable *vade mecum* for him who would trace a path through the thickets of Hebrew, and in Rabbi Solomon Klonitzki-Kline he finds an unerring guide, a guide who has already led many readers to view 'The Treasures of Talmudical Interpretations' published several years ago. We do not hesitate to recommend this volume to all who are interested in the subject; its perusal will most certainly reward the effort. Truly these are words fitly spoken, of which Solomon said, they were like apples of gold in pictures of silver.

We cannot refrain from adding – no doubt in a spirit of local pride – that this work by the venerable and scholarly Rabbi is dedicated to his children, among whom is Mrs. Nathan B. Cohen, of Montreal. It is a dedication to be envied.

The Snows of Yesteryear

Review of *Burning Lights* by Bella Chagall   6 December 1946

Recently there came off the presses of an American publishing house a sadly de luxe volume whose purpose it was lugubriously to record and to illustrate those of the renowned art-treasures of Europe which now, in the lurid aftermath of war, lived only in the architecture raised by their dust. In its pages, photograph of castle followed photograph of church, bristling battlement gave way to roseate facade, equestrian statue curvetted before marble monument – and of all of these artifacts, poignantly it was noted that they were now ruins, total or partial. It was, indeed, a dismal volume to leaf; its tragedy – the works of genius reduced to rubble – haunted one long after the book was closed. Long after, the mind stayed filled with the shadows of an architecture and the mirrors of an art which now were lost, perhaps, forever. The thought that these losses were unnecessary was an additional tourniquet about the heart.

But the memorial volume which now lies before us – Bella Chagall's tribute to a *life*, a way of life which sustained and inspirited millions, and which now, with those millions, is but the vanished smoke of crematoria – evokes from the reader an infinitely greater pathos than that of the melancholy treatise upon shattered sculpture. For the latter, after all, was concerned with but sticks and stones, things fashioned, precious objects, but mere objects nonetheless, and these – these burning lights – shine for the multitudes of humans who are no more, and for that poetry of their lives which at once glows and shadows in every one of these pages. It is not a museum, but a culture and a civilization, which rises from these paragraphs; and the description of its beauty only serves to accentuate the tragedy of its loss.

One feels it almost a sacrilege to attempt to assess this book by invoking the purely literary standards of criticism – so much has holiness gone into it – but even by these standards, Bella Chagall's book must remain a classic in its kind. Seeking to communicate both the gusto and the spirituality of typical Jewish life in Vitebsk, the writer has adopted the calendar and its coloured days as the motif of her table of contents; and what a beautiful year it is she leads us through! How touchingly, and with what a sensitivity, the folkways of her people are described! The memoirs of Gluckel of Hameln – which have their own honoured place in our thesaurus – are prosaic and gross in comparison to these sketches recording the reactions of a little poetess let loose to watch and estimate the picturesque protagonists of her environment.

This is, indeed, a unique book. First, and upon the most obvious plane, it is unique in that, in a literature in which the subject – life in 'the old country' – is almost entirely the preserve of men – here, for once, and, alas for a last time – it is through a woman's eyes that those lovely interiors of Jewish life are seen. Thus not only are freshness and novelty achieved, but also avoided are those vices of masculine writing on the subject – emphasis upon things theological, or nationalistic, or – at the other extreme – revolt from both the strictures and sanctities of the life described.

Unique, too, is the book in that it is obviously the product of a sensitive and poetic spirit. Again and again, under her hand themes the most palpable become etherealized, transubstantiated into elements that belong to the realm of pure poetry. I take as an example – and I tread gingerly in the precincts – the chapter on 'The Bath.' I doubt whether any other subject has, in our literature, as often been the butt of ribald humour as this of the 'ritualarium.' The *Mikveh*! Merely to utter the word is to conjure, upon the lips of even the most refined, a non–Mona Lisa smile. But how like a sanctum does this poor *mikveh* appear as it emerges from the prose of Bella Chagall! Not a suggestion of the vulgar or the sensual will one find here; here is spirituality all compact! A sacred place! With tenderness and delicacy, full of awe and wonder about the mysterious rite, full of pity and sympathy for its functioners, the chapter reads like some idyll laid in a scene of clouds and vapours. It is a singular achievement. Anybody can be poetic about roses and nightingales; it takes talent – and a love of one's subject – to make a lyric out of steam.

Indeed, it is as a book of poetry that this volume is really to be appreciated. The procession of Bella Chagall's year, fundamentally, follows the chosen path; it is the *luach* of all of Israel that she has used. Only – she has seen differently. A fascinating anthology of imagist poems, indeed, could be compiled out of the sights and insights of her prose. Of card games on Chanuka: 'The knaves who are younger want to show off with their skilfully twisted mustaches. Sometimes the two knaves on one card appear to be pushing each other with their sawed-off legs.' A winter scene: 'Over the roofs the chimney smoke roams freely, like a drunken goy.' Fauna and Flora on the New Year: 'No one knows whence the pineapple comes. With its scaly skin it looks like a strange fish.' An *esrog*: 'The yellow citron, plump and big, is sprawled like a Pharaoh on a soft bed in the middle of the silver sugar box.' A still life: 'Glazed Sabbath loaves, sitting like empresses.' Of the Reader's intonation of the name of Haman: 'He nods to me – he seems to be trying to indicate to me that Haman has run out of the scroll and that I am to hit him, kill him on the spot ... And under the reader's chant Esther walks down the stairs of spaced lines.'

These quotations, moreover, leave unillustrated the quiet humour, and the sense of wonder, and the true daughter-like love which pervade a book which is almost altogether delightful. We say *almost* because unfortunately we can not look forward to more writing of the same quality, unless it already exists in manuscript. For the 'Burning Lights' burn also for Bella Chagall who passed away on September 2, 1944.

The volume is also distinguished by thirty-six drawings done by Marc Chagall. They are a fitting complement to the text; the poetry of line and the poetry of paragraph harmonize; the creatures of Chagall's imagination, more-over – the three-fingered men, the beards within parabolas or beneath wings, the pointillated caps, the *Shaloch Monos* lad with head awry amidst the staggering houses, the girl dreaming within the grandfather clock – conceptions which Chagall always endowed with an other-worldly character, have with the passage of time taken on a new reality; the other-worldly has, in sorry truth, become vivid and actual. The wings, to-day, are photographic.

The translation from the Yiddish by Norbert Guterman leaves nothing to be desired. Overcoming the natural difficulty of translating the idiom of one language into that of another, Guterman has admirably succeeded in preserving the gist and essence of the original. He has avoided, too, that stilted pseudo-literary quality with which so many translations from the Yiddish come shackled into the world.

This, we understand, is the first of a number of publications of Judaica and books kin to Judaica, which are to be published by the well-known Schocken Books, now functioning also upon this continent. It is an auspicious beginning and establishes a standard worthy of all who have participated in the making of a memorable book.

Look on This Picture and on This ...

Review of *A Palestine Picture Book* by Jacob Rosner and Alfred
Bernheim and *Polish Jews: A Pictorial Record* by Roman Vishniac
22 August 1947

The publication of these two volumes – one of photographs of a world passed
by and the other of photographs of a world in process of rebirth – constitutes
a valuable addition to the library of Judaica which Schocken Books has been
building up zealously and fastidiously, for the benefit of English-speaking
Jewry. Coming, as they do, after the publication, under the Schocken impri-
matur, of a number of distinguished books on varied aspects of Jewish life, it
is as if to illustrate through the camera some of the themes which the Schocken
writers have hitherto merely adumbrated with words, that these bound port-
folios now appear. In this object they succeed admirably.

It cannot be gainsaid, of course, that a great deal of the fascination of
these photographs arises out of the very objects upon which the camera has
been focussed. Any photograph of the Warsaw which is no more would reach
the spectator with an irresistible pathos; even those blurred prints which befog,
and yet illustrate, the recent Black Books, are full of a tragedy which emerges,
perhaps more pitiable, through their very inarticulateness. Any photograph
of any part of Erez seen in the act of becoming, cannot but fill the reader with
elation; even those palpably propagandist shots that appear on Zionist cal-
endars, often move the on-looker, not only with their days, but also with
their works. But the photographs in these volumes are more than merely
their sub-titles; there is nothing about them that is haphazard; all reveal, not
only an interesting subject before the camera, but also an intelligence behind it.

This is not to say that the photographers have excessively intruded their
own personalities into their photographs. This is simply to say that these
photographs are selective, and are significant. They are, if I may be permitted
to use the Catholic metaphor secularized by Joyce – 'epiphanies' – revelations,
'inscapes' – more is seen than meets the eye. In the Palestine book, the very
first picture, for example, has this quality. The camera shows the coast-line
of Palestine – the Mediterranean, the beach, and a rising mountain. In the
centre, pigmy silhouettes. But one cannot tell whether these silhouettes have
issued from the land to swim in the sea, or have just emerged from the sea
to begin their entry into the land ... On page 12 Rosner has caught an almost
complete reminiscence of Van Gogh. From page 120, a full commentary on
Jewish history emerges: a Yemenite Jew is seen poring over what is obviously

a sacred volume; behind him is a blank wall, where, suspended from two hooks, are his *tallis*, his coat, and his staff: *impedimenta*.

The effects, it is to be noted, are achieved, first, through the naturalness of the persons photographed; they do not appear posed; and second, through the artist's selectivity. It was an inspiration to include in that Yemenite picture the hanging *tallis* and cane. A lesser eye would have made the picture out of the picturesqueness of the sitter's face. One is thankful also that in this volume the angle-shot, that last infirmity of the photographer-artist, is not to be found. The Jordan is definitely not viewed through the clefts of five fingers. Rosner and Vishniac are not at pains to prove themselves – through their photographs – acrobats. They shoot – like Michelangelo's Moses – from the forehead; not from the hip, or from recumbence, or from a chimney-pot. To this rule there are two exceptions, both functionally justifiable – on page 48 where the hydro-electric potentialities of the Jordan are considered from a crow's nest; and on page 56 where the harbour at Haifa is photographed from a height: harbours are not to be photographed from the Plimsoll line.

I regretted about the Palestine book only that there was about it a certain quality which can best be identified as that of the Fitzpatrick travelogue: it is beautifully panoramic; unrelievedly idyllic (Rosner should have resisted the temptation on page 15 – pictures of massed fleecy sheep are to art what verses about roses and nightingales are to poetry); and, in a sense, *too* selective (not once does an Arab come within snapping distance of the camera). It suffers from the vice opposite to that of the biblic spies: it reports that there are absolutely no giants in the land. But while in Fitzpatrick this attitude is unpardonable – for Fitzpatrick the earth and the fullness thereof are but sunshine and leisure, – in Rosner, face to face with both the intoxicating memory of the Palestinian past and the epic grandeur of present reconstruction, this emphasis upon the positive – the only White Paper in the book is marginal – is easily understood.

Vishniac's volume, on the other hand, suffers from a different one-sidedness. For him Polish Jewry is orthodox Polish Jewry. This is an approach which, perhaps, makes for picturesqueness – *shtreimel*, earlocks, caftans, beards, – but not for truth. If from Graetz's *History* one gets the impression that the two principal activities of our people were (a) the writing of books, and (b) being persecuted, from Vishniac's portraits one must gather that the two themes of Polish Jewish life were (a) religion, and (b) poverty. This is largely, but not wholly, true. An analysis of the Vishniac pictures would thus seem to indicate that no Jews were eligible for immortalization by his camera unless they were bearded; it is only in mass-scenes that the unshaven are permitted. The poverty theme, too, – and this is not to underestimate the abysmal penury in which Polish Jewry languished – is carried to lengths which tend to deprive that poverty of its pity: six pictures of Jewish merchants appear in the book;

the first shows a storekeeper apparently making change (very small change) with an air which is composite of general meditation and specific melancholy – his exposed stock consists mainly of shoelaces and pins; the second is a storekeeper without even the saving consolation of a customer; the third is a fish-vendor, pathetic and cold in December weather, his hand is on a metallic container, and his hand is not gloved; the fourth, a female stallkeeper lugubriously viewing the approach of a tax-collector; the fifth, a Jew hopefully offering for sale two turnipy horse-radishes; and the sixth – a storekeeper with nothing to sell! Each of these pictures standing alone would be a full and bitter commentary upon the plight of Polish Jewry; but to use six of them, and to make these six consecutive – this is defeatful of the purpose of each and all of them. It is as if one were making a hyperbolical anecdote out of what was a true and savage actuality. How much more effective – for the obvious purpose of the compiler – is the picture on page 6: Synagogue Court in Vilna. At first glance it looks like a light-hearted, almost comic scene: upon the doorsteps of a synagogue a happy-go-lucky boy is seen entertaining his only partially attentive audience; there is certainly no heavy drama here; but the air of listlessness, unconcern, despair, not to speak of the mad irrelevancy of the boy's gesture, has the aura of a premonitory nightmare.

Of course the Vishniac book is one which we are glad to have; it may have failed to indicate the part which Polish Jewry played in Polish life, of their school systems (other than that of the *cheder*), of the radical Jewish movements, of Sejm representation, etc., but what it portrays it portrays well. It almost lives up to the essay by Abraham J. Heschel which introduces the book, an essay full of understanding and love, a classic of its kind. Certainly the inclusion, in a book of pictures every one of which contains human beings, of two 'still lifes' – if the term can be applied either to the *Bet Midrash* library – tattered volumes of the Living Law, pictured on page 24, or to the gravestone photographed on page 31 – was a masterly stroke, a gesture whose symbolism lingers in the memory long after the book is closed.

Although picture-books, these are not books to leaf through, and leave. The faces of the one will haunt, the faces of the other will elate the reader for many hours after he has left them, and on many occasions when he least suspected that they walked his memory. I left them with an alternative regret that the process of photography was not invented centuries ago, – that the Second Commandment had inhibited our artists; for records such as these, I felt, of all the fathers that begat us, in all their generations, would be no mean legacy.

Only Half the Language of Faith

Review of *The Language of Faith: Selected Jewish Prayers* edited by
Nahum N. Glatzer   10 October 1947

'*The Language of Faith,*' says the introductory first page of this little volume,
'is the first publication of the Schocken Library series. It is based on a reverence
for the great classical traditions of Judaism and a conviction of their contemporary significance. Its selection as the first publication of the series represents
a declaration of the intentions of the Schocken Library in the field of Jewish
literature.'

It should be stated forthwith that these intentions are honourable. Like
all the other publications which have issued from the House of Schocken, this
one, too, appears to be the result – in format, design, and typography – of a
labour of love. The man who made possible the publication of this beautiful
anthology of prayers surely was not interested in launching a best-seller.
There are easier ways to grow rich on royalties than via the printing and sale
of unprescribed liturgies. Schocken Books is more a patron than a publisher
of Jewish literature. With the exception about to be indicated, everything
about this book – its clear print, its pony text, its sanguine rubrics, its eclectic
editing – is designed for the greater glory of Hebrew letters.

The character of the volume is admirably described in Mr. Glatzer's
epilogue. 'In this book,' he says, 'a community of diverse voices has been
assembled: We hear a herdsman pray in his own humble way; a sufferer who
continues to aspire to his God; a community imperiled, awaiting the Messiah;
a mystic, lonely with the Lonely, in love with the source of Love; worshippers
assembled at the dawn and the close of the Day of Atonement; a traveler
starting out upon his journey. We hear a simple woman pray for her husband
and her children; a congregation longing for Zion and the establishment of
the kingdom of God on earth ... About one half of the selections is from the
liturgy of Ashkenazic Jewry. The other half consists of private devotions,
ranging from the talmudic masters to Nahman of Bratzlav (*ca.* 1800), the
great hasidic master.'

Insofar as the Hebrew and Yiddish texts are concerned, therefore, *The
Language of Faith* is truly worthy of the aforementioned labour and love
expended upon it. We must regret, however, that the English translations, in
many cases, are far from adequate to the challenges flung across to them from
their opposite Hebrew pages. Time and again one encounters in the Hebrew
prayer an inspired idiom, some word-play which summarizes an entire context,

and one looks to see whether the English rendition is equal, in force, or ingenuity, or succinctness to the Hebrew original; and time and again one is disappointed. *Ha-maariv arovim* (p. 13) surely should have been Englished by something more singular than 'who makes evening fall.' The translation on page 16 ought surely to have shown, by syntactical arrangement, that the word *Yisrael* was the nexus of the prayer translated. *Ho-emes l'amitoi* (p. 33) is worthy of something better than 'innermost truth.' *V'chol shachar l'sha-chair* (p. 55) – which must have pleased Yehuda Halevi since he made it his climactic phrase – remains a challenge ignored. One would have liked also to see *l'ha'avir gilulim* (p. 107) translated by some word other than 'idols,' some word which would suggest the primary connotation of *gilulim* ... But perhaps the same delicacy which impelled the editor to omit the first paragraph of this prayer also prevailed upon the translator to content himself with the clean sculptured word: 'idols.'

Another possibility which has been totally ignored is that which might have been afforded by the acceptance of the challenge of the various dialects in which these prayers are written. A prayer from the Aramaic, we think, ought to be rendered in an idiom different from that which is used to render a psalm; that idiom is usually either a legalistic one, or a mystical one; there should be something in the flavour of the English translation to indicate the tang of this particular poured wine. Even the Hebrew of Yehuda Halevi differs substantially from that of David Sweetsinger; translations should attempt to show the difference. Similarly, it is incongruous to render eighteenth-century Yiddish (p. 15), which is far more archaic than the mere two centuries' lapse would suggest, in an English which is in all respects of to-day, – so much so that *un' du bleibst immer un' eivig* is rendered, almost colloquially, 'but you are there, you will always be there.'

The key to all of these lost opportunities, is, we think, a mistaken notion held by the translators touching the uses of simplicity. Simplicity, we agree, is a literary virtue; but in the translation of prayers it can be carried to an extreme fatal to the genre. Not that God finds unacceptable the prayers of simplicity – see page 78, the prayer of a shepherd who did not know how to pray, yet here, strangely enough, the translator puts into the mouth of the rustic a locution straight from the lawyer's writ: 'It is apparent and known unto you' – but prayer, forming part of a Divine Service, as most of these prayers do, is ritual, and ritual is formal. The prayers in Aramaic, in fact, are so formal, they are hieratic. In any event, the present book is addressed to readers, and only mediately to God; this reader, at least, expects from a composed prayer not only a petition, but also the ceremonial of petition.

To what a pass this attitude can lead the translator is perhaps best illustrated by his rendering of Psalm 130, 'De Profundis,' to which, of course, a standard of comparison exists. This is the Authorized Version, – followed also in the version of the Jewish Publication Society.

Out of the depths have I cried unto thee, O Lord.
Lord, hear my voice: let thine ears be attentive to the voice of my
supplications.
If thou, O Lord, shouldest mark iniquities, O Lord, who shall stand?

The version before us reads:

From the depths I called thee,
Adonai,
My Lord, heed thou my voice,
attentive be thine ears
to my pleading voice.
If, God, thou keep sins in mind,
My Lord, who would endure?

His is a hardy spirit who would seek, except on theological grounds, to
improve upon the Authorized Version; yet that hardiness of spirit surely
would be excusable if it did actually result in some bettering of the text. The
lines before us, however, far from improving on King James's book, actually
introduce elements that are as uncouth as they are unnecessary. The intensive
'de' – *out* of the depths – is omitted, – without warrant. The translation,
moreover, is addressed not to the Lord, who requires no further identification,
but to a named deity – Adonai. The editor, it appears, is responsible for this
appellation. 'The *Adonai* of the English translation is the name the Jew substitutes for YHWH, the unutterable holy name of God.' This certainly is to
carry the inhibition of the tetragrammaton to an absurd. Does not Mr. Glatzer,
when he translates YHWH into Yiddish, say *Gott*, and not *Adonai*? Does not,
in fact, the attribution of a surname to the Lord, as if He were some tribal
godling, detract from Divinity? One is at a loss also to understand what
prompted the translator to improve upon the unarticled Lord of the A.V. by
adding the possessive adjective to His name to make Him a member of the
judiciary. 'If, God, thou keep sins in mind' – really, this is an avoidance of
the archaic which is too much. Surely if the second person singular 'thou'
can enter the translation, then the verb should accord, should be 'keepest.'
What special virtue issues from his solecism? Nor is the translation consistent;
elsewhere (p. 20) he condescends to a verb's second person singular, and says,
quite properly, 'thou hast called,' and not 'thou have called.' On page 84,
however, he relapses again into the language of Browning's Caliban:

Well I know, Adonai,
I was nought, and thou made me.
Thou formed and founded me,
a deed of life and mercy doing with me.

It is to the credit of the translator that when he comes to Psalm 23 (p. 108) he attempts no improvements.

This insistence upon a plain style of translation leads also to other homeliness. What other translators render as 'manifold mercies' is here, with scientific precision, rendered *'multiple* compassion.' The temple is not, as others would have it, 'the great and holy house'; it is 'the *grand* and holy house.' And yet, – despite the undeclared principles of plainness and modernity – the translators do perpetrate, almost against their wills, a number of archaisms. 'You bethink you how the world was made' is the opening line on page 38, a page in which God is first addressed as 'You,' and then, presumably on greater intimacy, thee'd and thou'd. On page 56, the translator, elsewhere ascetic, affords himself the luxury of 'goodly years.' What prompted the literalism: 'May the will come from thee,' we shall never know; the phrase is usually, and adequately translated, 'May it be acceptable unto thee'; in fact on page 60, the translator forgets herself and so renders the idiom. Clumsy inversions, reminiscent of Matthew Arnold's comic 'I you thank,' also occur to show that the translator is not always one with his traductive credo:

My God,
the soul you have placed in me
pure is.

Pure is! We must mention too that the Hebrew verbs for 'hope' and 'trust' are improved upon by being translated 'aspired.' 'Though He cut me down, to him shall I aspire' – this (p. 58) the reader will be interested to learn, is to substitute: 'Yea, though he slay me, yet will I trust in him.' We fear that this use of the verb 'aspire,' as also the use thereof on page 34, is designed not so much to better the language as to improve and refine the religious concept involved.

We think, finally, that it was the translators' philosophy of translation rather than any deficiency in their parts which produced this failure. Olga Marx has translated other books for Schocken, and done them well. Mr. Sloan is a talented poet; the challenge of these prayers is surely not beyond his means. Here and there, throughout the volume, there do occur lines of remarkable felicity. 'You who favour the earthling with knowledge' (p. 40); 'Blessed is He whose utterance created skies' (p. 52); *yoitzair braishis* rendered 'shaper of origins' (p. 20); 'to prosper our goal with hope and future' (p. 28); 'That we may rise in the morning and find / our heart waiting to fear thy name' (p. 28).

But, alas, 'twas the principle that destroyed the practice.

Baedeker: Kasrilevke

Review of *Inside Kasrilevke* by Sholom Aleichem, translated from the
Yiddish by Isidore Goldstick   16 April 1948

When the great metropolises in which Jewry, in successive centuries, fashioned
for itself its own specific mode of life, come to be counted, Kasrilevke, too,
we feel sure, will have to be taken into the tally. It is true, of course, that at
no time did Kasrilevke wax to the stature of a capital; there are some who
would not even credit it a city; some there are who go so far as to question
Kasrilevke's reality; nonetheless Kasrilevke remains, as the Hebrew phrase
would have it, a 'mother in Israel.' It was; and in the imagination still persists.
Its very fictiveness gives it authenticity; in the Czar's domains there never
was a hamlet, a town, or a city called Kasrilevke; upon the maps it is nowhere
dotted; yet because Sholom Aleichem's Kasrilevke reveals the typical architecture, the peculiar residents, and the unique mores of all the Russian-Jewish
townlets of his time, this composite municipality is a locus much more factual
than any of the many named congregations of the Pale.

This is so because Kasrilevke, unlike the decadent Ottoman Empire, its
contemporary, was ever more than 'a mere geographical expression.' Kasrilevke was a way of life, a way of life which Sholom Aleichem, in these his
light cursory pen-sketches, captured in their ineluctable typicality. *Fuit Ilium*;
Kasrilevke is no more; but that which gave Kasrilevke its character – namely,
its Jewry – still moves, joking or sighing, through the pages of Sholom Aleichem. Of course there are other cities builded of the imagination of this
great Jewish architect; Yehupetz is not to be scorned; and even Boiberik,
though set upon mud, is not to be omitted from the catalogue of the cities of
refuge. But all three – Kasrilevke, Yehupetz, Boiberik, – owe whatever immortality is vouchsafed to them to the life and habits, the struggles and hopes,
the Jews and *shabbas-goyim*, that they sheltered.

It is for this reason, perhaps, that the pieces – *Dos Naye Kasrilevke* and
Kasrilevke Nisrofim – do not seem to carry as much conviction as issues from
the other of Sholom Aleichem's investigations into the Kasrilevke psyche.
Inside Kasrilevke, in fact, is too literally a *vade mecum*; the author discusses,
seriatim, its transportation, hotels, restaurants, liquor, theatre, etc.; the emphasis is thrown primarily upon the inanimate place, only incidentally upon
the human situation. In other writings of Sholom Aleichem, Kasrilevke, the
habitat, emerges as the ambience of a way of life; here it is the *Ding an sich*.
The result is the essays appear factitious; as if the author were saying to

himself, now that I have done the hotels, what shall I do? Why, of course, the restaurants! And having done the restaurants, etc. The nexus is occupational, not human.

The point is effectively illustrated both in the story of Reb Yosifl's challenge to God and in the story of Reb Yosifl's challenge to the building contractor. In both instances, the narrative rises above the level of tourist description to the altitude of eternal verity. This is because in Reb Yosifl we see *life and personality*, and in the other sketches only an address.

For a bird's eye view, however – the bird being a *yom kippur* rooster – the rotatory conspectus of *Inside Kasrilevke* is more than adequate. Time and again, despite the method of inventory, the spirit of Sholom Aleichem, in a remark, a phrase, an anecdote, humanizes his subject and Kasrilevke again appears, as it was intended to appear, in the image of a people. This occurs most frequently when in a given situation a Sholom Aleichem worthy speaks in the idiom of the folk. Then it is as if the accreted wisdom of the ages, the omnisecular experience of Jewry, were being brought to bear upon the author's material; and then it is that one sees again the aptness of Rabinovitch's pen-name – Sholom Aleichem, the Jew's hello; the individual writer, in his very signature announces the approach of the total heritage: Sholom Aleichem – here come all of us!

Thus when someone speaks ironically of the week-day quiet of the river Sambation, or of the posthumous achievement of a golden tombstone, the words are the words of a Sholom Aleichem character, the script is Sholom Aleichem's; but the primal ventriloquist is the Jewish folk-imagination. Of the same primitive source are the colourful maledictions, in prose and in verse; and of the same ultimate authorship, the Kasrilevke metropolitan boast: when it comes to carcasses, Kasrilevke too is counted with the cattle.

In this volume the peculiar genius of Sholom Aleichem emerges rather in single lines than three-dimensionally. Apart from Reb Yosifl and Rochel of the hotel (very grossly burlesqued), the dramatis personae, as we have indicated above, are auxiliary rather than central to the writing. The result is that a great number of minor personages flit through the pages of the book; with an epithet the author makes caricatures of them; they remain remembered. Of this company are 'the fellow with red whiskers and a blue wart on his nose'; 'an asthmatic with a sparkle in his eye'; the clown 'with whiskers on one side of his face'; 'a man at odds with all the world who kept spitting'; 'the contractor with his explosive laugh he-he-he'; the young man 'with a bifurcated little beard'; and the 'red-cheeked females who were busy cracking sunflower seeds.' Nor must one forget the keepers of the bath, fittingly named Adam and Eve. These creatures are not really persons; they are personified idiosyncrasies; they reveal the author more than his object, but they reveal him at his most perspicacious and in the exercise of a talent which is basic to his work: it is the talent of summing up the whole in the part. *Inside Kasrilevke*, too, is, after a fashion, a summation of Sholom Aleichem's theme, of a theme which is further synopsized in the paragraph with which the book ends: 'This has ever been the fate of the little folk of Kasrilevke: when they dream of good things to eat – they haven't a spoon; when they have a spoon – they don't dream of good things to eat.' This work, therefore, may well serve as a liminal introduction to Sholom Aleichem, his life and laughters.

It is of special interest to Canadian readers that the translation of this book has been done by Dr. Isidore Goldstick, who, among many distinctions, is perhaps best known as a leader of Canadian Zionism. Beyond the boundaries of his own country, Dr. Goldstick is cherished for the felicity of his translations of both Yiddish prose and poetry. Indeed, some of the poems of Yehoash have been by no one better Englished than by Goldstick; and his achievement with regard to these sketches of Sholom Aleichem is of a comparable success.

It is a cliché of the bilingual criticism of Sholom Aleichem translations that Sholom Aleichem cannot be translated; like all clichés – including the present one – it is only partially true. Every pouring of wine from one bottle to another entails some loss by evaporation; in this sense the Latin and Greek classics, too, are untranslatable. The translator, alas, can only render an equivalence, an approximation of the original text; both the aura which hovers about any given vocabulary and the larger cultural context which surrounds any given paragraph of a literary work must of necessity vanish, or at least be diminished, when substituted by words which in their own language have gathered their own historic and literary associations. But these strictures apply to all translations, and not only to those from the works of Rabinovitch. The most that one may concede in the case of Sholom Aleichem is relative difficulty – not absolute impossibility. Often we suspect that the myth of the untranslatability of Sholom Aleichem is a notion fostered (a) by those who have tried and failed, and (b) by Jews to whom Sholom Aleichem is so precious and private a possession that they begrudge the goy even a re-cooked slice of this leviathan, and (c) by those who so revere the man's memory that they fain would consider all Sholom Aleichem translations as *yayin nesech*.

Dr. Goldstick, we think, has by example exploded this myth. His translation is in all respects adequate, and in many respects, admirable. His rendering of Sholom Aleichem's parody of a post-conflagration appeal for funds – Kasrilevke burned down, and biblic poeticism invoked to wring the hearts of the compassionate sons of the compassionate – leaves nothing to be desired. Even typography is used as a mode of translation: a Kasrilevke theatre playbill is translated, and reproduced in all respects, including the misprint, in the typographical style current at the beginning of this century. It is true that there may be, here and there, instances where some might prefer a phrase, or a word, other than the word or phrase used by Dr. Goldstick; upon a translation, any translation, total and unreserved agreement is impossible. Such agreement, in fact, has never again ensued since the miracle of the Septuagint. But the next best thing – agreement not miraculous in its totality – that, certainly, Dr. Goldstick's translation must elicit.

The Dybbuk

Text of a Trans-Canada Radio Talk   23–30 July 1948

I think it may safely be stated that there is no other play in the repertoire of the Yiddish theatre which has enjoyed so continuous a popularity and so world-wide a reputation as Anski's *Dybbuk*. Its premiere having taken place in Warsaw on the ninth of December 1920, exactly thirty days after the death of its fifty-seven year old author, it has since been staged, with varying interpretations, an untold number of times. Maurice Schwartz of the Jewish Art Theatre played it in 1921; in Russia after Stanislavsky had toyed with it, the Moscow Art Theatre finally produced it, but as a sort of burlesque of the irrational; Max Reinhardt, too, brought his genius to bear upon it. In Eastern and Western Europe various acting troupes for more than a decade – until a more dangerous dybbuk entered the soul of that continent – made it part of their repertoire. The Habima players, in Europe and in Palestine, alone performed it more than a thousand times; at this moment the same group is giving the play a successful revival in New York. Nor have the productions of *The Dybbuk* been confined to the Yiddish or the Hebrew language; there have been French, German, Polish, Danish renderings; there has been translation into the Scandinavian, and it is rumoured that there is extant a version in Japanese.

In English *The Dybbuk* was first produced by the Neighborhood Playhouse in 1925, and in Canada it was first seen when Rupert Caplan, who directs to-night's performance, produced it on the stage of His Majesty's Theatre in Montreal. In whatever language produced, *The Dybbuk* has evoked universal enthusiasm, an enthusiasm which may be explained not only by the intrinsic merit of its drama, but also by the inescapable appeal of the great mystical verities it enunciates.

A first glance of the play, it must be admitted, might lead one to question its suitability for modern performance. Certainly the non-Jewish auditor and the twentieth-century Jewish auditor too, must find strange and often outlandish the world of dark custom and flashing apocalypse which is revealed as the play progresses from act to act. Much of the terminology of *The Dybbuk* no longer has any currency save in circles devoted to the study of Cabbala and folklore; many of its traditions belong to a way of life that has vanished; the very atmosphere of mysticism in which *The Dybbuk* moves and has its being must be remote, indeed, from the appreciation of a public which these many years have been nurtured upon the dry biscuit of realism. Who to-day can make the wandering departed spirit, sojourning among the living and from a living body speaking out its complaint, credible otherwise than as whimsy? Which of our contemporary dramatists, appropriating his 'slice of life,' would dare stage before the attention of a sceptical audience a trial scene in which the plaintiff is a soul roused and summoned from its eternal rest to give evidence in a court of law? Yet despite these obstacles to credibility the play does engage the emotion of its audience; does elicit that suspension of disbelief without which every poetic work must remain unviable, still-born; and does move the hearts of men with intimations of immortality, inklings of the supernatural, vague communion with truths inarticulate.

And because this nostalgia for truth which transcends the boundaries of the mundane is common to all mankind, – because even the superstitious beliefs which give motive and meaning to the action of the protagonist find some counterpart in the general pattern of the minds of the human race, minds even the most sophisticate, *The Dybbuk* in whatever tongue presented meets ready comprehension and response.

Shortly you will be listening to the play yourself, and because I do not wish to put myself in the category of those people who introduce an anecdote by giving you its punch-line, I forbear from expatiating upon its action and argument. I do think, however, that the interest of the listener would be served if something were said about some of the rather technical terms which recur again and again in the text of the Anski classic. What, for example, is a Dybbuk? Literally the word means adhesion, something which adheres, and refers to the belief that there are departing souls which unreconciled to their fate, seek out that living soul to which they feel an affinity and so adhere to it as completely to change the personality – in our play, even the voice – of their chosen host. Strangely as this doctrine may strike the ear of atomic man, it is not peculiar to the lore of the eighteenth-century community described in *The Dybbuk*. Under the more grandiloquent title of metempsychosis, the notion has been entertained by men in all times and all ages. Early Hindu religion speaks of the thousands of reincarnations through which the individual soul may go. Herodotus attributes the idea to the Egyptians; Pythagoras made it popular in Greece. Into western civilization this concept enters mainly through the work of Plato. It is of course a central tenet of the Cabbala, and persists in contemporary theosophy. To this day it is believed in Tibet that the soul of the deceased Dalai Lama enters into that of a boy, his successor, born exactly nine months after his death. And in as recent a work as James

Joyce's *Ulysses* we find both Stephen Dedalus and Leopold Bloom pondering reincarnations throughout that famous Dublin day. That this belief is not subject to proof by syllogism is irrelevant; for the reader it is not necessary that he believe it; it is only necessary that he believe others believed it.

In a world in which *The Dybbuk* receives an accredited if unnaturalized acceptance, many other things undreamed of by pragmatic philosophers may occur. Here is this world between two worlds – the play *The Dybbuk* was at first called *Between Two Worlds* – the characters are moved by considerations which have but little to do with the profit and the loss, with the possessions and rewards of this valley of the shadow. The real scene of *The Dybbuk* is a bridge – the bridge which joins this life to the next. Almost throughout, the atmosphere is oppressive with judgment, broods with divinity. Chanan, the hero, wrestles with the secrets of the Cabbala; as he dies, the occult book *Raziel* falls from his hands. The Thirty-Six – the thirty-six anonymous worthies, water carriers and mendicants whose true holiness is not recognized by man – the thirty-six for whose sake alone God stays His hand and His wrath from a sinful world, – the thirty-six whose number is twice eighteen, the number of life – they are nowhere seen, everywhere present. In this milieu, the scholars of the synagogue stand engaged in calculating the value of every single letter in Holy Writ, attributing to each a number, one to the Aleph, two to the Bet, – even as we count C for a hundred and M for a thousand – and do from these calculations and equations seek to wrest some hidden meaning out of the Sacred Scriptures. The word of the greatest potency, of course, is the tetragrammaton, the four-lettered name of Jehovah, forbidden to be uttered save by the purest of the pure. For those who refuse to obey the laws of Torah there are no police sanctions; there is only, both for the parents who compact together that their children shall wed and then reject the compact, and for the student transgressing the proper limits of inquiry, there is only the instrument of excommunication with its black candles and white robes and ram's horn blown to shatter the air with anathema.

It is obvious that such elements in a play at once make for picturesqueness and stimulate the imagination, and there is no doubt but that not a little of *The Dybbuk*'s appeal lies in the charm of its unfamiliar properties. If, however, it was only the fascination for the esoteric which *The Dybbuk* answered, the play would be merely a piece of quaintness, an exercise in the antique, and only part of its attractiveness would have been explained. It is rather because the action of *The Dybbuk* appeals – although in a stylized form – to the perennial longings of men, that the play is perennially popular. The quarrel between the family of Chanan and the family of Leah belongs, though clothed in different vesture, to the same class as that between the Montagues and the Capulets. Pacts between parents touching their children, since they reach right into the heart of human relations, have ever engaged the interest of the spectator; they are a staple of the drama. Trial scenes – the whole world, – except its litigants, – loves trial scenes. The Messenger – the mysterious emissary from nowhere who interrupts the action with his melancholy ambiguous oracles – he, too, is of those who direct themselves to that appetite for wonder which in the human race is basic and ubiquitous. Thus it is in more than one sense that Anski's paradoxical description of the play is justified; *The Dybbuk*, said Anski, was a piece of realism about mysticism.

Of the total meaning of the play, the interpretations are as varied in their tendencies as are the interpreters in their temperaments and convictions. Some producers, smug and superior in their sceptic enlightenment, have sought to present *The Dybbuk* as if it were a satire upon superstition. Others have again attempted to direct into the play meanings economic and political; for them the scene in which the beggars appear is full of social significance; for them the so-called outmoded beliefs are but the natural corollaries of an outmoded economic system; and for them it is the messenger, offering the parable of the mirror and the window-pane who carries the full weight of the play's meaning, as he intones: 'Behold – in the window there is glass and in the mirror there is glass. But the glass of the mirror is covered with a little silver, and no sooner is the silver added than you cease to see *others* and see only *yourself.*'

Still other directors, attracted to the symbolism of *The Dybbuk* settings, have gallantly reduced the spoken play almost to a pantomime, a staging of formal gesture, hieratic stance, earlocked and caftan'd attitudinizing. Others again have emphasized the national moral inherent in the play's argument – the lesson that the individual interest, in a rightly ordered world, must cede to the public welfare. Says Rabbi Azrael, addressing himself to a Dybbuk who is not entirely without justification: 'I command you to leave the body of this maiden that a living branch of the tree of Israel may not be blasted!' And finally there are those who are particularly taken by the mystic overtones of this Chassidic masterpiece, by the truths but tentatively grasped which emerge from it, by the blurred but nonetheless gratifying glimpses of landscape beyond the bourne from which no traveller returns. If the necessary ingredients of classic tragedy are purpose, passion, and perception, certainly *The Dybbuk*, with its manifold purpose, its great purging passion, and its final and reconciling perception, qualifies for the characterization.

Of the performance that you are now about to listen to, it may even in advance be stated that it is unique at least in that it marks the first time that *The Dybbuk* is presented on the air. It is a notion for which Mr. Rupert Caplan, and Mr. Mac Shoub who adapted the script for radio, may well be congratulated. There is, I think, a special appropriateness in having a play which is so much concerned with spirits and the ethereal bring its message to the listener through the medium of the air-wave and the disembodied voice.

Thus is there added to Anski's realism about mysticism yet another element of the realistic: the burden of *Between Two Worlds* is actually carried through the space between the worlds. We are made eavesdroppers of interplanetary conversation; the choir and orchestra singing and playing the far-away melodies of Chassidism do but provide a sort of music of the spheres. And yet such is the marvel of the play that though its time is that of centuries past, and its locus the no-man's land of the terrible transition from life to death, from death to life, its appeal is to that Dybbuk, that secondary soul in all of us – the sense of beauty and of truth – which not all the incantations known to Cabbala can ever utterly cast out. It is a play of truths sempiternal, of longings immortal. Well might *The Dybbuk* take for its own epigraph the mystical utterance of William Butler Yeats who, sailing to his own Cabbalistic Byzantium, thus addressed the higher powers touching the soul and its agonized plight:

> O sages standing in God's holy fire
> As in the gold mosaic of a wall,
> Come from the holy fire, perne in a gyre,
> And be the singing-masters of my soul.
> Consume my heart away; sick with desire
> And fastened to a dying animal
> It knows not what it is; and gather me
> Into the artifice of eternity.

Somewhat of that artifice, somewhat of that eternity is offered by the drama you are about to hear.

A Chassidic Anthology

Review of *Tales of the Hasidim: The Later Masters* by Martin Buber
3 December 1948

OF HOMILIES

One wonders, as one reads through the collection of wisdom and piety which makes up this book, why so many of these anecdotes and aphorisms, evidently chosen from among many others by the distinguished Martin Buber, remain, at least to the reader, flat, stale, and unacceptable. Certainly it is not because through our veins there flows the inky blood of *Misnagdim*; for generations our ancestors have sworn by the holiness of 'him who should live.' Nor is it that we have been infected by Graetz's supercilious attitude towards the Besht and all his works; that quirk of the great historian we have always considered his sad deficiency.

It is, we fear, because a subtler poison has entered our constitution that so many of these excerpts fail to move us except with impatience or annoyance. Alas, we find ourselves – with many of our contemporaries – of that company which cannot appreciate sacred literature unless it has in it something of the novel, the paradoxical, the witty, or, better still, something of that shuddering naiveté, that startling innocence which transcends in religious effect all the ingenuities of all the pilpulists of all the academies.

Too many of the parables before us have none of these qualities. Too often they constitute but solemn reiterations of platitudes, and sometimes, downright vulgarisms. It is true that audacity in religious expression is sometimes a merit; but comparing the service of the Lord to the servicing of Bathsheba (p. 51) is audacity which merges right into chutzpa, if not worse. Nor is one tremendously impressed by the Sadagoran contribution:

'What can we learn from a train?'
'That because of one second one can miss everything.'
'And from the telegraph?'
'That every word is counted and charged.'
'And the telephone?'
'That what we say here is heard there.'

The truth of these truisms is incontrovertible, but, since they compare the greater to the lesser, – God's works to those of a.t. & t. – they constitute an exegetical solecism. And they lack the true religious note.

Martin Buber, it appears, has gone to the opposite extreme: where Graetz uniformly scoffed, Buber invariably prays. But his zadicolatry is not always convincing.

Indeed, at times one is inclined to suspect that some of these anecdotes were smuggled and sabotaged into the collection by some cross-brained Litvak *Misnagid*. Thus Rabbi Mendel of Rymanov is alleged to have said: 'If a thousand believing *hasidim* were to gather around a block of wood, it too would work miracles!'

OF THE SLAVIC

It is more than merely Slavic place-names that the Chassidic movement has introduced into our hagiography, although even that contribution is not without its colour and fascination. How otherwise would our heaven have been enriched, as with some new eighteenth-century constellations, with seraphs of Strelisk, cherubs of Kalev, and sundry luminaries of Tchortkov, Sadagora, Probishtch, Zlotchov, and Tchernobl? How else, save through the grace of saintly intercession, could such a moujik nomenclature become naturalized among the appellatives of Amos and Isaiah?

But it is also for that it re-introduced into our exilic culture the elements of the proletarian and the peasant that the Chassidic movement is notable. So many of these anecdotes of pipe-smoking rabbis, of saints consorting with teamster and gipsy, possess the true flavour of the soil, so much of this wisdom is farmer's wisdom, that it constitutes a refreshing interlude after the cloistered hemmed-in airless disquisitions of Talmudic legalists.

Indeed, in this entry of Slavic folklore into our own eastern culture, the process of religious and intellectual influence comes full circle. There is no doubt but that concealed beneath the surface of Russian peasant culture there lies, impalpable but extant, a considerable number of eastern vestiges: one has only to listen to some Caucasian melodies to assure oneself of this affinity; the introduction of the Slavic to the Judaic is, in a sense, therefore, a return of the eastern to the eastern.

OF TRANSLATION

We move for the establishment of an Anglo-Jewish Academy, one whose business it will be, among other things, to determine and set down what are the proper Englishings (and transliterations) for our specialized Hebrew and Yiddish ecclesiastical vocabulary. We doubt whether forty immortals will be sufficient for this task; a complete Sanhedrin seems necessary; but the work is certainly one which requires to be done.

Why is this volume titled 'Tales of the *Hasidim*'? Is it thought that American Jews suffer laryngeal occlusions? Is Chassidism really unpronounceable to Anglicized Jewry? How about Loch Lomond?

Olga Marx, who does a generally fine job of translating, here renders *Kol Nidre* as 'All Vows.' This, of course, is literally correct; but surely the phrase 'All Vows' is much too reminiscent of 'All Saints,' and therefore objectionable as a gentilizing of our halidom? Surely it would have been better to leave it as *Kol Nidre*, which if not completely naturalized, is well on the way with first papers.

'The Ten Days of Contrition' are referred to as 'The Ten Days of Turning.' This is, again, a literalism, but a literalism with much to recommend it. The notion that turning is equivalent to repentance – compare Eliot: 'Because I do not hope to turn again ...' – is not an esoteric one; but it isn't a common one, either. 'Evil Urge' for *Soton Hora* seems singularly weak, and 'Quorum' for *Minyan*, while corporatively exact, lacks the necessary religious connotations: can it be said that wherever there is a quorum the Shekinah abides?

What, then, should have been the proper translations? We are not an Academy.

Melech Grafstein's Sholom Aleichem

Review of *A Sholom Aleichem Panorama* edited by Melech Grafstein
21 January 1949

The impelling causes which prompt publishers and editors to put out books of one kind rather than of another are often very difficult to fathom. Sometimes it is the greed of the publisher that lies palpable on every page; everywhere one sees that the publisher thought he had hit upon a novel notion and was determined to cash in on it. Other occasions there are when it is the publisher's vanity that preens itself through every editorial gesture; you can almost feel him storming the gates of immortality. Such motives, of course, infect the given opus with the taint of corruption even at the outset. Fortunately, the pain which publications thus impelled inflict upon the reader are compensated by those of the third category – the works which see the light of day because behind them stood a man encompassed and overwhelmed by a great love.

It is to this third category that Melech Grafstein's *Sholom Aleichem Panorama* belongs. From the first page to the very last of this splendid-looking volume, the indicia of Grafstein's worship of the memory of Sholom Aleichem, a worship which almost reaches the thither side of idolatry, shine before the reader like the details of a prolonged and impressive religious ceremonial. To Melech Grafstein every obiter dictum, every single aside of the Great Master is precious and sacred; is there extant somewhere an old programme of an early Sholom Aleichem theatre performance, behold it here photostated and gloriously framed. The humorist's handwriting, his musical experiments, his letters, his photographs – a complete album of Sholom Aleichem at different times of his life and with various friends, both great and humble – all are preserved, with love and boundless affection – in the pages of this book. The result is that we get the impression, not of an editorial job assigned for a wage to some dryasdust scholar, but of the presentation of some dearly beloved cult by some priest or minister fearful lest the memory of his adored one be not properly esteemed. The only comparable things that we know of are the volumes of Dickensiana which now appear not so often as they used to; the veneration, the love, the cherishing which goes beyond mere literary appreciation, is the same in both.

Nor is it difficult to understand. Melech Grafstein associates the flourishing of Sholom Aleichem and of Peretz with the days of his youth – then it was that both these masters counted for something in the Jewish world, the world of Eastern Europe, and, by echo and reverberation, the world abroad. That youth Grafstein would recapture, hence this act of tribute which for 415 pages brightens the *Sholom Aleichem Panorama*. It is, moreover, a celebration not without its tragedy, – for they who were the readers of Sholom Aleichem, they and their children, six million of them, are no more. Grafstein's plight is therefore like that of the minister, devotee of the ancient worship, who knows that the first congregation has disappeared; passionately, he looks about him for another; – and he has Sholom Aleichem translated into English.

One does not expect such a book to be produced by one man, no matter how many translators and collaborators he can command. Such a book usually issues from an organization, or from an academy, if not of forty immortals, at least of forty mortals. We are happy that it had no such genesis. Academy editions usually pay for their greater authority by a diminished enthusiasm. We are happy that in London, Ontario, there abides a man, King Grafstein by name – that name demands to be translated – who, indulging in a remembrance of things past, has seen fit, by his own effort and at his own cost, to offer to the present this resplendent vision of a glory that he would not see vanish.

But books born out of love, like love itself, carry their own penalty. Love being blind, many things which are obvious to the undimmed eye are not perceivable by the infatuated one. Hence some slips of taste which, to this reader at least, though he recognizes them for slips of taste, provide a certain quaint and outmoded charm. One may perhaps quarrel with the necessity which prompted such a superabundance of photographs; one may perhaps question the pertinence of some of these insertions; one may even feel a little uncomfortable before the naive excess of some of the laudations; but all this is a very small price – if price at all – to pay for the great riches here contained.

We spoke of the peculiar charm of the general make-up of the book. It is a charm difficult to describe – partly it is made up of the nostalgia of album-reading – here are all one's uncles and aunts, here are the typical attitudes and poses (including baskets of flowers) which once, long ago, were the *dernier cri*; it is as if one were looking at a 1914 movie, but a movie in which the dear remembered names of one's family constituted the cast. Perhaps another editor, another publisher, would, in putting out this volume, have called upon the entire apparatus of 1948 modernism: surrealist drawings, pseudo-impartial estimates, wild and daring typography. If this had been done, loss would have been suffered. We would have had the nice hygiene and synthetic flavour of an up-to-date beverage, – but not, alas, the bouquet and aroma of heritage wine.

Of the verbal contents it can only be said that in such an universality, unevenness was inevitable. Some of the essays, as some of the translations, are good; some are better; some, neither. Those which are good are very good, indeed; those which are not declare their deficiency after the first paragraph. In a volume such as this, however, it is the total impression which counts, and that total impression is here sufficiently favourable to cover all blots and blemishes. We have here, in truth, a panorama – essays, short stories, sketches, verses, plays, etc. – of the world of Sholom Aleichem. For opening that vista to the eyes of many who would not otherwise be blessed with such vision, Melech Grafstein deserves from Yiddish literature an interpreter's reward, from English writing a debt of gratitude. He has done them both a service, and more than the service he perhaps intended; for he intended a panorama and an anthology, and has fashioned also a documentary and a monument – a monument of love to the memory of Sholom Aleichem. That is why the slips and errors do not count; love conquers all.

Poet of a World Passed By

Review of *Sefer Yiddish* [in Yiddish] by J.I. Segal   9 June 1950

After reading, with a pleasure which was largely made up of lyric pain, the almost six hundred pages of this volume, I could see its author in no other guise but as a sort of inspired last survivor of some vanished tribe, a melancholy bard walking among the ruins of his burned-down village, pausing to recall a former felicity associated with this landmark, an historic incident associated with that other, calling to the empty air, and finally turning aside, determined to fashion in words the monument and image of his destroyed birthplace.

For it is in this volume, so full of contemporary poignancy, and yet so eloquent with timeless statement, that Segal emerges as the devoted elegist of all that was fine and beautiful in the life of Eastern Europe in general, and in particular, in the life of the typically Chassidic hamlet from which he hails. The poems, it is true, are concerned with numerous subjects, yet one is the theme to which they are sung – a threnodic ululation for a world that once shone with piety and humility, and now beyond humbleness lies in ruin and rubble.

As if Koretz were itself a Torah and Segal himself following the injunction of Ben Bag-Bag, he turns it 'about and about.' Above all he recalls with a self-associating nostalgia its beggars, its secret saints, its paupers. It is clear, moreover, as one reads these lines all of pathos compact that it is not only a compulsion to mourn another's death – the passing of the six million

– that impels the poet on from elegy to elegy; he mourns also his own childhood whose very image now lies like a broken toy before him.

Above all Segal mourns what he fears to be the demise of a language. Certainly his loveliest and most touching lyrics are dedicated to the praise of Yiddish, the speech itself; he caresses it, he soothes it, he would with a mere act of will bring it back to its original currency, its pristine glory.

He even sanctifies the language. He achieves this sanctification through a technique indicated in the very title of the book: he Hebraizes as much as possible of the Yiddish vernacular. To a language which already boasts at least a ten-per-cent solution of Hebrew, Segal through neologism, through adaptation, adds more and more. After the *Sefer Yiddish* is read, the language itself emerges as a second *loshon koidesh*, holy speech.

Through these poems there march, in reminiscent sequence, the worthies of Koretz, Segal's uncles and aunts, the town-characters, its recognized rabbins, its hidden saints. Here, too, the symbols of Jewish folklore take on a new life and vividness – the bearded and pathetic goat, the golden parrot, those ineffable raisins and almonds.

Segal's matter, then, is fit subject for poetry – the beauty and colour of a unique culture, the tragedy of its uprooting and destruction. To this theme the poet brings a temperament and a technique equal to its challenge. It is difficult to illustrate in English the linguistic felicities and ingenuities which Segal is able to manipulate – suffice it to say that in his hands the Yiddish language, despite its alleged moribundity, becomes a ring of fire, vivid, chatoyant, protean. He is its master; it is as if Segal were privy to some verbal jiu-jitsu whereby he could make its words leap into whatever stances, contortions, and attitudes he devised for them.

Yet an evocative theme and virtuosity galore are not enough – there must also be manifest, if the poem is to be poem and not mere treatise, the fashioning imagination. Segal's is one of the most fanciful, one of the most tropical, in contemporary Yiddish literature. Even his saddest songs admit to a certain gaiety – the gaiety of the imagination with its own imaginings consoling itself among the ruins.

It is the imagination, in truth, which strews the pages with wealth. It is this which makes possible, in a literature where the Queen Sabbath has been sung almost ad nauseam, a 'Song of Praise for the Dull Level Mid-week'; it is this which transforms the beggar come from distant parts into a king travelling incognito; or this which makes possible that most revealing and most heart-breaking of images – the one in which Segal compares the Yiddish poem to the grandfather's answering *Amen* to his grandson's *kaddish* ...

In many of Segal's poems there is allusion to the paintings of Chagall. The reference is not accidental. Segal is the Chagall of poets – his village is

Chagall's village, his distortion, his marvels and wonders are kin to those of that genial artist.

There is no doubt but that the *Sefer Yiddish* is an event in contemporary Jewish literature.

The Art of Hertz Grosbard   4 April 1952

Whoever has not heard Hertz Grosbard reading, reciting, elocuting, – these verbs are but pale descriptions of his performance – whoever has not heard him rendering from the masterpieces of Yiddish literature, not seen him flash forth its gems, vivify its printed pages, such a one has not ever really known the power and beauty of human expression.

Last week I went to listen to this wizard who turns into magic the simplest of words. It was an experience.

It was with misgiving that I went. Elocution can be such a dire deadly art. A man – and women are even worse offenders – get him upon a stage, a sheaf of papers in his hand, or a burden of books weighing him down, he pauses before the microphone, he surveys his audience, and then – methodically, relentlessly, he either pursues his listener with a sickening drip of prissiness, or drowns him in a sea of monotony, or seeks to tear him to shreds, passion by ranted passion. One keeps looking at one's watch.

Not thus Grosbard.

For Grosbard brings to his recital, over and above a multitude of other talents, one paramount excellence: intelligence. He so studies his text that he himself is woven into its texture. He does not comment upon the selections he includes in his repertoire; his reading is the commentary. As, garbed in formal dress, he moves from reading to reading, pausing a space between the varied selections, he so transforms his manner that it is as if one were watching him go through a special kind of make-up, right upon the stage, – only the make-up is a make-up of personality, of changed articulation, and not of raiment or beard.

In heavy pondrous voice he announces the title of the piece he is about to read – you *see* the bold-face capital letters.

He raises his eyebrows – you *know* that what he is reading is in italics.

Even the commas in his text are somehow expressed.

Those three significant dots that so frequently appear at the end of literary sentences, – with a gesture, a shrug of the shoulders, a crinkled nose, he pronounces them.

The result is – protean. Last week he read about fifteen selections – and the stage was peopled with over a score of characters, each different from the other, and all owing their existence and personality to the articulation of Grosbard's voice, to his subtle and subdued mimesis.

And these characters, they were not routine. They hailed from the kingdoms human, animal, vegetable, mineral.

Yes, he endowed with a personality and a typical mode of expression even the cat in the fable by Steinberg. That cat, it doesn't simply meow; it takes all of its sentences – as Grosbard reads them – and makes them feline; it me-ollifies the Yiddish language.

Take his reading of Lutzky's piece about the contents of a cooking-pot. Under Grosbard's specially devised mode of reading, these contents, onion and bean and long thin *loksh*, all are made to speak with accents bean-bold, onion-involved, loksh-like.

Many can mimick human speech. Grosbard ventriloquizes vegetables.

His reading is not simply a reading, it is an animation of the inanimate, – a Disney cartoon in words.

As one recalls his varied program, – monologue, dialogue, mass *mise-en-scène*, fanciful fable and Chassidic tale, exercise in naiveté, nostalgic poem, parody, satire, – one hears him again reciting, intoning, whispering, sneering between the hyphens, weeping, almost-weeping, thundering, confiding, even neighing. (Did you ever hear a horse neigh Yiddish? A talking horse? A horse talking Yiddish with inflections truly equine?) Grosbard does all that; and then, in the next poem, he will show you how a sentence actually dreams.

To achieve these virtuosities, Grosbard comes admirably endowed. A fine presence; a face wonderfully expressive, it is like some rugged landscape over which cloud and sunshine play hide-and-seek; a resonant voice, agile in transformations; eyes like the ancient mariner's; and above all – intelligence.

And these are not simply physical traits; they are, each of them, actors in a cast, directed by Grosbard, obedient to his bidding.

Hertz Grosbard has been in this country but a short time, and has already given a number of his word-concerts, everywhere bravo'd and encore'd. In Europe he enjoyed a far-flung reputation as *diseur*; his performances were rightly considered events.

Alas, the Jewish audiences of Europe are no more, and Grosbard must perforce seek his auditors upon this continent. I think he ought to be given the widest hearing possible; his is a cultural contribution of the first order.

Is it necessary to understand Yiddish to appreciate Grosbard? It helps, of course, but it is not essential. I venture to believe that even those *totally* ignorant of that language may find in his readings much that is at once entertaining and rewarding. For at the very same time Grosbard is pronouncing Yiddish, he is – in tone, in gesture, in inflection – communicating speech universal. He converts, by mere reading, Yiddish into an already-understood Esperanto.

His program, it is to be noted, is chosen with the same intelligence that he brings to his reading. Large portions thereof are pure entertainment – humour and parody and satire, fun with significance, gaiety that does not evaporate with its laughs. When I consider the wandering lecturers on Jewish humour, peddling, as much too often they do, their parcels of vulgarity to Jewish centres, or the Jewish impresarios of skits and revues, that bring to the face a blush as red as the borsht they sing, and contrast this fare with that which Grosbard provides – I am unable printably to complete this sentence.

Elocutionist? Reader? *Diseur*? Actor? Grosbard is all of these; he is also, this Grosbard, bard. Bard is he not only in that he brings his own poetic addition to his texts, but bard also in his *métier* and the manner thereof. For he makes real and vivid again the old tradition, that of the bard wandering among the folk, meeting in camp after camp with gathered tribesmen, and there reading to them, reciting before them, tales of tragedy or of high exploit, song of love, epic of enemy resisted, – the remembered treasures of the heritage.

Such a bard is in our midst again. Let the tribesmen gather.

Poems of Yehoash

Review of *Poems of Yehoash* selected and translated by Isidore Goldstick, with a biographical sketch by Evlin Yehoash Dworkin

26 September 1952

This is a beautiful book that lies before us, of an immaculate candour, its whiteness enhanced by its letters of gold, a truly pure and pious memorial to a great Yiddish poet, absent from among mortals these twenty-five years, now in the high company he keeps immortal.

Immortal, one says of Yehoash, and upon the utterance of the lavish epithet no anxieties follow; here is no doubt. For Yehoash has made himself the most wonderful prophylactic against oblivion; he has translated the Bible. He has bound himself to a Book Eternal. As long as Yiddish is spoken, or remembered, so long will the name and work of Yehoash be spoken and remembered, for in Yiddish his version of the Bible is sole, unique, without rival; it admits no parallel text. What the Mendelssohn version is to German, what the 1611 version is to English, that Yehoash is to Yiddish. Not a book, but a testament; not a work, but a monument.

Yehoash's translation, a great good in itself, brought to his native tongue a double felicity. It rendered the Old Testament accessible even to those of his co-religionists who had no Hebrew; it gave to the Yiddish language itself a classical ring, a sublimity it had hitherto lacked. Such consummations are usually the result of a combined effort (one thinks of the seventy elders, each in his cubicle, labouring at the Septuagint); entire academies, assembled synods, conclaves convoked – these are the usual instruments of Bible translation. Yehoash laboured alone. He laboured, moreover, in the constant shadow of death. Until his very last day, disease eating his lungs, stifling his breath, he stood, at his work, giving to the book of Life the life of a new language.

These are the facts and memoirs, this is the admiration, which give to his daughter's brief memoir the poignant pathos that it communicates. As one reads from paragraph to paragraph one is moved by the dauntless spirit of the poet, touched by the love and loyalty of his house. 'It was my task to read aloud from his translation, as he walked back and forth with a *Tanach* in his hand, listening to the cadence of the Yiddish and comparing it with the original.' How reminiscent of the midnight sessions in the home of Milton, his daughters reading him Aramaic – with these differences, Milton's daughters read but knew not what they read, Milton was all austerity and dourness, while Yehoash moved in a circle of love.

There is yet another sadness which issues from these pages. The commemoration of the twenty-fifth anniversary of the passing of the Bible's Yiddish translator finds six million of those Yiddish-speaking readers no longer among the living. It is as if some sorcerer, moved by the illnesses of his kith and kin, set himself to discover the elixir of life, and discovering it, runs posthaste back to his native town only to learn so many of his kinsmen perished.

There is, then, a great justice in Dr. Isidore Goldstick's translations from Yehoash's poems. For the Yiddish-speaking readers that Yehoash lost so grievously, they provide – dire compensation – an English-speaking public. Goldstick's Englishings, moreover, demonstrate that Yehoash was not only a translator of the Bible, superb distinction though that is, but also himself a poet worthy to be translated.

And Goldstick, to whom Yiddish and Yiddish literature are already indebted for many loyal and resourceful services rendered, does well by Yehoash. He is no easy poet to translate. There is in Yehoash's lines a certain delicate fragility which often will not bear up under the torsions of translation. One must move carefully about them, lest they flake, or even break. It is to the credit of Goldstick as a translator, to his honour as a man, that he has approached these tenuous artifacts with care, piety, precision, and has achieved in a number of these translations the translator's ideal, to wit, the translation that reads like an original.

Of Hebrew Calligraphy

Review of *The Israel Art Haggadah* hand-lettered and ornamented by
Jacob Zim   8 May 1953

It may seem a curious thing to our readers that the following excursus on
Hebrew calligraphy, for which it is a Passover Haggadah that serves as point
of departure, should appear in our columns at a date closer to the pentecostal
than to the paschal festival. It is, indeed, true that more than a month has
passed since the larceny of the *afikomen*; still, the anachronism of present
publication, we think, is more apparent than real. In the first place, it is not
a review of the Haggadah that we intend – that composition has already passed
the muster of the centuries – but some notes on Hebrew typography, a subject
ever timely. The text of Mr. Zim's Haggadah is here presented simply as
model and exemplar. We feel certain, moreover, that our readers, imbued
with that spirit of kindliness which we have learned to expect from them, will
set these paragraphs down, not as one month belated, but as eleven months
anticipatory.

Mr. Zim, originally Zimberknopf, is descended, we are informed, from
a long line of scribes and calligraphists. The hereditary talent, it appears on
every page, has not forsaken him. Calligraphy has ever been a greatly honoured, though not always greatly rewarded, profession in Jewry; cases indeed
have there been when Jews distinguished either in the courts of Spain or in
the chancellories of the East, have owed their eminence to precisely this talent;
it has traditions at once religious and secular; it provides one of the few, very
few opportunities whereby the artistic inclination among Jews, the second
Commandment notwithstanding, may be exercised, not only with impunity,
but to the greater glory of God; and of art, pursued in this tradition, Mr.
Zim is an inspired practitioner.

Nor are they the illustrations, the vignettes, the border pieces, the eyelets
and the fleurons, with which the scribe occasionally ornaments his pages,
which have elicited our especial admiration; it is his sense of symmetry, his
ordering of the single page, his shaping and manipulation of the Hebrew letter,
it is on these things which he should be judged and these which proclaim him
master of his craft. Labouring against the prohibition which forbids the making
of images, the Hebrew scribe converts, even as does the Arabic calligraphist,
his challenge into a virtuosity, and turns mere geometry, the squares and
blocks of his alphabet, into a most singular art-form, abstract, pure, spiritual.
Shapes, human or animal, here are an intrusion; it is the ancestral letter itself,

each so rich in saecular association, which is to be so designed, lengthened or widened, thicken'd or etherealized, as to convey the scribe's secret silent commentary to his text.

As the tradition requires, Mr. Zim's letters are full of *taggin*, the so-called pot-hooks and hangers, the filaments of diadem which crown the letters of our Scrolls of the Law; but with Mr. Zim these quiddities are not merely ornamental but functional in their purpose. They provide, out of the very body of his founts, a running commentary to the narrative and doxology of the Haggadah. Thus his page 63, topped by four lines of Hosanna, is so fimbriated with hair-line ascension, so rarefied with their broken, medial horizontals, that the paragraph, though heavily set, appears as a levitation, an ascension, an exaltation of scripture. Again, on page 69, the scribe achieves an ingenious transposition of piety: two paragraphs there are, each beginning with a *yud* – these Mr. Zim so arranges that they shoot from the page like the two iotas of God's name!

His reading of the text, indeed, is most perceptive. Noting that the classic passage, *dayenu*, consists of a series of protases ('if God had only ...') and apodoses ('... and had not ...'), and that the introductory phrases *illu* and *v'loi* are made up of the same letters, *aleph, lamed,* and *vav,* he shapes his two pages to a symmetry at once visual and logical. The French idiom, *sauter aux yeux,* is here given vivid exemplification; the meaning of the poem does in truth 'jump at the eyes.' His spacing, of course, is measured and calculated; yet, on page 49, third line, there appears to be a lacuna; one suspects at first that Zim has nodded until one observes that this seeming error is preceded by text touching 'God's open hand,' and one realizes that the scribe is illustrating this divine quality – by means of empty space!

Equally ingenious is the scribe in the shaping of ligatures, letters that are combined either because of the exigencies of space or the imperatives of meaning. On page 47, in the word *olam* ('the world') a *mem* thus nestles in the shadow of a *lamed,* and one is at a loss to know whether it was the stricture of the line-length or some mysterious connotation concerning the ways of the world which compelled this joinder: one ends up by suspecting both causes as being operative here. A similar ligature, this time between *mem* and *resh,* in the word *shene'amar* ('as it is written') is effected twice on page 27 – they are things to be pondered over.

One of the tests of the scribe is his manipulation of the *litterae dilatibiles,* the dilatable letters, letters that may be widened or narrowed, as the page requires. Skill in this technique of an extraordinary kind is displayed, on page 74, in the poem 'And it happened in the mid of night,' where the scribe plays with a fascinating versatility on the letters *lamed* and *hai* of the word *lailah* – 'night.'

The book contains an untold number of such calligraphic felicities. These may be compared, in a sense, to the commentatorial beauties which frequently occur in the cantorial art; cantors, even as scribes, are wont to make, these with their trills and tremolos as those with their lines and ornamentations, their interpretations of text. Here, however, is not the place to annotate the annotator. Let the reader peruse this text at his leisure – he need not wait until next Passover – and he will find therein, in the seemingly barren mould of mere type, in the very configuration of Mr. Zim's *aleph* and *bais*, much to please the eye and much to engage and edify the mind.

In Memoriam: J.I. Segal   12 March 1954

With the sudden snatching-away, at the early age of 53, of the poet J.I. Segal, Yiddish literature has suffered a loss most grievous, – irreparable. For Segal was not just another rhymester toying with the echoes of sound, a bard by mere avocation. Poetry for him, the faithful guardian of an antique tradition, was not only a calling to be followed; it was a call to be answered. That call came to him across the generations by way of an unbroken sacred legacy, bequeathed at first by the Baal Shem Tov, cherished by the Bratzlaver, and at last transmitted from his favorite Koretz to this latter-day Levite 'making great song for a little clan.' At the ark and covenant of his verse he served his office well. Much music might yet have issued from those lips that Death has so prematurely stilled. With that sixth sense which is the special, and sometimes terrible, gift that God bestows upon all poets, Segal had his premonitions. More than a decade ago, he wrote, touching the perpetual conflict between the world's contending lesser gods:

> The God of Lies shows two sharp oxen-horns,
> But the horns of the God of Truth are small and sorry ...
> And the God of Beauty, with the antlers of a deer,
> Stands in a quiet wood, as in a dream,
> And, wondering at the light of the young day,
> Drinks the dew in with his large, mild, brown eyes.
>
> But the God of Death – that sable haggard hunter! –
> Hidden behind a tree, has drawn his bow.
> O, all the trees and saplings hold their breath!

In the time which was given to him, however, he himself created a great legacy of verse. The language in which he wrote has fallen upon evil days, the halidoms which he served are almost universally disregarded; nonetheless, alone, and in an alien environment, he stood protector over them, – to a tongue which seemed archaic, adding his own neologisms; to a tradition that was waning, contributing the afflatus of his genius. That tradition, brought here from his forefathers, he thought of as 'Old Gold':

> Even as a great country withers, and goes to rot,
> And a peaceful tribe is broken, and falls at last –
> Such was the falling of that poor small hut,
> My grandfather's, whose memory be blessed!
>
> Seven the generations beneath that roof,
> And the roof was cracked, and let in rain and day ...
> I took, then, bag and baggage, warp and woof,
> And, a lost exile, went forth on my way.
>
> O, the dear folksong ambled after me,
> Riding upon that famous little goat
> Which shook its beard in the golden melody,
> And shook the crib in the marvellous anecdote!
>
> The ship in the harbour waited, twilight-hooded.
> Upon the masts hung seagulls, timorous.
> Upon the shore the silent twilight brooded ...
> Then ... slid into that waiting ship with us ...

With such bag and baggage come into a milieu which either knew them not, or was fast forgetting them, Segal's portion was a difficult one, – doubly difficult, first, in the choice of his craft, poetry, and second, and that to him was rightly more important, in the view of life which he sought to telescope through his work. In one of his introspective poems, so poignant to read now, he says:

> For whom am I these things recounting?
> For my most welcome guest, Reb Death,
> Come now to ask of me accounting
> For my exhaled and squandered breath,
>
> For all my doubts and hesitations,
> And all my foolish fears and sighs,
> And for these sorrowful collations
> Over the which I spent my eyes.

I never did become a scholar,
And no doubt never grew more smart,
While all the wise ones, the connivers,
Lorded it in the public mart.

Of course I have been hurt by these things,
By seeing the sated rich men kick
Good folk about, themselves all pompous
Behind silk stomach and gold stick.

But I, I certainly have gathered
The little that to my way came,
And with my measured days, allotted,
Played the right proper bitter game.

And now the little period passes:
What is the small change I owe you?
O write it down among the grasses;
It will be paid, whatever's due.

There is nothing due. It is the world that is in his debt, not he in its.
For, as labours of love and acts of piety, he enriched the literature of his
people; he preserved, shaped, and renewed its language; in his poetry, he
fashioned works of an enduring worth; in his prose, he enunciated principles
and established criteria that will long hold sway; and in all these endeavours
he stood the unfee'd custodian of a culture. With his passing that culture is
depleted.

With a special anguish will his loss be felt by his family and friends;
his family whose portraits shine through every volume of his poems:

My child has just begun to walk,
I watch her every little step.
I hold her by her left hand,
And God by her right ...

and his friends, among whom the writer of these lines was proud to count
himself, and for whom Segal's company – alas, no more! – was a constant
delight. His fine convivial spirit, his *bons mots*, his sage anecdotes, his quiet
sense of humour, and, above all, his great human sympathies, these made up
a personality such as one rarely encounters. One thought, sometimes, whether
as one leaf'd through the pages of his books and saw revealed there his all-
absorbing pity for the hopeless and helpless of this world, the pauper, the
beggar, the hunchback, the child, or whether as one listened to his subdued

speech, speech in which the name of the Bratzlaver joined, through some transcendent concord, the name of Rilke, one thought that this poet, this Segal of the two iotas, was, perhaps, one of those thirty-six for whose sake God stays His angry hand.

Certainly the major motifs of his life as of his work were understanding and compassion. Jewish literature will celebrate him; the Jewish community will record him; we will remember him. We will remember him for our many and long sessions, in which we mingled the parables of Rabbi Pinchas of Koretz with the visions of William Blake, and both with spring and summer weather; we will remember him for the seriousness of his inner thought and for the gaiety of his outward expression; and always remembered will he be for the words of compassion with which he ever sought to console those who dwelt in the windy chillness of the valley. It was a compassion which went beyond sect, and clan, and race, and continent, it embraced mankind. Would that it had been given, if not to him, then to another, if not to one other, then to the united many, to achieve what Segal longed for in his 'Song':

World, I would take and lift you up,
Like a sheep lost in the dell,
And bear you to the high hill-top,
To the golden well!

Surely I know your tiredness,
Lamb fallen to the ground!
I, too, am weary and athirst,
And have no water found.

O, high upon the sunlit hill
That well is cool and deep ...
The sun washes her face in it
Before she goes to sleep.

World, I would take and lift you up,
(Sheep lost in the dell!)
And carry you to the high hill-top,
To the golden well!

2 / JEWISH FOLK CULTURE

Jewish Folk-Songs

Were all tomes and treatises on Jewish life in Eastern Europe to go up in incendiary or censorial smoke, there still would remain in the numerous folk-songs which haunt the epic memory of the Jew, sufficient material wherewith to conjure up, as by incantation, the phantom of that picturesque past. For there is hardly a phase of Jewish life which is not echoed or mimicked in the ubiquitous folk-song, written by an unseen hand, and sung by an impersonal voice. No scribbling dilettante, in search of a private immortality, penned the naive simplicities of these songs; out of the travail and pain, and out of the joy and jubilee which encompassed an entire nation were these little cherry-stone masterpieces born. From the mind of a multitude they sprang; they found refuge in the heart of a people. A song was sung, and as by a miracle, an entire ghetto, from rabbi to sexton, throbbed in harmony. In a world of private property, our folk-songs were the first assets to be nationalized.

The folk-song runs the complete gamut of the lyric, and twangs harmoniously from every heart-string. There are the wistful self-commiserating songs of dowerless old maids waiting for belated lovers until, as the proverb has it, their braids grow grey; boisterous carousal-hymns; ditties for teamsters; melodies for the lovelorn; epithalamia, and their logical aftermath in lullabies; Chassidic ecstasies tunefully rendered; satiric thrusts at the atheist and the heterodox; and pithy graveyard commentaries. They are a catalogue of folk-emotions, and upon all of them lies the national signature. For the sorrow is not of the spinster, but of spinsterdom; and the joy not of the single *Chassid*, but of the entire *Bet Hamidrash*.

To translate these Yiddish melodies into Anglo-Saxon gutturals is no easy task. In no matter how impeccable a translation, the nuance is always absent; and what reads in the original as a cry from the heart, becomes in translation as the virtuosity of a ventriloquist. When it is intended, moreover, that the translated verse be sung to the tune of melodies untranslatable, the incongruity between the tongue that Shakespeare spake and the *niggun* that Reb Levi Yitschok hummed becomes glaringly apparent. The nameless authors of the songs must in their graves resent this pouring of old wine into new bottles; *qui traduit, traduce*. At best, translation can give but the import and intent of the original song; its inflection and subtlety can never be linguistically naturalized into an alien tongue. It is like the rough texture of the reverse side of a Persian carpet; the pattern is there, but the artistry is missing. For the translations which follow, therefore, we apologise to anonymity.

There are some folk-songs, moreover, which defy translation even within the limits charily outlined above. One can not put into English metre the lullaby which croons that under Yankele's cradle there stands a white goat which departs to traffic in almonds and raisins; and which, after having sent the bearded goat upon his commercial ventures in the sale of the toothsomest of delicates, goes on to prophesy that Yankele will learn Torah, for Torah is the best of wares. And yet a powerful *argumentum ad parvulam* is wrapped in this lullaby. The good graces of the child are won by the mention of the national sweetmeats and by the reference to his sincerest crony, the domestic goat; a whimsical partnership is then indicated in which the billy becomes a merchant and Yankele a scholar, dealer in merchandise far more precious, – a partnership like that of Zebulun the seafarer, and Issachar, dweller in tents. No other people, we think, has ever expressed sentiments like these in its lullabies. The German suckling listens to songs of soldiers on the Rhine; the British infant is lulled to sleep with chanties about mariners braving the foam; but Israel's child, combining piety with pity, dreams of sage Talmudists and lugubrious goats.

And indeed this uncommon lullaby is the beginning of what would be judged by romantic standards to be a commonplace life. For in the ghetto existence of the eighteenth and nineteenth centuries there was no room for the Shakespearian division of life into seven poetic ages. In the following song one will look in vain for the whining schoolboy; here is no lover sighing like a furnace; here no soldier full of strange oaths.

> When he has frolicked for a little
> He will learn Torah, jot and tittle;
> The child will con his daily verses,
> And we will hear the town rehearse his
> Sweet merits; and at his own wedding
> Acute *Responsa* he'll be threading.
> The whole world will eke out a pleasure
> From bridegroom, bride, and dowry-treasure.
> A dowry-purse of worth exceeding,
> And such a family of breeding!!
> The groom will dwell there, without payment,
> For three good years, in food and raiment.

Such was the pre-ordained level of the days of a not penurious son. There are, however, lullabies that penniless mothers sang to pauper babes, songs from which there springs a poignant anguish culminating in a Yiddish resignation. In the days when the hand that rocked the cradle was the man's, while the wife went a-bargaining, it is thuswise that a father in Israel hums to his cradle-Kaddish:

> On the attic sleeps a roof,
> Decked with shingles, split and small;
> In the cradle dreams a child,
> Naked, with no clothes at all.
>   Hop, hop, even so,
> From the thatch the goat pulls straw,
>   Hop, hop, even so.

Immediately the impression of poverty is made indelible. The child lies in the cradle without even the luxury of diapers; and the goat, unable to find sustenance in fodder, is forced to pull straw from the thatched roof. Then, symbolism:

> In the attic stands a crib,
> In it swings a spider, who
> Draws my life-blood out of me,
> Leaves me bitterness and rue.

Follows the refrain in which the hop-hop echoes the to-and-fro action of a cradle pushed by a masculine foot. Then, finally, an ingenious and typical solution of the problem of an empty pantry:

> On the roof the rooster crows,
> And his comb is fiery red –
> Let my wife go borrow aught,
> Let her buy the children bread.

In after years the youngster now lulled to sleep with songs of poverty will, if the spirit moves him, also study the Torah of the Lord, even as his more affluent brother of the substantial dowry. But he, in all likelihood, will either eat 'days' at the home of some Jewish patron, or sojourn at a boarding-house. Upon neither prospect can Jeshurun wax fat. If he eats 'days' his precarious sustenance is assigned on Wednesday to the kind intercession of Reb Shmerl, on Thursday to the equally benignant munificence of Reb Beril, but in the final analysis 'to eat days' meant literally to swallow the vacuum of one's twenty-four hours, to live upon insubstantial air, to devour one's life with gaping but unfed mouth. And even a boarding-house was no paradise. The following is a description of the Barmecide banquets of those days:

> We ask our boarding-mistress –
> When will you set the table?
> She strolls here, she strolls there,

We might as well talk Babel ...

We tell our boarding-mistress
The dinner hour's nearing –
She strolls here, she strolls there,
She is most hard of hearing ...

Our boarding-mistress tells us
Eat, children, eat in plenty ...
And to herself she murmurs –
Each glutton crams for twenty ...

When one realizes the high esteem in which religious learning was held, one can easily understand the sacrifices that were made to acquire it. Certainly secular learning could hold no candle to the light of the Torah. Here is a ditty replete with comparisons the most odious:

Better a Hebrew teacher,
Though he be a hothead,
Than a college student
With his clothes all blotted ...

Better a Bible tutor
With half-a-dozen tots
Than a medical doctor,
His hat split in nine spots ...

Better a Talmud student,
Though not of the first water,
Than wise apothecaries
Who fry their meat in butter ...

But not all Jewry, of course, preferred the yarmulka'd head above others. Fond mothers might pray that their children become leaders in Israel; proud fathers might hope that their sons become beacons of the exile; but there were fastidious maidens, however, who had different tastes. The heroine of this folk-song discusses her suitors with her father, and by a process of elimination in which she spares no opprobrious epithet it is upon a Big Business man that she sets her heart. For:

A cobbler's apprentice now hammers his leather,
And now beats his wife, in fair or foul weather;

A journeyman-carpenter hammers his casket,
And if his wife hungers for food, she must ask it ...
A baker's apprentice bakes bread upon bread;
Thrice daily his wife must declare herself dead.
A scholar-lad sits all day long, and he squeezes
His benches; his wife dines and sups on diseases.
A merchant makes money from fauna and flora,
And kisses his wife, like a holy Torah.

Another folk-song records the high and mighty manner of some beautiful daughter of Israel. The blush of modesty does not rise to her already roseate cheeks when she sings of herself:

Lovely am I, O lovely, and lovely is my name;
Matchmakers seek to wed me to rabbis of great fame;
How much a rabbi knows, 'tis true, no other knows,
But I am to my mother her dearly-cherished rose.

Her methods of dealing with undesirable suitors are drastic:

Water in the chamber, and sticks in the shed,
If I do not like a lad, he'll have these on his head.

But not all the unwedded are as fortunate as the aforementioned coquette. Here, an old maid bewails her dreary fate:

I sit me down upon a stone;
I weep; I sorrow; I make moan;
For all the virgins get them spouses
But only I remain alone.
Alackaday! O star of sorrow,
When shall I become a bride?
On this day? or on the morrow?
Surely I am not so funny;
And all the world knows, we have money!

When a wedding did occur, however, it was usually accompanied by prolonged festivals at which wine flowed like water. In a famous drinking song a bridegroom reminisces:

And I recall at my espousals
There were most heathenish carousals;

And when they broke the destined platter,
We all bibbed wine, and none drank water,
And though I was the bridegroom, I
Permitted not my throat to dry.

When I was wedded, I remember
Wine made blood fire, and bone an ember,
The Rabbi said his benediction, –
The contents of the cup was fiction,
And I stood by, and licked my cup,
I licked it down, I licked it up.

But after the broken platter and the empty plate of the wedding feast
there comes the prosaic post-nuptial life, entailing the care of mewling children
and preposterous mothers-in-law. The mother-in-law, of course, has been the
butt of numerous witticisms; and she has lived up to her reputation. In the
following the hard-beset daughter-in-law complains of the continual criticism
of her mother-in-law:

When I knead the dough
She cries – too much water!

When I chop the fish
She screams – it is bitter.

When I make the bed
She yells – far too high!

When I heat the oven
There is smoke in her eye.

When I walk slowly:
'Look, how she rolls!'

When I walk quickly:
'She ruins her soles.'

Yet all the fret and fume of life has but one conclusion; and the end of
the matter is vanity. Poverty is forgotten, forgotten the slings and slurs of
outrageous fortune; the wedding feast is only an empty memory; the old
maid's anguish is no more, even the mother-in-law's tongue-lashings no

longer hurt. For seated on a stone all of these with a gesture of Jewish resignation do hum the final folk epilogue:

And when one burns – one burns brandy,
And when one bakes – one bakes bread.
And when one dies,
One lies dead ...

Waxen candles
Drop their grime;
And when one dies, one
Dies in time ...

Of Hebrew Humor
November 1935

Doubtless he knew Semitics, who in a mood of professorial abstraction dog-matically announced that 'les Juifs n'ont pas ni la faculté de la curiosité ni de rire'; but Semites he most certainly knew not. That the Hebrews are a folk wanting in curiosity is a statement which stands confounded both by the intellectual gropings of Jewish scientists and by the inquisitive gossipings of Jewish housewives; and that they are a people bereft of a sense of humor is an accusation that may be straightway refuted by the incontrovertible logic of a rude and undisciplined cachination. To disprove such a slander one has merely to laugh it out of court. The zealous picker-up of learning's crumbs, however, will not be content with an argument which releases itself with a trumpeting of cacophonies and a marshalling of teeth; he may bid you to consider the hyena, how he jokes not, neither does he smile, yet laughs a laugh like the Olympian in all his glory. He may even continue to observe that minced noise and the countenance wrinkled by a pleasant emotion do not of necessity prove a soul highly susceptible to the nuances of civilized wit. And reason and wisdom may be his. He will desire, therefore, signs and wonders other than the loud paroxysm of mirth to convince him of the Hebraic sense of humor, now suffering suspicion of non-existence.

Those who hold the Word of God, as it is recorded in the Book of Genesis, in high esteem will be impressed no doubt by the scriptural fact that the second Patriarch owed his very name to the faculty of laughter. When Mother Sarah smiled with an inner knowledge at the prophecy of the three strangers who assured her that after the passing of time her womb would open and be fruitful, she was reacting in a manner somewhat understandable in a matron of ninety to that humor which lies in the counterpresentiment of fertile fancy and sterile reality ... Unless we consider Cain's rhetorical question as to the relationship between himself and his brother a species of wit, the incident which resulted in the circumcision of Isaac is the first example of conscious Hebrew humor in Holy Writ; and even if Cain's impertinent interrogation be considered, under the circumstances, cruelly humorous and pregnant with dramatic irony, the staunch nationalist, remembering the past of the man who most un-Jewishly slaughtered a quarter of the world, and in consequence asserting the cosmopolitanism of Cain, will hardly be enthusiastic of holding him up as an exponent of anything Hebrew. Upon second reflection, and overcome with a spirit of compassion, one may even welcome to the anthology of wit, Cain's classic question, recognizing that in it lies one of the first principles of Hebrew humor, namely, that two interrogations make an affirmation.

If there still be those who with an obdurate glumness stay unimpressed by this biblical citation, we bid them go to the medium, the lineal descendant of the Witch of En-dor, and there in her darkened chamber invoke the spirits of eld. Samson will appear there, the riddle-monger and trickster, he, who having with the jawbone of an ass assailed masses, in puns commemorated his exploits against the Philistines; solemn Isaiah, whose flame-touched lips burned with satire malefic; Nathan, shrewd prophet, who in pastoral metaphor parabled the most notorious of King David's amours; Elijah, who conceived of divine Baal as a prey to the ordinary weaknesses of the flesh, specifically somnolence and hard-hearing; Solomon, husband of several hundred concubines, and perforce a man of supreme good-humor. Other ghosts, too, of ticklish parts will hover about in the darkness: Jael may be there, grasping a blood-bespattered mallet, and Judith, holding the head of Holofernes, witnesses of a grim and ghastly humor.

Surely these may testify, even to the most skeptical, that the Hebrew diaphragm has not from want of laughter fallen into desuetude, that the Hebrew tongue still doth retain as it ever hath a sharpness and a cunning, and that the Hebrew rib, though tampered with at creation, still will respond to the pointed, be it in event or in phrase ...

It may be admitted without lessening from the vindication of Hebrew humor that the Talmudic theologians for a time muzzled the pure and unadulterated giggle. Unseemly it was for one aspiring to celestial honors to comport himself with that lack of dignity and indecorous abandon which laughter implies. The good life was a serious business which did not allow for undue frivolity; a people burdened with six hundred and thirteen Mosaic injunctions to which were appended multitudinous rabbinic fardels, must, lest it infringe upon the melancholy prohibition, hesitate before it lost itself in flippancy, unethical and almost blasphemous. A familiarity with godhead was in no way conducive to the lighter arts; no man could look upon His face and smile thereafter ... The high seriousness which is reputed to be the Hebraic virtue *par excellence*, served in no small degree to lengthen the features of a face already elongated by a nose of proverbial proportions. If one wished to enter the palace of the King of Kings, one did not approach the gateway performing the antics which hearty laughter necessitates; one did not send up by way of hallelujah and hosannah a loud and gusty guffawing, nor did one serenade the Angel Gabriel with a well-modulated and most musical ha-ha. One maintained, contrariwise, as serious an attitude then as when one assuaged the importunities of the flesh to the end that the Children of Israel might be as the stars in the heavens and the sands of the sea, or as staid a demeanor as when, on the Day of Atonement, one mortified that same flesh for the soul's redemption.

Was it not Rabbi Akiba who asserted that laughter and lightheadedness accustom man to the abominable? And was it not a rabbin of equal piety who declared that he who jests brings annihilation to the world, afflictions do come upon him, and in the end he descends to Gehenna? We still shudder to recall how Rabbi Jochanan smote with a single glance his pupil Kahana for that the latter, unable to properly close his lips, seemed to be continually smiling.

Another Talmudic authority on the divine reactions to comedy lays down the following maxim: In this world it is forbidden to fill one's mouth with laughter. The implication of this doleful dictum – mirth as a pleasure reserved for the beyond – has apocalyptic potentialities; the imagination already pictures in one corner of heaven Zebulun, let us say, nudging Issachar in the ribs, his eyes wrinkled with the zest of a travelling salesman's story, and in another the three patriarchs, the good kings of Israel, and all the saintly who have a portion in Paradise, sitting about the heavenly throne, their crowns tilted rakishly on their heads, holding both their wings, ambrosial tears trickling from their gleeful eyes, enjoying, as a reward for a godly life, the bliss of a continual and uproarious hilarity.

Yet here one must pause to record the inevitable exception. Not entirely were the rabbis a lugubrious lot; though the vertical lines ran dismally down their countenances publishing to the world at large, and informing the secretarial angels, that they were in mourning for the sins of the valley of the shadow, it would be a libellous misstatement to say that a horizontal smile never crossed their lips to cancel the parallels of gloom. Averse they were, it is true, to that humor which manifests itself rollickingly in the bumptious lark, or heathenishly in the obstreperous prank, yet even to these there were exceptions. To behold a staid and dignified pillar of the synagogue on the Feast of Rejoicing hop about the pulpit cuddling a scroll of the Torah; or to behold him on Purim, after he had, according to pious though rash injunction, so tipsified himself as not to be able to distinguish the curse of Haman from the blessing of Mordecai, to behold him then cavorting about in religious ecstasies, a truly God-intoxicated Jew, was to dispel any illusions which one might have as to the matter of Hebrew puritanism.

At this juncture we feel ourselves bound to split yet another dialectic hair. The rabbis, as was demonstrated above, did set their faces against all humor in the active sense. They objected to un-Hebraic rowdyism and unrestrained tomfoolery; they frowned upon the aping antic and the mimicry which involved a loosening of man's dignified and erect composure. If the body was to be brought from its serene exaltation to any sort of emotional epilepsy it would be only in the following-out of the psalmist's exhortation that all one's bones should tell the glory of God. Yet despite the rigid and humorless comportment of the body, the mind might, according to Talmudic examples, go upon its intellectual sprees. It was in the realm of mental acrobatics, therefore, that the rabbis, adept in sophistry, and in the art, as the Yiddish byword has it, of arranging a love-match between two diametrically opposite walls, released what one might call the suppressed desire for the witty and fantastic.

Hence the theologians, discussing the quantity of semen in mighty Samson's philistinish ejections; hence, according to *Sanhedrin*, the appearance of Resh Lakish, whose past be it remembered would not bear investigation, and his witticisms on the bachelor life; hence, according to the same tractate, Rabbi Isaac on Adam's unmentionable diversions during the season of his loneliness; and hence in *Moed Katan*, Rabbi Paupa on the alleged dimensions of Pharaoh's uncovenanted member. One might, if one were cut out to be a scavenger or a censor, multiply instances with such profusion, as to bring the subject of Talmudic humor to the attention of all right-thinking, bawdfearing gentlemen; but with due regard for the morals of one's sister, who might chance, as they invariably do, upon this *Index Expurgatorious*, one politely desists.

The rabbis had moments, too, that were not dedicated to the sweet release of scriptural ribaldry. The Talmud is replete with finely phrased anecdote, cryptic parable, and ably-concocted sententious epigram. Even *Haggadah* has usually a hard husk of morality about a palatable kernel of wit. If brevity, as the long-winded Polonius was wont to say, is the soul of wit, the abbreviated and compactly set dicta of the Gemara, and the almost asthmatic nature of Tannaitic enunciation hold a suggestion of what might have been without the aforesaid strictures against undue levity.

It is difficult to analyze the nature of wit; even such thinkers as Bergson and Freud, issuing *ex cathedra* utterances on this high matter, have failed to bring conviction to any save those their disciples avowed through thick and thin. For the subject is indeed elusive, as is evidenced by the common counsel which enjoins one not to explicate a joke rewarded by its auditors with an unruffled expectancy, inasmuch as a joke explained is a joke no longer. Yet all alchemists of wit manifest a singular unanimity maintaining its kinship with intellectual acrobatics; a witticism is a sudden and almost miraculous revelation of the obvious, a double-jointed exercise in the mental, a cerebral gymnastic, a prestidigitation which elicits from the capacious robes of the sublime the nimble rabbits of the ridiculous; a sneeze, as Heine called it, of the intellect ... Measured by these standards, the Talmud is full of potential humor, and displays in every quotation the faculty that draws distant analogies, and achieves, Euclid notwithstanding, the meeting of the parallels.

Exile, it need hardly be recorded, ruthlessly wiped off even the first faint glimmerings of a smile from the face of the Jew, and substituted for the facetious twinkle of the Hebraic eye the ever-triturating tear. King John of England, drawing out the teeth of the recalcitrant Jewish tax-payer of Bristol, is a symbol of the physical deletion of the Hebraic smile. By foreign waters and in strange lands, he remembered not the songs of Zion, nor did he recall the answers to the riddle of Timnath. Too preoccupied was he attempting to explain the properties of that dramatic irony which had converted him, in a night illuminated by Roman torches, from the primogeniture of God to the bastardy of the world, to study the intricacies of humor. From being a hawker of jokes, he had become himself a butt for all the indelicate quips of Christian wits; journeying in his covenantal caravan from perilous land to land more perilous he furnished sport, high and low, alike to rustic and burgher, serf and suzerain. He set all of Europe laughing with a ribald and cruel laughter, gloating over his antics, as he acrobatically tossed upon the horns of ghetto dilemmas.

In Rome he appeared in his toga with *tzitzis,* and by the very pathos of his condition supplied feeble satirists with jests ready-made. In Spain he performed, unwillingly again, a comedy in slapstick upon a tragic stage whose crimson curtain fell to the music of crackling faggots, the while his agonized grimaces produced much slapping of Christian thighs and much shaking of godly paunches. It is not recorded whether the crucifixes smiled. In Poland, newly-brought into the fold, humiliatingly he parodied himself dancing his dances of painful pantomime, for the delectation of his hospitable and jovial patrons. In Italy he was fattened and compelled to run a race with prostitutes so that the spectators might draw a moral therefrom, and the text of the Pentateuch about a corpulent and stiff-necked Israel be emended to read: And Jeshurun waxed fat, and ran. In domains Slavic and Teuton, in all places whither the word of the Gospel had traveled, appreciative audiences demanded encores of his self-abasing travesties. He was the court-jester of Europe, wearing a *yarmulke* for foolscap, and flaunting a *lulav* as bauble.

The Jew, it is seen, blessed the bored peasant and the blasé priest of the Dark Ages with a form of recreation. The circus was in town; and happy were the

good burghers and burgesses to sally forth to regard this gypsy folk that wore,
beside the tatters which were the disguise of their riches, long eight-threaded
pendules, and curious talismans, and spiral side-curls, and unrazored jowls;
to regard them, and perhaps if the spirit moved and the word of God exhorted,
to enjoy the creative zest of adding to the play some local color mixed mainly
of native mud and indigenous mire. Assuredly this was a quaint people, tickling
the rib of Christian Europe; and not without their meed. Even at the sanctified
hands of gracious Popes, with their cardinals in conclave assembled, he received
worthy recognition as a jester, and was duly awarded the badge of saffron,
and dubbed with the cornute cap. From the *première* of the wry comedy on
Tisha B'av of the year seventy and throughout the whole series of the presentations of the Hebrew Nights' Entertainment, the world was titillated by
these frisky clowns hopping about in agony, making gestures intended to be
heroic, and uttering the unconscious gags of martyrdom.

For a space, these miserable targets of Gentile archery were stricken
pitifully dumb, dumb beyond repartee. Evidently the clown himself had been
dulled beyond the appreciation of his own absurdity. Glumly he did forego
his sense of humor; his sole answer to the saintly jeers, the fanatical index-
fingers, the quivering of the orthodox bellies, was a mournful silence, ghetto
vertebrae, and sufferance that was the badge of all his tribe. Others there
were, however, of greater irrepressibleness and of spirit more elastic, who,
despite tears and turbulence about them, continued to crack, much with the
same placidity as a monkey his nuts, their literary and biblical jokes.

The humorists were recruited chiefly from the aristocracy of learning,
worthies who spent a sing-song existence puzzling out the lacunae of the
Lawgiver. For the ordinary Jew, non-erudite but pious, went about his business
dutifully and with no titillating interruptions, gathering through industry
ducats in this world, and acquiring through virtue liens on property in the
next. The typical Hebrew anecdote, as it was later to spring full-armored from
the head of folk-humorists, was as yet beating imperceptibly beneath the
burdened carapace of the masses. In some especially ascetic moment, a Jew,
we doubt not, may have indulged in self-flagellating witticism, but for the
most part the melancholy cloudiness of his countenance was unbroken by the
levin of anecdote. The writings of the period are particularly barren of the
bright badinage of the plebs. Unlike voyagers of a later day, Benjamin of
Tudela did not sprinkle his travelogues with reminiscent accounts of anecdotes
told to him by members of the lower classes.

Actively, therefore, the humor of the Hebrew proletariat existed not; it
had suffered a sudden and temporary demise, destined at some future day to
be gloriously resurrected. Yet passively, there still lingered on in their minds
a subtle appreciation of the farcical; still could the Jew indulge, though secretly,
in a sly dig at fate, a sardonic smile at inquisitorial busybodies, a word satiric.

For the bearded scapegoat whose undignified stampings broke the monotony of the Middle Ages was not, the theologian and threnodist Zunz notwithstanding, always weeping behind the buffoon's mask, by duress imposed. Not always did he pass through the vale of tears attired in sackcloth and covered with ashes; even in the midst of tragedy itself, tragedy that by some lunatic wilfulness of mad actors had worked itself into comedy, there flickered in his life a suggestion of heavenly humor, a suspicion that perhaps, after all the chortling and tittering, the joke was not entirely at his expense.

One ventures here a mimetic interpretation of history. The Holy One, Himself in Dignity and in Person, sits in His heaven amusing himself by writing, with a quill plucked from Lucifer's wing, the multitudinous permutations of irony. His mannikins below strive for the ultimate haw-haw, for the last and therefore the victorious cachination. The ambitions of monarchs, the intrigues of statesmen, the scribblings of poets, all of these have as their goal but one end – to have out upon time and humanity the last laugh. The Holy One smiles as pensively He bites His quill, remembering that the last laugh is inevitably the decorous chuckle of the sexton plying a spade. But his mannikins persist, they must have their puny jokes. In such manner, accordingly, do the devotees of conflicting creeds boil one another with gusto that all surveying may applaud their especial favor with deity by a self-laudatory grin. The Jew, however, it was impossible to laugh out of existence: most exasperatingly would he find, even while his tormentors were writhing in ribald paroxysms, some flaw in the syntax of the joke, some loophole that proved him not entirely the ridiculous butt. Thus passively, and by that marvellous process of adaptation which consists of grinning and bearing it, did he prove a discomfiture to his enemies.

Elastically drawn upon the rack, he chuckled to himself at the sight of fanatic fools who for so brief a pleasure lost the Kingdom of Heaven; tortured by strange devices and broken by ingenious engines, his soul smiled at so easy a method in inheriting a portion in Paradise. For martyrdom was a prank in which one climbed a tree to rob a nest of mysterious contents. The foe of Israel imposed upon him all the indignities of the lugubriously ludicrous, while Israel, in turn, revenged itself, with the violence of the proverbial snuff-box bandit, by a self-assurance that the torturers were really doing no more than committing spiritual suicide. Being the especial protégés of deity, it behooved deity, they felt certain, to espouse their cause, blessing them that blessed and cursing them that cursed. So, amidst all their discomforts, into their gaberdine-sleeves they laughed.

It was in the eighteenth and nineteenth centuries that the Jewish anecdote, at long last, regained its speech. Born in the hearts of a people gradually released from ghetto-gloom, and nurtured by frequent repetition, it soon grew to babbling adolescence. After centuries of frigid melancholy, finally it thawed out, and seemed to draw from its prolonged hibernation a renewed vigor. In Russian hamlet, and in German town, in Polish city, and in Galician village, the anecdote came to be hawked, like merchandise, in provincial dialects of multitudinous varieties. The poor had once more inherited their own particular *conte*; they adorned it with proverb; they ornamented it with idiom. Wit and humor were no longer the enviable prerogatives of the learned; the water-carrier, as well as the *Talmid-chochem* could now toy with quips and pranks. The Jewish joke, an *enfant terrible*, gesticulating and slyly grimacing, thumbing its nose at pomposity, now, with the passage of time acquired respectability and tradition; it flourished and waxed great.

The academic satirists, the cultured wit mongers, of course, still continued to shock and to amuse. Heinrich Heine when he gave over for a space the praising of roses in poetry, dedicated himself to the cultivation of thorns in prose. Isaac Erter edified his contemporaries with such eschatological revelations as those disclosed in the Complaint of Sani, Sansani, and Smengaloff, revelations the purport of which was that 'there ain't no such animal' as a demon. With subtler wit, but more platitude, Judah Loeb Gordon exploded the current fallacies of his co-religionists. More genial, and much more intimately in touch with the masses, Sholom Aleichem, whose very disguise was a *nom de paix*, repeated, with many variations, the tragi-comedy of being both poor and a Jew. Moishe Nadir, the lapidary of wit, even today makes bread out of throwing stones. Yet this jolly company, though perforce mentioned, do not properly belong in our treatise, concerned as it is, not so much with literary wit, as with folk humor.

The scenes of the mental parturitions of the commonalty were manifold. A *Mithnagid*, heatedly inveighing against the shams of Chassidism, might regale his cronies in the *Vilna Klaus* with fictitious tales of ludicrous miracles and questionable wonders that befell some mythical *rebbe*; – how, as the folk-song has it, the Master of the Name went dry into the water, and *mirabile dictu* came out a great deal wetter; how the *Rebbe*, may he live, could gaze from Galicia right into Erez Israel with his admirable glass, his schnapps glass; and how, indeed, were wonderful other marvels of his working. Or, perhaps, old and decrepit Jews, *batlanim* of the synagogue, sitting of a winter's afternoon in the twilight after *Mincha*, whiling away the moments before *Maariv*, warming themselves at the synagogal stove, would recount one to the other anecdotes and gags that would set their old ribs quaking with senile laughter. Or, robuster ones, congregating in the *Mikveh* on Fridays, undergoing the hebdomadal sweat-bath, while the attendant with his twiggen broom lazily flogged away the oncoming languors, might exchange, as they meditatively murdered a louse, some spicy witticism, some gay narratives, not entirely in harmony with the pious ablutions they were performing. Or again, flown with liturgy and with wine, after a Purim feast or a circumcision ceremony, the tale would pass around with the bottle and there would be no surcease until all dignities had been somewhat punctured with perforating mockeries. Or the scene would shift to the fairs and the market-places, where as-yet-penurious but still potential Rothschilds would tell tales of ingenious business cunning, and build up upon the example of their clever cousins, fabulous but phantom fortunes. Or still again – to cover with a miraculous diminishing of distance the route from Novgorod to Volozhin, we would chance upon pale and anaemic *yeshiva bachurim*, wearied with the tortuous logic of Abbaya and Rabba, finding a temporary recreation in the rather obscene yet finely-phrased anecdotes, since become proverbial satires, on the buxom daughters of ignorant innkeepers, quotations from sacred lore unfortunately fraught with indelicate ambiguity, *pilpul* rotating with ceremonial gyrations about a single member, essentially Judaic.

In such corners and under such circumstances, was the anecdote Hebraic born, born to inflict upon its victims the thirty-nine lashes that are the proper due of the transgressor. Good-humoredly it poked fun at the petty and forever ill-starred shop-keeper, devising strange plans to outwit the shrewd custom of poverty. Superiorly it confounded with his own scepticisms the omniscient atheist, who flaunted the signed affidavit of God's non-existence. It ridiculed almost with venom, the pious and punctilious heaven-regarding fanatic, who wore the phylacteries prescribed both by Rashi and Rabbenu Tam. With urbane impartiality it revealed the foibles alike of pauper and of millionaire. It laughed the somniloquent *maggid* out of the *almemar*. It toyed with the oriental hyperboles of the *shadchan*, and in one fell swoop set to naught the match-maker and his match. It scortulated the religious fakir, sponging upon the sweated roubles of the credulous. Ignorance it flayed in high places and Vulgarity in low. It reduced the abracadabra of the legalist to its ultimate meaninglessness; and the sham ecstasies of the ostentatiously-transported, it derided. It spared not the mighty, nor did it have compassion on the mean. In fine, it held up, as the phrase has it, the mirror to life.

And it was a mirror of the people's own rude making, a mirror where the laws of optics were put to shame by ridiculous perspective and uncomely gaunt elongations. The proof of the *kugel*, as everyone knows, is in the digestion thereof; and the best criterion of the sociological implications of the Hebrew joke is in the number of types which it embraces. In it every phase of Jewish life is grotesquely reflected. It is of no small significance that there are comparatively few stories of Jewish ladies of pleasure; she was, despite the persistence with which mediaeval municipal authorities located their brothels in the heart of the ghettos, an unknown person in Hebrew life. In comparison with the *contes* which we have collected among the thesauri of other nations, the tales of the Hebrew 'strange women' appear as a shamefaced minority. And this literary phenomenon is but a reflection of a vital fact.

It was in such corners and under such circumstances, too, that the metropolitan Chelm, city of fools and simpletons, rose resplendent in the imagination of Israel. The Jewish Encyclopaedia says with prosaic exactitude and with an utter indifference to the splendid role that Chelm plays in Jewish folk-lore, that it is a town in the government of Kovno, population forty-two thousand, all of whom, with the exception of three hundred – presumably hewers of wood and kindlers of sabbath-fires – are Jews. Most of these, the writer goes on to say, are engaged in mercantile pursuits, only about one thousand five hundred and forty-nine being artisans. Notes on the educational and philanthropic institutions of the town follow.

Not for its traffic in flax and in lumber, not for its synagogues exalting every lane, not for these is Chelm renowned among the cities of the world, but for that it is the Hebrew Gotham, a city whose census is taken under tabulations headed dolt, addle-pate, numskull, blockhead, and all the other varying degrees of nitwitry.

This indeed is the metropolis that, in defiance of all architectural rules, was built from its roofs down, the city in which common sense was heavily and outrageously taxed, the capital in which – but let the poet take the reader within its precincts, there to proffer him the keys of the City, and there to abandon him, knowing full well that he who can unlock the gates of Chelm can have access to all the remote corners of Jewish humor.

On a little brown pony, a little boy rides
Over cobblestone roads through strange countrysides;
He rides to and fro, and he rides up and down,
Asks milkmaids and blacksmiths how far 'tis to town,
          To topsy-turvy town ...

His grandfather told him that would he be wise
He must see the fool's town with his very own eyes,
See Jews catch the moon in a bucket for cheese,
And find the next night that moon stuck in the trees –
          That moon stuck in the trees.

See the simpleton settling high matters of state;
The rabbi a-scratching his dubious pate,
Watch the baker knead rolls out of dough made of lime,
Since it never turned sour, and kept a long time,
          Because it kept a long time.

And hear the philosopher in the town-hall
Drone nothing is nothing and that is all.
And also the poet who bawled out a song

Which proved that the heat stretched the summer day long,
    Did stretch the summer day long ...

So into the hamlet the little boy rides –
O even his pony is holding its sides!
The little boy smiles to the Jews of the realm,
Nods right and nods left to the burghers of Chelm,
    The simple burghers of Chelm.

On Translating the Yiddish Folk-Song   30 August 1946

The Yiddish folk-song, like all folk-songs, is essentially a simple thing; certainly it is not weighted either with the rhetoric or the cerebralism which, for the most part, characterize the personal poetic artifact. The sentiments which it expresses are, indeed, so common to the folk way, that here, if anywhere, one may suspect that joint communal creativity which literary historians postulate for all folk-songs. Here the reader will encounter none of those complicated metaphors which bespeak the individual poet seeking to affix his signature within the body of the poem; the sophisticated search for *le mot juste* is nowhere in evidence; and even the rhymes, which in many instances, significantly enough, are faulty rhymes, – faulty rhymes, not assonances, – intrude themselves into the song merely as so many aids to memory. The rhythms, too, do not seem to have gone to school; not a few are but approximations of the rhythm of the pre-existing melody for which they supply the text.

    In a word, the Yiddish folk-song is exactly what it sets out to be: a simple and direct utterance, expressing in forthright speech some touching aspect of an emotional situation. This situation may arise either out of the relations between man and God, or of those between man and man, – and as the Negro preacher said, the brethren include the sistern, – but in either event, they seek to focus within the limit of the given song, an intense, and primitively clear illumination of a particular plight, a ceremony, or attitude.

    This simplicity, of course, does very well for the original poem – whatever subtlety or suggestiveness is required is supplied by the music; but for the translator, paradoxically enough, the unornamented lines are as binding as wire. By the very exiguity of the original, no scope is afforded for those Houdini wrigglings which are the translator's usual means of transit from one vessel to another; between the reproduction of the sense and the echoing of the rhyme, he enjoys but small latitude, indeed; and were it not for the fact that so many English words share a common ancestry with the Yiddish counterparts, the task would seem maddening, if not impossible. When to these difficulties, there is added the altogether gratuitous one – that of falsifying the rhythm to tally with the music – one gets the suspicion that the cabal of authors who devised these songs never really wanted them to be translated.

If so, one can understand their fears, fears which no doubt would centre mainly on the question of vocabulary, where the greatest difficulty arises out of the difference in the cultural backgrounds which lie behind the translated and the translating tongues. To render from French into Italian may be no easy undertaking, but the difficulty would be mainly etymological, not cultural. The cultural history of the two peoples is, in its large outlines, identical; but to speak in English of things which move and have their being only in a Jewish milieu, and that milieu full of Slavic influences, is to be compelled not only to translate, but also to explain. In verse-translations, such a procedure, when not impossible, is still undesirable.

How, for example, is one to translate *l'chaim, rebbe*? Obviously, the *rebbe*, like all titles and designations, remains unchanged in English, but the *l'chaim*? Is one to acknowledge the Hebrew and translate 'To life!' much as one would bid the sedentary *rebbe* – 'To horse!'? Even 'To your life!' paralleled on 'To your health!' will not do, for the word is idiomatic, like *skoal!* and *prosit!* and like them should not be translated. *L'chaim, rebbe* must perforce remain: *l'chaim, rebbe*! Any other version would be a perversion.

Or take – may it not harm you! – the exclamation, *Oy veh!* Bold, indeed, would he be who sought to transliterate this *cri du coeur* with a lorryman's 'O, woe!' It is true that the words are essentially onomatopoetic, and, therefore, should be translated by a similar onomatopoeia, but the fact denies the theorem. The personal and historic associations, which vibrate from the phrase, cannot be Englished. The epic memory which is evoked by the two monosyllables is not conjured by any English equivalent. One does not translate a groan. A groan? *Oy veh!* is so to our manner born that not always does its utterance imply connotations of woe. The tragedy which invented the phrase has, indeed, been so constant that *Oy veh*, as often in the folk-songs, is uttered in the presence of something exciting though not unpleasant, by way of mere reflex. How, then, to show the distinction? It cannot be done. *Oy veh* remains ineluctably *Oy veh*, and only its context shows the nuance.

Gewald! That is another one. The exclamation is a cry for help, as when one is beset by thieves; it is also a mere expression of exuberance. Some of the Chassidic folk songs, it will be noted, do begin with these afflative outcries; they are made in the very presence of the *rebbe*; they are not intended as cries for help. But neither can they be rendered, when the translator bursts in upon the sacred assembly, by an Englishman's ejaculations, no matter how high-spirited. 'Heigh-ho'? Imagine *Chassidim* shouting 'heigh-ho!' ... *Gewald*, what is the world coming to!

Concepts, names and articles, indigenous to our culture, are equally untranslatable. *Moishe Rabbeinu* is not, certainly not in a folk-song, ever to be rendered as 'Moses our Teacher.' The latter phrase evokes a pedant, the former a prophet, a patriarch, a member of our family. Upon the Yiddish tongue, which forgets that the talk is Hebrew, it is as if *Rabbeinu* were a surname. And *kugel* – to descend from Sinai to Kasrilevke – is, with one exception, always and in all languages, *kugel*. The exception is when it is *kigel*. *Bokser*, too, is rebellious, like its namesake, against translation. Upon the market-place, it is known as St. John's bread. But that is obviously impossible! *Chassidim* and St. John, *l'havdil*! And even to call it the fruit of the carob is no great aid to digestion.

There is yet another peculiarity to these songs which must surely tax the translator. Often they are bilingual, Hebrew and Yiddish, and sometimes, trilingual, with Russian thrown in. Certainly the translator would be unfaithful to the original if his version went English, English all the way, and failed to indicate, in the text itself, that more than one language was involved. Some translators have sought to achieve the necessary authenticity by substituting for the Hebrew, Latin equivalents. This method, we fear, gives an impression altogether too Gregorian. It is safer, we imagine, to leave the Hebrew intact, pure, and by translation undefiled. Certainly, if it is communication that is intended, Latin is a dubious medium; it is, in fact, merely to substitute the unknown for the esoteric. Moreover, in most of the songs the Yiddish translates the Hebrew, anyway.

It would seem from the foregoing that our subject has really been the non-translation of the Yiddish folk-song. This is in large measure true. The best that one can do is to convey, as far as is possible, the simple meanings of the original into the translation, and let the music do the work of commentary. For the truth is that these songs owe their survival almost entirely to their music; if they stood by themselves, without benefit of staff notation, we doubt very much whether they could win themselves a place in anything but an anthology of folklore and social mores; it is only by virtue of the fact that these words trip from the tongue to the accompaniment of ancestral melody that they still constitute a living part of the culture. At the same time the music would be but music were it not for the verbal commentary which accompanies *it*.

As for the translator's role in this collaboration between song and music, he has done his duty if, without injury to the text or mayhem to the music, he has, in some measure, reproduced in the English versicles, some of the gaiety, the pathos, the humour, and the mountain-moving faith which characterized a way of life which though still extant, has altered its form and lost the intensity that made it so unique and strong in the old country in the old times.

The Yiddish Proverb   28 November 1952–2 January 1953

Who does not know one? Everybody, surely, who has ever had a grandmother knows a proverb. No proverb, moreover, is ever anywhere adduced without another rising to confute it: our grandmothers interrupt our conversations. For they are inalienable elements of our national heritage, these pieces of 'old-said sooth,' legacies handed down to us without burden of succession duty, quaint mirrors of memento that send across the centuries their sudden flashes of sharp, prismatic illumination.

Because they have come down to us from sources humble and unsophisticated, because they are couched in a language now falling into desuetude and in an idiom earthy if not vulgar, we are inclined to treat them as of but small cultural worth, little heirloom knick-knacks that one humours with a passing smile. They are not literary; they smell of the kitchen; despite their truth and wisdom, they are often so embarrassingly primitive. The lore of the rabbis, the subtleties of the academies of Eastern Europe, the *belles lettres* of Warsaw and Vilna, these, we are likely to say, are of the proper corpus of our Diaspora culture; but these old wives' sayings ...

Yet the Yiddish proverb, offering, as it almost invariably does, a true reflection of the pattern of the Jewish mind, is not so summarily to be dismissed. It constitutes an important and most rewarding element in our cultural thesaurus. Its typical form, its peculiar wisdom, its very language, mark it as one of the great cultural products of Jewish life in the Diaspora.

It is true that of recent years there has arisen, particularly in Israel, a sect of philosophers, narrow, intransigent, insular, who, dismissing the little that the Diaspora (they concede) did produce, would treat all of Jewish exilic history as one vast cultural blank; only that will they recognize as authentically Jewish which has issued out of Israel, out of 'the air,' as the Talmud has it, 'of the land that maketh wise,' all else being but expense of spirit, and sheer loss; but these parochial views, it must be asserted, are as unseemly as they are blind. The Talmud, without which rabbinic Judaism is nothing, was written in Aramaic, not Hebrew, – was a garden grown in Babylon. The classic of mediaeval Judaism, Maimonides' *Guide to the Perplexed*, is Spanish in origin,

Arabic in language. The Torah itself, one is startled to realize, descending, as it did, from Sinai, is extra-territorial and no local Palestinian product!

The Yiddish proverb, too, may be forgiven its Diaspora provenance; and this all the more since it represents elements – imagination and insight – that are constant in the Jewish psyche. When to these intellectual characteristics of the proverb there is added the fact that the vessel into which it is poured – the Yiddish language – is a language incomparably suited both to its mood and tenor, then is that proverb seen in its utter originality and uniqueness. This is not to say that Yiddish proverbs are without their duplicates in other tongues; common sense is common heritage; but the nuances are never alike.

The principal cause of this individuality, of course, is language. The Yiddish language is not a mere variant of German; nor is it, despite its fifteen per cent Semitic vocabulary, a kind of watered-down Hebrew. It has a character all its own, a character born in large measure of the experiences which it was called upon to communicate; pathos is the word for Yiddish. The very lilt of its articulation, its sing-song inflections, its dialects distinguished one from the other by slight but meaningful phonetic changes, all of these announce in music, as it were, not only the dominating mood but also the running history of this language.

Some examples may serve to illustrate this point. Mediaeval medicine recognized, as elements determinative of human temperament, the existence of four cordial humours – blood, phlegm, choler, and melancholy or black choler. The predominance of one of these humours over the others determined a person's disposition, whether he was gay or sad, stolid or energetic. In English – such has been the happy history of the people whose island has never been invaded – three of these words have left but a small mark on the language; only the word 'humour' persists – and invariably it connotes a humour gay and jovial. The distinctions have been lost. Yiddish, too, has preserved in its current vocabulary but one of the four humours – *mara shchorah* – the black humour, melancholy!

The very pronunciation of a word throws light on this subject. Take the word *yos'm* – an orphan. The word is Hebrew naturalized into Yiddish. Now with the establishment of the State of Israel, there was introduced into that country the Sephardic pronunciation of Hebrew. This is a pronunciation which is as removed from the Ashkenazic which prevails in the Diaspora as Arabic is from Italian. The first is hard, clipped, guttural, the pronunciation of a people afraid to catch sand in its throat; the second is soft, caressing, it lingers over its vocables, it has a rise and fall. Thus the Sephardic Israeli will refer to an orphan as *y'toim* (who will pity a *y'toim*?) while Yiddish over the fatherless one bends and sighs *yosim'l* ...

It is not surprising that a language so rich in the connotations of inflection should often resort to what the professors call onomatopoeia – imitative sound.

Oi is a Yiddish exclamation; it may serve also as an evening's commentary. Of a man who is neither among the world's mighty nor yet of its dispossessed, the Yiddish proverb says that 'he is not *ai! ai!* nor yet *oi! oi!*'

Although Yiddish speech has been current upon the lips of Jews for centuries, it was only recently that there was published in the United States – a thesaurus of that language. It is indeed this ponderous volume which prompts the reflections on the proverb which follow.

Compiled by Mr. Stutchkov, who has apparently taken Roget's classic work as model, the book at once stimulates both pride and sorrow – pride in the wealth of its vocabulary, the variety and subtlety of its concepts, the magic of its linguistic transformations; and sorrow at the thought of its so belated, its almost posthumous, appearance. Among other peoples, books such as Stutchkov's are edited and published on the occasion of their language's widest dissemination and triumph, at the peak of its renaissance, in the flush of its greatest acceptance and glory. Stutchkov's volume steals upon the world like a remote and indistinguishable echo.

For its voice is the voice of the memorialist rather than that of the lexicographer. The tongue whose synonyms and idioms it tabulates is to-day a tongue that falters; the millions whose native and habitual speech it once was have vanished; themselves, and their language, are no more. Nor is there elsewhere a flourishing to compensate for the silence that hangs heavy over the European air. Decline is universal. Stutchkov's book, ordered and arranged like a dictionary, reads, in fact, like an archive.

It is from the thousand pages of this archive that there spring to the eye pictures and conjurations of a world and a way of life that once throbbed with beauty and potency not altogether destroyed. This is no philologist's treatise, and so this is not the place to dwell upon the cosmopolitan colours that give to Yiddish almost all the shades and hues of the map of Europe. There is hardly a concept or an idea about which this language cannot display borrowings Hebraic, additions from the Slavic, French derivatives, modifications from the German, recollections of the Latin. For encrusted within the strata of Yiddish lie the varying indicia of Jewish wandering: tally up these Stutchkov paragraphs and you will discover in each of them the verbal mementos of Jewish peregrination and vicissitude.

The proverbs, however, derive largely from the sojourn in Eastern Europe. In form, they own to the characteristics common to all proverbs: they are short; they show sense; they have salt. A proverb is no proverb if it is long-winded; it is, then, a discourse, or a sermon, or a bore. A proverb is a brevity; even a stutterer should be able to render it with *éclat*.

The soil of the proverb is common sense; not esoteric wisdom: that makes for visions; not paradoxical insight: that produces the epigram; but plain ordinary common sense, truth convincing to both philosopher and peasant. Rightly has the proverb been termed 'the ready money of human experience'; it is, in fact, a kind of sparkling small change, less valuable, perhaps, than the banknotes of science, less impressive, to be sure, than the drafts of philosophy, but money, certainly, more current with the merchant.

And without salt, the proverb is but an oatmeal truism, a flat and unsmiling platitude, noodles of the 'nudnick,' the diet of bores.

Leafing through the pages of Stutchkov, one soon discovers that the Yiddish proverb possesses these aforementioned qualities to an eminent degree. It is, above all, a piece of shrewdness, full of sage and pithy counsel; it eschews analysis, it urges the practical. It observes, for example, and all who intend acrimony should take this advice to heart, that 'when the miller quarrels with the chimneysweep, he, the miller, leaves the quarrel black, the chimneysweep leaves it white.' The osmosis of insult has never been more vividly illustrated. 'When you quarrel,' says another proverb, 'quarrel, but only up to that point where you may still be able to make up.' It is a *vade mecum* for diplomats: the first rule is never to issue a final ultimatum.

Many of the Yiddish proverbs receive not a little of their wit and punch from the fact that they are couched in rhyme. Rhyme serves not only as mnemonic; it gives to the proverb so dogmatic a turn and snap that contradiction seems thereby to be discountenanced. We transliterate: *Ein mol is shein, tzvei mol is chein; drei mol – hak ois di tzein.* This is a counsel against the repetitive, and may, perhaps, be rendered as follows: 'Once – is nice; not bad – twice; thrice is a vice.'

Appetite comes with eating. This was observed even in Eastern Europe where there were not many occasions for experimentation: *Der ershter bissen iz an egber; der zweiter macht a loch; der dritter shreit, Gib noch;* which is to say: 'The first bite a hole does bore; the second and third cry, More, more.'

Women giggling, women weeping – the proverb's rhymester did not let them go unnoticed: *Veinen un lachen zenen bei veiber gringe zachen.* It is a conclusion irrefutable: 'For women either to laugh or to cry – both easy as pie.'

In an impoverished economy, an edible which supplied its own condiment was a God-send. Therefore the proverb rejoices: *Tzu a herring badarf men nit kein zaltz, un tzu griven kein shmaltz.* Which is to say that one does not add salt to herring, nor fats to *griven.* A Nobel Prize awaits him who will render *griven* into English.

Yet another characteristic of the Yiddish proverb is its apparent nonsensicality. At first reading the proverb sounds palpably absurd; one pauses to gather whether what one has read is actually that which has been said; and one is aware, suddenly, that an apocalypse has issued out of a solecism, an optical distortion has yielded a vision. The nonsense makes sense. It were as if an Irish bull had calved.

'If someone is fated to be drowned,' says the proverb, 'he'll not get killed.' True, but truer than it sounds. 'A person is like a shoemaker: a shoemaker lives and lives, and then dies; likewise a person.' Incontestable; but more is meant than meets the ear.

Sometimes the witty effect is the result of a non-sequitur. 'From drinking an overbrimming cup of hot tea,' the proverb, in its homely fashion, warns, 'one may scald – the knee.' The picture that is conjured up is a moving picture; it is, in fact, 'a double take:' For one had expected that the peril against which the proverb was issuing its warning was the peril of scalded lips; the scene that had been induced was that of a man charily touching lips to the rim of a cup, and suddenly all is changed, distorted, overturned. The tea has spilled, the man is bent double, the locus of calorification is elsewhere. What had begun as a sentence of etiquette is suddenly seen to be a counsel of self-preservation.

What is the difference, it has been asked, between a *shlemiel* and a *shlimazel*? The answer evokes a similar situation. Imagine once again the drinker and his cup of tea, only this time he is being served by a waiter, and once again the tea spills. The action provides the distinctions: the waiter is beyond doubt and unquestionably a *shlemiel*; the tea-drinker, he is *shlimazel* proper.

Often the Yiddish proverb is misogynist in sentiment; here, too, however, it is discreet enough to couch its scorn in sentences of nonsense. 'Where a Jewess (read *Yiddine*) is illiterate and can't read her prayerbook, she will at least count the windowpanes in the synagogue.' Such comment upon her fenestral devotions was suffered, no doubt, in silence; but what a jargoning there must have been heard where the proverb announced that 'women in company will speak all at once because they know in advance there's nothing to listen to'?

Because liturgy was an important element in Jewish daily, and not merely festival, life, the Yiddish proverb took for its own many of the locutions of the prayerbook. The result is a literary allusiveness unique among folk-proverbs. It is as if a peasant were heard to be quoting Latin in the midst of his homely sayings. On the one hand a pontifical Hebrew quotation, on the other a piece of culinary wisdom – the effect is most disconcerting. *Adam yesoidoi m'ofor v'soifoi l'ofor; baintayim chapt er a blintchik.* Only a combination of obituary and advertising English may do justice to the original: 'Ashes to ashes, and dust to dust – but, in the meantime, blintzes are a *must.*'

Frequently they are not complete proverbs but ingenious similes, startling metaphors, illuminating comparisons, upon which the folk imagination spends its fire. Of something startlingly inappropriate, the idiom will say that it suits 'like ear-rings on a sow' or – to move to another realm – 'like *tzitzith* on a Cossack.' Something of no importance is to be heeded 'like last year's snows.' The diminutive is described as being the size of 'the liver and lights of a flea'; a man of small stature is said to 'go promenading under a table.' Ugliness has the appearance of 'my troubles on the left side.' That which is superlative is said to be, if of feminine beauty, a *tzimes*; if of commercial yield – *shmaltz*; and if of aristocratic provenance – *smetena* (cream). The adjective 'good' is compared: *good, better*, and *p-s-sh*, – the final valve-exhaust expressing the *ne plus ultra*, the ineffable beyond which nothing.

A peculiar expression, throwing much light on Jewish psychology, is that which describes a timid person as one 'whose heart beats like that of a bandit.' (*Es klapt ihm dos hartz vie bei a gazlen.*) A curious sublimation – the victim of the bandit is attributing to the bandit his own reactions were he to pursue the bandit's vocation! For of Jewish highwaymen in Eastern Europe there is no record, save the following:

> There was a Jewish bandit who lived in a wood,
> He never did much evil, nor ever did much good,
> For he would halt a merchant, quivering to his toes,
> And in a gruff voice whisper: 'You'll pay through the nose!'
> And then he'd search his person, having bid him pray,
> And snatch his broken snuff-box, and sneeze himself away.

If the last expression is an instance of the proverb's pity, – pity for the bandit – instances of its irony, too, are not wanting. The impossible, the proverb promises, will happen on 'the week-days between Pentecost' (a non-sense), or 'when heaven will hold a fair,' or 'where nails will blossom.' In a complete and telling *mise-en-scène*, the miser is satirized: *A karger zipt yoich mit a goppel, un traiselt noch opp.* 'The miser takes his soup with a fork, – and shakes off the overflow ...'

Better than any treatise in sociology, the Yiddish proverb serves to illuminate, both through its direct statements and its chosen images, the realities of Jewish life in Eastern Europe. Here, from the subject-matter of the proverb and from its wisdom, one can learn what the Jew held dear, what terms of reference were constants in his life, what were the true and basic patterns into which he wove his comments upon daily experience. An examination of the proverbs with this end in view must lead inevitably to a realization of the part which religion played, not only in the festive and ceremonial life of the Jew, but in his everyday thoughts and reactions.

Though flung across the centuries far from his ancestral home, he still lived, it appears, within the geography of the Bible. Of the mileage between Warsaw and Moscow he might have only the vaguest of notions, but the itinerary of his forefathers through the wilderness was known to him, even up to its forty-two halts and sojournings, as if it were a trip he had just made with the teamster from Boiberik. Indeed, his whole life, week by week, was a sightseeing tour through the Scriptures. That is why he would say, if he wished to express a great distance, not that such and such a thing extended from London to Petrograd, but that it reached *m'Hoidoo v'ad Kush*, 'from India even unto Ethiopia.' Here, too, certainly, he did not have any clear idea of routes and distances; from the first verse of the Book of Esther he did know, however, that these two termini encompassed 'over one hundred and seven and twenty provinces.' Sometimes he felt that even such an expression of distance, though biblic, was a concept too gross and mathematical; then he would say, in terms liturgic rather than geographic, that the expanse was 'from *baruch sh'omar* to *adon olam*,' that is, from the initiatory to the concluding prayers of the morning service. This everybody understood.

Similarly, if he wished to give his listener an idea of something violently vibrative, he did not vulgarly compare it to jelly on a cold and frosty morning; he chose his image from the South; the thing shook, he said, like a *lulav*, a palmleaf. Or again, if something was to be described as wet, moist, sweaty, it was not from the field of labour that the comparison was selected; the nature of Hassidic devotion supplied it: the object was as wet 'as the phylacteries on the brow of a Hassid,' – the Hassid being one who prayed with might and main, a very lather of liturgy, 'all his bones,' as the Psalmist enjoined, 'declaring the glory of God.'

Frustration, dispossession – these notions, too, proved their equations in the obsessive rites of religion. Forlorn he was 'like a Jew deprived of *Mincha* (the afternoon service),' frustrated 'like a tailor who has failed to get his *aliyah* (summoning to the Reading of the Law),' such summonings being rare sumptuosities in the life of the proletariat. Even the notions of barter and exchange were expressed in terms drawn from a more scriptural context, – nugatory and futile transaction being described as 'an exchange of last year's *luach* (religious calendar) for a discarded myrtle,' this lower-case myrtle being one of the plants forming part of the religious paraphernalia of the Feast of Tabernacles.

Of a more homely origin, but hardly more frequently encountered, are the proverbs which attach their precepts to food and eating. If something is weak and fragile, it is said to have the power of an *eyerkuchel*, literally, an egg-cookie; if it is *passé*, exhausted, it is said to be 'like a blown-out egg.' The same *mise-en-scène* suggested the observation (the appetizing requires no effort) that, 'for the consumption of *borsht*, teeth are not required.' The kitchen continues with its oracles: 'From an ordinary potato,' it asserts, 'one may make a fine pancake.' Here asceticism is out of place: *Fun al chett, vert men nisht fett*; which, roughly rendered, means: 'From "I have sinned" all you get is – thinned.'

It was well that the kitchen's leaven came to attenuate the high and other-worldly aspirations of the synagogue. The result was a view of life here below that saw things clearly and saw them whole, that penetrated through the sham and the hypocritical and emerged with wisdom that was hard, matter-of-fact, almost cynical. 'The world,' says the proverb, 'is beautiful; it is people who make it ugly.' 'Where you hear the barking of dogs,' says another proverb, as shrewd as it is devastating, 'there humans live too.' Not all are aware of these truths: 'The worm snuggles in his horseradish, and thinks there's nothing sweeter.' Everyone to his taste, and his fate: 'The same sun bleaches linen white and tans the gypsy black.' Each, also, to his temperament: *A menschen derkennt men b'kisoi, b'kasoi, b'koisoi* – 'A man may be judged by his portion, his passion, his potion.'

It would be fatuous to seek to build a philosophy of life out of two proverbs, yet two proverbs there are which summarize, as it were, the weltanschauung with which most of the aphorisms are weighted. 'Life is no more than a dream,' says one, but adds: 'Don't wake me up.' The other expressed faith in God. *Az Gott lozt leben, muz er dertzu mo'ois geben.* 'God gives us past, present, and future – the three tenses; He has to give us also for expenses.'

One of the most ingratiating of the qualities of the Yiddish proverb is its capacity to poke fun at its makers. Sometimes that capacity goes to such extremes that one is tempted to suspect in these proverbs the presence of some antisemitic pith; their authorship, of course, exonerates these from such suspicion. For their denigrations are not the result of hate but of realism – a talent for seeing things as they are. 'Of everything,' says the proverb, 'Jews think they have too little – only of brains they think they have enough.' The sting of this comment is removed, of course, by the obvious implication that the proverb's author, a Jew, does not share this high opinion of Jewish wisdom. Equally cynical is he of Jewish, or of all other, virtue. 'Don't cast suspicion on a Jew,' he says, 'because you're probably right.' Self-analysis goes even further and divides the Jewish psyche according to a scheme of percentages. 'A Jew is made up of 28% caution, 70% *chutzpah*, and 2% sugar.' And, should any arise to controvert these assertions, there's a proverb for that, too: 'Contrary is the Jew – greet him with *Sholom Aleichem*, he'll always answer, *Aleichem Sholom.*' For those not familiar with the manner of Jewish courtesy, it should be stated that this reversal of the greeting is the usual and formal response; an etymological, though not a semantic parallel, would be provided if one were to answer 'Hello' with 'O, hell!'

Even the attitude towards love was most realistic. It is true that the Yiddish language enjoys a multiplicity of synonyms for the rapturous passion; one speaks of 'conducting a love affair,' of 'having an inclination towards,' of 'burning,' 'glowing,' 'flaming,' 'crackling' (*flakeren*), of 'having someone baked into one's heart,' and – there the sound conveys the sense – 'of being *ferchlopsjed*'; nonetheless, the proverb asserting that 'Love is sweet' hastens to add 'but sweeter still with bread.' The proverb does not speak of butter; that, it seems, was a saccharinity beyond the farthest concepts of the poverty-smitten masses of Eastern Europe.

And of proverbs on poverty there is a wealth. This, on the lips of the submerged ghettos, seems to have been a constant; here was a subject ever ready to hand. For the poor man's diet, according to our anonymous proverb-makers, comes from a strange and highly imaginative menu. 'On what,' ask the commentators, 'does the pauper live?' And make answer: 'On fainting drops.' With sniffs and inhalations, as it were, did he sustain himself, for should he have betaken himself to foods more solid, his banquet was bound to be suspect, evocative, indeed, of ambiguous sympathy. 'If you see a poor man eating chicken, then one of two things is true – either he is sick, or the chicken was.'

That hence should ensue an awareness of class-distinctions was inevitable. 'The poor man sings, the rich man but gives ear.' (*Zingen zingt der ariman, der reicher hert zich nor tzu.*) Yet was not the pauper altogether abashed; music, after all, was his; and the proverb, moreover, brought him the parable of 'the man who was as rich as Korah but had not a *groschen* (penny) to buy a candle by the light of which he might count his wealth.'

Buffeted by fortune, driven from pillar to post, the humble anonymous *kabtzan* (pauper), having nothing else to study, studied the nuances of his plight. He knew, first, that his poverty, like the title of some Spanish grandee, could be encompassed by no less than seven Hebraic synonyms; he knew that for the blows of misfortune he was ever on the receiving end; and he made himself, not morosely but with a kind of verbalizing joy, a vocabulary to communicate the gradations of these buffetings. Thus in Yiddish, the following are some of the words for 'blow' – *stusack, buchtza, patch, lyap, flaska, frask, flam, matnas-yad* (a fiver), *gob, kulak, psak, knobel* (garlic), *kail,* and *fierdige kofel-shmoinedige petch,* which latter, literally translated, means a double-octuple lambasting. Sufferance was not only the badge, it was the very gaberdine of the tribe.

So accustomed and so inured, to him even death held no terrors. He greeted it with cheer and jeer. *Abi gezunt,* he said, *dos leben ken men zich alein nemen*: 'As long as one's healthy, no matter – one's life one can take one's self.' As for worldly goods, in the grave all were alike: 'Winding-sheets have no pockets.' Only one anguish really troubled him, and that was the curriculum of death itself. *Dos shtarben vi dos shtarben, das bagrobben leight in dr'erd*: 'Dying – never mind the dying – it's the burial that gets you down.'

Were there, then, in this ambience no consolations to attenuate anguish, affliction, and hard times? There were, and not the least of these prophylactics was the well-rounded curse. The Irish and the Jews run neck and neck in this talent for malediction; to the Jew it was a kind of secret weapon. Armaments he had not, bucklers and shields none, turned was his back to the oppressor, but one weapon still was his – the oath full-mouthed breathing execration. 'The nightmare that I nightmared last night,' he mumbled under his breath, 'and the night before, and all the nights of the year, on the enemy's life and limbs may they descend!' Or 'May God bless him with three servants – one to curry him, the other to hurry him, and the third to bury him!' Again, for the two-fold foe: 'May each one swallow the other, and each with the other choke!' A special case: 'May all his teeth fall out, except one – for toothache!' And finally, – at least for the time being – a permanent commination: 'May he be transformed into a candelabrum – by day to hang, to burn by night.'

But it was not in the consoling anecdote nor in the glib malediction that the Jew found his strength. He found it in his faith in God. For the Jew's relationships with Deity were not of the aloof and formal nature so characteristic of so many other religions. The easy familiarity which Rabbi Levi Yitschok of Berditchev adopted towards his maker, summoning Him, as he does in the folk-song, to a law-suit to answer for His treatment of Jewry, constitutes a forwardness which, in the eyes of devotees of other religions, verges on blasphemy. For the Jew, however, such intimacies had in them nothing of the audacious; was not God a constant Presence, a present help? His rabbis were more than rabbis, they were cronies of the Lord, familiars in heaven, able to address the *Rebono Shel Olam* in the second person singular: I will sing thee, says Rabbi Levi Yitschok of Berditchev, a *thou*-song. 'Le bon Dieu, – ils le tutoyaient.'

The same abiding faith, the almost personal assurance of salvation, manifests itself again and again in the language of the Yiddish proverb. 'He who has provided teeth, He will provide also bread.' One is never totally helpless: 'God willing, a broom shoots.' (One of the tragedies of East European Jewry, it appears, was a deficiency of brooms.) Nor was even Deity immune to the ironies of His faithful servants: 'God helps the pauper, He preserves him from expensive transgressions.' Sometimes it appeared that the mills, though they ground fine, ground slow; this thought the Yiddish proverb expressed, naturally enough, in the language of commerce. 'God's is a good account – but He's a slow payer.' Despite these familiarities, the distinction between the human and the divine was never lost. 'Fear God,' enjoins the proverb, 'but of men – beware!'

Such the social relationship, such the philosophic concepts, and such the attitude to God, which emerge from the Yiddish proverb. They conjure up, these scattered apothegms, these saws and random instances, a complete and coherent world. Alas, it is a world passed by. The far-flung Jewish hamlets on the shores of the Vistula, the Volga, the Danube, among the Carpathian Heights, are no more; they have been emptied of their Jewish folk. Their way of life persists only in memory, is proverb only in some now rarely read book of *Responsa*; flashes forth in the sudden recollection of some Yiddish maxim, some haunting lullaby, some folk-song eloquent of things of long ago.

We cast, then, through the quaint far-seeing spectacles of the proverb, a last retrospective glance over this vanished world. Not sovereign, it was, nevertheless, a domain, a kind of a-political polity. It had its capital, this comic-tragic principality, – the city of Chelm, that Gotham of Jewry the houses of which were built from the roof down, whose cheeses were made out of moonshine churned in a pail, the boards of whose bath-house were laid, with a shrewd municipal perspicacity, splinter-side up, so that no-one should slip.

It had its own economics, not the dismal science known of the professors, but a love of faith, a way of life in which the people 'starved thrice a day, not counting supper, – and thanked God for a decent respectable living'; its own class divisions – 'the rich puffed and puffed, the poor grew swollen'; and its own utopia – 'winding-sheets have no pockets.' A superficially grim world, yet not without its gaieties and compensations, – the joys of festival, Purim and its pious intoxications, Chanukah and its vicarious heroisms; the high afflatus of scholarship, the Yeshiva prodigies for the delectation of their audiences simultaneously juggling the contents of all the tractates of the Talmud to produce a mirage of subtlety and wisdom; and, on a lower level, the antics of its professional wits, its *schnorrers*, *badchanim*, wedding-entertainers, its Hershel Ostropolyer, Shaika Feifer, Motka Chabad.

It had its national mascot, this mingled world of dream and hard reality, 'the little white goat' which was to be found beneath every Jewish cradle, a silent bearded auditor of the mother's lullaby promising the drowsy child great distinction in Torah in days to come. Its own national bird, too, it had, *die goldene pawe*, the golden parrot, winging its way to the ghetto from lands remote, from some mighty monarch's palace, and bearing in its beak a letter full of most happy tidings.

Discrete, scattered, and isolated as these items were, they served nonetheless to create a world that was composite. The dreams of that world break out here and there in the nostalgias of the proverb. Elsewhere they go to fashion that phenomenon known as Yiddish literature, the sage wisdom of Mendele Moicher Sforim, the more sophisticated insights of I.L. Peretz, the all-encompassing humour of Sholom Aleichem.

The renowned cities and villages of the world have been wiped off the map. Boiberik is now a comic reference, Yehupetz as desolate as Samarkand, Kasrilevka a fallen crown. But the contribution which these metropolises of the mind made to the long epos of Jewry, though not as alive and vibrant as aforetime, is still to be felt, here in some gesture, there in some spontaneous response, almost everywhere as an impalpable but nonetheless effective influence. And nothing can serve better as an index of that influence than the Thesaurus of Jewry's Proverbs.

3 / THE BIBLE

Among the uninitiated there is an erroneous impression that the Bible is a book reserved for learned rabbis and pious ministers, a book as uninteresting as a sermon and as uninviting as a textbook. You need only open its covers to dispel that illusion and to become entranced in a romance containing every form of art from the narrative to the philosophic and offering in a most attractive form its mental pabulum. It is not surprising, therefore, that Heinrich Heine speaks of the Bible thus: 'The Bible – what a book! Large and wise as the world, based on the abysses of creation, and towering aloft into the blue secrets of heaven. Sunrise and sunset, promise and fulfillment, birth and death – the whole drama of humanity – are contained in this one book.'

Similar is the phraseology of Walt Whitman, who says: 'How many ages and generations have brooded and wept and agonized over this book. What untellable joys and ecstasies, what support to martyrs at the stake, from it! Translated in all languages, how it has united this diverse world! Of its thousands, there is not a verse, not a word but is thick-studded with human emotion.'

The Frenchman Jean-Jacques Rousseau and the German Goethe unite in singing its praise. Says the one: 'Peruse the books of philosophers with all their pomp of diction. How meagre, how contemptible are they, when compared with the Scriptures!' Says the other: 'The greater the intellectual progress of the ages, the more fully will it be possible to comprehend the Bible not only as foundation but as the instrument of education.'

Such is the consensus of opinion about a book which to the Greeks was *the* book – Biblion – a book which has already run into a circulation which numbers millions; its editions are legion; its commentaries defy enumeration. From the original scrolls to the Greek Septuagint and from that to the version of King James, 1611, it has been translated into every known language and has received explanation and exegesis from sources so different as Rashi and Thomas Paine; it has even won the immortality of textbook perpetuation. It has kept one people together for ages; for ages it has moulded the thought of the universe. From it men have taken their life and for it have laid that same life down. It is a testament which has at all times appeared in its wisdom old and in its utility ever new. To the aged it has brought consolation; and to the young, counsel. From its pages religions have sprung; from its chapters philosophies have been formulated; in its treatises Truth has received deification. It has been and still is the encyclopedia of the soul.

One turns its pages at random. One seeks to give an example of its heartening solace and so many are there, that one knows not where to begin; an example of its ever-useful advice, one begins and knows not where to end; of its truth and one feels constrained to quote it whole.

Apart, however, from its highly moral and ethical teachings, the Bible is couched in a most literary language and contains possibly every form of literary style that can be imagined.

As Ernest Sutherland Bates says: 'Though the Hebrews may have used an elementary metre in their verse, their main principle of versification was a parallelism of word, phrase and strophe, which, though distinct from the structure of prose, was very close to it, supplying through the King James translation the ultimate basis for the free verse of Walt Whitman and the polyphonic prose of Amy Lowell. So in these various ways the Bible might be said to be almost contemporary.'

LYRIC

As is well known, Bible poetry makes use only on rare occasions of rhyme. Its poetry is distinguished from its prose by the peculiar parallel construction. Thus the famous last word and testament of Jacob given in highly exalted and poetic language begins as follows (Genesis, Chapter 49):

> Gather yourselves together, and hear, ye sons of Jacob;
> And hearken unto Israel your father.

Indeed from this swan song of Jacob, rich in metaphor and pregnant with prophecy, many a poetic cameo is gleaned. Thus:

> The sceptre shall not depart from Judah,
> Nor a lawgiver from between his feet,
> Until Shiloh come;
> And unto him shall the gathering of the people be.

> Binding his foal unto the vine,
> And his ass's colt unto the choice vine;
> He washed his garments in wine,
> And his clothes in the blood of grapes.
> His eyes shall be red with wine,
> And his teeth white with milk.

Another remarkable poem – a chant of victory – issues from the mouth of Moses (Exodus, Chapter 15):

> The enemy said,

> I will pursue, I will overtake, I will divide the spoil;
> My lust shall be satisfied upon them;
> I will draw my sword, my hand shall destroy them.
>
> Thou didst blow with thy wind!
> The sea covered them; they sank
> As lead in the mighty waters.

Nor do we believe that any finer example of free verse can be gleaned even from the most ultra-modern periodical than this from the song of Deborah, exalted and exultant, in which she describes the death of Sisera (Judges, Chapter 5):

> At her feet he bowed, he fell, he lay down;
> At her feet he bowed, he fell;
> Where he bowed, he fell down
> Dead.

What finer anthem could there be uttered in exile than Psalm 137:

> By the rivers of Babylon,
> There we sat down, yea, we wept,
> When we remembered Zion.
> We hanged our harps
> Upon the willows in the midst thereof.
> For there they that carried us away captive required of us a song,
> And they that wasted us required of us mirth, saying,
> 'Sing us one of the songs of Zion.'
> How shall we sing the Lord's song
> In a strange land?
> If I forget thee, O Jerusalem,
> Let my right hand forget her cunning.
> If I do not remember thee,
> Let my tongue cleave to the roof of my mouth;
> If I prefer not Jerusalem above my chief joy.

Many have written in poignant language about the ravages of old age but none have caught the heart with anguish as the author of Ecclesiastes in his Chapter 12:

> Remember also thy Creator in the days of thy youth,
> Or ever the evil days come,
> And the years draw nigh, when thou shalt say,

'I have no pleasure in them'
Or ever the sun, and the light,
And the moon, and the stars, be darkened,
And the clouds return after the rain:
In the day when the keepers of the house shall tremble,
And the strong men shall bow themselves,
And the grinders cease because they are few,
And those that look out of the windows be darkened,
And the doors shall be shut in the street;
When the sound of the grinding is low,
And one shall rise up at the voice of a bird,
And all the daughters of music shall be brought low;
Yea, they shall be afraid of that which is high,
And terrors shall be in the way;
And the almond tree shall blossom,
And the grasshopper shall be a burden,
And the caper-berry shall fail:
Because man goeth to his long home,
And the mourners go about the streets:
Or ever the silver cord be loosed,
Or the golden bowl be broken,
Or the pitcher be broken at the fountain,
Or the wheel broken at the cistern;
And the dust return to the earth as it was,
And the spirit return unto God who gave it.

The highly poetic language, the reference to the spinal column as 'the silver cord,' the brain as 'the golden bowl,' the arms as 'the keepers of the house,' the teeth as the grinders which 'cease because they are few,' these, coupled with the deep and sincere feeling of the disillusioned Koheleth, render this section one of the finest expressions of resigned sorrow in all literature.

I do not refer to the Song of Songs which is in itself a complete anthology of love poems, and to which, when he desired to define poetry, Keats pointed.

EPIC

The wanderings of the Jews in the wilderness, suffering their reverses and successes narrated in the Pentateuch, is an Odyssey which makes the travels of Ulysses pale and those of Aeneas peregrinations without purpose. Here are no petty gods squabbling among themselves for the gaining of an ephemeral and illicit pleasure. Here is rather an omnipotent power working out the destiny of a great people, lofty in conception and perpetual in time. This is an epic, moreover, which is not a mere work of romance, the dream of a blind bard, which to-day has vanished, but an epic of realism, the last chapter of which has yet to be written.

IRONY

Though he may have been a professor of Semitics, Ernest Renan certainly showed no great knowledge of Jews when he said: 'Les Juifs n'ont ni la capacité de la curiosité ni de rire.' The Bible is full of satirical thrusts and ironic counterpoint; one of our great forefathers, indeed, got his name from the capacity of laughter. Thus out of the bitterness of Job consoled with empty words comes this:

> No doubt but that ye are the people and wisdom shall die with you.

Job had already manifested an epigrammatic turn of mind when he called one of his daughters 'Keren Hapuch' – cosmetic box.

And out of the divine assurance of Elijah comes this challenge to the heathen, calling in vain upon his god:

> Cry aloud for he is a god; either he is talking,
> or he is pursuing, or he is on a journey, or
> peradventure he sleepeth, and must be waked.

Even the pun finds utterance on the victorious lips of Samson when he reports: בלחי החמור חמור חמרתים which roughly rendered would be: With the jaw-bone of an ass, I have assailed masses.

One soon realizes that quotation would prolong analysis interminably. It suffices to say that from the biblical books of Kings and Chronicles, replete with fact which is significant and with legend which is even more so, down to the sophisticated aphorism contained in the Books of Prophets and the poetical metaphysics of Job, including, in the intervening passages, the cynical reflections of Koheleth, the faithful verse of the authors of the Psalms and the idyllic descriptions of the Book of Ruth, the lamentations of Jeremiah, in which the sorrow of a nation becomes the sorrow of one, and that sorrow of one, a weltschmerz in itself, including also the apocalyptical revelations of Ezekiel and the humanitarian prophesies of Isaiah, all these books, we say, have never been surpassed, have never been equalled, only imitated.

LANGUAGE

Nor is it in entire poems in which the authors of the Bible excel but here and there in its pages there will flash before the eye a phrase, a simile, a metaphor, so effective that in many cases it has entered into the currency of daily speech. Thus:

> We have been with pain, and we have been with child, and we have brought forth wind.
> ...
> Sift the nation with the sieve of vanity.
> ...
> The heavens shall be rolled together as a scroll.
> ...
> Behold I have graven thee on the palm of my hand.
> ...
> A man of sorrows and much acquainted with grief.
> ...
> The stone which the builders refused has become the headstone of the corner.
> ...
> If I ascend up into heaven, thou art there;
> If I make my bed in hell, behold, thou art there;
> If I take the wings of the morning, and dwell in the uttermost parts of the sea,
> Even there shall thy hand lead me and thy right hand hold me.
> ...
> Who hath gathered the wind in his fists?
> Who hath bound the waters in a garment?
> ...
> Cast thy bread upon the waters, and thou shalt find it after many days.

History, anecdote, tale, genealogy, poetry, play, epigram, – all are to be found in these pages. Well did the members of the Great Synagogue say when they did enjoin: 'Go over it and over it, for everything is in it!'

The Gesture of the Bible   16 July 1948

It has been noted by others, and particularly by Ernest Renan, that the language of the Old Testament is pre-eminently a language of concrete images, and, as such, a language designed to appeal more to the senses than to the ratiocinating mind. The athletic metaphors of field and farm are everywhere; abstract terms are kept at a minimum, and when they do occur are, like the word *truth*, of a nature the most elementary; even moral concepts are rendered in a vocabulary whose first approach is to the eye or to the touch. Almost throughout, thoughts are communicated in terms of things.

It is this aspect of biblic speech, of course, which endows the Scriptures with the highly poetic quality they have. There is no philosophizing in the Bible, although much philosophy; here and there you may encounter an Aristotelian syllogism; but it will be a syllogism of ordinary human relations and not of the schools; dialectics are left for the Talmudic descendants of the Book's people. In fact, there is hardly a statement, and this includes ethical injunction, which is not couched in terms evoking both the *person* and the *thing*, the person in the act of doing, and the thing in the state of being shown. And these verbal traits are of the essence of poetry.

Many theories have been advanced to explain this scriptural predilection for the concrete image. Mr. Renan, for example, seizes upon the obvious and deduces from the absence of a philosophic jargon in the Bible the judgment that the Hebrews had no talent for philosophy. Like most seizures upon the obvious, it fails to take into consideration a number of facts which make Renan's entire generalization suspect. If philosophy was beyond the Hebraic scope, how did it happen that the descendants of these same unmetaphysical primitives were able to produce a Maimonides, a Spinoza, a Bergson? Moreover, what *philosophic* truth stands greater than the discovery of monotheism, a discovery made without benefit of subtle talk about phenomenon and noumenon? The fact would seem to be rather, that the ancient Hebrews achieved a *tour de force* beyond the capacity of latter-day metaphysicians, namely, the enunciation of the most abstruse verities in a language which even peasants and shepherds could understand!

That this was the technique of the Bible with regard to the more complicated processes of thought did not escape the acute observation of Maimonides who in his *Guide to the Perplexed* paused to comment upon the use of such anthropomorphic terms as 'hand of God,' 'finger of God,' etc. Certainly in a creed which insisted upon the incorporeality of the Lord, the attribution of such physical details to Deity was a practice which seemed to verge upon blasphemy. Why then were they used? Says Maimonides: *l'shabair es ha-ozen,*– to shatter the ear, that is idiomatically to say, to accustom the ear by slow and familiar steps to the general concept of Divinity. Concrete phraseology to express abstract thought, therefore, is used so as to lead the mind by slow degrees from the primitive towards the ethereal.

With the cultivation of the Freudian doctrine, yet another hypothesis is advanced to explain the ubiquity in the Old Testament of words having reference to things rather than to thoughts. This hypothesis suggests that the whole vocabulary of the Bible is part of an attempt to escape from the aesthetic suppressions occasioned by the Second Commandment: 'Thou shalt not make unto thee any graven image, or any likeness of anything that is in heaven above, or that is in the earth beneath, or that is in the water under the earth.' To this stricture the Children of Israel, with the unfortunate exception of the Golden Calf affair, carefully adhered – neither in sculpture nor in painting did Hebrew chisel or brush create the forbidden image. But the soul, it would appear, hungers toward such creativity; where such creativity is impeded, frustration ensues.

But frustration always seeks some way out. For the ancient Hebrew the way out of the prohibition of the Second Commandment was – to make images in words. Only *graven* images were forbidden, not verbal ones; thus the writers of the Bible were able both to observe the Commandments and still satisfy their artistic longings.

It is an interesting and appealing hypothesis, attractive not only for the light it throws upon the antique style but also for the quaintness of a procedure which takes old Isaiah's psyche upon the confessional couch. To our mind it is an hypothesis not without merit, and much more evidence in its support could be brought forward than has hitherto been adduced.

We think, for example, that the metrical form which characterizes biblic poetry – the *parallelismus membrorum* – might also be analyzed with a view to discovering whether it, too, stems from the same nostalgia for image-making born by resistance out of the Second Commandment. Whenever the Scriptures move towards direct poetic utterance, it will be remembered, they follow a definite form – phrases are made parallel one to the other, what is said on the one hand is invariably repeated on the other, thus: 'Give ear, O ye heavens, and I will speak; and hear, O earth, the words of my mouth. My doctrine shall drop as the rain, my speech shall distil as the dew, as the small rain upon the tender herb, and as the showers upon the grass.'

It will be seen that what Moses is stating in the first verse is simply the fact that he is about to speak and wishes the world to listen. But he must state it ambidextrously. In the next verse the same thought – doctrine equals rain – is four times repeated. These duplications, triplications, quadruplications persist throughout the Bible.

It will, of course, suggest itself that the parallel construction is to be explained as a basic rhythmical form, a form in which the rhythm is made by the *thought* more than by the *mere number of syllables* in the phrase. (This is one of the reasons why the poetry of the Bible is translatable into so many languages without that loss which a syllabic prosody invariably suffers.) Yet such an explanation, while paying tribute to the rhythm, would not explain why *this* particular rhythm. It seems to us that here, too, we find a corollary to the Freudian theorem: the *parallelismus membrorum* is to prosody what the image is to sculpture and painting. Like the human body, it is two-armed, two-legged, two-eyed, double-eared; or three-legged; or quadrupedal; in any event, it is, as its name indicates, a form which has limbs and members. Like the graphic arts, it acknowledges the one dominant principle, symmetry; and like those things prohibited in the Second Commandment, it is concerned with likeness. The likeness, however, is auditory, and not visual, and thus the prohibition is foiled.

The Bible Manuscripts   28 September–26 October 1951

Is not our ethic based on hearsay? Is it not because of the echoing of the reverberations of the thundering upon Sinai that we have shaped our moralities even as they are, such and not otherwise? For what is this civilization which one vaunts – Jew, Muslim, or Nazarite – but the particularized elaboration of those ten behests and prohibits, the far-flung vibrations unceasing of those ten mighty thunderbolts, rumbling menace, sounding promise? From them, the decimals of the Lord, issue recurrent the Laws and the Prophets. Wise with inspired surmisal, that rabbin, who deduced from the simple decalogue all of the six hundred and thirteen commands and foregoings of Holy Writ. Yet as he did, did even the less wise: pandects and codes entire have from these ten been fashioned; the continents would be guided by them; upon the high seas the black flag blenches at their mentioning; and on the isles of the sea, remote, solitary amidst the waste or warmth of waters, rise spire and dome shining, mirroring Sinai's lightning.

The large currents of the heart, their tides, their direction, are by these ten moons governed. Set on a cloud the muezzin sends forth shrill the thunder of the One. The Jew before his couch, whether for night or for millenium, cries *Hear!* and in one long breath proclaims the One. Even the Christian, thrilled by threes, joins and consubstantiates them One. One! and Alone! Unique! Sole! Singular! First! Last! Eternal! Sempiternal! One! Thunder it One, the ten. And the pagan on the heath, the painted pygmy burst from jungle-leaf at last knows One: the idols go gangrenous; the jewelled puppets fall, are wood, are rotted punk, the fetishes are flown.

Because of the ten affection rises by degrees, and glows familial; because of the ten the hearth is warm. Venerable the father, respected, honoured; cherished the mother, her children are not ever weaned.

The wife is husbanded.

And the earth's weary know rest, its seventh part. Six days they labour and toil; oh, wearing and laborous the toil of those who from the dawn unto the dusk put burning hands against the sun to roll it slow, so slow, over the rounded humped sky! But see! upon the Sabbath, that heavy fiery sun benign – it moves itself!

More, it preserves from pillage the weak, and from untimely death, – that dict from the mountain. Had the news of it not come down to us, what rapes! what murders! what ravaging by banditti, ambushes, despoliations, slaughters! Had the Voice from Sinai not been reported, in what had consisted man's excellence over the beasts of the field? In nothing; for all had then been a pacing, a stalking, a questing for quarry. Only because the decagon hems us in, is order, such as is; had the news of it not come down to us –

And here the mind halts, as before a precipice. Who brought the news of the Decalogue? Is it not within the coils of ten *rumours* that we are coiled? Is the news to be believed? Is there a script from an eyewitness? A testament has been adduced; what probate confirmed it? Is there record contemporaneous with the event?

Answers fidelity: But of course, there are the Tables of the Law! Where?

They are reported as having been brought down from the mount:

> And Moses turned, and went down from the mount, and the two tables of the testimony were in his hand: the tables were written on both their sides; on the one side and on the other were they written. And the tables were the work of God, and the writing was the writing of God, graven upon the tables.

Yes, but read on:

> And it came to pass, as soon as he came nigh unto the camp, that he saw the calf, and the dancing: and Moses' anger waxed hot, and he cast the tables out of his hands, and broke them beneath the mount.

Ah, but there was a duplicate; read *you* on:

And the Lord said unto Moses, Hew thee two tables of stone like unto the
first, and I will write upon these tables the words which were in the first
tables, which thou brakest ... And it came to pass, when Moses came down
from Mount Sinai with the two tables of testimony in Moses' hand, when
he came down from the mount, that Moses wist not that the skin of his face
shone while he talked with him.

Where, then, are these second tables, written, not in God's hand, but
in the hand of Moses?

The Book of Kings records them, recording the dedication of the temple
of Solomon:

And the priests brought in the ark of the covenant ... There was nothing in
the ark save the two tables of stone, which Moses put there at Horeb, when
the Lord made a covenant with the children of Israel, when they came out
of the land of Egypt.

These tables, are they extant?

No.

What! lost? Misplaced? These tables which tradition says weighed forty
seah and were of sapphire quarried from the solar disc – lost?

Lost, buried, crumbled, transfigured – no man knows, even as none
knows the place where lie the bones of Moses who did hew them.

Who did hew them? How is that known? Failing exhibit of the stone
tables, how is it known that they ever were?

From Scripture.

But the scripture in our hands, which attests to the existence and the
disappearance of its own original, is but a transcript. Who made it? And if,
at the time of its making, its master stone was lost, how indeed was it made?
Have we the name of the copyist? Was he a man to be vouched for? Was he,
like its first transcriber, a man meek, one who would put down that and that
only which was dictated, or was he – world-destroying thought! – of that
tribe of copyists who would themselves be authors, who add to their texts
what in their arrogance they deem to have been overlooked (by Omniscience!)
and subtract therefrom what in their obtuseness they deem to be superfluous?
Can it be – recognize Satan by his interrogatives – can it be that this writ we
cherish is not at all the reportage of God's Sinai, but the feigning, the invention
of some petty molehill of a Sinai, a scribe's secret megalomania?

The scribes of Israel are above reproach. Labouring in poverty, from
piety, no worldly suspicions attach to them. For not for wealth – that corrupter
of texts – chose they their vocation, nor for the glory of authorship, nor for
the forging of hallowed exhibit to justify secular power, but for the power
and glory of God; one impulse driving them: that from each at least once in

his stay upon earth there issue, counted, contemplated, shaped, the words that Jehovah Himself dictated to the hand of Moses. This was, continues to be, their reward; no other ... Did not the rabbis observe twenty-four fast days to petition the Lord that the scribes of Israel wax not rich lest in their affluence they spurn the parchment and despise the pen?

Of record: petition granted in all cases.

Poor they were, these calligraphists, for the pittance inscribing phylacteries, sanctifying with the *Shema* the door's lintel, raising with their script the vile vellum to dignity celestial, all for their bread and salt, poor they were – yet not without emolument. The grace of holy vocation. The confidences of angels. Serenity from heaven. And more mundane – the artist's skill, Bar Kamza's skill, Bar Kamza upon whose hand God fixed such blessing that he was able to manipulate four pens between five fingers to write with the one stroke the quadriliteral word!

Consider, indeed, the rules and disciplines which the scribes to their scriptures brought! Remember, always, they were mere copyists, duplicators, fashioners of facsimile; yet for their copying they made them these rules which authors striving toward a work's perfection, geniuses murmuring inspiration, might well take to heart. An epic poet's *vade mecum*, not that of simple clerk.

1. *Writing to be done upon parchment.* The hides of *clean* beasts must they be, – not pigskin (*absit nomen!*). One does not consecrate on ground profane.

2. *Before writing, meditate.* He is a scribbler and no scribe who falls palms forward on his sheet, submits to runaway pen and fingers' epilepsy, and only after the page is black, discovers what it is he wrote. Alas, then it is too late, for –

3. *No erasures.* If error has crept into the text, if the scribe's nodding shows, alas; the words are not expungeable. Ugly, in truth sacrilegious, are deletions, outmarkings, defacements, over-writings, erasures, for it is Holy Writ. Rather that the entire sheet be removed (not destroyed; despite flaw, it has been touched by holiness) and hidden away, preserved, garnered to some *genizah*, until, its days full-numbered, it is ripe for burial in some sacred tomb.

4. *And the ink – indelible.* These are not notations of the week's dealings at the bazaars, things that may be permitted to fade to faint mnemonic of a sometime importance. This is script eterne, text imprescriptible!

5. *Before writing, every word pronounce.* Let them float on the air, the divine syllables, and then, of their own weight, settle in place; for these are words intended to have currency among humans, all humans; test it, therefore, with voice and through ear. In the midst of air-waves pulsating with God's words, the scribe writes.

6. *And before the writing of the names of God – pause, pronounce, ponder.*

7. *No writing downward.* The lines straight, parallel, on a level. Who writes down, blasphemes.

8. *And no gilding of letters.* Shall one dare to gild what is already beyond gold? There was a scribe in Alexandria who thought to give lustre to his scroll by gilding; his scroll, it shone with aureate tetragrammatons! The rabbis condemned it.

9. *No piercing of letters, either.* The sheets written, ready to be sewn together with a thread of dried tendon of clean beast, beware the perforation of the letter!

10. *Count letters; do not add; omit not.* For he who omits so much as one iota from the prescribed text brings thereby dis-harmony, if not destruction, to the world.

With such rule did they fence themselves, and with the fear of the Lord. Read the colophon appended, not to a Scroll of the Law, but to less holy Mahzor by Moshe ben Asher, the glory of Tiberias, and learn therefrom of the fear and trembling with which Jewry's scribes made themselves the Lord's amanuenses:

> Whoever alters a word of this Mahzor, or of this writing, or erases from it a letter, or tears off from it a leaf – saving he knows for certain that there is in it a word in which we have erred, whether in transcription, or in punctuation, or in Masorah, or in defective or in plene, – let neither pardon nor forgiveness be his! Not ever let him be granted the vision of the beauty of the Lord, nor ever know the blessings God reserves for those who fear him! Be he like a woman in impurity, like a leper isolate, that his limbs be crushed, the pride of his power broken, his flesh consumed away that it be not seen, and his bones that are not seen stick out!

Who, then, would hazard, against such caveat and curse, to tamper with this script, this paradise, that the sword-wielding angels defend?

Hagbah! Raise aloft this scroll in your own synagogue cherished, or the scroll the great museum boasts, or any other scroll of any of the Jewries, capital or hamlet, to-day's or of a thousand years ago, – is a more meticulous script possible, a penmanship more fastidious? Looking, the eye itself must fall in love with Holy Writ and know ever thereafter all of nature numinous with that vision! And can such perfection have issued from scribe careless, scribe forger, scribe garbling Sinai's grand locution?

There, in square panoplied array, the letters march, by columns, forty-two lines to a column – memento of Israel's two and forty desert journeyings – each column heralded and led, vanguarded by the initial *vav*, erect, at attention, lance-bearers of those holy hosts! God's warriors, these letters, they stand firm, fixed, weariness not leaning on its neighbour, but each separate from the next, – all mustered and marshalled, embattled against evil, that blaspheming foe. And their weapons beside them.

This *mem* – dark powers fly before its square; this *ches*, it can cover iniquity as under a mound. Like a leader of thirties, this *lamed* runs; the *gimel* readies its kick. Beware the *zayin* – its cutting edge! Beware the knived chariot – the *aleph*! Satan, beware and beware, the *tauf's* explosive retort, the *ayin's* double-edged sword!

Aligned, arrayed, the letters march, – the valour of Israel. No terror affrights them, whether of the open field, of the secret ambush or of the overwhelming sea. See, in their staunch formations how they cross the Red Sea; they make out of themselves the bricks of a wall; the walls rise on either side; on either side the sea rages, raging at the dry-shod Israelites.

Then in full armour emerge again. Proud they march, with their crowns upon them, their *tagin*, those delicate diadems. Behold the *shin*, beautiful as the stag, antlered! The *tess*, with coronet! The crested *samech*! With crown and dignity, the puissant *pai*!

Soldiers of the Lord, with their captains and officers, they advance against the regiments of evil. Their swords are raised against corruption, they would strike down vileness, evil is the enemy, their adversary and sworn foe.

And shall he who provisions such an army against such a foe – the strategist scribe – shall such be deemed dishonest sutler?

Glilah! Roll up the scroll, and see the army tented!

Now is the scroll girded with silk; and mantled. Rich and ornate its vesture, of velvet or samite, gorgeous in design, encrusted with scripture, – a needle cantillatory threaded its singing words. Its two rollers – trees of life! – project ivory, and on them, royal, the Crown of the Law, silver, behung with hushed bells, like flowercups. Upon the mantle itself – thoracic the Breastplate, chased or embossed, saltant with banners, triangle, eagles volant, rampant lions. Dangles from silver links upon the Breastplate – the *Yad*, the silver pointer, – finger of righteousness, precious index!

With endearments, with caressings, with embellishments, with a great trembling care, the scribes esteemed and honoured Torah. Nothing was omitted from their worship thereof; all that could serve to magnify, majestatize, to its glory they brought it. Shall, then, such be held under suspicion, and their scroll's authenticity doubted?

It would seem, then, that this document is beyond question; that in this writ we have the exact image, the very visual photograph, of the writ which came from Moses' hand, of God's primordial glyph. Mirror flashing against mirror – from the Table of Moses to the Stone of Joshua to the Scroll in the Ark to the writings of Aristeas to the calligraphy of the youngest scribe – the image is repeated and the latest is facsimile of the first. The tradition, then, is an unbroken tradition, we can take our oath upon this Bible that this Bible is the Book.

Yet questions arise, and bewilderments. Why – in this scroll before us – are there these texts which look suspiciously so like emendations? Why is this letter huge and majuscule, and that one minuscule reduced, concealed between the branches of its neighbour? Is this erraticism of the original, or is it some redactor's variant? And here, where the narrative calls for *kalail* – to curse, who euphemized it *baruch* – to bless? Do our eyes see right, here in the twenty-fifth chapter of Numbers, the twelfth verse thereof, a bisected *vav*? A bisected *vav*! Was it so also upon the Tables, or is this a vestige of their breaking? Roll back Numbers, Chapter 10, – what have we here? A topsy-turvy *neun*? The *neun* stood on its head! Surely this must be an error, some one scribe's peculiar oculism! But the next scroll has it, too. Did the first?

And now consider it, the most startling, the most shattering of the idiosyncrasies of these scribes. For here, and here, and here again, the word's writ one way, and tradition bids you read another. *Ketib* – thus it is written, but *Keri* – you must read it thus. Nor is it a simple innocuous ambiguity which thence ensues, but often – and this is the most un-hinging thought of all – downright negation. For the word is written *lo*, with an *aleph*, meaning 'no'; it is read *lo*, with a *vav*, meaning 'to him.' A no has been nullified! The Bible's *no*, Sinai's prohibitory *no!* has been argued, edited away; the *nay* is converted into *yea!* What follows? Volcanic are the implications, the earth's foundations tremble, seismic is the human heart ...

Comes the scholar to soothe and to pacify: These variants and emendations, the stigmata of these dots and the cleavage of those letters, these marginalia that seem to distort the text and these juxtapositions that profess to simulate – do not be alarmed, they are not the result of a wicked tampering. No demons with inked claws did hop these errors onto the sacred page. This is the work of the Masoretes.

The Masoretes, anonymous immortal guild! Who through the centuries, from the redeeming days of the Hasmoneans to the days when the scions of Rashi brought distinctness and distinction to Talmud, did labour in the garden of Torah, comparing, collating, gathering a tradition that lingered in Aleppo, garnering a reading known in Troyes, to fashion the text definitive, that is to say, the text primitive, as issued at Sinai, as remembered by Ezra and the Men of the Great Synagogue. Forgers of fetters some have called them, thereby meaning to belaud their achievement as a guarding against deviation; keepers of the tradition, of the *masorah*, others have dubbed them, meaning thereby to dignify their scholarship as a thesaurus handed over in unbroken succession from Moses himself; but whether as smiths of an unbreakable text or as custodians of a treasured heritage, it is to them that there is ascribed those peculiarities that so widened the eye and shuddered the soul.

Thus is there the Numerical Masorah which, like a miser with his gems, counts and numbers and computes and takes toll of the words, the letters, that Holy Writ contains; cabbalistic, it announces that it is precisely at the word *vayishchat* (grim omen!) in the twenty-third verse of the eighth chapter of Leviticus that the Bible reaches its middle point!

The Grammatical Masorah – which to a text made up entirely of consonants, – as if Law and Holiness came to the world in one grand impetuous expostulation! – added vowels; and to a text without punctuation – as if all in level voice had been said – gave accents; inspired, it endows divine utterance with human articulation.

And the Exegetical Masorah, which reveals at length why these dots, that strange pointillation is gathered about the verb which tells that Esau did kiss Jacob. Say the exegetes: An ambiguous kiss it was, a biting rather than an osculation; and those dots – they are Esau's teeth ravenous above the kissing word!

These, then, are not tamperings and contradictions, but system designed for the text's protection. Proof? Since the Masoretes ceased their labours, no other changes have accrued; their scholarly prophylaxis has kept the text intact.

But they did make changes? Upon whose authority? Why, upon the authority of tradition, Moses ben Asher having received it from Asher ben Moses who in turn received it from the elder Moses, who had it from his father Asher, who was told it by a yet earlier Moses to whom it had been entrusted by a still earlier Asher, back and back and back, to the very first Moses!

And who asserts this?

Alas, the Masoretes themselves. They only. Shall this, then, be called evidence?

Let them be brought, the earlier witnesses, the manuscripts from before the time of the Masoretes, so that we may see with our own eyes – best evidence! – what and where they emended. Evoke the earlier codices, that codex Muggeh that the Masoretes so fondly quote; the codex Hilleli, praised of Zacuto, by Kimchi placed in Toledo; the codex Sanbuki – was it not written on the banks of the Tigris in the very light of the Babylonian wisdom? – the codex of Jerusalem seen in Saragossa; that of Jericho, excellent in accents; the codex Great Mahzor said to have been divided for reading on the Sabbaths of the year; the codex Babylon. Let us place them, these versions of a great antiquity, side by side, that we may read in the sanct library the text cherished before the makers of fetters to their smithies repaired.

Alas, these scripts will never again be seen. They have perished from the earth. They have been dust these many years, lost in some catastrophe, burned by vandals, swallowed by whales, or buried no man knows where. They live only in the memory recorded of later authors; this rabbi saw the codex there, another had it reported that it was seen. But the eyes of to-day will not ever look upon them; they are one with the scroll once treasured in the Temple, one with the splinters from the shards of Moses' broken tables. Unless a miracle take place and in some remoteness the unsuspected *Genizah* be uncovered, the illustriousness of these codices must remain but matter of rumour and frustrated search.

Let us console ourselves then with what is attainable, reachable, seeable. Which are the oldest Bible manuscripts extant?

Not older than one poor millenium. The scholars have ransacked the libraries, the archaelogists have rummaged in the tombs; Firkowitch has journeyed far and wide, and Schechter, clambering into the sealed attic, has seen his beard grow grey with the powder of old parchment; but no one – not a one – brought back manuscript, or scroll, or codex, that dated earlier than the tenth century of the gentile era.

Go to the Bodleian, or the Ambrosian, the British Museum or the Vatican, or any sanctuaries bibliothecal of our day – there is not a maker of catalogues who can boast you an antiquer writ. For when to that dark century we come, all vanishes, all in a cloud of dust is puffed away, and it is as if the Word had never been, as if it were in that tenth century, then, and not until then, that the Decalogue had numbered *its* ten, its ten and the law of Moses!

The which is blasphemy.

The oldest manuscript extant? It is that which is to be found in the collection at Leningrad – MS. Heb. B.3 (but where is Sinai's catalogue number?) – hight the Codex Babylonicus Petropolitanus; and it is dated as of 916 of the era of Man who came to add neither jot nor tittle. 916! – and before that all is emptiness, a blank, a deathly silent desert, uncoded, de-scrolled! Almost one would say that the Voice sounded millennia back at Sinai had fallen upon a world of deafmen, deaf-mutes who regained their hearing, and then their writ, only in 916!

The which is absurd.

Scrolls there were – certainly, most certainly – before that famous date. For before that date one finds it quoted, translated; religions and hierarchies are founded upon it; often its text as argument did lead to death; always its text as guidance led to life. Yet the tantalizing question, unresolved, abides: Were those earlier texts exactly like the ones before us? In all respects? Even like the Codex Babylonicus that the Soviet Godless so zealously in their archives hold?

No answer.

Nor does there issue a light from the kindlings of the dragomans, the translators and their polyglot. No light – but rather confusion, shadow misconstruing shadow, until the whole is but a variegated darkness. For they all fell victim, these translators, to the translator's vice – traduction. In place after place they do render the text and do rend it, patching it into a harmony – with the quilts of their own minds. Not translators, but smugglers of commentary. 'He who renders a verse' – say they, making an ethic out of their distortions – 'as it reads, with strict literalness, lies!' But many forms has falsehood.

Hence the insidious recension of translation, where anthropomorphism is paraphrased away (God does not give ear; it is heard), and the shunning of the personification of the inanimate (the sword does not come, but murderers bearing swords), and the too vivid eschewed (Ezekiel does not eat the scroll, he listens attentively to its contents). It is the translator who eats the scroll. And with gusty appetite, for he gorges, he believes, in a good cause – the impersonality of God, the honour of Israel. Was it imagined that Moses had married a Cushite woman? Go to the translator, and discover her 'pretty.' Was Rachel's god-handling of her father's household gods set down as theft? A grievous error; the translator puts things right – he renders 'she took,' not 'she stole.'

But, ah, the Codex Vaticanus – the translation of the seventy of the Septuagint, translation whose manuscript is five centuries earlier than the earliest of the originals, that Codex Babylonicus, yclept of Leningrad! Surely here must be enlightenment, so much nearer is it to Sinai, so much more authoritative since an academy of seventy, and not one errant man alone, did labour upon it?

Not so thought the Talmudists: they did liken the day of the appearance of this Septuagint to the day of the fashioning of the golden calf! Indignant, they charged these Hebrew Greeks with having introduced into Holy Writ not less than thirteen deliberate alterations! Some, for base motive. Sheer slavish sycophancy, they charge, rendered the 'hare' of Leviticus a 'roughfoot,' and not, as was right and correct, a *lagos* – for *lagos*, the seventy brave translators feared, might offend the honour and dignity of the royal Ptolemaic family, surnamed the *Lagi*! Thus was the word of the King of kings made to falter before a kinglet, a rabbit-prince, mere mortal!

No, these *pseudo*-Jonathans and these *blind* Rab Josephs – they aid us not. Rather do they confirm us in our suspicion of sacrilegious emendation and blasphemous editing. The impertinence of them! The writ reads thus and so, and these double-tongued interpreters dare, for the correction of the Lord's metaphysics, for the improvement of His etiquette, to traduce it so and thus!

Remains, then, the original query: How do we know, how are we sure that the text before us is that that came down from the mountain? Can it be that all these centuries when we have conformed, we conformed to the edict of a forgery? And when we sinned, the sin was but an illusion, an error in a reading?

The question sends earthquakes under the world's foundations. The dynasties tremble. The question distils poison in the brain – the moralists shake in a chill, the philosophers go mad.

The Bible's Archetypical Poet   6–20 March 1953

There are many who could qualify for the distinction. First in time if in nothing else, there is the famous Jubal, he who in the fourth chapter of Genesis is designated 'the father of all such as handle the harp and the organ.' There can be no doubt but that here we hear for the first time the lyre trembling in our midst. Winning, perhaps, the suffrages of most, there is King David, right royal psalmodist, of whose kingly titles brightest was that which dubbed him 'sweet-singer in Israel'; and there is his son, prolific also of writings, who under the name of Solomon wrote of love that is immortal and under the name of Qoheleth wrote of mortality and all its emptinesses vain. The prophets, major and even minor, are not without their claims; touched with fire upon the lips, their words, like sparks, fly upward, and are winged words. As between these to choose for the apple of typicality is to choose as between the invention of an instrument and the composition of a manuscript, as between the prophet-rhetorician's happy phrase and the poet-pietist's inspired utterance. It is a choice that implies comparisons in texts; it takes for granted the assumption that all of the candidates are poets and then challenges itself to declare which one of them is of the greatest eminence. With the exception of Jubal's virtuosity, no longer heard, the choice involves a weighing of the ethereal, a measuring of the elusive subtle, in a word, a study in literature.

Literature, not life. What we are here primarily concerned to discover, however, is not so much the Bible's texts of all-excelling poetry as that instance of biography, that scriptural *curriculum vitae* that would best illustrate, with the very sanction of Holy Writ, the typical role and function of the poet. And that biography we have found, we think, in the record of one to whom not a single strophe, not a versicle, has ever been ascribed. It is, to our mind, the young Joseph whose life presents the coveted paradigm.

He begins scion of an ancestry worthy of his vocation: he is the son of a father who wrestled with angels. So were they all, it will be said, so were all twelve – but it was Jacob himself who marked differences; his preference is made explicit: *Now Israel loved Joseph more than all his children.* Nor was the special tenderness, noted as having taken place when Joseph was seventeen years old, but a passing predilection; it persisted to the old Patriarch's very last day. Says Jacob in the famous testamentary chapter penultimate to the closing of the Book of Genesis: *The blessings of thy father have prevailed above the blessings of my progenitors unto the utmost bound of the everlasting hills: they shall be on the head of Joseph, and on the crown of the head of him that was separate from his brethren*. In that grand hyperbole about the utmost bounds of the everlasting hills, the father, speaking himself like a poet, recognizes in his Joseph a son apart.

Against the drabness of his brothers, Joseph like a rainbow shone, for his father made him, it is written, a coat of many colours. *Sic literatim*. But it is Joseph's mind that is truly of the thousand peacock hues; a myriad facets does it have; it flashes similitude, image, colour. It was this chatoyant quality of his son's imagination, no doubt, which prompted the doting Jacob to array him outwardly as he was inwardly arrayed.

Wrapped, then, in the garment of imagination, behold, the dreamer cometh. For this, indeed, this epithet, this is the key to Joseph's craft. He is not a mere coiner of phrases, a fashioner of verses, a compiler of stanzas; he is a dreamer and, what is infinitely more important, an interpreter of dreams. He takes the universe for the matter of his dream, the sun and moon and stars eleven, standing corn and kine in the field, and derives from them things past, things passing, and things yet to come. To his brothers he seems to live as if in another world, yet it is his world which proves to be, in the fulness of time, a world of solid and true substance. They mock him, his father rebukes him, but it is his dream which abides.

Yet, though dreamer, it is not to things fanciful and fantastic, that Joseph gives interpretations. His feet are ever planted firmly on the soil; a time would come, indeed, when in the pit he would be even more firmly grounded. He dreams, but through the haze of the dream, he grasps reality. He never loses touch with it. What were the two great interpretations which led eventually to his elevation to the palace of the Pharaoh? They were interpretations touching food and drink – the dreams of the baker and the butler. It is significant that it was the latter, the dreamer of the inspiriting vine, budding, blossoming, shooting forth its clusters of ripe grapes, who remembering his faults that day, spoke up for the imprisoned poet.

He never loses touch with things; he never loses touch with people. Though of Joseph it is written that he brought to his father the evil report of his brothers – all poetry is comment – though he conjured up imaginations of arrogance in which he beheld his kith and kin making obeisance to him, yet it is not those incidents which illustrate his typical attitude. Not many of the reported utterances of Joseph, though poet, are memorable, but two there are which have throbbed with their humanity across the centuries. The second, which without tears can be read only by an only child, takes place in the court of Pharaoh. Joseph can no longer conceal himself from his brothers: *And he cried, Cause every man to go out from me. And there stood no man with him, while Joseph made himself known to his brethren. And he wept aloud ... And he said unto his brethren, I am Joseph; doth my father yet live?* But it is the first which, though not so dramatically couched, presents the whole theme and tenor of the poet's work. It is in Shechem where Joseph is found by a certain man: *And behold, Joseph was wandering in the fields and the man asked him, saying, What seekest thou?* The answer casually made that day on that solitary sunlit road resounds down the ages. It is Joseph's central impulse, to be exemplified again and again in his career: *And Joseph said, I seek my brethren.*

Yet, although all of Joseph's efforts are towards a recognition – a recognition of his brothers – a recognition that was to come, after much sorrow and anguish, only at the end of the Joseph story – a heavy haze, a thick veil, almost an inscrutable curtain hangs between them. They are consumed with envy, the eleven of the one. Every time old Jacob in affection casts his regard upon Joseph, it is as if eleven daggers pierced the hearts of the others. And what they particularly abominate are those cursed dreams of his: How he preens himself on his imaginings; how he struts about after every inspired visitation! You would think that he, and he alone, had been singled out for divine communications, favorite not only of his father on earth, but favorite and chosen vessel for his Father in heaven. The dreams, then, they resented, but they resented even more the implication that flowed from them, – the assumption that upon the head of Joseph there rested some special kind of grace. They hated him.

Therefore, *when they saw him afar off, even before he came near unto them, they conspired to slay him.* Had they waited his near approach, had they but given him opportunity to utter his first words of greeting, perhaps the conspiracy had altogether been nullified; but he was afar off; the brothers knew only their own hearts, Joseph's they knew not. The course of the conspiracy made a pattern that was to be followed all too frequently in the history of human brotherhood. As if they were reading an indictment, they in hatred proclaimed him dreamer. They flung him into a pit – he who in his mind had elevated himself to the highest of the sun and the moon now lay lower than the level of the earth. They would surely have killed him outright had it not been for the intervention of Reuben, Reuben whom his father was later to characterize as of 'excellency of dignity.' Reuben vainly thought thus to be able later to save his brother and to deliver him to his father again; but he, too, was deceived in the fraternity.

But before the brothers dispose of Joseph, they execute the gesture which bespeaks the whole source and origin of their hate. They strip him, says the Bible, out of his coat, and, to make the point explicit, the Bible continues: *his coat of many colours that was on him*. Now let it be seen how gloriously arrayed this poet is!

Him they leave in the pit, without water; themselves they sit down to eat bread. That bread tastes good – it is seasoned with revenge.

And, behold, a company of Ishmeelites came from Gilead with their camels bearing spicery and balm and myrrh. To the motive of revenge there is now added the motive of profit – the poet destroyed may yet be used. Joseph is sold to the Ishmeelites – for twenty pieces of silver. Thus was Joseph not simply sold – he was undersold.

At this point Reuben returns, he who had thought by some device to save his brother harmless from the plot. *And behold Joseph was not in the pit, and Reuben rent his clothes*. Returning to his brothers, the tragedy bursts forth from his lips in few pathetic words: *The child is not!*

The opening ceremonial of hatred, the stripping of Joseph's coat, is now converted into a technique of closing alibi. A goat is killed, and the coat is dipped in its blood, *the coat of many colours that was on him*. And old Jacob, who knows not the truth that lies before him – that it was his son Joseph that was the scapegoat – cries out, deceived, yet speaking truth: *An evil beast hath devoured him!*

It is impossible to preserve this story, detail after symbolic detail, without realizing that here we have encountered the classic design figuring the relation between the poet and his fellows. Described in its bare and epic outlines in the Book of Genesis, it is a design which repeats itself down through the ages. The dictionaries of national biography are replete with it. Every generation sees its repetition, every clime has its counterpart. It is a design which, beginning with misunderstanding and envy, moves on towards conspiracy, suggests, at first, a mere humiliating of its victim, then, feeding upon its own thoughts, soon clamours for revenge, and thus, by its own clamorous blood encompassed, broods on the ultimate: murder. From that ultimate it recoils; it cannot bring itself to strike the killing blow, but by this time, the distinction is purely technical: *The child is not*.

It is true that the brothers walk away from the scene of their crime without an awareness of the seriousness of that crime. Nowhere in Holy Writ is mention anywhere made of regret or remorse. Only when at last they find themselves in the court of Pharaoh, their brother revealed to them, only then are they troubled; and even then, they are troubled 'at his presence.' In his absence they are able, no doubt, to summon up a dozen exculpatory reasons. They meant only to teach him a lesson, no more. He was altogether too arrogant and had it coming to him. They didn't kill him, after all, did they? They killed only a goat. And besides (hypocrisy's last outcry) wasn't it for his own good? Didn't he as a result end up as viceroy of Egypt?

But the child was not.

It is as Jacob calls his sons together to bestow upon them his prophetic benedictions (*Gather yourselves together that I may tell you that which shall
befall you in the last days*) that we learn, from Joseph's special benediction,
as recalled in the forty-ninth chapter of Genesis, what the vocation of poet
really means. We have done with the patterned incidents of the poetic life;
Joseph has suffered his trials and agonies.

He has been lifted out of the dungeon: *And he shaved himself, and
changed his raiment, and came in unto Pharaoh.*

He has learned humility, not only with regard to his brothers, but also
with regard to himself: *And Pharaoh said unto Joseph, I have dreamed a
dream, and there is none that can interpret it: and I have heard say of thee,
that thou canst understand a dream to interpret it. And Joseph answered
Pharaoh, saying, It is not in me: God shall give Pharaoh an answer of peace.*

He has, despite antipathy, come to a closer understanding of his brothers:
*And Joseph saw his brethren, and he knew them, but made himself strange
unto them, and spake roughly unto them; and he said unto them, Whence
come ye? And they said, From the land of Canaan to buy food. And Joseph
knew his brethren, but they knew not him.*

His own children have reconciled him to his fate: *And Joseph called the
name of the first born Manasseh: For God, said he, hath made me forget all
my toil, and all my father's house. And the name of the second called he
Ephraim: For God hath caused me to be fruitful in the land of my affliction.*

And now Jacob speaks of futurities, and this speaking provides in outline
the central inspiration and attitude of the poet: *Joseph is a fruitful bough,
even a fruitful bough by a well; whose branches run over the wall: The
archers have sorely grieved him, and shot at him, and hated him: But his
bow abode in strength, and the arms of his hands were made strong by the
hands of the mighty God of Jacob.*

Here, then, we find, issuing from the lips of Jacob, a blessing, the benign
visitation whereof must go to make the poet complete. He must be, first, a
fruitful bough, must have natural talent, be a poet born. No amount of study
will here avail to fashion a creator out of him who lacks the spark; analysis
is vain, and imitation is to none effect. The parrot parrots, and the ape does
ape; only the human speaks, only the human's gestures are his own.

But even the bough, naturally fruitful, cannot forever draw sustenance
from itself. Wherefore is Joseph blessed to be *even a fruitful bough by a well.*
Not isolated, not alone, not altogether self-sustained, does the poet live; he
lives hard by a refreshing and ever renewed source of water; he lives and
labours within a tradition. The spider weaves entirely from his entrails; but

all he creates is a web. The ant, to whom one bids all sluggards go, the ant, no mean maker of artifacts, he works within a society. Thus Jacob, addressing Joseph, conceals his unspoken reproach within the very heart of his blessing, and by indirection enjoins his favorite son from sundering himself from his brothers, themselves, in their way, the makers of a tradition. The bough is fruitful only near the well; removed therefrom, it thirsts, is parched, one withers away.

But to rest within a tradition, to remain content thereby, and not to seek to bring to it originality and innovation – this, too, would be a denial of the poet's devotion. He who merely repeats is no poet; he adds nothing to the catalogue of created beauty; his are but pale duplicates of a brighter original. The true poet is he who, nourished upon the ancestral heritage, yet – if only in the slightest – deviates therefrom. Rooted in the common soil, he turns his eyes to new directions. He is, indeed, a fruitful bough; he springs from earth fed secretly by a well; but his branches run over the wall. Thus are the ideas of convention and revolt, of tradition and innovation, conjured up in the single image of Jacob's benediction.

The reader, we trust, will forgive us for having at such great length and with such close interpretation sermonized upon the career and heritage of Joseph. Certainly we did not intend, after the manner of Thomas Mann, a three-articled trilogy touching this great mystic personage. We have wished but to point to the paradigmatic implications of this biblic narrative to draw out of its individual instances some universal law of recurrence, to extract from its peroration in the forty-ninth chapter some insights as to the poetic impulse and craft. No doubt much remains within those freighted verses of Genesis which might yield yet further parallels and additional lessons. The Bible, as Ben Bag-Bag was wont to say, 'is a Book that may be turned about and about, for all is in it.' We are content to have drawn the outline. Let fruitful imagination – the moving spirit of each reader – fill in the gaps with commentary and ornamentation best suited to each particular temperament and to the constant theme.

4 / LITERATURE AND THE ARTS

WORSE VERSE

The rhyme is out of joint – O cursed spite
That ever I was born to set it right!

To counteract the penchant of modern publishing which attempts to make cheaper literature great, there has of late been a tendency to make great literature cheap. Thus it is that the silvertongued Shakespeare is sold in the market-place for a nickel; and *Paradise Regained* for the same sum. Thus was it also that for seven cents we purchased an anthology of modern verse which it was our original intention to scan but which, through intrinsic handicap, we were forced merely to read; and to read in the manner of a celestial laundryman – up and down. After an assiduous perusal we come to the conclusion that we have overpaid at least seven cents.

It is with free verse that we propose to-day to be free. Had there been existent in the twentieth century a school of poetic satire we might have been spared this purgatorial office, and this incumbent chastisement would have been superfluous; as it is, however, satirists live while satire is dead. The scurrilous felicities peculiar to Dryden have been bowdlerized from criticism by an impure Puritanism; the papal interdictions characteristic of Pope are no more invoked; the iambic diatribes proceeding from a Byronic spleen, too, are no longer in vogue; no more is it heroic to exchange Billingsgate in couplets of that name. It is therefore through this column, pillar of society as it is, that we are obliged to free verse from prose.

It is impossible to speak of the general current of free verse; mud has no current. This edifying simile is indicative both of its clarity and its cleanliness. Ezra Pound senses no compunction of his aesthetic conscience when he fertilizes the poetic field with his genius and with adjectives manurial. D.H. Lawrence, endowed with a poet's licentiousness, also takes liberties with the Muses and apostrophizes them in hortatives concupiscent; he renders the abode of the Graces a moral disgrace. Sandburg, too, upholds the hold-up character of Chicago in bombastic vociferations of which the following ethereality is a typical one:

Hog Butcher for the World,
Tool Maker, Stacker of Wheat.

Evelyn Scott, a woman, mark, is the perpetrator of the following:

> The moon is as complacent as a frog.

She further opines that (by some marvelous metempsychosis) she is

> A woman holding up her dress
> So that her white belly shines
> Haughty
> Impregnable
> Ridiculous.

Our criticism is climaxed in the final attribute. To multiply such citations would be to compile an index of immorality, and to contribute to the juvenile delinquency of this college. It is sufficient to state that if ever there was a vocabulary of prurience compared to which the mouthings of Rabelais are as Sunday-school speech, [...] of the vers-librists. If these poetasters have a wide circulation it is that they are read by virtue of their vice. The cavaliers of Pegasus are dead; the stableboys have mounted in their stead.

The ambition of these versifiers is not to write poetry; rather is it to write new poetry. The contention that it is poetry can, of course, be banished with a gesture; it is as absurd as would be a statement to the effect that the staccato ejections of the laconic Jingle of the *Pickwick Papers* is inspired expression. If it is anything it is expired expression. Free verse is merely prose in the hands of an insane compositor.

The supposition of the superficial, however, that the vers libre is a phenomenon of modernity is the most unfounded of inexactitudes. What today is heralded as imagist is no more than a reactionary reversal to the rebus intelligence, a degeneration into the concrete, an acceptance of the nous of the noun – it is attempt to say nothings with things. Considered leniently it is no more than a system of higher hieroglyphics. It was in free verse that our prehistoric progenitors made vigorous love to the un-Platonic cavewoman. As Whitman admits, with more truth than poetry, his is a 'barbaric yawping.' To parody the dictum of Rousseau: Verse was born free and free for all.

It is the swollen smugness of the vers-librist which causes him to search for new deformities. He is above rhyme, he is below reason; intuition and an introspective mysticism are his inspirations. He is the singer of solipsism. That rhyme is a melodious symbiosis, an acoustical congratulation, a zygote of sound, and a gemination of harmony, he utterly and fundamentally denies. Heard melodies are sweet, he says, but melodies unheard are sweeter. With a challenging vociferation he asserts his eternal greatness. Byron awoke and found himself famous; he finds himself famous, but never awakes.

Having murdered melody, they organize the mutilation of form. True poetry is a dream; free verse is a nightmare. The vers-librist being revolutionary in character, primarily abolishes capitals. Furthermore, in a spirit of lacerating asceticism and humble self-suppression he decapitates his ego into a small i. Thus this contorted typography, often scattered in a zigzag geometry, leads the uninitiated to suspect that the milk of Hippocrene has fermented into extra-American beer. Thus it is that with the exaggeration of their super-sophistication they show themselves no more educated than the unlettered. In fact, we can speak of this phase of literary production as modern illiterature.

Not only have capitals, punctuation and logical printing been abolished but even words are being dispensed with. Their place is being taken by a necessary accoutrement of typographical paraphernalia of the poeticule – dots. This is supposed to introduce a new period in modern verse. The trinity of dots is fraught with oracular connotations; in it the profoundest of philosophies are rounded out. The whole abracadabra of abstruseness is concentrated in these dotted triplets. They are the unwritten constitution of the cult of the occult. Their intellectual stand implies a desire not to be understood.

We are now awaiting further developments of free verse. We have seen it dispense with capitals, punctuation, and part of the human vocabulary; we are anticipating, eagerly and earnestly, the time when free verse will reach the culminating realization of its ideals when, in a last extremity, it will abolish thoroughly and entirely all words, idle words, and will compose its lucubrations with a completeness of dots; and free verse will become a grand hiatus.

G.K. CHESTERTON

None of our contemporaries illustrates the liaison of the corpulent and the spiritual so well as that monstrous monarch of the fairies, G.K. Chesterton. Born in 1874, he is still alive and at large; witness two hundred avoirdupois pounds of incarnate paradoxy. The lightest jugglings of this colossus of obesity must perforce carry weight; here is a literatus who truly deserves to speak in the editorial plural. One has never associated physical fatness with intellectual leanness; here, however, is a prodigy of plumpness who astounds us with the nimbleness of his dialectic; in fact this ever-alert embonpoint leads us to assert that Chesterton is both wide and awake.

Of Chesterton we cannot write that his early youth was spent in such and such congenial surroundings, or like Dickens', wasted upon such and such a useless toil; for the simple reason that his early youth was never spent; it still clings to him. A story of his youth is a story of his life. Chesterton will never see the beginning of his second childhood because he will never see the end of his first one. We submit this apologetic explanation that we are by no means insinuating that he still has an infantile attachment for the rattle, but we do say that he treats this noisy sphere as if it were a rattle. We feel in fact, that even if he were to die a greybeard nonagenarian we would be justified in announcing in our obituary notices that Gilbert Keith Chesterton had been cut off in the prime of his youth ...

If, as Byron opined, 'The days of our youth are the days of our glory,' then Chesterton's existence is one of perennial glory. The juvenile pleasure in life, the youthful gusto, and the unconquerable *joie de vivre*, are still his own; we are certain that Chesterton moribund will still prove with a paradox that Death is Life. Never has he with a superior gesture characteristic of the aged and the experienced waved aside childish things. Without intending to canonize him we quote Wordsworth's apostrophe to the Child:

> Thou best philosopher, thou Eye among the blind,
> That, deaf and silent, readst the eternal deep,
> Haunted forever by the eternal mind,
> Mighty Prophet! Seer Blest!

This, with omission of the deaf and the silent, is the Child Chesterton; this the enfant terrible of orthodoxy. He seems to possess the secret of perpetual youth, if not of the body, at any rate of the spirit; he knows how to be young without suggesting monkeys, or their glands. 'The Child is the father of the Man.' Chesterton is the trinity of the Father, the Child and the Man.

It is this everlasting immunity to age that explains the unquenchable optimism of Chesterton, his philosophic quibblings and his intellectual flippancy. Platitudinous would it be to remark that there are two kinds of optimisms, just as there are two kinds of pessimisms, – the morbid and the beautiful. The optimism of an inflamed cerebellar membrane is as hopeless as a pessimism kept alive with dyspepsia and absinthe. Sunrise may be regarded as the symbol of the truly aesthetic optimism, and sunset of the truly worthy pessimism. Chesterton, to use the pagan term, is therefore the worshipper of the sunrise. Just as one can never imagine Pickwick without his pot of port, so can one never alienate the picture of Chesterton from wine when it is red. He has been called the hale and hearty poet – he mixes his ale with his art. The animal spirits tabernacled in this tenth-of-a-ton of rotundity can be none other than those of fat Falstaff re-incarnated. He is not, however, like the sceptical Omar or the credulous Verlaine who drink for the sake of forgetting sorrow; Chesterton drinks for the sake of remembering happier things. With him the wine induces laughter, enjoyment; and the spirit of good-will is related to the Wine of the Eucharist.

In one of his books Chesterton speaks of the man who was Thursday. It seems to us that every man can, with some pardonable exaggeration, be assigned the name of some specific day. The Pessimist awaiting the Doomsday every minute of his existence lives one long Doomsday; the Optimist welcoming the Millenium has his life marked by the blessedness of that alleged state; the Ascetic believes life to be one long day of Atonement; the Decadent, considering how his days are spent, thinks of a series of polygamous nuptials; the Communist [...] in the red of one May-day; and lunatics and lovers ponder over life as the suffering of a prolonged Moon-day. In fact, every man, like every dog, has his day ... Chesterton is the Man who is Sunday, and unlike the usual preacher of the Sabbath, he has preserved the Sun in Sunday. He is the defender of the people; his philosophy is not to laugh at the common people; his philosophy is that people should laugh in common. He is in fact the laughing philosopher of the proletariat, he is the democratic Democritus.

Also is he a poet, priest, politician and buffoon. The incongruity of this is that he will appear at a meeting of the Actor's Union in the vestments of a priest, and will address the Theological Seminary in the motley of a patch; he will talk on high matters of state with the rampant imagery of the poet, and will criticize poetasters with the practicability of a politician. He is too often the square peg in the round hole; but there is this to say in his favour – the peg is always on the square.

Chesterton revels in paradoxes. Unsympathetic critics, therefore, have accused him of standing on his head for the sake of being different. Let us here assert that there is no opprobrium attached to the standing on one's head; Benjamin Disraeli, wishing to declare the mental independence of the Jew, alleged the same thing of them. Furthermore, being different does not necessarily mean being wrong; the history of reform shows that it often means being right. The privilege that athletes enjoy in the performance of corporal somersaults for their physical health, Chesterton enjoys in the performance of mental somersaults for his spiritual health, for he believes that a rush of blood to the brain – the blood which is the life – will be a rush of life to the brain.

VERBUM SAT

With sadness and with a sense of incumbent duty, we propose to celebrate the funeral of one who has, with the connivance of the printer's devil, found sanctuary in the consecrated columns of 'The McGilliad'; we purpose in a transport of contrition to smother that arrant merry-andrew masquerading in an alphabetic domino; in a Dr. Jekyll–Mr. Hyde transformation we intend to throttle our very alter ego, one A.M.K. And this for many reasons. But for these especially: that he has attempted to noose our tongue in sesquipedalian circumlocution, that he has essayed to hasten premature insanity with labyrinthine dialectic, that he has concocted a beverage which inebriates with the multiplicity of its components; and that with a fiat of prolixity he has created a world which possesses longitude without latitude. For these low crimes and misdemeanours do we take him to task; so much as that we are inclined to draw disparaging comparisons between our literary umbra and the notorious Johnson. Upon second thought, however, we discover that the relation is one of contrast. Johnson incorporated his opinions in his dictionary; A.M.K. incorporates his dictionary in his opinions.

Being physically allied to A.M.K., we know where lies the fuse which sets ablaze the pyrotechnics of his vocabulary. It is, My Lords, in his immoral inclinations, inclinations which emanate from the very centre of his being. He preaches polygamy in polysyllables; and in an abstruse and symbolic phraseology clothes the nakedness of his ambitions; it is because he has a complex that he speaks not simply. Inveterately averse to the staccato sound, he opines that the Yellow Peril is really its monosyllables. To express this vernacularly, he does not believe in monosyllables; that is why, we presume, slanderous tongues have it that he does not believe in God. This, however, is no gossiping rumour; it is evident that A.M.K., with malice aforethought, is attempting to conceal lubricity in his thesaurus, to wrap concupiscence in verbiage. In vain. The Board of Censors, men steeped in the lore of Priapus, acquainted with the technicalities of Havelock Ellis, and endowed with an imagination excelling even that of Freud, shall not be duped. Your least innuendo, A.M.K., shall not be passed un-noticed by these versatile gentlemen.

No doubt you will argue, much-respected shadow, that your lengthened lingo snares complete epistemological entities in the intricacy of a polysyllable, and that in the amalgamation of several verbs into a single philological essence you expound the conceptions of an ordinary paragraph; that, in short, you make a word suffice. Sophistry, brother, sophistry ... You appear to me, swallowing as you do the immeasurability of words, no different from the Italian sucking spaghetti from the apparent infinity of a bowl. Are you then not aware that brevity is the soul of wit, that brevity is a consummation greatly to be sought even in the single word?

– What, A.M.K. (interposes A.M.K.) – what, is it your intention to defend that untenable dictum of Bill's, a dictum than which there is none more misleading nor tending more to corrupt a human logic? In the first instance, I have in my Opus 13 long ago demonstrated the non-existence of a soul, ergo, the soul of wit. Furthermore, the full absurdity of the syllogism of Shakespeare is realized only then when we apply to it that most infallible method, recommended by Euclid and sponsored by all those who have reason in mind, the *reductio ad absurdum*. Thus, if brevity is the soul of wit then it follows as the female the male that the briefer a statement the wittier. The ultimate of brevity is nihility, which by premise, must therefore be the ultimate of wit. This, O better half, is as preposterous as a statement to the effect that the greatest wit is the nit-wit. Evidently Shakespeare erred; I am divine; I forgive ...

– With due deference to the fact that you, Sir, are my spiritual twin, I assert that you are a farceur of flippant fallacy, a dispenser of quibbling quodlibets, a monger of perverted antitheses, a pundit of puny puns, a –

– And such I intend to remain. I frame no apologia for my peccadillos; with blatant spitefulness shall I proceed on my faulty ways, and with a stiff-necked obstinacy on the path of sin. I will persist in amazing with maziness; I will continue to make myself clear through an enlightened obscurantism; and still shall I puncture morons with oxymorons – my preciosity is precious ... What! Are not my lengthy polysyllables a manifestation of a love of letters?

O may the gods wreak a just vengeance upon you A.M.K. May they afflict you with an unconquerable stutter and visit you with a chronic asthma ...

THE TREASON OF TRADITION

We have yet to listen to a perennial paean of this Canada of ours which omits from its chorus an account of the nobility of our traditions and the pedigree of our institutions. Every flattering demagogue regards tradition as part of a magical bombast with which he ingratiates himself with a class whose tranquillity is in fact stagnation. The politician attempting to magnetize the votes of the so-called lower classes assures them that their poverty is nothing ... for they may console themselves with a wealthy heritage – of tradition; generals, too, desiring to inspire in their subordinates the ideal of suicide, generally assert that wars are fought to preserve a noble institution – war; in short, it has become a tradition to eulogize tradition ... The musty opinions of our ancestors are foisted upon us as part of an enduring legacy; for us, if they have any value at all, it is as antiques ...

The leading protagonist of tradition in present days is that modern anachronism Chesterton. A clear thinker, though a paradox-manufacturer, he nevertheless is the author of some immortal blunders: he writes a book called *The Man Who Knew Too Much* and signs it – Chesterton; he publishes a history of his country in which he devotes several pages to the psychological reactions of top-hats and the national importance of pantaloons; and he is continually crying that Jews are running away with England, while it is his imagination that is running away with him. Furthermore, he attempts to defend tradition in a catch-phrase. With his customary sensationalism, he maintains that tradition is not a reactionary movement, as is usually asserted, but rather an ultra-radical one; it is granting the franchise not only to all the living but also to all the dead.

The equivocation is charming; its flaws, however, are detected as soon as the metaphor is continued to its ultimate implication. It seems to us that it is trifling with the franchise to grant every ghost in Cock-Lane a vote; how, for example, can spirits vote on Prohibition? Dead men can belong to either of two constituencies: the Kingdom of Heaven, where, we are informed by the divines, the votes are cast in pacific unanimity; or to the other place, where elections are carried on with fiery vehemence ... There, to banish celestial boredom, they may make laws to their hearts' content; let the dead bury the dead ... This, however, is certain: they who rest in peace cannot legislate on war. By derivation, a 'vote' is a will; the only will we allow the deceased is the testamentary one ...

Tradition, therefore, is an attempt to liven up current politics by inviting to its open forum all the denizens of the city of the dead ... The antiquated doctrines, the moth-eaten customs, and the prehistoric rites of our forefathers ought, in our opinion, to have died with them ... The judgments of our progenitors can at best be disreputably second-hand. Tradition, like vinegar, sours with age. If it is an injunction to remember the dead, it is also an injunction to remember to die; – it is a memento mori. Dead men tell no tales – they should not be given that opportunity. We fail to see why the attitude of those who have been gathered to a happier race should still prevail in the conduct of mundane affairs. Our fathers themselves attempting to free themselves from the governmental tyranny of their elders adopted this as their slogan: No taxation without representation. We, seeking emancipation from the spiritual suzerainty of our fathers, adopt as our slogan: No representation without taxation ...

Thus it is that Chesterton's dictum suggests a fantasia from which one awakens as from a nightmare. To endow the spiritual proxies of our forefathers with a legislative power in the formation of our laws and in the regulation of our every-day life, would, even if that power is only an advisory one, be to give the sepulchres their say; we insinuate that those sepulchres may be whited ones ... Tradition, in enfranchising corpses, virtually creates in the cemetery a Lower House ... We submit that it is blasphemy to make out of the House of the Dead a poll room; we maintain that it is sacrilege to make out of coffins a political platform ... We object to the introduction in our social organization of that which we are pleased to call necropolitics ... Tradition, let us repeat, gives the dead a vote – so do telegraphers ...

It seems to us that it is of no little significance that the word institution (which is imposed upon us as a finality) etymologically means the commencement; and that the word treason is in the same way a doublet of the word tradition ... The respect shown to the fossilized customs of conventionality is nothing but an exaggerated form of father-worshipping, an idolatry of the household gods ... We may walk in trodden paths so often that they be worn into elongated graves ... To conclude, tradition, in pursuing Chesterton's superficiality, is a visitation of the iniquities of the fathers upon the children, unto even more than the third and fourth generation ...

WONDERLUST

One of the chief faults which all potential reformers find with the present organization of society is that it is monotonously unromantic. They point to the specialization of industry and declare that a man, the sole activity of whose working day consists of plying a single screw, will, in the course of time, surely degenerate – and that even a professor must perforce become a bore through the very nature of his labors: he drills ... They maintain, perhaps with a platitudinous sincerity, that the Age of Machinery has not so much invented machines as it has transformed men into such. The concatenations of social circumstance, they assert, have so brought it about that it has become the lofty ideal and the sole purpose of those who still believe in the fiction of the dignity of labor, to dedicate the greater part of an existence of three-score-and-ten to, using a classical example, the making of button-holes ... Cynically they insinuate that even religion has become a financial entity: that the common creed of today is money-theism ... Produce! Produce! Produce! cried Carlyle, and Tennyson, quite unconsciously perhaps, mumbled something about the 'one increasing purpose.' Both, say the reformers, spoke the same – Working for a living, they asseverate, one bores oneself to death ... It seems to us that there is no small amount of truth in their statements, but –

One need only venture forth to find adventure. With the traffic which is the concomitant of that very industry whose influence is alleged so baneful there is high enterprise and hair-breadth escape merely in the crossing of a street ... Every step one takes may hurtle one in the great adventure of the infinite. The very attempt to detect in life purpose, as the philosophers are wont to do, makes life a detective story. It is not necessary to travel to the gardens of Italy, or to the orchards of Spain, to the vineyards of Provence, or to the rose-fields of Roumania, to seek romance; it is not necessary to go to the Romance countries to find it. A truism it is that the spirit of poetry depends not on the place but on the poet. A prosaic Philistine may visit all the paradises aforementioned and yet return with impressions, not of gardens but of garlic, not of orchards but of onions, not of wine but of vinegar, not of attar of roses, but of ashes of roses. It is obvious therefore that it is the manner in which we look at things that determines their character; it is the way we regard them that sets our regard for them. Wonderlust does not necessarily express itself in wanderlust; one need not tour to the four corners of the world to be filled with a spirit of strangeness – the street corner will suffice ... There, the red letter-box stands, a confessional holier than any other; there, a rushing fire-engine straightway conjures up a vision of a dragon with blazing eyes, fuming and tearing through the streets; and there a telegraph pole reared up to the heavens evokes the biblical exclamation – Lo! the finger of God! The adventurous is not necessarily the picaresque.

There is an unsolved riddle in the repeated questionings of every day, and in the commonplaces of a routine existence there is something intriguingly mysterious. A bread to us is not so many calories of food-energy but a martyred field of waving wheat in tabloid form ... flowers are not pre-eminently subjects for the botanists, rather are they the princes of the earth taking their morning airing, wearing their coronets of silver or gold or ruby or sapphire ... a pen is not a stick of wood but a gun which shoots feathers of consolation or fusilades of satire, and today ink is to the soul what water is to the soil ... a gramophone is not merely a jazz-container; it may be a nightingale's nest ... and snow is not congealed water but white grass growing downward from heaven to earth. The only solution to monotony therefore lies in the creative faculty of the mind; a rampage of imagination, a stampede of the fantasy, a capering of the inventive spirit, ingenuity let loose, prancing – these are the rescues from boredom. If we can make an existence pure in no other way, we will make it so with the white lie ...

The Age of Miracles is not past. Every event is a miracle; what would be the greatest miracle would be the cessation of them. Scientifically, we suppose that the sun rises because of a natural law; emotionally, we believe it is because of a supernatural awe. God uttered His *Fiat Lux* this morning just as he did on the first dim day of creation:

The unwearied sun from day to day
Does his Creator's power display,
And publishes to every land
The work of an almighty hand.

Scientists attempt to explain biblical miracles with scientific facts; we attribute to all facts a miraculous accompaniment. Show us a sign, cried the Unbeliever, shutting his eyes to the manifold symbols about him. The wonders of ancient times repeat themselves with the generality of history. When one turns on the tap and water pours forth, the act is accompanied with as much sanctity as that of the smitten rock gushing its stream; and when one beholds the Papuan speed across the waves on his surf-board one understands the walking on the water. Even money, that article most slandered by the Romanticists, can itself work miracles. In fact in our more fantastic moments we have associated money with manna, which is said to have had whatever taste one wished it to have ... And as for the incident of Balaam's ass, all we can say is that even today we are constantly, through no fault of our own, listening to asses speak ... Every day the first chapter of Genesis is being repeated and every day are we privy to the visions of Ezekiel and the revelation of St. John. Thus, to exile monotony it behooves us to consider ourselves Alecs and Alices in Wonderland. We therefore conclude our sermon with the elaboration of a simile: life has been likened to a play; it is in fact – a miracle play ...

Proletarian Poetry   5 August 1932

In the Centenary Issue of the *Canadian Jewish Eagle*, the great Jewish critic Sh. Niger comments on the proletarian elements which have recently invaded Yiddish literature. He deplores the passing of the 'art for art's sake' slogan, and regrets the advance of the new theory, so enthusiastically espoused by Soviet writers and so vociferously heralded by Marxian propagandists, that literature is not literature unless it ends with a revolutionary moral. Although it must be admitted that one of the functions of art, though certainly not the only one, is to rouse the reader to a realization of existing injustice and current oppression, it still is to be doubted whether this need be achieved only through the perversion of letters into a series of political phrases and economic clichés. There are, of course, other subjects for the writer which in no way touch the ever-present class-struggle; there are eternal verities, truths which belong to all ages and to all people, axioms which should not be taken out of the province of the artist, nor, if magnanimously permitted, be squeezed into a preordained ideological mould. The whole theory, as a matter of fact, lends itself easily to a *reductio ad absurdum*, especially when it is meticulously applied to the art poetic.

We suggest, therefore, to Comrade Lunacharsky, ex-Minister of Education in Russia and renowned protagonist of proletarian literature, that he dedicate the days of his retirement to the compilation of a primer for party bards. In this work, we counsel, the romantic poets should be derided; the religious bardlings condemned, in virtue of Marx's famous dictum about opium and faith, as traffickers in narcotics; Shakespeare, who knew not class-consciousness, stigmatized a bourgeois; and Keats, the son of a stableman, who wrote about handsome Greeks and the mythical horse Pegasus, sentenced to a languishing oblivion in his ivory tower. For the edificiation of the versifiers of the future, moreover, a new *Ars Poetica* should be appended to the aforementioned primer. Herein rhymes are to be eschewed; their search is a waste of time and energy, impeding the poetic five-year-plan which we advise in connection with the proletarian renaissance. We urge the Minister, too, to urge the cultivation of free verse, renamed, for 'free' is a democratic concept, 'verse-dictatorial.' He ought also to put a ban on the mention of leprechauns, invention of Irish Nationalists, and on the mention of nymphs, creation of Hellenic oligarchs. Odes to lilies ought also to be interdicted, for are they not white, and therefore counter-revolutionary? Let there be heard in poetry only the whirr of machinery and the riveting of skyscrapers; let birds be condemned to silence in atonement for the joy which they brought to a capitalistic regime; let only the robin, clad in crimson overalls, sing unrestrained.

We need not multiply the restrictions and laws upon the art of poetry. The school of Lunacharsky, adept at these things, can add to them themselves *ad infinitum* and *ad nauseam*. We wish only to append a note to the future publisher of this suggested masterpiece. Its jacket must at all costs bear in vorticist symbolism the sun as hammer-head and the crescent moon as scythe; and its title, for we remember that all poetry must in the new system reflect the teachings of the author of *Das Kapital*, must imperatively be: *Carol, Marx*.

We hope that this advice will not be treated with the scorn which it merits ... Our suggestion is in fullest harmony with the policy of Moscow, where Stalin shows that he is wiser than even Plato. For Plato banished poets from his republic; but Stalin uses them.

National Anthems   31 December 1943

Probably the most static element in a people's culture is its repertoire of national anthems. Its social mores may develop, its laws may suffer amendment, its general outlook may undergo the inevitable changes brought about by the march of time, but its songs seem always to remain the same. With undiminished gusto the sons sing the songs the fathers sang. Indeed, an anthem may have lost much of its original significance; the feelings it expresses may no longer have validity for the choirs which utter them, even the words may have become obsolete and archaic; nonetheless, though the significance is gone, the melody lingers on.

It was no doubt with this in mind that Mr. George Bernard Shaw recently suggested an amendment to the words of the second stanza of 'God Save the King.' The suggestion, be it noted, was sensational on two counts. That someone, without prior Buckingham Palace approval, should dare to lay metric hands upon the royal song, a song which had been sanctified by the centuries and whose tune had been adopted by many European countries for their national anthems, was boldness of the first order. That that someone should be G.B. Shaw, who has throughout the three score and ten years of his life never expressed any great concern either about God or the King, seemed yet another marvellous phenomenon of our age. Could it be that Shaw's black girl in search of her God had at last found Him in a song? Or were Shaw's corrections suggested by way of an appendix to his *Intelligent Woman's Guide to Socialism?*

Frankly, we are not very impressed by the Shavian improvements. The original version of the suspect stanza reads:

O Lord our God, arise,
Scatter his enemies
And make them fall.
Confound their politics,
Frustrate their knavish tricks,
On Thee our hopes we fix –
God save us all.

This version of Mr. Harry Corey's has much to recommend it. Piety it does not lack – the great determinant of human destiny is ever God. But it also has the human qualities of vigour, picturesqueness, and self-interest. The defeat of the enemy is vividly described, he is scattered and he falls; the source of his confusion is indicated – his 'knavish tricks'; and the climax of the anthem is almost epigrammatic: with the Lord's saving of the King, He saves us all. It is the anthem of a soldier of The King, my boys.

Mr. Shaw's version, however, reads like the fastidious versification of the Archbishop of Canterbury:

> O Lord our God, arise,
> All our salvation lies
> In Thy great hands.
> Centre his thoughts on Thee,
> Let him God's captain be, Thine to eternity –
> God save the King.

No one can really quarrel with these lines. But, as they say out West, them's not fighting words. Religious they are, almost theocratic in fact – a rhymed sermon. Where vigour was, there is now doctrine; where picturesqueness, idealism; and in the last line, Shaw the Fabian leaves the singers out.

We doubt, therefore, whether Mr. Shaw's poetic effort will really revolutionize public song. We are inclined to believe that it will still be the old version of the second stanza of 'God Save the King' which people will omit to chant.

It is to be noted that this amendment to our national anthem comes hard upon the heels of a declaration by the Russian Government that 'The Internationale' is to be abandoned by the Soviets. A new song is to be sung by the Russian masses, with words by one Sergei Mikhailov and music by V.V. Aleksandrov. According to official pronouncement, couched in the usual language announcing rationalized change, '"The Internationale" no longer reflects in its contents the fundamental changes which have taken place in our country as result of the victory of the Soviet regime and does not express the essence of the Soviet state.' The fact is that this change is but a corollary to the action of the Soviet Government which some time ago ordered the Comintern to announce that it no longer existed. The result of the transaction is that not only has the Third International received sudden burial; in future its *el moleh rachmim* is also to be omitted. It is, of course, a matter of complete indifference to the democracies of the world with what songs the Russian allies march into battle – as long as they succeed in killing Germans. That is the music that counts. If now the further attacks upon the fleeing Nazi forces are to be accompanied to verses in praise of 'the republic of the free,' 'our motherland to glory,' 'Stalin is faithful to the people,' the whole put to music of bomb and shell – why, good luck to them!

But those who have regarded Russia as a potential protector of the world working-class, as a country motivated by a concern for the 'wretched of the earth' and 'the prisoners of starvation' wherever they may be found, will no doubt be disappointed by this symbolic innovation. It is an innovation which proclaims once again the fact that the Soviets are to-day primarily concerned with the national interest of Russia; if the wretched of the earth and the prisoners of starvation don't know enough to rise without being told to do so in a song, they will have to suffer themselves the consequences of their own inertia.

Nor is this trend in Soviet policy a new one. The dissolution of the Comintern has already been adverted to. Other phenomena in recent Soviet history have also emphasized the fact that Stalin, the realist, is fully aware that nationalism – despite years of internationalist indoctrination, is a powerful force. Thus, the Ukrainians were recently and dubiously flattered by having a city named after their own Chmelnitzky, a character who was by no means a revolutionary hero. Thus, too, indirect warnings have been recently issued to the Yevsektzia, whose days, it is to be hoped, are numbered. Nationalism is the order of the day; and that is as it should be. The right to exercise one's full individuality is a right which belongs to nations, as well as to persons. We trust that those comrades who were wont grandiloquently to proclaim the world their fatherland, and to look upon Zionist aspiration as a piece of re-actionary nostalgia, will now regard their own idol before they blaspheme against another's devotion.

It would appear, therefore, that Russia is to-day *'mit leiten gleich.'* In fact the dialectic of history has resulted in a superb irony – while the capitalist countries proclaim this war as a war of liberation, an effort which is to end when democracy will be accorded to all the conquered peoples of Europe, it is Russia which adopts a policy tantamount to 'Sinn Fein' – ourselves alone. The Communist doctrine is not for export; one is not, of course, responsible for the acts of intellectual smugglers.

The amendment to 'God Save the King' suggested by Bernard Shaw, it is to be noted, was made the day after 'The Internationale' received its coup de grâce. We have already indicated how naturally strange it is that Shaw should concern himself with patriotic ditties. It must not be forgotten, how-ever, that Shaw is a Fabian Socialist to whom 'The Internationale' is second only to his prayers, which practically gives it first place. He surely must have felt a pang of anguish at the Soviet relegation of his favorite hymn. Could it be, then, that his 'God Save the King' improvements are primarily intended as an ironical commentary upon the fate of 'The Internationale'? If you, he seems to say, are going to move from internationalism to nationalism, then I will move from monarchism to theocracy!

We may add – we hope the mighty powers of the earth will forgive this intrusion – that it is also high time that the 'Hatikvah' be relegated to the same position which 'The Internationale' occupies. We know of no song among the anthems of the nations of the world which is more lugubrious or less soul-stirring than the strains of the 'Hatikvah.' We find no fault with the words, – but the music! It is a marvel that the Zionist movement has been able to advance as far as it has, hampered as it has been by a song whose music is a lullaby rather than a march. It is not to be wondered that in Eretz Israel it is not the 'Hatikvah' but 'Techsakna' which is anthemized. Besides, the melody of the 'Hatikvah' is really a Czech folk-song. Let us, in harmony with the world principle of restitution, give it back to them.

Queen Mab and Mickey Mouse   18 January 1946

No doubt there have been occasions – and those both many and double-featured – when the Hollywood impresario has richly deserved the leisurely concocted slurs which outraged Art has levelled against him; nor should one, considering the bankable and most consolatory rewards which are given to the mogul in the hours of his disgrace, be moved to defend him, were it not for the fact that, left unchidden, the slur-slinging tends too often to take on the character of a mere conditioned reflex: *The Movies, The Aesthete – Nausea, real or simulated.* It is a situation, of course, which is as undesirable in the craft of criticism as to the 'industry' of Art.

Nor is it solitary in the star-filled night, this cat-calling. Indeed, out of denigration unabating, some writers, it is observed, do make themselves envying careers. Faithfully attending all the premières, they look upon the two hours' traffic, and with a perverse godliness, invariably see it as 'not good.' They rush to their typewriters and gleefully announce to the world that the MGM lion, as was to be expected – made with the mouth to roar, but only yawned. Once more Hollywood, they report, has failed to reach the standard which would win their not-too-easily-granted approval. Thus do they earn themselves reputations for fastidiousness, and thus heckle out their living.

And, it must be admitted, this feud which the snob conducts against the mob is at times entertaining, if not altogether edifying. One *can* watch it with amusement, or with unconcern. One is not tempted to intervene; one is not impressed, but one hopes: Perhaps out of the gall may come forth strength. But surely, when in their impetuous vituperation, the critics leap from the

Lion onto the Mouse, and spare not even Mickey – surely then it is time to cry: 'Hold, enough! Thus far may ye go; ye shall not venture farther!'

For if the moving picture industry has in anything justified itself as a medium of art, it has indubitably done so in the Walt Disney film, a form of creative expression which more than any other follows in the great tradition of graphic literature. It is true that certain moralistic cavillings have lately been heard reprimanding Mickey Mouse for his violences; apparently the manner in which the protagonist elasticates his enemies, the Homeric battles in which he indulges, his ingenious devastations, and the slam-bang denouements he invariably achieves – apparently these are deemed to run counter to proper morality. Perhaps; but not to life, all of which, if we believe Darwin, is based on conflict; and not to literature, where struggle is of the essence. The point which the critics, moreover, ignore is that in the Disney film, the violence is always made ridiculous; morality could receive no greater tribute. To enjoy all the excitements which violence arouses, and not to be moved by it to mimesis – it is a consummation which only a great and moral art could achieve.

The most important distinction of the Mickey Mouse saga, however, is not its illustration of sweetness and fright, but rather its satisfaction of the longings of our generation for poetry. It need hardly be stated that the moviegoer who ventures into the palace to acquaint himself with Mickey's latest doings is but seldom aware of the fact that he has come in search of poetry! He would, indeed, repudiate the suggestion as shameful. He does not read poetry; he associates the thing with persons and interests with which he has no sympathy. Yet the pleasures he derives out of watching the antics of the human mouse – whether he realizes it or not – are definitely, primarily, and perhaps solely poetic.

That Mickey Mouse is the first star upon the Hollywood firmament is a fact which need not be labored. No other shadow upon the screen, except his, ever moves audiences to applause. It is a great compliment; for the crowds sitting in the dark certainly do not applaud, as one applauds a stage actor, for flattery. Theirs is rather Gratitude's pure gesture; the hand-clapping of sheer delight. And in this the hands that are involved number twice the statistics of the box office.

One asks oneself, therefore, what is the nature of the magic that so moves people? And one analyzes the conventions of Disney artifact. One observes, first of all, that its varied instalments follow the tradition already established by the great story-tellers of the past; they move about single incidents in the life of the same hero; and the incident has connotations which go beyond the mere narrative. They are, in a word, fables, like those of Aesop, fabliaux, like those which had Reynard the Fox as their ubiquitous character.

And they appeal to the human through the animal.

That this is so, that this had to be so, both because of the nature of the communication which Disney sought to make – copy-book lessons which would have been resented if they had sprung from the life of people, and not beasts – and because of the medium – superimposed cartoons seeking to give the impression of total action – is best evidenced by the failure of 'Snow White and the Seven Dwarfs.' Here the suspension of disbelief failed to operate; the human protagonist lacked verisimilitude. The audience, observing how Snow White never walked, but always floated, as if propelled from one draft to another, refused, alas, to believe in her. It is, of course, possible that Mickey Mouse's locomotion is also as unreal; but humans, who know the animal mainly from other *cartoons*, would not know. On that subject, it would seem, only mice can speak with authority.

But the principal characteristic of the cartoon film is its use of the metaphor. What the poet seems to achieve by an appeal to the imagination, Disney makes visual and audible. When the script speaks of bluebells ringing, forthwith the flowers are drawn in all points like a bell, and they do tintinnabulate; when a character in the film is so surprised that you can knock him over with a feather, behold a feather lays him low. The film becomes the universal imagination in action; and Mickey Mouse *le Byron de nos jours*.

It is, in fact, precisely because the movie-visitants enter the theatre desiring to be regaled by ingenious metaphors, far-fetched similes, picturalized conceits, that they so willingly suspend disbelief as to accept the most fantastic of happenings occurring to the most unlikely of creatures. Worlds impossible then become possible; size loses its limitations; the big is made small, the small big. How often, indeed, have we sat watching the little activities of animal creatures, foreshortening themselves so that they travel all over the body of some human, uncouthly drawn, then leaping into delightfully conceived vehicles, all rustic-made, where the spokes are fashioned out of insects' legs, and the cover out of their transparent wings, and the whip out of snails' antennae, and the vehicles move, and they are all so mahogany-rich for they are hazel-nuts! The mind is refreshed, is satisfied; the similarity between the dissimilar has been painlessly established; the hunger for new worlds, by metaphors made, is appeased. And as one watches this hebdomadally-repeated scene, always with its inspired variations, one wonders, Has one seen it before, Has one imagined it before, and one suddenly, suddenly remembers Queen Mab:

> She is the fairies' midwife; and she comes
> In shape no bigger than an agate stone
> On the forefinger of an alderman,

Drawn with a team of little atomies
Athwart men's noses as they lie asleep.
Her waggon spokes made of long spinners' legs;
The cover, of the wings of grasshoppers;
The traces of the smallest spider web;
The collars, of the moonshine's wat'ry beams;
Her whip, of cricket's bone; the lash, of film;
Her waggoner, a small gray-coated gnat;
Her chariot is an empty hazel-nut
Made by the joiner squirrel, or old grub,
Time out of mind the fairies' coach-makers.

It is in reply to this speech of Mercutio's that Romeo says:

Peace, peace, Mercutio, peace,
Thou talk'st of nothing.

To which he makes reply:

True, I talk of dreams.

Annotation on Shapiro's *Essay on Rime*

22–29 March 1946

THE THESIS:

In these two thousand lines of 'classic English decasyllables,' Karl Shapiro, having earlier demonstrated his unchallengeable authority as a poet – was he not Pulitzer'd and Guggenheim'd? – now presents himself, though still in buskin shod, as an essayist. His purpose, as stated in the Foreword – also in classic English decasyllables – is to consider the unhappy plight of contemporary poetry, a poetry which he sees as by three confusions confounded: a confusion in prosody; a confusion in language; and a confusion in belief. It would have been easier for me, as for other readers, to synopsize these indictments if Shapiro had been both more specific and more coherent as to the nature of the confusions he was deploring; unfortunately the poet, dividing his essay into three main sections – one for each Babel – contents himself merely with passing eclectic judgment upon the various techniques of modern verse; but nowhere does he say, except in the most general pejorative terms – what is being confused with what.

For Shapiro's section on the confusion in prosody – despite its *ex cathedra* manner and pseudo-erudite tone – finally proves only that the types of versification are many – information which one could have gleaned from any primer on the subject. So much pomposity and affectation – Shapiro insists on referring to *The* Christabel, *The* Paradise, *The* Science (Lanier's *Science of English Verse*) – was hardly necessary, one feels, to accentuate the positive. Throughout the entire essay, in fact, Shapiro is continually bringing forth *clichés* with the air of one who is producing apocalypses. On page 36, for example, he discovers – so that all henceforward may know – that language invariably precedes grammar; on page 33, he kindly reveals that '*style* was originally the implement of writing'; elsewhere he devotes one hundred lines to establish the fact that when Joyce was writing *Ulysses* he was a poet! Three-quarters of the book, I regret to say, is made up of such supererogatory truism; as for the assertions of the remaining quarter, these, to put it peaceably, are debatable.

Thus Shapiro makes a great to-do about the distinction between lines which scan by count of eye and those which scan by count of ear. No new approach to versification is here effected; this is mere glossary; all that Shapiro has done is to apply an anatomical metaphor to an old and not always pertinent analysis, a metaphor, by the way, which is no more and no less valid than saying 'by count of finger and by count of toe.' Both adumbrate the difference between statistics and rhythm. I say *not always pertinent* because it is a contrast which itself is subject to amplification; when Shapiro writes

> To study metric in the Paradise
> Is one precise approach to count of eye,

he is arbitrarily prohibiting his ear from hearing what his eye is counting; for the force and melody of Milton's pentametre is due precisely to the acoustic variations effected within the uniform scope of his ten syllables. Shapiro himself seems to realize the absurdity of attaching to myopic Milton – of all people – the count of eye technique; he writes therefore, of Milton's masterpiece: '... written in blindness, and by count of eye'; and then hopes that self-refutation will be taken for paradox – but it is a paradox lost. I may add, by way of *argumentum ad personam*, that with Shapiro's instruction on the optic-acoustic modes of scansion, I was unable, even after weighing the cadences of prose speech, to make his line 86 a decasyllable; it reads:

> General and personal; second, personality

Of the confusion in language, Shapiro, without enunciating criteria, cites examples. The language of science intruded into poems; reportage sliced into verses; inversions and other poeticisms; grammatical constructions borrowed from alien speech; the use of portmanteau words like *luck, history* – all of these illustrate, somewhat unscientifically, his meaning. For the most part these judgments are sound; one would only like to add to the words *luck* and *history* also that other magical factotum *love*, a word used with such promiscuity that it has lost all meaning, as in the case of Shapiro's last lines:

> I have tried to indicate no more than that
> The aftermath of poetry should be love.

What signification, to use one of Shapiro's class-words, does *love* have in this context? Does it mean that the end-purpose of poetry is the cementing of closer human relations? But a work on technics can hardly be made to point such moral. The truth is that these lines are definitely a *non-sequitur*, a facile imitation of 'L'amor che move il sol e l'altre stelle,' here evoked solely for the sake of a grandiloquent peroration.

The third section speaks of the confusion in belief. Lest the reader imagine that Shapiro is charging his contemporaries with a lack of ideals in general, Shapiro soon makes it clear that he means *belief* literally – credo, ritual, hermeneutics. The trouble with modern poets, Shapiro evangelizes, is that they ain't got religion.

ITS ORGANIZATION:

I have had some difficulty in communicating the outline of Shapiro's thought because Shapiro, it would seem, has, by empathy! himself become not a little confused. What he has written is not really an essay but a series of observations whose relationship one to the other consists solely in the fact that all of them are comments upon a single theme, the art of writing poetry. Their sequence is factitious, their division the arbitrary one of *form* and *content*, here, for prestidigitation, made into a trinity. Table-talk it is, chit-chat, literary tripotage made cohesive by categories out of Roget. The essayist does not – as his purpose surely required – enunciate standards or values; he proclaims no principles; he simply catalogues his likes and dislikes, and then sets them up according as to whether they relate to his victim's or protégé's scansions, solecisms, heterodoxies.

The result is, first of all – and this, taken by and for itself, is all to the good – that Shapiro provides himself with an opportunity to recall and publish his uncollected *bons mots*. Commenting upon E.E. Cummings' poem-patterns, he says: 'The composer becomes a compositor'; discussing the Objectivists, he writes: 'An asterisk becomes an electric light!' or parodying Rimbaud, he speaks of the curve of 'e,' rhythm of 'm,' astonishment of 'o.' Of our prosodic debt to classic literature, he admirably remarks:

> We know that from the mansions of antiquity
> Much has been looted, and not all of marble.

To such epigrammatic felicities, he adds technical ones, instance the onoma-topoeia so dear to professors:

> how by a shift of weight
> Cliffs and enormous fragments of the verse
> Are hurled headlong, or brought to rest, or stopped.

or

> Though usage sets pronunciation, pitch
> May modify or flatten the accent.

Ingeniously he demonstrates his skill in the technique of breaking a sentence to achieve surprise:

> The bread and butter verses of the poor
> In talent ...

It is a sweet trick; but Shapiro, unfortunately, sours it by repetition:

> The anxious protestations of the poor
> In faith ...

These charming quiddities all have the air of *obiter scripta*; and for the most part are both entertaining and shrewd. But enthusiasm often leads astray, and Shapiro, with pontifications afflated, too often permits himself to make assertions which will not stand examination. 'Hopkins' influence,' he says, 'is actually small in metric, as in belief.' I don't know about belief, but the spokesman for the influenced, C. Day Lewis, writing in *A Hope for Poetry* on behalf of Auden & Co. (including subsidiaries) seems much more grateful. Something, or other, sneers Shapiro, 'no more scans than Hebrew' – a half-truth; Hebrew poetry has scanned – except line 86 of the Hebrew poet Shapiro – at least since the days of Immanuel of Rome, contemporary of Dante. As for biblical poetry, that is governed by a different prosodic principle, the *parallelismus membrorum*. Shapiro, therefore, is wrong again when, referring to 'the fad of showing parts of the Bible versified and hacked to lines of even length,' he declares that

> Nothing could be
> More typical of the new vulgarity.

Not the new vulgarity, but the old dispensation. For in the manuscript editions of the Pentateuch it is precisely to such a hacking that the lines are subjected, the Song of Moses (Exodus, Chapter 15) moreover, being so spaced as to simulate the dividing of the waters. But through such matters, Shapiro has evidently passed dry-shod.

And what does Shapiro mean when in the section on prosody – prosody, not belief – he asks: 'But *morally* considered, is it not a danger to atomize the language ... and beget brain-poems of such a nature?' What standard of morals is involved in the making of such mere verbal decisions? Are orthography and orthodoxy really twin-concepts? And how – speaking in contempt of the pony text – does Shapiro, in this latter day, hold up Murray – with his brazen interpolations – and Lang – with his Wardour Street English – as ideal translators?

By disguising a personal anthology as a well-dressed essay, Shapiro succumbs to yet another methodological risk. Both because he is weak in logic – must a poet be one who boasts five sensitive senses, and small sense? – and poor in the organization of his material, his essay does not avoid those self-contradictions which ever hover over the unscientific mind. Thus, on page 22, he denigrates Spender because that poet, allegedly, 'doubles his tracks in all the poetry / Subsequent to his earliest'; but Eliot, 'personal in the highest and best sense,' he praises (line 1126) because he has a 'style which signs its name at every even pause ...'

Elsewhere, Shapiro takes to task the poets 'who grovel for allusion, / The point of reference and the authority' (line 1565). Nothing, I imagine, illustrates the allusive technique better than Eliot's *Waste Land* – that ingenious scenario: costumes by the Elizabethans; music by Wagner; dialogue by Bartlett; from an idea by Miss Weston. Yet having so despised the method, Shapiro hails its product as (line 436) 'our world-weary masterpiece!' And the allusive master, it is seen, is one who *forges* a name at every even pause.

Again, in line 37, the poet states: 'To science belongs / The isolation of knowledge, to art belongs / The isolation of beauty,' a much too facile dichotomy which Shapiro supports with a fallacious illustration from natural lore, as invented by poets: 'The owl,' he pointedly avers, 'has many thoughts, the woodlark only songs.' But certainly, for the purposes of syllogism, it still has to be proved – demonstrations equally difficult – both that the owl has thoughts, and that the woodlark hasn't. Nor may this reference to popular mythology be defended as a poetic license; when a poet *argues*, he forgoes his right to the suspension of disbelief. But no matter; Shapiro soon forgets the non-rational sources of song to write (line 656): 'The fountain of rime wells from a central source, / The language of understanding.'

Indeed, apart from this concession to the language of understanding, what emerges most blatantly from Shapiro's thesis is an anti-intellectual bias, and, as corollary, a distaste for analytical literary criticism. *Bellum contra cerebellum*. It is significant that in an essay discussing poetry and criticism in the twentieth century he finds no occasion to mention the name of I.A. Richards. It is true that he does speak, in line 34, of 'the squawking chickens of semantics,' bethinking himself in line 1376 to deride only pseudo-semantics, but nowhere does he indicate the slightest appreciation of Richards' tremendous contribution to the contemporary critical approach. In general he seems to shy at anything which resembles the shadow of a thought; the dialectic, he avers, forgetting Donne, is the foe of poetry; the owl is inferior to the woodlark; and it is regrettable that to-day there is not 'more poetry of the kind that Yeats bequeathed and less verse of the mind.' One wonders by what ratiocination Shapiro comes to consider Yeats's Byzantium poems mindless. Shapiro's cerebrophobia goes even further; he applies it not only to literature but also to life. 'The Age of Reason,' he affirms (line 1598 *et seq.*), 'walked beside the Age of Progress toward the Age of War!' The holocaust, one is to imagine, was the result of too much thinking, and in the Dark Ages, one is to suppose, all was love and affection.

And, finally (lines 1466–1484), Shapiro doesn't like critics.

THE METRIC:

The metric, as has already been indicated, is 'made upon the classic English decasyllable, / Adapted to the cadence of prose speech.' In this form are couched not only the essay proper, but also the Foreword, and even the postscript gratitudes:

> I wish to make acknowledgment to Doctor
> David Lovett of Baltimore, to whom ...

The prose speech is further emphasized by a frequent resort to the vernacular. 'In one of the most widely circulated' ... 'And vice versa' ... 'Perhaps the current interest' ... language of the *causerie* introduced to give an informal and anti-poetic authenticity to his remarks. It cannot be gainsaid that a certain air of sincerity is thus established, but not without penalty; too many of the lines read like that notorious exemplar of blank verse: 'A Mr. Wilkinson, a clergyman ...'

Although they do not display frequent end-rhymes, Shapiro's lines are not blank verse. Like Pope's, his essay is rhymed, but unlike Pope's, the rhyme-scheme is most erratic:

> Nor is it accurate to *charge* the great
> With misconstruing metric; by and *large*
> Whether they write for eye or ear or *both*,
> True poets are *loath* to probe their own designs.

It is a pegleg prosody, and in adopting it, Shapiro seems to think that he is implementing Lanier's prophecy (lines 218–220) 'that rime / Will *mate* with prose and probably *create* / A yet-undreamed-of measure for our verse.' The truth is, of course, that this measure has been nightmared before, in children's books, in the barbarisms of Cicero's un-classic verse: 'O fortu*natam natam* me consule Ro*mam*,' and by A.E. Coppard, to mention but several instances; but it is a measure generally and rightly regarded as pastiche.

A DIAGNOSIS:

One may wonder why Shapiro ever wrote this essay at all, or, having written, permitted it to be published. Certainly it represents a distinct falling-off from the high standard of his work both in *Person, Place and Thing* and in *V-Letter*. I venture a surmisal.

It seems to me that this essay was primarily written for the purpose of whistling away the anxieties which apparently trouble the author. They are, as Shapiro says in another connection, the result of being 'sensitive to mistakes,' and they divide themselves as follows:

(a) A touchiness about his own literary style, its authenticity, and its alleged derivation from Auden. (For one of many examples, see 'Guineapig,' *Person, Place and Thing*, page 12.) How does one defend oneself against such a suspicion, often articulated by book-reviewers? Shapiro has his answer: First, one attributes to Auden a multiple style – and so, presumably, no style at all, and, therefore, nothing that can be imitated – and then (lines 910 *et seq.*) one attacks what is left, simple or multiplex. One attacks also his 'signatures,' such as his all-cover use of a word like *history*; one's own sin in that connection (*P.P.T.*, page 18) is thus atoned. And finally, having murdered, in full view of all, the poet allegedly imitated – so runs the logic of the anxious one – who will now charge him with affinities?

It is significant, too, that another of Shapiro's major influences, Delmore Schwartz, is not even mentioned, not by name reviled – an evasion amounting to a taboo.

(b) An uncertainty about his position as a Jew in American letters. I have had earlier occasion to point out that this feeling of alien-ness greatly disturbs Shapiro, disturbs him so much that it takes on a pathogenic form. In *Person, Place and Thing* there are a half-dozen references to Jews, all, all self-denigratory to the point of masochism. And in *The Essay*, the feeling persists. Freud – consider it! – is dubbed 'this great *German*.' Seeing that Freud was not a German, but an Austrian; and not only an Austrian but a Jew; and that, in any event, Freud's nationality is entirely irrelevant to the point Shapiro is making (lines 1640 *et seq.*) this is a most peculiar identification. But perhaps, it is poetically just; Freud, in his time, made Moses into an Egyptian.

It is in discussing the confusion in belief that Shapiro most embarrassingly reveals his unsureness. If only the poets of to-day had some religion, he says, any religion; and he enumerates 'the six heads of the Hindu Lady, The Blessed Virgin, or the Greek Aphrodite.' Jehovah his enumeration ignores. As for Christianity, he regrets, '*our* purely literary use of Christ in painting, prose, and rime.' Can it be that *Ash Wednesday* has indeed had the effect upon Shapiro which he attributes to it:

> but hear
> How every step enjoins the heart to follow
> Whether it will or not, or start or stay,
> Or turn again, or kneel and genuflect?

Or are they lines 1770 *et seq.* which explain Shapiro's stance:

> Poetry insofar as it depends
> Upon belief succeeds in ratio
> To the success of the belief itself.

And Christianity, obviously, is a more 'successful' belief than Judaism.

Equally typical of Shapiro's sense of insecurity is his tirade against foreign influences in contemporary English poetry. 'That English style has suffered,' he mourns, 'through the adoption / Of forms somehow derived from alien speech / Cannot be overlooked.' I offer no comment on the statement itself – although I cannot help but remember Chaucer's and Conrad's French importations, Johnson's and Milton's Latin, Carlyle's German, none of which killed Cock Robin – I note only the identity of him who makes it, and think of the French patriot out of Corsica, the Irish one out of Spain, and the German one out of Austria.

(c) Misgivings about the craft of poetry in general, and in particular his own participation therein. This evidences itself by a number of instances. Realizing that most of his own poems are static – persons, places, and things; Buick, Library, Hospital – Shapiro naturally scorns 'the dialectic which is the foe of poetry.' But the agenbite bites deeper than that – seeking to disarm the reader, Shapiro invokes a typical defense. The poets I have discussed, he says,

> Are those who seem the best to illustrate
> Our errors; *covertly, I have employed*
> *My own poems freely as examples.*

Purgation by confession is then followed by repudiation, and the essayist speaks knowingly of some poets and 'their infamous hatred of the thing they write.' Then ensues the plea in extenuation: poems 'in the main' are 'beneficent and harmless forms'; that, says Shapiro, is the view 'of a sane perspective.' The effective suicide of Hart Crane and the virtual one of Arthur Rimbaud also seem to give the poet some uneasy paragraphs.

I think that The Rime, except as a personal notebook or as a submission in psychoanalysis, should never have been essayed.

A Definition of Poetry?

A Reply to a Request   19 April 1946

Dear John,

But no, you don't! Not me will you inveigle into your space-filling trap! Symposia on the nature, essence, character, and qualities of poetry, are, of course, all very good in their way, certainly can do no harm, often, in fact, stimulate, if only *a contrario*, towards analysis and discovery; in a magazine of rationed proportions, such as yours, they serve to extrude much bad verse, and do, therefore, *pro tanto*, justify themselves. But *definition* of poetry – that is a Pegasus of a different color. I'll not mount him!

Too many before me, John, have come a buttock-battering cropper for me – unpadded, bony – not to take heed. Definitions of poetry, you know, have been heard of before; indeed, they were no mean persons who invented them. And it is when I consider these definitions, and note how all of them do either from lack of logic or stint of sensibility, crumble to powder, that I must recoil from your arachnoid invitation. Not me!

Let me call these witnesses, the cloud of witnesses, in numbers thick, in testimony nebulous. They come – mark you! – from the finest families. Wordsworth, for example: 'Poetry is the spontaneous overflow of powerful feelings; it takes its origin from emotion recollected in tranquillity.' Yes, you

heard it before; every schoolmarm puts W's daffodils into this vase. Now I
don't want to enter into a learned disquisition – even if I could – into a word-
by-word parsing of this so innocent-looking declaration; but do take its key-
words: *spontaneous, emotion, recollection, tranquillity.* Was E.A. Poe, la-
boring for six months upon the acoustics of 'The Raven' – admittedly a bad
poem, but not for protracted parturition bad – spontaneous? The adjective, in
fact, is a typical piece of romanticism. Its implications are vatic – they evoke
the picture of the poet as a chosen but helpless vessel, selected by powers
above him, for the communication of wisdom which the said powers have at
last decided to make privy to man. The poet as oracle, seated above the fuming
pit, and speaking with a voice not his own.

The second half of the definition, moreover, contradicts the first. If the
overflow of these feelings, dubbed powerful, is really spontaneous, then it
results, no doubt, out of some irresistible compulsion. Yet it is recollected in
tranquillity! A tranquil compulsion!

As for W's notion that poetry is written with the memory, he maligns
the art. He reduces it to accountancy; he confuses it with reportage. Nor is
it from emotion – except in the most inclusive sense of the word – that it
originates.

Consider, now, to what conclusion this definition leads us. It provides
us with a formula, and the formula provides the poem. Here it is: 'Not guilty'
– the plea of the innocent accused. It is spontaneous, believe me; it originates
from emotion; it is founded upon recollection; and considering the circumstances of its utterance, is said in comparative tranquillity. 'Not guilty' – prize
poem, according to plans and specifications.

And you want a definition from me, who never enjoyed intimations of
immortality?

Nor does Coleridge, who criticized his pal's slipshod vocabulary, do any
better himself. 'The best words in the best order' – that, he said, with some
diffidence it is true, was poetry. Prose, on the other hand, was only 'words
in their best order.' Here second-best, apparently, would do. (Mental association prompts a riddle: In what way is Prose like Shakespeare's wife?)

Now apart from the fact that its undefined superlative begs the question,
the definition also fails to make clear why the *best words* are so wantonly
withheld from prose, and why it must content itself with *ersatz*, albeit best-
ordered. On the other hand, are Hopkins' words – 'what with dread,' 'Brim,
in a flash, full' – in the best order? Or is this not fair, since Coleridge is not
to be judged by poetry published after he ceased from defining?

O, that this definition might be subjected to the test empiric! Into a
foreign country send a secret agent, he armed only with a knowledge of its
language, its grammar, and Coleridge's definition. Nothing more. Mission?
To report on the state of poetry in the said realm. Such a report, John, I *would*

publish; 'twould be worth, both in positive entertainment and negative edi-
fication, ten symposia!

Sad Shelley, too – they fly to this business like moths to the flame –
leaves his stanzas written in dejection long enough to announce that poetry
is 'the record of the best and happiest moments of the best minds!' This time,
you observe, the question is thrice begged. And when Shelley, I would have
you know, says 'happiest,' he means, as the rest of his defense shows –
happiest! Not merely felicitous, in the literary sense, but happiest, full of a
sweet content. Shelley, of course, realizes how funny this must sound to
readers who attend to what they are reading, so he attempts some highfalutin
hocuspocus to indicate that he means happiest *sub specie aeternitatis*. But
under the aspect of eternity, all are happy, and not only poets. And as for
the 'best minds' – that must have choked you, too. Some of these best minds
were lodged in the crania of lunatics. I think it was Housman who pointed
out the fact that the four most distinguished poets of the xviiith century –
Collins, Cowper, Smart, and Blake – all, at one time or other, bedded at
Bedlam.

You see Shelley plain – do you think I'll put myself in like case?

But those, after all, were poets, and, as we see, knew not what they did.
The critic, the educator – there's the man to go to. Quoth Matthew Arnold:
'Poetry is the most beautiful, impressive, and widely effective mode of saying
things.' But what is beautiful? How is effectiveness judged? By circulation,
perhaps? If I recall correctly, it was almost in the same words that the son of
Mussolini defined his bombing of the Ethiopians: the most beautiful – their
flesh, he rhapsodized, burst like flowers – impressive – and how! – and widely
effective mode of saying things! No, this is not a definition, no more than
was his father's who simplified the Ablative by calling it the Quale-Quare-
Quidditive Case. Matthew, too, was a poet.

It must be stated, however, that not all of the professional definers
remained as temeritous as these classic ones. They soon caught on to the fact
that what they were seeking to answer was really a trick question. So of late
they have countered with trick answers – alas, transparently tricky. Mr. E. A.
Robinson, therefore, poker-facedly informs us that poetry is a language that
tells us something that cannot be said! If anybody wishes to be persuaded by
this kind of double-talk, it is, of course, their privilege so to be persuaded;
but really, this is not definition, this is rhetoric, and rhetoric which requires
what not even poetry requires, namely, a suspension of logic; of logic, not
merely of disbelief. To the same class of pretty-pretty characterization – full
of a tantalizing meaninglessness, as inscrutable as a Mona Lisa pasted onto
the muzzle of the Sphinx – is Untermeyer's coy utterance: Poetry is the power
to define the indefinable in terms of the unforgettable. How much this seems
to say, and how paltrily informative it is! In justice to its author, I do point

out that while in a 1932 edition of one of his numerous poetry books, he claims the charming definition for his own, in 1942 – ten years and one thought later – he bethinks himself, and attributes the thing to one Michael Lewis. (Lewis, no doubt for Louis, and Michael for Myer, who being *unter* is placed first!)

Now, John, are these the quiddities you want to elicit from our Eisteddfod? Spare yourself the trouble, and save the postage. Take your Roget's thesaurus, gather the antonyms, and scramble – by the living Lord, you'll get yourself an oxymoronic definition that will surely flabbergast your readers!

But I have not ended my tale of discomfiture beheld and example noted. There are some, apparently, who find Robinson's and Untermeyer's definitions unacceptable as being too dazzlingly illuminating. Mr. Sandburg, otherwise a straight-shooter and a forthright talker, also goes mystical – becomes a Houdini of explication, a Blackstone of poesy. Poetry, he says, so that you should henceforth know what it is, poetry is the opening and closing of a door, leaving those who look through to guess what is seen during a moment. Not clear? He continues: Poetry is the synthesis of hyacinths and biscuits. I trust that you are properly grateful for this information; with this standard your editorial function should now weigh lightly upon you.

Or perhaps you would be interested – if you don't see it in the window, ask for it – in some other stock we have on hand – some priceless rare definitionry of a diagnostic order – some *materia medica poetica*? That, too, is available. Attend: Housman *loquitur*: 'I can no more define poetry than a terrier can define a rat, but I recognize the object by the symptoms it provokes in me. One of the symptoms was described in connection with another object by Eliphaz the Temanite: "A spirit passed before my face, and the hairs of my flesh stood up ..." Experience has taught me when I am shaving of a morning to keep watch over my thoughts, because if a line of poetry strays into my memory, my skin bristles so that the razor ceases to act.'

Not bad empirics; but how can women, and other beardless minions, tell?

However, there is also a female diagnostic. 'If I read a book,' said Emily, 'and it makes my whole body so cold no fire can warm it, I know that it is poetry. If I feel physically as if the top of my head were taken off, I know that is poetry. These are the only ways I know it. Is there any other?'

Is there? I hate to oppose the heavy-weighted Dr. Johnson against the delicate Dickinson, but his pontification is pertinent, pertinent both as indicating the impossibility of the task, and the undesirability of undertaking it. 'What is poetry? Why, Madam (or Sir), it is much easier to say what it is not. We all know what *light* is, but it is not easy to *tell* what it is.'

I cannot tell, and until I can, I will resist your blandishments. Should it be granted me some fine day, to reduce poetry to a formula, to make the subject as precise as, let us say, atomic physics, you shall hear from me. For the time being, however, my atomic prosody has discovered only the perfect onomatopoeia – boom! – I'll let you know when I develop the rest.

Sha! Sha! Shostakovitch! 20 February 1948

We must frankly admit that in this journal music is not within our jurisdiction. Its prerogatives belong rather to Mr. I.R. of the *Jewish Daily Eagle*, who has only to speak of the mixolydian modes to convince us of our abysmal ignorance. This unfamiliarity with the esoteric techniques of this art, however, does not mar our enjoyment of it. We know what we like; we know, above all, that music is one of the purest of the arts, and that our enjoyment of any example of it, like our enjoyment of a mathematical proposition, need never be marred by either composer's political convictions, or by insinuations lurking between the bars.

Alas, we have been disillusioned. From Moscow issues news that both Shostakovitch and Prokofieff have been put in the dog-house – where they may bark, but not in staves – as composers of music that is essentially bourgeois. It is a communication that is difficult to fathom. In the first place, how does one tell bourgeois music from communist music? Does the octave imply political loyalties? Is F-flat revolutionary and G-sharp counter-revolutionary? Or is it that the scale itself, based as it is upon a hierarchy of notes, is bourgeois inasmuch as it insists upon class distinctions? Or is it a question of modes, – the minor being considered Trotskyite and deviationist?

Upon these matters, there is no light from Moscow. All that we are told is that Prokofieff is not a fit composer for the Soviet Union. Why? It is not revealed. Perhaps a secret code has been discovered hiding among the instruments of *Peter and the Wolf*, a parable whereby Peter the Great is opposed to his successor, thus uncomplimentarily designated. But, then, Shostakovitch – he has no Peters and no wolves. Moreover, there was a time when both of these composers were hailed everywhere, in Russia and abroad, as the foremost exponents of Russian music, as the finest instances of the heights to which art could rise under Soviet patronage. What has brought about the change?

We strongly suspect that no change has really ensued. Even in the days of their glory, both Prokofieff and Shostakovitch did not exact the whole-hearted approval of Stalin. Stalin, – it is no longer a state secret – loves a simple melody, something that you can carry in your head and hum. This cerebral music, these designed cacophonies, these prearranged discordances, –

he could live, and live very well, without them. Up to now Stalin, it appears, was too busy to express his opinion; besides, the citizens of the allied countries seemed to have a taste for this kind of noise, seemed to think that it showed some musical advance – so let Prokofieff have his day and the ally his impression. Such an accommodating attitude, of course, now belongs to the past – *exeunt* Shostakovitch and Prokofieff.

One is left only to contemplate what would have happened to Russian music if Stalin, like Truman, had had a daughter who sang.

Marginalia   11 June 1948–28 January 1949

TOWARDS AN AESTHETIC

Whence better than from the original blueprint, the first formula, Genesis, Chapter 1?

First described is the condition before Creation: *Now the earth was without form, and void, and darkness was upon the face of the deep.*

Whence it is to be deduced that there are three requisites to an artifact: (a) form, (b) content, (c) light. By the last one must understand internal light – radiance; external light is already assumed in the concept of form.

It was from his God, therefore, that the Angelic Doctor learned that 'Ad pulchritudinem tria requiruntur: integritas, consonantia, claritas.'

Genesis 1 then proceeds to indicate a series of steps which must be taken before the Creator can rest from his work, and say, finally, It is good.

(1) The establishment of two lights, one for day and one for night. This is to teach us that all created things are worthy of their Creator only if they can be appreciated on two levels; if in a poem, everything is as clear as daylight, it might as well have been written in prose; if, on the other hand, its moonlight radiance, shrouded in shadows, threatens to remain so forever, it is a light again unsatisfying; it thwarts the natural desire for clear and complete vision. The compromise consists in the alternation of the two kinds of light; one mystical, the other apocalyptic.

(2) The division of the waters: Divine grammar and syntax.

(3) The making of grass, herb-yielding seeds, and fruit-trees bearing fruit. The world's vocabulary, which does not live unless it comes alive, unless it reproduces itself, unless it connotes.

(4) The declaration of the seasons: In art, in law, time is of the essence.

(5) *Let the waters swarm with living creatures, and let fowl fly above*

the earth: Art dynamic, not static; protean, not uniform; self-multiplying, not sterile.

(6) The making of man in God's image: This is the poet's signature. In his creation, it is He who must be seen. The artist is a creator completely surrounded by mirrors.

THE POEM AS CIRCULAR FORCE

(a) Centripetal: Where the mind of the reader, at the conclusion of the poem, is drawn back into the poem's vortex. The compulsion is to burrow, to seek the centre. Most of Rilke's poems are of this kind.

> The leaves are falling, falling as from way off
> as though far gardens withered in the skies;
> they are falling with denying gestures.
>
> And in the night the heavy earth is falling
> from all the stars down into loneliness.
>
> We all are falling. This hand falls.
> And look at others: it is in them all.
>
> And yet there is one who holds this falling
> endlessly gently in his hands.

At the conclusion of this poem, the reader will not be launched, as he will be in case (b), upon a series of tangential thoughts. The last line here is not, as it will be in case (b), a point of departure, but a curve for return. The reader, at the end of the poem, finds himself impelled to retrace his steps, seeking once more the heart of the poem, this time confident that he may open it for now he owns the key to the mystery, found in the last stanza. He sees now how he who holds this falling endlessly gently in his hands, thus holds the autumnal leaves, and the heavy earth – endlessly gentle: 32 ft. per sec. per sec., not more, not less – and mankind itself. All the vibrations of the poem throb within the poem itself.

(b) Centrifugal: Where the poem, raising the reader to a speed of exaltation, at its conclusion, launches him forth with accumulated circular force, from a tangent into space. The poem, though an experience in itself, becomes the immediate cause of further experiences whose content is postulated, not by the poem's content, but by its mood. The final lines of Keats's poems provide illustration:

Silent, upon a peak in Darien.

It is at this point of elevation that for the reader the real poem begins. The other thirteen were but a climbing – with exhilaration, it is true – to this height.

Fled is that music: do I wake or sleep?

The insistence upon mood is explicit. At this point the reader, if worthy of the poem, begins himself to muse.

And gathering swallows twitter in the skies.

It is as if 'from a tangent into space' were being geometrically demonstrated. Up to this point the poet confined himself to images which could be kept within the limits of his stanzaic canvas; here release takes place; and the mind, too, is set winging with the swallows in the skies.

See also the sonnets of José-Maria de Heredia. Almost all of them depend for their effect upon the liberty of flight afforded by the last line, a flight whose direction, of course, has been subtly predetermined in the opening lines.

(c) The wheel static:

Life is real! Life is earnest!
And the grave is not its goal;
Dust thou art, to dust returnest,
Was not spoken of the soul.

The wheel is at rest; you count the spokes, its rhymes, and you see the hub, its meaning. And what you see and count there is; there is no more.

BROWNING'S BLASPHEMY

And God's in his heaven –
All's right with the world!

Sophisticated pessimists condemn these lines and indeed the entire song as a failure because, they say, the optimism expressed is facile, unearned. It is difficult to agree with this criticism; it is obvious that the poet set out to be optimistic in an easy light-hearted fashion; if such is the impression which the poem finally gives, certainly the poem must be admitted a success.

But it is rather because he has *not* succeeded in giving us the clean wholesome thought he had in mind that this poem must be judged a failure. Any one for whom words are meanings, and not mere incantations, must be at a loss to understand the total poem, to make peace with a climax which after insisting that 'God's in his heaven,' proclaims that, therefore – or what's the dash there for? – therefore 'all's right with the world.' As long as He confines himself to heaven! As long as He does not intrude upon earth!

It is clear that this implication was unintentional. That 'seven' had to find its echo. Hence, the failure. Thus does a rhyme compel a sacrilege.

ROBERT FROST AND THE FIVE SENSES

Much has already been written about the fact that most writers, as one judges from the evidence of their texts, seemed to be possessed of one special sense more developed and keener than the rest. Thus Émile Zola demonstrates in almost all of his writing the extraordinary sensitivity of his nose. His *weltanschauung*, very largely, is a sense of smell. Thus Swinburne receives experience as through a conch, through a murmuring of sound in meaning remote. In Keats it is the metaphor of taste – the grape crushed against the palate – which recurs again and again. Other poets lean – and an entire school of critics uses this predilection as a touchstone – to the image purely visual. One ventures to suppose, moreover, that if one made a statistical analysis of the writings of the blind, it would be the tactile reaction – the tapping stick – which would predominate. It would appear, in fact, that there is no writer, and for that matter no person, in whom the five sensitivities are equably distributed.

Measured by purely pragmatic standards, this maldistribution must be regarded a serious handicap. Aesthetically, of course, it has its compensations – often it affords, precisely because one-sided, a sharper view, or touch, or hearing of the thing to which attention is being given. The focus narrowed, the illumination increased. But from any such view, however, four-fifths is necessarily omitted. It may be very intriguing to get an artist's communication all in terms of smell, very titillating to learn about the world through the fingertips; also very inadequate. The whole person is not engaged.

If such are the dangers to which communication is subject at the moment of utterance, what is one to say touching the difficulties of human conversation when one realizes that still further perils await that communication at the moment of its receptior. The reader, too, has his idiosyncrasies. He, too, may suffer from an overdeveloped single sense. To the poet of the specialized sense, he, for his part, may be listening all ears, or all tongue, or all thumbs.

It is daily that we see exemplified before us the fable of the blind men arguing about the shape of the elephant.

The music of her face – Lovelace's daring metaphor, taken out of context

– may well be used for clinical experiment; and it is not difficult to imagine five different readers, each suffering from a weighted sense, attaching different connotations to this very simple image. Thus:

The auditor: He, obviously, would take the phrase as an appeal to his sense of hearing and would read it as a compliment to the general harmony of the lady's features. By its very composition this face is musical, even when silent.

The voyeur: The term is used in preference to 'seer' – encumbered, as it is, with intimations of prophecy – but without the specialized meaning it has in Kraft-Ebbing. The voyeur, with a cartoonist's imagination endowed, sees 'the music of her face' very vividly indeed: minims for eyes; the nose a quaver; the ear a clef; the mouth a pause, a rest.

The palpator: To him music provides as much pleasure through the ivory smoothness of the piano-keys as through the sweet vibrations of the piano-strings. He reads 'the music of her face,' therefore, as a tactile tribute, even as in the Song of Songs he reads: Thy breasts are like two doves.

The gustator: This subject is a man of taste unmetaphorical. Naturally his reactions are primitive; the world and all that is therein are subject for ingestion. The music is dinner-music. The phrase to him is of a sexual significance. Cf. Cleopatra's fear, in Shaw's *Antony and Cleopatra*, of being eaten by a man. Both Freud and the anthropologists corroborate this association.

The olfactor: To such an one, a face is memorable and dear because of the odour of its cosmetics, the sweetness of the breath of its mouth; nor is it unusual that such an one should synesthetize his evocations and call them music.

No wonder Robert Frost makes sure:

Essence of winter sleep is on the night,
The scent of apples: I am drowsing off.
I cannot rub the strangeness from my sight
I got from looking through a pane of glass
I skimmed this morning from the drinking trough
And held against the world of hoary grass.
It melted, and I let it fall and break.
But I was well
Upon my way to sleep before it fell,
And I could tell
What form my dreaming was about to take.
Magnified apples appear and disappear,
Stem-end and blossom-end,
And every fleck of russet showing clear.

My instep arch not only keeps the ache,
It keeps the pressure of a ladder-round.
I feel the ladder sway as the boughs bend,
And I keep hearing from the cellar bin
The rumbling sound
Of load on load of apples coming in.

Here all the senses – with the exception of that of taste, which is subsequently suggested in the word 'cider-apple' – are adverted to. The scent of apples, explicitly; sound – both by direct reference and onomatapoetic effect in 'load on load of apples coming in'; sight – recurrent throughout; and touch – wonderfully, lingeringly evoked through after-pressure. The sense of orientation, too, is not forgotten. 'I feel the ladder sway as the boughs bend.'

Above all, this poem, like a great number of Frost's poems, is remarkable also for the suggestion of the presence of a sixth sense. For although the poet seems to be describing merely the sensations he feels during the procedures of apple-picking in the fall, actually he is discoursing on life and immortality, discoursing not pedantically, not obviously, but by implication, and so subtly that one cannot affirm that the implication is there. The implication seems born in the mind of the reader; the reader is made poet. But of course the seed for the implication was planted by Frost:

One can see what will trouble
This sleep of mine, whatever sleep it is.
Were he not gone,
The woodchuck could say whether it's like his
Long sleep, as I describe its coming on,
Or just some human sleep.

OF JAPANESE POETS

Poets in Japan, it appears, are not born; they get that way when they are about to die. Thus, it is reported, almost all of the samurai warlords recently condemned for their participation in the criminal promotion of the late hostilities have been moved in their penultimate days to court the muse. In this they afford yet another element of gratifying contrast to their opposite numbers in Europe; the Nazi convicts, it will be recalled, beguiled the imminence of their mortality in prose, crass ugly prose which either frothed with hatred's desperate spittle, or crawled in mean obsequious hypocrite retraction. How different is the sublime indifference, the designed irrelevance, with which the Japanese indite their epitaphs.

Writes the notorious Tojo:

For many generations the cold moon has shone until to-day.

It is a splendid simple sentence. Reading like some lesson out of a child's copybook, it yet throbs with oracular connotations. We all know what Tojo has in mind: though prating of the moon, he is no lunatic: he means in his very polite Japanese manner to comment upon the war-trials which condemned him criminal, and he means to say that from time immemorial the cold moon (war) was accepted as a natural phenomenon, a moon, – until to-day. But good poet that life, or death, has made him, Tojo will not condescend to make an explicit statement. He utters instead a simple parable: its premises may be all wrong, its philosophy all distorted, – but its utterance is truly poetic, and – considering the personal position of its author, – truly tragic.

These remarks, however, are not to be considered as expressive of sympathy for Tojo the warmonger; our attitude to him is the same as our attitude to all poets personally reprehensible; it is an attitude learned from the Japanese treatment of the silkworm: keep the silk, and throw the worm away.

OF POEMS ABOUT BABIES

There should be a law against them. The writing of baby-poems (extra! extra! all about the pitter-patter of little feet, the ineffable beauty of pink toes, the charm and mystery of inarticulate goo) should be made a criminal offense, subject to the same penalties as other forms of obscenity. For we have yet to encounter an example of this type of art which was both honest and successful; every instance we have beheld – and the women's magazines are full of them – appeared meretricious to an extreme. The poetess – she was usually a poetess – invariably wrote as if she was certain that her subject was irresistible; only an ogre, she knew, would look critically at an artifact in praise of bambinos; she did not find it necessary, therefore, to exert herself too strenuously about the poetry. Why, the word *baby* itself, she felt, was a poem. We agree; and would prefer to consider the poem at its title completed.

There are in English literature, it is true, some memorable verses about infants; but they are all – it is with trepidation that we point this out – about infants that didn't survive. There come to mind, in this connection, Milton's wonderful little threnody on a child who died of a cough, Jonson's touching lines on Salathiel Pavy – not quite a babe, a babe protracted – and in recent days Dylan Thomas's 'Refusal to Mourn the Death, by Fire, of a Child in London.' Even Stevenson's verses on the milky theme – so coy, so goody-good, leave much to be desired.

No, the practitioner should start at the other end. For juvenilia he should write poems about old age – some of the most successful expressions on this subject have been by youngsters – then work backwards until in the full maturity of his life he may venture his last and greatest challenge – the poem on a babe. So, in his last years did Joyce, writing the best of his shorter poems, 'Ecce Puer'; and a better master to follow there has not been.

A CONVERSATION

– This poem has no form? I agree. That is what I intended. It is a modern poem and was meant to mirror contemporary life which – you will not deny – is itself formless.

– I neither deny nor confirm. For the moment I wish to consider this poem, not contemporary life. But even assuming that contemporary life – which, by the way, has been going on from time immemorial – is actually formless, am I correct in saying that the reader of your poem is intended through its formlessness to obtain an image of our contemporary chaos? The chaos of life is equated by the chaos of the poem? Is that right?

– That is exactly what I meant.

– Is it not true that this equation is possible only if we assign to chaos itself some characteristic recognizable form?

– I beg your pardon?

– Is it not correct to say that chaos, and every part of chaos, is like every other part of chaos?

– Certainly, since it is all chaotic.

– Then would not any series of unintelligible syllables, any scrambling of the letters of the alphabet, in a word, any other literary chaos, do just as well to mirror the chaos of contemporary life?

– No, because – this is obvious – in a mere chaotic scramble, the artist's intention is lost. The intention is to simulate a particular chaos.

– Then one chaos may after all be different from another? There are *particular* chaoses. Under what aspect do these differ? Is it not under the aspect of their – form?

– Well, after all, in a poem one can't reproduce all chaos. The permutations are infinite. One must select.

– Your poem, then, is one which is selective of chaos. Does a mirror select?

– A false analogy. The man who focuses the mirror selects. I am that man.

– But on what basis does he focus his mirror?

– He seeks a *typical* scene. A part which will represent the whole.

– Then, since he seeks the representative, he is really in search of form, is he not?

– There is a distinction. It is a distinction between intellectual forms – the significances of the things seen – and technical forms – the shape of things seen. They ought not to be confused.

– But you are the one who is confounding them. You were the one who sought to equate intellectual formlessness with technical formlessness.

– What's the use? You are a sophist. You go at poetry as if it was something sensible. Give me back my poem. I *know* I'm right.

– Not you, but Plato, expulsive Plato, he was right.

THE POEM OF THE AGE

Certain critics there be who are never content merely with the poetry of a poem; enjoying a large philosophical appetite, they seek everywhere that special flavour and tang – 'the spirit of the age.' Unless the poem under examination provides that peculiar condiment, they invariably thrust it, unsatisfied, away.

Alas, this epicurean taste is one which is but rarely appeased. It is not every day, it is not even every age, which produces the masterpiece which at once exists qua masterpiece, and as summation of the cosmic view of a particular time and place. Such *chef d'oeuvres–cum–summa theologica* may, in the world's history, be counted on the fingers of one hand; the Bible is such a work; such a work is Dante's *Comedy.*

Our own age, of course, has not yet produced its definitive expression. This is not at all surprising since the age we speak of began only four years ago with the detonation over Hiroshima. But already one may venture some surmisals as to the form and nature of its representative work, if and when that work is written.

Its technique, I think, will consist largely of an application to literature of the dominating techniques of contemporary science. Surely the time has come to put a stop to Newtonian *belles lettres*; atomic is the era's word. Nor can the writer of the future afford to ignore the new psychological frontiers of the mind; the truth is that the manner of most contemporary writing has already established it as a truism that no author can approach the criticism of life without a Freudian-et-al. apparatus.

This being the technique – a sort of radio-activated sublimation – the subject matter of the age's classic, too, seems equally preconditioned and predetermined. Let not the reader smile when we name that subject – love. It is the compelling necessity of our time – this social love which causeth even the evangelizers to stammer.

For, insofar as love is concerned, the principal problem of the age is a scientific one: the filling of the vacuum. Even the invention of the terrors of the atom bomb has been based on a somewhat amended version of the physicist's maxim: Nature adores a vacuum. To-day the dialectic must be pre-cipitated to bring back the first fine careless abhorrence.

What will this great poem of the future look like? If we knew, we would write it. We venture, however, the formula for a minuscule exemplar. Take the word: *Love*, and proceed first of all by chain-reaction. What two other words does it suggest? Put them down. Then what two words does each of love's suggestibilities bring to your mind? Put them down. You will advance, thus, in a geometric progression, simulating, on your way, the repercussions of the chain-reaction, invoking, as you go along, the associational promptings of our common psychology – and you will be surprised to what a point you will come. When you stop. But you need not stop. The charm of this game is its infinite possibilities.

I doubt whether in so factitious a fashion you will achieve that master-piece which our great critics long for; but its modus you may, if you have enough talent, perhaps adumbrate.

[UNTITLED]

[...] colours to the vowels – *A black and E blue*, and so on, is a locus classicus in modern criticism. It marks the first artistic exploitation of synaesthesia – the intentional derangement and confusion of the senses, perpetrated not to diminish but to increase the scope of the five pleasures. It is true that many have questioned the exactness of Rimbaud's identifications; to some it is the sound A that is blue, and the sound E that is black; the important thing – important because by compounding it adds a new sense to man's faculties – the important thing is that the auditory should be spoken of in terms of the pictorial.

Yet Rimbaud in daring to go so far seems not to have dared enough. The vowels are given their rainbow. But are the consonants really colourless? Do not the sounds, too, evoke, in the mind of one susceptible to such expe-rience, their own tints and colours? Is there not also a hue after the cry of the consonants? Surely S is blue, as it is the sky and its constellations, B the boldness of brown, and F something soft and shaded? Nor is it only of colour that the consonantal sounds speak, but shapes and forms, too, are conjured at their utterance. R is the very essence of waviness, and T pointillist's precision itself.

But not here is the place to go through the alphabet. Such experimen-tation we leave to the psychologists and their laboratory statistics. The which we await.

FREE VERSE

Poetry which abuses its latitude to obtain its longitude.

COMMENTARY

In poetry it is without comment that one makes commentary.

THE CLICHÉ

Every decade has one – the word, the phrase, the shibboleth, which having gained for itself a certain currency in intellectual or literary circles, is then wantonly exploited by the incompetent for the purpose of winning easy victories. Thus not long after Auden in the thirties discovered that 'history was to blame' – Joyce noted it earlier, in *Ulysses*, en passant – every poetaster of the decade made it a habit to conclude his versified lamentations with some snide comment about 'history.' The use of this word, it seemed, gave the poet who introduced it reluctant into his opus a sort of Spenglerian status. Here was a man who was not content merely to fashion lyrics for the hour, poems for the day – *his* work enjoyed scope and sweep – did he not speak of history?

The same kind of treatment was accorded to the word *luck*. Let Fitzgerald rhyme about *Kismet*, and Hugo verbalize about *Anangke* – the contemporary poet was set on making something small and intimate, something philosophically casual of this large concept. The number of luck poems, we need hardly say, is legion.

History no longer serving, and luck somewhat faded, a new counter has appeared in the market: myth. It is the same old grandiloquence, dressed, this time, like an anthropologist.

It has been years, we think, since someone has thought of using the name of God for the thrill of an easy effect. Apparently it doesn't work, as it used to. There was a time, however, when one could have earned a lifetime reputation on a strategy of exclamatory Gods. See the works of Robert Browning.

A good poet, we think, is one who makes conviction issue from his work without sending irresponsible summonses to God and History and Luck to testify on his behalf. Such witnesses may of course be summoned, but they are not, to use the lawyer's term, compellable.

Book Reviewing, in Seven Easy Lessons

10 December 1948

The great day of the book reviewer, as of the bard, is gone, belongs to the past, seems destined never to return again. In the place of those authoritative and exhaustive pronouncements which the nineteenth-century reviewer was wont to indite whenever a reviewable book came complimentary to his desk – the essays which Macaulay upon such occasion penned have not yet been supplanted, either for judgment or for style – in that yawning place the gentle, much too gentle reader to-day meets only the most attenuated of substitutes: 'paragraph comment,' 'briefly noted,' 'books received.' Moreover it is somewhat furtively that even these nods to the literary are introduced into the periodicals in which they do appear; surreptitiously placed at the end of the magazine to be seen only after the really important has been read; hidden away, like some adolescent's pornography, among the end pages of a worthier volume.

At times, indeed, the low esteem in which the editor holds the book reviewer's craft becomes embarrassingly explicit. 'Send me,' he writes, 'a book review of two-and-a-half inches.' It is true that very often a book can be characterized in a sentence, dismissed in one tenth of an inch; but such brevity should be the book reviewer's privilege, not the linotypist's *diktat*.

However, recalcitrant as reviewers may be, it is the editorial majesty which prevails. The result is that the contemporary book review is a production altogether *sui generis*, and, depending upon the temperament or ignorance of the book reviewer, may be categorized as follows:

The title commentator: This man finds it sufficient for his purpose to read the name and surmise the subject of the book under review. Such labour expended, he launches forth into his own essay or squib (space is of the essence) on the same subject. Thus every book received is but a point of departure, a springboard, in a sense an inspiration to write your own. This is, moreover, a technique which is eminently satisfactory to all concerned: to the author, for he has received a free ad, and in the process has not even been explicitly insulted; to the editor, for his lines have been preserved; and to the critic, for he has been more than a critic, he has been creative, he has shown that on whatever subject any writer chooses, he, too, could write his book if he would.

The table-of-contents authority: More industrious than the first – this man does wade forward to the third page of the work under review – he is also more modest. He spares the reader his private disquisition; no essayist, he. Instead he devotes his column, or half column, to telling the reader what the book is about, information which he himself has gathered from an exhaustive study and a detailed analysis of the table of contents. It is in such reviews that we encounter those startling revelations which inform us that the biography discussed moves logically from *Early Years* to *Adolescence* to *Maturity* to *The Final Period*. Possessing a mind at once chronological and mathematical, this critic, unlike the more sophisticated members of his fraternity, never confuses his reader; him he who counts may read. Indeed, him he who counts to eleven may outstrip.

The index browser: Whether it is some secret semitic influence which is at work in his critical procedures, or a peculiarity of temperament, or a sense of the economical, it is difficult to say, but this pundit reads his reviewed books backwards. He starts from the index; wildly he runs through the alphabet until his finger settles upon some familiar word; he looks it up in the page referred to; and he's off. If he doesn't find the word in the place to which it is referred, he writes a scathing denunciation of the index-maker. To this critic there should be given for review only dictionaries.

The blurb-blabber: Here we must for a moment withdraw from our pursuit of the bookworms above described, bookworms who introduce themselves into either the front or the back cover, to consider those critics who remain delicately poised on the book's jacket, crawling, like flies, over the blurb's expanse, crossing a *t* there, and dotting, like flies, an *i* here. All simplicity and accommodation, the blurb critic finds himself indebted to the publisher not only for his book, but also for his book review. Who is he, he seems to ask himself, that he should contradict the man who not only read the manuscript but also laid out good money to have it set up and bound?

O, for some gallant and enterprising publisher who would paginate and bind his blurb, and wrap it in a jacket made out of his book!

The rave-reviewer: This is a well-known genus and does not require much description. He is the reviewer on the make, he who seeks an opportunity to praise so vehemently that even the publisher may get wind of his review, arrange to have the review read to him (the publisher), and then include him (the critic) on the jacket. If the book becomes a best seller, the author makes a fortune and the critic a reputation. With a reputation so made, the critic then proceeds onto radio programs, lecture tours, etc. On second thought, we really do not know why this kind of review should be called a 'rave-review'; the 'rave-reviewer' is by no means as crazy as he sounds.

The snarler: The snarler doesn't care for money, he wants fame; and the heights of fame, he has discovered, can often be reached over the corpses of mutilated authors. Accordingly he spends his spare time inventing witticisms, any witticisms, witticisms *in abstracto*. And then he waits. Soon enough a book comes along for review; then, relevant or irrelevant, bang go all the wisecracks! The result is that Snarler is quoted, the author, not.

The book that wasn't there: And finally there is the critic who seems eternally unhappy – he never gets for review the books he would really like to read. Invariably his book review discusses either the better book that the writer might have written, or the other subject which would have been much more pertinent to the times. The book before him, however, is never it. When 'It' finally arrives, the times have changed, and it is another it that the critic languishes for.

What a tribe!

The Usurper   14 January 1949

There is no more pathetic reading in the whole realm of literature than the dusty bound volumes of the 'little magazines' of yesteryear. As one thumbs these pages, hectic with manifesto and ever fretful like the porpentine, one's heart is heavied by this spectacle of rebellions which overthrew nobody but their authors, of world-shaking pronunciamentos recorded by no real seismograph, of new movements too soon paralyzed, of frustration mightily flexing its muscles only to collapse, after one or two performances, into a meek and silent inertia. One wonders, indeed, at the ever undaunted perseverance of each new masthead of editors, all unmindful of the quick oblivion which overtook their predecessors, persisting – despite the bleached incunabula bestrewing their paths – in following the cruel and deluding gleam.

Nor can it be said of these intrepid ones that they know not what they do. They know only too tragically and too well what they do. Not an issue of these valiant periodicals but it is prefaced by a statement of policy, that is to say, three paragraphs lamenting the present plight of poesy, how that the writer is scorned and menial, how this condition of disregard has worked upon the poet himself to corrupt his matter and enfeeble his manner, how the bourgeoisie, or the philistine, or the bureaucrat, etc., etc. – a threnody which having been uttered is then followed by three paragraphs of defiance and determination. What happens to the defiance is a matter of sorry record; it is upon the reiterated jeremiad that we would pause.

The poet is no more, these say. He has vanished from our society.

But none of these manifestos, we have observed, is troubled to inquire touching the vanishing poet: Where has he gone to? The poet 'who does not count' – his whereabouts one knows. On a monthly lease he resides in the little magazines. The little magazine, however, is by definition not a part of society; it expresses rather a revolt against society; it is, in fact, for want of patronage that it is little. But the poet who made his peace with society – where is *he*?

It was in vain that, infected by the bewilderment of an avant-garde which, with respect to society at large, always occupied a flanking position, in vain that we sought him in his usual haunts. In the usual haunts one found only – the contributors to 'little mags' (note the abbreviation of endearment; thus do the rejected cling to and caress their spurned possession). Of the writer who was at home in the great societal mansion, there was neither sign nor symbol.

And then – by accident – as if by the machination of some Dramatist who was making drama out of the lesser mortal ones – we found him. In the most unlikely of places. Who would have thought to look for him on the exchange, in a mart, in a marketplace? Yet there we found the missing one – the poet who had absconded, and had, under a new name made himself a new life in a new world.

We really should have been able, at the first suspicion of his disappearance, to fathom his identity – his alias was almost – almost, but how far from quite! – a paraphrase. For the vanished poet was now in an advertising agency, a copywriter!

It was, as we have said, to be expected. Hitherto he had dealt in words, but profitlessly, and without fame; what more natural than that he should forsake the milieu of his futility to move into a sphere where words, though issued anonymously, at least were rewarded with coin of the realm, – and much of it. How he had once laboured over a sonnet, building octave and sestet, polishing its rhymes, spending hour upon hour to audition to himself its varied euphonies, transfusing its clichés, setting its climax – and for what? Rewards? There were none. Kudos? To be read by the editor and the proof-reader. How different things were now when but an ingenious zeugma: *He took the Switzer watch and his time*: provided a week's salary! An apt allusion: *The Old Gold Rush of '49*: – that, and no more – was enough to win him a bonus. Indeed, he had but to call upon 'alliteration's artful aid,' and the metaphor's support, and a slogan simile or two – the bag of tricks which in the old days had got him nothing but the sneers of his rivals – to win him the much-desired twenty-five thousand dollar laureateship.

He had been lost; and had found himself. Prodigal poet, now he 'belonged.' Appearing now, in two colours, in the advertising columns of those very slick-paper magazines, the big mags, whose literary columns he had once despised, it was as an integral part of an all-embracing system that he now functioned.

Moreover, together with rewards – the generous stipend, the sense of affinity – there was yet another advantage which he enjoyed. Like the diplomat's, his also was the privilege of immunity. No more reviews! The copy written, no arrogant critic ever dared, as he did in the blue period, unmask his plagiarisms, or laugh his images to scorn, or question his taste; or pierce him with the ten thousand other arrows that quivered in his quiver.

Thus did we find him, the mislaid poet. Not being the editor of a little mag, we did not bother to point out to him the error of his ways. We forewent the pleasure of needling him about the lackey-role he played. We did not reproach him for that he took sacred things – and prostituted them to a peddler's purpose and profit. We were far above showing him that the skill he once enjoyed had degenerated among the easy ephemera he daily created. These taunts and reproaches, we knew, would avail nothing as against the weekly pay-check which in his mind shone more resplendent than all the golden lyrics of the ages. We left him in his cubicle, where he said he belonged, to his solecisms and his fees.

We left him – but not without having stumbled upon the method whereby the usurper might be dethroned. We offer it to all editors of little mags, present and to come. Let there be an end to these periodicals and to their family feuds and coterie quarrels. Such internecine warfare serves only to weaken and scatter the true bearers of the tradition. *Voilà l'ennemi!* The copy-writer, he it is who has usurped and degraded the true function. And while the fine, the honest ones languish in poverty because they ever and ever seek The Word, in wealth it is that he wallows, the copy-writer, the debaucher of words.

Since his chief concern is the reward, strike at him where he is most vulnerable. Review him! Let his employer see what a third-rater trying to be a second-rater his employee is, and let him bethink himself of the first-rate salary he pays him. Instead of the pedantic review of the slim volume of the latest experimentalist, let the little mag publish a detailed analysis of the current ads, their absurdities, their grammatical errors, their pathos, their general incompetence. It would not be long before the tycoon 'who pays for all this' would be bursting a blood-vessel, and pushing a button.

Exit the copy-writer. Enter the next one. Repeat the dose. *Karthago est delenda!*

In Memoriam: Alexander Bercovitch   12 January 1951

The sudden passing, in circumstances at once tragic and dramatic, of the artist Alexander Bercovitch, removes from the Jewish and indeed the Canadian scene a personality who was as picturesque as the most vivid of his very colourful and talented paintings. His death, which took place suddenly on Sunday afternoon, was surrounded by ironies and contrasts such as one finds only in the most ingeniously contrived novels of the artistic life. On Sunday night, Bercovitch was supposed to have been present at the opening of an exhibition of his paintings at the new 'Y' building. The portraits, the landscapes, yes, and the still-lifes, duly shone down from their frames. A considerable audience circulated about the walls illuminated with Bercovitch's talent, expressing pleasure, admiration, and intending purchase. That evening would have been for Alexander Bercovitch a triumph which he had well deserved, richly earned. But there was no sign of Bercovitch; he was momentarily awaited. Someone, perhaps, even joked about 'the late Mr. Bercovitch.'

The late Mr. Bercovitch, indeed! At that moment the artist Alexander Bercovitch was lying 'unrecognized' upon a slab in the morgue! He had collapsed dead on the corner of St. Lawrence and Mount Royal, in the heart of the Jewish district; and before anyone could come forward to identify him, his mortal remains were removed to the macabre place. Not until much later – his genius having been praised, his absence having been first regretted, and then 'understood' as but an artistic eccentricity – was it learned that Bercovitch – the man – was no longer among the living.

Remained the artist.

What a parable we have here of the lot of the god-gifted man, creator of images! At the very moment when the audacity of his creativeness is about to be rewarded, the laurels by the jealous gods are snatched from him! And when he perishes, he perishes in the midst of the people, unknown and unrecognized!

But Recognition, slow to focus its sight, is sure at last to see. Bercovitch has deserved well of our people, to whom he brought distinction and renown, and deserved well of our country whose landscapes he did with so much loving care transpose to vibrant canvas. Many are the places where he has made forever enduring, forever bright, the seascapes of Gaspé, the paysage of the Laurentians. The little pieces of world he gathered up – cosmos shaped out of chaos – and brought together with his artist's fiat into the confines of a frame, endure.

He will be remembered. He will be remembered, not only by his friends who will always recall his shy, his naif personality, his mosaic hesitations in speech, his inarticulate verbal descriptions, but by all lovers of art who will cherish before their eyes the uninhibited eloquence of his palette, the brightness he brought down from the sky, the hundreds of days wherein, like Joshua, he told the sun to stand still.

Honour to his memory! Glory to his art!

The Case of Jascha Heifetz

1 May 1953

Let it be stated at the outset that we are all for freedom. We believe, in fact, that he who limits the freedoms to but four seeks merely to establish a kind of viable minimum, and that freedom, as the true liberation insists, is a thing essentially unconfined. It is protean; it is ubiquitous; the number and the variety of its epiphanies are past telling; wherever life throbs, there freedom justly invokes its prerogatives. It embarrasses us to have to assert, therefore, at this late date – though assert it we must – that we are all for it.

Let it be stated also that we intend no apologia for the hoodlum who, presumably in anger at Mr. Heifetz's performance of Strauss music in Jerusalem, assaulted the virtuoso with an iron bar. His act was worse than reprehensible, it was indictable, and no doubt the Jerusalmite authorities are pursuing the matter further. Though for freedom we are – how ironic that one should have to emphasize one's possession of the obviously virtuous attitudes! – we are also for law and order.

The above hazards of misconstruction having been cleared, Heifetz's own postion may now be surveyed in its proper perspective. Mr. Heifetz, it will be remembered, came to Israel to regale its inhabitants with his incomparable talent. He was to bring to them the delights of music; from the depths of austerity, from the strictures of hard times, he was to release and lift them to the serene altitudes, the pure empyrean of ineffable sound. His coming was enthusiastically hailed; his arrival warmly greeted.

And then he announced that at his first concert he intended to include in his program a work by the late German composer Richard Strauss. This genius was not unknown to the music-lovers of Israel; the recently-arrived refugees from Europe, indeed, knew that worthy well – Strauss had been, under Goebbels, the gauleiter of harmonics of the Third German Reich! The announcement aroused a storm of protest; both the radio and the press warned the performer against his intended performance; the Government requested the deletion of the affronting piece.

Mr. Heifetz, however, persisted in his plan. At his first concert, every number he played was received with loud ovation. The Strauss sonata met dead silence. This happened in Haifa; in Jerusalem Heifetz did it again – here the lights went out as Strauss's first notes came on. Heifetz completed the number in darkness.

Explicit protest, then demonstrative silence, then ominous darkness – were these things not enough to cause Mr. Heifetz to reconsider his position? Ah, but the artist was asserting a high principle, the principle of freedom of expression! He had a right to select his own music, even as a speaker had a right to choose his own words. Error rampant! – to which the late Mr. Justice Holmes had long ago given quietus when he declared that the principle of freedom of speech still did not accord to a person in a crowded public hall the right to cry *Fire!* where no fire was.

Yes, but there is a distinction between words and music! Music, the aesthete will declare, rises above the barriers of race and nation, exists on a plane above the contentions and quarrels of man, is mere sound, unargumentative, and, therefore, pure. Fatal fallacy – for sounds, too, have their conventions. Words are but sound; there is nothing more innocuous than the articulation of the consonant g; the letter p, too, is by itself harmless; yet should a vowel be placed between these two consonants, and the pronounced result flung at some auditor, surely assault, if not mayhem, may ensue! Why? Because, by convention, the word has associations, and these constitute the head and body of offense.

To Heifetz's listeners, Strauss music meant only one thing – the noise of the Third Reich. Some, in fact, may have even heard that music played, as was the notorious custom, in concentration camps, as background for torture and execution. The Pavlovian reaction could easily have been foretold. This was not music to soothe the savage breast; this was music to agonize the human soul.

Why, then, did Mr. Heifetz persist? What prompted him to offer to his eager audiences, so full of good-will towards him, these wantonly cruel recollections? Certainly Mr. Toscanini, a non-Jew, had a finer sense of proportion and taste.

Mr. Heifetz, it is reported, left Israel in high dudgeon to continue his tour in Europe. He is scheduled to appear in Paris: will he there play *Deutschland Uber Alles?* ... 'There is,' said Mr. Browning, 'no truer truth obtainable by Man than comes of music.' It is to be hoped that Mr. Heifetz has obtained it.

5 / CANADIAN LITERATURE

Mortal Coils

Review of *The Shrouding* by Leo Kennedy   5 January 1934

From the melancholy frontispical text quoting *The Duchess of Malfy* to its last black solemn cover, this skeletonic volume of verse bonily rattles out its dire threnodies, incomparably done. In Canadian poetry Kennedy's book presents a precious ossuary of poems, a macabre necropolis of phrases, a mausoleum of gilded verse. Howbeit, one must not be led astray by the fact that *The Shrouding*, in its 59 pages, contains about a dozen references to the dead, about half a dozen mentions of burials, and a couple of casual invocations of moles, earthworms, and sextons. Yet he who would surmise from these superficialities that the poet is a sorry wight, a gaunt ascetic, a morose monk treading cemeteries and eking out small consolation from epitaphal intimations of resurrection, would miss the entire point of the book, implied in the author's 'Self Epitaph.'

> His head was brittle,
> His wits were scattered;
> He wrote of dying
> As though life mattered.

For this is precisely the inference to be drawn from Kennedy's continual preoccupation with the departed and their dismal doom. Death is so beautifully and poignantly tragic only because life has such varied pleasures and such delicate delights.

> This the grim irony, that brain and bone
> Should have no subtler value than a stone.

Moreover, if we may use a psychological yardstick for poetic feet, to Kennedy, still in his twenties, Death by its very remoteness, is as yet a romantic subject. Old men seldom speak of the Dark Angel; and then, only in circumlocutory euphemisms; but the young, in the temerity of their inexperience, refer to him with impunity. 'Now more than ever seems it rich to die!' cried young Keats in a moment of sublime ecstasy brought on by the music of the nightingale. It is such sensual delights, such joie de vivre that renders Kennedy

half in love with easeful Death
Calling him soft names in many a musèd rhyme.

The jettatura of the Angel of the Thousand Eyes, moreover, is alleviated by Kennedy's firm belief in resurrection, a creed of Catholic origin and pantheistic development. It is because the poet regards the pale flowers stirring underground, these Men of April undergoing their perennial renaissance, that Death is diminished of its terrors.

He did not deserve the anonymity which he bears, who said, 'Si vous voulez savoir si un homme est poète, demandez lui ce qu'il pense et ce qu'il sent au sujet de la nature, de l'amour et de la mort.' The last is Kennedy's all-engrossing theme, a theme which by corollary includes them all. Parallel to this choice of subject, moreover, runs the author's use of adverb, adjective, and verb. It would not be pedantic to say that he who would write well of Nature must first train his adjectives for the duties which they must perform. A talent for the descriptive, an aptitude for the embellishing phrase, these, in the poetry of Nature, require the perfected adjective. In love, life and literature teach us, it is not the content or the object, but the style, the mode and manner, which captures the imagination and whatever else there is to capture; in fine, Cupid's darts are all adverbs. But in Death, the be-all and the end-all, the verb's the thing.

Consider, then, Kennedy's remarkable use of this part of speech in the poem 'Soliloquy for Bells.' These 'drip with sound,' 'dully toll,' 'fling ecstatic peals,' 'stammer through the Angelus,' 'drowse out the Vesper notes,' and 'flute their matins.' Again in 'Epithalamium before Frost':

Now that leaves shudder from the hazel limb,
And poppies pod, and maples whirl their seed,
And squirrels dart from private stores to slim
The oak of acorns ...

Occasionally, of course, Kennedy will obtain his effects by a few deftly turned adverbs and adjectives. Thus in his 'Litany for These Days' the words mire, slime, polluted, miasmic, corruption, rot, foetid, and stagnant, create an atmosphere of unrelieved decadence unrivalled since Baudelaire. His facility with words is further illustrated by his fashioning of unforgettably apt phrases. 'The brown casket of its root,' 'the censorship of frost,' 'quilted lip,' 'measured stitches of the spade,' 'rapturous earthworms eager to be fatter,' 'tall palace of my flesh,' 'loungers in loose vests of wood,' 'the crucible of death' – these coinages bear the stamp authentic of no counterfeiter's die.

As a Canadian volume, Kennedy's is the first of its kind. It establishes, we hope, the advent of a new era; it marks a definite departure from that mollycoddle imitative school of Dominion poetasters, who have been variously dubbed as quasi-semi-pseudo-Victorian. For here is a Canadian book which –

mirabile dictu – holds no references either to pine or to maple; here no call of the Yukon breaks the stillness of the icy air; and here no Indian brave to vigorous iambs prances. Death in a hundred shapes, as Virgil would say, stalks through these lines, and women's societies, sipping tea and nibbling cake, desire better appetizers than poems on life and death.

Not only does Kennedy deviate from the standard themes and eroded clichés of our national poesy, but he also avoids subjects purely contemporary and ephemeral. The reader will look in vain for textual indices to date these verses. Apart from the copyright notice and nominal reference to four as yet insignificant contemporaries, *The Shrouding* contains no age-marks. For all the internal evidence, these poems may have been written by the metaphysical poets, or they may be from the Gregorian chants, or translations from the Greek. The sociological interpeters of literature will find little here to substantiate their theses. Here is singing for sweet singing's sake, raptures, careless and fine, inspired by no scientific sol-fa, prompted by no political staff notation. Here is pure poetry, for the robin, though dight in red, need no Marxian be.

Pure poetry, and though the flame of emotion is here, it burns incandescent in a mental glass. A great deal of Kennedy's poetry is cerebral; it lives up to that best of definitions of poetry – thought in blossom. The apotheosis of intelligence can go no further than this:

> The small activity of mice,
> The velvet passing of a moth,
> And one grey spider's cautious tread
> Make thunder in this shed:
> Where God has stored his tightened drum –
> A mind inside a head!

The book is a fine piece of workmanship, done in admirably-chosen type. The gaunt portrait of Kennedy by Ernst Neumann is fitting and excellently done. *The Shrouding* is a book to be kept for literary and historical value; it marks the resurrection of Canadian poetry.

'The Decencies Had Perished with the Stukas'

Review of *Dunkirk* by E.J. Pratt   19 December 1941

The great conflict which at this writing has embraced practically the entire world has not, singularly enough, produced as yet, any great war poetry. One would have expected that it would have been otherwise; that out of the tragedy and agony of the world-shaking events which we witness to-day, there would have arisen, by way of compensation – O so inadequate! – some inspired utterance, some winged words which would be remembered long after the dust had settled, and the smoke had vanished into thin but again breathable air. Certainly there was ample precedent for such an expectation. The slaughter of Troy is immortal, not because of the extent of the carnage, or the matters which were at stake, but because a divine poet sang of them in numbers which echo through the ages. Even the last war is to-day remembered, not so much in the military strategy which characterized it, as in the principles for which it was fought, principles which have received their finest utterance in the verse of Rupert Brooke, or Siegfried Sassoon, or W.W. Gibson, or Isaac Rosenberg.

With the exception of the little masterpiece upon which we are about to comment, we have noted, in the literary production of the last two years, no work which rose to the demands of the swelling theme. Recently there was published in England a volume of anonymous war verse; the contents of the book indicate that the publishers need not have taken the superfluous precaution: the reputation of no one is made therein. The anthology of air-poetry – The Poetry of Flight – prepared by Mr. Selden Rodman is an indication of the trend which future poetry is likely to take; but a trend is not an achievement. As a matter of fact, it has been left to the orators and rhetoricians to give speech to the moving ideology of the war. Certainly no one will gainsay the fact that Winston Churchill's addresses, his pithy synopses, his classic allusions, his bold Elizabethan vocabulary have put all the bardlings and poetasters who have touched the subject, ignominiously in the shade.

This may be due in part to the fact that this is a people's war. No aristocratic poet, sitting in an ivory tower, can hope to understand the emotion which agitates a subterranean bomb-shelter. Only one who has caught the spirit of an indomitable people, one between whom and his nation runs the electric current of mutual understanding and common endeavor, can hope to express those folk-sentiments which are of the essence of poetry. It is also true – and this supplies an additional reason for the inarticulateness of the contemporary poet – that events have moved with such speed that many of the poets – who, alas, are not political animals – have been unable to keep pace with them. The third decade of this century was one which was characterized in its literature by a too often indiscriminate worshipping of letters 'of social significance.' Too often, indeed, the poets have been what Mr. Archibald MacLeish has so aptly called 'the camp-followers' of an ideology. The war, and the alignment of war has wrought havoc with the cut-and-dried intellectual compartments of the red robins, piping social significance.

Dr. E.J. Pratt is one of Canada's outstanding poets; it has been given to him to achieve the first memorable poetic utterance of this era. The poem *Dunkirk* is a short one; yet it has all the sweep and compass of an epic. Nor is this due merely because the theme is epical; it is the approach, the manner of treatment, the memorable phrase, the immortal thought which give to the work a longevity equal to the memory of Dunkirk itself. Here the author has caught, and penned in a phrase, revealed in a calculated understatement the spirit which stood the heroes of Dunkirk in such good stead, and which turned defeat into victory, disaster impending into glorious salvage. Here too Dr. Pratt has held up, in a line, in a stanza, the nature of the opponents, and here above all, he has evoked the great unbroken tradition of British fighting men, fighting the wickedness of the foe, and the impartial cruelty of the elements.

Pratt pays tribute to the outlook which came to life and power with the advent of Churchill and Bevin. 'Appeasement is in its grave,' and 'Honour,' to use the phrase of Rupert Brooke, 'walks in our ways again.'

> Churchill and Bevin have the floor,
> Whipping snarling nouns and action-verbs
> Out of their lairs in the lexicon,
> Bull-necked adversatives that bit and clawed,
> An age before gentility was cubbed.

Dr. Pratt is a poet of the sea; but he is not a maritime poet such as Mr. Masefield. Dr. Pratt's ships are not sailing boats; they are the mechanical leviathans of our generation. Throughout his writings Dr. Pratt shows a keen awareness of the scientific and mechanical aspects of contemporary life, aspects which the pedestrian mind considers essentially prosaic, but which the pen of Pratt reveals as of the same, indeed a greater grandeur than Homer's navigational catalogues. Dr. Pratt no doubt enjoys a tar's holiday when he begins to enumerate the types and kinds of vessels which participated in the relief of Dunkirk; the very names of the ships, the very names of the volunteers, Britons of all classes and walks of life, reads like a true cross-section of British life, terrene and maritime. To a landlubber like the writer, the tour-de-force is as overwhelming as – is that the phrase? – a strong nor'wester.

As for the character of battle, here is no chivalric gallantry, no Eton regulations, no Queensberry rules. The enemy is ruthless.

> Inside the brain of the planner
> No tolerance befogged the reason –
> The *reason* with its clear-swept halls,
> Its brilliant corridors,
> Where no recesses with their healing dusk

Offered asylum for a fugitive.

...

The bird's right to dodge the barrels on the wing,
The start for the hare,
The chance for the fox to cross his scent,
For the teeth to snap at the end of the chase,
Did not belong to this tally-ho.

...

The last civil rag was torn from the body of war –
The decencies had perished with the Stukas.

The Briton, however – including Dr. Pratt – still thinks, even at this writing, of the blood-thirsty struggle as a spring competition. One of his most powerful sections is called 'Regatta and Crew,' and here it is, in perhaps the finest lines of the entire poem, that he summarizes what may be called the 'British tradition.' It is achieved, it is true, by a conjuring with great names, but it is no mere incantation of abracadabra. He speaks of the dawn of time and those who had been 'as sacrifices upon the mortuary slabs of Stonehenge,'

of Caractacus
Taking his toll of the invaders
In his retreat to the fens and hills;
Boadicea,
The storming of Londinium and Verulamium,
And the annihilation of the Roman ninth.

'Social significance' there is, too:

They had fought the poll-tax and burned
The manor rolls under Ball and Tyler.
They had led the riots against the Enclosures.
They had sung ballads to the rhythms of the gibbets.
The welts had been around their necks and ankles.

The Adventurer – note the Morgan-mouthed alliteration – 'had carved with curse and cutlass Castilian grandees in the Caribbean.'

Freedom to them was like the diver's lust for air.
Children of oaths and madrigals,
They had shambled out of caves
To write the clauses of the Charters,

To paint the Channel mists,
To stand hushed before the Canterbury tapers.

One final quotation, a quotation which is an example of the epic theme treated in biblic style. Readers will no doubt remember the fortieth chapter of Job which in masterly and unforgettable language describes Leviathan. Because the weapons of this war are as the behemoth, it is thus that Dr. Pratt describes them:

Born on the blueprints,
They are fed by fire.
They grow their skin from carburized steel.
They are put together by cranes.
Their hearts are engines that do not know fatigue
In the perfection of their valves,
In the might of their systolic thrusts.
Their blood is petrol: Oil bathes their joints.
Their nerves are wire.

We recommend the book unreservedly to our readers. It is both an aesthetic achievement and a source of inspiration. It is proof paramount that patriotism and poetry – the cynics notwithstanding – are not incompatible concepts.

The Poetry of A.J.M. Smith

Review of *News of the Phoenix* by A.J.M. Smith   February 1944

It was with a self-immolating modesty that Smith, in his recent anthology, *The Book of Canadian Poetry*, prefaced his own poems with a biographical note so reticent of information that one gleaned from it only the knowledge that the poet-anthologist had been born and had not died. This well-bred restraint – of a piece with that chivalrous taciturnity which caused him also to omit the ages of the anthology's elder poetesses – does him serious injustice. While the work of other poets in the volume is heralded by paragraphs announcing their respective precedence in Canadian poetry, no such 'sennet heard without' announces the advent of Smith. Yet, for almost two decades Smith has been one of the major influences not only upon that sodality known as the Montreal Group, but upon all of the younger Canadian writers of verse. It is an influence which he has exerted through the medium of his essays in criticism, but more particularly through the example of his own craftsmanship. For no other poet of our country and our generation has been so faithful to the standards of his calling, and no other so self-critical. He has cut and polished his own texts until in their penultimate version – in his lifetime there is no ultimate one – they have shone 'like jewels on the stretched fore-finger of Time.' Never has he admitted any version of his verse to be the final one, always has he sought some new perfection, so that not merely the latest, but all of his poems, like his own skin, have grown with him. In Canadian poetry, he is, as Eliot said of Pound, il fabbro miglior – the better smith.

An appreciation of Smith's craftsmanship – his hammered gold on gold enamelling – is not to be taken, however, as underestimating the content and essence of his verse. It is true that Smith's poems are never editorial; he is sybilline, not megaphonic; but the purposefulness of his writing cannot be gainsaid. He has hewed to the aesthetic line with a consistency and a devotion which is reminiscent only of Rilke; he has taken for his themes the grand verities and not the minuscule ephemera; and he has written of them in a manner which is never dated, only with difficulty placed, and always inalien-ably personal. Himself he has taken his advice 'To a Young Poet'; in his work he has treasured, above all,

> ... the worth of a hard thing done
> Perfectly, as though without care.

But it is only the finished poem which looks as if it has been done 'without care.' The fact is that Smith's carelessness is studied, and his economy a planned one.

News of the Phoenix, Smith's long-awaited first volume, illustrates on every page this his fastidious manner, his subtle tone. Here, indeed, are a hundred felicities, each in its nature technical, but each serving the purpose of enhancing and intensifying the experience which prompted it. The rhyme-scheme of 'Two Sides of a Drum' – altogether a faultless thing – where 'blossom' is echoed by 'bosom,' and answered by 'dream' and finalized by 'drum' – the vibrating progression of oncoming sleep; 'Yet shadows I have seen, of me deemed deeper' – the effect of emphasis and contrast seems careless until one notices that here are four long e's, following one another, like a violin playing the same sweet note, loath to forsake it; the use of the present participle in 'Prothalamium'; the word 'girl' to designate the 'cold goddess Pride'; the sonnet on Proteus where the language itself becomes protean so that one grasps at a cornet only to discover it to be a coronet, a head only to find it a 'river-source'; his adjectives – unfailing touchstones – : ashen rain, gummy April, alluvial dreams; these, and many other instances, testify to a creative force, original in its conceptions, impeccable in its execution. They manifest, in their transmutation of ordinary sensitive reactions into extraordinary intellectual experience, that it is his own method which he urges upon 'The Christian Doctors,' a method

> Whose end it is to burn sensation's load
> With animal intensity, to Mind.

The poems in *News of the Phoenix*, though not arranged in any definite order, may be divided into three categories – metaphysical poems, poems of Greek inspiration, and, in a third group, poems of a strange new quality – of a hard-boiled classicism, an amalgam of Hellenic allusion, Elizabethan sonority, and vernacular cliché. Touching the first group, there is no doubt but that Smith, who under Professor Grierson had made a close study of the religious poets of the seventeenth century, has adapted the metaphysical manner and made it peculiarly his own. That there is in this *weltanschauung* something which is closely akin to that of the temper of our own age is evidenced, among other things, by the aptness with which Hemingway recently stole a sermon from Donne to point a contemporary moral. Smith, too, has found that he who preached 'from a cloud in Paul's' preached doctrine suitable to both his own ethics and aesthetics. Moreover, Smith is, albeit in no orthodox sense, of 'a true religious heart'; like a renaissance pope, he may or may not believe in God; but all His saints he venerates. It is the piety which endows with their effectiveness such poems as 'The Offices of the First and the Second Hour,' 'Calvary,' 'The Cry,' 'The Shrouding,' and above all, 'Good Friday' – one of the most poignant of religious poems, shaming the hymnals, and admirable, I believe, even to men of little faith.

Of the 'Hellenic' verse, it must be said forthwith that it is neither Keats nor Landor. Yet is it to the true Greek manner born. Thus, in 'Hellenica I,' there is, after the manner of the Greek Anthology, an antithesis, but unlike the Palatinate, it is an antithesis at second remove; for when 'swallows *swerving* over the waters of Mitylene,' recall 'the faint *curve* of Iope's sweet mouth,' it is sotto voce that the epigram is uttered. It is to be noted, too, that Smith's strictly Canadian poems – the paysage is unmistakable – are, in their economy of language and in their imagist precision, essentially Greek. They are

> sharpness cutting sharpness
> arrows of direction
> spears of speed.

The mise-en-scène, of course, is undeniably Canadian. It is the chorus which is Greek; which is to say that the maples are maples, and not maple-syrup.

To readers in search of new caviar, it will perhaps be the third group which will be found most interesting. It is in this group that we find such lines as: 'Or zero's shears at paper window-pane,' 'In minds as polite as a mezzanine floor,' 'The great black Othello of a thing is undone by the nice clean pockethandkerchief of 6 a.m.' For here Smith has taken the language of modern life and naturalized it into his classic lines. When, in 'A Portrait, and a Prophecy' symbolic phrases like 'love to the tiger' sit cheek by jowl with colloquial ones, like 'let the faults of youth go hang,' and when these suddenly culminate in

And now, by God! he has fallen in love with Penitence!

it is as if Dr. John Donne were speaking out of the corner of his mouth. The sentiment may perhaps be xviith century; the articulation is up-to-the-minute. Again, when in 'Ode: The Eumenides,' a mythological veil is thrown over a personal lyric, replete with such phrases as 'the bold front,' 'the bright line,' 'We have a date in another wood' (Nous n'irons plus au bois, les lauriers sont coupés), the effect is the same: a new frisson has been achieved; an ancient myth has been given new meaning. Nor is this technique adopted merely for the sake of novel confection; it has a purpose – to make feelings which in another context might be considered literary or romantic appear for what they are – true, realistic, a piece of vital experience.

Taken all in all, *News of the Phoenix* constitutes a historic contribution to Canadian letters. The record of an austere spirit, at once sensitive and intellectual, it marks the closest step a Canadian has taken towards a 'pure poetry,' a poetry which is pure yet does not live in a vacuum.

New Writers Series, No. 1

Review of *Here and Now* by Irving Layton   8 June 1945

For the past four years there has been functioning in the city of Montreal a group of young writers who, despite the double rationing of paper and talent which prevails in our Dominion, have managed periodically to publish a literary magazine which bears the modest and somewhat diffident title: *First Statement*. As if tomorrow there is likely to be an *Afterthought*. While this publication has not yet shattered the foundations of the earth, nor even, we fear, made a slight dent in the Laurentian plateau, it has already won the admiration of many who have been impressed by both the courage and logic of its editorial policy, a policy illustrated in the magazine's contents rather than manifested beneath its mast-head. Ambivalent, it is a policy which cherishes the Canadian tradition, but reserves the right to look critically upon the work of all of those who in the past have spoken in the name of that tradition; at the same time, it fosters the new and the creative, reserving, here again, the right to look critically upon that which has nothing but newness to recommend it, the merely novel, the pure fantastical. Steering a path between the Scylla of the c.a.a. and the Charybdis of the cults, its two capable pilots, John Sutherland and Irving Layton (with the help of its bos'n Louis Dudek, now of New York), have successfully piloted their craft, unescorted by dreadnoughts of philanthropy, through the forty-eight war-months of its life.

Now, encouraged by success achieved, and unabashed by the multitudes who are so sunk in darkness as to be unaware of its existence, *First Statement* has undertaken, in addition to its magazine, the publication, in book-form, of the work of a number of young Canadian writers. No. 1 in this series is the poetry of Irving Layton which, with emphatic up-to-dateness and accentuated indigenity, appears under the title *Here and Now*.

As was to be expected from the varied callings which, according to the book's jacket, Mr. Layton has followed – busboy, waiter, insurance agent, salesman, clerk, boxing instructor, proofreader, and B.Sc. (Agr.) Macdonald College, – his hereness and nowness are both filled with versatility and adventure. This sense of adventure, spiced with a refreshing cynicism, and enhanced by our city's local colour, Layton admirably communicates to his poems. Like the admirers of Sir Christopher Wren, one has only to look about one to see this volume's table of contents. (Is that why the table is omitted?) A gent's furnishing store, a restaurant de luxe, a boarding house, De Bullion Street, the waterfront, the Jewish fishmarket, his own vocations, – all, so near, so dear, are subject for his writing, and to all he brings a keen perception, a sensitive personality, an active intelligence, and a fine literary skill. The result is that there are some poems in this volume which are classics of their kind. 'Newsboy' is one, its companion-piece 'Proofreader' another; the epigrams, too, show Layton at his forte – observation followed by laconic explosiveness.

As for Layton's talent, it manifests itself, even in his poorer poems, by the telltale phrase, the signature locution. Describing the stock-in-trade of a newsboy, he grandiloquizes his plebeian métier into something rich and Marlovian:

> For him the mitred cardinals sweat in
> Conclaves domed; the spy is shot. Empiric;

> And obstreperous confidant of kings,
> Rude despiser of the anonymous,
> Danubes of blood wash up his bulletins ...

Or, again, in the same tone:

> For at my back daily the compositors –
> Aproned morticians that with lacquered sticks
> Lay out the columns like coffins – hammer
> Upon the bones of heretics, martyrs,
> Nepmen and the conquerors ...

These, surely, are lines which give to things contemporary a grandeur Elizabethan. They make, because sifted through the poet's imagination, illuminated by his insights, poetry out of what nine out of ten would consider material crass and prosaic. It is this same very personal view which sees a street as 'reptilian ... whose scaly limbs are crooked stairways,' or notices, of a watch, 'that the gold shine *wets* his cheeks,' or observing how fatal are the consequences of geometry as utilized in death-dealing instruments, remarks 'I marvel how Lord Euclid's dream can stiffen a boy.'

This last quotation, indeed, illustrates a technique which Layton uses with most telling effect – the technique of 'the coiled phrase.' This is usually a concept expressed in words which at first reading looks innocent enough – that is, if innocence consists in saying what one means – but upon second examination, and this is not a matter of time but of mental reflexes, upon second examination it springs at the reader with meanings hitherto unsuspected. Because of their suddenness, moreover, they strike with added impact. Certainly it is only after analysis and reflection that one can find the association between Lord Euclid and a war casualty. Similarly, in 'Stolen Watch,' the lines

> Behind the limp and legless coats
> His heart races the seal's

first involve hesitation in the search for meaning, followed suddenly, with eureka-joy, by the shock of recognition.

This is not to give the impression that Layton is abstruse and esoteric. He is just not simple. When, however, he wishes to convey an image with immediacy, he knows how. 'Minutes drop like dandruff' ... 'Suburban Westmount that squats upon a slum' ... 'Barns [seen from a moving train] collapse like real estate models.' In all of these locutions, the imaginative fiat has worked to put the reader behind the eyeballs of the poet.

Mr. Layton, as has no doubt been already suspected both from some of the titles of his poems and the multiplicity of his callings, is a Jew. It is regrettable that this particular aspect of Layton's heritage is the theme only of two of the poems published in this volume, one of which is unworthy of inclusion, and the other clearly shows what sombre richness this orebody can offer to Layton's prospecting:

> Old Jews with memories of pogroms
> Shuffle across menacing doorways;
> They go fearfully, quietly.
> They do not wish to disturb
> The knapsack of their sorrows.

Perhaps Layton's Jewishness manifests itself more in his approach to a subject than in the subject itself. Nothing illustrates this better than the neat cerebration with which he fashions his epigrams, the pilpulistic antitheses, the wit double-jointed. Thus, with unconcealed pleasure he chisels a stone for a wit:

> O you who read my epitaph,
> Approve this final jest and laugh;
> For if I stood where now stand you,
> Believe me, friend, I would laugh too.

This is a first volume of verse; as such, it of necessity shows some of the symptoms of the primiparous. Thus, in 'Returning with an Annual Passion,' a poem about April, Layton concludes:

> April winds suck buds, and Christ,
> Christ in a fox-hole
> Cannot save my soul.

It does seem to us that the evocation of Christ, in the poem of a Jew, and of one who is described as 'Marxist in outlook,' lacks conviction.

But these are trivia. *Here and Now* reveals an unmistakable talent, a power of expression which is unique and personal, and a social awareness which endows poetic utterance with base and substance. Layton can certainly take his place in the Canadian pleiad, not like a twinkling little star, but as one of unquestioned brightness and constancy.

Writing in Canada

A Reply to a Questionnaire   22 February–1 March 1946

Dear Raymond Souster,

I am delighted to join your socratic symposium. I love quizzes. It is my vocational disease; no doubt the result of early exposure to the techniques of cross-examination. In fact, it is everybody's disease: for always at our backs we hear the graphs and chartings galluping near. Your five-pointed catechism, moreover, is, I think, particularly timely now; for all will agree that now, as we stand on the threshold, or precipice, of some kind of new era – atomic or atomicate – self-examination is a proper penultimate discipline. And such an examination, of course, must include that consideration of both the influence and the ideologies of the serious writers in our country, to which you direct yourself. Gladly entering your antiphony, I ponder the responses.

1. *From your own experience would you say that the audience for serious writing has appreciably increased in Canada over the past five years?*

You will agree with me, no doubt, that the absence from the question of a definition of 'serious writing' constitutes a serious semantic oversight. I presume that it was intended that the symposiacs should furnish their own critical apparatus, should bring along, as to a symposium they ought, their own bonded liquor. For the purposes of this question, therefore, I take 'serious writing' to mean writing which is designed to satisfy more than the merely seasonal interest, writing that either sensitively reflects significant experience, or better still, that in itself constitutes such experience, writing, in a word, that may enter the corpus of lasting literature. Obviously I exclude the publishers' puff-ball, the Book of the Week; hammock literature – the novel which is concerned either with the gematria of the unsolved murder or with the geometry of the recurrent love-triangle; verse written in support of National Loans; poesy that versifies slogans or puts party eloquence into rhyme; – all of them, in a sense, serious writing, deadly serious – but not in the sense in which I understand your question. Now, whether the Canadian public has, during the last lustrum, begun to hunger for such writing, it is difficult for me to tell; first, because they have not had much on which to satisfy such hunger, if it existed; and second, because the accurate answer to such a question can be gleaned only from publishers' account books, and not from casual observation.

This, however, I will state: Canadians to-day are more inclined to receive serious writing than they ever were before. Two causes have militated toward this end. First, the experience of the last war, which brought everyone closer – excuse the expression – to the eternal verities; witness the spate of religious tracts – Maugham's *Razor*, Huxley's *Time Must Have a Stop*, Douglas's *Robe*, Asch's *Apostle*, Isherwood's *Vedas* – which sought to evangelize our generation; and, second, the position which Canada now occupies in world affairs, a position which brings with it a sense of importance, strength, confidence – the twentieth century, as Laurier prophesied, may yet be ours. (Whatever that means.) Certainly our geography has changed; geopolitics has converted our country from a flanking colony to a central state. Our national economy, too, has been altered; we are no longer concerned merely with what we can grow, but also with what we can make. Our physical make-up is different; once we were a land which consisted only of a double spinal column, our two railways; the air-plane has since provided ribs and girth. In international affairs, too, we have grown; our diplomats speak modestly of a Middle-Power. We are even worth spying upon. All has changed; our sinews, our muscles, our thinking; only the voice, as yet, is not commensurate with the body.

2. Have you tended to be influenced by English writers rather than American writers? And which of the two do you think is the healthiest influence for Canadians?

I have never really made a distinction – except for the Customs department – between the one and the other. I have considered all English writing – Australian, South African, Canadian, and American – H.L. Mencken to the contrary notwithstanding – as a single entity. They all stem from the same tradition, though each is subjected, of course, to local modification. The distinction between them is neither linguistic nor cultural (except for philologists who think that the difference between a lift and an elevator is schismatic), the distinction is merely political, organizational. Can one, without benefit of biography, distinguish between a poem written by T.S. Eliot before his British naturalization, and one after? Ah, in Britain Eliot got religion. So Auden got it in America. Churchill's mingling of the waters of the Thames and the Mississippi was not, it seems to me, mere rhetorical hyperbole.

As for myself, I am influenced – forward or backward – by everything I read, or see. I do not distinguish reading from living; that mirror metaphor is phoney. A writer speaking to me from print – if he's a good writer – is as real as himself in the flesh; and often more acceptable; I don't have to take the worse with the better. I get the silk and throw the worm away. Moreover, since what I seek is the human, I do not confine myself to writing English or American. The good Lord granted the gift of speech also to others – for example – in a bilingual country this may be mentioned – also to the French.

I cannot leave this question without noting that the term 'healthier influence' is an irrelevancy. There are no influences characterized by place of origin which can be deemed either healthy or unhealthy. In the final analysis, a writer gets influenced by those things which do best harmonize with his own temperament. For Milton even Hebrew influence was healthy.

3. *Do you consider it important in your writing to stress Canadian backgrounds, with a definite reference to cities, streets, place-names, etc.?*

The very form of the question, I must say, exposes the naiveté of the philosophy of those who go out of their way to *stress* Canadian backgrounds. The writer who is concerned with his writing, and not with his passport, neither stresses nor ignores that background; inevitably, if he is honest and sensitive, it will emerge in the totality of his work. This business of indicating longitudes and postal addresses is a procedure so superficial that far from stressing the Canadian background, it merely caresses it. Not in this way does one give a literature a national identity; in this way one writes only Baedekers.

If the question means: Should the Canadian writer write about the Canadian scene? the answer is, Of course, if he feels so impelled to write. But it is what he writes which will interest us in him as a writer, and not the emergent fact of his Canadian citizenship. Nor need he be any the less Canadian because his short story has failed to mention Yonge Street, or his poem the Laurentians. Shakespeare – I do not mean to conjure with big names, but he illustrates my point – Shakespeare is not mistaken for a Venetian because he laid a scene upon the Rialto. This serious writer, in fact, is only incidentally interested in geography, as when he gives Bohemia seacoasts. What a Czech nationalist he would have made! Nonetheless, no one – with the exception of some German professors – will question his Englishry; and, of course, when the Bard was so moved, he 'referred' to Sherwood Forest. But the play was the thing, not the forest.

Was Dante – since I am dealing with the big shots – was Dante, who gave his countrymen speech, a poor Italian because he wrote of purgatories and not peninsulas? I venture to say that even in that remote work, he was palpably Italian, and this not simply because he peopled hell with Florentines.

The proper study of mankind is Man – not paysage. Paysage is important only insofar as it affects the man upon it; but Man, he is the measure. The literature emanating from Windsor, Ont. – you will agree with me – cannot be very different from that of Detroit, Mich. You may object, however: The literature of New Orleans will certainly be different from Windsor's. And I agree. As different as Windsor's from that of Dawson City, or Yamachiche, or Louisiana's from that of Oregon. To make writing rotate about geography, rather than admit geography as one of the many aspects of the creative process – is to pervert the purpose of our craft. Also, it leads to comic conclusions, as when one gathers from the opera of Kipling, first, that this is the best of all worlds, second, that in it the British Empire is the best of all possible Empires, third, that in the said Empire, England is the best of all possible countries, and fourth, that in the aforementioned England, Sussex, and only Sussex, is the earthly paradise. Love of one's environment, I admit, is a laudable and highly convenient virtue; but about it, one builds, at best, only minor literature. For a factitiously nationalist – reference to cities, streets, etc. – literature must inevitably end up by being parochial.

How, then, does a national character emerge in a literature? Mainly, I think, through the force of character, the personality of its writers; and for this emergence, it is necessary only that they possess talent. A tremendous *only*. Wanting that, not all the city directories or geographical surveys, will succeed in giving their work a Canadian, or Torontonian, or North-West, or, indeed, *any* character. Possessing that, the author's novel about a Mr. X. moving in an unnamed country may be received, quite properly, as an honorable addition to our literature.

Am I to be taken as saying that the Canadian, to assert his humanity, ought to eschew the theme purely Canadian? I put the question only to afford myself the opportunity of repudiating its suggestion. Neither peace nor war, neither eschew nor sedulously seek out. The writer's argument, if I may use an old-fashioned word, wells up from his temperament, his interest, the things that do inwardly move or trouble him. Excepting one who is motivated by a desire to please an already-organized claque, or to conform to a previously-prepared criticism, in vacuo, as it were – the writer's, the honest writer's conformities are incidental, accidental, and not of the essence.

It well may be – and I look forward to its demonstration – that a writer may be prompted to choose his Canadian subject so that his universal attitudes, since confined to a given locale, may be accentuated the more. The problem of man's aloneness on the face of the earth – is there a better milieu for its exposition than our wide grain-filled or snow-filled spaces? Man's relationship to his different fellow – a bilingual culture seems made to order for such a theme! The universal desire for adventure, conquest over nature – we who sit on the roof of the world ought to be able to see further these possibilities than others. The new orientation of geography, an orientation which makes us neighbor to the hitherto remote, which emphasizes the oneness of this globe – the dialectic comes around full circle – is also ironically enough, a Canadian theme! But whatever the writing, it will be its seriousness, and not its local color, which will give it whatever character it may have.

I can not leave this question without referring to an occasion when this pseudo-regionalism, this doctrine of autochthonous picturesqueness, was, quite unconsciously, brought to its *reductio ad absurdum*. This happened at the last convention of the Canadian Authors' Association where a gentleman, and no doubt a scholar, delivered a paper on – *Canadian Poetry and the Tourist Trade!*

4. Are you satisfied with the standard of reviewing in Canada? Do you feel that commercialism has invaded the literary field to a highly dangerous degree?

The term 'invaded,' I must say, is here, not quite *le mot juste*. It implies that until a certain date the field of literary criticism was occupied by other than commercial reviewers. This is an inexactitude. Apart from the occasional annual survey of letters in Canada, and the occasional review in *The Canadian Forum* and the little mags, there is no literary criticism in Canada.

Examine the book pages of our leading metropolitan newspapers. These journals, after all, wield a much greater influence – via circulation – than do the more fastidious periodicals sans A.B.C. rating. And what do these reviews consist of? Pure unadulterated verbiage, mere bubbling blurb; no literary discrimination, no standards, certainly no literary conscience. Often, in fact, the reviews of two different books are practically interchangeable. One paean is as good as another – both lack relevance to the book discussed. I say paeans, because most of the reviews, with rare exception, are laudatory – and for good and ignoble reason. The reviewer, it soon appears, is working hand in hand with the bookseller; every time his leading review is published, behold, as if by inspired coincidence, an ad from the local bookseller, announcing, with a suitable quote from the reviewer, the said book's qualities as mighty 'must' literature. The critic, obviously, is assisting, not the reader, but the merchant; he has consented to abdicate his position as censor of letters to take up the function of expediter of inventories.

Now such criticism – whether prompted by a desire for co-operation between the literary arts and the business techniques, or moved, impurely and not simply, by financial considerations – is not criticism. It is log-rolling, copy-writing, huckstering, book-selling, anything – but it is not criticism.

Consider it: we have, at this date, no outstanding literary critic in Canada. I except A.J.M. Smith's literary estimates in his *Book of Canadian Poetry* and E.K. Brown's essays on the same subject. But the writings of these men are in no way in a position to compete with the sickening clichés and meaningless laudations of the contemporary book-reviewing press. Perhaps it is a naive question, but who is our Edmund Wilson, who our T.S. Eliot?

There are, of course, factors other than commercialism which militate against an adequate Canadian criticism. One of these is provincialism – provincialism of a different kind from that adverted to above, but still, its natural corollary – a provincialism which, either through obtuseness or wilfulness, segregates itself from the more advanced literary influences. The poetry of

Dylan Thomas or of T.S. Eliot still evoke the fatuous sneer in the contemporary press. *Ulysses, the* masterpiece of our century – note how Joyce has made a saecular pattern out of a single day, a spatial universe out of the environs of Dublin – is still not legally purchaseable in our country. And there is, finally, a pervasive scorn which is directed against men of letters by men of affairs. At best – such seems to be the attitude of the manager – those writing fellows are employables – to be employed by advertising agencies, or bureaux of information; here, at least, they may be useful for the higher purposes of national enterprise; for the rest, God save my son from becoming a writer. That kind of stuff, he maintains, is for the wife. Indeed, he seems to proclaim a combined feminist-democratic principle for writing – of women, by women, for women.

Is this, you ask, dangerous? To have great poets, said Walt Whitman, and *Poetry Magazine* has repeated it for over twenty years – to have great poets, one must have great audiences. On the Canadian scene, both the audience and its greatness are as yet, mere potentialities. And our critics are not doing much to convert the potential to the actual.

5. *What Canadian writer do you think has best expressed the Canadian consciousness? Are there any writers you would name as having been undeservedly neglected through public apathy or poor critical judgment?*

Considering my earlier remarks about the Canadian 'consciousness,' I am at a loss to answer your question. I do not think that we have yet arrived, in writing, at a 'Canadian consciousness.' Thus far all we have had is a Canadian subconsciousness – made up of colonialism, Victorianism, etc. – and that has been illustrated, not expressed – it takes more skill to express the subconsciousness than the consciousness – by all our organized bardlings and psittacean rhapsodists. As for the neglected – you wring an agony out of my heart – aren't we all? Is there one writer upon whom the Canadian public dotes, whom it delights to honor, whom it laureates and subsidizes, while all the others look on, envious and unappeased? There is none. The apathy of our public is general and impartial; when it abandons that impartiality, it does so only to neglect one more than the other. You will forgive me if I resist the temptation to draw up a hierarchic list of the rejected. These 'pitches of littleness,' as the Anglo-Saxon purist could call them, are not to my taste.

A Curse on Columbus

Review of *Jews Without Money* by Michael Gold   18 April 1930

Judging by the products of a prolific press, the Jew is becoming a literary vogue. Novelist and historian, essayist and biographer, all who can blithely tattoo a typewriter have begun to toy with Semitic heroes. The brothers Tharaud, for example, have developed a prosperous custom for that literary museum of theirs, wherein the Jew is picturesque wax-work and pathetic anachronism. Books about the Jews, like the Jews themselves in Egypt, have fructified and multiplied and filled the land. An avid public, eager to devour the curiosities of this peculiar people, insists that the writer betake himself to the Jew. Three million introspective Hebrews, moreover, assure the magnum opus a success. Two types of literature have thus been developed – on the one hand a literature that seriously attempts to discern the intriguing psychology of our people, that studies the temperament behind the gesticulation, that analyses customs, not costumes; and on the other hand a supercilious literature that from a lofty pedestal surveys the nation of rag-pickers, emphasizes antic instead of gesture, and in discussing the Jew has to go slumming.

Michael Gold's book is of the first type; to study his characters he does not have to go to the slums – he lives there. His knowledge of New York's East Side has not been fleetingly gleaned from a sight-seeing bus; he was brought up in vulgar intimacy with Chrystie Street, and New York is his step-motherland. It is because the metropolis has been so familiar and yet so strange to him, that the very title of his book flaunts a challenge. The Sombartian economist who imagines that every Jew is intimately associated with Pluto and Plutocracy, stands confounded before the jacket which weeps – Jews without money; the anti-Semite who pictures this folk as lilies that toil not, neither do they spin, yet go arrayed like Solomon in all his glory, receives a shock at the idea of a penniless Hebrew; and the average man who believes that Jews study calculus from the cradle, and that every little Abie lisps in numbers for the numbers come, is amazed at the sight of this East Side poorhouse. For here are paupers in a golden land and here penury stalks in a hundred shapes.

Despite the fact that he was brought up in a Jewish home, Michael Gold seems to know more about its social condition that about its ethnic customs. Judaica seems to be a closed book to him, or rather a book rarely opened. When he describes a feast where cheese blintzes and chicken are eaten at the same table, we suspect serious heresy, and when he speaks of the three Passover nights and their banquets, we wonder at the ultra-piety; when he explains that the Zaddiks are descended from the Thirty-Six Wise Men of Israel, we feel that he is confusing *Chassid* with *Lamed Vav-nik*, and when he declares that the *Chassidim* revolted some three hundred years ago, we are skeptical of his chronology. But even Homer nods, so why blame Mike if he takes an occasional literary nap?

After all, to know Jews, one does not necessarily have to swallow the *Shulchan Aruch*. And Gold knows his Jews; he knows their thoughts and he knows their language. He has, moreover, rendered this language into English in such a way that it lives with very brightness. Such delightful anathema as 'may his nose be eaten by pox,' or 'may the worms find him,' such Semitic similes as 'he swelled up like a turkey,' 'he was sapped dry as a herring,' and such a vivid epithet as 'iron frost' – all direct translations from the Yiddish, endow the book with a native and poetic vigour. Gold has learned not only to infuse a Jewish spirit into his writing, but he also has learned to write English. His previous books have been written as badly as Upton Sinclair's; his present one shows style and strength, marred by no moralizing, no pro-letarian propaganda, save in obiter dicta and in apostrophes à la Bodenheim. Nonetheless, there are certain constructions that betray him: 'nostrils like a camel,' 'they lived in the slime and horror of the trenches, knowing why as little as soldiers,' – with what gloating pleasure the pedant would draw his red pencil through this. We pass them over for the greater and more fun-damental aspects of the book.

The characters are splendidly done; the story, if there is one, is una-dornedly yet effectively told. No one with discrimination can read this book and thereafter continue to mouth capitalistic clichés. The Shakespearian will lay it aside with a sense of something rotten in the state of Denmark, and the Jew will shrug his shoulders and sigh, 'Ach, America.'

The Jew in English Poetry   March 1932

The theory that the English are the Ten Lost Tribes, a theory supported by the flimsy suppositions that Saxon is allegedly Isaacson, that British is *Ish Brit* (Man of the Covenant), and that the House of Windsor is descended from the House of David, finds equally flimsy confirmation in the fact that English literary men, up to the modern period, have treated the Jew with that vilifying meanness which one only accords a poor relative. There is hardly a reference to Jews of the pre-expulsion date which does not repeat, at least in paraphrase, that delightful tid-bit of the monkish chronicler who spoke about 'dogs and their vomit.'

And in this, Christian literature was a true mirror of Christian life. The Jews, who together with the cream of English aristocracy can boast that they came over with the Conqueror, had hardly been in the country for eight decades when the first ritual blood accusation was levelled against them in Norwich. Richard, who slandered the beast when he dubbed himself Lion-hearted, celebrated his marriage with a massacre of Jews who came bringing him wedding gifts. John Lackland, the monarch who signed Magna Charta, combined his Department of Public Health with his Chancellory of the Exchequer when he extracted the teeth (healthy) of Abraham of Bristol in an effort to make the latter cough up 60,000 marks. In 1219, Stephen Langton, Archbishop of Canterbury, instituted dress reform among Jews with the imposition of the historic badge. As a gratifying exception, we hear that King Henry in a special charter declared the oath of one Jew equivalent to that of twelve Christians. This seemingly inexplicable compliment becomes clear when we realize that the Jews occupied a position akin to that of the king's tax-gatherers.

Throughout this period English literature consisted mainly of legal documents in which the Jew usually played the unpopular role of creditor. The Star Chamber, so notorious in history, derives its name from the Hebrew *Shtar*, a deed. This function in society exercised by Jews certainly did not tend to render them beloved among the pawning masses, and even His Majesty, usually the protector of Jews, his chattels, was beginning to alienate his affections. The final divorce, a canonic one, came when Edward the Confessor, combining piety with profit, cleansed his Christian state of Jews, and confiscated their property.

The most scurrilous attacks upon Jews in English literature occurred when the Jews were unknown in England. Chaucer, whom Tennyson calls 'the first warbler of sweet breath,' set the tradition. In his Prioress' Tale, this is how he warbled:

> Amonge Cristen folk, a Jewerye
> For foul usure and lucre vilanye ...

or

> Our firste foe, the serpent Sathanas
> That hath in Jewes heart his waspes nest.

The story is of how the Jews did murder innocent Hugh of Lincoln, how they were discovered, and how his slit throat sang piously:

Therefor with wilde hors he did them [the Jews] draw
And after that he hang them by the lawe.

But Chaucer, be it said in justice, was no fanatic. He realized that even among his own brethren practice did not harmonize with theory. His pen therefore slips into this confession:

This abbot which that was an holy man
As monkes been, or elles oughten be ...

The Morality Plays, which followed later, drew their main topics from the Bible, and it sounds somewhat ludicrous to read in them of how the patriarchs, Abraham, Isaac and Jacob, spoke with a perfect and almost prophetic knowledge of Christian theology. The only Jews who could ever be admitted to the virtues of Christianity, according to these plays, seem to be dead ones.

The chief crime with which later literature charges Jews is that of usury, a practice into which Jews were driven by their exclusion from almost all other trades, but which is certainly contrary to all Hebraic ethics. The Bible prohibits interest; and the Talmud places the usurer on a level with the pervert and blasphemer.

It may be noted, however, that whereas no Jews were in England between 1290 and 1648 at least, there were acts passed against usury in England in 1487, 1546, 1552, and 1571; and then in 1578 a Royal Commission still had to be appointed to investigate. In the same year, however, Euphues set the fashion by using the word 'Jew' contemptuously. With reference to the practice of making verbs out of nationalities, we mention in passing, the repartee of the Hebrew who was accused by an American of attempting to 'Jew him down,' that he would not have done so had the other not sought to 'Yank him up.'

The man who glorified this accusation into a classic was Kit Marlowe, who saved himself from being hanged (a warrant was out for his arrest) by being killed in a drunken brawl. He created in his 'Jew of Malta' a monster by the name of Barabbas (note the reprehensible reference) who incarnated all the vices then known to civilization. The play is full of all the melodramatic props of the era: forged letters, blackmail, murdered friars, disguised musicians, poisoned rice, secret nunneries, seething cauldrons, rebellious daughters, etc. Barabbas, indeed, is so wicked that the Talmud does not suffice him for knavish quotations, and the Jew has to resort to Latin, as a philosophy of life: 'Ego mihimet semper proximus' – I am my best friend. The only way in which Barabbas is different from the general bogey-man conception of the Jew, his only individuality, indeed, is that his nose is not crooked; with an inspiration of originality, Marlowe made him 'Bottle-nosed.'

In Shakespeare, apart from his Merchant of Venice, there are only about six references to Jews. It is the play of the myriad-minded one, however, which has most puzzled the commentators. It is said that the reason for the work was the fact that Lopez, a Jew and physician to Queen Elizabeth, had recently been executed. Nonetheless it seems surprising that Shakespeare should have undertaken to write a play prejudicial to a nation whose members he knew not, nor ever saw. Coleridge, great Shakespeare scholar, and friend of the Jews, from whom he always borrowed ideas, but never money, omitted this play from his lectures on Shakespeare.

The play, however, seems to have been written hurriedly to meet popular demand, and was in fact modelled upon Marlowe. Despite the fact that near-divinity hedges Shakespeare, critics have pointed out numerous flaws in this work. The law of the pound of flesh is derived from the Roman Law of the Twelve Tables, and not from Jewish law. Shakespeare, though laying his scene on the Rialto, knew nothing about the laws of Venice. The court scene, in which everyone seems to forget Venetian Law, is guilty, not of injustice, but of crass stupidity. Shakespeare's speech: 'Hath not a Jew eyes ...' is hardly the thing Shylock would have argued, for the same plea, even to the detail of laughter, can be made of a hyena. Shakespeare too errs in Judaica and in composition when he sends Shylock to eat with a Christian, even after Shylock had, in a previous act, declared: 'I will not eat with you.' That Lancelot Gobbo should be Shylock's servant is also inexplicable inasmuch as Jews were not allowed to employ Christian servants. Furthermore, Lancelot is hardly the person to have around in the same house as the beauteous Jessica. Moreover, the court scene does not speak well for Christian solidarity, for whereas it appears that Antonio could get none of his friends to loan him the money to pay his debt, even when he is on the verge of losing a pound of flesh, Tubal and Shylock stand by one another throughout the play. And finally, Shakespeare defeats his own purpose, for in the end Shylock is unconsciously made out to be a martyr.

In 1611 there appeared the King James authorized version of the Bible. This book, more than any other, has exerted an influence upon the thought and diction of the English people. Its idiom has become part of the language, and its typically Hebraic philosophy has moulded English minds. In the nineteenth century when a Jew translated Shakespeare into Hebrew, this is what Peretz Smolenskin wrote: 'The English took our Bible and translated it into all the languages of the world; we in revenge have taken their Shakespeare and translated it into the Hebrew language.'

John Milton, 'the God-gifted organ-voice of England,' was thoroughly imbued with Hebraic sentiment and erudition. He could read Hebrew, and rendered into English verse Psalms 80–88. He wrote a poem on circumcision. Blind, it was only in the geography of the Bible that he travelled with ease. Of his *Paradise Lost*, Nahum Sokolow writes: 'This most glorious cosmological epic of the world's literature could have been written only by a man who knew the Bible by heart and whose verse, when he so chose, could consist solely of combinations of texts from the Bible or images influenced by biblical ideas.'

The year 1648 is memorable in Jewish history for three events: the Messianic announcement of Shabbathai Zvi; the massacres of Chmelnitzki; and the negotiations between Manasseh ben Israel, a Dutch Jew, and Oliver Cromwell for the re-admission of Jews into England. One of the curious arguments which Manasseh used was the fact that the millenium, according to biblical prophecy, would come only then when the Jews were dispersed all over the world; they were now almost all over the world, even in America; one had merely to allow the Jews into England to complete the dispersion, and usher in the millenium in which Cromwell and his Puritans devoutly believed. Nothing definite came of these discussions, but in 1657 we already read of a Jewish cemetery in London.

John Dryden's poetry is replete with biblical references and knowledge of Jewish customs. His political poem 'Absalom and Achitophel' flogs English institutions with the cat-o'-nine-tails of biblical verse. He comments thus:

> But when the chosen people grew more strong
> The rightful cause at length became the wrong ...

or

> In Israel's courts ne'er sat an ab-beth-din
> With more discerning eyes or hands more clean.

Alexander Pope was much interested in the Hebraic theme. His poem 'Messiah' has been translated into Hebrew by Hogan, who had been a censor of the Hebrew press in Russia, and who became an apostate in England. Pope's other works have but passing references to Jews; thus –

> On her white breast a sparkling cross she wore
> Which Jews might kiss, and infidels adore

or

> out-usure Jews or Irishmen out-swear.

Shelley, apart from a chance remark on the Wandering Jew, expresses his generally anti-semitic sentiments in 'Swellfoot the Tyrant':

Call in the Jews, Solomon the court porkman,
Moses the sow-gelder, and Zephaniah
The hog-butcher.

But these epithets of Shelley's were not born of any prejudice against
Jews. It was merely his radicalism which prompted him to express himself in
the above terms, for Shelley was like the Emperor Frederick – he believed
that Jesus, Mohammed and Moses were all alike, imposters ...

Wordsworth has written several poems about Jews of a sympathetic but
sentimental nature. It is to Byron that, as Sokolow avers, Zionist poetry owes
more than to any other Gentile poet. His poetic drama *Cain* draws its poetic
inspiration from the Bible and his 'Hebrew Melodies,' which are among the
most popular of his poems, were written to music composed by his Jewish
friend Isaac Nathan, from whom he used to receive 'seasonal bequests in the
form of *matzo*.' Byron's great sympathy for the Jews, as for other oppressed
people (the Greeks, for example), is evident from the lines:

Tribes of the wandering foot and weary breast,
How shall ye flee away, and be at rest!
The wild-dove hath her nest, the fox his cave,
Mankind his country – Israel but the grave!

Keats has but one reference to Jews and that lives up, as his entire work
does, to Elizabethan tradition:

Like two close Hebrews in the inspired land.

As for Coleridge, the nearest he came to writing on Jewish themes was
that he contemplated an epic on the destruction of Jerusalem. However, he
satisfied his ambition by translating into bad English the worse Hebrew of
Hyman Horowitz's elegy on the death of Princess Charlotte.

Tennyson, in whose work the biblical influence is very apparent, used
to read the Bible in the original. In her journal of 1867, Lady Tennyson writes:
'Alfred is reading Hebrew, Job, Song of Songs, and Genesis.' Browning, too,
was thoroughly steeped in Hebraic lore as do witness his poems 'Holy Cross
Day,' 'Ben Karshook's Wisdom' and 'Rabbi Ben Ezra.' Some of his Hebrew,
however, is astonishing and Browning owed his familiarity with it to a little-
read edition of the *Itinerary of Benjamin of Tudela*.

Through the centuries the treatment which Jews have received at the
hands of English poets has continually improved. The accusation of usury has
entirely disappeared, and with it the entire literature which battened on it.

The true English spirit is much more manifest, culturally and politically, in the prophetic lines of William Blake:

> I will not cease from mental fight
> Nor shall my sword sleep in my hand
> Till we have built Jerusalem
> In England's green and pleasant land.

Robinson Jeffers – Poet-Fascist?

Review of *Be Angry at the Sun* by Robinson Jeffers   6 February 1942

Mr. Robinson Jeffers is in many quarters deemed to be America's outstanding poet. Even Miss Edna St. Vincent Millay, no mean Sappho herself, accords to the hermit of the California coast, the laurels of pre-eminence. This tribute, it is readily admitted, is not surprising; Mr. Jeffers' vigor of diction and violence of opinion are such that they cannot fail to draw attention always, admiration often. Pre-occupied with elemental nature – the sea, the wind, the stars – and not in a sentimental authors-association fashion – the verse of Robinson Jeffers is itself characterized by elemental strength. Whitmanesque only in the shape of his lines, the content of his writing is much more powerful than anything the good bearded democrat ever wrote.

Indeed, there is about the work of this bard a quality which can only be called aristocratic; far from the madding crowd, and fleeing what Chaucer called 'the presse,' Robinson Jeffers keeps himself confined, not to any ivory tower, but to a real one, made of rocks drawn from the mount on which he dwells, and builded by himself. Here, monarch of all he surveys, the poet communes with the great forces of Nature – not in any Wordsworthian sense – and breathing the pure air of his altitudes, and thinking the great thoughts of his solitude, he looks down upon the lesser breed below, and adopts, with reference to their fate, an attitude of Olympian aloofness, the godly unconcern about the destiny of mere workers. It is no doubt pure coincidence, but this hawk-faced man has chosen as his most frequent ornithological image the hawk, which rises to heights, and looks upon 'the other birds' as no more than winged edibles.

It is in his latest book, *Be Angry at the Sun*, that this Nietzschean complex comes to the fore. Here his writing is based upon the premise that the poet is bound to think only in eternities – like God – and that therefore, the pain and agony of war or social revolution are simply laws of Nature, and but another example of the mysterious workings of Providence. In vain will the reader look for some touch of sympathy, some suspicion of fellow-feeling in the references to the holocaust about him. What is the individual, compared to the cosmic history? Jeffers will not condescend to think in terms of anything less than cosmic. Accordingly, it follows that the duty of the poet in this day and age, is to be a spectator – and if he is located on top of a high hill where he can get a better and more comfortable view – why, so much the better for him. Like Nietzsche, he is 'Beyond Good and Evil.'

To tell the truth, it is difficult sometimes to surmise whether Jeffers' poems on the present war are prompted by pacifism – that he hates the shedding of blood – or by an ultra-militarism – there is not enough shed to please him. Confusion of thought, indeed, is apparent in more than one instance. Consider this of 'Great Men,' sentiments admirably expressed – but what sentiments:

> Consider greatness.
> A great man must have a following, whether he gain it
> Like Roosevelt by grandiose good intentions, cajolery
> And public funds, or like Hitler by fanatic
> Patriotism, frank lies, genius and terror.

To Jeffers apparently there is no difference between the two men, save in the means which they used to achieve power; and of the means employed, Hitler's seem to be the more laudable!

In fact, Adolf seems to have a sincere admirer in the great 'American' poet. Writing on September 19, 1939 – after the rape of Austria, and the mutilation of Czechoslovakia and during the onslaught upon Poland – he says:

> This morning Hitler spoke in Danzig, we heard his voice.
> A man of genius: that is, of amazing
> Ability, courage, devotion, cored on a sick child's soul.

Do you note the thrill in 'We heard his voice,' and the compassionate pity in 'cored on a sick child's soul'? Goebbels could not have done better.

It is no wonder, therefore, that Jeffers now enjoys the dubious distinction of being the first English-speaking poet to write a play or whatever it is – with Adolf Hitler as the hero, and in a sympathetic role, a latter-day Napoleon, a great patriot, an impotent father of his people. Generously, he puts into the Fuehrer's mouth the announcement that 'I hate gambling with German lives' ... 'I hate blood.' Like a translator for the Potsdam publishing house, he makes one of the characters say: 'Democracy ... Did you ever hear a prosier word? Democracy: the clay life-belt that sank Athens, and is sinking France. Blood and soil are poetry, you can fight for them; democracy is pure prose, abstract, indefinite, and, as they use it, dishonest.' Of liberty, there is this precious gem:

> I have heard a story about freedom, a vain vain tale
> Told by some Greeks, by some slave-holding Greeks
> And a few Roman authors, Rome being the greatest
> Slave-driver in the world before Spain and Britain.

It is not intended, by quoting these lines, to imply that the opinions of the characters are those of the author. One cannot, however, avoid the suspicion, a suspicion induced by the fact that the really purple patches are the pro-fascist ones, that the poet's sympathy lies largely with the 'strong, fierce, clean' ideology of the Nazis; and that even if he is somewhat shocked at German ruthlessness, he feels bound to tolerate it as being merely the strength of the superior animal, the blond beast. Otherwise, where did Jeffers pick up the epithets with which he characterizes the leading personalities of the democracies – 'Churchill, the bloody-minded amateur, Roosevelt and his playboys.' It is true that it is Hitler who is so characterizing them, but the words are particularly Jeffersian – not Jeffersonian.

As late as May 28, 1940 – Jeffers conveniently dates his verse – the poet regards the conflict between Britain and Germany with sublime indifference:

> And why do you cry, my dear, why do you cry?
> It is all in the whirling circles of time.
> If millions are born, millions will die;
> In bed or in battle is no great matter
> In the long orbits of time.
> If England goes down and Germany up
> The stronger dog will still be on top,
> All in the turning of time.

Is it not marvellous to be able, in these days to summon up such godlike apathy? Does it not speak for the greatness of Mr. Jeffers that he can survey, without pain or annoyance, the death-agony of millions? It is true that these poems were written during the period of American isolationism. Even then, it was only the Lindberghs and the Coughlins who were isolationist. For them Jeffers wrote his poetical philosophy:

> I have often in weak moments thought of this people as something
> higher than the natural run of the earth.
> I was quite wrong; we are lower. We are the people who hope to win
> wars with money as we win elections.

Now, thoroughly compromised, we aim at world rule, like Assyria,
Rome, Britain, Germany, to inherit those hordes
Of guilt and doom. I am American, what can I say but again, 'Shine,
perishing republic' ... Shine, empire.

Indeed, what can he say? What can he say now, after Pearl Harbor?
What can he say now that his own little tower is menaced on the California
coast, his own tower, and not that of millions of 'mish-mash blood'? Will he
still continue his insulated attitude of aloofness, his production of mighty
utterance in a vacuum?

Mr. Jeffers, of course, was well aware of the danger that history might
catch up with him. In his preface, he seeks to forestall such *ex post facto*
criticism. Says he:

Yet it is right that a man's views should be expressed, though the poetry
suffer for it. Poetry should represent the whole mind; if part of the mind is
occupied unhappily, so much the worse. And no use postponing the verse to a
time when these storms may have passed, for I think we have but seen a
beginning of them; the calm to look for is the calm at the whirlwind's heart.

The battle has reached the whirlwind's heart, but it is doubtful whether
one will find calmness there.

We must admit, by way of final word, that we regret having to judge
a poet's work for the opinions which it expresses. The fact remains that .
Robinson Jeffers still remains master of a peerless utterance, still, from a
technical viewpoint, an incomparable poet. Our remarks are prompted only
by a recollection of something we had read somewhere to the effect that a
poet must possess a sense of common humanity; this we sought in the writing
of Mr. Jeffers; and failed to find. We are angry, therefore, not at Apollo, but
at Mrs. Jeffers' son.

Is This the Jew the Authors Drew?   3 July 1942

There has just come to our hand the monumental work of H.L. Mencken: *A
New Dictionary of Quotations*, sprawling, in double column, over thirteen
hundred pages. It appears from the introduction that Mr. Mencken, who for
many years was the *enfant terrible* of American letters, did not content himself, in his labors, with merely fashioning immortal dicta of his own; for the

last twenty years, he has also been collecting, and arranging in alphabetical order, the wit and wisdom of the ages. It is a work at once scholarly and entertaining, revealing in its approach both the erudition which characterized his *American Language*, and the cynicism which informed his *Prejudices*.

There have been, of course, other collections of apothegmic wisdom. There is, for example, Bartlett's, and Stevenson's *Home Book of Quotations*. But while these latter are replete with proverbs and purple patches which in the final analysis turn out to be but blushing platitudes, the sophisticated collection of Mencken contains but a minimum of such copy-book maxims. Everywhere Mencken has sought to catalogue only those sayings which are touched with some attic salt, or some tang of irony, or with the sour-sweetness of paradox. The pedestrian locution gets no lift in his omnibus; the merely moral injunction thumbs in vain to be included.

The result of this principle of selection – the survival of the slickest – is that the *Dictionary* becomes more than simply a reference book, to be used by rhetoricians in search of a telling phrase or a borrowed verbal tuxedo. In fact, orators will be well-advised to eschew this book; its remarks on statesmanship, or politicians, or democracy, are not all of the kind which will find favor in the eyes of the electorate. Nor will those who seek the golden compliment find it in Mencken's ore; rather is his property a mine for the unearthing and resurrection of the biting sarcasm, the rapier insult. Indeed, among the headings of his subjects – in greatest part consisting of adjectives and common nouns – Mencken has included the proper names of some of the world's great ones, and what other great ones have thought of them. With rare exception, it turns out that the more they thought of them, the less they thought of them.

We are doubtful, therefore, whether this book will add any harmony to the music of the spheres. But that it will add to the gaiety of nations cannot be denied. Turn its pages at random; wherever your finger lands, you will find, not only sageness, and good worldly sense, but subtle wit, and humor not quite gentle, and entertainment in all its hundred guffaws. It is made for instruction; and it can serve for parlor-games. It is this book, indeed, which this writer would wish to have with him upon that desert island, so beloved of publishers' advertising-men; for here is not only the best authors, but the best of all the best authors. After all, upon the desert island, one longs for no rational system or *weltanschauung* – a pleasant dictum can charm away the afternoon.

We do not propose to review this book. We are not made of the stuff of that scholarly gentleman who once sat down to write a review of the *Encyclopaedia Britannica*, and won immortality in Clifton Fadiman's *Reading I've Liked*. The fact is that the only proper review of a dictionary is a larger dictionary.

But, modest as we are, we can review a single word. The word is 'Jew.' We are given to understand that certain scribes of the Yiddish press have already visited their maledictions upon Mencken's head for the choice of quotations which he has made. We believe that gnashing of teeth is entirely uncalled for. The reader, no doubt, will already have surmised, from what has been said above, that Mencken's Judaica could not be all honey and saccharine. It isn't. It is about evenly divided between quotations which declare the Jew lower than the worm, and laudations which pronounce him higher than the angels. It is, in its nine columns of collated epigrams, half *shimpf-lexicon,* and half sheepskin *magna cum laude.* Thus the proverbs anent Jewry emanating from Germany and Czarist Russia and the Ukraine could hardly be expected to be complimentary; to the masters of pogroms, an insulting proverb is the least of sins. They enjoy, however, a certain currency – alas, a currency much too great; not Mencken is the man to ignore them.

Mencken, moreover, includes also dicta of Jews about Jews. He quotes: 'No more vicious antisemite than a Jewish antisemite.' 'A Galician Jew is worse than a Christian' (authorship – German Jews) and the return compliment 'German Jews are half Christians' (authorship – Galician Jews).

One notes, too, from this collection that the German science of Jew-hating was developed long before Hitler. When you hear Goebbels rant about Jewish war-mongering, he is only echoing Werner Sombart: 'Wars are the Jew's harvests.' When Hitler speaks about Jewish egotism, his lie is not original. Said Christian Lassen: 'The point of view of the Semite is subjective and egoistic. His poetry is lyrical, and hence subjective. In his religion he is self-seeking and exclusive.' And even Martin Luther is quoted as follows: 'Jews and papists are ungodly wretches; they are two stockings made of one piece of cloth.'

On the other hand Mencken quotes also the following. From Zunz: 'If the duration of afflictions and the patience with which they are borne ennoble, the Jews may vie with the aristocracy of any land. If a literature which owns a few classical tragedies is deemed rich, what place should be assigned to a tragedy which extends over fifteen centuries and in which the poets and actors were also the heroes.' From Disraeli: 'They are an ancient people, a famous people, and a people who in the end have generally attained their objects. I hope Parliament may endure for ever, and sometimes I think it will; but I cannot help remembering that the Jews have outlived Assyrian kings, Egyptian Pharaohs, Roman Caesars and Arabian Caliphs.' From Balfour – The Balfour Declaration. From Elbert Hubbard: 'The Jew may hang on to a dollar when dealing with the enemy, but he does not dole out pittances to his wife, alternately humor and cuff his children, nor request, by his manner, that elderly people who are not up to date, get off the earth.' From J.R. Lowell: 'A race in which ability seems as natural and hereditary as the curve of their noses.'

From Chaim Weizmann: 'The world is divided into two groups of nations – those which want to expel the Jews and those which do not want to receive them.' And from Pope Pius XI: 'It is not possible for Christians to take part in Antisemitism. We are all Semites spiritually.'

It is true, of course, that Mencken's collection contains also some of the 'pearls' of Antisemitism. The fact is that the book is not his book, but a compilation of excerpts from other books; moreover, the heading *Antisemitism* refers the reader to *the Jew* so that both subjects are treated together. His is indeed, a too hopeful soul who would expect Mencken to draw the curtain of silence over these abominable dicta for the sake of sparing the feelings of a Jewish reader. In the final analysis, these Jew-baiting utterances reveal the character of their utterers and not that of their targets. Thus the Spanish inquisitor is quoted: 'Innocent or not, let the Jew be fried.' Thus the German proverb: 'Beat my Jew, and I'll beat your Jew.'

In justice to Mr. Mencken, it must be pointed out that his quotations about other nationalities constitute similarly an amalgam of favorable and unfavorable, the unfavorable predominating because the wittier. Neither the Englishman, nor the Frenchman, nor the German emerge from his columns unscathed. Perhaps the key to the situation is given in one of the final epigrams anonymously quoted by the Baltimore sage: 'Jews are like everybody else, only more so.' Even their objection to the quotations is a confirmation of this truth.

The Heart of Europe

Review of *Heart of Europe* edited by Klaus Mann and Hermann Kesten 4 February 1944

It is the tacit irony of this fascinating volume of prose and poetry written by European writers during the last two decades that most of the heart of Europe is to-day removed from its body. That part which is still constricted within the continental boundaries, obviously suffers from angina – one can tell that by the blueness of the patient's lips, the dyspnoea of his utterances, and his general sense of impending death. As for the rest – the exiled and transplanted heart – it is a macabre and cathartic sight: a heart whose cardiac palpitations, whose systole and diastole expands and contracts in an habitat not naturally its own, and feeds not the body for which it was intended. It is the symbolic heart of the frog, persisting in its nerveless activity, in the foreign thorax of a laboratory jar.

Although not all of the authors included in this volume are exiles, – some, unfortunately, are still 'there,' and some, fortunately, are dead, – all of the selections are translations. The British Isles, apparently, are not part of Europe; there is no original English literature in the book. This is explained by the apology that to have included English texts would have swelled still further the bulk of the volume. It does not seem a good excuse, inasmuch as the geographical and political facts of England's appositeness to Europe cannot be contradicted; and another sheaf of pages would have made no great difference in the size of the book, already quasi-encyclopaedic. It is not out of patriotism that we insist upon this point; but we do think that the absence of so European a writer as James Joyce is a serious flaw in the 'totalitarianism' of its content. In the final summation, such arbitrary omissions do Britain a grave literary injustice. American anthologies, although written in an American frequently recognized as English, do not as a matter of course, include British writing. Now Europe, too, excludes it. It would seem as if Great Britain must seek refuge in an anthology to be called 'The Isles of the Sea,' which would, presumably, include England, Iceland, Anticosti, Montreal, and Oceania.

With regard 'to European authors as such' – to use a European phrase – there are also some serious omissions. We note that Lion Feuchtwanger is conspicuous by his absence; it has been suspected that the editors gave way to an anti-communist bias. We venture to say that very few European writers were so widely read as Feuchtwanger. Emil Ludwig, too, is not to be found among the immortals. Moreover, if the 'heart of Europe' here electrocardiographed is to be authentic, it should have included also the personification of its thromboses – its Hamsuns, its Spenglers, – these included, of course, with the necessary diagnostic comment.

But having done with this carping criticism, it must be said that this volume has provided this writer with several evenings of engrossing and profitable reading. By and large, we have found the prose much more palatable than the poetry; this is no doubt due to the difficulties of translating from this medium. As typical example we take a poem of Ivan Goll translated by William Carlos Williams; unfortunately Goll's original is rhymed, and Mr. Williams is not adept at rhyming, enjoying, as he does, other qualities as a poet. A line from Holst is translated: 'I will *enthought* you ever *deeplier*, Death.' This inefficiency, to put it mildly, in translation is of course not characteristic of all the poetry, but it does suffice to give the impression that the European prosateurs are superior to its poets; and there is reason to suspect, from other versions, that this is not so.

The Heart of Europe contains quite a number of wonderful things. Paul Valéry's essay on Homo Europaeus sets the tone, in a way, for the general spirit which pervades this volume, although it is true that logically the essay, a curious combination of platitude and epigram, will not hold water. Silone's story of Peppino Goriano is done with that writer's usual effects of irony and revolutionary insight. Karel Čapek does a cute little essay on literature and Ernst Weiss describes a heart operation – Cardiac Suture – in a manner and with a technique which makes it probably the most exciting and breathless thing in the book. The selections from Kafka are typical, and therefore good. Probably the most pathetic, the most touching, the most sensitive in the European connotation of the word is the story by Stefan Zweig: 'The Invisible Collection.' Among the Italians it is Italo Svevo's piece which is the most readable – the Italian section including a chunk of heavy Croce, ponderous and unsympathetic Borgese, and evangelical Salvemini.

At the same time, 'The Bulletproof Hidalgo,' written with consummate skill by Franz Werfel, is, after all, only a synthetic tour de force. Jean Cocteau's is not a style, but a mannerism. Ilya Ehrenburg has done much better things than 'The Zaddik.' Brandão's 'The Thief and His Little Daughter' is really not tragedy, but dime-novel sentimentality. Unamuno's 'Religion of Quixotism' is a literary blurb for Spanish nationalism – but we are not, forsooth, awarding marks and diplomas.

For the principal value of this collection is its eclectic nature. There is something here to suit every taste, to evoke the proper reaction from almost every temperament. In the final analysis, literary pleasure is the result of a co-operation between author and reader. Frequently a lack of appreciation will result not from any intrinsic defect in the writer, but rather from a prejudice, a bias, even a previous conditioning of the reader.

One thing is certain – the heartbeat of this book is authentic Europe. Time and time again one will observe in its paragraphs a sentence, an obiter dictum, which reflects the quintessentially European. Something is said or thought which could not have been said or thought either in Asia or America. We are given to understand that the number of plots which a writer can make use of total, in their final skeletonic reduction, no more than thirty-seven. It would, indeed, constitute a most interesting tour de force for some future anthologist to compile a collection of stories showing how the essential themes are treated in Asiatic, European, and American literature.

The compiler of the biographical and bibliographical sketches deserves to be complimented both for the information and entertainment he relayed. They, together with the introductory sections to each national group, make an excellent contribution to the contents of the volume. We were surprised to note how many Jews were represented in this book; what it proves, we do not know.

Maimonides in Hollywood

Review of *A Guide for the Bedevilled* by Ben Hecht   13 April 1944

The last thing one ever expected Ben Hecht, manufacturer of scenarios and expert in the plastics of epigram, to do was to paraphrase for the title of his own book, one borrowed from the works of the illustrious Rambam. Little, indeed, was there in the previous career of Hecht which would suggest that he and Maimonides were related either by blood or alliance. In general, it was not Judaica which one associated with the name of Hecht. As the author himself indicates, he was well in his prime – lucky egregious Jew! – before he encountered personally the problem of anti-semitism. With him, too, strife began at forty.

While this comfortable – though temporary – immunity from the blights of Judaeophobia has, when one sets out to write a book about the disease, its obvious disadvantages, its compensations, too, are not to be overlooked. To the phenomenon of anti-semitism, therefore, Hecht brings the fresh unspotted gaze of one who first descries some new bacteria under a microscope. Certainly Hecht does not appear to be hampered by the natural inhibitions which characterize the ghetto-Jew talking about anti-semitism. The latter usually contents himself with speaking about 'the eternal hatred of the eternal people,'. or if he is sociologically minded, 'the dislike for the unlike'; he speaks, he sighs, and there is an end to the matter. Hecht, however, still cherishes the unabated indignation of the man who has just discovered that he is hated for being a Jew. The revelation is doubly shattering; it is not pleasant to realize that one is disliked; and furthermore, he had never thought of himself as specifically a Jew.

Indeed, with a frankness which is one of the many charms of his book, Hecht admits, and proves, that throughout his life, he, like Shakespeare, knew little Hebrew and less Yiddish. After years of assimilation, even his own kith and kin seem strange and outlandish to him; to his father's brothers he refers as 'those dialect comedians who were my uncles.' Until Jew-baiting in these United States uncovered his shame, he always was under the illusion that he was an unhyphenated American. His indignation, therefore, is more than that of a Jew being called a Jew; it is the indignation of a *goy* being miscalled a Jew. Hecht never heard that sufferance was the badge of his tribe.

From this attitude, and from his right Jewish temperament, – all lack of Jewish education to the contrary notwithstanding, – there ensues a text which is one of the most brilliant indictments of anti-semitism we have ever

read – a continuously entertaining source of pleasure and consolation, a virtuoso's exercise in wit and passion. It is true that here the reader will look in
vain for those ponderous analyses of the causes and cures of anti-semitism;
here are no statistics about the incidence of unemployment upon Jew-hating,
no graphs illustrating the parallel curves of inflected accents and inflected
noses, no excursi upon racialism and the purity of western civilization. Many,
no doubt, will find these lacunae a source of disappointment; they will come
for theses and walk away only with *bons mots*.

A book, however, should be esteemed or otherwise for what it sets out
to be, and not for what the reader would have liked it to be. Of the tomes
treating anti-semitism from the point of view of economics, religion, or political science, there is no end; it is refreshing, therefore, to find a writer who
eschews these trodden paths, and propounds a purely psychological – if not a
totally personal – view of the great hatred. Hecht does just that, and if, at
times, his paragraphs lead to nihilist conclusions, they nonetheless have the
sincerity and the effectiveness of a talented man conversing brilliantly about
the skeleton – not in his – but in his neighbour's closet.

For brilliant the book certainly is. Studded with epigrams, shrewd insights, novel suggestions, imaginative writing, it bears the reader impetuously
through its pages, torn between admiration for the author's wit, and catharsis
at the author's passion. It is this scintillating quality which is at once the
book's asset and its liability. While it leaves the reader without any large piece
of retainable exposition – firecrackers startle but do not illuminate – it fills
him with those quotable tid-bits which are the chief delight of a book of this
kind. Says Hecht of philosophers: 'journalists in search of an abstract scandal';
of the loon who discovered that anti-semitism is a *weltanschauung*: 'he goes
around feeling himself a mob'; of the lack of sympathy for the colossally
tragic plight of the Jew: 'a dead Jew remains a historic figure – never quite a
human corpse'; of the comparative nature of alien-ness: 'a man has only to
travel three hours in an aeroplane to find himself full of characteristics considered outlandish'; and of the history of the Jews: 'like a trick done by Houdini
– they are captured, bound in chairs, bashed with hammers, pierced with
knives, jammed in a trunk, and the trunk lowered to the bottom of the sea;
after an impressive interval, the trunk is hoisted to the surface, the lid unbound
and opened – whereupon the Jew steps out – refreshed.'

Unfortunately, out of the very tropicalness of its author's talent, the
book suffers from the defects of its virtues. These are two-fold. In the first
place, the passionate intensity all too frequently degenerates into melodrama.
It is admitted, – certainly by this writer, who is of the Covenant and who,
though younger than Hecht, heard of anti-semitism much earlier than he did
– that his theme, the present sorry plight of our people, is such as to make
the angels weep. This, however, does not justify Mr. Hecht, prompted no

doubt by the anguish of his soul, pursuing, like a Jewish Javert, a race-hatred of his own, directed, naturally enough, against Germans and all things Germanic, with the possible exception of the Berlin Dadaists, now mainly extinct. In this phobia, he out-Emilates Ludwig, out-Vansittarts Vansittart. It is an attitude which while emotionally understandable is scientifically untenable.

The second penalty for his skill is that Mr. Hecht, impeccable prestidigitator with words, becomes so fascinated by his verbal felicities that he lingers too long upon his several subjects, embellishing, concocting wisecracks, indulging in masochistic ironies, and generally squeezing to the last drop whatever cuteness there is in tragedy. He appears in fact to have taken too literally the advice which Shmarya Levin gave him: If you want to write of Jews, make jokes.

But these are small failings compared to the great values of the book. These values are such as to cause us to forgive even the ostentatious display of Hecht ignorance as where he refers to Bialik's *'Tzipor'* as the Eagle – 'twas a bird of a different feather – or when he seems to imply that a lack of education in *Hebrew* prevented him from reading Sholom Aleichem and Hirshbein. For it is something that Hecht should take time off from his murder-mysteries and his bedroom-dialogue to concern himself about the Jewish problem. The position which he occupies and the power of his utterance are two assets which all those who wish to unmask the anti-semitic goon for what he really is, must heartily welcome. One who tilled other vineyards has returned to his own for some latter-day pruning. He is a churl and an inverted snob who would not greet such a one into the ranks of fighting Jewry.

Moreover, there are a number of things said in this book which only Ben Hecht could have said to give them the force of inside information. His attack upon those Jews who sedulously eschew the Jewish question, and particularly upon the Jewish moguls of Hollywood who will produce pictures about the struggle of all peoples, from the Kamchatkans to the Madagascars, but not about Jews, must remain a *locus classicus* in our literature. Good things, too, are his scenario for a play about Semmelweiss, his psychoanalysis of Belloc, and his character sketches of the Goon, the Loon, and the Gutter Napoleon. It is a book which we heartily recommend to our readers; if you fail to buy it, contact the person who has one – he is bound to quote it to you piecemeal.

Grand Invective

Review of *The Tempering of Russia* by Ilya Ehrenburg

22 September 1944

This book is a collection of newspaper articles, written by the author during the early ordeals of Russian defense, and published from occasion to occasion in the *Red Star*, *Pravda*, and *Izvestia*. Obviously indited without an eye for book-publication – that is quite apparently an afterthought – but for day-to-day circulation, these essays of hatred rise time and again above the mere level of journalism to take their proper position upon the higher altitudes of enduring philippic. No other writer, indeed, has been able during the past four years to give to his columns, arising out of what superficially looked like the ephemera of warfare, quite that permanent quality which inheres in Ehrenburg's fire and brimstone. Certainly here is a work, written with passionate intensity, which may sometimes repeat itself but never diminishes in vigour, its temper maintained always at high pitch, and its persuasions continually irresistible.

Two themes run throughout the volume: first, the implacable determination of Russia to defend itself at all costs, and second, the subnormal savage *untermensch* character of the German invader. With reference to the first it is worthwhile noting that not once throughout the three hundred and fifty-six pages of the collected articles does there appear any reference to Marxian dialectics or Hegelian philosophy. Indeed, to have put the quarrel with the Hitlerite invader on such a plane would have been to pay too great a compliment to the Fascist hordes; it would have implied that here was a conflict between two philosophies of life; the fact is that Hitlerism is no philosophy, and the battle was purely and simply between man and beast. Time and again Ehrenburg insists upon this point; one cannot help but reflect, as one considers the early analyses of Hitlerism current in this country, that the Russian approach was both the truer and the more pragmatic.

It is for this reason, indeed, that the appeals to the army and the partisans published by Ehrenburg are almost invariably based upon the argument patriotic. It is the Russian soil which is to be defended and not some particular economic notion; it is the Russian soul which is to react against the invader, and not merely a set of indoctrinated syllogisms. So essential a part of Ehrenburg's approach is this appeal to Russian history and Russian geography, that he cannot write about them without waxing lyrical. These lyrics in praise of the Russian spirit, indeed, constitute the only relief to an otherwise continuously tense diatribe against the German race.

No other writer, we believe, has unmasked the character of that people and culture – which consists, to use the author's phrase, 'of faces scarred in sabre-duels, fat-rumped Valkyrie, and spider-swastikas on houses' – with that prosecutor's vigour that informs Ehrenburg's series of coruscating *J'accuses*. Basing himself in large measure on interviews which he had with German prisoners of war and on letters found on German corpses, Ehrenburg uses these conversations and this correspondence as opportunities to reveal the true import of the New Order. Written with bitter irony, with unpitying realism, with implacable hatred, one gets the feeling, as one reads these essays in prophetic fury, that the ink must have been of blood, and that the paper should have been of asbestos.

One cannot avoid a comparison between Ehrenburg's treatment of the Germans and their culture and Vansittart's. Both, to put it mildly, dislike Hitlerites. But while Vansittart the English diplomat expresses his hatred in nice official language, fit for state memoranda, witty, embellished with poetic quotation and classical allusion, Ehrenburg is the Jew who writes with passion, with the memory of atrocity perpetrated against his kith and kin, with invective and malediction last heard of only in the *tochacho* pages of Deuteronomy. When the Nazis register a victory, he does not despair; he proceeds to write an article on the Hitlerite love of death – one of the most brilliant analyses of Goebbels' theory and practice that has ever been penned. When they suffer a reverse, he does not stand silently by; he gloats, he rejoices, he makes satisfying jokes about their unpitiable plight. Retreating before General Winter, he describes their disappointment: 'You would have thought them so many tourists deceived by a travel bureau.' Discovering the frozen bodies of Nazis, he writes paragraphs about the manner of their death, so that all may read and know that the supermen are not invincible, seeing that they are vulnerable even by weather. All the time, moreover, in defeat and in triumph, his writing vibrates with an undeviating belief in the eventual annihilation of the Beast. The words of an old rabbi, saved from the Gestapo, he takes for his own, for the world's: 'Green grass lives longer than Nebuchadnezzar.'

In his foreword, Ehrenburg admits that when he was writing these sulphuric articles he was 'not thinking about objective truth.' It could have been not otherwise; Ehrenburg, throughout the concocting of these bottles of vitriol, never considered himself merely a history-professor; he was a warrior, a warrior with a pen which could stir a Molotov cocktail with the best of them. This is not to say that the articles deviate from truth; surely that was not the meaning of Ehrenburg's admission. All that phrase could mean is that the intensity of the indictment is uniformly so high-pitched as to leave no room for the extenuating circumstances so beloved of the theorist miles away from the scene of the crime.

The book is full of many good things, truth, righteous indignation, patriotic fervor, wit. Mannerheim, for example, is spoken of as the man who would annex to Helsinki – the Urals. 'Laval up the lamp-post, sing the children of Paris. To be sure, he won't give any light, but it will be bright.' Of Franco's gift to Hitler – 'an army composed mainly of law students and bootblacks.' Of the motivation of German armies in Russian weather: 'Tenants marching to get warm rooms.'

The book includes also letters from Russian soldiers addressed to the author. Here one can see definitely the effect which Ehrenburg's writings had upon the military front; the voice receives its echo, and the echo is sounded by cannon.

A great debt is owed in this war to those masters of rhetoric whose inspiring periods stiffened morale and gave meaning and will to the United Nations crusade. Considered now, four years after their utterance, the speeches of Churchill read like what they truly were – the expression of the Englishman's will-to-freedom, articulated in immortal language. In this respect, the metronomic style of Stalin's speech is at a decided disadvantage; that disadvantage, however, is amply compensated for by the articles of Ehrenburg, which in a personal style succeeded in expressing the total personality of the Russian people, their indomitable will, their boundless courage, their love of country.

The translation by Alexander Kaun appears to us to be without fault. We judge this by no comparison with the original – alas, we know no Russian – but by the fact that the translation reads like an original, and that is always a good measure of a translation's success.

Those Who Should Have Been Ours   16 November 1945

With the exception of the Yishuv, whose voice is padded by censorship and sealed with White Papers, it is, it would seem, only the English-speaking Jewries who today, in our traumatic muteness, might perhaps supply our people with utterance that is direct and authentic. Certainly it would be a long time before the Jewries of Europe regain their speech; even for those who have survived, the memory of horror still paralyzes the tongue. One would have imagined, therefore, that American-Jewish writers, at least those of the last decade, would, with compelling impulse, have seized upon what obviously appeared to be their destined function. The disappointing fact, however, is that as one calls the roll of the younger generation of Jewish writers in this country, and as one looks into the themes which evoke and the spirit which moves their efforts, one is shocked to discover that these men, whose undoubted talents might certainly have contributed something towards the preservation and advancement of the tradition in which they remain, whether they would or not, inextricably involved, are upon the subject of their heritage, either singularly silent, or, if outspoken, outspoken to most self-deprecatory effect.

I speak specifically of the younger writers, because the older ones, with some notable exceptions, are already too firmly and indeed irrevocably committed to the thesis that the less Jewish they appear, the more American they will be. They are, to vary a notorious formula of the last century, Americans by Jewish dissuasion. They think that by travelling incognito, they will be mistaken for royal, or at least New England, personages. They delude themselves into believing that in the guise of crypto-Jews in American letters, they have arrived; the truth is, of course, that having nothing original to contribute, they have not arrived, but only landed. As a consequence, they are relegated to the secondary roles in literature; they become either the anthologists, like Louis Untermeyer, of better men's writing, or the commission-agents, like Clifton Fadiman, of this week's 'literary special.' Even in these functions, it is to be noted, they persist in the *marrano* attitude, and refuse to give nod or beck to anything which might, by a too informed appreciation, betray their own affinity with Jews or Judaism. As for the rest of these worthies, tongue-tied by the inhibitions arising out of their own imposture, and bereft of the heritage which might provide a real and sincere basis for self-expression, they fill Hollywood with their synthetic scripts. They 'make' with the dialogue; they study the curiosities of the early American. They write. But they do not create. One cannot create with another's genitals. Hence *ersatz* and mimicry.

The younger writers, however, though seemingly lost to their fathers, at least display a troubled conscience. Some time ago there was published in *The Contemporary Jewish Record* a symposium by Jewish authors who were at pains – in this instance, that is precisely *le mot juste* – to reveal what their Judaism meant to them. As if to imply – so, at least, I had hoped – that life began thereafter, the symposium was confined to writers 'under forty.' With the exception of one contributor, all agreed that their Jewish origin, or heritage, had only a negative meaning to them – *lucus a non lucendo*; and the sole dissenting one, son of a rabbi, esteemed his Jewishness because it drove him to a greater and more scholarly interest – in Scottish literature! As a whole, it was pathetic to watch the symposiacs get themselves *aliyoth*, and then stand, stuttering and embarrassed, incapable of uttering the proper benediction.

Nor are these negative determinations the result of an absence of good-will. One of the most talented of this group, a subtle and sensitive poet, Delmore Schwartz, concluded his essay with the following: 'And thus I have to say (with gratitude and yet diffidence because it has been so different for other Jews, different to the point of death) that the fact of Jewishness has been nothing but an ever-growing good to me, and it seems clear to me now that it can be, at least for me, nothing but a fruitful and inexhaustible inheritance.' Indeed, for Schwartz, whose major theme is the ubiquitous sense of alienation, his Jewishness is but so much more grist to the mill. Both his *Shenandoah* and his *Genesis* are written in this spirit. It is, of course, regrettable that limitations of background so hamper his work that his 'inexhaustible inheritance' conveys only negations, and no positive values. These limitations are evidenced by such Jewish solecisms in his work as the confusion, in *Genesis*, of the laws touching *chalitza*, or the appearance in the same place, of an uncle called Ishmael. Not in the modern centuries has a Jew been dubbed Ishmael; he might as well have been named Esau. But even negativisms can emerge as positive contribution; witness the Decalogue. Schwartz, at least, recognizes in his work that the point he recently made about T.S. Eliot may apply, with even greater aptness, to the contemporary American-Jewish writer: 'The protagonist of *Gerontion* uses one of the most significant phrases in Eliot's work when he speaks of himself as living in a *rented* house; which is to say, not in the house where his forbears lived.'

To what a pass the escapism of the contemporary American-Jewish writer may lead him is best evidenced by the case of Karl Shapiro, who, though under forty, was somehow not a collaborator in the symposium. I had seen some of Shapiro's poems when they had first appeared in the pages of *Poetry: A Magazine of Verse*, and subsequently when they were published in books called *Person, Place and Thing* and *V-Letter*. There was no doubt, as one read any of the poems, that here was an original, a powerful talent. A voice such as his had not been heard in American poetry – a perfect, an impeccable recreation in words of the very sound and texture of the American scene, together with a rich sensuality, reminiscent only of Keats – if Keats had lived in an age of department stores. Here was a combination which was strange, yet real; fascinating, yet, in its last analysis, factual.

Who, other than copy-writers, had ever written a poem in praise of a Buick? One would have thought that this theme could never rid itself of the smell of gasoline. Yet Shapiro's 'Buick' emerges as a most precious and vital thing, a slim ecstasy, pure motion, a motored Pegasus. A similar miracle he achieves with so crass a subject as moving-day, hitherto considered as of interest solely to transport companies; his 'October 1' is more than a poem; it is a piece of biography, made to stand still, with all its pathos and poignancy, for the hour of its action, for the minutes of its reading, for the days vibrating with its recollection. Drug-stores he sings, and the color and perfumes of barber-shops; mongolian idiots are his argument and the strangeness and intimacy of twins. 'Cokes' and not hippocrene, is the beverage of his Muse; neon flashes through his verse. Others, of course, have noticed before this that the American scene is somewhat peculiar; it was left to Shapiro to endow these pedestrian quotidian things with a richness and vividness which one had hitherto associated only with mediaeval pageantry as floridly painted by Keats.

All of which is to say that Karl Jay Shapiro is already one of our major poets, and quite properly Pulitzer'd and Guggenheim'd. To this we need hardly add that Shapiro is a Jew; the name, of good Talmudic derivation, is one which no goy to goydom born has ever to our knowledge assumed. Moreover, any doubts on the subject are immediately dispelled upon an examination of the text of *Person, Place and Thing*; only a Jew could be author of the numerous references to Jews which appear in the book; and studying the nature of these references, we must add, only a Jew or an antisemite.

For in the space of eighty-eight sparsely printed pages, Shapiro adverts frequently to the race from which he sprang. I am ready to overlook his Christmas carols, his poem to Evelyn 'whose great heart comes over him like sound of Christmas'! After all, if Sholem Asch may, so may Shapiro. But why must every reference to Jewry, made by Shapiro, invariably be uncomplimentary? Why must 'the scions of important Jews' have eyes 'whose gaze like marbles searched her dress, and paid'? Are these eyes not ever used for any other purpose? Time was when the eyes of the scions of important Jews were associated with learning and with the small script of Rashi. Moreover, is it only the sons of important Jews who so wickedly roll their eyes? Are the optics of the gentiles ever demure and downcast?

Again, on page 35, 'he trained his joys to be obsequious Jews.' So Jews are not only lascivious, they are also servile. To consummate his indictment, his climax of self-hatred, he coins an adjective, genial in all respects save its implications, the adjective 'hebroid.' Writing of the poet, presumably himself, he says (p. 88):

He is the business man, on beauty trades,
Dealer in arts and thoughts who, like the Jew,
Shall rise from slums and hated dialects.

'Like the Jew' – he *is* a Jew. The dialects of his forefathers are as hateful to him as the slums of their habitat. That this is so is seen again in his poem about his grandmother whom he pities because history has moved her 'through strange lands and many houses, confusing the tongues and tasks of her children's children.'

The cause of this confusion is quite obvious. It is obvious not only from the things which Shapiro has said about his people, but also from those which he has failed to say. There is not any indication anywhere that the poet is aware of the rich cultural heritage which should have been his; he who succeeds in lending glamor to a soft drink emporium can find nothing worthy of reference in a culture which has spanned the centuries and covered the continents. It is the grandson who is to be pitied, and not the grandmother. Shapiro may feel at home with the American person – although that is doubtful (does he not say: 'To hate the Negro and to shun the Jew, is the curriculum'?)

– and the American thing; but in the American place, he is definitely an alien. And without the sanctuary of internal cultural resources.

It is a pity. It were no pity if Shapiro were merely a poetaster; but he is a poet. Let us not be misunderstood; it is not the function of the creative artist to be a public relations counsel for his people, though it is no disgrace if he is. But surely Shapiro's poetry is in no way enhanced, his Americanism in no way made more authentic, by this studied – and unalleviated – denigration of his own. It is not necessary, in speaking the tongue that Shakespeare spake, also to assume that Shylock is part of its syntax. Escape has led to *selbsthass*. What Shapiro's future is likely to be can be surmised from an article in *Poetry Magazine* which speaks of his flirtations with the creed of the majority. The rebel, despite his satire on the American middle-class, is about to surrender to it unconditionally.

But to return to the symposium. Although its apologetic lucubrations made dismal reading, it was gratifying, nonetheless, to observe that most of the contributors were permeated by a sense of shame which expressed itself either by a formal genuflection to 'the Jewish heritage' whose legacies the writer was gracefully rejecting; or by an exculpatory reference to parents' neglect; or by a ringing and somehow dubious asseveration that the apologist loved not Jews the less, but human beings more; or by the downright brazenness of the Second Son of the Haggadah. At least two of the writers felt themselves constrained to speak in derogatory terms of Ludwig Lewisohn; thus the true personification of their conscience was recognized. Howard Fast, indeed, went so far as to say that 'he could not, nor did he desire to go groping back into a Jewish past and rear the dangerous and always vulnerable walls of an *Island Within*.' Apart from begging one question – why must it be the past? is the present tragedy of Jewry too trifling for consideration? – and answering another wrongly – the Jew does not rear the walls; he finds them ready-made – the blood-brother of Paul Revere apparently feels himself more at home in the past he excerpts from the archives of the D.A.R. But for the most part, one sensed the sting of conscience. These writers did not deny their feeling of alienation; they acknowledged it, but only as one of several exiles they were suffering. They did not feel prompted to place greater emphasis upon the atypicalness of their Jewish origin than upon the singularity, for example, of their calling.

Such is the mood which apparently prevails among contemporary Jewish writers. Whether the sense of uneasiness adverted to above will eventually resolve itself into a more positive consideration of the uniqueness of their own position, there is no way of foretelling. Will the plight of their race, recovering now from an ordeal which has cruelly lopped it to two-thirds its size, evoke in Jews, in artists whose trade is sensitivity, a feeling of oneness with the persecuted, tragedy shared with kith and kin? Will the inspiration of Palestine banish their sense of inferiority? Will the supercilious glaze fall from their eyes, as in the light of current history they survey again the treasures of their heritage – a heritage which consists not of a vague *mystique*, but of a recorded culture and a discernible *Weltanschauung*? Will these talents at last come to realize the alternative that faces them: that they are ours – or nobody's? I do not know. I only pose the question. I abide, from others, the answer.

Rilke and His Translators

Review of *Thirty-one Poems by Rainer Maria Rilke* translated by
Ludwig Lewisohn   2 August 1946

'The large body of poetry he left is quite solitary. It is near to earth and to God; it is remote from all the ugly and tumultuous preoccupations that keep man from both earth and God. All those who amid the heavy, hideous dreams of these preoccupations awaken with a yearning for purity and oneness will seek out the work of Rainer Maria Rilke ...' It is in these eloquent, and almost devout, terms that Ludwig Lewisohn, in the introduction to this volume of translations, speaks of the German-writing poet whose wonderful lyrics he has so wonderfully Englished. And this tribute, morever, is not to be read as an apology; while it is true that some time ago the Palestinian press seemed much agitated about the question as to whether it would be morally right for Jewish writers, ever again, to have truck or traffic with anything written in the language of our mortal enemy, the majority of the participants in that controversy, one is proud to report, were against a boycott directed against an alphabet; and the eminently civilized translator of the poems, too, takes it for granted that one quarrels, not with the lexicon of a writer, but rather – if one quarrels at all – with the sentences he makes out of that lexicon.

This being so, there can be no quarrel with Rilke. The truth is that it was the Germans of Goebbels' ilk who quarrelled with all that Rilke stood for, and – so great was their revulsion to anything that was fine, even poems politically innocuous – they more than merely quarrelled with Rilke's admirers. In a report on the present status of German culture, I read, touching the fate of Rilkiana under the Nazis: 'An interest in Rilke's work and ideas was considered, in the last years of the regime, to be a symptom of resistance to Nazidom. Groups of Rilke-lovers who met to study his poetry were closely watched by the Gestapo, and Hermann Kanisch is rumoured to have been put into a concentration camp shortly after the publication of his remarkable study of the poet's esthetic assumptions.' One may entertain, of course, one's own opinion about a 'resistance-movement' whose dynamic exhausts itself in a passion for the poet in the princess' tower; the quotation is adduced solely to indicate that the Gestapo recognized an alien when it saw one, even though that alien wrote a German most inspired. Perhaps, – remembering Adolf's grammar – because ...

In any event, Rilke, probably one of the greatest, and certainly the subtlest and most sensitive poet of this century, Rilke stands as the direct antithesis of everything for which the Fuehrer stood. Where that one was loud, shrill, hysterical, and vulgar, Rilke was soft, subdued, meditative, aristocratic; where the Fuehrer went orgiastic before the spectacle of massed battalions, Rilke – one recalls the account of his unhappy stay at the military academy – couldn't endure a uniform. And where the Nazi archetype addressed himself to the bestiary, Rilke invoked angels. Indeed, it must have been one of those who providentially spirited him away eight years before the monster came to power, sparing him the ordeal of seeing the language he himself used to such God-like purpose, depraved into a medium for recording the 'inventories' of crematoria.

However, it is not Rilke, anti-Fascist by prolepsis, but his poems, English by translation, with which we are here concerned. It is to be noted forthwith that this is not the first time that these poems have been rendered into English; during the past decade quite a Rilke cult has grown up, and many hands have been laid upon his lines. We say *lines* advisedly, for almost all of these translators, invoking and making a fetish out of the ideal of *verbal* and *linear* exactness, have confined themselves to rendering into English the sets of lines which go to make up a Rilke poem. The result has been that in these translations the rhymes and metres, upon which Rilke obviously labored, disappear, get lost in the shuffle, go *spurlos versunken*; what is left is a dictionary, word-for-word rendition, much in the style of the classical cribs; it is as if one were to advance as a serious literary translation the sing-song of the *cheder*: *Shir* – a song – *hashirim* – of songs – *lishlomo* – of Solomon!

No doubt this type of pseudo-translation is mainly the result of a mistaken notion as to the proper use of the pony text – that excess of riches which on one side of the opened book gives you the original authentic poem, and on the other a line by line equivalent, so that if you wish you may read both pages simultaneously.

Now this may be all very well for prose; although even here it is a moot question. But certainly a ballad is no ballad in translation if it does not translate, in addition to the words, also the conventions of definite metre and definite rhyme. To render his lines, one by one, and without re-establishing in the translation the image of the formal pattern used by the author, is as much a treason of translation as to add, for the sake of rhyme or of padding – the faithful translator's usual pitfalls – connotations not contained in the original version.

It is argued by the Englishers of whom I am writing – the Nortons, Lemonts, Leishmanns – that they seek, in their fashion, to avoid 'those deviations in translation which occur when the translator is faced by the problem of rhyme scheme and rhythm.' But that problem – is it rude to point out? – faced also the original poet; he, too, just didn't sit down to convey his meaning in one first careless rapture and forthwith saw that it was fine; he, too, like Jacob with the angels, wrestled. To make his intention prevail over the intrusion of unwanted words and the stiff-neckedness of unmalleable ones, he struggled. He fought to achieve the form; for the form and the poem are one and indivisible.

Surely, if the subjected author had wanted the effects of a linear translation – and effects there may thuswise be had, albeit irrelevant effects – he would have written the originals differently. In fact – *o hysteron-proteron!* – it is to be noticed among the younger British poets that some of them are writing original poems in a manner which owes its technique, not to a derivativeness from Rilke himself, but to a derivativeness from the Rilke translations. It is Mrs. Norton who is *chère maîtresse*. Thus, the English fame of Rilke, as carried in these translations, exemplifies Rilke's definition of fame. Fame, he said, writing of Rodin, is ultimately but the summary of all *misunderstandings* that crystallize about a new name.

Well, Dr. Lewisohn is not like one of these. In the collection before us, gleaned from the various volumes of Rilke, Lewisohn gives us *poems*, complete *poems*, not lines. The rhymes, the metre, the pattern, the form, come to life again, and we see Rilke's stanzas as he intended us to see them. Lewisohn deals in artifacts, not equations. There is not a subtlety, not a nuance which the translator has missed, or failed to convey in his versions. The true test of a good translator is, of course, this: Does it read like an original? These thirty-one do.

What we have been saying is that there are translations and there are translations. Let us illustrate. Here is Mrs. Norton, in a blow-by-blow report of a Rilke sonnet:

> Even though the world keeps changing
> quickly as cloud-shapes,
> all things perfected fall
> home to the age-old.
>
> Over the changing and passing,
> wider and freer,
> still lasts your leading-song,
> God with the lyre.

Not understood are the sufferings.
Neither has love been learned,
and what removes us in death
is not unveiled.
Only song over the land
hallows and celebrates.

Reference to the original will immediately show that all the words have been used. Indubitably, they have been rendered, and one may say, rendered forthrightly and with precision. But where are the rhymes, the masculine and feminine rhymes so ingeniously and effectively placed in the original? Where is the song? Where, in fact, is the sonnet?

Here it is, and it is Lewisohn who gives it to us, as its maker intended it to be:

Swift though the world change like wrack
Of clouds dividing,
All that is perfect melts back
In the abiding.

Above the flowing of things
Freer and higher,
Lasting thy music rings,
God of the lyre.

Ill are our sorrows known;
Love we have not learned well;
Death the inscrutable

Darkly conceals us;
Song o'er earth rising alone
Hallows and heals us.

Here, then, the sonnet lives again. The effects willed by Rilke enjoy a reincarnation; where he wanted feminine rhymes to give a touch of lightness to his speech, such rhymes appear; when the text requires a solemn peroration, a slowing of movement, he achieves it by a use of heavier consonants – 'Song o'er earth rising alone' – *Einzig das lied überm Land* – and where the original sets the tone of final irrefutable triumph – *heiligt und feiert* – the translation 'hallows and heals us.'

Everywhere these translations of Dr. Lewisohn's manifest both a faithful adherence to the letter of the original poem, and what is more important still, a faithful understanding and transmutation of its spirit. Carefulness, precision, subtleness, are everywhere in evidence; these poems were not dashed off with the speed of a sight translation; we note that two of thirty-one appeared as early as 1929 in Van Doren's *Anthology of World Poetry*. Altogether it is a splendid and precious collection in which the distinguished novelist takes time off from his prose to worship awhile at the more flaming altar of poetry. And it is gratifying to see that his devotions are at least thrice rewarded: they constitute, first, a reassertion of the affinity between the cultured of the world, regardless of their race; they give again a glowing reflection of a great spirit in communion with himself and his worlds, angelic and human; and they bring back again, into proper perspective, the true function and the whole duty of the translator. They demonstrate once more that only he can translate another's poetry who is himself a poet.

Departure and Arrival

Review of *Thieves in the Night* by Arthur Koestler

22 November 1946

THE NOVEL

Once again Mr. Arthur Koestler adopts that story-telling technique, – he has almost perfected it to a formula, – with which he has for the last decade at once represented and edified the intellectuals and liberals of his generation. The technique is as easy to analyze as it is difficult to synthesize; one takes for major theme – the one increasing purpose of the novel – some problem, or ideology, which is agitating the public mind – these things used to be called 'subjects of social significance,' and one organizes and transforms the pros and cons of the matter in hand into such incidents happening to such characters as will most effectively bring out the underlying polemic which motivated the book. In this fashion intellectual debate is converted into personal conflict. The essence of the book is thus not its 'argument' in the old sense, but its arguments, its controversies, its special pleadings.

It cannot be gainsaid but that in the skill with which Koestler manipulates his briefs-concealed-in-narrative, he stands to-day unsurpassed, indeed, unequalled. For he brings to his métier endowments and experiences which have admirably fitted him for his chosen tasks. In the first place, he has himself, ever since he came to manhood, stood *in medias res*. He is himself the intellectual, the radical crusader imprisoned in Spain, the disillusioned Marxist, the pathetic refugee, about whom he writes. In this sense, almost all of his writing is autobiographical; and inasmuch as it is the autobiography of an interesting person involved in important things, it necessarily engages the attention and sympathy of contemporaries who although perhaps not touched by the personal plights which he describes, are still affected by the philosophies and the movements which these situations illustrate.

In addition, Koestler brings to his work a mental apparatus which gives to his writing not only the polish of a fine style – the usual hallmark of the liberal education – but also the profundity of an analytic mind – the end-product of a sound scientific training. His books are immediately recognizable, even in their obiter dicta – as the books of a twentieth-century mind. Thus, while earlier writers – with the possible exception of Aldous Huxley, and in his case, no doubt, one is really, in this connection, listening to the voice of his brother Julian – invariably choose their images, parallels, and parables, from the realm of classical literature, Koestler goes to the world of science, and to the latest science, for his thought patterns. In this fashion, his characters will refer, as they do in this novel, to the weight of the denizens of Jupiter and to the possibility of Caesarean operations upon cattle; and their epigrams will read like parodies on text-book definitions (Jews are an extreme condition of life. The Dead Sea a symbol of Jewry – oversalted; overspiced; saturated. A clinical note on a hand-grenade: it is typically Jewish – oversensitive and neurotic.).

It is a method which is not to be despised. It serves to accentuate the contemporaneity of Koestler's novels, and it comes as a pleasant and realistic relief after those timeless (*sic*) novels which read as if they might have been written at any period after the seizin of the classic heritage.

How well this technique – the story as debate – and these modern- [...] ators, could serve the purpose of their master is impeccably illustrated in Koestler's *Darkness at Noon*. This no doubt was due to the fact that in this novel all the action rotates about a debate – to confess or not to confess – the novel *is* the debate; the very title is a polemic. In *Arrival and Departure*, however, the method begins to show its weakness: the argumentative skeleton about which the book is built begins to show its bones; the reader recognizes – as he does not in *Darkness at Noon* – the points of transition where the narrative ceases and the essay begins.

Thieves in the Night – which, since it concerns itself with the Palestine problem, the White Paper and its exclusion of refugees from the Holy Land, might have been called: *Departure and Arrival*, – suffers we fear, from the fault of its predecessor in reverse. Apparently, Mr. Koestler desired to project into his novel all of the conflicting philosophies which have made Palestine both their laboratory and their forum; unfortunately, he devised for this purpose, the very un-subtle and un-realistic method of injecting into each of his characters one of the pertinent points of view which, as total cast, make up the entire argument. The result is that the characters are not *personae* but protagonists. The *Chalutz* is like all *Chalutzim*; the *Mukhtar* like all *Mukhtarim*; the Englishman and the Englishwoman might have walked out of one of those syllable-swallowing plays; and the American, like the type American abroad, is quixotic and unmannerly. The method is reduced to its own absurd in Koestler's description of Jewish femininity; they are all, in Koestler's eyes, and he looks at them an untold number of times, callipyginous.

A TRACT FOR THE TIMES

However, if the book, as novel, leaves much to be desired, it is nonetheless a most eloquent and well-informed analysis of the Palestine situation. One would have preferred, indeed, if Mr. Koestler had done his job as straight reporting; had given, without benefit of synthetic climaxes and prearranged denouements, his inimitable descriptions of the protagonists in the Palestine drama, and his shrewd surmisals of the motives which impel them. For Koestler does bring a fresh view and an original personality to bear upon the problem; he sees that in Palestine to-day, 'everybody seems to be walking with sunstroke,' when they are not upset by the *Khamsin*; he estimates the latter-day Lawrences who flit from sheik to sheik at their proper value: pansies chasing about in Bedouin dress; he understands the impulse behind Jewish self-hatred – 'a form of Jewish patriotism'; and for an ex-Marxist brought up in the school which confuses all nationalism with chauvinism, he is bold to say that 'Nationalism is only comic in others – like being seasick or in love.' He epitomizes the philosophy of the Irgun: 'A nation of conscientious objectors cannot survive.' Moreover, these epigrams, illuminating as they are, give no inkling of the passionate intensity with which Koestler pleads the cause of those who have fled from Europe – 'the thing to forget' – and reach the shores of Palestine only to hear 'honourable members invited to sit on drowning men's heads.'

We doubt very much whether any other contemporary writer can excel Koestler in the lucid and forceful explication and exposé of political philosophy. These talents are everywhere apparent in this book (Koestler does *not* do injustice to the Arab point of view); and although the author finally converts his novel into an *apologia pro Arieh Stern* – the only atypical thing about it – the last page sees all the pro-Jewish, pro-Arab, and quasi-British arguments thoroughly exhausted. The column of figures is complete, and all that remains is to make the addition.

THE JUDAICA

By way of postscript, we might suggest that for its second edition – and this book ought to have more than one edition – some editing might be done so as to eliminate those solecisms which dog the steps of a writer who like Koestler, had left his subject for twenty years. *Anu yivneh ha-Galil* is bad Hebrew grammar. 'Oh, Moses our Rabbi,' says one character, 'I wish you hadn't.' The words *Moishe Rabbenu* are not a substitute for 'Christ! I wish you hadn't.' We think, moreover, that the name of Wabash – 'old Wabash' – one of the elders of the kibbutz, is particularly ill-advised. Even if his name was actually Wabash. Its American connotations are too distracting, and succeed in giving the old man an unintended comical character. The gentleman on page fourteen, who is presented as an authority on the Hebrew language, ought also to be corrected; he states, so as to make a dubious point, that the Hebrew language knows no higher figure than a thousand. He must have forgotten *r'vovo*. Equally erroneous are the prosodic opinions on page 151 – 'our lyrics stopped with the Song of Songs' – 'tis a slander upon the memory of at least Yehuda Ha-Levi.

Knut Hamsun   26 December 1947

At last justice has caught up with the genial Hamsun. This Hamsun, it will be remembered, did in the heyday of his youth and fame, pen novels touching the plight of the world's scorned and dispossessed; his great sympathy for the underdog, as evidenced through the easy catharsis of his literature, won him international fame. One got to regard Knut Hamsun as more than a mere novelist; many looked upon him as a sort of articulate conscience, a spokesman for the dumb, the incoherent, the muzzled.

Alas, he turned out to be but an idol with feet of clay. When subjected to the pressure of the Nazi machine, – if indeed pressure there was – Knut Hamsun went over to the camp of the oppressor. The winner of the 1920 Nobel prize descended to a function the most ignoble of all – Hitler's lackey; the author of *Hunger* became a collaborator in its designed and systematic spread through Europe; the shoemaker's apprentice of Bodo in North Norway returned full circle to his first vocation – a polisher of Nazi boots.

This collapse and degeneration of what once looked like a great personality was all the more depressing in that it occurred in a country in which the rest of the population – thousands by no means as richly endowed as Knut

– were putting up a valiant resistance against the invader. While the Norwegian masses were groaning beneath the yoke of the invader, Knut Hamsun, who should have constituted himself head and forefront of their resistance, consented – for money – to become a scribbler of Nazi propaganda.

The last word, however, was to be uttered by the Norwegian people. Brought to trial for collaboration with the enemy, the pitiable nonagenarian was convicted and condemned to pay a fine of 85,000 dollars. Hamsun is thus the beneficiary of judicial lenience. He is merely being made to give back his ill-gotten gains. The fine, moreover, is to be used for the support of Norwegians widowed and orphaned by Hamsun's employers.

No doubt it was Hamsun's age which saved him from a severer penalty. The trick is that death, which must come to all traitors, long ago came to Hamsun, that corpse of his former self, the decomposing cadaver, the Death-in-Life, of what once was a man.

Isaak Babel

Review of *Benya Krik, the Gangster, and Other Stories* by Isaak Babel   10 September 1948

Since 1931 very little has been heard of Isaak Emmanuilovich Babel, the extremely talented Russian-Jewish writer who sprang into fame during the first years following the Revolution. Approved and sponsored by Maxim Gorki, to whose encouragement Babel gratefully attributes the course which his life was to take, his short stories and sketches, scattered through various periodicals, took his contemporaries by storm. The Revolution was in search of a voice that would give to the great adventure a more intimate, a more personally stirring tone than could be heard either in the dryasdust dialectics of its theoreticians or the uncouth sloganeering of its pamphleteers. In Alexander Blok it heard that voice, but it spoke poetry, caviar to the general; in Isaak Babel it heard it in narrative, in a prose racy of the marketplace, the inn sharp with the smell of vodka, the barracks.

Red Cavalry, his first published volume, is already indicative of the principal characteristics of his writing. Its subject matter is the saga of Budyenny's soldiery; it dwells largely upon incidents as fierce as the Cossack General's mustaches; upon the eastern front all is certainly not quiet. Out of this gory picaresqueness, however, – out of the raids, the confiscations, the killings of fathers by sons – there does somehow emerge an impression of the idealism which prompts – and according to Babel, subsequently a Cheka member, excuses – the bloodshed and rapine. From this altogether too one-sided description of the sketches it might appear that Babel was but another votary of that cult of violence which has so transmogrified literature since the twenties; but it is precisely here that Babel's manner is individual and unique.

For hard-boiled though he is, he is not uniformly hard-boiled. When the reader least expects it, in the very shambles of a paragraph, suddenly his style will lift to something high, heroic, lyrical. The lyrical, on the other hand, seldom persists to the degree of nausea; as soon as it approaches that dangerous point, behold! Babel is again speaking like a man, a Cossack, a Cossack and drunk.

It is impossible to overemphasize the importance of this trait. The hard-boiled, persistently cultivated, too soon degenerates into the callous; 'deaths in the afternoon' tend to deprive both life and death of meaning, and insensitivity, whether faked or real, takes from the most moral of all occupations – literature – the standard of values which is basic. On the other hand sentiment inordinately prolonged becomes sentimentality, and one is overwhelmed by such a riches of standards that discrimination becomes difficult, if not impossible. It is between such a Scylla and Charybdis that Babel steers his expert mariner's course. The two attitudes are strategically alternated, and one feels in the reading of his stories as one feels in life, – now high, now low, never wholly in the abyss, never wholly in the empyrean.

To the device which accomplishes these saving juxtapositions, the rhetoricians of old gave a name – zeugma, the yoke, and for Babel the zeugma is the key, key not only to his style, but key to his political position, key to his heart. Nowhere is this better illustrated than in his most distinguished short story, fourth in the volume under review: 'The History of My Dovecote.' It is a story of a pogrom, but the word 'pogrom' is used only once, it is its very last word. The story is one of violence and murder; but its dominating symbol is a pigeon. It builds to a climax, but the course of building appears casual, and is only subsequently revealed for the masterly artifice that it is. The central actions are those of theft and killing, described with an almost literal realism; but the tone – even amidst the scattered feathers and the sprawling corpse – is lyrical, lyrical with the sad lyricism of a Hebrew violin. The result? The very lyricism double-dyes murder to the darkest blackest sable.

A similar ambivalence – though in a different mood – is apparent in the story called 'Karl Yankel.' It is the story of a *mohel* arrested for having perpetrated a circumcision, it is the story of little Karl Yankel (Karl after Karl Marx) and the heavy machinery of justice set in motion for the protection of his life and limb. There is no doubt but that the Jew Babel's sympathies are with the parents and the *mohel*; the subtle satire which he directs at the pompous prosecutor makes this amply clear. But it is also obvious that Babel's revolutionary sympathies are with the code under which the *mohel* is being prosecuted; the last paragraph of the story makes *that* clear. To maintain both sympathies in the same story, we need hardly point out, requires a narrative technique of the highest order.

Babel's models, strangely enough for the poet and drummer-boy of the Civil War, are models in the classic tradition – de Maupassant for structure, Flaubert for *le mot juste*. French culture was very popular in the Odessa of Babel's youth, and Babel early succumbed to its charm. In the workmanship of his stories, and even of his sketches, the example of de Maupassant is everywhere apparent: they are – supreme French compliment! – universally well-made. Nothing is casual, accidental, or padded; the parenthesis of paragraph one makes the climax of paragraph the last. As for the single phrase, the isolated word, Babel eschews the hackneyed like the cholera. Even fish, when the exigencies of his story require it, even fish – disgusting clammy creatures – are made attractive, the fishmonger's hands 'are covered with fish scales, reeking with the odors of beautiful, chilly worlds.'

The collection of stories edited by Avrahm Yarmolinsky is divided into three sections, each section containing examples of different aspects of Babel's interests. The first, touching Benya Krik the gangster – the hero is formed on an actual prototype, the unlamented Mishka Yoponchik – is the poorest of the lot, the effects are too easy, and the reader's tribute is paid rather to the curriculum vitae of Benya than to any unusual skill in his biographer. It is the stories which rotate about the Jewish way of life in Russia, the old giving way to the new, the new still retaining an embarrassing nostalgia for the old, which are most likely to survive. Certainly no anthology of world Jewish literature can ever afford to ignore 'The History of the Dovecote.'

One wonders as one reads with gratitude these priceless stories of two decades ago which Schocken now makes available to the English reading public, one wonders as to what kind of thing Babel, were he still among the articulate, would be doing now. Why he has not been heard from – it is stated that he is still alive – remains one of those riddles with which the Soviets delight to tantalize western curiosity. Some there are who put his silence down to a crisis in his own temperament; at the age of thirty-seven he is supposed, like Rimbaud, to have given it all up. Others purport to see in the very ambivalence of his style the cause and reason for his abdication; under the Stalinite regime, these say, only Stalin can be ambivalent; the rest must speak out (in one sense) or shut up (in all senses). Zaslowsky and Ehrenburg, they point out, do not practise ambiguities. They further point out that in *Red Cavalry* there are altogether too many '*mon général*' references to Trotsky. Whatever the reason for Babel's silence, it is a great pity.

That Rank Picture

17 September 1948

It is difficult to imagine what convoluted motives could possibly have impelled Mr. J. Arthur Rank, the British movie mogul who came to his vocation through an interest in educational church-films, to 'present,' as the magnanimous phrase has it, 'the world's most treasured story, *Oliver Twist*,' and it is even more difficult to fathom the dubious lovingkindness which prompted him to emphasize, in that priceless tale, the ugly caricature of its arch-villain Fagin, a Jew. We must confess that we would never have suspected, had we not read it explicitly stated in *The Eagle Lion's* advertising copy, that this particular opus of Dickens was 'the world's most treasured story'; its distinction seems to have escaped also the notice of all those other movie-producers who might have snatched at a masterpiece upon which no royalties were payable; though first published in 1837, O.T. (not Old Testament) had to wait more than a century until – blessed day! – Arthur Rank appeared 'brilliantly to bring to the screen all the excitement, suspense, and gripping drama of the world's most treasured story!'

And to bring a portrayal of one of the most despicable of Jew-caricatures in all of English literature! In justice to the memory of Charles Dickens it ought at this point to be stated that insofar as he was concerned the perpetration of Fagin was accomplished in comparative innocence. How the odious picture came to be drawn is variously told. Some say that Dickens was moved to include this gruesome cartoon in his *dramatis personae* by a desire to win some of the popularity which had recently attended the production of *Barney Fence*, a play in which a knave of Fagin's breed and calling had also been held up to hatred, contempt, and ridicule. George Cruikshank, famous illustrator of the Dickensian, takes the credit (*sic*) all to himself. It was he, he boasts, who suggested to Dickens, as the latter stood among the serial instalments of his novel, the creation of a character like Fagin, one who incorporated in his person all manner of villainy, and one who, as both the exigencies of the novel and of justice demanded, would eventually come to a bad end in Newgate. In anticipation of such an opportunity, Cruikshank had already made some macabre sketches of Newgate's interior, and now awaited, his background prepared, only for the personage worthy of it, that is to say, a personage amenable to his own lurid and melodramatic style of drawing. When one adds to the revelation of this anecdote Dickens' own penchant for the grotesque, the creation of Fagin – given the pervasive and insidious prejudices of the time – is not as surprising as it might otherwise seem.

Nonetheless, there were some who were both surprised and shocked. Thus a Mrs. Eliza Davis, to whom Dickens sold his Tavistock House, was prompted to write to him: 'It has been said that Charles Dickens, the large-hearted, whose works plead so eloquently for the oppressed of his country, has encouraged a vile prejudice against the despised Hebrew. Fagin, I fear, admits of only one interpretation ... But Charles Dickens lives. The author can justify himself or atone for a great wrong on a whole scattered nation.'

In reply to this letter Dickens wrote disclaiming any malicious intention. Specifically he defended himself by pointing out that other characters in *Oliver Twist* were equally wicked and that therefore the presentation of Fagin could not be considered invidious. He added – somewhat ingenuously – that Fagin is called a Jew not because of his religion but because of his race. How ironical, how tragically ironical this second argument appears in the light of subsequent history!

Despite his attempt at self-exculpation, the matter of Fagin still continued to trouble Dickens' conscience, and large-hearted man that he was, he sought an opportunity to make amends. In 1865 there appeared *Our Mutual Friend*, in which there figured a Jew. This was a Mr. Riah, who was now seen to be as good as Fagin was bad, a paragon of virtue, a model of long-suffering, all the saints of the calendar rolled into one. As a gesture of atonement, Mr. Riah is admirable, but as a character – incredible, almost, indeed, as incredible as Mr. Fagin.

Such, in brief, is the history of the relation between Mr. Dickens and Mr. Fagin. It is clearly seen that in these relations Dickens was in no way prompted by malice and that the worst that could be said of him was that he succumbed to the attractions of what he mistakenly considered a picturesque and didactic character. The truth is that Fagin is not even a creation; he is an evocation, a nineteenth-century recall of the stage-Jew of the Middle Ages, the red-headed monster of the morality-play.

But no such defense can be made for Mr. Rank. He 'presents' Fagin and makes him one of the three principal characters of the movie – after having had the benefit of Dickens' experience. Even if Mr. Rank, religious man, were as 'whole in life and free from guilt' as some of his apologists contend, he still had sufficient warning of the dangerous possibilities of his film in the very place – the life and works of Dickens – where he discovered his text. What that danger is has been eloquently and pathetically exposed by Dickens himself, speaking through the mouth of Mr. Riah: 'Men find the bad among us [Jews] easily enough. They take the worst of us as samples of the best; they take the lowest of us as presentations of the highest, and they say: All Jews are alike.'

If this peril was perceptible in Dickens' time, how much more so in an age which follows immediately after the decade of the Nazi phobia. Goebbels,

Nazi maestro of movies, certainly would have welcomed Fagin to his repertoire of Jewish characters. How, then, does it happen that Mr. Rank, votary of the dim religious light in both cinema-house and chapel, remained so blind to the obvious?

Can it be that with the production of *Oliver Twist* Mr. Rank was seeking to exploit the unfriendly feelings prevalent in England as a result of the Palestine trouble? Is it possible that through the presentation of this film Mr. Rank was attempting to settle a score with his Hollywood rivals, most of whom are reported to be Jews? It would indeed be a sad, a sorry and shameful state of affairs if the answers to these questions were in the affirmative.

It is argued in defence of the film that no real objection to the portrayal of Fagin can be taken because Fagin, the villain, is found in the company of Christian villains. This is, it will be remembered, the defence which Dickens attempted to make and which left him still with an uneasy conscience. No wonder; the distinction is so apparent it can escape the attention only of the wilfully blind. For it is all a question of circumstances, of ambience; Fagin belongs to a minority; to hold up a single member of a minority to hatred is automatically to encourage and incite the majority against the entire group. Nor is it an answer to say that one shows also Christian reprobates. They are among those whom kinship will impel to forgive. Thus there are Jewish villains depicted on the stage at Tel Aviv; but no one cries: Antisemite. We venture to suggest, indeed, that if *Oliver Twist*, Rank's *Oliver Twist*, were presented in that city, not only would the character of Fagin pass uncommented, save for its clumsiness, but the film as a whole might even be received enthusiastically. But *Oliver Twist*'s parable – the parable of the lad who, given a meagre mandate, dared to ask for more and was whipped – that certainly would leave its impression.

Cantabile

Review of *The Cantos of Ezra Pound*   September–October 1948

De litteris, et de armis, praestantibusque ingeniis

And when they brought him back
the fibbiest fabricator of them all
          il miglior fabbro
they didn't know what to do with him
          at the customs he had had nothing to declare
saving and except a number of synonyms, to wit:

zhid, sheeny, jewboy, youpin, kike, yitt, shweef.
                              and the ballad
    But bye and rade the Black Douglas
    And wow but he was rough!
    For he pulled up the bonny brier
    And flang't in St. Mary's Lough.

didn't know what to do with him ... hang him?
old, *exhaussé*, a poet, there was a question of ethics, moreover
            one kuddent make a martyr of him, cood one?
                              St. Ezra Benedict

So the seven psychiatrists feigned insanity
committed him.

USURA: that his offence
that he sought to extract an exorbitant interest
                              from a limited talent.
speculated in the culture exchanges
passed off
              χρύσω   χρυσοτέρα
the Dante coinage, Provençal, Chinese yen
not as his own, but his for increment.

It must be admitted, however, that as a pawnbroker
he was distinguished.
He invented a new way to ring a coin on the table
was expert in the bite for counterfeit,
trafficked only in the best mdse. and to his friends gave discounts
for the rest was fierce, bearded like the pard, like his Jew.

            Pound   Libra   £

USURA

The cantos? 'The art of conversation' said Tate (Allen) meaning
small talk shouted.
80 of them 80
anecdote, persiflage, ideogram, traduction
              traductore – tradittore
all to the same if any effect – the syphilisation of our gonorera
                  and Pound its thunder clap,
a good role but the wrong actor.

Don't you think said the lady from Idaho on tour at Rapallo
that he will be remembered?   Yes

As the author of a Gradus ad parnassum
  " a compiler of several don'ts
  " a perpetrator of ditto
  " a dropper-down of learning's crumbs
and as the stoic of the empty portals.

Otherwise, as Jimmy, quoting himself and poor Mr. Breen
      E.P.: E P
      'EP.   *Est Perditus*

Of Jewish Existentialism

Review of *Antisemite and Jew* by Jean-Paul Sartre   5 November 1948

I began the reading of this book, I must confess, with a certain amount of
prejudice both against its author and against his subject. I felt, first of all, that
the fame of M. Sartre, father of existentialism, had been entirely too factitious
a creation; that what had happened was that the post-war intellectual, bereft
of his gods, disillusioned with his ideologies, and in eager search of new altars,
had accepted M. Sartre's definitions only because a better set appeared to him
to be wanting; that those definitions, where they were new, were false, and
where they were true, were old; and that the novelty which did seem to inhere
in the existentialist system, issued only from the use of new synonyms to
substitute for old concepts. Never before, it appeared to me, had so much
tribute been paid to a thesaurus. Existentialism, I suspected, was nothing more
than the Da-da, aftermath of the First World War, only now it was arrayed
in a respectable (because it covered more) New Look. I felt too a certain disdain
for the credo of existentialism: a religion which feared to incur the expense
of a god. Nor did the palaver about 'anxieties,' 'situations,' 'essences' – scientific and up-to-date though it sounded – effect conversion; one had heard
it before. All the adulation seemed most unjustified; and one wondered at
Sartre's skill in feigning greatness.

  The subject of the book, too, was not ingratiating. What contribution
could Sartre, even Sartre, at this late date make to the study of Antisemitism?
What could a goy, 'an ethnic' as the old manuscripts say, tell me or any other
Schocken reader about a matter of which we had not only personal, but also
hereditary knowledge? And anyway, didn't *Gentleman's Agreement* exhaust
(*sic*) the subject?

  Sartre's book confirms most of the anticipations adverted to; but adds
one compensating revelation – Sartre writes brilliantly. All the old clichés are

here, but they are so polished and shined up, so closely integrated into acute ratiocinating paragraphs that when they do emerge, they do so with flash and fanfare and are justifiably mistaken for epigrams. Even that old chestnut – 'Antisemitism is not a Jewish problem, it is a Christian problem!' (I don't think there ever has been a goodwill meeting which has not been regaled by this piece of wisdom) – issues, after an excursus of close reasoning, like an apocalypse. Sartre also has a very interesting and beautifully developed section on the mystical nature of Jew-hatred; but says no more than Maurice Samuel has said, with equal wit and pertness, on the same subject. Sartre makes distinctions between authentic Jews and inauthentic Jews, which are remarkable only in that they are made by a non-Jew. Sartre comes to the conclusion that if the Jew did not exist, the Antisemite would invent him – which again is but a sentence written to synopsize the theme of 'The City Without Jews.' Sartre states that Antisemitism is the poor man's snobbery – a variation of the old definition that Antisemitism is the Socialism of fools. Sartre observes the connection between obscenity and Antisemitism – an observation that could not be avoided by anyone who ever saw a copy of Streicher's *Stuermer*. And so on, and so on, through all the age-old diagnostic.

What, then, makes this long essay, originally published as *Réflexions sur la Question Juive*, the classic contribution it incontestably is? It is the style of the man, a strange and refreshing combination of polemical vigour with metaphysical closeness. In philosophical *belles lettres* – where the well-written so often lacks profundity, and the profound, style – it is a gratification to come upon a treatise which is at once as readable as an essay and as analytical as a critique. For this is Sartre's manner: he begins with basic definitions – in truth his contribution has really ended with the enunciation of these definitions – and then draws, with inescapable logic, all his conclusions from his premises. If he did only this, however, one would praise his book of theorems, and be done; but Sartre does more; he dresses his theorems in living language, he adduces example, he employs – most non-Euclidean! – a delicate irony, he plays with paradox, he juggles epigram. And all the time does not deviate from his logical pattern! He sartorializes philosophy. He doesn't scintillate, he glows, like a mind which is a flame, not a flint.

Like almost all tracts on Antisemitism, Sartre's too, is better in its diagnosis than in its cure. At one moment, in the penultimate chapter, it looks as if Sartre is insisting upon Jewish authenticity, an acceptance by the Jew of his lot and not a flight from it, and a consequent self-development within the given situation. The espousal of such a solution, of course, would bring Sartre into the camp of Rabbi Mordecai Kaplan, and would make out of the *Partisan Review* but a supplement of *The Reconstructionist*. Naturally the suggestion is made but to be rejected. There is another solution to the Jewish problem; it is, it is – one expects thunder and lightning – it is Socialism; and again Sartre runs true to form: one had awaited the Messiah, one had even heard the ram's horn; but all one sees on the horizon is the old familiar donkey. Forsooth, I do not intend an aspersion upon Socialism, some of my best trends are Socialistic, but Socialism – it is clear from Sartre's exposition – involves assimilation, the loss of distinction, the unified amalgam, and thus the solution is, after all, but the dissolution one was seeking to avoid. Of such a solution, in which the Jewish is lost, lost not vainly, but for the enhancement of the human, but lost nonetheless, of such an *existenz*, the authentic Jew can only ask: Do you call this living?

T.S. Eliot and the Nobel Prize   12–26 November 1948

> Lights, lights,
> She entertains Sir Ferdinand
> Klein.

The news that Mr. T.S. Eliot had been awarded the Nobel Prize did not, it must be admitted, fill any of the members of the Klein clan, esquire or sir, with the same feeling of elation which it seems to have aroused in other quarters. It is true that one was gratified that a poet, any poet, should suddenly find himself a man of substance; it is equally true that one was pleased that the chosen one should be of His Majesty's subjects; but it was somewhat disturbing that one should discover, first, that the esoteric art of Mr. Eliot had become, with the passage of time, so hackneyed that it could even be submitted to the Nobel Committee, and second, that once submitted and presumably understood, the masters of the world's greatest literary award should see fit to bestow it upon a writer of the limited talents (within that limit, it is granted, excelling) and of the even more limited views of Mr. Eliot.

Let it be said immediately that we are not quarrelling with the literary tastes of the Nobel Committee. It is resignedly that one accepts them. An institution which has honoured the mediocre and ignored the first-rate, patronized Hesse and snubbed James Joyce, – it is not altogether with reference to literary standards that such an institution is to be judged. Bearing in mind both the will of the man who established the prize and the manner in which his executors have awarded it, it appears clearly that the Committee has often been impressed by large general considerations, human or national, rather than by the particular qualities of the elected genius. Too often has The Award been an act of piety where it should have been an act of discrimination. Surely it was because of his martyrdom – and hardly because he resembled Goethe

– that Karl von Ossietzky in his day was accoladed. The Swiss writer Hesse, say people who are at a loss to find a better reason, got It – because he was, in a time of war, of a neutral country! Indeed, one has only to read through the obituaries of the ennobled immortals to perceive that in almost every case it was either the man's patriotism, or his idealism, or his humanitarianism, and not his style, imaginative strength, verbal felicity which the Committee sought to flatter and reward.

This is not to say, forsooth, that the Noble Judges completely ignore their darlings' professional competence. They certainly do not; they weigh and consider; one can safely assume that before issuing judgment they make sure that the recipient is, or is known as, a writer. But it is to be doubted whether they go much beyond that laudable precaution.

With regard to the Scandinavian apotheosis, therefore, Mr. Eliot's merit (or deserts) are not to be measured by the criteria which one ordinarily uses in the ranking of literature. That would be grossly unfair – as unfair as it would be to apply to the lives of the gods the actuarial tables of the Prudential Insurance Company. It is by the standards which the Nobel Committee itself has seemed hitherto to have used that the matter should properly be judged.

In the case of Mr. Eliot these standards, we think, have been either ignored or very laxly applied.

Since the Nobel Prize is one which by definition recognizes only titans, it may be pertinent, first of all, to inquire whether Mr. Eliot is a major or a minor writer. Mr. Eliot himself has acknowledged these categories, and, in one of his essays, has even ventured the principle of distinction: the major writer, he says (our paraphrase), is simply one who, *ceteris paribus*, has written *more* than the minor writer. The talent being the same, it is the quantity which determines pre-eminence. The one is master of a substantial *corpus*; the other – if we may be permitted – of only a brilliant corpuscle. This latter has not what Eliot, in his essay on Thomas Heywood, called 'the dignity of an *oeuvre*.'

Now, Mr. Eliot is a poet. He has written, it is true, many distinguished essays, but these essays, it shortly will be shown, are for the most part the result of a shrewd glossatorial strategy, are really but disguised annotations to his poems, are supplements to those poems, and, though couched in a feigned professorial impersonality, are personal apologetics. Moreover, it is as a poet, and not as an essayist, that Mr. Eliot will stand robed in the august presence of the King of Sweden. And as a poet, Eliot has written extraordinarily little. One can number his lines, let alone his poems. Largely his reputation rests on *The Waste Land* (1922), typical in that it contains the one idea (borrowed) which is encountered again and again in his exiguous *corpus*, and in that it illustrates the one technique (borrowed) which he contributed to English poetry. And *The Waste Land* is, as epics are measured, no epic; it has altogether 403 lines, of which at least 25% are not the author's own, but excerpts from popular songs, and quotations from 35 different writers, in six languages, including the Sanskrit. Moreover, *The Waste Land*'s ingredients, linguistic, allusive, theological, may well serve as an objective correlative to Eliot's poems. The proportions, we venture to say without having taken a count, are practically the same. The only difference is that in the later *Four Quartets*, Eliot's allusions – to which he has not bothered, as he did with *The Waste Land*, to supply ten pages of notes – are even more restricted and personal.

It is not carpingly, therefore, that one asks, touching these macaronic reiterations: Is this *scope*? Is a man with so quantitatively modest an achievement to be hailed as a writer whom the *world*, through its Nobel Committee, is to delight to honour? It is no answer to say that what he *has* written is brilliant and by its own standards impeccable; one does not award the Nobel Prize to the coiner, no matter how gifted, of an epigram. Nor is it an answer to point out that Eliot has achieved world-stature by having been translated into many languages. In the first place, that was not difficult; his poems were already written in six tongues; and, in the second, translation, it is generally agreed, does not enhance but reduces the value of a work of literary art. Not his universality, surely, has merited Mr. T.S. Eliot the Nobel Prize.

It may also be questioned whether T.S. Eliot's is entirely an original talent. The fact is that the thing which struck Eliot's contemporaries as particularly novel was – the frankness of his derivativeness. He made out of quotation a poetic technique. Selecting the subject of his poem, *The Waste Land* for instance, he permitted Dante, Shakespeare, Baudelaire, Laforgue, Gautier, Webster, Ovid, Goldsmith, Spenser – to name but the men in the upper brackets – to write the poem for him. With such collaboration, felicity was inevitable. Eliot is thus a truly modern poet, an entrepreneur-poet, a poet-executive, one who knows how, as they say, to delegate duties.

It is true that Eliot's poetry, though admittedly derivative, came to his English audience as something fresh and strange. This was because Eliot very shrewdly derived himself from either the locally unknown or the temporarily forgotten, Laforgue or John Donne. Indeed, after having made a success out of the concealment of his literary antecedents, Eliot felt himself free to pass on to his disciples the secret of that success: 'One of the surest of tests is the way in which a poet borrows ... A good poet will usually borrow from authors remote in time, or alien in language, or diverse in interest' ('Philip Massinger').

We have referred to the essays as commentaries not so much on the authors whom they purport to discuss as on Eliot's own poetic practice. It is a device which is illustrated time and again, and has in it something which is at once pathetic and comic. Thus *Journey of the Magi* begins

> A cold coming we had of it,
> Just the worst time of the year
> For a journey, and such a long journey:
> The ways deep and the weather sharp,
> The very dead of winter.

But lest the reader miss the true nature of the allusion and remain unappreciative of the felicity of Eliot's manipulation of it, Eliot writes an essay on Lancelot Andrewes in which, casually, he quotes the following excerpt from a sermon delivered in 1621: 'It was no summer progress. A cold coming they had of it at this time of the year, just the worst time of the year to take a journey, and specially a long journey in. The ways deep, the weather sharp, the days short, the sun farthest off, *in solstitio brumali*, "the very dead of winter".'

The Waste Land, Ash Wednesday, and many of the early poems are full of allusions to *The Divine Comedy*. Obligingly, Eliot has written an essay on Dante in which somehow the explication of his matter requires quotation of precisely those lines which throw light on his (Eliot's) poetry. Almost every one of the essays provides examples of the system of annotation by *obiter dicta*.

The result, of course, is that one is tremendously impressed by both the extent and the esoteric nature of the great writings which Eliot has digested. If it is to the world's most distinguished *reader* of literature that the Nobel Prize is awarded, then Eliot has richly deserved it.

Moreover, even here – here in the originality of his derivativeness and the catholicity of his anthologies – it is a moot question whether Eliot is entirely unique, *sui generis*. Obviously it is not to be suggested that Eliot's prize should have been shared by the descendants (if any) of Dante and Laforgue; these are, technically speaking, *hors de combat*; but there *is* a man alive who, though he permitted himself the discretion of withdrawing his own work from competition, might still have laid claim for a part of Eliot's award. That man is Ezra Pound. He it was to whom *The Waste Land* was dedicated as to *il miglior fabbro* – the better craftsman. He, it is said, was the man responsible for reducing that *Waste Land* from a work of 700 lines to one of 400 lines – criticism showing that the art of deletion, especially in poetry, is often superior to that of composition. And Pound it was who introduced Eliot to the fame and exploitability of many of his dead collaborators. Pound's imprint, in fact, is to be found everywhere in Eliot's work.

This is true not only of the technical instruction which Eliot took from Pound, but manifests itself also in choice of theme, and even in echo of phrasing. Pound writes *Portrait d'une femme*; Eliot writes *Portrait of a Lady*. Pound invents a Mr. Sycorax; Eliot discovers his relative, Mr. Apollinax; Pound does an Antisemitic squib about a Mr. Brennbaum; Eliot does likewise with Mr. Bleistein.

It really is not fair; the booty should have been divided.

Nor can it be said that Eliot, though derivative in manner, was a world-shaker in thought. The theme that runs through all of his work is the orthodox doctrine of Anglican Christianity. They are the old truths which our poet reiterates; nor does he refresh them, like Kierkegaard, with new insights. When Eliot, in that famous passage, identified himself as a royalist in politics, a classicist in literature, and an Anglican in religion, he took the trouble to define the first two terms, but of the third stated that it was not for him to say what it was. It is in this sense that his entire work shows the hereditary strain; it was the poet's grandfather, the Rev. William Greenleaf Eliot, D.D., who wrote a remembered sermon on 'Suffering Considered as Discipline.' Hand in hand with this acceptance of authority runs a subsidiary or correlated theme: the praise of the past. The whole of *The Waste Land* bears the un-mistakeable mark of the *laudator temporis acti* – the man who sings the good old days gone by. Most people will agree, I think, that a man with a mind which is continually reverting to the superiority of the past over the present is a bore; it is Eliot's virtue that he converts this platitudinous attitude into something vigorous and almost revolutionary. But the attitude remains fun-damentally what it is – one of reaction. Eliot's choice of the final standard whereby one can identify the truly [...] Baudelaire is he who has 'a sense of his own age' – he always [...] seemed to use as a singular inept strategy on the part of an essayist every one of whose essays is a critical tactic. For by that standard, Eliot doesn't belong in the twentieth century at all. All his writings show an antipathy to everything the twentieth century stands for; sympathy he appears to have had only for that which in the modern age was still mediaeval.

It is to be doubted, however, whether Eliot's orthodoxy was the moti-vating consideration of the Swedish Academy. Piety – though a laudable quality – hardly is relevant to the making of literature; if it were, it would be the Pope or the Archbishop of Canterbury who would be receiving the annual awards.

Moreover, T.S. Eliot did not always figure as the champion of Chris-tianity. It is one of the ironies of criticism that Eliot's reputation was made by *The Waste Land* – a work which for a decade continued to be praised for its nihilism and decadence. Indeed, it was these features of the poem – su-perficial ones, it is true, but at the time no others were appreciated – which so strongly appealed to the first post-war generation. In Eliot the critics of the twenties heard a poet who darkly muttered the decline of capitalism, the contemporary negation of values, the way the world ended, not with a bang but a whimper. He did, at that moment, appear to have a sense of his own age. And then in the thirties came the revelation –

> That was not what he meant at all.
> That was not it, at all.

Eliot, far from being a revolutionary exponent of the modern and the avant-garde, was really no more than a latter-day purveyor of the ancient Christian verity and velleity.

Yet without the misapprehension of the twenties Eliot might have remained but another metaphysical experimenter, a somewhat donnish essayist, a writer for church circles. Once he had been hailed, however, as the spokesman for his generation, withdrawal from that position – now that it was revealed through the retroactive effect of *Ash Wednesday* and *The Four Quartets* that he was but the usual Christian – was extremely difficult. A reputation was thus built upon a misunderstanding and the writer who had become famous as a typical son of his generation eventually appears before the Swedish Academy as an early Father of the Church.

All of which is but of minor interest to the Nobel Committee. That committee never makes reputations; it endorses reputations already made. The half century of literary awards of the Swedish Academy affords not a single instance in which that body by its sole gesture raised to world fame some genius unrecognized and languishing in obscurity. The man perforce had first to be translated into the Scandinavian; and in such translation, naturally, much of the real essence of a man's work is lost.

The Nobel Award thus continues, by all the standards invoked, a riddle. It is known, however, that the co-operative Swedes often confer their distinction upon a writer for no other reason than that he qualifies as a 'humanitarian.' Does Eliot, even by this easy standard, really qualify?

The truth is that our poet, despite his constant preaching of the Christian virtues, remains, in his attitudes as revealed in his work, a prig and a snob. With what a self-satisfying superiority he speaks of 'the damp souls of housemaids'! How troubled his aesthetic is by 'the smell of steaks in passageways'! How the personality of Apeneck Sweeney mars the Bostonian calm of his meditations! The 'young man carbuncular,' 'the small house agent's clerk' evokes his well-bred scorn; he is 'one of the low on whom assurance sits / As a silk hat on a Bradford millionaire.' Again and again Eliot's Christianity gives itself away, until one is convinced that here, too, he has borrowed from Pound:

> For I am homesick after my own kind,
> And ordinary people touch me not.

Perhaps the final test of a man's religion and humanity is his attitude to minorities. The minority with whom Eliot seems to have been obsessed are the Jews – and here, too, his 'poetic' utterances are such as to make one question again whether the Nobel Committee really knew what it was doing.

The old man in *Gerontion* – who is presumably a personification of European civilization – complains thus (only the rhythm differs from Hitler's lucubrations):

> My house is a decayed house,
> And the Jew squats on the window sill, the owner,
> Spawned in some estaminet of Antwerp,
> Blistered in Brussels, patched and peeled in London.

The Streicher caricature is also exemplified:

> But this or such was Bleistein's way:
> A saggy bending of the knees
> And elbows, with palms turned out,
> Chicago Semite Viennese.
>   (*Burbank with a Baedeker*)

Capitalism is, of course, Jewish:

> I shall not want Capital in Heaven
> For I shall meet Sir Alfred Mond.
> We two shall lie together, lapt
> In a five per cent Exchequer Bond.
>   (*A Cooking Egg*)

He even descends to the Antisemitism of the music hall joke. When a Jewess eats, she eats thus:

> Rachel, *née* Rabinovitch
> Tears at the grapes with murderous paws;
>   (*Sweeney among the Nightingales*)

It is, indeed, an interesting speculation to consider what might have developed out of Eliot's occasional flirtations with Fascism had not the 1939 declaration of war taught him discretion. Certainly in the thirties Eliot was writing of what he called classicism in a vein most suspect: 'Yet there is a tendency – discernible even in art – toward a higher and clearer conception of Reason, and a more severe and severe control of the emotions by Reason ... I will mention a few books, not all very recent, which to my mind exemplify this tendency ...' and then he leads off with Georges Sorel's *Réflexions sur la violence* – a classic text-book of fascism!

The war, we said, thwarted the growth of Eliot's 'classicism' – but he found a way out. He edited a selection from Kipling, the author who ornamented his collected works with swastikas. One has only to consider Eliot's literary standards as enunciated in his early essays to realize how strange a choice this was – obviously the element of affinity between Kipling and Eliot was something other than a common aesthetic code. Despite the pathetic effort which Eliot makes in the introduction to that book to prove Kipling a considerable poet, the feeling remains that it is K's xenophobia which is the real catalytic agent.

No, the motives behind the Nobel Prize award for 1948 remain inscrutable. It can only be assumed that in the Swedish Academy Eliot has at last found his ideal readers: 'I myself should like,' said Eliot in *The Uses of Poetry*, 'an audience which could not read nor write.' Perhaps this is too unkind a quotation; perhaps it is another which could apply – 'Poetry can communicate before it is understood.'

Or perhaps it was a year in which the awards were all pragmatic – D.D.T. and T.S. Eliot.

Hemlock and Marijuana

Review of *In the Penal Colony: Stories and Short Pieces* by Franz Kafka   17 December 1948

It is already a cliché of contemporary literary explication that the works of Franz Kafka are intended to be understood on several levels. Indeed, it does not take much perspicacity to recognize that in almost every one of Kafka's stories there lies concealed some parable, some adumbration of a verity which transcends the mere data of the narrative. For here, invariably, more is meant than meets the eye; the story may be a story of Devil's Island, but its meaning encompasses the globe; it is, in truth, a nineteenth-century *Maggid-of-Dubnow* who speaks, with a sophistication unknown to the Preacher, and of the Preacher's faith utterly bereft, through these essentially simple anecdotes of insights and realizations touching nothing less than the human situation. Of that situation he has one terrible assertion to make – its perplexedness; through the labyrinth of his prose, with its windings and retractions, its provisos, its however's, its perpetual tentativeness, issues the devastating question: What is truth?

The question is put without jesting.

It is in this sense that Kafka is a sort of latter-day Maimonides, but it is no *Guide* to the Perplexed that he writes. His entire opus is the *Song of Perplexity* itself.

Kafka's critics, unwilling to remain in a condition of continuous suspension-of-significance, have each sought frantically to attach some meaning to K's myriad-faceted parables. Thus there are those who bring to K's works an annotating apparatus compounded all of Freud and Jung; The father! The father! they cry, as if Kafka were the result only of his immediate father; others purport to read into Kafka's complicated paragraphs a search for some religion, even a flirtation with Christianity; none are content to remain with the impression of the obvious – the sense of overwhelming alienation which rises from every one of Kafka's pages like some poisonous vapour unbalancing the reader.

The meaning lies – in the ambiguity.

This is true, not only of the general tenor of his work, it is true also of its particular components. Choose at random, and examine as for syntax, any paragraph in Kafka. A positive statement, a bold bald assertion, is as rare as the worm of Asmodeus. There is nothing which cuts straight. No sooner does Kafka find himself on the brink of an affirmative, but he retreats, hedges, somersaults backwards. Over that precipice he will not fall. The genius of his writing lies in that his phobia is contagious.

The Kafkan attitude is nowhere better illustrated than in the volume before us. While in *The Castle* ambivalence is carried to such lengths that often it appears that K is parodying himself, here both the philosophy and the method go just as far as permissible, but not beyond, – right up to, and not over, the Sabbath limit of literary perambulation. It is, to change the image, as if Kafka were being presented *in vitro*: 'The Metamorphosis' and 'In the Penal Colony' – a microcosm of the Kafka world.

'The Penal Colony' is a story shattering and horrendous. When I first read it in *Partisan Review* several years ago, its terrible impact for weeks unfitted me from any further reading, anywhere; in other books I could only dabble and browse; after the ordeal of that experience everything else seemed trivial, an artifact and pointless. The tang of 'The Penal Colony,' the tang of the true hemlock, lingered upon my palate for days. Of justice here below, its callous drama and its tragic farce, I walked for days familiar.

But 'The Penal Colony' diminishes to the proportions of some colonial civil servant's anecdote in comparison with the quiet more-than-murder of

'The Metamorphosis.' Where the first pointed up the terror of some single human institution – justice – the second points up the peril, the uncertainty, the sheer unreality of the total human situation. And this quality it is which raises the Kafka story – considered purely and simply as a horror story – shivering altitudes above anything Edgar Allan Poe at his macabrest could conceive.

For Poe's stories are melodrama; their horrors, by definition, occur only to people who are not minding their own business; in a sense, therefore, their horrors are justified, and while we shudder, we do not completely dissolve. The calamity of the Kafka story, however, is likely to fall upon anyone at all, even upon the unobtrusive, even upon insignificance reduced to an initial (K), even upon you and me. In Poe, the reader is largely a spectator, in Kafka, he is personally involved.

'The Metamorphosis' is based upon a single frightening postulate; a travelling salesman (i.e., a nobody) wakes up in his bed one morning to find that he has been transformed into a gigantic insect! Acceptance of this opening sentence is the sole suspension of disbelief which the story demands; after this sentence, everything is – I say it, but with a changed voice – reasonable, logical, inevitable. Indeed, after that sentence and for the entire space of sixty pages, the *word* 'insect' is not again mentioned. But with what a cathartic indirection the *fact* of insectitude is brought home to the reader (himself involved) time and again. I haven't paused to make a paradigm of the story, but I venture to suspect that if it were schematically analyzed it would be found to consist of a series of alternations: an instance in which Gregor Samsa considers the symptoms of insectality followed by an instance illustrative of his human, all too human, thought; this in its turn – lest the reader forget because of Gregor's sensitive meditations the true shape in which Gregor finds himself – this in its turn followed by some little event which again brings out the harrowing fact of metamorphosis; and so on, and so on. This, in fine, is the essential horror of the story: every time we begin to think of Gregor Samsa as a human, comes the sly phrase with the abhorred turn to set us crawling centipedestrian again.

Horror spawns horror; the obvious revulsion of the plight described is, after all, merely the beginning of this nightmare narrative. The sense of alienation; the kick of rejection (symbolized by the father's large, very large soles); the deprivation of love (symbolized by the removal of the picture showing the lady with her arm elbow-deep in a fur muff); the final nullification (without loss) – these are the stages and stations of an ordeal which begins like a simple piece of ingenuity and ends as a Dantesque 'human comedy.'

The bite of 'The Metamorphosis' is due, of course, to its hemlock philosophy (Samsa, like Socrates, just lies down and dies). But the effect is due to yet another toxic element. Poe's stories, it has been asserted, owe much of their strangeness to the fact that they were written while the author was under the influence of drugs. Kafka's stories are not caused by, but do have the effect, of drugs. Not much happens in a K. story, but time is so slowed down, motion is so lentitized, that in the space of one story one appears to have lived a lifetime. From what I am told of that notorious herb, it is the very marijuana manner. It is a manner which Kafka – without benefit of smoke – illustrates, on a minor scale, in his 'Meditations' and with incomparable effect in 'The Metamorphosis.'

This is a book unreservedly recommended. It is for adults, in their adulthood. Children, curious about metamorphosis, may be given Ovid.

Old Ez and His Blankets   4 March 1949

> Old Ez folded his blankets
> Neither Eos nor Hesperus has suffered wrong at my hands
> – Canto LXXIX

It was not without some qualms of conscience that the Bollingen election committee, which includes among its members Conrad Aiken, W.H. Auden, T.S. Eliot, Robert Lowell and Katherine Anne Porter, decided to give its one thousand dollar prize (thirty-three and a third times the usual thirty pieces of silver) to Ezra Pound. Awarding this prize to the renegade poet for 'the highest achievement in American poetry' as displayed in *The Pisan Cantos*, the Committee blandly announced that 'it was aware that objections might be made.' However, 'to permit other considerations than that of poetic achievement to sway the decision would destroy the significance of the award, and would, in principle, deny the validity of that objective perception of value on which any civilized society must rest.'

I have examined these leaning cantos of Pisa and must confess myself at a loss to understand how any such phraseology as 'objective perception of value ... civilized society ...' can be related to the erratic and often vicious outpourings which now constitute this 'highest achievement in American poetry.'

I venture to say, first of all, that I doubt whether any of the members of the distinguished committee – with all due respect to their titanic mentalities – can actually follow the sequence and the meaning of Cantos LXXII–LXXXIV. Much too frequently these cantos give the impression of an old man mumbling into his unkempt beard the gossip of two decades ago, the tag-ends of an outmoded pedantry, the dirty snivelling jokes of senile impotence. Frequently, too, that beard becomes frothy with malice, the spittle of hatred and frustration running down its matted clots. But a totally coherent statement never is made – what the old knave is actually saying is never made clear. It is just as well.

Passages here and there, however, are explicit – and we wonder whether it is upon these that the Bollingen critics have exercised their 'objective perception of value.' Is it really a mark of genius when a man combines the two phrases 'cat in the bag,' 'nigger in the woodpile' to speak with devastating novelty of 'the cat in the woodshed'? Is it wit beyond the compass of Walter Winchell when Ezra Pound refers to the French ambassador as 'the frogbassador'? Is it a contribution to the highest in American thought when Ezra quotes 'the guard as not thinking that the Führer had started it'? Is it poetic achievement to write:

(I heard it in the s.h.   a suitable place
to hear that the war was over)?

Is it American achievement to write of American achievement as follows:

(O Mercury god of thieves, your caduceus
is now used by the American army
                as witness this packing case)?

Or the American flag: 'the bacon-rind banner alias the Washington arms'?
Is there really a relationship between 'civilized society' and remarks such as these:

(a) Pétain defended Verdun while Blum
      was defending a bidet

(b) the yidd is a stimulant and the goyim are cattle
      in gt / proportion and go to saleable slaughter
      with the maximum of docility

(c) So that in the synagogue in Gibraltar
      the sense of humour seemed to prevail
      during the preliminary parts of the whatever
      but they respected at least the scrolls of the law
      from it, by it, redemption
      @ $8.50, @ $8.67 buy the field with good money

(d) And Churchill's return to Midas broadcast by his liary

(e) And the goyim are undoubtedly in great numbers cattle
    whereas a jew will receive information

All the cantos, it must be said, are made up of such delightful tidbits. It is true that here and there a neat epigram, a witty comment, a profound thought, a fine-sounding line of poetry, will obtrude through the tangle of cockatoo gibberish – but the felicities, it will be discovered, are invariably quotations, another man's wisdom, another's wit. Of his own Ezra contributes the usual exercises in the transliteration of dialect: '''The Hound of Heaven'' / a modddun opohem he had read'; the usual thievings from James Joyce, as witness the reference to peripla and Ulysses; the usual opinion about the origin of the last war: 'Knecht gegen Knecht / to the sound of the bumm drum, to eat remnants / for a usurer's holiday to change the / price of a currency'; the usual chinoiseries, all duly explained at the end of Canto 77; and the usual Pound against Shylock.

Some attempt has been made by reviewers to use quotations from these cantos to evoke sympathy and compassion for a poor poet, betrayed by belief in his own metaphor. These reviewers excerpt isolated lines to prove that Pound was really no more than 'a conscientious objector' opposed to all wars; unfortunately for this point of view there are extant cullings from Pound's Italian radio broadcasts which are by no means anaemic. Much is made also of the pathos of various lines in the Pisan Cantos; and indeed the spectacle of a megalomaniac traitor at last discomfited is a pathetic one. Great to-do also over the rhymes in which he calls to

> Pull down thy vanity,
> Rathe to destroy, niggard in charity,
> Pull down thy vanity,
>   I say pull down.

But, as is obvious from the context, the contrition is temporary and evanescent.

If, then, on the strength of these cantos, Ezra Pound deserved the Bollingen Prize, Goebbels posthumously should be awarded the Pulitzer. It is false to say that the Pisan Cantos constitute a high American poetic achievement; technically, these cantos are no better – intrinsically, much worse – than those which preceded them and which went unhailed and unprized by these same Aikens and Anne Porters. That Eliot should feel that Pound ought to be honoured is not surprising; as a poet he no doubt has an uneasy conscience about the Nobel Prize; he knows, moreover, that ideologically Pound is but an Eliot-plus-temerity. But that Auden – the milk-of-human-kindness Auden

– and Lowell, singer of fish and Fridays, – that these should seek to honour the man who prostituted his talent to the designs of the blackshirts and the bullyboys – this is something that cannot be understood except platonically, that is to say, in the light of that thinker who would banish all poets from his republic.

One can only assume, to explain the otherwise inexplicable, that it was a kind of vanity which taking possession of these critics, prompted them to bestow the monied accolade upon this very undeserving man. It is as if they said: 'Lesser spirits may be prejudiced by the man's treasonable activities, but we, aesthetes, pure and impartial, are above such merely political considerations; smaller souls might hold it against him that at a critical moment in the world's history, he was on the side of the hangmen and the kindlers in crematoria, but we – we measure only the length of his lines, not his rope. Let the crass and the uninitiate judge the irrelevant; the fact that the poet is now in an insane asylum serves only to give authenticity to his genius; and that he did not see eye to eye with the thousands who perished in the last war only emphasizes the fact that we are face to face with an independent spirit.'

Some such words the Bollingen critics must have addressed to themselves; made the award; and then gone off to bed, snug in the assurance that they were better, more broad-minded, more deeply sensitive than their brutish calculating fellows. Whether in their sleep they dreamed of the thousands tortured and murdered to the music of Ezra Pound's radio-broadcasts, whipped and broken to the rhythm of Ezra Pound's mellifluities, laundered to his Chinese, buried and lime-pitted to his incantatory Latin and Greek – only these sensitive poets can tell. If their sleep was indeed troubled they had but to rouse themselves, turn to Canto 79, and read:

> Old Ez has folded his blankets
> Neither Eos nor Hesperus has suffered wrong at my hands.

Neither Eos nor Hesperus.

The Masked Yeats

Review of *Yeats: The Man and the Masks* by Richard Ellmann, *The Golden Nightingale* by Donald Stauffer, and *The Permanence of Yeats* edited by James Hall and Martin Steinmann   June–July 1950

No great poet of our time has sought oftener to reveal himself, whether through autobiography, technical essay, or confidential letter, than did William Butler Yeats. And none has remained more enigmatic.

This is the result of a number of causes. One is confused, first of all, by the plurality of the man. The Collected Works contain at least four poets called Yeats: there is the aesthetic bow-tied willowy Yeats of the nineties; there is the patrioteering Yeats at once participant and critic of Irish Nationalism; the Yeats mystical, gyring about some Byzantium that never was on land or sea; and finally, for one short rejuvenated spell, Yeats the gay old blade. It is as if the poet were phoenix and in a single lifetime achieved four saltations from his own prolific ash.

No other contemporary poet has been so myriad-minded, so multifaceted. Nor can these transformations be attributed to a long-lived man's plagiarism – he is phoenix, not parakeet – for through all of them there runs the indelible bold line of his own personality.

There is also, to confound the makers of formulae, the strange un-twentieth-century biography of the man, his psychic researches, his dabbling in magic. Is one to consider as having something listenable to say a man who writes, seriously, the following meditation:

> Imagine yourself as being led through a forest or other wild place at nightfall by the light of a star – the only star visible – this is the morning star or the evening star – the star of the side of the vault through which the initiate enters – you come to a mountainside. This mountain, the central mountain of the world, is represented in old prints as having a flat top on which is Eden, a great walled garden. The birds of the night cry one by one ... You make the sign of the rending of the veil, and say Pawketh. There is a light suddenly and mouth of cave appears which shines with light. You approach the cave and cry out the word Shieh and make the sign, O and T. The cave is seven-sided and the walls are carved with Egyptian or earlier figures ... You make the sign of 5 = 6 and lie down in the pastos. Around are three figures, one of whom places on the breast the rose, one places in the right hand the tree sign and one in the left the lotus. You gaze upward at the rose and say 'O

Rose of Rubis grant to me the knowledge of 7 earth keys and the power over these. Let me know what I have been – what I am and what I shall become.'

As if this obfuscation were not enough there is the later darkness of *The Vision*, with its significant moons and apocalyptic masks, its complicated ravelling explanations.

If out of these eccentricities the critic is able to fashion some coherent pattern of behaviour, enters William Butler Yeats, the Senator!

He is, to use his own epithet, a public man. His vocabulary, however, still remains esoterically private, with oracular and evocative talk of towers, cones, gyres, mummies, winding-sheets, dolphins, tinctures.

It is this difficulty – difficulty in the man rather than in the poet – which perhaps explains the continuing appearance of the many books on Yeats. It is Yeats's own explanations of his intention which have made further explanation necessary. This poet's autobiographical style affords an outstanding example of uncommunicative garrulity. Read any paragraph at random. He seems to be taking you into his confidence, you are about to hear the key turn in his heart, and then – by an insidious modification, an intrinsic diffidence, the whole is nullified, and you are left as much the outsider as you were before. You go on to the next paragraph, and the next – again and again you will be most intimately excluded. These are not revelations, they are the motions of a fan dance.

Each of the books above, all published by Macmillan, attempts in its own way to resolve some of the difficulties to which we have alluded. *The Permanence of Yeats* seeks to do this by way of symposium; the editors, James Hall and Martin Steinmann, bringing together between the covers of one book a number of disparate essays on Yeats, seem to hope that thus a complete portrait may emerge. Unfortunately not all of the contributions to the symposium are of equal value. Many, it appears, were selected because they were written by distinguished critics; but not everything that a distinguished critic writes is distinguished; often, like lesser mortals he must meet a book reviewer's deadline, often he feels himself constrained to write simply because he has not yet made his statement on Yeats, and often he is just not at his best, and nods.

Mr. Ellmann's book, however, justifies the Macmillan proliferation. One of the most sensible books on the subject, it proceeds through a series of paradoxes towards a total, though necessarily ambivalent, picture of the man. Certainly it affords a refreshing contrast to MacNeice's inconclusive conversation piece on the same subject. Mr. Ellmann, moreover, adduces new data, facts not hitherto adverted to either by Hone or Jeffares. Perhaps this critic's principal merit is that he treats Yeats in Yeats's own terms, judging him as I imagine every artist would wish to be judged – in the context of his own texts

– and not by some arbitrary standards, as of social significance, aesthetic theory, political relevance, etc.

It was Professor Stauffer's book, however, which afforded real delight. *The Golden Nightingale* is a tour de force. Here Dr. Stauffer deduces with brilliance, and with charm expounds a theory of poetry based entirely on Yeats's praxis. Professorial often, he is nowhere pedantic, and provides in these essays a salutary antidote to some of the cerebral *pilpul* which passes for criticism. His reading of 'The Wild Swans at Coole,' so eruditely yet smoothly prepared for in the earlier chapters, moves from stanza to stanza with the grace and inevitability of its subject.

Homage to Ludwig Lewisohn 29 May 1952

We are happy to join with the many thousands who are to-day extending greetings and good wishes to Dr. Ludwig Lewisohn on the occasion of his seventieth birthday. From our recent conversation with Dr. Lewisohn we certainly had not suspected that the undone years had been so many, for everything about him – his career, his attitudes, his philosophy – bespeaks youth, vigour, recurrent juvenescence.

What does, indeed, indicate that the decades have stomped by is the great record of achievement which is Lewisohn's. For Lewisohn stands to-day, as he has stood for many years, as an unchallenged pre-eminence in the domain of Anglo-Jewish letters. Poet, novelist, translator, critic, philosopher – he has touched nothing that he has not enhanced. Gifted with a style at once fastidious and lucid, endowed with perceptions at once shrewd and sensitive, he strode onto the field of international literature – an heir of irrefutable title entering upon his heritage. His books upon the poets of modern France, the drama in Germany, his classic work on American literature, his deceptively easy but profoundly knowing essays on contemporary literary trends and values – all of these evoked comparison with the wide sweep of a Taine, the far-flung erudition of a Brandes.

But drawn by ancestral nostalgias, caught in the ineluctable net of racial memory and national tradition, Lewisohn kept forsaking his wide estates for that corner that is forever Israel's. This wilful dedication is all the more startling when one recalls the fact that this great Jewish mentor of our times spent his early years in an environment entirely assimilatory. Yet, as the late Shmaryahu Levin pointed out when he made comparisons between Herzl and Moses, there is something eminently right and just in such incongruity. 'For had it been otherwise, had Moses been brought up in Amram's right Jewish home,' – the peroration is Levin's – 'men would have said that his ideal of national integrity was but the result of the lullabies, the folk-lore, the hearth-pride, of his family, – no, amidst the very alienation of Pharaoh's palace, Moses came to his conclusions!'

Who wishes to learn the path by which Lewisohn came to the intellectual leadership of his generation has but to read the record of that odyssey, in three volumes recounted: *The Island Within, Up-Stream, Mid-Channel*. The very titles proclaim them a trilogy which might well have been called: *By the Waters of Babylon*.

To-day, Lewisohn's varied roles merge into one – the latter-day prophet. One of the earliest proponents of Zionism – he made the pilgrimage in 1925 – he sees the first flashes of that dream fulfilled. But politics is not all. Lewisohn entertains for his people higher aspirations, loftier ambitions – he dreams of a great cultural renaissance, a resurgence of that grand creative impulse, that visionary élan, by which in times past our ancestors kindled the minds and warmed the hearts of mankind; and in the vanguard of that movement, pointing a Promised Land, he stands himself. Disciples following him are not yet to be counted in myriads; alas, an entire generation, the generation that went whoring after strange gods, was lost; but others will come, as already they have come. It cannot be otherwise; the validity of his theses, the power of his monitions, the warmth of his personality, these make the burden of this prophet irresistible. Be his, then, many long and fruitful years to come, hosts of disciples, and the prophet's uniqueness, to wit, the thing conceived as vision seen as sight!

7 / JAMES JOYCE'S *ULYSSES*

The Oxen of the Sun

In a letter dated Trieste, the second of March, 1920, James Joyce wrote to his friend Frank Budgen:

> Am working hard at *Oxen of the Sun*, the idea being the crime committed against fecundity by sterilizing the act of coition. Scene: lying-in hospital. Technique: a nineparted episode without divisions introduced by a Sallustian-Tacitean prelude (the unfertilized ovum), then by way of earliest English and alliterative and monosyllabic and Anglo-Saxon ('Before born the babe had bliss. Within the womb he won worship.' 'Bloom dull dreamy heard: in held hat stony staring'), then by way of Mandeville ('then came forth a scholar of medicine that men clepen etc.'), then Malory's *Morte d'Arthur* ('but that franklin Lenehan was prompt ever to pour them so that at the least way mirth should not lack'), then the Elizabethan chronicle style ('about that present time Stephen filled all cups'), then a passage solemn uses Milton, Taylor, and Hooker, followed by a choppy Latin-gossipy bit, style of Burton-Browne, then a passage Bunyanesque ('the reason was that in the way he fell in with a certain whore whose name she said is Bird in the Hand'), after a diarystyle bit Pepys-Evelyn ('Bloom sitting snug with a party of wags, among them Dixon jun., Sa. Lynch, Doc. Madden and Stephen D. for a languor he had before and was now better, he having dreamed to-night a strange fancy, and Mrs. Purefoy there to be delivered, poor body, two days past her time and the midwives hard put to it, God send her quick issue') and so on through Defoe-Swift and Steele-Addison-Sterne, and Landor-Pater-Newman until it ends in a frightful jumble of pidgin English, nigger English, Cockney, with Bowery slang and broken doggerel. This progression is also linked back at each part subtly with some foregoing episode of the day and besides this, with the natural stages of development in the embryo, and the periods of formal evolution in general. The double thudding Anglo-Saxon motives recur from time to time ('Loth to move from Horne's house') to give the sense of the hoofs of oxen. Bloom is the spermatozoon, the hospital the womb, the nurse the ovum, Stephen the embryo.
>
> How's that for high?[1]

That this famous chapter in *Ulysses* is made up of a progress of parodies has been noted before. Stuart Gilbert, whose *James Joyce's 'Ulysses': A Study* (1930) remains to this day the commentary *par excellence*, devotes some interesting, if not exhaustive, pages to a discussion of the manner and the matter of these virtuoso exercises. Harry Levin, in a necessarily abbreviated work, adverts to them, and Frank Budgen in *James Joyce and the Making of 'Ulysses'* (1934) affords some glosses reported as issuing from conversations with Joyce. On pp. 223–9 of his book Budgen obviously makes use of the letter here excerpted to head this essay, but beyond the bare repetition of some of its phrases – Sallustian-Tacitean prelude, ninefold division – he essays no explication. Fourteen years have passed since the printing of Budgen's book, twenty-eight since the receipt of the Trieste letter, and Joyce's indication of his intent with regard to the *Oxen of the Sun* still reads like an enigma, almost like a practical joke.

What follows is an attempt – in some aspects tentative but in large outline final and of the writer's conviction – to give meaning to, and afford illustration of, the 'nineparted episode without divisions' and of the progression which is 'linked back at each part subtly with some foregoing episode of the day and besides this, with the natural stages of development in the embryo and the periods of formal evolution in general.'

THE STAGES OF THE EMBRYO

The first two pages (377, 378)[2] do not enter into the embryonic framework. The Sallustian-Tacitean paragraphs, as the letter states, constitute a prelude, are ovum unfertilized, are English as English might have been written had the Roman conquest remained permanent: *Britannia capta Romam cepit*. It is a section which quite properly may be dubbed gerundive both in that it is concerned with things about to become to be and in that its phraseology is frequently gerundival: 'that they her by anticipation went seeing mother'(378), 'suddenly to be about to be cherished had been begun'(378).

The First Month: This, although pre-indicated in the preceding paragraphs, begins with: 'Some man that wayfaring was'(378). This is Bloom – the motile wayfaring spermatazoon. The nurse, says Joyce, is the ovum, hence 'swire ywimpled'(379). The moment of fertilization takes place immediately after she 'him drew that he would rathe infare under her thatch'(379). Even the name of the proprietor of the hospital plays to Joyce's purpose: Horne, that is to say, an inlet of the sea (cf. Golden Horn), that is, the cervix; wherefore 'that man her will wotting worthful went in Horne's house'(379). See also 'in Cape Horn ... they have a rain'(398).

During this month the zygote, the single cell, develops by mitosis into two cells called blastomeres, which break up into four, eight, sixteen, etc., until the blastula is formed: 'Expecting each moment to be her next'(381). This multiplication of cells is accomplished by 'a warlock with his breath that he blares into them like to bubbles'(381). On the same page the swelling up 'wondrously like to a vast mountain' – a Mandevillian exaggeration – is proleptic.

The language of this section – Old English, alliterative – is to be considered, in biological terms, as unicellular, amoeboid.

It should be stated here, to avail throughout, that often the point where one month ends and the other begins cannot be indicated with precision. These liminal ambiguities, moreover, are intentional; it is 'a nineparted episode *without divisions*' that Joyce is writing; and he writes thus to imitate embryological life where the indicia of the second month, for example, do not always wait for a complete lunar revolution to elapse before they make themselves manifest. Sometimes they come earlier, sometimes later, but in the general nine-month progression they are identifiable month by month.[3]

The indicia adduced throughout this essay to establish identities in embryology, recapitulation, and evolution are by no means exhaustive. Many others will occur to the reader as, warned to look for them, he parses his way through the relevant paragraphs.

The Second Month: This stage is explicitly indicated: 'how at the end of the second month a human soul was infused'(383), but the month – as will be seen later from the chapter-correspondences – goes back to the previous page where references to the 'cup' show that invagination preliminary to the fashioning of the gastrula has taken place.

During the second month, the head of the embryo is disproportionately large: 'In colour whereof they waxed hot upon that head'(383).

External genitalia appear, but sex cannot be differentiated: 'and nature has other ends than we. Then said Dixon junior to Punch Costello wist he what ends'(383).

The Third Month: This, too, is explicitly announced in Punch Costello's song: '*The first three months she was not well, Staboo*'(385), but the month begins earlier on p. 384. This is the month when centres of ossification appear: 'A wariness of mind he would answer as fitted all and, laying hand to jaw'(384).

The appearance of the embryo at this stage prompts the series of epithets: 'thou chuff, thou puny ... thou abortion thou'(386).

The Fourth Month: This is not named by number; it is, however, the month in which sex can be differentiated; hence the 'anthem *Ut novetur sexus omnis corporis mysterium*'(386).

The Fifth Month: During this month, heart sounds are for the first time perceptible: 'Came now the storm that hist his heart,' 'and his heart shook within the cage of his breast'(388).

In the same month, foetal movements are usually felt by the mother. These acrobatics in the womb are equated with post-natal womb-acrobatics on p. 389 where we read about the positions Pickaback and Topsyturvy and Shameface (the typical embryonic attitude) and Cheek by Jowl! Joyce writing to Pound about his obtuse reviewers: 'Why didn't they at least say that the book was *damn funny*?'

The style is the style of Bunyan: *Grace Abounding*.

The Sixth Month: One hesitates to affirm that allusion to this month is to be found in 'So Thursday *six*teenth June Patk. Dignam laid in clay'(390). But there are other indicia: first, the reference to 'Mal M's brother will stay a month'(390) and second, the reference to children dying at birth: "Tis her ninth chick to live'(391). If born during sixth month, foetus never survives.

The Seventh Month: Upon this month Joyce dwells at greater length than upon any of the others. This is because the embryo at this stage may be born, and live. Indeed, as will be seen from the analysis of the chapter-correspondences, this section by itself is made to recapitulate the previous sections. But, of that later.

The seventh month is noted numerically in three different places; and the triplication is as far as Joyce will go to let the reader suspect that something unusual is taking place. On p. 394 one reads of the 'old whoremaster that kept seven trulls in his house,' on p. 398 it pours 'seven showers,' and on p. 399 Kitty has been 'wardmaid these seven months.'

The possibility of birth during the seventh month is alluded to when my Lord Harry, in a totally different context, 'slapped ... posteriors very soundly'(393). Also on p. 392: 'he took the bit between his teeth like a raw colt.' Again p. 398: 'I thank Thee as the Author of my days!'

Such babies often require special treatment; hence '*Mr Malachi Mulligan, Fertiliser and Incubator*'(395). One descries the babe's appearance, moreover, in the characterization of the Scotch student: 'a little fume of a fellow'(397).

The disappearance of the pupillary membrane is implied: 'wiped his eye,' 'claps eyes on her'(398).

A potential birth is described: 'Which of us did not feel his flesh creep?' 'An instant later his head appeared in the door opposite'(405).

The Eighth Month: Birth during the seventh month is only a possibility; embryonic progression continues, and then 'quite an altogether different complexion' is put 'on the proceedings'(410). A simile asserts the continuation: 'as mutually innocent of as the babe unborn'(410).

In this month the eyes are entirely free of their pupillary membranes, lost in the seventh: 'Visual organs ... commencing to exhibit symptoms of animation'(409).

The eighth, this is 'the little old man' month; the senescence of the foetus is adverted to in 'the stigmata of early depravity and premature wisdom'(410). If born, the child with proper care may live – hence the discussion on infant mortality, p. 411, on the 'seemingly healthy child'(412), and on 'staggering bob'(413) – the flesh of a calf newly dropped from its mother.

The Ninth Month: To identify this month, of course, Joyce need not have taken any special pains. Once the eight are recognized, the rest belongs to the ninth. Nonetheless distinctions are to be made. To the ninth month is attributable the passage (introduced by letting the cat into the bag – presumably with its nine lives) on p. 413: 'Meanwhile the skill and patience ... *accouchement*' up to 'All off for a buster, armstrong'(417). In this passage we read of the 'motherlight'(413) and 'the cry, and a tag and bobtail of all of them after'(415). One sees, too, in the glistering of 'life essence celestial'(416) and 'The door! It is open? Ha! They are out tumultuously ... all bravely legging it'(415) – the final parturition. The actual point of beginning of this month, as the recapitulations will show, is: 'It had better be stated here and now ...'(411).

I note also that the children of the Purefoys, named by name, p. 414, number – including the new Purefoy – nine. In this connection it is interesting to observe the same device applied to the same mystical number on p. 47 (*Proteus*) where in the last sentence of the second paragraph Joyce, thinking about the ninth wave, composes a wave-like sentence consisting of exactly nine clauses! Other significant nines abound throughout *Ulysses* in general and *The Oxen of the Sun* in particular.

The last pages, pp. 417–21, technically part of the ninth month, take the particular form they do because they represent the after-birth, the cleansing of the womb of blood and flesh and fluid not any longer required for the creature. These dregs, in linguistic terms, are the slang-speech of various groups and centuries. It is for this reason, too, that one finds in the text such terms as 'Chuckingout time'(417), 'There's hair'(418), 'Most deciduously'(418), and finally, 'Pflaap!' 'Pflaaaap!'(420, 421) – the act of vomiting: obstetric rendered emetic.

THE CHAPTER CORRESPONDENCES

Dividing the nine sections as they have been divided, they are now related, for reasons about to be given, to the following earlier chapters in *Ulysses* which they evoke.

The First Month: Calypso: The echoes of this chapter are signalized by references to the kidney: 'they make a compost out of fecund wheat kidneys out of Chaldee'(381); to Bloom's wife and daughter: 'dear wife and lovesome daughter that then over land and sea-floor nine years had long outwandered'(379); and to Bloom's session in the privy, p. 68: 'that him so heavied in bowels ruthful'(379) and 'anon full privily he voided the more part in his neighbour glass'(381); and to the bee, p. 68, which has become a 'dreadful dragon'(380).

The reference moreover is most fittingly made to Calypso for here the nurse – the ovum – plays Calypso's role; there couldn't be in fact a beginning without Calypso.

The Second Month: Telemachus: The section pullulates with the brood of mockers. The discussion, p. 383, is intended to pass for theological. The collector of prepuces, p. 15, is provided material: Malachi's praise of the unicorn 'how once in the millenium he cometh by his horn the other all this while pricked forward'(383). 'He who stealeth from the poor lendeth to the Lord'(384).

It is to be remembered that at this stage the head is disproportionately large.

The Third Month: Nestor: Here the two pound nineteen shillings (obtained from Mr Deasy) are the 'glistering coins of the tribute'(384); the Blake allusions: 'time's ruins build eternity's mansions'(385) recall p. 25, and *'vergine madre figlia di tuo figlio'*(385) equates *'Amor matris'*(29).

The abortion images of the embryological analysis apply aptly to a chapter in which the gracelessness of the Sargent boy, p. 29, prompts so many of Stephen's thoughts.

The Fourth Month: Scylla and Charybdis: The Elizabethan references are ubiquitous. 'Life,' as in the reference to Dowden, 'ran very high'(387). The Shakespeare-Hamlet tragedy, of course, is in the secondbest bed. Anne Hathaway's way is alluded to in 'thou ... broughtest in a stranger to my gates to commit fornication'(387) – but indeed throughout the page the correspondence is made explicit. Even the university of Oxtail (387) echoes the manner of Oxenford (215).

The Fifth Month: Cyclops: This section is identified largely on the evidence of the personified Phenomenon, p. 389: 'And then he starts with his jawbreakers about phenomenon and science and this phenomenon and the other phenomenon'(299).

The four tickets – Pickaback, Topsyturvy, etc. – referring as they do to foetal movements – constitute another example of the gigantism which marks the Cyclops' chapter.

Finally, to characterize Understanding as a tube, p. 389, is to think in the mon-ocular concepts of a Cyclops. The identification is brought out into full Cyclopean light in the phrase 'which forth to bring *brenningly* biddeth'(390).

The Sixth Month: The Wandering Rocks: The technique of the *Wandering Rocks* is the labyrinth, and here it is duplicated in the runnels of rain, and in the pellmell scampering of men and womenfolk (390). The locus of the *Wandering Rocks* is 'the streets' – here explicitly pointed at: 'In Ely place, Baggot street, Duke's lawn ... Holles street'(390). The symbol is 'Citizens'; and many are named (390,391). The *Wandering Rocks* motif is kept up, in fact, until entry into the seventh month: he 'hankered about the coffeehouses and low taverns with crimps, ostlers, bookies, Paul's men, runners, etc.'(391,392).

The Seventh Month: Proteus: The analysis of this correspondence presented most difficulty. The embryonic scheme, indicated above, showed the seventh month beginning on p. 392 and the eighth occurring on p. 409 – an interval of 17 pages. All the other months are disposed of in two or three pages. Something strange, surely, was happening here.

The importance of the seventh month as one in which an infant is likely to be born, and live, has already been stressed. The problem now is to discover a principle which will give coherence to the multifarious allusions which fill pp. 392–409.

The principle, it is submitted – and illustration seems to confirm the surmisal – is stated on p. 406: 'He is young Leopold, as in a retrospective arrangement, a mirror within a mirror ... he beholdeth himself.' The seventh month, it is affirmed, is, in its chapter correspondences *and* additional embryonic allusions, a retrospective arrangement, a mirroring within the seventh of all of the features of the first six. Thus:

THE MIRRORS WITHIN THE MIRROR

7:1:a *First Month Retrospected: Nestor.* Pp. 392–4: The allusions are obvious – cows, cattle, Doctor Rinderpest, bulls, Irish bull in an English chinashop, pp. 392, 393, 394.

That this is also a retrospection of the first embryonic month and of the act of conception appears from the references to 'hanging his bulliness in daisychains,' 'the finest strapping young ravisher in all the four fields of Ireland,' 'rapeseed,' etc.

7:1:b *Second Month Retrospected: Telemachus.* Pp. 395–7: Mr Mulligan, as in chapter one, here holds the scene again. Omphalos (396) sends us back to omphalos (9). And Mother Grogan, p. 397, completes the picture.

Embryonically, this is the month when violent cell multiplication is taking place: '*a pod or two* of capsicum chillies'(396) and when the external genitalia appear: '*testibus ponderosis atque excelsis erectionibus*'(396).

7:1:c *Third Month in Retrospection: Calypso.* Pp. 397–8: 'How great and universal must be that sweetest of Thy tyrannies which can hold in thrall the free and the bond'(398). One knows also that Mr Alec Bannon has established contact with Milly Bloom, p. 66, and now pays tribute to her, p. 398.

That it is the third month, '*Thrice happy he will be*'(398) corroborates.

A foetus born at this time, says Williams, may make spontaneous movements if still within the amniotic sac or immersed in warm saline solution. This truth is adumbrated: 'clapping hand to his forehead,' 'A drenching of that violence ... has sent more than one luckless fellow'(398), and 'dance in a deluge'(399).

The first three months *Calypso, Telemachus, Nestor* are thus mirrored *Nestor, Telemachus, Calypso.*

7:1:d *Fourth Month in Retrospection: Scylla and Charybdis.* Pp. 399– 400: The whole scene is reminiscent of the talk and action in the Library. Mr

Moore is alluded to again; as in the library, one of the protagonists is inter-rupted in his discourse: 'but at this point a bell tinkling in the hall'(399). The librarian's manner of speaking is repeated here: 'having spoken a few words in a low tone ... a profound bow to the company.' The squirmings on p. 399 are John Eglinton's shiftings of the body on p. 186. The dialectic? – 'Bless me, I'm all of a wibblywobbly'(399). The young surgeon, p. 399, like Mr Best, is at one moment called upon to withdraw from the company. The theological echoes are produced through pious references to the Deity (400) and to the son of the true fold (400). The defence of Miss Callan is the defence of Ann Hathaway.

The number of the month is apocalyptically concealed in 'May this pot of four half choke me'(399).

'Gad's bud,' no doubt, is the composite of theology and embryology, not to say botany.

'The presence ... among a party of debauchees of a woman'(399) is a typical fourth-month recognition of sex.

7:1:e *Fifth Month: Cyclops.* Pp. 400–1: This is recognized by 'the impudent mocks' to which Bloom is subjected, p. 400; and by the opprobrious epithets to him applied, p. 400.

That it is the fifth month is grandiloquently disclosed: 'It was now for more than the middle span of our allotted years'(400), a Dantesque application to foetal time.

The fifth month sees the body covered entirely with lanugo: 'overgrown children'(400).

7:1:f *Sixth Month: Wandering Rocks.* P. 401: This is suggested by the notion 'that *another than her conjugal* had been the man in the gap'(401) – a confusion in identification which occurs throughout the *Wandering Rocks* section. The 'itinerant vendor'(402), of course, combines in allusion the streets, the citizens, and the labyrinth. The imminence of birth is suggested: 'I bade him hold himself in readiness for that the event would burst anon'(401).

It is to be noted that the order of months, four, five and six, is the same, *Scylla-Charybdis, Cyclops, Wandering Rocks*, in the sub-series as in the first series: the negating mirrors negate themselves.

But one is not done with the self-multiplicative seventh month. Here on p. 402 the retrospective arrangement begins all over again – a second subsection, a mirror mirroring a mirrored mirror – and this time, all compacted into a single paragraph! – 'But with what fitness ... inoperative.' Thus:

1 *Cyclops*	'But with what fitness ... has this alien'
2 *Scylla-Charybdis*	'During the recent war ... granados ... four per cents.' Granados is a Shakespearean evocation, and

	the four per cents is read as a subtle back-reference to the preceding fourth month, namely 7 and 7:1:d, i.e., *Scylla-Charybdis*.
3 *Calypso*	'Far be it from candour to violate the bedchamber ... daughter of a gallant major'
4 *Telemachus*	'He says this, a censor of morals, a very pelican in his piety.' Christ as Pelican: cf. Dante, '*nostro Pelicane*'
5 *Nestor*	'In the question of the grazing lands.'
6 *W.R.*	'If he must dispense his balm of Gilead in nostrums.' Like an itinerant vendor.

Embryological correspondences are here difficult to establish; it would seem that the paragraph, like Bloom himself, is here 'oblivious of the ties of nature'(402).

Nature, and nature oblivious, having been illustrated, a new twist is now introduced. It is alluded to on p. 411: 'a mixture of both? This would be tantamount to a cooperation (one of nature's favourite devices).' But it is a twist with curlicues: the single paragraph just analyzed representing the multigeminal, we are now about to see exemplifications of triplets and twins, and even of one set of quadruplets. Thus:

'The news was imparted ... Sublime Porte ... second female infirmarian'(403). This *second* infirmarian is to let us know that the paragraph on p. 402 must be considered as the first of a series of six, and that there will now be only five more multiple-chapter correspondences to consider. (That this *is* so and *must* be so, will be shown when p. 409 is reached.)

The correspondences are as follows:

7:3:b Triplets:	*Wandering Rocks & Telemachus & Calypso*: running from 'The news was imparted'(403) to 'What God has joined'(405).

The allusions are:

Telemachus:	'Heir had been born'(403), 'Mr. Coadjutor *Deacon Dedalus*'(405), 'to put asunder what God has joined'(405), etc.
Calypso:	The woman's apartment (403), 'secretary of state for domestic affairs'(403), 'Mr Canvasser Bloom' etc.
Wandering Rocks:	This is reproduced through 'the strife of tongues' (403) but particularly through the catalogue of obstetric problems appearing on both p. 403 and p. 404. There are also allusions to minor incidents

	which happened in the *Wandering Rocks* chapter, such as the examination of the illustrations to an edition of Aristotle, p. 232.
7:3:c Triplets:	*Scylla-Charybdis & Nestor & Telemachus.* The second set of triplets. The paragraph on p. 405:
Scylla-Charybdis:	'portfolio full of Celtic literature,' 'what way would I be resting at all' a parody of Synge's prose, reminiscent of Malachi on p. 197; 'rookshooting,' 'his sceptre stalks me,' 'Mananaan,' etc. 'The sentimentalist is he who'(197), 'the chinless chinaman Chin Con Eg Lin Ton'(213).
Telemachus:	'The black panther,' 'Haines,' 'the Erse language' (Mother Grogan on Gaelic), 'camping out,' 'Samuel' Hebrew for 'His name is God.'
Nestor:	'for which, it seems, history is to blame.' 'Ah! Destruction!' ('Shattered glass and toppling masonry' [25]), etc.

The reference to the Childs murder must not mislead. It is not an allusion to either Hades or Aeolus, which are the ninth and eighth months; there cannot be a retrospection in the seventh of the eighth and ninth; the Childs is but a pun, maieutic, and as p. 416 will establish, Christological.

The score – that this is section C – is shown in 'Haines was the *third* brother.'

Now for the twins:

7:3:d Twins:	*Wandering Rocks & Calypso.* P. 406:
Wandering Rocks:	Bloom, in his various ages (a living embryo!) seen walking, travelling, canvassing.
Calypso:	The mirror is a recall of the little mirror in Professor Goodwin's hat (63); the theme of reincarnation and metempsychosis (64); Mr Bloom's walk from Dlugascz's, etc. The reference to Hatch Street is, of course, another pun.
7:3:e Quadruplets:	*Scylla-Charybdis & Calypso & Nestor & Telemachus.* P. 407:
Scylla-Charybdis:	The Shakespearean allusion inheres principally in the de Quincy description of the heavens, and is reminiscent of 'A star, a daystar, a firedrake rose at his birth'(207). It inheres also in 'the *ghosts* of beasts'(407).
Telemachus:	The wafting of the soul; the house of Virgo (*Jubilantium te virginum*); 'All is gone'(407) (Stephen

on his mother); 'Ominous, revengeful zodiacal
host!'(407) is echo of the host on p. 22.

Nestor: This is obvious: Nestor's cattle, horses and oxen
stampede through the paragraph.[4]

Calypso: Agendath Netaim, Lacus Mortis both from p. 61,
Millicent, etc. That this is the fifth month is adumbrated thus: 'in the penultimate antelucan hour,'
penultimate to a series of six. It is to be observed
also that the quadruplets find themselves in paragraphs where 'twilight' is twice repeated!

7:3:f Triplets: *Wandering Rocks & Telemachus & Cyclops.* Pp.
407, 408, 409:

Wandering Rocks: Apparent throughout. 'He was walking by the
hedge, reading'(409, 220); 'Periplepomenos' (of the
log-book); 'All desire to see you bring forth the
work you meditate'(408, 246).

Cyclops: The racing talk (408), the drinking (409), 'his gad-
ding hair'(408) belong to Mrs Vinegadding (321).
Above all, note that Glaucon, Alcibiades, Pisistra-
tus, p. 408, constitute – as a triplet! – the Man in
the G-A-P! (292).

Telemachus: Stephen clearly forms subject of comment throughout. That this sixth month is one of triplets and the
fifth of quadruplets is adverted to on this p. 408:
'Four winners yesterday and three today.'

One has now come out of this terrible seventh month, and Joyce affords
us (409) a test to determine whether our calculations have been correct. Twice
on that page the figure *four* occurs; at the top: 'she lay ill, four days on the
couch ... She was more taking then'; and in the last paragraph: 'During the
past four minutes or thereabouts he had been staring.' This is to let us know
that at this point we should have completed in the seventh month four sets
of six, and then some ('or thereabouts' 'she was more taking then'); this we
have done, thus:

Pp. 393–402	—	6	chapter-correspondences	
402	—	6	"	"
403–4	—	3	"	"
405	—	3	"	"
406	—	2	"	"
407	—	4	"	"
407, 408, 409	—	3	"	"
		27	"	" that is, four sets of six plus

'thereabouts,' and 'more taken!'

Before entering back into the main stream to go on to the chapter-correspondences of the eighth and ninth months, one pauses not so much to dwell upon the virtuosity of this seventh section, although compared to these sets of six, which are to prose what the sestina is to verse, it is Swinburne's double sestinas that are Child's play, but to marvel for the nth time upon Joyce's inspired ingenuities, especially as illustrated in the twin, triplet, quadruplet, and multigeminal divisions. Consider how he has practised his composite chapter correspondences: every one of the five is made to include either *Scylla-Charybdis* or *Wandering Rocks*! This is admirably appropriate. In illustrating monsters and multiple births, nothing could be more fitting than to evoke the whirlpool, the flying stone, and the rock wandering! *Wildfleisch* with a vengeance!

Here is the place also to recall that this entire seventh month, holus-bolus, has been set down as a correspondence to *Proteus*. What with its apparitions and changes – embryos that are single, and then double – embryos that get born and then slide back into the womb to form part of a sequence of nine – mirrors, metamorphoses, phantoms – it is a section just as Protean as the third chapter of the book itself.

The Eighth Month: Aeolus. Pp. 409 and 410 up to 411, 'Lafayette,' etc.: The chapter correspondences for the first six months, as will be remembered, were single. It was only when one was one-third way through the seventh that the multiplicative correspondences began. We are now in the eighth. Is one to revert to the system of the single allusion per month? The answer is yes and no; the entire section is allusive to but one chapter, but the section itself is to be constructed of allusions to the seven which preceded. To this effect we are warned, as we come through 'some description of a doldrums'(409) which was the seventh, of the existence of 'a certain amount of number *one* Bass bottled' – (bottled Bass – a zoologico-embryological pun) – 'which happened to be situated amongst a lot of others right opposite to where he was.' Right opposite is the eighth month. It is a set of seven, but has *one* overall designation: *Aeolus.*

1	Entirely due to a misconception; not the case at all; in the wrong shop (409); quite an altogether different complexion.	Proteus
2	Debaters ... keenest; theme ... *loftiest and most vital*	Telemachus
3	Crotthers ... Highland garb	Nestor (tartan fillibegs, 32)
4	The salted cowhide brogues ...	Cyclops (p. 291)
5	The convivial atmosphere of Socratic discussion	Scylla-Charybdis

| 6 | Fresh from the hippodrome, and that vig-
ilant wanderer, soiled by the dust of
travel | Wandering Rocks |
| 7 | Image of voluptuous loveliness. | Calypso (Lafayette – a
Dublin photographer) |

The whole paragraph, a parody of Macaulay – the seven-littered Warren is Hasting! – is concerned with oratory and rhetoric. The colour of Aeolus is red, which is the scarlet appearance of Bass's No 1 (410). And 'the language so encyclopedic'(410).

   The Ninth Period: Hades. Pp. 411–21: It is not called the ninth *month* because it involves more than thirty days, as both Nature and Joyce indicate. Joyce, however, insists, and in hushed numbers indicates his insistence, that it be considered the ninth. It, too, consists of recapitulations.

I

1	Mr S. Dedalus (Div. Scep.)	Telemachus
2	tangible phenomena ...	Cyclops
3	man in the street ...	Wandering Rocks
4	Mr L. Bloom (Pubb. Canv.) regarding the future determination of sex (Martha's)	Cyclops
5	Empedocles of Trinacria ... assert others ...	Scylla-Charybdis
6	A happily chosen position	Nestor (I am happier than you are, p. 35)
7	Infant mortality	Aeolus (Child's murder?)
8	It is interesting ... born the same way, die different.	Proteus
9	Infant mortality	Hades (also Aeolus: 'a mix- ture of both')

II

1	Mr M. Mulligan ... gray-lunged citizens	Telemachus
2	These factors ... spectacles offered by streets ...	Wandering Rocks
3	Kalipedia ... graces of life, classical statues	Scylla-Charybdis

4	Marital discipline in the home.	Calypso
5	Although the former (we are thinking of neglect); forgotten sponges ...	Proteus
6	*Deliveries* going off well; things balked (the trouble S. has getting his anecdote told in Aeolus)	Aeolus
7	Everything in nature, lunar phases, tidal movements, nature's vast workshop (a sentence of gigantism)	Cyclops
8	A child of normally healthy parents, seeming healthy, i.e. Sargent	Nestor
9	Immortality ... survival of the fittest ... give us pause	Hades

The third series runs all in one sentence!

III

1	Mr S. Dedalus (Div. Scep.)	Telemachus
2	Or should it be called an interruption	Proteus
3	Masticate, deglute, etc. pass through	Calypso, p. 68
4	Pluterperfect imperturbability	Nestor (the letter, p. 34)
5	Multifarious aliments, etc.	Wandering Rocks
6	Corpulent professional gentlemen	Cyclops
7	Not to speak of jaundiced politicians	Aeolus
8	Reveals as nought she could, in a very unsavoury light	Scylla-Charybdis (Stephen on Ann Hathaway)
9	The tendency above alluded to	Hades. (See previous sentence.)

IV

1	For the enlightenment of those who are *not so intimately acquainted.*	Telemachus
2	With the minutiae of the municipal	Wandering Rocks
3	Morbidminded esthete	Scylla-Charybdis
4	For his overweening bumptiousness	Aeolus
5	Can scarcely distinguish	Proteus
6	In the vile parlance of our lower class	Hades

7 Licensed victuallers	Cyclops, p. 289 et seq.
8 Cookable and eatable flesh	Calypso
9 Of a calf	Nestor

v

1 In a recent public controversy	Aeolus
2 With Mr L. Bloom (Pubb. Canv.)	Wandering Rocks
3 Dr A. Horne (Lic. in Midw.)	Scylla-Charybdis, p. 188. Socrates' mother.
4 Reported by *eye*witnesses	Cyclops
5 Cat into the bag, sexual congress	Proteus
6 Women who let the cat into the bag	Calypso
7 Woman let ... aesthetic allusion	Nestor, p. 35
8 She must let it out again	Hades. Contrast to 'or give it life.'
9 She must give it life	Telemachus

The reader will not have failed to have noticed that at this point one final sentence of the paragraph is unaccounted for: 'At the risk of her own was the telling rejoinder ... delivered.' It is, as if one were being plagued 'by laws of numeration as yet unascertained.' But the explanation is to be found on p. 411: we have before us the nemasperm (*nema* – a thread, a worm) which after the *misus formativus* (formative labour) is placed in front of the *succubitus felix*. And *succubitus felix* is *happy accouchement*!

Now we are in the next paragraph. The key is given in the numerals – 'one more blessing,' 'the conscientious second accountant' and 'the influential third cousin'(414). This will be shown to mean that there now follow three sets of nine. The triplication, it is suggested, is intended to accord with the wearisome repetitions of Dickens – weary, weary while, very very happy, and so on.

I

1 weary weary while	Hades
2 that surgical skill could *do* was *done*	Scylla-Charybdis. This is the porno-dynamic 'Do, do' of Hamlet in Scylla-Charybdis.
3 the brave *woman had man*-fully	Proteus

4 fought the good fight, very happy — Nestor. Ulster will fight; jousts; am happier than you, etc.

5 passed on, who have gone before — Wandering Rocks
6 gaze down — Cyclops
7 Reverently, One Above — Telemachus
8 first *bloom* of her new motherhood and — Calypso

9 is that loose sentence above. — Aeolus: 'telling rejoinder,' 'interlocutor,' delivered!

II

1 babe ... blessing — Telemachus
2 Doady there with her to share her joy — Calypso
3 God's clay — Hades
4 you and I may whisper it — Scylla-Charybdis (Library conversation)

5 trifle stooped in the shoulders — Cyclops (Doran's bottle shoulders)
6 whirligig of years — Wandering Rocks
7 grave dignity had come to ... accountant — Proteus
8 faroff time of the roses! — Aeolus (Rose of Castille!)
9 grouped in her imagination — Nestor ('Framed around the wall images of vanished horses,' all royal and du-cal names, 33)

III

1 Young hopeful will be christened — Telemachus
2 time wags on — Wandering Rocks
3 no sigh break — Aeolus
4 from that bosom — Calypso
5 knock the ashes from your pipe — Cyclops
6 curfew rings, distant day — Hades
7 dout the light whereby you read — Scylla-Charybdis: the noble substance dout. *Hamlet*
8 fought the good fight — Proteus. *Doady* in labour pain!
9 Well done, thou good and faithful servant! — Nestor

The next two paragraphs together make up a series of nine, four in the first paragraph and five in the second: 'A lad of four or five'(415); but there is an additional nuance – every one of the nine correspondences is accompanied also by a Protean allusion – it is 'A lad of four or five in *linseywoolsey*'(415). Thus:

1	darkest places of the heart	Hades (heart is its symbol)	1 Hidden away, call them as the world calls them	Proteus
2	all but persuade himself	Aeolus	2 As though they had not been, were otherwise	Proteus
3	most various circumstances	Wandering Rocks	3 Call them forth a vision or dream	Proteus
4	to insult over him	Cyclops	4 Shrouded in the vesture of the past	Proteus
5	an unhealthiness, a *flair*	Telemachus	5 Fare calm, as it seemed	Proteus
6	homeliness, immediate pleasures	Calypso	6 A scene disengages itself, as if	Proteus
7	the game, run, shock	Nestor, 33	7 Run, collide, stop	Proteus
8	darker friend, foreign warmth	Calypso (Floey-Atty-Tiny remind us that she is F.A.T. There are other instances of notarika in *Ulysses*)	8 I know not what, cool ardent	Proteus
9	linseywoolsey	Scylla-Charybdis (dialectic)	9 Blossomtime-gathered & hutched	Proteus

It will be observed that Calypso is *twice* referred to – she is the Lady of a Comely *Brace* of cherries. Joyce had to do this because Proteus is omitted from the catalogue in the first column; pairing Proteus with Proteus would be the very sudor of supererogation.

Again one is left with a pendent sentence; it belongs to the series of nine of the next paragraph, for we are enjoined to 'mark this farther.' It is also Protean throughout.

Thus we have

1 this young man ... too conscious enjoyment ... mother watches from the piazzetta (see p. 7)	Telemachus	1 Perhaps, faint shadow, remoteness	Proteus

2 The end comes	Hades	2 Suddenly	Proteus
3 antechamber ... studious	Scylla-Charybdis	3 Nothing it seems *there*	Proteus
4 of rash or violent	Cyclops	4 Nothing it seems	Proteus
5 Quietude of custody ... in that house	Calypso	5 Rather	Proteus
6 watch of shepherds and of angels	Wandering Rocks	6 Rather	Proteus
7 Shepherds ... crib	Nestor	7 Rather	Proteus
8 of Juda long ago	Aeolus (p. 141)	8 Rather	Proteus

('Mark ... and remember.' Remember what? That Proteus cannot be paired with Proteus, and that therefore one of the series will be duplicated; Telemachus is repeated.)

9 in Bethlehem	Telemachus	9 Rather	Proteus

And now, once more, the whole in one sentence.

1 the serried stormclouds	Wandering Rocks
2 in swollen masses turgidly distended	Calypso
3 compass earth and sky	Cyclops, p. 339, 'Ascend to the glory of the brightness at an angle of 45 degrees'
4 drowsy oxen	Nestor
5 blighted growth	Hades
6 with the reverberation	Aeolus
7 *rives* their centres	Scylla-Charybdis
8 transformation	Proteus
9 the Word	Telemachus

And yet again, two series in *one* sentence. A cry (of six) and a tag (of nine)!

I

1 Burke's!	Hades (to burke is to mur-

der. Burke's is, of course, the tavern. On yet another level, this lets one know that the baby is issuing: to burke is to garrotte.)

2	Outflings	Cyclops, p. 339
3	my lord Stephen	Telemachus
4	Giving the cry	Aeolus
5	cry and a tag	Scylla-Charybdis
6	of all them	Wandering Rocks

II

1	cockerel	Cyclops
2	welsher	Nestor ('I pay my debts!')
3	bilbos	Scylla-Charybdis (The Mutines in the Bilboes. *Hamlet*)
4	punctual Bloom	Calypso
5	Bloom at heels	Aeolus (the youngsters following him)
6	headgear, etc.	Wandering Rocks
7	universal grabbing	Hades
8	ashplants	Telemachus
9	what not	Proteus

A tag and a bobtail; in fact, a tag and four bobtails 'of all them after.'

I

1	A dedale	Telemachus
2	A dedale of youth	Wandering Rocks
3	lusty youth, noble every student	Nestor (Mr Deasy's school)
4	Nurse Callan	Calypso
5	taken aback in the hallway	Scylla-Charybdis
6	*news* of placentation	Aeolus
7	ended	Hades
8	a full pound	Cyclops (gigantism)
9	a full pound if a milligramme	Proteus

Now for bobtails:

A

1	They hark him on.	Nestor
2	The door! it is open?	Aeolus
3	out tumultuously	Cyclops
4	all bravely legging it	Wandering Rocks
5	Burke's, Holles	Scylla-Charybdis (Dialectic: house of death, house of life)
6	their ulterior goal	Hades

B

1	sharp language	Cyclops
2	raps out an oath	Aeolus (Myles Crawford's oath)
3	and on	Wandering Rocks
4	Bloom stays	Calypso
5	a thought	Proteus
6	up there	Telemachus

C

1	Doctor Diet & Doctor Quiet	Scylla-Charybdis
2	Dr Quiet	Hades
3	not other now?	Proteus
4	Ward of watching	Calypso
5	told its tale	Aeolus
6	washedout pallor	Nestor (Sargent boy)

D

1	Them all being gone	Hades
2	Them all being gone	Nestor (Interview Deasy)
3	a glance of motherwit	Aeolus
4	a glance	Proteus
5	helping he whispers	Scylla-Charybdis
6	Madam, storkbird	Calypso

It will be observed that in the above a new trick has been added: the single word or phrase, whether alone or with other words, connotes more than the single chapter-correspondence.

The next paragraph, up to the sentence 'A truce to threnes and trentals,' will have 9 sets of 9 – a ninth month's nonary:

I

1 The air	Aeolus
2 air without	Nestor (the playing field)
3 impregnated	Calypso
4 *raindew moisture*	Proteus
5 life essence celestial	Telemachus
6 glistering	Cyclops
7 Dublin Stone	Wandering Rocks
8 starshiny	Scylla-Charybdis (p. 207)
9 *coelum*	Hades (Lucifer: 'Heaven is hell')

II

1 God's air	Telemachus
2 Allfather's air	Nestor ('That is god!' [35] – a viconian allusion)
3 scintillant	Cyclops
4 circumambient	Wandering Rocks
5 cessile	Calypso
6 Breathe it deep	Proteus (40)
7 deep	Hades
8 scintillant circumambient	Scylla-Charybdis (p. 207)
9 air	Aeolus

III

1 By heaven	Hades (see above)
2 Theodore Purefoy	Telemachus
3 doughty deed	Nestor (the good fight, etc.)
4 Botch	Proteus
5 I vow	Calypso
6 remarkablest progenitor	Cyclops (hyperbole)
7 chaffering	Scylla-Charybdis
8 allincluding most farraginous	Wandering Rocks
9 chronicle	Aeolus (newspaper office)

IV

1 Astounding!	Cyclops
2 In her lay	Calypso
3 God*framed*	Nestor (p. 33 – framed around the walls images, etc.)
4 Godgiven	Telemachus
5 Preformed possibility	Proteus
6 Cleave to her!	Scylla-Charybdis (an allusion to the disjunctive and cohesive meanings of the word *cleave*)
7 Serve! Toil on!	Wandering Rocks
8 scholarment	Aeolus
9 go hang	Hades

V

1 all their daddies	Cyclops (hyperbole)
2 Theodore	Telemachus
3 Art drooping under	Aeolus (bag of wind)
4 bills, ingots	Scylla-Charybdis (accounts payable, accounts receivable)
5 ingots ... in the countinghouse?	Nestor
6 not thine!	Proteus
7 Head up!	Hades ('More room if they buried them standing' [107].)
8 every newbegotten thou shalt gather	Wandering Rocks
9 homer of ripe wheat	Calypso (Eve, wheatbellied)

VI

1 thy fleece is drenched	Telemachus (the fleece of the Lamb of God)
2 Darby and Joan	Scylla-Charybdis
3 Joan	Calypso
4 canting, curdog	Proteus (46, 47, 48)
5 all their progeny	Wandering Rocks
6 Pshaw, I tell thee!	Aeolus (p. 136)

7 He is a mule	Nestor
8 a dead	Hades
9 dead mule … kreutzer	Cyclops (general denigration hyperbolically expressed)

VII

1 Copulation without population!	Calypso
2 No, say I	Proteus
3 Herod's	Telemachus
4 slaughter	Hades
5 Vegetables	Cyclops (p. 289)
6 forsooth	Scylla-Charybdis
7 beefsteaks	Nestor
8 red	Aeolus (colour of chapter)
9 bleeding!	Wandering Rocks (circulatory system)

VIII & IX

One sentence.

1 She	Calypso
2 She is a hoary	Scylla-Charybdis (reference to Mrs Shakespeare's seniority)
3 pandemonium	Hades
4 pandemonium of ills	Telemachus
5 enlarged glands	Cyclops (gigantism)
6 mumps	Proteus (this affliction sometimes unsexes)
7 quinsy	Aeolus (cf. Auden's 'the liar's quinsy')
8 bunions	Wandering Rocks
9 hayfever	Nestor

1 bedsores	Proteus (p. 40)
2 ringworm	Cyclops (cycle)
3 floating kidney	Calypso
4 Derbyshire neck	Nestor
5 warts	Wandering Rocks

6 bilious attacks	Telemachus (His mother's 'greensluggish bile,' p. 7)
7 gallstones	Scylla-Charybdis (*sekel* – Hebrew, a stone)
8 cold feet	Hades
9 varicose veins	Aeolus (the vein in which they speak, distended)

And now – 'A truce to threnes and trentals and jeremies.' This is a signpost; this, in addition to being an appeal to Theodore Purefoy to cease lamentation over his lot, is also information that the threne (threen, 3's) and the trentals (30's – thirty days hath, etc.) and the jeremies (9's) have ended. (Jeremiah is reputed the author of Lamentations, written after the destruction of the Temple, which took place on the *ninth* day of Ab, and is still a fast-day in the Jewish calendar.)

There is also a clear mathematical check-up. 'Twenty years of it, regret them not.' This is to hint that since the last summation in the seventh month (the 27) one should have performed 20 × 12 recapitulations. Let us see, then, whether we really have 240.

Recall of seventh month, Proteus, not included in last addition	1
Eighth month, its name Aeolus and seven recalls, pp. 409–10	8
'It had better be stated'(411) to 'tendency above alluded to'(413).	27
'For enlightenment ... give up life to save her own'(413).	18
'It had been a weary weary while'(413) to 'Well done, thou ... faithful servant'(414).	27
Linsey-woolsey section (Newman & Pater parody)	9
Linsey-woolsey section (Ruskin parody)	18
Overall Proteus recall of last two groups	2
'Burke's'(415) to 'stork bird comes for thee'(416)	48
'The air without'(416) to 'varicose veins.'	81
Overall name of ninth section: Hades	1
	240

Now, if we add to this 240 the 6 recalls of the first six months plus the 27 of the seventh month we get 273, that is 9 × 30 + 3, a jeremy of trentals and a threne![5]

It should also be noted here that Joyce has taken into consideration the difference between lunar months (28 days) and calendar months. He exploits for this purpose the address of the National Maternal Hospital: 29, 30, 31

Holles St. – the heliotic digits being precisely those supernumerary to the lunar!

The rest of the chapter is also full of correspondences; certainly it is not the chaos that it appears to be; for the purpose of this essay, however, it is here that, together with Joyce, one should call a truce.

One can now understand the intoxication of Joyce's query: 'How's that for high?' It is high, high and deep and reminiscent of Hopkins' tribute to *The* Creator

> Who hews mountain and continent,
> Earth, all, out; who, *with trickling increment*,
> Veins violets, and tall trees makes more and more.

One is quite conscious of the fact that this exegesis, precisely because of its complication, may prompt some readers to incredulity and resistance. It may be contended that the foregoing analysis is the result, not of Joyce's intention, but of a forced ingenuity on the part of the commentator. It is a compliment which is here regrettably unacceptable. There is, *imprimis*, Joyce's letter declaring his subtle intention; there is, *secundo*, that plethora of allusion which, while it may be the result of accident in one or two or three or four or five of its instances, cannot be merely coincidental in three hundred and more; and there is, *tertio*, the mathematical evidence. It is a rule touching the interpretation of documents that a document ought to be understood in that sense whereby *all* of its words receive meaning; without the above explication, most of the numbers occurring in the *Oxen of the Sun* appear to be arbitrarily chosen; with it, every figure – at the least – is given purpose and significance.

What is much more serious, however, is that hostile critics may now use the evidence here adduced as further substantiation for the general charge of Alexandrinism levelled against *Ulysses*. To do so, however, would be really to misunderstand Joyce's intention. Complicated and macaronic as the structure of this chapter is, it is certainly not a mere *tour de force*. It is functionalism, and not ornamentation, which is its principal objective. Even those who considered in this chapter only its parody styles could not escape the impression that what Joyce was doing was illustrating Haeckel's 'fundamental biogenetic law' (on it Haeckel established his whole *History of Creation*[6]) that ontogeny is a recapitulation of phylogeny. That intention – realized through the labour pains of chapter-correspondences which come first at intervals of ten minutes, then five, then two, then every second – emerges even more clearly, more functionally, now.

The method is functional also in the larger sense. In a book in which the parallels are Homeric, the cycles Viconian – 'cycles of cycles of generations that have lived' – and theosophical the continuums, it would have been a serious oversight if historic evolution and individual gestation had been ignored.

It is functional, again, in relation to the structure of the entire work. *Ulysses* is the labyrinth fashioned by Daedalus Joyce; it is reasonable that the most complicated, the most labyrinthine part thereof should be that part in which is to be found the equivalent of the Minotaur: *The Oxen of the Sun*.

The revealed architecture of the chapter, moreover, not only supplements, but throws new light on the parodies themselves. Miss Rebecca West, one recalls, dared in an early review to characterize Joyce's parodies as pastiche. As late as 1947 the young Toynbee writing of this chapter speaks of 'everything [being] deliberately artificial.' How ludicrous this now seems! Pastiche? As the human body, *effigo Dei*, is pastiche. Artificial? Like an embryo!

The difficult is not necessarily artificial. A birth, too, is laboured. No one will gainsay that the *Oxen of the Sun*, next to the *Scylla-Charybdis* chapter, is an exemplum in the taking of pains. How tightly disciplined was the work in this chapter only a consideration of the various self-imposed technical strictures can adequately reveal: tied to the exigency of narrative coherence and bound by the compact with Homeric allusion, Joyce, Houdini-like, permitted himself yet further to be trussed up in embryological reference, shackled with linked recapitulations, fettered by parody, bilbo'd by evolution, and, at the end (through nine encores) escapes alive!

The recapitulation method also introduces, I think, a new form to literature: 'the voice in the cellar' heard either in cachinnation or exegesis. What a fine irony it is, fine in that it is not accompanied by the usual lifting of the eyebrow, that the section of the ninth month, bringing the child into the world, should be dubbed, *Hades*! The 'perverted transcendentalism' of p. 411 thus takes on a new meaning: resurrection from the womb. And how hilarious the equation of the eighth month with *Aeolus*, belly full of wind! And so on, and so on; the catalogues of the preceding pages are full of such illuminating incongruities.

Equally revealing is the roll of the chapters upon which Joyce has not conferred the dignity of correspondence. The Lotus Eaters? The *fainéant* do not produce children; that chapter, moreover, ends with a description of 'a father of thousands' which is 'limp.' The Lestrygonians? They were cannibals, eaters, not makers, of human flesh. The Sirens? The embryo is always a deaf-mute. Nausicaa? Its principal event is a sterile onanism.

Are there then no phrases throughout the *Oxen of the Sun* which can be construed as allusions to the four omitted chapters? Indeed there are, but they are isolated, do not fit into any system, and are frequently also allusive to the recapitulated chapters. Such ambiguity, considering the different levels upon which Joyce wrote, was unavoidable; it was, like miscarriage, an occupational risk. What is of the essence, and finally persuasive, is the overwhelming weight of concordant reference.

The chapter-correspondence technique affords Joyce yet another advantage. It provides him with the means to abandon – without aesthetic loss – the aloof impersonal attitude he elsewhere declares to be the only one possible for the creative writer (... paring his fingernail, *Portrait of the Artist*). For once, Joyce asserts himself, bids defiance to the world, tells it what he thinks of it and what he thinks of himself. The paragraph about to be quoted is practically the transcript of a letter addressed by Joyce to himself. Reference to the recapitulations will show that the name Theodore Purefoy is equated with Telemachus. This is no accident. Theodore (Godgiven) Purefoy (of the true faith) *is* Telemachus, is Stephen Dedalus, is James Joyce. The identification, moreover, is not mere critical metaphor; through chapter-correspondence and actual text it is made precise and explicit. I transcribe:

By heaven, Theodore Purefoy, thou hast done a doughty deed and no botch! Thou art, I vow, the remarkablest progenitor barring none in this chaffering allincluding most farraginous chronicle. The right of paternity is copyright. *Thou art all their daddies, Theodore. Art drooping, bemoiled with butcher's bills at home* – Joyce, in the early years – *and ingots (not thine!) in the countinghouse?* Joyce in the bank at Trieste. *Thou shalt gather thy homer of ripe wheat.* Homer: a Greek poet, a Hebrew quantity: Ulysses Bloom. *See, thy fleece is drenched.* Of the knightly order of the Golden Fleece, most distinguished order in Europe. *Pshaw, I tell thee!* This pshaw is not simply an exclamation. It is a retort, in answer to the question on p. 136: *What have you now like John Philpot Curran? Pshaw!* Joyce is setting himself up against that other Irishman George B. Shaw. For other examples of silent p's, see p. 173: 'Ptake some ptarmigan.' *Enlarged glands, mumps, etc.* When Joyce looks for a disease or ailment to evoke Cyclops, the one-eyed, he finds enlarged glands and ringworm. He carefully avoids anything pertaining to deficiency in eyesight. Eugene Jolas reports that Joyce 'seemed to resent the constant macabre preoccupations with the condition of his eyes. '*Twenty years of it, regret them not* – 1902 to 1922 an approximation. Twice the ten years of p. 246. *Thou sawest thy America, thy lifetask,* etc. Literally true. *Mother's milk,* etc.: The nature of his work is indicated: first, *milk of human kin,* then *milk of the stars* – the stars of *Scylla-Charybdis; punch milk,* a Cyclopean pun; *milk of madness* – the race is not wholly to Swift; *the honeymilk of Canaan's land* – the desert is to Bloom. And far from being a renegade and blasphemer, Joyce is, *sub specie aeternitatis,* a true *old patriarch!* A reverend father *Pap!* A man whose epithet has enough P's for at least three *parish priests!*

'AND THE PERIODS OF FORMAL EVOLUTION IN GENERAL'

This is all that Joyce says in his letter about evolutionary progression; it is moreover 'evolution in general' that he will use as his framework. He could not do otherwise; the data here are by no means as specific as they are in embryology or chapter-correspondences. Darwin describes the situation as follows:

'I look at the geological record as a history of the world imperfectly kept and written in a changing dialect; of this history we possess the last volume alone, relating only to two or three centuries. Of this volume only here and there a short chapter has been preserved; and of each page only here and there a few lines. Each word of the slowly changing language, more or less different in the successive chapters, may represent the forms of life which are entombed in our successive formations, and which falsely appear to us to have been abruptly introduced.'

The language of this quotation may well serve as a description of Joyce's method in this chapter.

I

The First Month: In the beginning was the Sun. The exordium of the chapter, aptly enough, is an invocation to the light one, the bright one, Horhorn.

The second paragraph on p. 377 has been described by Stuart Gilbert as 'diplodocan.' If this word conveyed merely an idea of shape it would be, no doubt, an adequate description of the top-heavy Latin syntax; the word, however, carries also connotations of time, and in this sense its use is definitely misleading. We have not yet reached the age of the diplodocus; in fact, what we are witnessing in this paragraph is the scientific illustration of the creation of the world. The style gives the impression of whirling masses – the whole paragraph consists of two long syntactically-complicated sentences, one declarative, the other interrogative – and resembles nothing so much as the motion of matter broken from the sun, a vortex in space. It is the sun which is the 'exhortator and admonisher of his semblables'(377). The world now subsists on its own. It is as if – the fancy is not attributed to Joyce – it is as if the world ablated from the sun and made absolute were best spoken of in ablative absolutes, in groups of phrases which have to be gathered up to be understood.

The world crystallizes and we are now among the Azoic Rocks, rocks in which one does not find even the dead signs of life. The Archaeozoic period, I think, ends with 'term up'(378) and leads us into the Proterozoic. Since the Azoic contained no life, it is equated with unfertilized ovum and included in the first section.[7] The remarks on the gerundive are equally applicable here.

In the Proterozoic we find the earliest trace of life, worm-like creatures; our text reproduces them, I think, as 'eft rising' (another pun – eft, a minuscule newt). That most of the earth's surface is covered with water is alluded to in 'Full she dread that God the Wreaker all mankind would fordo with water'(370). Bloom's daughter is described as having been nine years 'on land and seafloor!'

Archaic English helps Joyce out: Bloom 'had on got his weeds'(371). Progression from land to water, however, is beginning to take place: 'tidings are sent from far coast.' And the tiding, too, has its ebb and flow of meaning.

At this time, too, there were creatures called trilobites which, some scientists surmise, were probably related to the American king-crab of to-day. This phenomenon of the Palaeozoic is alluded to in the 'bellycrab' of p. 379. The age of the invertebrates is over.

II

With *The Second Month* we enter the Mesozoic, the Secondary. Here we find the bones of giant reptiles and the like – they are 'the horrible and dreadful dragons'(380), the brontosaurus, the diplodocus. 'The fishes withouten heads'? I think these are the Ammonites, a division of creatures like squids with *coiled* shells, multitudes of which have been left in the strata of the Mesozoic.

'The entwining serpents with scales'(381) are, of course, the winged reptiles (the pterodactyls), reptiles whose scales became fronds, and, at a much later stage, grew feathers.

It is to be noted finally that in this age there appear the highest insects, such as *bees*, etc. (380).

III

The Third Month: This, naturally, is the Tertiary Period – geologically containing the Eocene, Oligocene, Miocene and Pliocene periods. By this time, flowers have appeared: 'the flower of the flock'(384); on p. 385 the march of evolution is thus described: 'time's ruins build eternity's mansions. What means this? Desire's wind blasts the thorntree but after it becomes from a bramblebush to be *a rose* upon the rood of time.' Later it is 'the flower of quiet margerain gentle'(386). It is also the Age of Mammals; we are not surprised to find therefore that the corselet is 'of lamb's wool.' It is in the later part of this period, too, that one encounters the ape-ancestors of man – 'the curse of God ape'(386).

IV

The Fourth Month: the Quaternary Period. We have reached a new stage in evolution, of course, and 'life runs very high in these days.' Geologists, however, are not very clear about the nature of the ape-man produced in this period: 'all is hidden when we would backward see from what region of remoteness the whatness of our whoness hath fetched his whenceness'(388). It is also during this period, and certainly in the next, that man begins to bury his dead; 'an occulted sepulchre amid the conclamation of the hillcat and the ossifrage'(388). The ossifrage gets its name from the fact that it is a 'bone-breaker'; it is from the evidence of broken bones that much touching the habits of ancient man is learned.

The period ends with the Ice Age which gets backward mention only in the sixth month: p. 390, 'the big wind of last February a year.'

V

The Fifth Month: This, the beginning of the Early Palaeolithic (sub-human) takes us right into Genesis 1, and is a prelude to the Flood of the sixth month: 'Wisdom (Sophia-God) hath built herself a house, this vast majestic long-stablished vault, the crystal palace of the Creator, all in applepie (Eve: dietician) order.' Shortly after creation men turned to wickedness and stood very much in need of Calmer's advice (389). Their wickedness, moreover, consisted of Carnal Concupiscence (Genesis 6:1–7). It is the period when Pithecanthropus will lead to a higher man: 'Mr Ape Swillale' to 'Mr Sometimes Godly'(390).

It is to be noted that early investigation attributed the character of Pleistocene rock to floods – the diluvial hypothesis. The ice-sheet hypothesis followed later.

VI

The Sixth Month: the late Palaeolithic (fully human). This is the Age of the Neanderthal Man, he who has evolved far beyond Eoanthropus. Here, too, the Deluge appears. Under the description of the storm of June 16th, the references to the Flood are unambiguous. The Ark is shadowed in Bloom 'sitting snug with a covey of wags,' and one hesitates to say, but cannot resist saying that 'the bright pair of Turkey trunks of Mrs Moll' is the rainbow of Genesis 9!

Saint Swithin is, of course, a useful saint, and rice-slop, 'a shrewd drier,' a pertinent allusion.

VII

The Seventh Month: The beginning of the Age of Cultivation: 'Joseph Cuffe's live stock'(392) and meadows, etc. Animals are domesticated: 'choking chickens behind a hedge,' 'the bearpit,' 'the cocking main'(392), and 'the farmyard drake'(396). There is breeding of cattle, p. 393. Grass makes plains and prairies: 'green is the grass that grows on the ground'(394). Agriculture is again referred to in 'the sowing of rapeseed'(394) and in the use of pitchforks (for rowing!). Some kind of river-navigation begins; it is not very good, it gets all its terms mixed up: 'manned the yards, sprang their luff ... ported her helm,' etc. (pp. 394–5).

The ages are now alluded to retrospectively.

First, Azoic, Proterozoic: 'There's as good fish in this tin'(392); 'some salty sprats'(392); 'farmer Nicholas that was a eunuch'(393). Life emergent from water: 'Then, with the water running off him'(394).

Second, Mesozoic: 'A gale of laughter at his smalls'(397) (culottes), i.e., a variation of 'the dwarfmen of Finlandy,' an allusion to the short-legged (smalls) monsters of this age. 'A salient point'(397). A reference to the kangaroo motion (saltus) of some of the Mesozoic creatures.

Third, Tertiary: Monsters belong to the past: 'so amiable a creature'(398). Early man, a hairy thing: 'slicked his hair'(398).

Fourth, Quaternary: This is the Age of Mammals: 'a fine bit of cow-flesh!'(399). And of flowering plants: 'Gad's bud'(399).

Fifth, Palaeolithic: The Age of Pithecanthropus: 'An age which knows not pity'(400). The whole paragraph – 'testiness, outrageous mots' is descriptive of Mr Ape Swillale. The identification is given police accuracy: 'a cropeared creature of a misshapen gibbosity'(400), etc. 'the missing link of creation's chain'(400) is still 'a man of a rare forecast'(401), and tends toward 'the Supreme Being'(401).

Sixth, Late Palaeolithic: The Neanderthal Man – 'the man in the gap,' 'a linkboy'(401); he has the 'wonderful faculty of metempsychosis'(401), that is, to change the ape into man.

Second recapitulation: Here we proceed in one paragraph on p. 402 from 'the lowest strata' to the 'ranching of Mr Cuffe' to 'seedfield and ploughshare.'

The third recapitulation: We begin here, as previously indicated, with the second month, and find

Second, pp. 403–4: a minotaur, which is a monster, and therefore typical of the Mesozoic.

Third, p. 405: a creature that begins to look like a human: 'This is the appearance is on me.' It is 'camping out.' The ancestors of apes and men issue from the Eocene of the Tertiary.

Fourth, This is the period penultimate to the recall of Genesis: 'And in an instant (fiat!).' The very illuminating record of quaternary rock is fittingly harmonized with the retrospective style of Lamb.

Fifth, Early Palaeolithic: p. 407: 'Grey twilight' and 'sagegreen pasture-fields'(407). The mammals, as we know them, have been fully developed: 'slim shapely haunches, tendonous neck'(407). And the monsters are 'ghosts of beasts' now to be found only in *Lacus Mortis*; they are flooded fossils. The 'equine portent' is the horse evolved from Eohippus in the Eocene to Equus in the Pleistocene.

Sixth, The Late Palaeolithic: p. 408: Animals are being domesticated 'by the bullockbefriending bard.' Man rides both 'the camel and the boisterous buffalo.' The mare has developed and 'is not the filly that she was.' The first true man is about to appear: 'A gate of access to the incorruptible eon of the Gods'(409).

And now back into the mainstream:

The Eighth Month: This, it will be recalled, is 'the little old man month,' p. 410: In evolutionary history it is what is known as the epoch of 'The Old Man' – the first True Man as patriarch, maker of family tabus, etc. Grant Allen, in his *Evolution of the Idea of God,* lays stress chiefly on the posthumous worship of 'The Old Man.'

Lynch's countenance already bears 'the stigmata of premature wisdom'(410). 'Townbred manners' appear. At the head of the board is Mr S. Dedalus – the old man, 'remarkablest progenitor barring none.'

The Ninth Month: Period of civilization culminating with The Incarnation, pp. 411–16: Here we encounter the beginnings of religion: 'religious ministers of all denominations'(411); art: 'plastercast reproductions of the classical statues'(411); civics: 'municipal abattoir'; some science: 'which can scarcely distinguish an acid from an alkali'(413); landscaping: 'a shaven space of lawn'(414); advanced agriculture: 'thoughtful irrigation'(415). And finally – Christianity – the Word, Logos! Indeed it is 'the silent night, the holy night' that is rendered in typical Carlylese: 'The air without is impregnated with raindew moisture, life essence celestial ... there under starshiny. *coelum.*'[8]

It is to be noted, also, that in this evolutionary march, Joyce has not forgotten the coloured races of mankind. The white race, is, of course, everywhere: Purefoy is white; the colour of this chapter is white. The Mongolian, however, is evoked on p. 400 in 'the chinless Chinaman'; the negro in 'negro's inkle,' p. 404; the red man in 'the strawberry mark,' and the mixed and intermediary races in 'portwine stain'(404).

Space does not allow for a discussion of the relationship between the parody styles and the various schemata analysed above. It is a relationship which is most revealing. The description of the Deluge, for example, is done after the manner of Pepys, a perfect harmony: 'waters, and the Clerk of the King's Ships.' The eighth month, 'the little old man' month, is done, fittingly enough, in the manner of Thomas Babington Macaulay. And Joyce's autobiographical letter on p. 417 is written, most justifiably, in the style of the author of *On Heroes, and Hero-Worship, And the Heroic in History.*

NOTES

1 This letter is in the possession of Mr John J. Slocum, president of the James Joyce Society. I am indebted to Ellsworth G. Mason for drawing its existence

to my attention and for providing me with a transcript.

2 All references are to the pagination of the Random House edition of *Ulysses*.

3 The month by month characteristics of the foetus are gleaned from Williams, *Obstetrics* (edited by Henricus J. Stander, 1941). The editions of Williams run back as early as 1903.

4 Assuming, as Joyce in large measure assumed, that Victor Berard's thesis is correct – that the Homeric saga is an anthropomorphised Phoenician logbook – the Oxen of the Sun as a symbol of fertility may be linguistically established through Semitic speech: *por*, an ox, provides the root for *pru*, multiply (Genesis 1: 28); and *shemesh*, the sun, becomes the verb *shamaish*, to serve, and is converted into the noun *tashmish* – copulation. Another word for ox, *aleph*, which gives us the originally bicornate alpha, leads to *eleph*, a thousand.

5 Wahl, quoted in Williams, *op. cit.*, p. 258, calculates the actual duration of gestation to be 273 to 274 days.

6 *Readings in Evolution, Genetics, and Eugenics*, by Horatio Hacket Newman.

7 For the purpose of this analysis, Wells' *Outline of History* is sufficient reference. Newman (*op. cit.*, p. 68) reproduces, after Osborn, a useful geologic time scale.

8 What S. Foster Damon, in an article in *The Hound and Horn* (Fall 1929), sensed intuitively – that a great Christian parable is concealed in *Ulysses* – is thus, through the manifold techniques here discussed, explicitly stated.

The Oxen of the Sun: The Labyrinth Charted

MONTH	PAGINATION	EMBRYOLOGICAL INDICIA	RECAPITULATION	EVOLUTIONARY STAGE	PARODY STYLE
Prelude	377–8			Creation of World / Azoic	Sallustian-Tacitean
The First	378: 'Some man' ... to 381: 'Almighty God'	Fertilization and Mitotic development	Calypso	Proterozoic: Archaeozoic	Old English Wayfarer and Traveller poems. Mandeville
The Second	381: 'This meanwhile' to 384: 'About that present time'	External genitalia appear	Telemachus	Mesozoic	Malory's *Morte d'Arthur*
The Third	384–6: To be short, this passage	Centres of ossification	Nestor	Tertiary	Elizabethan Chronicles
The Fourth	386–8: Thereto Punch Costello ... pea	Sex differentiated	Scylla-Charybdis	Quaternary	Milton / Taylor Browne / Hooker
The Fifth	388–90: brenningly biddeth	Heart sounds heard	Cyclops	Early Palaeolithic	Bunyan
The Sixth	390–2	Foetus, if born, dies	Wandering Rocks	Late Palaeolithic / Neanderthal Man / The Flood	Pepys Evelyn

The Seventh	392–409	Child may be born and live	Proteus	The Age of Cultivation	Defoe-Swift to Landor
7:1:a First	392–5: for a' that	Ravishing, Rapeseed	Nestor	Azoic / Archaeozoic	Defoe-Swift
7:1:b Second	395–7: larum in the antechamber	Pod or Two Testibus ponderosis	Telemachus	Mesozoic	Steele-Addison
7:1:c Third	397–9: store of knowledge	Spontaneous movements Amniotic Fluid	Calypso	Tertiary	Sterne
7:1:d Fourth	399–400: with … a heart	Recognition of sex	Scylla-Charybdis	Quaternary	Goldsmith
7:1:e Fifth	400–1: Supreme Being	Lanugo	Cyclops	Early Palaeolithic	Burke
7:1:f Sixth	401–2: … laugh together	'In readiness to burst anon'	Wandering Rocks	Late Palaeolithic	Sheridan
7:2:a First	402	'Oblivious of ties of nature'	Cyclops	'Lowest strata … to seedfield and ploughshare'	Junius
7:2:b Second			Scylla-Charybdis		
7:2:c Third	to		Calypso		
7:2:d Fourth			Telemachus		

The Oxen of the Sun: The Labyrinth Charted

MONTH	PAGINATION	EMBRYOLOGICAL INDICIA	RECAPITULATION	EVOLUTIONARY STAGE	PARODY STYLE
7:2:e Fifth			Nestor		
7:2:f Sixth	402: acid and inoperative		Wandering Rocks		
7:3:b	403–5: whom God has joined	Triplets	W.R. / Telemachus / Calypso	Mesozoic	Gibbon
7:3:c	405	Triplets	Telemachus Nestor / S-C	Tertiary	Walpole
7:3:d	406	Twins	W.R. / Calypso	Quaternary	Lamb
7:3:e	407 to Taurus	Quadruplets	S-C / Calypso Nestor / Telem.	Early Palaeolithic	de Quincey
7:3:f	407–9: … constellation	Triplets	W.R. / Telemachus / Cyclops	Late Palaeolithic	Landor
The Eighth	410–11: Lafayette	'Little Old Man'	Aeolus (7 recapitulations)	The Age of The Old Man	Macaulay

The Ninth	411–21	Parturition	Hades		Civilization / The Incarnation	Huxley to Carlyle
	411–13: to save her own		45 recapitulations			Huxley
	413–14: good and faithful servant		27 recapitulations			Dickens
	414: 'There are sins' to 'silent, remote, reproachful'		4 plus 5 recaps	Proteus	CIVILIZATION / THE INCARNATION	Newman Pater
	415: 'He frowns a little' to 'utterance of The Word'		18 recaps			Ruskin
	415: 'Burke's!' to 416: 'A truce to'		Par. I: 48 recaps Par. II: 81 recaps			Carlyle
THE NINTH		PARTURITION	HADES			

The Black Panther

A Study in Technique   1950

Imitatio Dei

The art of the first chapter of *Ulysses*, the commentators agree, is theology; and in support of their assertion they point with an obvious pertinence to the great number of ecclesiastic gestures and theological terms in which the chapter abounds. Buck Mulligan speaks in 'a preacher's tone,' he is 'untonsured,' his face and jowl 'recall a prelate.' Allusions to the saints are frequent, and frequent the meditations upon the church and its triumphs over heresy. Benedictions are uttered, the sign of the cross is made, and there is much counting by threes. God, whether as Essence or expletive, is everywhere.

This proof of the chapter's concern with things sacred does seem, however, to postulate a method of equation much too facile for it to have recommended itself to the fastidious and paradigmatic mind of James Joyce. Throughout the text haphazardly to sow religious symbols and then to proclaim that text as of texture theologic is not at all Joyce's way of encompassing his ends. To him, as numerous instances show, design and pattern are of a primary importance: the text sometimes may appear incoherent, the structure never is.

Moreover, complaisance with so easy a theory of the theological process in *Telemachus* must inevitably leave in the text a number of difficulties embarrassingly unresolved. Who is Seymour? Who is Clive Kempthorpe? What is the pertinence of the remark about the red Carlisle girl, Lily? After this chapter, none of these persons will be mentioned again. Why is the Englishman, whose real name, as Dr. Gogarty recalls, was Trench, here rendered Haines? What is the aesthetic compulsion which motivates the reference to the black panther? Upon what principles are selected the various quotations of poetry and verse? Is it only verbal association which dictates the lengthy interior monologues, or is there here some other element at play? And what kind of nickname, in 1904, is Kinch? Or epithet: *dogsbody*? Why is Kinch a knifeblade?

These, and an entire catechism of questions which will present themselves, as their answers in the following paragraphs are suggested, can be met, it is submitted, not through the adding up of a list of discrete allusions, but only through the acceptance of a theological hypothesis, consistent and complete, – only through a recognition of the daring, and – were it more explicit

– the blasphemous, adumbration which casts its cruciform shadow over the entire chapter.

For behind its comparatively innocent and routine action, behind the small talk and big words of *Telemachus*, there is figured, in abbreviated form, a contemporary counterpart of the life of Christ, an *Imitatio Dei* of the year 1904. In this re-enactment there appear three *personae*: Stephen Dedalus, in whose attitude and language the genuine Christine is subsumed; Malachi Mulligan, né Oliver *St. John* Gogarty, who takes on the role and performs the action of the original St. John the Baptist; and Haines.

In this light, many of Malachi's gestures acquire a new significance. Like St. John, he is the announcer, the messenger, in Hebrew – a *malach*. He is at once the last echo of the Old Testament and the first cry of the New. When he sweeps his mirror a half circle in the air, *it is to flash tidings abroad in sunlight now radiant on the sea* (page 8). It is he who permits himself to say to Stephen, in language most reminiscent: *And to think of your having to beg from these swine. I'm the only one who knows what you are* (9). On page 10, when he offers his characterization of Stephen, he defines that knowledge: *O, an impossible person*. And on page 12 the dialogue describes that relationship explicitly:

> – Dedalus, come down, like a good mosey.
> – I'm coming, Stephen said, turning.
> – Do, for Jesus' sake, Buck Mulligan said. For my sake and for all our sakes.

Thus while the dialogue reads like a synoptic version of the Gospels, the relationship of the New Testament to the Old – 'like a good mosey' – is not forgotten.

The life of St. John, moreover, affords additional parallels. The meal that is eaten in the tower includes honey: *And his meat was locusts and wild honey* (St. Matthew 3:4). Like John, Malachi wears a girdle about his loins; like John he is arrayed in garments of a hairy texture: for the Baptist's camel hair, his own *lovely pair with a hair stripe* (8). The gift of a pair of shoes to Stephen is also designed to echo Holy Writ: *But he that cometh after me is mightier than I, whose shoes I am not worthy to bear* (ibid.).

The final scene, of course, discovers Malachi Mulligan in an actual act of baptism. And the last word of the chapter marks him, as in the Gospel according to St. John, 'usurper': *He was not that Light, but he was sent to bear witness of that Light* (St. John 1:8).

Stephen's adversary, however, is not Mulligan: it is Haines. Since Stephen is, at second remove, Love, it is not surprising that he should be opposed by one whose name is an Anglicization of the French word for 'hate'. Joyce plays fair with his reader; he warns him of the connection: says the old woman to Haines, *Is it French you are talking, sir?* (16). Haines, then, is Hatred as opposed to Love; Haines is Satan. Moreover, Haines brought along to the tower by Mulligan is again in fulfilment of Scripture: *For John came neither eating nor drinking, and they say, He hath a devil* (St. Matthew 11:18).

What we find *sub rosa* in this chapter, therefore, is, among other things, a dialogue between Christ and Satan, a re-enactment of the Temptation. On the very second page, Mulligan's reply to Stephen, *Yes, my love*, is now seen to be not an epithet but an appellation. The next sentence, in antonymal sequence, moves from *my love* to Haines. Of Satan *alias* Haines it is stated that, *He can't make you* [Stephen] *out.* 'Twas ever so. Haines, moreover, is of the opinion that Stephen is 'not a gentleman'; it is obvious that Haines is very conscious of Sir John Suckling's compliment to the prince of darkness. Of Haines Stephen says: *There's nothing wrong with him except at night* – an ancient opinion of the devil. When Mulligan swears, he invokes the name of God; not so Haines: *By Jove, it is tea, Haines said* (14).

And Haines wakes up raving and moaning after having dreamt of a black panther. 'One summer night,' writes Dr. Gogarty in *Mourning Becomes Mrs. Spendlove*, 'when it was too hot to sleep although the door was open, shortly after midnight Trench, who had been dozing, awoke suddenly and screamed, "The black panther!" He produced a revolver and fired two or three shots in the direction of the grate.' This well may have been; but Joyce, in making *Haines* dream the dream, aimed at more than mere reportage. The black panther, as the old bestiaries have it, is a symbol of Christ.[1] In his dream to Satan Christ comes as nightmare. Stephen, then, is Love. Stephen's mother, little knowing, *laughed with others when old Royce sang*:

> I am the boy
> That can enjoy
> Invisibility.

Stephen's brooding upon *Love's bitter mystery* (11) is thus an act of introspection, and his abstruse proofs syllogisms of self-justification:

> Pooh! Buck Mulligan said. He proves by algebra that Hamlet's grandson is Shakespeare's grandfather and that he himself is the ghost of his own father.
> What? Haines said, beginning to point at Stephen. He himself?

Under an earlier aspect Stephen is Kinch, 'toothless' Kinch, as in *kinchincove*, that is to say, the Babe, the Bambino. There is a moment, however, when he belies his identification: he asks, *Would I make money by it?* (17). It is a question which issues more properly from the mouth of the Adversary than from that of Stephen. Mulligan's comment put things straight again: *You put your hoof in it now, says Mulligan. What did you say that for?* (18).

The actual Temptation takes place on pages 21 and 22. It is prepared for by the series of innuendoes already referred to and by allusions to the forty-foot hole: *And he was in the wilderness forty days, tempted of Satan: and was with the wild beasts* (St. Mark 1:13).

On page 19 Stephen tells Haines that he pays rent for the tower *twelve quid to the secretary of state for war* – (unto Caesar – Caesar's), and two pages later there follow the things which are God's. Out of the very text the colloquy between Satan and his intended victim may thus be rendered:

SATAN: (*After the recitation of Mulligan's sacrilegious verse*) We oughtn't to laugh, I suppose. He's rather blasphemous. I'm not a believer myself, that is to say. Still his gaiety takes the harm out of it somehow, doesn't it? ... You're not a believer, are you? I mean, a believer in the narrow sense of the word. Creation from nothing and miracles and a personal God.

STEPHEN: There's only one sense of the word, it seems to me.

SATAN: (*Offering Stephen some fire from a tinderbox – for Stephen's ciga-rette*) Yes, of course. Either you believe or you don't, isn't it? Personally I couldn't stomach that idea of a personal God. You don't stand for that, I suppose?

STEPHEN: You behold in me a horrible example of free thought.

The answer, as tradition required, was ambiguous. Free thought was confessed but was declared horrible. Despite his insinuating understatements, his 'rathers' and his 'somehows,' his feigned concession, his willingness, nay eagerness, to meet his interlocutor halfway, Satan is no further advanced than when he began his seduction. *Stephen walks on* (21). *Satanas retro!* For Stephen knows with whom he is dealing; as he makes ready to go he looks back at the smiling Haines, and remembers an Irish proverb: *Horns of a bull, hoof of a horse, smile of a Saxon.* Thus is the devil, horn and hoof, revealed an Englishman.

All the accounts of the Temptation (Matthew 4:1–10; Mark 1:12–13; Luke 4:1–13) are followed by descriptions of Jesus, walking by the sea of Galilee where he beholds two brethren, Simon called Peter, and Andrew his brother, casting a net into the sea. He asks them to follow him, for he will make them fishers of men. In *Telemachus* these fishers of men are to be found standing at the verge of the cliff, waiting for the man that was drowned (23).

Nor is the Temptation and its aftermath the sole event in the life of Christ which is interlinearly parallelled. Christ purging the temple of mon-eychangers is also recalled, and this by means of the debagging scene which is conjured up on page 9. If Haines makes any noise, Malachi promises, he'll bring down Seymour and they'll give him a ragging worse than they gave Clive Kempthorpe. Seymour, it must be asserted in the light of concordant evidence, is but another name for Christ, being, as some say it is, an Englishing of St. Amour, via St. Maur. Kempthorpe, though a name somewhat more cryptic, surrenders its meaning to etymology: *the hamlet of the beards* (thorpe – hamlet; kemp – a knot in wool, from the Norse word for beard), that is, Jerusalem. Kempthorpe's first name, Clive, is equally appropriate, – from the root 'to cleave' meaning 'to separate,' even as Pharisee is from the Hebrew root *paroish* meaning the same thing.

In the gospel according to St. John (2:13–15) the scene is described as follows:

> And Jesus went up to Jerusalem.
> And found in the temple those that sold oxen and sheep and doves, and the changers of money sitting:
> And when he had made a scourge of small cords he drove them all out of the temple, and the sheep and the oxen; and passed out the changers' money, and overthrew the tables.

In *Telemachus* it is thus transposed to Oxford, and imagined:

> Young shouts of moneyed voices in Clive Kempthorpe's rooms. Palefaces: they hold their ribs with laughter, one clasping another. O, I shall expire! Break the news to her gently, Aubrey. I shall die! With slit ribbons of his shirt whipping the air he hops and hobbles round the table, with trousers down at heels, chased by Ades of Magdalen with the tailor's shears. A scared calf's face gilded with marmalade. I don't want to be debagged. Don't you play the giddy ox with me!

It is all there, hell let loose through Ades of the nine devils (Ades of Magdalen – another communicative *hapax legomenon*), the premonition of the end (*O, I shall expire!*), the table, the scourge, the oxen, the money-changers and their Golden Calf (*gilded with marmalade*).

Also recalled is Mother Eve, for whose sin Christ came to atone, recalled in the shape of the milkwoman who, upon another level of interpretation, is the personification of Ireland, Poor Old Woman, and on yet a third level, *la vieille*, about whom more will be said later. Mother Eve, she enters *from a morning world*, and imitating the clichés of that morning world *she praises the goodness of the milk* (*And he saw that it was good* [Genesis 1]). Eden becomes *a lush field*, and the woman whence came our woe a *wandering crone*, *lowly form of an immortal serving her conqueror and her gay betrayer.* She is *of man's flesh made not in God's likeness, the serpent's prey* (16).

The chapter ends with the Revelation of St. John the Divine. *Seymour* [read *Christ*] *is back in town* (23), according to the announcement of the young man grasping a spur of rock (*petros*). He has *chucked medicine* (given up miraculous cures) *and gone in for the army* (the church militant). Mulligan, a Protestant, is then prompted to recall the Babylonian Woman and he mentions the red Carlisle girl, Lily. Lily's original is in Revelations (17:4): *And the woman was arrayed in purple and scarlet colour, and decked with gold and precious stones and pearls, having a golden cup in her hand full of abominations and filthiness of her fornication.* This explains both the remark about *going over next week to stew* (23) and the reference to *red-headed women who buck like goats* (24). *Spooning with him on the pier* (23) – that is to equate *the waters where the whore sitteth* (*ibid.*, 17:15).

The theological content of *Telemachus*, it is thus shown, is made up of more than merely aspersed religious reference. It has evangelical coherence. Coherence of narrative, however, though superior to the random techniques the commentators originally supposed, is not a consummation with which Joyce, one imagines, would content himself. Coherence is not pattern, but only an element in it. Pattern still remains to seek. Considering the christological background already sketched and noting certain clues in some places offered with a give-away explicitness – *Introibo ad altare Dei …* (5) *In nomine Patris et Filii et Spiritus Sancti* (14) – it will not now come as a startling surprise if it is suggested that the basic structure of this chapter is that of the Ordinary and the Proper of the Mass.

THE MASS

It must be stated forthwith that it is no pious rite which is celebrated here; out of the parodies which the irreverent Malachi Mulligan perpetrates it is not the Blessed but the Black Mass which emerges. Mulligan, in the five required sacerdotal vestments arrayed, is dressed for his function: his *dressinggown, ungirdled* (5), is alb and cincture; his *primrose waistcoat* (19) – chasuble with Y orphrey; the amice, covering neck and shoulder, and having two long strings, is represented by *stiff collar and rebellious necktie* (18), subsequently described as *rippling over his shoulder* (23); the towel carried over his forearm is, of course, the maniple; it is finally converted into the remaining vestment, when, on page 19, he slings it *stolewise* round his neck.

The Buck, moreover, bears an epithet suitable to his role, a reminiscence of the greatest buck of them all, the Irish 'Buck' Whalley,[2] of whom it was whispered that he had acted as priest at a Black Mass. Mulligan's intention is not kept secret; again and again he makes pointed allusion to 'the mockery of it.'

Throughout the chapter the Mass is not only exemplified: its order is observed with precision and in sequence, as the parallel columns which follow will illustrate.

Part of the Mass. Its characteristics:	Its correspondence:
1 *Preparatory prayer at the foot of the altar.* The beginning of the Mass, it is preceded by the sign of the cross. The priest begins the Antiphon: *Introibo ad altare Dei* and is antiphonally answered by the Server.	The sign of the cross is seen in the position of the razor and mirror. The introit is explicitly uttered. Malachi gives a long low whistle of call and two strong shrill whistles answer (antiphonally) through the calm (5).
2 Psalm 42 (*Judica me*) is recited by the Priest alternating with the Server. It is a psalm which prays God to judge and distinguish the petitioner's cause from the nation that is not holy (*de gente non sancta*) and asks deliverance from the unjust and deceitful man. It says also: *They have conducted me and brought me unto thy holy mount ... Why art thou sad, O my soul, and why dost thou disquiet me?*	The nation that is not holy is for reasons indicated in the text, the *English, bursting with money and indigestion* (6). The holy mount and tabernacle is the Martello Tower. Disquieting is effected by Haines, raving and moaning.
3 *The Public Confession (Confiteor Deo).* This is an acknowledgment of guilt before God, a confession to the blessed Mary, the Archangel Michael, John the Baptist, the holy apostles Peter and Paul, and all the saints. The priest prays God that He forgive and grant absolution, 'turn again and quicken us.'	Malachi invites Stephen to *Look at yourself* (8). Stephen recalls his failure to kneel down when his dying mother asked him. The Virgin is adumbrated in *Our mighty mother* (7); John the Baptist is present; Sir Peter Teazle is there for a reason; and the saints follow in the train of St. Ursula, who led 11,000 of them.

Remission and absolution are equated by *It simply doesn't matter ... Look at the sea. What does it care about offences?*
And no more turn aside and brood echoes the priest's verse.

4 The priest ascends the altar and says: *Aufer a nobis, quaesumus Domine, iniquitates nostras: Take away from us our iniquities, we beseech thee.*
He refers to the saints *whose relics are here.*

No, mother, let me be, let me live. Her secrets: old feather fans, tasseled dancecards, etc. (11).

5 *The Introit.* This is a part which varies from feast to feast. It is assumed, for reasons already suggested and further proof to be adduced, that these variable parts are from the Mass for the Feast of Corpus Christi. Its introit is from Psalm 80:7: *He fed them with the fat of wheat, and filled them with honey out of the rock.* The priest enters the sanctuary to begin the Mass.

Breakfast is ready (12). It will be remembered this breakfast consisted in part of bread and honey.

Kinch, ahoy! ... Buck Mulligan's voice sang from within the tower (12).

6 *The Kyrie Eleison* (Lord, have mercy). A series of invocations addressed to each of the Three Divine Persons.

This is phonetically reproduced, the *kyrie eleison* being transformed *coronation* and thrice repeated, thus:

> *On coronation*
> *Coronation day?*
> *O won't we have a merry time*
> *On coronation day* (12).

7 *The Gloria in Excelsis* (Glory to God in the highest), the Angelic Hymn. In the cathedral at Lucca flames are kindled at the intonation of the *Gloria* whenever the archbishop pontificates.

In the gloomy domed livingroom of the tower (13).

Two shafts of soft daylight fell across the flagged floor (13).

8 *The Collect*, a short prayer said before the Epistle and having direct reference to the feast of the day. The Collect of the Feast of Corpus Christi speaks of the memorial of the Passion. Its last words are *Who livest*.

The resurrection of Christ on the third day is obliquely envisaged: *We'll be choked ... Open that door ... The key scraped round harshly twice and, when the heavy door had been set ajar, welcome light and bright air entered. Stephen haled his upended valise to the table* (13).

9 *The Epistle*. That for the Feast of Corpus Christi is from 1 Corinthians, 11:23–9: *Took bread, and giving thanks, broke and said, Take ye, and eat.*

Bread, butter, honey ... Bless us, O Lord, and these Thy gifts (13).

10 *The Gradual*. The fourth variable part of the Mass. It contains the prayer *Munda cor meum ac labia mea*, cleanse my heart and lips. It contains the alleluatic verse (*Alleluia*: praise God).

But hush, not a word more on the subject (13).

For the Feast of Corpus Christi, Psalm 145:16 recited: *Thou openest thy hand and fillest every living creature with thy blessing*. The priest intones: *In nomine Patris et Filii et Spiritus Sancti*.

The tea, sugar, eggs, fish, milk, lemon (14).

The Gradual of Corpus Christi is followed by a sequence.

Four lines of text and ten pages of notes (14).

11 *The Gospel*. This is the most solemn of the readings at the Mass because it tells a story of Christ whose words and deeds it recalls. On Corpus Christi Day it is from St. John 6:50–51. At High Mass the Gospel is sung. It concludes: *Gloria tíbi, Domine.*

This is most blasphemously rendered on page 15.

Glory be to God (15).

12 *The Credo*. The profession of faith drawn up in the General Council

The islanders speak frequently of God (15).

of Nice in 325 and Constantinople in 381, it asserts, among other doctrines, one God, and belief in Christ who 'for us men and for our salvation came down from heaven,' a faith in the Second Coming, and loyalty to the one holy, Catholic and Apostolic Church.

In the description of the milk-woman, Mother Eve recalled.

The milkwoman listens only to Buck Mulligan.

13 *The Offertory Verse.* This is a prayer of self-surrender and oblation; at this point bread and candles were once offered; the practice was discontinued at about the eleventh century; to a certain extent the collection has taken the place of candle and bread.

Heart of my heart, were it more, More would be laid at your feet (17). This is from a poem of Swinburne's called *The Oblation.*

The milkwoman collects her money.

14 *The Offering of the Bread and Wine.* The paten with the host is taken, and offering it up, the priest says: *Accept, O holy Father, this unspotted host ... which I offer for my innumerable sins, offences, and negligences.*

Yet here's a spot (17).

Agenbite of inwit. Conscience (17).

15 *The Incensing of the Offerings.* The incense is blessed. The priest prays: *Set a watch, O Lord, before my mouth, and a door round about my lips.*

I blow him out about you (18).

Stephen is reluctant to expatiate on Hamlet (17, 18).

16 *The Washing of the Hands.* The priest washes his fingers, reciting Psalm 25:6–12. *I will wash my hands ... and I will compass thine altar ... The wicked ... whose right hand is filled with gifts.*

They wash and tub and scrub (17).

Would I make money by it? (17).

17 *The Prayer to the Most Holy Trinity.*

From her or from him? From me (18).

18 *The Orate Fratres.* The priest, calling the congregation to prayer with him, says audibly: *Orate, fratres.* Brethren, pray.

Why don't you play them as I do? (18).

19 *The Secrets.* Said inaudibly, it ends with an ekphonesis. In it the priest recommends the offering just made.

He emptied his pockets on the table. There ... And there's your Latin quarter hat (18).

20 *The Preface* (a prayer of thanksgiving). That for Corpus Christi and its Octave acknowledged *God in visible form so that we may through Him be drawn to things invisible.* As the priest introduces the Preface, he holds both hands over the altar, then joins them before his breast, and finally, until he says the *Sanctus,* disjoins them.

Do I contradict myself? Very well, then, I contradict myself (18).

His hands plunged and rummaged (18).

21 *The Sanctus,* the triumphal hymn of the angels, which announces: *Blessed is He that cometh in the name of the Lord!*

And going forth he met Butterly[3] (18).

22 *The Prayers before the Consecration.* These invoke the Saints and implore their protection.

(St.) *Thomas Aquinas and his fifty-five reasons* (19).

23 *Oblation of the Victim to God.* The priest signs thrice the oblation with the Sign of the Cross. There follow (a) The Consecration of the Host, (b) The Consecration of the Wine, (c) The Oblation of the Victim to God.

You couldn't do it under three pints (19).
He proves ... that grandson ... is grandfather, and that he himself is the ghost of his own father. What? ... He himself? (19).
The sacred pint alone can unbind the tongue of Dedalus (20).
The Father and the Son idea. The Son striving to be atoned with the Father (20) (atoned – at-oned).

24   *Prayers after Consecration.* The priest offers the Body and Blood of Christ for the comfort of the souls in purgatory.

This is sacrilegiously rendered through the verses on pp. 20–21.

25   *The Pater Noster.* The Lord's Prayer. *Our Father who art in heaven ... forgive us our trespasses ... our daily bread.*

The idea of a personal God (21). *You don't stand for that* (21). *Now I eat his salt bread* (21).

26   *The Libera Nos,* prayer beseeching liberation from all evils, past, present, and to come.

Able to free yourself (22) from the Italian and British master.

27   The priest puts the Particle into the Chalice.

Haines detached ... some fibres (22).

28   *The Agnus Dei: Lamb of God, who takest away the sins of the world, have mercy on us.*

It seems history is to blame (22).

29   *The Prayers for Holy Communion.* These are prayers for peace, for sanctification, and for grace. They ask that the church be granted unity.

The entire paragraph beginning: *The proud potent titles ...* (22).

30   *The Prayers at the Communion.* Communion of the Body and the Blood.

The man that was drowned (23). *A swollen bundle ... Here I am* (23).

31   *Prayers during the Ablution.* The priest prays that 'the temporal gift may become to us an eternal remedy.'

Snapshot. Brief exposure (23).

32   *The Communion Verse: Dominus vobiscum.*

Ah, go to God (23).

33   *The Post Communion Verse.* That for Corpus Christi requests God that 'He make us to be filled with the eternal enjoyment of His Divinity.'

I'm the Uebermensch (24).

34   *The Dismissal: Ite, missa est.*   *I'm going, Mulligan, he said* (24).

35   *The Blessing.* The priest makes a
profound reverence. He turns to   *His plump body plunged* (24).
the faithful invoking upon them   *Turning the curve, he waved his*
the blessing of God.   *hand* (24).

36   *The Last Gospel.* The beginning of
the Gospel of St. John, which reads
in part: *There was a man sent from
God whose name was John ... He
was not the Light but he was to
testify concerning the Light.*   *Usurper* (24).

One can but recall, as one goes through this progress of subterranean reference, the remark of Arthur Symons, one of Joyce's early friends, concerning the Black Masses that are 'even now performed from time to time in a secrecy which is all but absolute.'4 At the same time one must be amused, too, by Thomas Merton's assertion5 that it was Joyce's *Ulysses* which was one of the influences which brought him into the bosom of the Church. Certainly it is in most mysterious ways that God His wonders works.

THE WITCHES' SABBATH

It is as a part of the Witches' Sabbath6 that the Black Mass finds its properly improper performance. The correlation was by Joyce not ignored. *Telemachus* is, clandestinely and all, such a Witches' Sabbath. Haines, it is now realized, is not simply a devil, content of St. John; he is the Devil. In Ireland he is, according to Lactantius, upon his rightful estate. Said that author: 'The Lord so divided the world with the devil that *occidens, septentrio, tenebrae, frigus* – The West [*Westmeath* (23)], the North [*I'm hyperborean as much as you* (7)], the Dark [*the awaking mountains* (5)], and the Cold [*the cold gaze* (22)], fell to the sphere of the Adversary.' In Dublin he is in his very capital; something, says Burns, 'is just as true as the deil's in hell, Or Dublin City.' The exact terrain of conflict is located between Kingstown (Christ's?) and Bray Head (the notorious vicar's?). Because of the unholy presence there proliferate throughout the chapter a herd of *beastly's, damn's,* and a *deuce* or two.

Other diabolic paraphernalia are also indicated. The aunt is 'to fork out' twenty quid; hoofs are barely concealed. It is not without significance that at his first approach to Haines, Mulligan is all but choked (13).

As in the Witches' Sabbath the first discovery of the Devil finds him already enthroned.7 A *tall figure* [Haines's] *rose from the hammock where it had been sitting* (13). The introduction of the old woman is prescribed procedure; she is *la vieille* (when the devil can do nothing, says the proverb, he sends an old woman); she is the heroine of the Sabbath and is expressly so described: *a witch on her toadstool* (15). Nor are her usual adjuncts forgotten: her broomstick flashes from the peculiar phrase about the Carlisle girl being 'up the pole' (23), and the necessary frog is shadowed forth in the young man moving *slowly frogwise his green legs* (23). Satan's mascot, the goat, is with a special appropriateness introduced into a chapter whose colour is given as gold-white; for it was traditionally the goat whose head was sculptured as a sign of forced servitude in the gold and ivory of the pastoral crozier.

The hidden ceremonial in *Telemachus* runs true to form. The manner in which the Mass is imitated only to be distorted has already been charted. It is pertinent to note that faithful (after their fashion) as are the echoes of the Mass, no sacring bell is ever heard; since bells drive away evil spirits Witches' Sabbaths shunned them. It will also have been noted that by the time Haines comes upon the scene, Mulligan's razor has gone out of sight; this is, among other reasons, because the devil is reputed to have an antipathy towards knives, an antipathy which gives deeper meaning to Mulligan's comment upon the relations between Haines and Stephen: *He* [Haines] *can't make you out. O, my name for you is the best: Kinch, the knifeblade* (6). A similar aversion the Destroyer entertains towards salt; he hates it, a preservative; he leaves it for Stephen to consume: *Now I eat his salt bread* (23).[8]

One of the most important rites of the Witches' Sabbath is its orgiastic dance which reaches so great a pitch of intensity that often it culminates in actual levitation and flight. The part is given to Mulligan: *running forward to a brow of the cliff* [he] *fluttered his hands at his sides like fins or wings of one about to rise in the air ... He capered before them ...* (20). Joyce, however, refrains from equating the gesture most revolting of the Witches' Sabbath, – the *osculatio ad anum diaboli*; as Mulligan, in language which preludes the action of page 719, keeps on making remarks about 'scutter' and 'noserags' and having *Haines up the nose ... against him* (9), this rite is suggested and, of course, repudiated.

The *Circe* chapter, as is well known, presents in large measure a transmogrification of the principal events of Bloom's day. Here, in Nighttown, all that has been hitherto restrained and inhibited is at last released; what during the day was implicit is now at midnight made explicit. From this treatment, *Telemachus* is not excepted. Page 583 discovers Father Malachi O'Flynn (the Father O'Flynn of the ballad 'who makes hares of them all'), in a long petticoat and reversed chasuble, his two left feet back to the front, celebrating camp mass. He is in the company of the Reverend Mr. Hugh C. Love, who apparently in the course of the day has acquired a middle name: Haines. Father Malachi O'Flynn intones: *Introibo ad altare diaboli*; the Reverend Mr. Haines

Love responds: *To the devil which hath made glad my young days*; and on the following page the Voice of all the Damned articulates the word God backwards.

Mulligan's address to Stephen, *Ah, poor dogsbody* (7) is at last explained.

Assuming as premise the situation revealed in the foregoing pages, one may now approach and, it is submitted, at last solve, a problem which has agitated the minds of Joyce scholars ever since *Ulysses* was first published: Why did Joyce, out of all the days of the calendar, choose precisely the sixteenth of June as his all-inclusive echoing microcosmic Day?

It is clear that uppermost in Joyce's thought, though nethermost in his utterance, was the equation between Stephen and Christ. That equation, indeed, he transcribes on page 674 in what was for Joyce speech unambiguous:

What were Stephen's and Bloom's quasisimultaneous volitional quasisensations of concealed identities?

Visually, Stephen's: The traditional figure of hypostasis, depicted by Johannes Damascenus, Lentulus Romanus and Epiphanius Monachus as leucodermic, sesquipedalian with winedark hair.[9]

Auditively, Bloom's: The traditional accent of the ecstasy of catastrophe.

Ulysses was in a sense intended, therefore, as the body of Christ, rendered literature. As late as his fiftieth birthday Joyce is still heard dropping hints – unheeded – as to the nature of his work. Reports Mr. Eugene Jolas, in *My Friend James Joyce*: 'On that occasion we gave a small dinner at our home in Paris attended by Mrs. Joyce, Thomas McGreevy, Samuel Beckett, Lucy and Paul Léon, Helen and Giorgio Joyce, and others. The birthday cake was decorated with an ingenious candy replica of a copy of *Ulysses*, in its blue jacket. Called on to cut the cake, Joyce looked at it a moment and said: *Accipite et manducate ex hoc omnes: Hoc est enim corpus meum.*'

This being so, the day that Joyce should have chosen was that of the Feast of Corpus Christi; in 1904 it fell on Thursday, the second of June. But Joyce, because he had in him the Jesuit strain, *only injected the wrong way* (10), desired also to fulfil his secondary intention – a Witches' Sabbath. This perverse desire may have suggested itself to him out of a contemplation of the data of his own biography. 'The main reunion of the witches,' writes Mr. Rudwin, 'occurred on May Eve (April 30) which was sometimes known as Toodmas in Great Britain and as Walpurgis Night in Germany, and on November Eve (October 31) called Hallowe'en. As a later addition, midway between the nights of power, we have witches' gatherings on Candlemas (February second).' February second was Joyce's birthday.

Now Witches' Sabbaths cannot be perpetrated on Feasts of Obligation; this is a rule which even the Devil observes. It is traditional, too, that they take place on a Thursday. 'It seemed,' pontificate Messieurs Garçon and Vinchon, 'that Sunday, the day of holy congregation and of prayer, which recalls the creation of the world and the resurrection of the Saviour, must necessarily be respected by the Devil; and similarly, Friday, the day of the Passion ... The Turks, says one author, celebrate Friday, the Jews Saturday, the Christians Sunday. The Devil has set himself in front of them all, and has taken Thursday in order to have the first celebration.'

The Feast of Corpus Christi, though invariably a Thursday, was therefore, as has been indicated, unsuitable for Joyce's complete purpose; it served only as his point of departure. It is true that he has used its Proper of the Mass, but in that he by no means contravened prescribed form, for the devil's tabu is against the day, not its liturgy. The most proximate Thursday, thereafter – the ninth of June – was also impossible; it belonged to the *Octave* of Corpus Christi. The earliest next opportunity was the Thursday following – that is to say, the sixteenth of June.

NOTES

1   Panter is an wilde der,
     Is none fairer on werlde her;
     He is blac so born of qual. .
     ...

     In his hole sithen stille
     Thre dages he slepen wille
     Than after the thridde dai
     He riseth and remeth lude so he mai
     Ut of his throte cumeth a smel
     Mid his rem forth over al
     That overcometh haliweie.
     ...

     The dragunes one ne stiren nout
     Wiles te panter rameth ogt,
     Oc daren stille in here pit
     Als so he weren of dethe offrigt.

     SIGNIFICACIO

     Crist is tokened thurg this der
     Wos kinde we have told gu her.
     For he is faier over alle men
     So evensterre over erthe fen.

2   Of him it is reported that he once made a bet to walk to Jerusalem – to play ball against its walls. He made it. It is also reported that on another

occasion 'Jerusalem' Whalley and his friend Col. St. John Leger set fire to the apartment in which they were besotting themselves so as to see how long they could stand, here on earth, the fires which for eternity awaited them. With University College, which Joyce attended, 'Buck' Whalley's name is associated as one of its earliest owners and residents.

3 Dr. Gogarty refers thus to Butterly: 'Going forth I met Butterly, a spruce little barrister ... who always seemed to be leaving in a hurry, though no one knew where he went or where he slept. He was now leaving the scene of one of his famous jokes.' *As I Was Going Down Sackville Street*, p. 65.

4 In *Figures of Several Centuries*.

5 In *The Seven Storey Mountain*.

6 It is not performed on the Sabbath, nor is it in any way related to the Day of Rest. The word is said to be derived from French *s'esbattre*, to frolic.

7 For relevant information on the devil and his orgies, see *The Devil*, by Maurice Garçon and Jean Vinchon; and *The Devil in Legend and Literature*, by Maximilian Rudwin. There is also – to stir the mind to wonder anew about Joyce's choice of the name Seymour – *Irish Demonology and Witchcraft*, by St. John Seymour (New York, 1913).

8 The whole phrase, of course, is an echo of Dante's *Purgatorio*, Canto XVII: 'How salt the savor is of others' bread.'

9 The reference is to a literary picture of Christ, by some attributed to Johannes Damascenus, by others to a fictitious character, Publius Lentulus by name.

A Shout in the Street

An Analysis of the Second Chapter of Joyce's *Ulysses*   1951

I would not pay overmuch attention to these theories [Vico's] beyond using them for all they are worth, but they have gradually forced themselves on me through the circumstances of my own life.[1]

These theories, enunciated principally in Vico's *Scienza Nuova*, which purports to provide 'the design for an ideal eternal history traversed in time by the histories of all nations,'[2] must of necessity here be stated briefly.

After the Flood, says Vico, the races of mankind 'were lost from one another by roving wild in the great forest of the earth, pursuing shy and indocile women, and fleeing from the wild animals with which the great ancient forest must have abounded. They were scattered further in search of water, and as the result of it all were reduced, at the end of a long period, to the conditions of beasts' (*Scienza Nuova*, par. 13).

This period of prolonged bestiality continues until for the first time after the Flood, 'the earth having dried,' a storm takes place and the sky rolls with thunder and flashes with lightning. Bestial man is filled with fear at this new appalling phenomenon; and out of this fear he fashions himself the idea of a god. This, says Vico (par. 191), gives the right sense to that saying: 'Fear first created gods in the world.'

Vico further supposes that the thunderblast finds primitive man under the open sky in the very act of fornication. Deeming the thunder at once menace and reproof, he drags his 'shy, indocile woman' into a cave, a place where they both may be hidden from the obvious wrath of heaven. Thus with fear there is born also the sense of shame, and thus, from now on, domesticity and legitimate union are established.

To the sound of thunder in the sky, man enters the Age of the Gods!

In these caves, continues Vico, 'settled with particular women, through fear of the apprehended divinity, in religious and chaste carnal unions, they [the once bestial men] solemnized marriages under cover and begot acknowledged children and so founded families. By long residence and burial of their dead, they come to found and divide the first dominions of the earth ... Hence they considered themselves noble, justly ascribing their nobility in that first state of human things to their having been humanly engendered in the fear of divinity ... The houses which had branched out into several families thus formed were called the first nations [*gentes*] because of such generation' (*ibid.*, par. 13).

These developments mark the entry of man into 'the age of heroes.' We have now come also upon the three most important Viconian principles of social organization: first, the discovering of God and the founding of religion, with altars and auspices controlled by the heroes; second, the practice of solemn matrimony; and third, the belief in the immortality of the soul as evidenced by the institution of burial. Says Vico (par. 333): 'We observe that all nations, barbarous as well as civilized, though separately founded because remote from each other in time and space, keep these three human customs: all have some religion, all contract solemn marriages, all bury their dead.'

Society having arrived at this stage, 'to the altars of the heroes, then, there come the impious-nomadic-weak, fleeing for their lives from the stranger, seeking refuge; the pious-strong kill the violent among them and take the weak under their protection. Since the latter bring with them nothing but their lives, they are accepted as *famuli*, and given the means of sustaining life' (*ibid.*, par. 18). The Age of Heroes, then, is characterized by the appearance of two classes, the protecting and the protected, the patricians and the plebeians.

But the plebeians are not content to remain forever subservient to the patricians. Envy prompts them. They long for the rights enjoyed by their superiors, particularly the right of association in the auspices which, legitimizing their marriages, would legitimize their children. They are not content with their fractional rights over property; full citizenship is what they desire. They seek equality. The patricians resist these demands and try to maintain their position through force. Conflict ensues. When this conflict, this curve in the cycle of historic progress is resolved, equality in society is established. The Age of Man is ushered in.

It is here (par. 300 et seq.) that Vico makes his summary of the three ages, their characteristics and identifying features.

	Age of Gods	Age of Heroes	Age of Men
Nature	Poetic, creative	Heroic	Human
Customs	Religious, pious	Choleric, punctilious	Enjoining duty
Government	Theocratic	Aristocratic	Human
Natural Law	Divine	Law of Force	Laws of Reason
Language	Mute; expression through religious act	Mute and articulate	Articulate
Written characters	Hieroglyphics	Symbols	Vulgar writing Demotic speech

It will have been noted that every step forward in this cycle of progress has been the result of an exercise of vice or weakness! Fear it was, and shame, that at the beginning lifted man from bestiality; arbitrary force it was which established the society of the heroes; and envy which preluded the Age of Man. Not the sage counsel of philosophers it is which founds societies, but providence working through the very weaknesses of man. 'Out of ferocity, avarice, and ambition, the three vices which run throughout the human race, it [legislation] creates the military, merchant, and governing classes, and thus the strength, riches and wisdom of commonwealths. Out of these three great vices, which could certainly destroy all mankind on the face of the earth, it makes civil happiness. This axiom proves that there is divine providence and further that it is a divine legislative mind. For out of the passions of men each bent on his private advantage, for the sake of which they would live like wild beasts in the wilderness, it has made the civil orders by which they may live in human society' (*ibid.*, par. 132, 133).

Vico's doctrine is thus a paradoxical one. His method of arriving at it also deviates from the usual norms of research. It is not from a study of chronology – here, says Vico, all is dark and obscure – but from philology, an analysis of the origins of basic words, that he comes to his conclusions. Philosophy, announces Vico in one of his opening paragraphs, is about to examine philology (*ibid.*, par. 7). Much attention, accordingly, is paid throughout the *New Science* to the derivations of names prominent either in early history or mythology. 'The names of the first family fathers,' says our author (par. 162), 'were given them because of the various properties which they had in the state of the families and of the first commonwealths, at the time when the nations were forming their languages. As far as our small erudition will permit, we shall make use of this vocabulary in all the matters we discuss.' Vico even pauses to inform us that 'to Adam ... God granted divine onomathesia, the giving of names to things according to the nature of each' (par. 401).

But society as developed up to the Age of Man does not remain static, a perpetual age of reason. Here Vico enunciates the law of recurrence (the ricorso), the crumbling of society back into a second age of barbarism, whence it rises once more according to the already-enunciated providential pattern, through the ages of gods, heroes, and men. The Age of Man frequently owes, says Vico, its stability to a monarch, but 'the monarchs mean to strengthen their own positions by debasing their subjects with all the vices of dissoluteness, and they dispose them to endure slavery at the hands of stronger nations. The nations mean to dissolve themselves, and their remnants flee for safety to the wilderness, whence, like the phoenix, they rise again' (par. 1108).

It remains, finally, to add that all of the above applies only to the histories of the gentile nations. To bring them to the age of reason and to the recognition of what is highest and best in religion, Providence has to work in spiral, ever upwards, from age to age; the Hebrews, on the other hand, were vouchsafed direct and immediate revelation. 'For whereas the gentile nations,' says Vico, 'had only the ordinary help of providence, the Hebrews had extraordinary help from the true God' (par. 313).

That in the writing of the *Nestor* chapter Joyce made frequent allusion to the Viconian philosophy cannot be gainsaid. 'The very atmosphere of Mr. Deasy's study,' says Mr. Stuart Gilbert, 'is "historical" – it bears for Stephen an impress of the "dingdong round" of cyclical return preconized by Vico. (It is significant that the name of Vico occurs in this episode, in a reference to "Vico Road, Dalkey."')[3]

One may note also that the Viconian doctrine is explicitly stated:

– The ways of the Creator are not our ways, Mr. Deasy said. All history moves towards one great goal, the manifestation of God.
Stephen jerked his thumb towards the window, saying:
– That is God.
Hooray! Ay! Whrrwhee!
– What? Mr. Deasy asked.
– A shout in the street, Stephen answered, shrugging his shoulders.

But not only is Vico's civilizing thunder heard; one encounters too, as the fox buries his grandmother under a hollybush, the rite of sepulture. The solemnity of marriage is adverted to by Mr. Deasy in his remark about faithless women and runaway wives. One is also conscious, in place after place throughout the chapter, of peculiarities in sentence structure which seem to suggest the hither and yon of Vico's ricorsi.

Is there more?

The following analysis is an attempt to show that the entire chapter, from beginning to end, has been shaped and influenced by Vico's paradigms of providence; that there is hardly a phrase which has not been, at least in its sequence in the text, predetermined by this pattern; that even the proper names occurring in this chapter find their place therein, not only in an order dictated by the course of the narrative, but also in an order dictated, in true Viconian style, by the nature of their etymologies; that every numeral appearing in the text has a significance which goes beyond its immediate one in relation to the narrative; and that the author, owner of the ash plant and master of divine auspices, speaks everywhere to the reader, not only in the explicit language of his composition, but also in that mute language so typical of his office. It will be shown, in fact, that throughout the chapter, in its very style and in the sequence of its paragraphs, the unrelenting winding workings of Providence are being continually simulated.

The table which follows, designed through its parallel columns to emphasize equation, is necessarily limited, for reasons of space, as to the scope of its explanatory notes. The reader will himself, we trust, find further instances in the text to corroborate our thesis.

1

The Age of Gods	Cochrane	The identification will be philologically justified when we reach Cycle 19.
	What city sent for him?	Cities, says Vico (par. 17), were called 'altars' throughout the ancient world of the gentiles.
The Age of Heroes	There was a battle, sir.	Conflict is the invariable characteristic of this age.

The text now informs us that there will be a delay before we reach The Age of Men, the boy's is a *blank face looking at a blank window*. The blank window consists of a paragraph in which the general Viconian law is paraphrased in Blakeian terminology. *Thud of Blake's wings of excess* is a reference to his famous dictum: 'The road of excess leads to the palace of wisdom,' and this is an exact parallel of Vico's assertion that it is through man's vices, his excesses, that Providence leads him toward civilization. We have here, too, a recall of the two Blake designs which were hung in The Royal Academy in 1784: *War Unchained by an Angel – Fire, Pestilence, and Famine Following* and *A Breach in the City – The Morning After a Battle.* The city and the battle appear within the first four lines; that he who announces the war, Cochrane, is herald angel will be shown later.

The Age of Men	Asculum	This identification, too, must await its confirmation in Cycle 27.
Ricorso	Another victory like that and we are done for.	Ricorsi will be signalized almost everywhere throughout the sequence by devices of repetition, as *another, again*, etc.

2

Of Gods	That phrase the world had remembered	The phrase of impatience, thud of wings, noise up above, thunder, which primitive man thought was God reproving his bestiality.
Of Heroes	A general speaking to his officers, leaned upon his spear.	The general, of course, is patrician. So is his weapon; Vico (paragraphs 112 and 562) makes a point of the fact that the Latin word for citizens, *quirites,* is from *quiris,* a spear.
	They lend ear	The Age of Heroes is characterized by articulate speech.
	You, Armstrong	In an age of force, the strong arm is noble.
	Ask me, sir, Comyn said. Wait.	The impetuous plebian is enjoined to wait his turn in the cycle of history. Then Armstrong is addressed and is asked if he knows anything about Pyrrhus. This is tantamount to asking him if he knows his bestial origin, for Pyrrhus is, in the present context, a homonym for Paris, which throughout the chapter is used to denote bes-

		tiality. Armstrong doesn't know; but the answer lies in his satchel: *figrolls*, one of many symbols to be found in this chapter which evoke the sense of rolling, the course onwards, from the age of the figleaf of shame. The sense of shame, says Vico (par. 504), builds nations.
	Welloff people, proud that their eldest son was in the navy	
	Aware of my lack of rule and of the fees their papas pay	Stephen is plebeian.
Of Men	Stephen poking the boy's shoulder	The plebs prodding the patrician.
	Pyrrhus, a pier	Pyrrhus, bestial man (the plebs believed to be of bestial origin, Vico, par. 414) – a peer!
Ricorso	A pier, sir, Armstrong said ... Kingstown pier, sir	A repetition

(In the next line, we will be told that we have accomplished two cycles: 'Two in the back bench whispered.')

3

Of Gods	A laugh: mirthless but with meaning	That is to say, a significant noise.
	Had never learned, nor ever been innocent	The state of primitive man
Of Heroes	With envy he watched	The usual plebeian attitude
	Edith, Ethel, Gertrude, Lily	Noble names all: Edith – rich gift; Ethel – noble; Gertrude – spear maid; Lily – a royal symbol.
Of Men	How, sir, Comyn asked	The common plebs gets its voice.
Ricorso	This cycle has none. Its bridge is 'a disappointed bridge.'	

4

God	For Haines's chapbook	Haines,[4] as has been shown in chapter one, is the devil. For his chapbook, the most desirable entry is – God.
		An equation for 'Noise in the street' is omitted in this instance because 'there is no one here to hear.'
Heroes	Deftly amid wild drink to pierce the polished mail	The plebeian, whose drink and talk is naturally wild, plans deftly to pierce, as Providence helps him to do, the patrician's polished mail. There is also a pun: wild talk (the bestial speech) will enter into polished mail (the age of letters).
	Indulged and disesteemed	The plebeian plight
Men	Winning a clement master's praise	'But finally,' says Vico (par. 29), 'as the free peoples could not by means of laws maintain themselves in civil equality because of the factions of the powerful … it came about naturally that … they sought protection under monarchies.'
Ricorso	Had Pyrrhus not fallen … Julius Caesar not been knifed	The whole paragraph is a paragraph of reflux.
	Weave, weaver of the wind	

5

| Gods | A ghoststory | A holyghoststory |
| | Where do you begin in this? Stephen asked, opening *another book.* | |

Heroes	Comyn intrudes, but it is Talbot who is told to 'go on'	'Behold the eagles, lions, talbots, bears, The badges of your famous ancestries.' – Drayton.
	The *breastwork* of his satchel	A military description
Men	Weep no more, woeful shepherd	
Ricorso	Weep no more ... weep no more It must be a movement then	

6

God	An actuality of the possible as possible. Aristotle's phrase formed itself within the gabbled verses	
		Something intelligible out of the onomatopoeia of the primitive savage
	Sheltered from the sin of Paris	When God is realized, man hides from his own bestiality. Paris – sin.
Heroes	A handbook of strategy	The author takes pains to state that the Siamese, a nationality associated with twinship, and therefore a natural evocation of the Age of Man, is not yet in that category; is still 'at his elbow.'
	Fed and feeding brains	Two classes
	Under glowlamps	Under the social order born out of lightning
	Faintly beating feelers	The plebs early resistance
Men	A sloth of the underworld ... shifting her dragon scaly folds	The plebs is moved (shifted) to another status. Dragon. Reference to the fable of Cadmus, sowing the dragon's teeth (Vico, par. 541).
Ricorso	Thought is the thought of thought	A repeat

7

God	Tranquil brightness	
Heroes	The soul is in a man- ner all that is.	To the manner born
Men	Tranquillity sudden, vast, candescent	The age of reason
Ricorso	Talbot repeated	

8

God	The dear might of Him	
Heroes	What sir? Talbot	
Men	asked simply, bend- ing forward	The patrician concedes.

This section, we are informed, is to be a short and empty one: 'Turn over,' Stephen said quickly, 'I don't see anything.'

Ricorso	He leaned back and went on again having just remembered.

9

God	Of Him that walked the waves	
Heroes	Craven hearts … scof- fer's heart and lips	Plebeians and patricians. The plebeians have only hearts; the patricians, being of articulate speech, have also lips.
	Eager faces … tribute	The plebs. See Vico on the census introduced by Servius Tullius (par. 25).
Men	To Caesar what is Caesar's, to God what is God's	Under a monarchy, the people free and the course of Provi- dence fulfilled. Darkness and shadows, says Vico (par. 7), symbolize antiquity. 'A long look from dark eyes … on the church's looms' is but another way of expressing the Viconian law of progress.

Ricorso	To be woven and
	  woven
	Riddle me, riddle
	  me ... Seeds to sow	

10

We are at this point informed that our calculations are correct: *Have I heard all? Stephen said. Yes sir. Hockey at ten, sir.*

God	Thursday	Thor's day. The day of the thunder-god

Heroes	They bundled their
	  books away, pencils
	  clacking, pages
	  rustling.	

Men	Crowding together	
Ricorso	Ask me, sir. O ask me, sir.	

11

God	The sky was blue	The French, notes Vico (par.
		  482), must have used *bleu* for
		  God in that impious oath of
		  theirs, *moure blue*, 'God's
		  death!'; and they still say *par-*
		  bleu! The Dawn is heralded by
		  cock-crow. It is this, and fur-
		  ther evidence, which gives sig-
		  nificance to Cochrane's name.
		  Cochrane, too, is cock-crow.
		  Rane, according to the N.E.D.,
		  is a prolonged cry or utterance.

Heroes	Bells in heaven	Gloria in excelsis

	Were striking eleven	Announcing imminence. The de-
		  vice is called proparoxyton, see
		  Ulysses p. 545, where it is
		  rendered 'the moment before
		  the next.' Another instance of
		  proparoxyton we have had in
		  Cycle 9. Ay: from A to Y, the
		  moment before Z. Z is the ri-
		  corso, Riddle me, riddle me,
		  etc.

Men	Poor soul in heaven	
Ricorso	What is that?	
	What, sir?	

12

Gods	We didn't hear	This means that something
Heroes		sounded.
Men	The lines were repeated	
Ricorso	What is that, sir?	
	We give it up.	

13

God		
Heroes	The fox burying his	The riddle made up Cycle 11; the
Men	grandmother under	answer, too, constitutes an en-
Ricorso	a hollybush	tire cycle.

14

God	A shout of nervous laughter	Like thunder, it 'echoes dismay.'
	A stick struck the door	
	A voice in the corridor	Noises in the street
Heroes	They broke asunder	Two classes, sidlers and leapers
Men	Sargent came forward slowly	Sargent – servant. His description bespeaks his lowly bestial origin: *tangled hair ... scraggy neck ... unreadiness ... misty ... weak eyes ... pleading.* He knows no writing – all he gets from ink is a stain; but the stain is date-shaped (the date is of the genus *Phoenix*) that is, pregnant with possibility.
Ricorso	A snail's bed	Whorled without end
	He held out his *copy* book	

15

God	The word Sums ... on headline	God's name as given to Moses: *Sum qui sum* (Exodus 3:14)

Heroes	Sloping figures A crooked signature A blot	The condescending patrician The plebs
Men	Cyril Sargent: his name and seal.	The plebian acquires the right of the patrician: a seal. Cyril – lordly; Sargent – servitor.
Ricorso	Mr. Deasy said I was to copy them off the board, sir.	Sargent has already said this.

We are now informed that our calculations were correct: *Numbers eleven to fifteen, Sargent said.*

16

| God | Can you do them
yourself? Stephen
asked. | *Them*, being Sums |

But unfortunately Sargent replies: 'No, sir.' Our cycle is thus frustrated, has become futile; we cannot move on to the Age of Heroes; we slide back, therefore, to the pre-historic period of bestiality. In Stephen's mind this period is associated with his mother. Why? Because Malachi has called her 'beastly dead.'

| Prehistoric
period of
bestiality | Yet someone had
loved him, borne
him in her arms
and in her heart ...
rosewood and wet-
ted ashes. | |
| | Was that then real?
The only true thing
in life? | Vico's theory: It is through
man's bestial vices, aided by
Providence, that he rises to
civilization. |

The frustration is now over. The 'bestial age' is gone, scarcely having been. We are ready now, after this misplaced ricorso (he 'listened, scraped, and scraped') and with the help of Stephen 'sitting at his side' to 'solve out the problem' for the discovery of God.

| God | A fox | See Cycle 13. The identification
is explicitly stated on p. 191,
Ulysses, line 10 – Christfox,
that is, Christ as quarry. |

	Shakespeare's ghost	See Cycle 5.
	Hockeysticks rat- tled ... the hollow knock of a ball ... calls from the field	Noises
Heroes	The symbols moved	
	The hockeysticks	
Men	Give hands, traverse, bow to partner	The classes are joined.
	Mummery – letters	The contradiction reconciled
Ricorso	Flashing in the mock- ing mirrors	A reflection
	A darkness shining in brightness which brightness	A repeat

That these three paragraphs constituted but one cycle is now confirmed. 'Can you work the second for yourself?'

17
God	The data	Both because they are the ele- ments of the *Sum*, and because *data* is primitive utterance, in several languages, for Father. See Vico, par. 448.
Heroes	The unsteady symbols	
	Waiting always for a word of help his hand moved faithfully	The plebs, still subservient. 'Shame flickering behind his dull skin' is, according to Vico, the emotion which impels to- ward civilization. Its hue, says Vico quoting Socrates, is 'the colour of virtue.'
Men	Tyrants willing to be dethroned.	
Ricorso	Secrets silent ... se- crets weary	

18
| God | The sum was done. |
| Heroes | You had better get
your stick |

Men	And go out to the others	
Ricorso	Stephen said as he followed towards the door	

19

God	His name was heard, called from the playfield	Mr. Deasy's voice calling, 'Sargent!'
Heroes	The scrappy field ... They were sorted in teams ... Voices contending	And here we see that Cochrane (cock-crow) and Halliday (holy-day) are on the same side.
Men	Will you wait ... till I restore order here	
Ricorso	As he stepped fussily back across the field	

20

God	His old man's voice cried sternly Their sharp voices cried out on all sides.	Mr. Deasy plays the part of Thor. We have been informed of this his role at the beginning of Cycle 10 where the boy says: 'Half day, sir. Thursday.' This we take as advance notice that No. 20, too, will be Deasy Thor, that Viking whose hair is 'bleached honey' and moustache 'angry white!'
	The smell of drab abraded leather	The age of bestiality is over.
Heroes	Stuart coins	Stuart – an administrator; patrician. *As it was in the beginning ... world without end* runs piecemeal through this paragraph-vividly to show Providence moving through the ages.
Men	To all the gentiles base treasure	Baseness and treasure together

Ricorso	A hasty step over the stone porch and in the corridor	

21

God	Blowing out his rare moustache Mr. Deasy halted	
Heroes	Two notes	Patricians and plebs
Men	One of joined halves	
Ricorso	Stowing his pocket-book away	

22

God	Two, he said	Mr. Deasy speaking. Having been informed where Cycle 20 was, we are now told that it is twenty plus two.
Heroes	Strongroom for the gold	
	An emir's turban	Patricians
	Hollow shells	Plebs
Men	Shells heaped ... emir's turban	Shells and emir's turban all in one heap. Sometimes this last age of men culminates in a monarchy; *a sovereign, bright and new.*
Ricorso	Turning his little savingsbox about	

23

God	Three, Mr. Deasy said.	On the three-furrowed thunderbolt, see Vico (par. 491).
Heroes	Sovereigns	Note the plural
	Shillings	The plebs
Men	Halfcrowns. And here crowns. See.	
Ricorso	I know. I know. If youth but knew.	

There were in this cycle three earlier ricorsi, but they were all frustrated:
a. Thank you, Stephen said. No thanks at all, Mr. Deasy said.

b. Symbols too of beauty and of power ... Symbols soiled by greed and misery.

c. The same room and hour, the same wisdom ... I can break them in this instant if I will.

At this point, Dedalus makes the count: *Three times now. Three nooses*, the nooses being Ricorsi.

24

God	Iago!	Because Iago, too, is a noise in the street. See Othello Act 1, Scene 1, line 69: *Proclaim in the streets*, and lines 74–81. Rod: Here is her father's house; I'll call aloud. Iago: Do; with like timorous accent and dire yell As when, by night and negligence, the fire Is spied in populous cities. Rod: What, ho, Brabantio! Signor Brabantio, ho! Iago: Awake! what ho ...
Heroes	The pride of the English ... The seas' ruler	
Men	On me and on my words, unhating	
Ricorso	Good man, good man. I paid my way ... I paid my way.	

If the monies mentioned in the account which follows in the next paragraph are added up, it will be discovered that they total 24.6 guineas, which figure corroborates the place we are at.

25

| God | Mulligan | The name Mulligan signifies monk. The priest has doffed his footwear. See Exodus 3:5. *Put off thy shoes from thy feet, for the place whereon thou standest is holy ground.* |

		The tie, as indicated in my analysis of Chapter One (see 'The Black Panther,' *Accent*, Spring 1950) is a religious vestment.
Heroes	Curran	Curran, Celtic for warrior, champion
	McCann	McCann – son of Cathun – Warrior
	Ryan	Ryan – Kinglet
	Temple	Name usually associated with place names of preceptories of Knights Templar
		Gets two lunches there
	Russell	For Russell, see cross-reference, *Ulysses*, p. 187:
		How now, sirrah, that pound he lent you when you were hungry?
		Marry, I want it.
		Take thou this noble.
	Cousins	Cousins – kinsmen, famuli, plebs
	Reynolds	Reynolds – faithful, loyal; liegemen.
	Kohler	Cabbages, as opposed to kings
	Mrs. McKernan	McKernan, son of the kern – ordinary foot soldiers. Plebs
Men	A generous people ... also just	The age of men has here been delayed.
		The lump I have [all in one] *is useless;* Stephen therefore, temporarily negates this period: *For the moment, no.*
Ricorso	Mr. Deasy ... putting back his savingsbox	
26		
God	Those big words	
Heroes	Albert Edward, Prince of Wales	
	Old fogey, old tory	Patrician
	O'Connell's time	O'Connell is derived from word for conflict
	Orange lodges	Of the ascendancy

Men	The union ... communion	
Ricorso	You fenians forget something.	

27
God	Glorious, pious, and immortal memory	
Heroes	Lodge of Diamond ... Armagh the splendid	
	Papishes	Papa – patres, patrician
	Croppies lie down	Plebs
Men	The union ... All Irish, all kings' sons	
	Alas, Stephen said.	All-ass, an anti-democratic sentiment. Observe that association of thought leads to *rectas*. It is now clear why Asculum, i.e., as-culum, i.e., all-ass, was deemed an equation for the age of man!
		Here it is pertinent to quote Vico on Homer: ' ... Delicacy is a small virtue and greatness naturally disdains all small things. Indeed, as a great rushing torrent cannot fail to carry turbid waters and roll stones and trunks along in the violence of its course, so his very greatness accounts for the low expressions we so often find in Homer' (par. 822).
Ricorso	From the Ards of Down	Ards – heights.

28
God	Lal the ral the ra	
	The rocky road to Dublin	A noise in the street
Heroes	Gruff squire on horseback ...	One of the liberal, that is, the noble arts, says Vico, is that of riding (par. 537).

	Sir John ... Day ... Day	Reply to plebs, unsirred

Here the cycle becomes stationary for a while: *Sit down a moment ...*
I have just to copy the end.

Men	The dictates of com- mon sense	
Ricorso	Sit down a mo- ment ... Sit down ... Just a moment	

29

God	Shaggy brows ... muttering	Deasy Thor muttering over a drum, in true Viconian fashion makes noise so as to erase an error!
Heroes	The princely presence Images of vanished horses stood in homage, their meek heads poised in air	
	Lord Hastings' Repulse,	The patricians are still resisting.
	The duke of Westminster's Shotover	Conflict continues.
Men	The duke of Beau- fort's Ceylon	A pun. Ceylon: Cinghalese Single Ease: Patrician.
	Prix de Paris, 1866	The aristocrat dukes and the ple- beian bestial pricks of Paris are joined (see Cycle 18 where 18 means the 'sum is done') to constitute an even dozen (6 and 6).
	Backing king's colours	Often this age features monarchy.
Ricorso	Full stop ... But prompt ventilation	

30

God	The bawls of bookies	Not only Gods, but testaments.

		From bestiality (amid 'mud-splashed brakes ... reek of the canteen,' i.e., the cellar) to thunder on its pitch, to God in one loud noise, is, indeed, getting rich quick.
Heroes	Ten to one the field	The ratio of plebians to patricians
	Fair Rebel	The usual conflict
	The vying caps and jackets	
Men	A butcher's dame, nuzzling her clove of orange	Pleb joined to patrician. The orange already has been used as a symbol of ascendancy.
Ricorso	We hurried by after the hoofs ... past the meatfaced woman	A cycle, from hoof (beast) to butcher's dame melled to orange (Age of Men) has been completed.

31

God	Again: a goal	*All history moves towards one great goal, the manifestation of God* (post., p. 35). That is why the hockeysticks are associated with the nobles, they are rods of divination, *litui*. See Vico (par. 25).
Heroes	Battling bodies, in a medley, the joust of life	Conflict
	That knockkneed mother's darling	Plebs
Men	Spear spikes baited with men's bloodied guts	Spears joined to guts.
Ricorso	Now then, Mr. Deasy said	Now – then

32

God	The matter in a nutshell	
Heroes	Foot and mouth disease	Social conflict between top and bottom
	No two opinions in the matter	Only one – that of the patrician

The next paragraph does not enter into the cycle; we have been enjoined to *just look through it*, to *laissez-faire*, informed that the *ring* is *jockeying*; that this *department* is *imperturbable*; and that only at length do we *come to the point at issue*.

	Foot and mouth disease	Still the Age of Heroes
	Koch's preparation	Koch – cook. Homer, says Vico, describes his heroes as always eating roast meat (par. 801).
	Serum and virus	Serum – watery liquid; virus, a stronger element
	Percentage of salted horses	Plebs. See Cycle 29. Salt of the earth – patricians
	Veterinary surgeons	Plebs, beastly
	Henry Blackwood Price	Deasy's cousin, kinsman, famulus
Men	Dictates of common sense	Dictate (patrician) common sense (plebeian). Combined in one phrase
	All important question	
	Hospitality of columns	The plebs received
Ricorso	And it can be cured. It is cured. By difficulties, by ... intrigues, by ... backstairs influence, by ...	
33		
God	He raised his forefinger and beat the air boldly before his voice spoke	Typical gesture of Deasy Thor
Heroes	In all the highest places	
	Old England is dying	The aristocrats give way
	Winding sheet	The next lines of Blake read: The winners' shout, the losers' curse,

		Dance before dead England's hearse.
	Goldskinned men ... maladroit silk	Pseudo-aristocrats
	Quoting prices	Price – kinsman. Seeking kinship
	Gabble of geese	But they are really plebs; speech still onomatapoetic.
	Uncouth ... maladroit ... Not theirs	
	Their full slow eyes belied the words	Dress and act like patricians, but are plebs.

The Age of Men never really happens in this cycle.

Men	The rancours massed	An illusion: all that is massed are rancours: they know their zeal is vain
	To heap and hoard	But it is a vain patience
Ricorso	Time surely would scatter all	
	Heap and hoard ... a hoard heaped	
	Passing on	

34

God	Who has not?	Who has not sinned against the light? Only God. But Deasy Thor finds this too subtle for him. What do you mean? he asks, and his underjaw falls sideways open uncertainly. Since Deasy still waits to hear from Stephen, Stephen gives him another, the usual, equation: the nightmare gives a back kick.
	Raised a shout. A whirring whistle: goal. That is God. Hooray! Ay! Whrrwhee! A shout in the street	

Heroes	Wings of his nose	Wings at the top of the rod signify eminent domain (V. 604), Wings on heels – ownership of field. Mr. Deasy's gaiters.
	Menelaus	Menelaus – withstanding men
	The Greeks made war	
	Brought the strangers	Plebs
	McMurroughs	Son of the warrior
	O'Rourke	The little friend. Plebs
	Brought Parnell low	
Men	Struggle now at the end of my days. But I will fight for the right	
Ricorso	For Ulster will fight And Ulster will be right.	

35		
God	I foresee, Mr. Deasy said	Divinari – to foretell the future. See Vico, par. 9.
Heroes	A teacher	
	A learner	Plebs. To learn, says Mr. Deasy, one must be humble.
	You have two copies there	Plebs and patricians
	I like to break a lance with you	The duel, an example of heroic virtue. Vico, par. 27.
Men	Mr. Field	
	Cattletraders at the City Arms	
	Answer letter from cousin	The famulus answered
Ricorso	That will do ... That will do.	
	Good morning, sir ... Good morning, sir, Stephen said again, bowing to his bent back	

36

God	Cries of voices and
	cracks of sticks
Heroes	The lions couchant on
	the pillar
	Help in the fight

We are about to reach the Age of Men but Mr. Deasy says: *Just one moment.* It never takes place, because insofar as the Jews are concerned 'she never let them in.' This, in Joyce's scheme, is not a piece of xenophobia, but another illustration (the first was in Cycle 33) of Vico's distinction between Jewish history and gentile history. The Jews, knowing God and His law through revelation, do not have to enter, as the gentiles do, the cycles of Providence to reach civilization. Insofar as Mr. Deasy is concerned he is conforming to what Vico calls (par. 610) 'the eternal property of not granting citizenship to a man of alien religion.'

Ricorso	She never let them
	in ... She never let
	them in

We have reached the conclusion of the chapter, and the end of Cycle 36. Is our count correct? See page 31 where Mr. Deasy counts out Stephen's pay, in crowns and shillings. Says Mr. Deasy: 'Three twelve. I think you'll find that's right.' Three twelve are thirty-six, and so is the addition of the numerals of the date of the Battle of Asculum – 27 plus 9, B plus C.

We leave Mr. Deasy, with dancing coins on his wise shoulders (all thirty-six of them) standing, as God, in the midst of a providential flux and reflux of history, a checkerwork of leaves.

And the sum is done. Vico, Dalkey, is indeed Vico – The Key. We now know, finally, how to accent and read the oracular statement which epigraphs this essay: 'I would not pay overmuch attention to these theories *beyond using them for all they are worth.*'

NOTES

1 From one of Joyce's letters in the collection of the New York Public Library.
2 All quotations from the *Scienza Nuova* are from the translation of Thomas Goddard Bergin and Max Harold Fisch, *The New Science of Giambattista Vico* (Cornell University Press, 1948).
3 *James Joyce's 'Ulysses': A Study* by Stuart Gilbert (New York: Alfred A. Knopf, 1930).
4 See 'The Black Panther,' *Accent*, Spring 1950.

Textual Notes and Emendations

The pieces gathered in this book represent a substantial portion – perhaps about two-thirds – of Klein's published writings on literature and the arts. It is impossible to speak of an exact percentage because there is no strict boundary to this part of Klein's corpus. In order to limit our selection to a manageable size, we have excluded those items that seemed to us the least valuable in terms of intrinsic quality or usefulness to students of Klein's work, as well as those that did not bear directly enough on the central concerns of this volume. In addition, we omitted a number of important pieces that were already easily available elsewhere, such as the satire on literary critics, 'And the Mome Raths Outgrabe,' which is included in Klein's *Short Stories* (University of Toronto Press 1983).

Readers interested in exploring more of Klein's published as well as unpublished writings on literature and the arts might begin by consulting the forthcoming A.M. Klein bibliography and index to manuscripts by Usher Caplan and Zailig Pollock in the ABCMA series published by ECW Press. An index to Klein's complete journalism, prepared by Zailig Pollock and Linda Rozmovits, is also due to be published in the near future. An earlier version of the Klein bibliography and index to manuscripts may be found in *The A.M. Klein Symposium* edited by Seymour Mayne (University of Ottawa Press 1975) as well as in Usher Caplan's 1976 dissertation, 'A.M. Klein: An Introduction,' available through University Microfilms.

The textual notes that follow provide information on the source of the copy text used for this edition, on the existence of other published and unpublished versions, and on significant emendations. Most of the pieces in this volume are from *The Canadian Jewish Chronicle*; only the exceptions are noted here. The dates of serialized articles are mentioned if they are not fully listed in the text proper.

Our basic principle has been to use the earliest printed version as the copy text; this generally tends to be the most reliable version. Variant texts have been used only as as a means of correcting misprints in the copy text.

However, we have systematically adopted all of Klein's own handwritten corrections and revisions on a number of tearsheets that he had saved, treating them as indications of final authorial intention. Such emendations are not listed here, but are covered simply by a general citation of the tearsheet, which serves in effect as the true copy text.

The original printed versions of many of the pieces appearing in this volume contain a fair number of typographical errors, grammatical slips, and inconsistencies of style – the combined results of hasty writing and inaccurate typing and typesetting. In dealing with these various flaws, our approach has been to interfere as little as possible in Klein's text and not attempt to improve on it. Obvious typographical errors, simple misspellings, and confusing mispunctuations have been emended silently. Emendations of a more intrusive sort are noted below.

In the emendations noted, that which precedes the bracket sign is the word or phrase established for use in this edition; that which follows the bracket sign is the word or phrase as it originally appeared in the copy text. [K] at the end of the line signifies that the emendation has been based on the author's own manuscript or typescript in the Klein Papers (Public Archives of Canada, Ottawa). Other sources of corrections are similarly noted at the end of the line within brackets. In a number of cases, an expression was listed not because any emendation was made but in order to suggest a possible alternative; such alternative readings are introduced by the phrase *sic, maybe*. The use of a solidus (/) in the emendation list indicates the end of a line in the original version.

There are a few cases where a portion of text seems to be missing – usually what appears to have been a line of Klein's manuscript or a line of newspaper type. Such gaps are represented in the text by a set of three dots within brackets.

At no point have the editors inserted the expression *sic* into the text itself. Where it appears, it is Klein's own expression.

Many emendations made by the editors have been based on a reconstruction of Klein's handwriting, which was sometimes misread by the typesetter. For example, a loop in his *w* can make it appear as *ev*, or two narrow *e*'s can become a *u*. In several instances, emendations have been based on the premise that Klein dictated a particular piece to a typist (often it was his wife) or typesetter, and that the word was not misread but rather misheard.

Errors in Klein's quotations from other works have been corrected only where it seemed necessary – that is to say, where the meaning would be affected. Insofar as possible, corrections were based on an examination of the source Klein was likely to have been quoting.

Klein's use of italics was somewhat inconsistent and his habits in that to standardize usage, at least within a given piece, but some inconsistencies remain.

Generally speaking, Klein's punctuation has not been tampered with, except in cases where clarity is seriously impaired. His punctuation sometimes reveals the use of outmoded forms, but more often it seems that he simply disregarded rules and punctuated according to the sound of the sentence as it might be spoken.

There are several different methods of transliterating Hebrew and Yiddish words into English, and in Hebrew there are different ways of pronouncing certain letters and vowel signs depending on dialect. As a rule, Klein's inconsistent spelling of transliterated Hebrew and Yiddish terms has been retained; the notes occasionally give variant spellings in parentheses.

Slight errors sometimes occur in Klein's use of other foreign languages, and where the errors appear to be his own solecisms they have generally been left intact.

Klein's inconsistent use of American and British spelling has been left unaltered.

KOHELETH
The Judaean II, 8 (May 1929)

BAAL SHEM IN MODERN DRESS
To draw] To / draw [*probably missing a line*] p 9 l 14

CHAIM NACHMAN BIALIK
The Canadian Zionist V, 3 (June 1937), where it is subtitled '1873–1934.' Klein's
    undated manuscript (probably 1936) is in the National Archives of the Can-
    adian Jewish Congress, Montreal (photocopy in Public Archives of Canada,
    Klein Papers, vol. 35). The essay is included with a selection of Klein's trans-
    lations in *Chaim Nachman Bialik*, an undated mimeographed pamphlet issued
    by the Hadassah Organization of Canada. It is also reprinted in *The Canadian
    Jewish Chronicle*, 7 July 1939. A related set of lecture notes dated 4 July
    1942 is in the Klein Papers, MS 6888–96. The Hadassah pamphlet was almost
    certainly typed from the manuscript; the printed versions were probably
    set from two different hand-corrected copies of the pamphlet.
consistently] constantly [K] p 16 l 4
this ultra-modern] the ultra-modern [K] p 17 l 10

imagines] images [K] p 19 l 11

MUSIC HATH CHARM
those other] these other p 20 l 19
wreaked upon the] wreaked upon this p 20 l 33

THE ART OF THE PASSOVER HAGGADAH
shtreimel and a long] *shtreimel,* a long p 24 l 34

THE LAST OF THE *BADCHANIM* – SHLOIME SHMULEVITZ
ever seen] even seen p 26 l 26

PALESTINE MOVING-PICTURES
of Eretz] of the Eretz p 40 l 2
warriors] worries p 40 l 29

THE SNOWS OF YESTERYEAR [RAVITCH]
mud] need p 48 l 13

THE POETRY WHICH IS PRAYER
learning] leaving p 50 l 14
aleph-bais] *Aleph* p 50 l 15

THE SNOWS OF YESTERYEAR [CHAGALL]
wonder] wonders p 58 l 33
gist] gust p 59 l 30

ONLY HALF THE LANGUAGE OF FAITH
master] writer [*restoring Glatzer's word*] p 63 l 31
thou, O Lord] *sic, Psalms has*: thou, Lord p 65 l 4

THE DYBBUK
do think] do not think p 71 l 25
Aleph] Alpha p 72 l 20
incantations] incarnations p 74 l 9

POEMS OF YEHOASH
The end of Klein's review is omitted here; in it he quotes in full two of Goldstick's
    translations: 'An Ancient Ballad' and 'The Haunting Eye.'
sessions] seasons p 84 l 17

OF HEBREW CALLIGRAPHY

Klein's corrections to some misprints are on a tearsheet in the Klein Papers, MS 25144.

IN MEMORIAM: J.I. SEGAL

waning] warning p 88 l 5
come] came p 88 l 23

JEWISH FOLK-SONGS

The Judaean v, 9 (June 1932). Reprinted in *The Canadian Jewish Chronicle*, 2 Sept. 1932 and 7 April 1944, with some misprints corrected.

OF HEBREW HUMOR

Opinion VI, 1 (Nov. 1935). Reprinted in *The Canadian Jewish Chronicle*, 25 Jan., 1, 18, and 15 Feb. 1946. A carbon copy of an early typescript is in the Klein Papers, MS 5107–32. The essay in *Opinion* is an edited version of this, with changes too numerous to list here. One large part (MS 5117–23) was taken out entirely.

and flaunting a] and a [K] p 103 l 40
may he live] may live [K] p 106 l 31

ON TRANSLATING THE YIDDISH FOLK-SONG

for those] for these p 109 l 33
mores] moves p 111 l 34

THE YIDDISH PROVERB

The Canadian Jewish Chronicle, 5, 12, 19, 26 Dec. 1952, and 2 Jan. 1953. A small excerpt was published in *Our Sense of Identity* (Toronto 1954), edited by Malcolm Ross. Klein's minor corrections and revisions are on tearsheets in the Klein Papers, MS 25116–26.

irony, too] irony, for p 117 l 21
precepts] percepts p 118 l 33
sham] storm p 119 l 3
flaska] sic, Stutchkov in Yiddish has: *flyask* p 120 l 27
its own] its even p 122 l 12

THE BIBLE AS LITERATURE

Also issued by the Hadassah Organization of Canada as a mimeographed pamphlet, undated but most likely from the 1930s. Much of the text first appeared in Klein's untitled review of a Jewish Publication Society edition of the Bible, *The Judaean* II, 5 (Feb. 1929).

to the Greek Septuagint and from that to] of the Greek Septuagint and from that of
[*The Judaean*] p 125 l 27
From it men have taken their life and for it have] For it men have [*Hadassah
pamphlet*] p 125 l 32

THE BIBLE MANUSCRIPTS
The Canadian Jewish Chronicle, 28 Sept., 5, 12, 19, and 26 Oct. 1951. Klein's
corrections to some misprints are on tearsheets in the Klein Papers, MS
25112–13.
quilts] guilts p 142 l 5
Can it be] Can it p 142 l 41

THE BIBLE'S ARCHETYPICAL POET
The Canadian Jewish Chronicle, 6, 13, and 20 March 1953. Related notes are in the
Klein Papers, MS 5063–6.
relation] relatives p 146 l 23
clime] chime p 146 l 27
draw] drain p 147 l 37

FROM *THE MCGILL DAILY*
The McGill Daily, 29 Oct., 5, 12, 19 Nov., and 10 Dec. 1927
as a frog] as p 152 l 2
speech, [...] of] speech, / It is sufficient to state that if ever / cone of p 152 l 13
G.K. Chesterton] *this piece untitled in* The McGill Daily p 153 title
He is in fact] He, in fact p 155 l 16
so much as that] *sic, maybe*: so much so that p 156 l 10
faulty] faculty p 157 l 16
that it is] that is p 159 l 2
Wonderlust] Wanderlust p 159 title
the course] that course p 159 l 21
have so 50] has so 50 p 159 l 26
with] worth p 160 l 34

QUEEN MAB AND MICKEY MOUSE
A very similar version of this piece, in the form of a handwritten draft letter to
'A.J.M.' concerning the latter's movie review in 'The Forum,' is in the Klein
Papers, MS 5211–16. The identity of 'A.J.M.' is unknown; it is evidently
not A.J.M. Smith. No clues could be found in issues of *The Canadian Forum*
from this period.

ANNOTATION ON SHAPIRO'S *ESSAY ON RIME*
Also published in *Northern Review* I, 3 (Oct.–Nov. 1946). Both versions were
 probably set from the same manuscript.
every even pause] even pause [*Northern Review*] p 173 l 27
Johnson's] *sic, maybe*: Jonson's p 176 l 31

A DEFINITION OF POETRY?
The manuscript is in the Klein Papers, MS 5073–7. There is also a related set of
 lecture notes, MS 6065–74, entitled 'The Definitions of Poetry.'
Poetry?] Poetry [K] p 177 title
unpadded, bony] bony [*the manuscript has*: unpadded – bony] p 177 l 26
in tranquillity] tranquillity [K] p 178 l 15
their best order] the best order [K] p 178 l 31

MARGINALIA
The Canadian Jewish Chronicle, 11, 25 June, 24 Dec. 1948, and 28 Jan. 1949. In the
 Klein Papers, among some mostly unpublished 'Marginalia' pieces, are manu-
 script versions of 'Towards an Aesthetic' (MS 5226-7), 'The Poem as Circular
 Force' (MS 5228-30), and 'A Conversation' (MS 5221-3).
Robert Frost and the Five Senses] *this piece untitled in* Chronicle; *title taken from
 Klein's reference to it, MS 7607* p 185 title
[...] *one or more lines missing* p 191 below title

THE USURPER
quite] quiet p 196 l 20

IN MEMORIAM: ALEXANDER BERCOVITCH
all lovers] all his lovers p 199 l 3

THE CASE OF JASCHA HEIFETZ
variety] vanity p 199 l 13

'THE DECENCIES HAD PERISHED WITH THE STUKAS'
finest] first p 206 l 11

THE POETRY OF A.J.M. SMITH
The Canadian Forum XXIII (Feb. 1944)

WRITING IN CANADA
Klein's minor corrections and revisions are on tearsheets in the Klein Papers, MS
 25045–58.

A CURSE ON COLUMBUS
YMHA Beacon v, 14 (18 April 1930)

THE JEW IN ENGLISH POETRY
The Judaean v, 6 (March 1932). Reprinted, with some slight revisions and with
subheadings removed, in *The Jewish Standard*, 10 June 1932, under the title
'When the Jew Was a Myth.' Also issued by the Hadassah Organization
of Canada as part of an undated mimeographed pamphlet on 'The Jews of
England.' *The Judaean* version was probably set from the pamphlet, with
some confusion resulting in the format of the subheadings; the format has
been standardized here, along the lines of *The Jewish Standard* version.

ROBINSON JEFFERS – POET-FASCIST?
cannot fail] cannot but fail p 232 l 13
poet communes with the great forces] forces communes with the great poets p 232 l 23

THE HEART OF EUROPE
Joyce is a serious] Jolce, serious p 239 l 11
is a literary] a literary p 240 l 16

GRAND INVECTIVE
cannot avoid] cannot but avoid p 245 l 12

THOSE WHO SHOULD HAVE BEEN OURS
New Palestine, 16 Nov. 1945. Also published in *The Canadian Jewish Chronicle*, 10
May 1946, under the title 'Talents That Should Have Been Ours.' A carbon
copy of the original typescript, with the latter title, is in the Klein Papers,
MS 5269–76. The *New Palestine* version is based on the typescript but contains
changes in diction and syntax, probably by an editor for the publication. The
Canadian Jewish Chronicle version is closer to the typescript, with only a
few slight changes by Klein himself. Klein took the section on Karl Shapiro
from his own earlier piece 'Jewish Self-Hatred' (a review of Shapiro's *Person,
Place and Thing*), *The Canadian Jewish Chronicle*, 14 Jan. 1944. A tearsheet
of that review, on which he drafted his adaptations for this article, is in the
Klein Papers, MS 24997–9.

RILKE AND HIS TRANSLATORS
confined] confused p 252 l 25
slowing] showing p 254 l 31

DEPARTURE AND ARRIVAL
those timeless] these timeless p 256 l 27
are not] is not p 258 l 7

KNUT HAMSUN
of what once] of once p 259 l 14

THAT RANK PICTURE
guilt] guile p 263 l 33

CANTABILE
Northern Review II, 3 (Sept.–Oct. 1948)

T.S. ELIOT AND THE NOBEL PRIZE
Noble Judges] *sic, maybe*: Nobel Judges p 269 l 8
showing] shown p 271 l 35

OLD EZ AND HIS BLANKETS
Slight corrections are on a tearsheet in the Klein Papers, MS 25099.

THE MASKED YEATS
Northern Review, II, 5 (June–July 1950)

THE OXEN OF THE SUN
Here and Now I, 3 (Jan. 1949). A preliminary draft of this article was sent by Klein
    to Ellsworth Mason on 21 June 1948; it is now in the Mason Papers at the
    Public Archives of Canada. A carbon copy sent to Leon Edel on 6 July is now
    in Edel's personal papers. There are numerous minor variations between the
    draft and the final article but no substantial difference in the basic argument.
    The article was probably set from a corrected copy of the draft version.
second of March] *sic; in Richard Ellmann's edition of Joyce's* Selected Letters *this
    item is dated the twentieth of March* p 289 l 2
Sa. Lynch] *sic; in Ellmann*: Ja. Lynch p 289 l 19
formal evolution] *sic; in Ellmann*: faunal evolution p 289 l 27
1: *Cyclops* ... 6: W.R.] *Klein should have numbered this list* 7:2:a ... 7:2:f, *as in
    his summary chart below* pp 297-8

THE BLACK PANTHER
Accent X, 3 (Spring 1950). Related notes on 'Telemachus' are in the Klein Papers,
    MS 5142–62.

A SHOUT IN THE STREET
New Directions 13 (1951).
Stephen said quickly] *sic; in Joyce*: Stephen said quietly p 351 l 15

Notes

Klein's writing is replete with literary and historical allusions, quotations from many sources, and expressions drawn from several different languages. The notes below attempt to aid the reader by supplying references, translations, and brief commentary where the context of the article itself does not adequately provide such information.

Deciding what to note and how much to note has not been easy. Names that would immediately be recognized by readers with a background in literary studies might well be unknown to others; many references that would be obvious to readers who are somewhat acquainted with Jewish culture might be meaningless to those who are not.

With foreign words and phrases, our policy has been to translate all of them in the notes, except for terms that might be considered sufficiently anglicized as to be part of the common language. Here, of course, it is difficult to know where to set a limit. A similar grey area exists in the annotation of quotations; those whose sources might be unfamiliar to most readers have, as a rule, been noted, but phrases from familiar quotations, or lines that echo familiar quotations – and there are hundreds of these in Klein – have not always been noted.

In order to keep the text as uncluttered as possible, the notes are placed here at the end of the volume and no note symbols or numbers have been inserted in the text. The notes to the three articles on Joyce's *Ulysses* are Klein's own, and they appear at the end of each article. The editors have not undertaken to annotate these articles; that task is best left to Joyce scholars.

When a foreign term is explained in the notes, the language of origin is normally shown in parentheses. It should be borne in mind that Yiddish contains a great many words and expressions borrowed from Hebrew. Usually what is indicated here is the Jewish language in which a given term originated, even if Klein might have been using it with the other language in mind.

KOHELETH

Klein's poem 'Koheleth' appeared in the same issue of *The Judaean* as this review.

Koheleth: (Heb.) Ecclesiastes

Judah L. Zlotnik (1887–1962): rabbi and writer. He came to Canada in 1920 and later moved to South Africa and then Israel, where he was known as Yehuda Leib Avida.

Abbasides: second great dynasty of the Arab-Muslim empire (750–1259)

Li-Tai-Po: eighth-century Chinese poet, considered one of China's greatest poets

Omar Khayyam: twelfth-century Persian poet and mathematician

Fitzgerald: Edward Fitzgerald (1809–83), English poet and translator of *The Rubaiyat of Omar Khayyam*

high seriousness: Arnold, 'The Study of Poetry'

The Judaean: monthly magazine of Young Judaea, a Zionist youth organization. Young Judaea of Canada had its headquarters in Montreal. Klein served as editor of the magazine and educational director from 1928 to 1932.

צופיל,: 'too much'

קיין קינד, קיין רינד : 'no children, no cattle' – ie, no family, no possessions (for Ecclesiastes 4:8)

'ars artem celare est': (Lat.) 'Art lies in concealing art.'

ענדליך... 'Finally – / Finally I woke to the realization, / I looked about and pondered / All that I achieved by my labours – / Vanity of vanities – / A meaningless dream! / Foolish and worthless / Your life and your striving, / Man, under the sun!' (for Ecclesiastes 2:11)

עולם וועלט — עולם אייביק : In his translation of Ecclesiastes 3:15 Zlotnik adds this line of his own in parentheses at the beginning. It says, in its terse way, that the Hebrew word *olam* has two meanings: 'world' and 'eternity.' It is a linguistic sidelight on the theme of the verse itself, that the world is always the same.

שמן and שם : 'ointment' and 'name' in Ecclesiastes 7:1

דאן האב איך... : The speaker addresses his own flesh and heart. 'Then I wanted to test life: / You, flesh – have some wine, / and you, heart – philosophize!' (for Ecclesiastes 2:3)

איינעם וואָס... : 'Someone who never put his hand into cold water,' ie, someone who never did a thing (2:21)

טאָ מיט וואָס... : 'So in what way does man have any more status than a dumb animal?' (3:19)

דער... וואָס פירט... : 'one who leads fools around by the nose' (9:17)

און עס נייען זיך... : 'and the eulogizers are sewing purses for themselves,' ie, they expect business – the reference being to hired eulogizers (12:5)

goluth: (Heb.) Diaspora, exile

אונזער געלעכטער... : 'Our laughter is mixed with tears, / And our happiness: *some* happiness!' (2:2)

כאַליאַסטרע : gang (2:7)

סאדזשעװוקעס : small lake (2:6)

BAAL SHEM IN MODERN DRESS

Villon: François Villon, fifteenth-century French poet

the Baal Shem: Israel Baal Shem Tov (1700–60), founder of Chassidism, a Jewish religious movement emphasizing joy in the service of God

the Bratzlaver: Rabbi Nachman of Bratzlav (1772–1811), famous Chassidic leader and teller of tales and parables

citrons redolent in cotton: referring to the *etrog* (Heb., citron), used in the ritual of the holiday of Succoth. To protect it from even the slightest damage, the *etrog* is stored in a bed of soft material such as cotton.

besomim-boxes: (Heb.) spice boxes, used in the Saturday evening ritual which marks the end of the Sabbath

Levi Yitschok of Berditchev (1740–1810): Chassidic leader. He stressed the element of joy in Chassidism and good that is in man. See Klein's poem 'Reb Levi Yitschok Talks to God.'

the Sanhedrin: the ancient Jewish supreme court and legislature

'been half in love …': Keats, 'Ode to a Nightingale'

Nahum-Ish-Gamsu (or Gamzu): first/second-century rabbinic scholar whose name supposedly derived from his habit of saying 'Gam zu le-tova' – (Heb.) 'this too is for the good'

'R'tsai Adonai': (Heb.) 'Accept, O Lord …' – the opening words of a daily prayer

shul: (Yid.) synagogue

gabbai: (Heb.) synagogue official

maggid: (Heb.) preacher

Blake: William Blake (1757–1827), English poet, painter, social critic, and religious visionary

Rebbe Alemelech: Elimelech of Lyzhansk (1717–87), early Chassidic leader and wonder worker, figure in a well-known Yiddish folk-song

Arim Melech: a poor king

Aza: such a

WHITE MAGIC

'true genius …': 'Great wits are sure to madness near allied' – Dryden, 'Absalom and Achitophel'

Shechina: (Heb.) Divine Presence

Zohar: the central text of the Cabbalah, a Jewish mystical system based on speculative and esoteric doctrines. *Zohar* in Hebrew means 'Splendour.'

Moses de Leon (1250–1305): renowned Cabbalist in Spain, regarded by most scholars as the true author of the Zohar

Simeon ben Yochai (or Bar Yochai): second-century sage, ascetic, and charismatic, to whom legend attributes the authorship of the Zohar

Leon de Modena (1571–1648): Italian rabbi who vigorously attacked Cabbalism

Jacob Emden (1697–1776): German Talmudic authority who suggested a late authorship for much of the Zohar

Ben Chasdai: Bension's ancestors, a famous Jewish family in twelfth-century Barcelona

Magic casements ...: Keats, 'Ode to a Nightingale'

Adam Kadmon: (Heb.) 'Primordial Man' – a Cabbalistic concept

Torah: In its basic meaning, Torah refers to the Pentateuch. In its wider sense, it includes all other sections of Holy Scriptures and rabbinic commentary.

with seventy faces: a reference to the Hebrew expression *Shivim panim la-Torah*, the Torah has seventy 'faces,' ie, numerous levels of meaning

thought in blossom: quoted from Heinrich Heine, nineteenth-century German-Jewish lyric poet and critic

A Robin ...: both quotations from Blake's 'Auguries of Innocence'

Great Holy Assembly: probably a reference to the *Knesseth Hagdola* (Heb., 'Great Assembly'), the supreme Jewish legislative assembly during the Second Temple period (538 BC–70 AD)

Seven Palaces: the seven *Heichalot* (Heb.), described in the Zohar as palaces in the celestial Garden of Eden

Sphiroth: forces of the Divine essence emanated from within the Godhead, through which Absolute Being reveals itself – a Cabbalistic concept

Pshat, Remez, Drash and *Sod*: the four levels of biblical exegesis – literal, allegorical, homiletical, and mystical – forming the acronym PRDS and pronounced *Pardess*, which is the Hebrew word for 'orchard' or 'garden,' symbol of paradise

I come ...: Shakespeare, *The Tempest* I, ii

CHAIM NACHMAN BIALIK

Mr. Rascoe: Arthur Burton Rascoe (1892–1957), American anthologist and writer, author of *Titans of Literature* (1932)

Dr. Coralnik: Abraham Coralnik (1883–1937), Yiddish journalist, critic, and philosopher

shofar: (Heb.) ram's horn, sounded on the High Holydays and on occasions of great national importance

Yehuda Halevi (c1075–1141): Spanish-Jewish poet and philosopher. See Klein's poem 'Yehuda Halevi, His Pilgrimage.'

magic casements opening on the Home: the Home being the 'Jewish national home,' ie, Palestine. Klein is playing on the line from Keats's 'Ode to a Nightingale' – 'magic casements opening on the foam.'

Achad Ha'am: pen-name (Heb., 'one of the people') of Asher Ginsberg (1856–1927), Russian-born Hebrew essayist, scholar, and editor, proponent of 'cultural Zionism'

The prophet is a fool ...: Hosea 9:7

piyyut: (Heb.) liturgical poem

gram-shmam: *Gram* is Yiddish for rhyme. This type of construction – echoing a

word, but with the sound *shm-* at the beginning – is a common Yiddish way
of expressing ridicule or dismissal.

Immanuel of Rome (c1261–1328): Italian Hebrew poet

Hermon: the highest mountain in Israel, near the Syrian and Lebanese border.
Klein couples it here with Parnassus, the mountain in Greece sacred to the
muses.

chalutzim (pl. of *chalutz*): (Heb.) pioneering Jewish settler in the land of Israel

Maimonides: Moses Maimonides (1135–1204), Spanish-born Jewish religious philosopher, legal scholar, and doctor, author of *Guide to the Perplexed*

the *Kuzari*: a philosophical dialogue by Yehuda Halevi (c1075–1141), outlining and
defending basic Jewish religious concepts

Yeshiva: (Heb.) Jewish traditional academy devoted primarily to the study of the
Talmud and rabbinic literature

Aleph: first letter of the Hebrew alphabet: א

Gimel: third letter of the Hebrew alphabet: ג

Ravnitsky: Yehoshua Ravnitsky (1859–1944), Hebrew journalist and publisher,
lifelong associate of Bialik. *Ha-Pardess* (Heb., 'The Orchard') was an annual
Zionist journal he published in Odessa in the 1890s.

Erez Israel (Eretz Israel): (Heb.) Land of Israel

zippor (*tzippor*): (Heb.) bird, apostrophized in one of Bialik's most famous lyrics

Oneg Shabbos: (Heb.) 'Sabbath enjoyment' or 'entertainment,' reception held on
the Sabbath, devoted to study and song

melitza: (Heb.) a type of flowery language, used by some of the earlier modern
Hebrew writers, imitating classical Hebrew

Herzl: Theodor Herzl (1860–1904), father of political Zionism, founder of the World
Zionist Organization

These I have loved ...: Rupert Brooke, 'The Great Lover'

דמעת לילי... : All my night-tears and my sighing, / Beat of heart and breath of
living, / Final dream of all my dreaming – / Let these be my heart's own
offerings / Brought to you until my dying. ('Just a Little Note She Wrote
Me' – transl. L.M. Herbert)

Maccabees: a priestly family that led the Jewish revolt against the Seleucid kingdom,
culminating in the re-conquest of Jerusalem in 164 BC

Kaddish: (Heb.) mourner's prayer for the departed

MUSIC HATH CHARM

Music Hath Charm: 'Music has charms to soothe a savage breast' – Congreve, *The
Mourning Bride* I, i

Gut Morgen: (Yid.) 'Good Morning'

Arcand: Adrien Arcand, Quebec Fascist leader, interned during World War II

nasty brutish animal: an echo of Hobbes's description of man's life in the state of
nature as 'solitary, poor, nasty, brutish and short' – *Leviathan* I, 14

Gemara *Berachoth*: a tractate of the Talmud dealing with prayers and benedictions

'a des raisons ...': (Fr.) 'The heart has reasons which reason has not' – a loose
    rendering of a quotation from Pascal, *Pensées*, 277
klesmer: (Yid.) musician
Al-hagittith: (Heb.) an obscure phrase appearing at the opening of Psalms 8, 81,
    and 84. It is probably a reference either to a musical instrument or to a kind
    of vintage song.
Saminsky: Lazure Saminsky (1882–1959), Russian-born Jewish composer in U.S.
Kol Nidre: (Aramaic) 'All Vows,' the name of a solemn musical prayer introducing
    the Day of Atonement service
Chad Gadya: (Aramaic) title of a traditional Passover song
And I could wish ...: Wordsworth, 'My Heart Leaps Up When I Behold'
Abraham Zvi Idelsohn (1882–1938): pre-eminent Jewish musicologist, lived mainly
    in Jerusalem
'a burst of music ...': L.W. Reese (1856–1935), 'Tears'
Anglo-Saxon lyrics: Middle English, to be correct
'Lo, the winter is past ...': Song of Songs (Song of Solomon) 2:11–12
tzilzail: (Heb.) in Psalm 150:5; generally taken to mean cymbals
Rabbi Shnayur Zalman of Lyadi (1745–1813): charismatic founder of Chabad
    (Lubavitcher) Chassidism
an English translation: Klein himself translated Rabinovitch's book, in instalments
    published in *The Canadian Jewish Chronicle*. The translation was later aug-
    mented and published in book form in 1952, under the title *Of Jewish Music,
    Ancient and Modern*.
The man who hath no music ... : Shakespeare, *The Merchant of Venice* v, i

THE ART OF THE PASSOVER HAGGADAH
Passover Haggadah: Passover is a spring festival commemorating the Exodus from
    Egypt. The Haggadah (Heb., 'Telling') is a narrative of the Exodus presented
    through a set form of benedictions, prayers, homilies, and psalms, recited at
    the Seder ritual on the night of Passover.
Midrash: (Heb.) a branch of rabbinic literature consisting primarily of hermeneutic
    commentary on the Bible and containing relevant homilies, tales, and
    anecdotes
Talmud: usually refers to the Babylonian Talmud (which differs in some respects
    from the Jerusalem Talmud), a compendium of commentaries on the Mishna
    by generations of scholars and jurists in many academies beginning in the
    third century and ending with its redaction at the end of the fifth century.
    Together with the Bible, it constitutes the basis of traditional Jewish law and
    culture.
Reconstructionists: followers of Reconstructionism, an American-Jewish movement
    founded in 1922, inspired by the liberal religious philosophy of Mordecai
    M. Kaplan (1881–1983)

yain nesach (*yayin nesech*): (Heb.) in its original meaning, 'libation wine,' wine consecrated by Gentiles for idol worship, and hence forbidden to Jews. Klein is thinking here of the associated interdiction (often referred to under the same category of *yain nesach*) against *any* non-Jewish wine, which at times even included Jewish wine that had merely been touched by Gentile hands.

the four questions: a part of the Passover Haggadah recited by the youngest child present

the Seder: (Heb.) the set of ceremonies, including the festival meal, observed in Jewish homes on the night of Passover

the third cup: Four ritual cups of wine are served during the Seder.

'hemstitched biscuits': ie, the *matzoh* (perforated, unleavened bread)

l'havdil: (Heb.) literally, 'to distinguish' – a way of saying 'may they be kept poles apart,' 'not to mention them in the same breath'

shtreimel: (Yid.) fur-edged hat traditionally worn by Chassidim

matzoh: (Heb.) specially prepared unleavened bread eaten on Passover

calculations of the plagues ... acronyms: the ten plagues of Egypt, listed by name and then by acronyms

afikomen: (Heb.) a special piece of *matzoh* eaten as a 'dessert' at the conclusion of the Seder meal. It is a custom (in Ashkenazic Jewish communities) for the children at the table to attempt to 'steal' it away from the person conducting the Seder, who therefore tries to 'hide' it from them. When it is stolen, the 'ransom' for its return is usually the promise of presents.

Elijah's visit: At one point during the Seder a cup of wine is poured for Elijah the prophet and the front door is opened to welcome him. In Jewish lore, Elijah is a herald of the Messiah.

chacham: (Heb.) wise one (of the four sons)

yarmulka'd dome: *yarmulka* – (Yid.) skull-cap

Rabbi Zlotnik: Judah L. Zlotnik; see Klein's review above, p 3.

bitter herbs: displayed and eaten during the Seder, as a memento of the bitterness of bondage in Egypt

'There was thick darkness ...': Exodus 10:22–3

THE LAST OF THE *BADCHANIM* – SHLOIME SHMULEVITZ

badchanim (pl. of *badchan*): (Heb.) jesters or merrymakers, particularly at traditional Jewish weddings in eastern Europe

I.J. Singer (1893–1944): distinguished Yiddish novelist and playwright whose works are largely concerned with depicting Jewish life in eastern Europe

Hershel of Ostropol: eighteenth-century Yiddish jester in Poland, popular figure in Jewish folklore. See Klein's play 'Hershel of Ostropol' (*The Canadian Jewish Chronicle*, 31 March and 13 September 1939) and his unpublished script titled 'Worse Visitors We Shouldn't Have' (Klein Papers, Public Archives of Canada).

'A Brivele der Mamen': (Yid.) 'A Little Letter to Mother'

Shomer: pen-name of Nachum Shaikevitch (1849–1905), Yiddish writer of popular plays and novels of suspense

'A Brivele dem Taten': (Yid.) 'A Little Letter to Father'

'Dos Talis'l': (Yid.) 'The Little Prayershawl'

'Dos Tillem'l': (Yid.) 'The Little Psalter'

'Yid'ele': (Yid.) 'little Jew'

Itzik Manger (1901–69): Yiddish poet, dramatist, and novelist

SAADYAH GAON

Gaon: (Heb.) head of academy in post-Talmudic period, particularly in Babylonia

Maimonides: Moses Maimonides (1135–1204), Spanish-born Jewish religious philosopher, legal scholar, and doctor, author of Guide to the Perplexed

genizah: (Heb.) depository for disused sacred books and ritual articles. A very old one often contains archival treasures.

Academy of Sura: one of the leading Jewish academies in Babylonia, from the third to eleventh century

triple-peaked mountains of the Hebrew verb: Hebrew verbs are usually constructed from triliteral roots.

tinnok shel bais rabbon: (Heb.) schoolchild

Midrashic: Midrash – a branch of rabbinic literature consisting primarily of herme-neutic commentary on the Bible and containing relevant homilies, tales, and anecdotes

paytanim: (Heb.) composers of liturgical poems

Amoraim: (Heb.) sages of the Talmud, scholars of the post-Mishnaic period, from about the third to sixth century

Resh Galutha: (Aramaic) exilarch, 'leader of the exile,' the lay head of Babylonian Jewry

Karaism: the doctrine of the Karaites, a Jewish sect, founded by Anan ben David in the eighth century, which rejected rabbinic Judaism and accepted only Scrip-ture as authoritative

Tannaim: (Heb.) rabbinic teachers of the Mishnaic period, from about the first to the early third century

'A little philosophy ...': Francis Bacon, 'Of Atheism,' Essays, 16

Moses Mendelssohn (1729–86): German-Jewish philosopher who attempted to rec-oncile eighteenth-century Enlightenment ideals with traditional Judaism

Kneseth Hagdola: (Heb.) 'Great Assembly,' the supreme Jewish legislative assembly during the Second Temple period (538 BC–70 AD). Klein's reference is anach-ronistic here.

BIALIK THOU SHOULDST BE LIVING AT THIS HOUR

Bialik Thou Shouldst ...: echoing 'Milton! thou should'st be living at this hour' –
   Wordsworth, 'London'

Yishuv: (Heb.) the Jewish community in Palestine

jewelled word: '... and jewels five-words-long / That on the stretched forefinger
   of all Time / Sparkle forever....' – Tennyson, 'The Princess'

'As to songs ...': Carlyle, *Life of John Sterling*

Beth-Ha-Midrash: (Heb.) the House of Study

Mathmid: (Heb.) an exceptionally diligent student wholly devoted to his studies;
   a *yeshiva* student who studies the Talmud day and night

Haganah: the clandestine military defence organization of the Jews in Palestine from
   1920 to the establishment of the State of Israel in 1948. *Haganah* in Hebrew
   means 'defence.'

Tel-Chai: Jewish settlement in Palestine where Joseph Trumpeldor was killed while
   defending it against an Arab attack in 1920

vox et praeterea nihil: (Lat.) 'a sound [or voice, or word] and nothing else.' The
   expression has its origin in Plutarch, *Moralia*, 'Sayings of the Spartans,' 233a,
   where it is said of a nightingale.

Vichyards: the French politicians who formed the wartime government at Vichy
   and collaborated with the Nazis

Their wreaths are willows ...: Shaemas O'Sheel, 'They Went Forth to Battle, but
   They Always Fell'

SAUL TCHERNICHOVSKY

window onto Europe: echoing Pushkin's comment (*The Bronze Horseman*, line 16)
   on Peter the Great's founding of St Petersburg

Yeshiva-bochur: (Heb.-Yid.) student at a Talmudic academy

Yehuda Halevi (c1075–1141): Spanish-Jewish poet and philosopher. See Klein's
   poem 'Yehuda Halevi, His Pilgrimage.'

Bar Kochba: leader of the unsuccessful second-century revolt in Judaea against
   Rome

Rabbi of Mayence: a reference to Tchernichovsky's poem 'Baruch of Mayence'

THE THIRTEENTH APOSTLE?

Sholem Asch (1880–1957): Polish-born Yiddish novelist. He lived in the U.S. after
   1938 and was the first Yiddish writer to enjoy an international vogue. His
   trilogy on the birth of Christianity was attacked in certain Jewish circles.

Hinc illae lachrymae (or *lacrimae*): (Lat.) 'Hence these tears' – Terence, *Andria*, and
   often quoted by others. The phrase is proverbial for 'That's the cause of it.'

parnassah: (Heb.) livelihood

PALESTINE MOVING-PICTURES
Eretz Israel: the land of Israel

HAD NOT THY TORAH BEEN MY DELIGHT ...
Rabbi Pinchos Hirshprung: See Klein's article on Hirshprung in *The Canadian
Jewish Chronicle*, 13 March 1942, reprinted in *Beyond Sambation*.
Responsa: (Lat.) replies to questions in Jewish law – a major form of rabbinic
literature
Haman: according to the Book of Esther, an official in the court of Ahasuerus and
author of an unsuccessful plot to murder all the Jews in the realm
the seed of Amalek: a reference to the Amalekites, a desert people who were hered-
itary enemies of Israel in biblical times. See Exodus 17:8–16.
Had not Thy Torah ... : Psalms 119:92
Sabbath candle upon a naughty world: 'How far that little candle throws his beams! /
So shines a good deed in a naughty world.' – Shakespeare, *The Merchant of
Venice* v, i

SOME PRAISE THE LORD – SOME PASS THE AMMUNITION
Some Praise the Lord ...: 'Praise the Lord and pass the ammunition' – the title of
a popular 1942 song by Frank Loesser. According to Bartlett, the expression
was originally that of Howell M. Forgy at Pearl Harbor. 'Forgy was serving
as chaplain on a cruiser at the time of the Japanese attack; the words were
said to a chain of men handling ammunition.'
Habent sua fata libelli: (Lat.) Books have their own destiny.
Saadyah and Amram: two Babylonian *Gaonim* (Heb., heads of academies) who
issued prayer-books still regarded as authoritative on the order of prayers for
all occasions. Saadyah died in 942 and Amram c875.
Tagore: Rabindranath Tagore (1861–1941), Bengali poet and mystic
Thirteen Principles: list of thirteen basic articles of Jewish faith formulated by
Moses Maimonides (1135–1204)
Emes v'Emunah: Titles of prayers (usually taken from their opening words) are not
translated in these notes unless the meaning is somewhat relevant to the
point Klein is making.
Eighteen Benedictions: known in Hebrew as *Shmoneh-Esreh* (Heb., 'The Eighteen')
or *Amidah* (Heb., 'Standing'), the central prayer in the three daily prayer
services. This prayer is recited silently while standing.
the *m'chayeh maisim*: (Heb.) the benediction which speaks of God's resurrecting
the dead
L'Chu N'ran'nah: (Heb.) 'Come, let us exult,' opening statement in the Sabbath-
welcoming prayer recited Friday evening
Uva l'Zion: (Heb.) 'And to Zion shall come [a redeemer]'

God will come as a redeemer: rather than the Messiah, which is the meaning
traditionally understood in the original

Aleinu ... : a Hebrew prayer proclaiming the sovereignty of God, and containing
some lines which Christians in the Middle Ages regarded as insulting to their
religion

Elohai, n'tzor l'shoini: (Heb.) 'Lord, guard my tongue [from speaking evil]'

Amidah: the Eighteen Benedictions. See note above, p 386.

Zangwill: Israel Zangwill (1864–1926), Anglo-Jewish author and translator

Jeremy Taylor (1613–67): English bishop, noted preacher and theologian

Maariv: (Heb.) the evening prayer

siddurim (pl. of *siddur*): (Heb.) prayer-books

Reconstructionist Movement: an offshoot of Conservative Judaism, founded in the
U.S. in the 1920s by Rabbi Mordecai M. Kaplan. Conservative Judaism is
less liberal than Reform Judaism but more liberal than Orthodox Judaism.

b'lachash: (Heb.) in a whisper

lishmo: (Heb.) 'for its own sake,' meaning for the sake of Heaven – a term to
characterize duties or virtuous acts performed for no ulterior motive but purely
out of devotion to God's law

Rabbi Judah: Judah ha-Nasi, redactor of the Mishna (early code of Jewish law)

sanhedrin ... katlonith: (Heb.) 'deadly Sanhedrin.' Klein is probably thinking of the
statements in Mishna *Makkot* 1:10 on the reluctance of the ancient Jewish
supreme court to sentence a man to death: 'A Sanhedrin that issues a death
sentence once in seven years is called a murderous one. Rabbi Eleazar ben
Azariah says, "Or even once in seventy years".'

He prayeth best ... : Coleridge, 'The Rime of the Ancient Mariner'

Baal Shem Tov: Israel Baal Shem Tov (1700–60), founder of Chassidism, a Jewish
religious movement emphasizing joy in the service of God

THE SNOWS OF YESTERYEAR [RAVITCH]

Snows of Yesteryear: 'Mais où sont les neiges d'antan?' (Fr., 'But where are the
snows of yesteryear?') – Villon, 'Ballade des Dames du Temps Jadis'

esquisses: (Fr.) sketches

Magna pars fui: (Lat.) 'I was a great part' – Vergil, *Aeneid* II, 6. The line actually
reads 'pars magna fui.'

'Lives of the Poets': an allusion to Samuel Johnson's *Lives of the English Poets*
(1781)

'like sheep ... staff': from the High Holy Day prayer *Un'sanne Tokef*, attributed to
Rabbi Amnon of Mayence, tenth century. See Klein's poem 'Address to the
Choirboys.'

cabin'd and confined: 'cabin'd, cribb'd, confin'd' – Shakespeare, *Macbeth* III, iv

caractères: pen-portraits. Klein is perhaps suggesting a comparison with the *Caractères* of the French satiric moralist La Bruyère.

Gemara-intonation: the sing-song intonation in which the Talmud is often read and studied. The Gemara is the compendium of commentaries on the Mishna, and the Mishna and Gemara together form the Talmud, though the term 'Gemara' alone is often used to mean the Talmud.

Ubi Sunt: (Lat.) 'Where are ...?' – an elegiac motif in medieval Latin poetry

PEN: International Association of Poets, Playwrights, Editors, Essayists and Novelists

Maidanek: one of the Nazi death camps

Chaim Lieberman (1890–1963): Yiddish literary critic and polemicist

Pilsudski-Beck: a reference to Polish political leaders between World Wars I and II

THE POETRY WHICH IS PRAYER

Siddur: (Heb.) prayer-book

Berditchever: Rabbi Levi Yitschok of Berditchev (1740–1810), Chassidic leader. He stressed the element of joy in Chassidism and good that is in man. See Klein's poem 'Reb Levi Yitschok Talks to God.'

Baal Shem Tov: Israel Baal Shem Tov (1700–60), founder of Chassidism, a Jewish religious movement emphasizing joy in the service of God

last of the Mohicans: title of a novel by James Fenimore Cooper (1789–1851)

Koretz: Segal's native town in the Ukraine

broigez-dance: *broigez-tanz*, a folk-dance in Jewish weddings in which a couple enacts quarrelling and reconciliation (*broigez* – Yid., angry)

volens-nolens: (Lat.) willy-nilly

Lamed Vovnik: (Yid.) a saintly person – 'one of the thirty-six.' According to a popular Jewish legend, there always exist thirty-six righteous persons, of unknown identity, on account of whose merit the world is preserved.

Francis Jammes (1868–1938): French poet who wrote with child-like simplicity about nature, animals, and commonplace events, often with deep religious feeling

aleph-bais: (Heb.) alphabet

Francis of Assisi (1181–1226): founder of the Franciscan Order

vade mecum: (Lat.) manual or handbook

pinkos: (Heb.) record book

Me'oras Hamachpelah: (Heb.) the cave of Machpelah, tomb of the biblical patriarchs and matriarchs in Hebron

Mani Leib: Mani-Leib Brahinsky (1883–1953), Yiddish neo-romantic poet

Moishe Leib Halpern (1886–1932): American Yiddish poet who, like Mani Leib, was one of the leading figures in Die Yunge ('the young ones'), a modernist Yiddish literary group centred in New York in the early twentieth century

Bratzlaver: Rabbi Nachman of Bratzlav (1772–1811), famous Chassidic leader and teller of tales and parables

Shir Ha-shirim: (Heb.) Song of Songs (Song of Solomon)

'bnai farnem': the phrase, combining Hebrew and Yiddish, would seem to mean 'people of scope'

shidduchim: (Heb.) matchmakings

traklin: (Heb.) parlour
Akiva (c50–135): foremost Jewish scholar of his age, patriot and martyr, of humble
origin, known for his modesty and kindness

AN ENCYCLOPEDIC WORK
Mishna: the earliest codification of Jewish law, redacted and arranged into six orders
by Judah ha-Nasi in the second century
Dmai: (Heb.) agricultural produce about which there exists some doubt as to whether
it has been duly tithed
Rabbi Israel Lipshitz (1782–1860): German rabbinic scholar, author of an important
commentary on the Mishna

'APPLES OF GOLD IN PICTURES OF SILVER'
apples of gold: Proverbs 25:11
paytanim: (Heb.) composers of liturgical poems
Symcha Petrushka (1893–1950): scholar and translator. He had settled in Montreal
in 1940. Petrushka completed his translation of the Mishna shortly before
he died.
ontogeny and ontology: Klein must mean here 'ontogeny and phylogeny' – terms
referring to the development of the individual and the species. In 'The Oxen
of the Sun' Klein refers to Joyce's use of Haeckel's principle that 'ontogeny
is a recapitulation of phylogeny.'
vade mecum: (Lat.) manual, handbook

THE SNOWS OF YESTERYEAR [CHAGALL]
Snows of Yesteryear: 'Mais où sont les neiges d'antan?' (But where are the snows
of yesteryear?) – Villon, 'Ballade des Dames du Temps Jadis'
Gluckel of Hameln (1645–1724): Yiddish memoirist
luach: (Heb.) calendar
goy: (Heb.) non-Jew, gentile
Chanuka: eight-day celebration commemorating the victory of the Maccabees over
the Syrian king Antiochus Epiphanes in 164 BC and the re-dedication of the
Temple in Jerusalem
esrog (etrog): (Heb.) citron used as a ritual object during the autumn festival of
Succoth
Reader's intonation ... Haman: The Book of Esther is recited publicly on the festival
of Purim. Whenever Haman's name occurs, the listeners, especially the
children, drown out the sound of his name with noisemakers.
Shaloch Monos: (Heb.-Yid.) gifts of delicacies delivered to friends on Purim

LOOK ON THIS PICTURE AND ON THIS
Look on This Picture ...: 'Look here upon this picture, and on this, / The counterfeit
presentment of two brothers.' – Shakespeare, *Hamlet* III, iv

Erez (Eretz): (Heb.) the Land, ie, of Israel

tallis: (Heb.) prayer shawl

White Paper: Klein is playing on this phrase by referring to the British White Paper of 1939, which tended to diminish or overlook Jewish claims to Palestine.

shtreimel: (Yid.) fur-edged hat traditionally worn by Chassidim

Graetz's *History*: monumental history of the Jews by Heinrich Graetz (1817–91)

cheder: (Heb.) Jewish elementary school

Sejm: Polish parliament

Bet Midrash: (Heb.) House of Study

ONLY HALF THE LANGUAGE OF FAITH

Ashkenazic: central or eastern European

hasidic (Chassidic): Chassidism – a Jewish religious movement, founded in eastern Europe in the eighteenth century, emphasizing joy in the service of God

Ha-maariv arovim: a phrase from the evening prayer service. There is a certain play on words in the Hebrew because the verb and the noun are derived from the same root.

Ho-emes l'amitoi: (Heb.) 'the truth in all its truth'

V'chol shachar l'shachair: (Heb.) 'and each dawn to seek out ...' Here, too, the noun and verb being derived from the same root, a play on words is effected.

Yehuda Halevi (c1075–1141): Spanish-Jewish poet and philosopher. See Klein's poem 'Yehuda Halevi, His Pilgrimage.'

l'ha'avir gilulim: (Heb.) 'to remove idols.' *Gilulim* (idols, abominations) comes from the Hebrew word for excrement.

David Sweetsinger: ie, King David, the Psalmist

Browning's Caliban: Caliban, a primitive character in Robert Browning's dramatic monologue 'Caliban upon Setebos,' derived from Shakespeare's *Tempest*

BAEDEKER: KASRILEVKE

Baedeker: a reference to the famous series of nineteenth-century guidebooks for travellers

Kasrilevke: imaginary town invented by Sholom Aleichem as a fictional archetype of Jewish towns in eastern Europe

Sholom Aleichem: pen-name of Sholom Rabinovitch (1859–1916), Yiddish author and humorist, one of the major figures of modern Yiddish literature. His realistic stories of Jewish life in eastern European villages are suffused with wry wit and compassion.

Isidore Goldstick (1890–1963): Jewish educator, journalist, editor, and translator of Yiddish literature. He lived in London, Ontario.

Pale: ie, Pale of Settlement, territory within the borders of Czarist Russia wherein Jews were legally permitted to reside

Fuit Ilium: (Lat.) 'Troy *has* been, is no more' – Vergil, *Aeneid* II, 325

shabbas-goyim: (Heb.-Yid.) non-Jews who perform for Jews tasks forbidden on the
    Jewish Sabbath, such as kindling a fire

vade mecum: (Lat.) manual, handbook

Ding an sich: (Ger.) thing in itself

yom kippur: (Heb.) Day of Atonement. There is a custom in which individuals
    symbolically transfer their sins to a rooster on the eve of Yom Kippur, and part
    of the ritual is to swing this 'scapefowl' about one's head. See Klein's poem
    'Plumaged Proxy.'

Sambation: the name of a legendary river that rages all week and is still only on
    the Sabbath. According to Jewish tradition, the ten lost tribes of Israel are
    exiled beyond this river.

goy: (Heb.) non-Jew, gentile

leviathan: legendary gigantic fish upon which the righteous will feed in the world
    to come

yayin nesech (*yain nesach*): (Heb.) in its original meaning, 'libation wine,' wine
    consecrated by Gentiles for idol worship, and hence forbidden to Jews. Klein
    is thinking here of the associated interdiction (often referred to under the
    same category of *yain nesach*) against *any* non-Jewish wine, which at times
    even included Jewish wine that had merely been touched by Gentile hands.
    The idea here is that the specialness of the Yiddish original would be defiled
    by translation.

compassionate sons of the compassionate: a literal translation of the Hebrew *rach-
    manim bnai rachmanim*, a proverbial expression describing Jews as excelling
    in compassion

miracle of the Septuagint: According to tradition, the seventy (some say seventy-
    two) scholars in the third century BC, commissioned to translate the Hebrew
    Bible and Apocrypha into Greek, all worked independently of one another
    and yet came up with precisely identical translations.

THE DYBBUK

Anski: S. Anski (An-Ski), pen-name of Solomon Rapaport (1863–1920), Russian-
    Jewish author and folklorist

Habima: Hebrew repertory theatre company founded in Moscow in 1918, moved
    to Tel Aviv in 1931

eighteen, the number of life: the word *chai* (Heb., live) is composed of two letters
    whose combined numerical equivalent is eighteen

Torah: In its basic meaning, Torah refers to the Pentateuch. In its wider sense, it
    includes all other sections of Holy Scriptures and rabbinic commentary.

Montagues ... Capulets: feuding families in Shakespeare's *Romeo and Juliet*

Chassidic: Chassidism – a Jewish religious movement, founded in eastern Europe
    in the eighteenth century, emphasizing joy in the service of God

O sages standing ... : Yeats, 'Sailing to Byzantium'

A CHASSIDIC ANTHOLOGY

Chassidic: Chassidism – a Jewish religious movement, founded in eastern Europe in the eighteenth century, emphasizing joy in the service of God

Misnagdim (pl. of Misnagid): (Heb.) Jews opposed to Chassidism

'him who should live': Klein is probably thinking of the expression she-yichye (Heb., [long] may he live), often used by Chassidim whenever the name of a revered rabbi is mentioned. See Klein's use of it on p 106.

Graetz: Heinrich Graetz (1817–91), Jewish historian

Besht: acronymic name of Israel Baal Shem Tov (1700–60), founder of Chassidism

pilpulists: pilpul – (Heb.) a method of Talmudic study involving sharp dialectical and often casuistic argumentation

Bathsheba: See 2 Samuel 11.

chutzpa: (Heb.) effrontery, nerve

Sadagoran: Abraham Yaakov of Sadagora

zadicolatry: The term is evidently Klein's coinage, meaning the excessive idolatry or worship of the zaddik (pl. zaddikim). A zaddik (literally, 'saintly person') is a leader of a community of Chassidim. Zaddikim tend to be venerated by their followers as holy persons. The tales in Buber's collection concern various zaddikim (the 'masters' in his title) and the legends surrounding them.

Litvak: (Yid.) Lithuanian. Lithuanian Jews were often caricatured by neighbouring Jewish communities as learned and sharp-witted, but emotionally dry.

moujik: Russian peasant

forty immortals: the Académie Française

Sanhedrin: the ancient Jewish supreme court and legislature

Kol Nidre: (Aramaic) 'All Vows,' the name of a solemn musical prayer introducing the Day of Atonement service

Ten Days of Contrition: between Rosh Hashanah (New Year) and Yom Kippur (Day of Atonement)

Because I do not hope ...: T.S. Eliot, 'Ash-Wednesday'

Soton Hora: literally, 'the evil Satan,' but there is apparently no such expression in Jewish lore. Klein probably meant to say Yetzer Hora – the Hebrew term for the 'evil urge,' a person's evil side, which leads to sin. The Yetzer Hora is sometimes almost personified as a tempter or bad angel, in opposition to the Yetzer Hatov, man's good or noble side.

Minyan: (Heb.) a group of ten male adults, the minimum required for communal prayer

Shekinah: (Heb.) Divine Presence

MELECH GRAFSTEIN'S SHOLOM ALEICHEM

Melech Grafstein (1893–1960): Yiddish author and journalist. Born in Poland, he lived in London, Ontario, from 1913. He was editor of The Jewish Observer.

Sholom Aleichem: pen-name of Sholom Rabinovitch (1859–1916), Yiddish author and humorist, one of the major figures of modern Yiddish literature. His realistic stories of Jewish life in eastern European villages are suffused with wry wit and compassion.

Peretz: Isaac Leib Peretz (1852–1915), a major figure in modern Yiddish literature, particularly noted as a short story writer

forty immortals: the Académie Française

King Grafstein: *Melech* is Hebrew for king. The hero of Klein's novel *The Second Scroll* is named Melech.

dernier cri: (Fr.) the latest style, the last word

POET OF A WORLD PASSED BY

Sefer Yiddish: (Heb.) Book of Yiddish

Koretz: Segal's native town in the Ukraine

Torah: In its basic meaning, Torah refers to the Pentateuch. In its wider sense, it includes all other sections of Holy Scriptures and rabbinic commentary.

Ben Bag-Bag: first-century scholar. His saying appears in *Ethics of the Fathers* 5:25.

loshon koidesh: (Heb.) 'holy tongue,' ie, Hebrew

kaddish: (Heb.) mourner's prayer for the departed

Chagall: Marc Chagall (1887–1985), artist, many of whose pictures are filled with images of eastern European Jewish village life

THE ART OF HERTZ GROSBARD

Steinberg: Klein means to refer to the Yiddish author Eliezer Steinberg (1880–1932).

Lutzky: A. Lutzky, pen-name of Aaron Zucker (1894–1957), Yiddish poet

loksh: (Yid.) noodle

POEMS OF YEHOASH

Yehoash: pen-name of Yehoash Solomon Bloomgarden (1872–1927), Yiddish poet and translator

Isidore Goldstick (1890–1963): Jewish educator, journalist, editor, and translator of Yiddish literature. He lived in London, Ontario.

whiteness ... gold: Klein is alluding here to the colours used on the cover of the book.

Tanach: the Hebrew Bible

OF HEBREW CALLIGRAPHY

Haggadah: (Heb.) a narrative of the Exodus presented through a set form of benedictions, prayers, homilies, and psalms, recited at the Seder, a family feast on the night of Passover

larceny of the *afikomen*: The *afikomen* (Heb.) is a special piece of *matzoh* (Heb., unleavened bread) eaten as a 'dessert' at the conclusion of the Seder meal. It is a custom (in Ashkenazic Jewish communities) for the children at the table to attempt to 'steal' it away from the person conducting the Seder, who therefore tries to 'hide' it from them. When it is stolen, the 'ransom' for its return is usually the promise of presents.

second Commandment: the second of the Ten Commandments, prohibiting the making of graven images

taggin (*tagin*): (Heb.) decorative and symbolic 'crowns' (formed of three flourishes) sometimes placed on Hebrew letters

yud: a letter in the Hebrew alphabet: ׳

two iotas: The *iota* is the Greek letter akin to the Hebrew *yud*. The word consisting of two *yuds* – impossible to pronounce as such, and instead spoken as if it were spelled the same as *Adonai* – is one of the sacred forms of the Divine name in Hebrew.

dayenu: (Heb.) 'it were enough for us' – the refrain of a Passover song enumerating all of God's deeds on behalf of the Jews in the Exodus from Egypt

aleph and *bais*: the first letters of the Hebrew alphabet

IN MEMORIAM: J.I. SEGAL

Baal Shem Tov: Israel Baal Shem Tov (1700–60), founder of Chassidism, a Jewish religious movement emphasizing joy in the service of God

Bratzlaver: Rabbi Nachman of Bratzlav (1772–1811), famous Chassidic leader and teller of tales and parables

latter-day Levite: The Levites provided song and music at the holy services in the ancient Temple in Jerusalem.

'making great song …': Keats, 'Fragment of an Ode to Maia, Written on May Day, 1818.' Ludwig Lewisohn quotes this line as a tribute to Klein in his introduction to Klein's *Hath Not a Jew....*

Reb: (Yid.) 'mister,' traditional title prefixed to a man's first name

Rilke: Rainer Maria Rilke (1875–1926), distinguished German poet

two iotas: Segal's initials are written with two *yuds*, which in Hebrew is one of the sacred forms of the Divine name.

those thirty-six: According to a popular Jewish legend, there always exist thirty-six righteous persons, of unknown identity, on account of whose merit the world is preserved.

Rabbi Pinchas of Koretz (1726–91): an early Chassidic leader known for his stress upon music

JEWISH FOLK-SONGS

Chassidic: Chassidism – a Jewish religious movement, founded in eastern Europe in the eighteenth century, emphasizing joy in the service of God

Bet Hamidrash: (Heb.) the House of Study

niggun: (Heb.) melody, traditional air

Reb Levi Yitschok: Levi Yitschok of Berditchev (1740–1810), Chassidic leader. He stressed the element of joy in Chassidism and good that is in man. See Klein's poem 'Reb Levi Yitschok Talks to God.'

qui traduit traduce: (Fr.) he who translates alters, or misrepresents; Klein evidently slipped up here, using the English word *traduce* instead of the appropriate French word *trahit*, to say 'he who translates, betrays.'

Torah: In its basic meaning, Torah refers to the Pentateuch. In its wider sense, it includes all other sections of Holy Scriptures and rabbinic commentary.

argumentum ad parvulam: (Lat.) argument directed at childhood

Zebulun ... Issachar: two sons of the biblical patriarch Jacob. According to a fanciful Midrashic tradition, they made an arrangement whereby Zebulun engaged in commerce, Issachar in Torah study, and they shared the rewards.

seven poetic ages: Shakespeare, *As You Like It* II, vii

Responsa: (Lat.) replies to questions in Jewish law – a major form of rabbinic literature

cradle-Kaddish: ie, male heir, the child who will recite the *kaddish* (Heb., the mourner's prayer) after the death of his father or mother

eat 'days': from the Yiddish, *es'n teg*, an arrangement whereby needy *yeshiva* students living away from home would eat meals as regular guests of assigned families on given days of each week

Jeshurun wax fat: Deuteronomy 32:15

Reb Shmerl ... Reb Beril: names used in the sense of 'somebody' or 'anybody' to illustrate a point

Barmecide banquet: feast on imaginary food – from *The Arabian Nights*

Talmud: usually refers to the Babylonian Talmud (which differs in some respects from the Jerusalem Talmud), a compendium of commentaries on the Mishna by generations of scholars and jurists in many academies beginning in the third century and ending with its redaction at the end of the fifth century. Together with the Bible, it constitutes the basis of traditional Jewish law and culture.

yarmulka'd: *yarmulka* – (Yid.) skull-cap

beacons of the exile: a term of praise applied to illustrious Diaspora Jews

OF HEBREW HUMOR

'les Juifs ...': (Fr.) 'Jews have neither the faculty for curiosity nor for laughter' – Ernest Renan

the second Patriarch: Isaac, whose name in Hebrew is associated with the word 'laugh.' See Genesis 18:12 and 21:6.

counterpresentiment: an expression occasionally used by Klein to mean some telling visual juxtaposition. There is no such word in English, but Klein apparently came to it through a faulty recollection of one of his favourite quotations

from Shakespeare: 'Look here upon this picture, and on this, / The counterfeit
   presentment of two brothers.' – *Hamlet* III, iv
Cain's rhetorical question: 'Am I my brother's keeper?' – Genesis 4:9
Witch of En-dor: 1 Samuel 28
with the jawbone of an ass assailed masses: Judges 15:16. Klein's play on the sound
   of 'ass' corresponds to the punning on that word in the Hebrew text of this
   verse.
flame-touched lips: Isaiah 6:5–7
Nathan: 2 Samuel 12:1–12
somnolence and hard-hearing: 1 Kings 18:27
Jael: Judges 4:21
Judith: heroine of the Apocryphal book of Judith
six hundred and thirteen: according to rabbinic teaching, the total number of biblical
   precepts and prohibitions
the stars ... the sands ...: Genesis 22:17
laughter and lightheadedness: *Ethics of the Fathers* 3:17
he who jests brings annihilation to the world: Talmud, *Avoda Zara* 18b
Rabbi Jochanan smote ... Kahana: Talmud, *Baba Kama* 117a. This and several other
   Talmudic references mentioned here also occur in Klein's poem 'Ave atque
   Vale.'
forbidden to fill one's mouth with laughter: Talmud, *Berachot* 31a
Zebulun ... Issachar: two sons of the biblical patriarch Jacob. According to a fanciful
   Midrashic tradition, they made an arrangement whereby Zebulun engaged
   in commerce, Issachar in Torah study, and they shared the rewards.
Feast of Rejoicing: ie, Simchat Torah, a festival of rejoicing in the Torah, in which
   Torah scrolls are carried around the synagogue with singing and merriment
Purim: feast day of the 14th of Adar, commemorating the deliverance of the Jews
   from Haman's plot to kill them, as narrated in the Book of Esther
Mordecai: the Jewish hero in the Purim story, opponent of Haman
Samson's philistinish ejections: Talmud, *Sotah* 10a
Resh Lakish: third-century Palestinian sage who in his youth was a brigand and
   a gladiator. The reference here is to Talmud, *Gittin* 47a.
Rabbi Isaac on Adam's unmentionable diversion: Talmud, *Yebamoth* 63a
Pharaoh's uncovenanted member: Talmud, *Moed Katan* 18a. However, users of the
   English edition of the Talmud published by Soncino will find this reference
   has been omitted.
Haggadah: (Heb.) variant spelling of *Aggadah*, denoting those sections of the
   Talmud containing homiletic expositions, stories, maxims, and folklore,
   as opposed to strictly legal material
brevity ... the soul of wit: Shakespeare, *Hamlet* II, ii
Gemara: the compendium of commentaries on the Mishna. The Mishna and Gemara

together form the Talmud, though the term 'Gemara' alone is often used to mean the Talmud.

Tannaitic: referring to the *Tannaim*, rabbinic teachers of the Mishnaic period, from about the first to the early third century

songs of Zion: echoing Psalms 137:1–3

riddle of Timnath: Samson's riddle in Judges 14

tzitzis (*tzitzit*): (Heb.) the eight-threaded tassels or fringes on the four corners of prayer shawls or other special four-cornered garments worn by religiously observant Jewish males. See Numbers 15:37–41 and Deuteronomy 22:12.

In Poland ... his dances: See Klein's poem 'Ballad of the Dancing Bear.'

Jeshurun waxed fat: Deuteronomy 32:15

yarmulka: (Yid.) skull-cap

lulav: (Heb.) palm branch, used as a ceremonial object on the festival of Succoth

Tisha B'av: (Heb.) the ninth day of the month of Av (or Ab), a day of mourning and fasting commemorating the destruction of the first and second Temples

Benjamin of Tudela: a twelfth-century Jewish traveller famous for his historically valuable travel book

Zunz: Leopold Zunz (1794–1886), German-Jewish scholar and historian

proverbial snuff-box bandit: See Klein's poem 'Bandit.'

Talmid-chochem: (Heb.) scholar, learned man

Heinrich Heine (1797–1856): German-Jewish poet and critic

Isaac Erter (1791–1851): Hebrew satirist

Judah Loeb Gordon (1831–92): Hebrew poet and critic

Sholom Aleichem: pen-name of Sholom Rabinovitch (1859–1916), Yiddish author and humorist, one of the major figures of modern Yiddish literature. His realistic stories of Jewish life in eastern European villages are suffused with wry wit and compassion. The expression *sholom aleichem* (literally, 'Peace unto you') is a popular Jewish greeting.

Moishe Nadir: pen-name of Isaac Reis (1885–1943), American Yiddish poet and humorist

Mithnagid: (Heb.) opponent of Chassidism

Klaus: (Yid.) synagogue

rebbe: (Yid.) rabbi, master; title of a leader of Chassidim

Master of the Name: a literal translation of the Hebrew *baal shem tov* – referring to Israel Baal Shem Tov (1700–60), founder of Chassidism, a Jewish religious movement emphasizing joy in the service of God

Erez Israel (Eretz Israel): (Heb.) the land of Israel

batlanim: (Heb.) idle frequenters of the synagogue

Mincha: (Heb.) afternoon prayer service

Maariv: (Heb.) evening prayer service

Mikveh: (Heb.) ritual bath

Volozhin: town in Belorussia, site of a famous Talmudic academy

yeshiva bachurim: (Heb.-Yid.) *yeshiva* boys, students in a Talmudic academy

Abbaya and Rabba: early-fourth-century Babylonian sages. Their agreements and
　　disagreements on various legal points constitute an important element of
　　the Talmud.

pilpul: (Heb.) a method of Talmudic study involving sharp dialectical and often
　　casuistic argumentation

phylacteries ... Rashi and Rabbenu Tam: Because of a difference of opinion between
　　Rashi and his grandson Rabbenu Tam (eleventh- and twelfth-century French
　　Talmudists) on the exact arrangement of the contents of the phylacteries,
　　a small number of punctilious Jews follow both opinions by donning two
　　different pairs of phylacteries.

maggid: (Heb.) preacher

almemar: (Heb.) synagogue pulpit

shadchan: (Heb.) matchmaker

kugel: (Yid.) pudding

On a little brown pony ...: Klein's poem 'Into the Town of Chelm'

ON TRANSLATING THE YIDDISH FOLK-SONG

Houdini: Harry Houdini (1874–1926), famous magician and escape artist

kugel ... kigel: variant Yiddish pronunciations of the word for 'pudding'

Kasrilevke: imaginary town invented by Sholom Aleichem as a fictional archetype
　　of Jewish towns in eastern Europe

l'havdil: (Heb.) literally, 'to distinguish' – a way of saying 'may they be kept poles
　　apart,' 'not to mention them in the same breath.'

THE YIDDISH PROVERB

sect of philosophers: See Klein's essay 'In Praise of the Diaspora,' *The Canadian
　　Jewish Chronicle*, 9 January–27 February 1953, reprinted in *Beyond
　　Sambation*.

Talmud: usually refers to the Babylonian Talmud (which differs in some respects
　　from the Jerusalem Talmud), a compendium of commentaries on the Mishna
　　by generations of scholars and jurists in many academies beginning in the
　　third century and ending with its redaction at the end of the fifth century.
　　Together with the Bible, it constitutes the basis of traditional Jewish law and
　　culture.

Maimonides: Moses Maimonides (1135–1204), Spanish-born Jewish religious phi-
　　losopher, legal scholar, and doctor, author of *Guide to the Perplexed*

Stutchkov: Nachum Stutchkov (Stutchkoff), author of the *Thesaurus of the Yiddish
　　Language* (New York: YIVO, 1950)

nudnik: (Yid.) boring or bothersome person

vade mecum: (Lat.) manual, handbook

We transliterate: While Klein's transliteration is a careful reproduction, his translation from the Yiddish is very free.

griven: (Yid.) 'cracklings' made from chicken or goose fat

tzitzis (tzitzit): (Heb.) the eight-threaded tassels or fringes on the four corners of prayer shawls or other special four-cornered garments worn by religiously observant Jewish males. See Numbers 15:37–41 and Deuteronomy 22:12.

tzimes: (Yid.) vegetable and/or fruit compote

shmaltz: (Yid.) animal fat (as food)

There was a Jewish bandit ...: Klein's poem 'Bandit'

'all his bones': Psalms 35:10

chutzpah: (Heb.) effrontery, nerve

Sholom Aleichem: literally, 'Peace unto you.' The common reply to this greeting is an inversion of the same expression – *Aleichem sholom*, 'Unto you, peace.'

the sound conveys the sense – 'of being *ferchlopsjed*': Stutchkov gives it as '*farchlyoptshen zich* (to fall in love).' Klein may have responded to the sound of the expression without exactly understanding it. It probably derives from the Polish *chlopiec* – fiancée, lover, sweetheart.

Korah: rebel against the authority of Moses in the desert (see Numbers 16), traditionally described as having been fabulously wealthy

Rabbi Levi Yitschok: Levi Yitschok of Berditchev (1740–1810), Chassidic leader. He stressed the element of joy in Chassidism and good that is in man. See Klein's poem 'Reb Levi Yitschok Talks to God' and his quotation from Levi Yitschok's 'Thou Song' (*A Dudele*) in the epigraph to *The Second Scroll*.

Rebono Shel Olam: (Heb.) 'Lord of the Universe' – a phrase often used colloquially in referring to or addressing God

Le bon dieu – ils le tutoyaient: (Fr.) 'The good Lord – they address him familiarly.'

Responsa: (Lat.) replies to questions in Jewish law – a major form of rabbinic literature

Yeshiva: (Heb.) Jewish traditional academy devoted primarily to the study of the Talmud and rabbinic literature

schnorrers: (Yid.) beggars, freeloaders

badchanim (pl. of *badchan*): (Heb.) jesters or merrymakers, particularly at traditional Jewish weddings in eastern Europe. See Klein's article 'The Last of the Badchanim – Shloime Shmulevitz,' p 26.

Hershel Ostropolyer, Shaika Feifer, Motka Chabad: legendary Jewish jesters

Boiberik ... Yehupetz ... Kasrilevka: fictional eastern European Jewish towns invented by Sholom Aleichem

THE BIBLE AS LITERATURE

This article is signed Ben Kalonimas, a pen-name occasionally used by Klein, mainly in the late 1920s and early 1930s – evidence that this essay may have been written much earlier than one might suppose from the date of publication. *Ben* in Hebrew means 'son' or 'son of'; the name Kalonymus is the correlative (probably Greek in origin) of the name Kalman. Klein's father was named Kalman, and this pen-name is therefore a coded version of 'son of Kalman.' Kalonymus occurs often as a Jewish name in Italy, France, and Germany in the medieval period, most notably as the name of an eminent family of scholars and poets that flourished in Germany from the ninth to the thirteenth century. Apparently unrelated but perhaps more famous was the Provençal philosopher and translator Kalonymus ben Kalonymus ben Meir (1286–after 1328).

Septuagint: the original, third-century-BC translation of the Hebrew Bible and Apocrypha into Greek. According to tradition, the seventy (some say seventy-two) scholars who were commissioned to produce it all worked independently of one another and yet came up with precisely identical translations.

Koheleth: (Heb.) Ecclesiastes – according to Jewish tradition, King Solomon

Ernest Renan (1823–92): French philologist and critic

great forefathers ... laughter: a reference to the patriarch Isaac. See Genesis 18:12, 21:6.

No doubt but that ye are the people: Job 12:2

'Keren Hapuch': Job 42:14

Cry aloud ...: 1 Kings 18:27

with the jaw-bone of an ass: Judges 15:16

'Go over it and over it ...': Ethics of the Fathers 5:25

THE GESTURE OF THE BIBLE

Ernest Renan (1823–92): French philologist and critic

Maimonides: Moses Maimonides (1135–1204), Spanish-born Jewish religious philosopher, legal scholar, and doctor, author of Guide to the Perplexed

Thou shalt not make ...: Exodus 20:4

parallelismus membrorum: (Lat.) parallelism of verses

Give ear ...: Deuteronomy 32:1-2

THE BIBLE MANUSCRIPTS

six hundred and thirteen commands: according to rabbinic teaching, the total number of commandments and prohibitions. The rabbi referred to is probably Saadyah Gaon, tenth-century biblical scholar.

And Moses turned ... tables: Exodus 32:15–16. The three subsequent quotations are from Exodus 32:19, 34:1, and 34:29.

And the priests ... Egypt: 1 Kings 8:9

seah: (Heb.) an ancient unit of volume, about 7.3 litres

scribes of Israel: For another treatment of this topic by Klein, see his short story 'The Seventh Scroll.'

Shema: (Heb.) 'Hear' – first word of the verse 'Hear, O Israel: The Lord our God is one Lord' – the proclamation of monotheism in Deuteronomy 6:4–9.
It is a central part of the Jewish liturgy, and is also stored in the *mezuzah*, a small case affixed to doorposts of Jewish homes.

Bar Kamza: Talmud, *Yoma* 38b. The reference is in fact to Ben Kamzar; Klein is confusing him with Bar Kamza, known as the man who was partly to blame for the destruction of the Temple.

the quadriliteral word: the tetragrammaton, God's proper name. In Hebrew it is composed of the four letters *yud, hai, vav, hai,* and is considered forbidden to pronounce; in English it is sometimes shown as YHWH or JHVH.

vade mecum: (Lat.) manual, handbook

absit nomen: (Lat.) perish the name

genizah: (Heb.) depository for disused sacred books and ritual articles. A very old one often contains archival treasures.

Mahzor (Machzor): (Heb.) festival prayer book

Moshe ben Asher: tenth-century Masoretic scholar from Tiberias whose carefully edited biblical text with accents and vowel markings became the basis for subsequent editions of the Bible

Masorah: (Heb.) literally, 'tradition' – textual notes entered in the margins of the Hebrew Bible, regarding spelling, writing, and proper reading, to safeguard correct transmission of the authoritative text

Hagbah: (Heb.) the ceremony of lifting up and displaying the Torah scroll after the reading in the synagogue

initial *vav*: The first word in each column of the Torah scroll usually begins with the letter *vav*.

vav: letter of the Hebrew alphabet: ו . Other letters mentioned in this essay – *mem*: מ , *ches* (chet): ח , *lamed*: ל , *gimel*: ג , *zayin*: ז , *aleph*: א , *tauf*: ת , *ayin*: ע , *shin*: ש , *tess* (tet): ט , *samech*: ס , *pai*: פ , *neun*: נ .

leader of thirties: The letter *lamed* has the numerical value of 30.

tagin (*taggin*): (Heb.) decorative and symbolic 'crowns' (formed of three flourishes) sometimes placed on Hebrew letters

Glilah: (Heb.) the ceremony of rolling up and closing the Torah scroll

Yad: (Heb.) 'hand' – the pointer used in reading the Torah scroll, often having a tip in the shape of a hand

writings of Aristeas: referring to the 'letter of Aristeas,' third century BC, in which the legendary origin of the Septuagint is described

Masoretes: scholars who established and preserved the *masorah*, the body of notes relating to the authorized text of the Hebrew Bible

Hasmoneans: Maccabees, Jewish royal family ruling Judaea from 167 to 37 BC

Rashi: Hebrew acronym for Rabbi Solomon ben Isaac (1040–1105), one of the most authoritative commentators on the Bible and Talmud. He lived in France.

Ezra: fifth-century-BC priest and scribe, key figure in the reconstruction of Jewish religious life in Israel and the building of the Second Temple

Great Synagogue: probably a reference to the *Knesseth Hagdola* ('Great Assembly'), the supreme Jewish legislative assembly during the Second Temple period (538 BC–70 AD)

vayishchat: (Heb.) 'and he slew'

Esau did kiss Jacob: Genesis 33:4

Firkowitch: Abraham Firkovich (1786–1874), Karaite leader and scholar who collected Bible manuscripts, mainly in Crimea

Schechter: Solomon Schechter (1847–1915), rabbinic scholar and founder of Conservative Judaism. He recovered a large part of the Cairo *genizah*.

yclept: (Mid. Eng.) called

this Septuagint ... golden calf: Talmud, *Sopherim* 1:7

pseudo-Jonathan: Targum Jonathan, Palestinian Aramaic translation of Prophets, accredited to Jonathan ben Uzziel (originated in early centuries AD)

blind Rab Joseph: Joseph ben Chiya (d. 333), Babylonian sage and exegete who left Aramaic translations of parts of the Bible. As indicated, he was blind.

THE BIBLE'S ARCHETYPICAL POET

The Bible's Archetypical Poet: See Klein's article 'Joseph and His Brethren,' *The Canadian Jewish Chronicle*, 20 April 1951, reprinted in *Beyond Sambation*.

wrote of love: a reference to Song of Songs (Song of Solomon)

Qoheleth (Koheleth): Ecclesiastes

Now Israel loved Joseph ...: Quotations in this essay are from Genesis 37, 41, 42, 45, and 49.

Sic literatim: (Lat.) literally thus; literally as quoted

Thomas Mann (1875–1955): German author, whose works included the tetralogy *Joseph and His Brethren* (1933–43)

Ben Bag Bag: *Ethics of the Fathers* 5:25

FROM *THE MCGILL DAILY*

During his second year at college, Klein contributed a series of columns to the student newspaper, the *McGill Daily*, under the heading 'The McGilliad.' He identified himself only by his initials – A.M.K.

The rhyme is out of joint ...: playing on the closing lines of Act I of Shakespeare's *Hamlet* – 'the time is out of joint ...'

Billingsgate: a term for coarse, abusive language, derived from a well-known London fishmarket

Hog Butcher for the World ...: Carl Sandburg, 'Chicago'

The moon is as complacent ...: Evelyn Scott, 'Autumn Night'

Whitman: 'I sound my barbaric yawp over the roofs of the world' – 'Song of Myself'

Rousseau: 'Man is born free, and everywhere he is in chains' – *Of the Social Contract*

Heard melodies are sweet ...: Keats, 'Ode on a Grecian Urn'

G.K. Chesterton (1874–1936): English novelist, essayist, and critic

'The days of our youth ...': Byron, 'Stanzas Written on the Road between Florence and Pisa'

Thou best philosopher ...: Wordsworth, 'Intimations of Immortality'

'The Child is the father ...': Wordsworth, 'My Heart Leaps Up When I Behold'

third and fourth generation: Exodus 34:7, Numbers 14:18

Priapus: Greek and Roman god of male sexual power

Havelock Ellis (1859–1939): British essayist and scientist noted for his studies in the psychology of sex

brevity is the soul of wit: Shakespeare, *Hamlet* II, ii

Produce, produce ...: *Sartor Resartus*, II, 9

'one increasing purpose': Tennyson, 'Locksley Hall'

Fiat Lux: (Lat.) 'Let there be light' – Genesis 1:3

The unwearied sun ...: stanza 2 of the hymn 'The spacious firmament on high' by Joseph Addison

smitten rock gushing: Numbers 20:11

Balaam's ass: Numbers 22

PROLETARIAN POETRY

Sh. Niger: Shmuel Niger (1883–1955), New York Yiddish literary critic

NATIONAL ANTHEMS

Shaw's black girl: a reference to Shaw's *Adventures of the Black Girl in Her Search for God* (1932)

el moleh rachmim: (Heb.) 'Lord, full of compassion' – opening words of the memorial prayer for the departed

Chmelnitzky: Bogdan Chmelnitzky (1595–1657), leader of Cossack massacres of eastern European Jewry in 1648

Yevsektzia: Jewish section of the propaganda department of the Russian Communist Party from 1918 to 1930

mit leiten gleich: (Yid.) 'on a par with others,' like people generally

'Hatikvah': (Heb.) literally, 'The Hope' – title of the Zionist national anthem

'Techsakna': (Heb.) the opening word and title of a Zionist patriotic song

QUEEN MAB AND MICKEY MOUSE

out of the gall: probably an echo of Samson's riddle, 'out of the strong came forth sweetness' – Judges 14:14

sweetness and fright: a play on Matthew Arnold's phrase 'sweetness and light' from *Culture and Anarchy*

She is the fairies' ...: Shakespeare, *Romeo and Juliet* I, iv

ANNOTATION ON SHAPIRO'S *ESSAY ON RIME*

style ... implement: the English word *style* comes from the Latin *stilus*, a pointed
implement

L'amor che move ...: (Ital.) 'the love that moves [the sun and the other stars]' –
Dante, *Paradiso* xxxiii. Often quoted by Klein; see his poem 'My Literati
Friends in Restaurants.'

obiter scripta: (Lat.) written comments made in passing

parallelismus membrorum: (Lat.) parallelism of verses

bellum contra cerebellum: (Lat.) a war against the brain

O fortunatam natam me consule Romam: (Lat.) 'O Rome fortunate to be founded
during my consulate,' a line frequently cited by the ancients as an example of
bad verse

I have had earlier occasion to point out: Klein is referring to his review of *Person,
Place and Thing* in *The Canadian Jewish Chronicle*, 14 January 1944. See
'Those Who Should Have Been Ours,' p 246.

Moses ... an Egyptian: in Freud's *Moses and Monotheism* (1939)

French patriot ... Irish ... German: Napoleon, De Valera (actually born in the U.S.),
Hitler

agenbite: (Old Eng.) remorse

A DEFINITION OF POETRY?

Dear John: presumably John Sutherland, literary critic and editor, one of the leading
figures in the *First Statement* group in Montreal in the 1940s

Shakespeare's wife: a reference to the line in Shakespeare's will in which he left his
wife his 'second best bed'

Houdini ... Blackstone: famous illusionists

Housman: A.E. Housman, *The Nature of Poetry* (1933)

A spirit passed ...: Job 4:15

SHA! SHA! SHOSTAKOVITCH

Sha! Sha! Shostakovitch: The theme of this editorial is elaborated upon in Klein's
novella of the early 1950s 'The Bells of Sobor Spasitula' (*Short Stories*,
University of Toronto Press 1983).

I.R.: Israel Rabinovitch, editor of the Montreal Yiddish daily *Der Kanader Adler*
(*The Canadian Jewish Eagle*), which was published alongside the weekly
Canadian Jewish Chronicle by the Eagle Publishing Company

MARGINALIA

Ad pulchritudinem ...: (Lat.) 'Three things are needed for beauty: wholeness,

harmony, and radiance' – from Thomas Aquinas, and quoted by Stephen
    Dedalus in Joyce's *Portrait of the Artist as a Young Man*
The leaves are falling ...: Rilke, 'Autumn'
Silent, upon a peak ...: Keats, 'On First Looking into Chapman's Homer'
Fled is that music ...: Keats, 'Ode to a Nightingale'
And gathering swallows: Keats, 'To Autumn'
Life is real ...: Longfellow, 'A Psalm of Life'
God's in his heaven ...: Browning, 'Pippa Passes'
Shaw's *Antony and Cleopatra*: Klein means *Caesar and Cleopatra*.
Essence of winter ...: Frost, 'After Apple-Picking'
A black and E blue: Arthur Rimbaud, French symbolist poet, in 'Voyelles'
Milton's ... threnody: 'On the Death of a Fair Infant Dying of a Cough' (1628)
Jonson's touching lines on Salathiel Pavy: actually Salomon Pavy, a boy actor
    mourned in Jonson's 'Epitaph on S.P. a Child of Q. El. Chappel'

BOOK REVIEWING, IN SEVEN EASY LESSONS
Macaulay: Thomas Babington Macaulay (1800–59), British essayist, historian, and
    statesman

THE USURPER
The Usurper: See Klein's treatment of this theme in his poem 'Portrait of the Poet
    as Nobody' (an early version of his better-known 'Portrait of the Poet as
    Landscape').
fretful like the porpentine: 'like quills upon the fretful porpentine' – Shakespeare,
    Hamlet I, v
Voilà l'ennemi: (Fr.) Behold the enemy
Karthago est delenda: Cato's famous expression, *Delenda est Carthago* – (Lat.)
    'Carthage must be destroyed'

IN MEMORIAM: ALEXANDER BERCOVITCH
Alexander Bercovitch (1891–1951): Russian-born Montreal artist
like Joshua: Joshua 10:12–13

THE CASE OF JASCHA HEIFETZ
gauleiter: Nazi district governor
Toscanini: Arturo Toscanini (1867–1957), famous symphony orchestra conductor
Deutschland Uber Alles: 'Germany over all,' opening words of the German national
    anthem in use from 1922 to 1945
'There is no truer truth ...': Browning, 'Charles Avison'

MORTAL COILS
Mortal Coils: echoing Shakespeare, *Hamlet* III, i

The Duchess of Malfy (usually *Malfi*): a tragedy of revenge by John Webster (1614)

jettatura: (Ital.) evil eye

'Si vous voulez ...': (Fr.) 'If you wish to know if a man is a poet, ask him what he
thinks and what he feels about nature, love, and death.'

Baudelaire: Pierre Charles Baudelaire (1821–67), major French poet and critic,
leading figure in the French symbolist movement

'Death in a hundred shapes ...': *Aeneid* II, 369 – 'plurima mortis imago'

Ernst Neumann (1907–56): Montreal artist and friend of Klein's

'THE DECENCIES HAD PERISHED WITH THE STUKAS'

Stukas: dive-bomber aircraft used by the Germans in the Spanish Civil War and
in World War II

Archibald MacLeish (1892–1982): American poet and critic

'Honor ... walks in our ways again': Rupert Brooke, '1914, III: The Dead.' The
line in the Brooke poem reads 'And Nobleness walks in our ways again.'

THE POETRY OF A.J.M. SMITH

Montreal Group: group of Montreal poets writing in the 1920s and 1930s, consisting
chiefly of F.R. Scott, A.J.M. Smith, Leo Kennedy, and A.M. Klein

'like jewels ... Time': '... and jewels five-words-long / That on the stretched fore-
finger of all Time / Sparkle forever....' – Tennyson, 'The Princess'

il fabbro miglior: or rather, *il miglior fabbro* (Ital.), the better maker or craftsman –
Dante, *Purgatorio* XXVI. T.S. Eliot uses the phrase in his dedication of *The
Waste Land* to Ezra Pound.

Professor Grierson: H.J.C. Grierson (1866–1960), scholar and critic, noted authority
on Donne and the metaphysical poets. Smith did his graduate work under
Grierson in Edinburgh in the late 1920s.

Hemingway: Ernest Hemingway (1898–1961), American novelist. The reference
is to the title of his novel *For Whom the Bell Tolls*.

Nous n'irons ...: (Fr.) 'We'll to the woods no more, the laurels all are cut' –
Théodore de Banville (1823–91), *Les Cariatides* (originally from a children's
circle-dance)

NEW WRITERS SERIES, NO. 1

C.A.A.: Canadian Authors' Association, often ridiculed by Klein's generation of poets
because it embraced 'refined' and sentimental versifiers

Sir Christopher Wren (1632–1723): British architect, designer of St Paul's Cathedral.
The inscription on his tomb there reads 'Si monumentum requiris circum-
spice' (Lat., 'If you would see the man's monument, look about you').

pilpulistic: *pilpul* – (Heb.) a method of Talmudic study involving sharp dialectical
and often casuistic argumentation

WRITING IN CANADA
Raymond Souster (b. 1921): Canadian poet and editor of verse
your Socratic symposium: The rest of Souster's symposium was apparently never
    published.
gematria: (Heb.) used here in the sense of 'deciphering.' *Gematria* is a method of
    disclosing hidden meanings of biblical or other texts by interpreting words
    according to the numerical value of their letters.
Laurier: Sir Wilfrid Laurier, Liberal prime minister of Canada from 1896 to 1911
Baedekers: famous series of nineteenth-century guidebooks for travellers

A CURSE ON COLUMBUS
A Curse on Columbus: This was at one time a proverbial Yiddish comment on the
    hardships and evils of life in the New World. See Klein's poem 'Dialogue.'
brothers Tharaud: Jerome (1874–1955) and Jean (1877–1952), reporters and novelists
    who wrote on current events and historical topics, including Jewish history
Sombartian economist: Werner Sombart (1863–1941), political economist who wrote
    two books in 1911–12 on the role of Jews in the rise of European capitalism
lisps in numbers: 'I lisped in numbers, for the numbers came' – Pope, 'Epistle to
    Dr Arbuthnot'
cheese blintzes and chicken: Jewish dietary laws forbid the eating of meat and dairy
    foods together.
three Passover nights: No more than two are celebrated.
Zaddiks (or more correctly, *zaddikim*): (Heb.) pl. of *zaddik*. A *zaddik* (literally,
    'saintly person') is a leader of a community of Chassidim, and often is vener-
    ated by his followers as a holy person.
Chassid (pl. *Chassidim*): (Heb.) follower of modern Chassidism, a Jewish religious
    movement founded in eastern Europe in the eighteenth century, emphasizing
    joy in the service of God
Lamed Vav-nik: (Yid.) a saintly person – literally, 'one of the thirty-six.' According
    to a popular Jewish legend, there always exist thirty-six righteous persons,
    of unknown identity, on account of whose merit the world is preserved.
Shulchan Aruch: widely accepted code of Jewish law, compiled and systematized by
    Joseph Caro in the sixteenth century
Upton Sinclair (1878–1968): American novelist and social critic
Bodenheim: Maxwell Bodenheim (1893–1954), American novelist who wrote realistic
    novels about New York's East Side

THE JEW IN ENGLISH POETRY
'dogs and their vomit': Proverbs 26:11
'the first warbler': Tennyson, 'The Dream of Fair Women'
'God-gifted organ-voice': Tennyson, 'Milton'

'On her white breast': Pope, 'The Rape of the Lock'

'out-usure': Pope, 'Second Satire of Doctor John Donne'

'tribes of the wandering foot': Byron, 'Oh, Weep for Those' (from 'Hebrew Melodies')

Benjamin of Tudela: a twelfth-century Jewish traveller famous for his historically valuable travel book

'I will not cease': Blake, 'Jerusalem'

IS THIS THE JEW THE AUTHORS DREW?

Is This the Jew ...: echoing 'This is the Jew / That Shakespeare drew' – attributed to Pope, of Macklin's performance in 1741 of Shylock in *The Merchant of Venice*

shimpflexicon (in correct German, *schimpflexikon*): dictionary of insults

MAIMONIDES IN HOLLYWOOD

Rambam: Hebrew acronymic name of Moses Maimonides (1135–1204), Spanish-born Jewish religious philosopher, legal scholar, and doctor, author of *Guide to the Perplexed*

like Shakespeare ... Yiddish: Klein is playing on Ben Jonson's comment that Shakespeare had 'small Latin and less Greek.'

goy: (Heb.) non-Jew, gentile

sufferance was the badge: 'sufferance is the badge' – Shakespeare, *The Merchant of Venice* I, iii

Javert: police officer in Victor Hugo's *Les Misérables* (1862) whose devotion to duty crushes all human feeling

German Dadaists: Dadaism – an early-twentieth-century art movement emphasizing the incongruous and haphazard

Ludwig ... Vansittart: Emil Ludwig (1881–1948), German-born biographer; Robert Vansittart (1881–1957), British diplomat, outspoken critic of Nazi Germany

Shmarya Levin (1867–1935): author and prominent Zionist leader

Sholom Aleichem and [Peretz] Hirshbein: both Yiddish authors

GRAND INVECTIVE

Ilya Ehrenburg (1891–1967): Soviet writer and propagandist

untermensch: (Ger.) sub-human creature, term used by the Nazis; opposite of *übermensch*, the superior man or superman, ie, the German Aryan

tochacho pages of Deuteronomy: the threatened curses catalogued in Deuteronomy 28:15–68 (*tochacho* – Heb., chastisement)

Nebuchadnezzar: king of Babylonia c604–561 BC, conqueror of Jerusalem

Mannerheim: Baron von Mannerheim, Finnish soldier and statesman, pro-German and anti-Russian during World War II

Laval: Pierre Laval, premier of France, collaborator with Nazi occupiers

THOSE WHO SHOULD HAVE BEEN OURS

Yishuv: (Heb.) the Jewish community in Palestine

Americans of Jewish dissuasion: echoing the German-Jewish assimilationists' self-description as 'Germans of the Mosaic persuasion'

marrano: general term for Jews who were compelled to renounce their religion and convert to Christianity during the Spanish Inquisition, and whose descendants in many cases continued secretly to practise the rites of Judaism through many generations

The Contemporary Jewish Record: The symposium, titled 'Under Forty,' appeared in the February 1944 issue.

lucus a non lucendo: (Lat.) 'a grove [is called a grove] because it excludes the light' – an etymology from Quintilian claiming that the word *lucus* is named for a quality it excludes. Klein uses it here to underline how these writers are, ironically, Jews only in a negative sense.

sole dissenting one: David Daiches

aliyoth: (Heb.) pl. of *aliyah*, 'going up,' here in the sense of *aliyah la-Torah*, 'going up to the Torah' – the honour of being summoned up to the lectern in the synagogue to recite the benediction upon the reading of the Torah or to perform one of the other functions connected with the reading

chalitza: (Heb.) the biblical ceremony permitting a childless widow to marry someone other than the brother of her late husband (Deuteronomy 25:5–10)

the case of Karl Shapiro: This part of Klein's article essentially duplicates an earlier piece, 'Jewish Self-Hatred' (a review of *Person, Place and Thing*), *The Canadian Jewish Chronicle*, 14 January 1944.

goy: (Heb.) non-Jew, gentile

small script of Rashi: Rashi is the Hebrew acronym for Rabbi Solomon ben Isaac (1040–1105), one of the most authoritative commentators on the Bible and Talmud. Rashi's commentary is traditionally printed in a small and quite distinctive Hebrew script.

selbsthass: (Ger.) self-hatred

Second Son of the Haggadah: the 'wicked' son spoken of in the Passover Haggadah who sneeringly excludes himself from the community of Jews

Island Within: an allusion to the title of a 1928 novel by Ludwig Lewisohn

D.A.R.: Daughters of the American Revolution, an élitist and ultra-patriotic society

RILKE AND HIS TRANSLATORS

Princess' Tower: Duino Castle, where Rilke began *The Duino Elegies*

spurlos versunken: (Ger.) sunk without trace

cheder: (Heb.) traditional Jewish religious elementary school *hysteron-proteron*: (Gr.) latter [put in place of] former, an inversion of the natural order

DEPARTURE AND ARRIVAL

in medias res: (Lat.) in, or into, the midst of things; usually describing the manner in which epics traditionally begin – Horace, *Ars Poetica*

Chalutz (pl. *Chalutzim*): (Heb.) pioneering Jewish settler in the land of Israel

Mukhtar (pl. *Mukhtarim*): (Arabic) village chief

Khamsin: (Arabic) sirocco, heat wave

Irgun: (Heb.) literally, 'organization,' short for Irgun Tsva'i Le'umi (National Military Organization, also known by its Hebrew acronym, Etsel), a Jewish underground armed organization founded in Palestine in 1931, an activist breakaway group from the official defence body, the Haganah

apologia pro: (Lat.) defence of

Arieh Stern: Klein evidently had in mind Avraham Stern (1907–42), a founding member of the Irgun who formed his own underground group during World War II.

Anu yivneh ha-Galil: The Hebrew should translate as 'we will build the Galilee' but the verb here is mistakenly conjugated in the third person singular – *yivneh* – instead of the first person plural – *nivneh*.

kibbutz: (Heb.) collective settlement in Israel

r'vovo: (Heb.) ten thousand, ie, myriad

Yehuda Halevi (c1075–1141): Spanish-Jewish poet and philosopher. See Klein's poem 'Yehuda Halevi, His Pilgrimage.'

ISAAK BABEL

Alexander Blok (1880–1921): Russian poet

Cheka: Soviet security service organized by Lenin in 1918

mohel: (Heb.) Jewish ritual circumcizer

Zaslowsky: David Zaslavsky (1880–1965), Soviet writer and journalist, Bundist. He opposed the Bolsheviks at first, then adhered to the party line.

Ehrenburg: Ilya Ehrenburg (1891–1967), Soviet writer and propagandist

THAT RANK PICTURE

whole in life and free from guilt: 'integer vitae scelerisque purus' – Horace, *Odes* I, 22

CANTABILE

In 1946, in his Modern American Poetry course at McGill, Klein had his students write parodies of Pound's verse (Klein Papers, Public Archives of Canada, MS 6648); this may have given him the idea of writing a review in the form of a parody. Klein abhorred Pound's anti-Semitic and fascist views (see 'Old

Ez and His Blankets' below), but he clearly knew Pound's poetry well; his library contained more books by Pound than by any other writer, with the exception of Joyce.

De litteris ... ingeniis: (Lat.) 'about books, arms, and men of unusual genius' – Pound, *Canto XI*. Pound quotes Platina (Bartolomeo Sacchi, 1421–81), who was imprisoned for conspiracy against Pope Paul II.

il miglior fabbro: (Ital.) 'the better maker' – Dante, *Purgatorio* xxvi. T.S. Eliot uses the phrase in his dedication of *The Waste Land* to Pound.

But bye ... St. Mary's Lough: the concluding stanza of the Scottish ballad 'The Douglas Tragedy.' The Black Douglas was an ally of Robert Bruce, who fiercely harassed the English in the north in the fourteenth century. Klein is also alluding to Major C.H. Douglas (1879–1952), founder of the Social Credit movement, of which Pound was an adherent. Douglas was a rancorous anti-Semite and a vehement critic of banks, interest, credit, and other related aspects of capitalism.

St. Ezra Benedict: an allusion to Benedict Arnold, a general in the American Revolutionary Army whose name has become proverbial for traitor. Pound treasonously broadcast propaganda for Mussolini during World War II.

USURA: Pound saw usury as the root of all evil. See in particular Canto XLV.

χρυσω χρυσοτερα : 'more golden than gold' – a fragment attributed to Sappho

bearded like the pard: Jacques' description of the *miles gloriosus* in his speech on the seven ages of man – Shakespeare, *As You Like It* II, vii

'The art of conversation' ... small talk shouted: a paraphrase of Allen Tate's essay 'Ezra Pound' – 'The secret of [Pound's] form is this: conversation. The *Cantos* are talk, talk, talk ... they are just rambling talk.'

traductore – tradittore: 'traduttore, traditore' – a translator is a traitor (Italian proverb), Klein's point being that Pound was, literally, both

syphilisation: In the 'Cyclops' episode of Joyce's *Ulysses*, the anti-Semitic 'citizen' responds to Leopold Bloom's defence of British civilization saying 'Their syphilisation, you mean.'

Rapallo: Pound lived in Rapallo, Italy, for many years.

Gradus ad parnassum: a Latin or Greek dictionary intended as an aid for students of Latin or Greek verse composition; the subtitle of Pound's *ABC of Reading*

a compiler of several don'ts: an allusion to Pound's article 'A Few Don'ts by an Imagiste'

Jimmy ... Breen ... EP: 'Jimmy' is James Joyce. 'Breen' is Dennis Breen, a pathetic lunatic mentioned in several chapters of *Ulysses*, including 'Cyclops'; he is upset at receiving a postcard with the message 'U.P.: UP,' which he interprets as an attack on his virility. 'E.P.' is, of course, Ezra Pound, with specific reference to 'E.P. Ode pour l'Election de Son Sepulchre,' the first section of Pound's autobiographical 'Hugh Selwyn Mauberley.'

'EP. *Est Perditus*: a reference to the originally medieval anti-Semitic taunt 'Hep' (the apostrophe in 'EP marking the elided *H*). Its true origin is obscure, but it has traditionally been considered an acronym for *Hierosolyma est perdita* (Lat., 'Jerusalem is lost').

OF JEWISH EXISTENTIALISM

Da-da: an early-twentieth-century art movement emphasizing the incongruous
    and haphazard
goy: (Heb.) non-Jew, gentile
Gentleman's Agreement: a novel by Laura Z. Hobson (1947) dealing with polite
    but pervasive anti-Semitism in the u.s.
Stuermer: the viciously anti-Semitic Nazi newspaper edited by Julius Streicher
Rabbi Mordecai Kaplan (1881–1983): American religious philosopher, founder of
    Reconstructionism, a liberal Jewish movement

T.S. ELIOT AND THE NOBEL PRIZE

Lights, lights ...: Eliot, 'Burbank with a Baedeker: Bleistein with a Cigar'
ceteris paribus: (Lat.) other things being equal
hors de combat: (Fr.) disabled, out of the fighting
the way the world ended: Eliot, 'The Hollow Men' (slightly altered)
That was not what he meant: Eliot, 'The Love Song of J. Alfred Prufrock' (slightly
    altered)
'damp souls of housemaids': Eliot, 'Morning at the Window'
'the smell of steaks in passageways': Eliot, 'Preludes I'
Apeneck Sweeney: Eliot, 'Sweeney among the Nightingales'
young man carbuncular ... house agent's clerk ... Bradford millionaire: Eliot,
    The Waste Land III, 231–4

HEMLOCK AND MARIJUANA

Maggid-of-Dubnow: Jacob Kranz (1741–1804), famous eastern European preacher
    and author of homiletic fables (*maggid* – Heb., preacher)
Maimonides: Moses Maimonides (1135–1204), Spanish-born Jewish religious phi-
    losopher, legal scholar, and doctor, author of *Guide to the Perplexed*
worm of Asmodeus: Asmodeus (*Ashmedai* in Hebrew) – the name of a demon in
    ancient Jewish legends. He alone knew the secret of where to find the legend-
    ary *shamir*, a worm whose mere touch could cleave rocks.
Sabbath limit: the distance beyond which a Jew may not walk on the Sabbath –
    2,000 cubits (approx. 1 kilometre) from the border of his town or settlement.
    See Exodus 16:29.
in vitro: (Lat.) literally, 'in glass' – isolated from the living organism and artificially
    maintained, as in a test-tube

OLD EZ AND HIS BLANKETS

Walter Winchell (1897–1972): popular American journalist and broadcaster, frequently sarcastic commentator on the news

Goebbels: Josef Goebbels (1897–1945), Nazi minister of propaganda

THE MASKED YEATS

pilpul: (Heb.) a method of Talmudic study involving sharp dialectical and often
casuistic argumentation

HOMAGE TO LUDWIG LEWISOHN

he has touched nothing that he has not enhanced: translation of Samuel Johnson's
Latin epitaph for Oliver Goldsmith – *nullum quod tetigit non ornavit*

Taine: Hippolyte Taine (1823–93), French literary critic and historian

Brandes: Georg Brandes (1842–1927), Danish critic and scholar

Shmaryahu (Shmarya) Levin (1867–1935): author and prominent Zionist leader

Herzl: Theodor Herzl (1860–1904), father of political Zionism and founder of the
World Zionist Organization

Amram: father of Moses

Index

Abbasides 3
Abraham of Bristol 227
Achad Ha'am 14, 16
Adam 102
Ad-writers 196–7
Aestheticism 33
Aesthetics 132, 169–77, 182–92
Aiken, Conrad 278, 280
Akiba, Rabbi 51, 101
Aleichem, Sholom. *See* Sholom Aleichem.
Aleksandrov, V.V. 164
Amram (scholar in Babylon) 43
Amram (biblical) 285
Andrewes, Lancelot 271
Anski, S. (Solomon Rapaport) 70–4
Anthems, national 163–6
Anti-semitism 225, 237–8, 241–3, 266–8; in English literature 226–32, 262–4, 272–4, 279–80; in epigram and quotation 235–8; as self-hatred 175–6, 249–51. *See also* Nazism, Holocaust.
Aquinas, Thomas 182
Arcand, Adrien 4, 20
Aristeas 138
Arnold, Matthew 4, 19, 66, 179
Art 23–6: as creation 182–3; and morality 167, 173; sentimentality in 27–8
Art-for-art's sake 16, 42, 161

Asch, Sholem 37–9, 217, 249
Assimilation, Jewish 18, 34–5, 241, 246–51, 268, 284–5
Auden, W.H. 172, 175, 192, 217, 278, 280

Baal Shem Tov, Rabbi Israel 6–7, 10, 46, 49, 52, 75, 87
Babel, Isaak 259–61
Bacon, Francis 31
Badchanim 26–9, 122
Balfour Declaration 237
Ballads 252
Bar Kamza 136
Bar Kochba 36
Bard 26–9, 83
Bates, Ernest Sutherland 126
Baudelaire, Charles-Pierre 204, 270, 272
Belloc, Hilaire 243
Ben Asher, Moshe 137, 140
Ben Bag-Bag 79, 148
Ben Chasdai 11
Ben Chiyah, Rab Joseph 142
Ben Isaac, Rabbi Solomon. *See* Rashi.
Ben Israel, Manasseh 230
Ben Moses, Asher 140
Ben Yochai, Simeon 11–13
Benjamin of Tudela 104, 377
Bension, Ariel 10–13
Bercovitch, Alexander 198–9

Berditchever. *See* Levi Yitschok.

Bergson, Henri 102, 131

Bernheim, Alfred 60–2

Besht. *See* Baal Shem Tov, Rabbi
  Israel.

Bialik, Chaim Nachman 13–19, 32–5,
  36, 43, 243

Bible 30–2, 50, 83–4, 117–18, 148, 161,
  190, 228, 229–31; humour 99–
  100, 129; Joseph as poet 143–8;
  King James Authorized
  Version 5, 64–5, 229; language
  and structure 127–30, 131–3,
  172–3; literature 125–30;
  manuscripts 133–43

Blake, William 9, 12–13, 90, 179, 232

Blok, Alexander 259

Bloomgarden, Yehoash Solomon. *See*
  Yehoash.

Bodenheim, Maxwell 226

Bollingen Foundation 278–81

Book reviewers 193–5, 220–1

Borgese, Giuseppe Antonio 240

Brandão, Raul 240

Brandes, Georg 284

Bratzlaver. *See* Nachman, Rabbi of
  Bratzlav.

Brooke, Rupert 17–18, 206–7

Brown, E.K. 220

Browning, Robert 65, 184, 192, 200,
  231

Buber, Martin 74–7

Budgen, Frank 289–90

Byron, Lord George Gordon 16, 151–2,
  154, 168, 231

Cabbalism 10–13, 15, 70–4, 140

Cain 100

Calligraphy 24, 85-7

Canadian Authors' Association
  (CAA) 213, 220

Canadian Forum, The 220

*Canadian Jewish Eagle, The. See The
  Jewish Daily Eagle.*

Canadian literature 203–31. *See also*
  poetry, Canadian.

Čapek, Karel 240

Caplan, Rupert 70–4

Carlyle, Thomas 33, 159, 176

Cartoons, film 166–9

Censorship 42, 151, 181–2, 199–200,
  261, 262–4

Chabad, Motke 122

Chagall, Bella 57–9

Chagall, Marc 59, 80–1

Chanuka 58, 122

Chassidism 49–50, 74–7, 93, 106,
  109–10, 118, 226

Chaucer, Geoffrey 176, 227-8, 232

Chelm 108, 122

Chesterton, G.K. 153–5, 158–9

Chmelnitzky, Bogdan 165, 230

Christian Herald, The 37

Christianity 37–9, 103–4, 176, 227–30,
  238; T.S. Eliot and Christianity
  272–3

Churchill, Winston 206, 212, 234, 246

Cicero 175

Cinematography, in Israel 40

Cliché 192

Cocteau, Jean 240

Cohen, Mrs Nathan 57

Coleridge, S.T. 46, 178, 229, 231

Collins, William 179

Conrad, Joseph 176

Contemporary Jewish Record, The 247

Coppard, A.E. 175

Coralnik, Abraham 14

Corey, Harry 163

Coughlin, Charles 234

Cowen, Mrs Philip 24

Cowper, William 179

Crane, Hart 177

Croce, Benedetto 240

Cromwell, Oliver 33, 230
Cruikshank, George 262
Cummings, E.E. 171–2
Curses 120–1, 137, 157, 245
Cynicism 3

Dadaism 243, 266
Daiches, David 247
Dante Alighieri 190, 218, 270–1, 277
David, King of Israel 14, 20, 33, 64,
      100, 143
Da Vinci, Leonardo 23
Davis, Mrs Eliza 263
Death 120, 203–4
Deborah (biblical) 127
Decalogue 11, 24, 132, 133–5, 141, 248
De Heredia, Jose-Maria 184
De Leon, Moses 11
De Maupassant, Guy 261
De Modena, Leon 11
Diaspora, humour 99–109; philosophy
      of life 4, 6; proverbs 112–22
Dickens, Charles 77, 152–3, 262–4
Dickinson, Emily 180
Disney, Walt 82, 166–9
Disraeli, Benjamin 155, 237
Donne, John 174, 211–12, 270
Dryden, John 151, 230
Dudek, Louis 213
Dybbuk, The 70–4

Ecclesiastes 3–6, 25, 127 ·
Edward the Confessor 227
Ehrenburg, Ilya 240, 244–6, 261
Eisenstein, Ira 43
Elijah 100, 129
Eliot, T.S. 173, 210, 217, 220–1, 248,
      268–75, 278, 280
Eliot, William Greenleaf 272
Eliphaz the Temanite 180
Ellis, Havelock 156
Ellmann, Richard 282–5

Emden, Jacob 11
Epicureanism 3
Erter, Isaac 106
Esau 140, 248
Euphues 228
Excommunication 43, 72
Existentialism 266–8
Ezekiel 142, 161
Ezra 139

Fable 167
Fadiman, Clifton 236, 247
Faith 50, 88, 97, 119, 121
Fanaticism, religious 43, 45–6
Fantasy 160, 168
Fascism: Jeffers 232–5; Eliot 274–5.
      See also Nazism.
Fast, Howard 250
Feast of Rejoicing 101
Feifer, Shaika 122
Feuchtwanger, Lion 239
Films. See cartoons, movies.
Firkovitch, Abraham 141
First Statement 212
Fitzgerald, Edward 3, 192
Flaubert, Gustave 261
Folk-songs, Jewish 26–9, 93–9, 109–12,
      122
Folklore 70, 80, 108
Forst, Siegmund 25
Francis of Assisi 50
Franco, Francisco 246
Free verse 4, 22, 126–7, 151–3, 162,
      192
Freud, Sigmund 102, 132–3, 156, 176,
      186, 190, 276
Frishman, David 43
Frost, Robert 185–7

Gautier, Théophile 270
Genesis, Book of 143, 161, 182–3
Gibson, W.W. 206

Gilbert, Stuart 289–90
Ginsberg, Asher. *See* Achad Ha'am.
Glatzer, Nahum 63–6
Goats, in folklore and biblical
    narrative 80, 88, 94, 95, 122, 146
God, personal relationship to 7, 9, 12,
    49, 66
Goebbels, Josef 199, 233, 237, 245,
    251, 263–4, 280
Goethe, J.W. 125, 269
Gold, Michael 225–6
Goldsmith, Oliver 270
Goldstick, Isidore 67–70, 83–4
Goll, Ivan 239
Gordon, Judah Loeb 106
Gorki, Maxim 259
Graetz, Heinrich 61, 75
Grafstein, Melech 77-9
Grammar, Hebrew 30, 54–7
Graphic arts, Jewish 23–6, 60–2, 85–7
Great Synagogue, The 32, 130, 139
Grierson, H.J.C. 211
Grosbard, Hertz 81–3
Guterman, Norbert 59

Ha'am, Achad. *See* Achad Ha'am.
Habima Players 70
Haganah 34
Haggadah 23–6, 85–7, 102, 250
Halevi, Yehuda 14, 33, 36, 64, 258
Hall, James 282–5
Halpern, Moishe Leib 50
Haman 42, 59, 101
Hamsun, Knut 239, 258–9
Hasidim. *See* Chassidism.
Hasmoneans 139
Hatikvah 166
Hebrew (language) 14, 16–17, 30, 54–
    7, 80, 85–7, 113, 130, 131, 137–
    8, 258. *See also* translation.
Hebrew (literature) 32–5, 36
Hecht, Ben 241–3

Hedonism 3
Heifetz, Jascha 199–200
Heine, Heinrich 29, 103, 106, 125
Hellenism 36, 211–12
Hemingway, Ernest 211
Henry, King of England 227
Hershel of Ostropol 26
Herzl, Theodor 284
Heschel, Abraham J. 62
Hesse, Herman 268–9
Hirshbein, Peretz 243
Hirshprung, Pinchos 41–2
Hitler, Adolph 233, 237, 244–6, 252,
    258, 274, 279
Hokkus 3
Holbein, Hans 26
Hollywood, movies 166–9, 243, 247
Holocaust 41–2, 52, 57–9, 78, 79, 246.
    See also Jews, in Europe, loss.
Holofernes 100
Holmes, Oliver Wendell 200
Hone, Joseph 283
Hopkins, Gerard Manley 172, 178
Horowitz, Hyman 231
Hosea 14
Houdini, Harry 242
Housman, A.E. 179, 180
Hubbard, Elbert 237
Hugo, Victor 192
Humour, Jewish 99–109, 115–22,
    129–30
Humours, the four cardinal 113
Huxley, Aldous 217, 256
Huxley, Julian 256

I.R. *See* Israel Rabinovitch.
Idelsohn, Abraham Zvi 21
Illustrations 23–6
Images, graven 132
Imagination 80, 144, 160, 168
Imagism 152
Immanuel of Rome 14, 172

'Internationale, The' 165–6
Irgun 257
Irony 10, 129
Isaac (biblical) 99–100, 129
Isaiah 18, 44, 100
Isherwood, Christopher 217
Ishmael 248
Issachar 94, 101

Jacob (biblical) 126, 140, 143–8, 253
Jael 100
Jammes, Francis 50
Japanese war criminals 187–8
Jeffares, Norman 283
Jeffers, Robinson 232–5
Jesus 37–8
Jewish Daily Eagle, The 20, 162, 181
Jews: in North America 225–6, 246–7;
    in England 226–32; in Europe
    60–2, 67–70, 75–6, 93, 106–8,
    117, 260–1; in literature 215,
    226–32, 235–8, 240, 262–4; loss
    of 41–2, 47–8, 52, 57–9, 60–2,
    78, 79–81, 82, 114, 121–2, 246;
    as objects of ribaldry 103–4;
    philosophy and theology 30–1,
    43–4; as writers 240, 246–51. See
    also art, folk songs, humour,
    proverbs.
Job 66, 129, 209
Johanan, Rabbi 101
John, King of England 103, 227
Johnson, Samuel 156, 176, 180
Jonson, Ben 188
Joseph, (biblical) 143–8
Joshua 198
Joyce, James 12, 60, 72, 170, 189, 192,
    221, 239, 268, 280; Ulysses
    analyses 289–366
Jubal 143
Judah Ha-Nasi 45
Judith (biblical) 100

Jung, Carl 276

Kabala. See cabbalism.
Kafka, Franz 240, 275–8
Kanisch, Hermann 251
Kaplan, Rabbi Mordecai 23, 42–6, 267
Karaism 31–2
Kasrilevke 67–70, 122
Kaun, Alexander 246
Keats, John 9, 12, 14, 128, 162, 183,
    185, 203–4, 211, 231, 248
Kennedy, Leo 203–5
Kesten, Hermann 238–40
Khayyam, Omar 3, 154
Kierkegaard, Soren 272
Kipling, Rudyard 219, 275
Klesmer 20
Klonitzki-Kline, Solomon 54–7
Koestler, Arthur 255–8
Koheleth 3–6, 128, 143
Kohn, Eugene 42–6
Koretz 49, 79, 87

Laforgue, Jules 270–1
Lamed Vovnik 50, 72, 90, 225–6
Landor, W.S. 18, 211
Lang, Andrew 173
Langton, Stephen, Archbishop of
    Canterbury 227
Language, poetic 170–1. See also
    Hebrew language, Yiddish.
Lanier, Sidney 175
Lassen, Christian 237
Laurier, Sir Wilfrid 217
Laval, Pierre 246
Lawrence, D.H. 151
Layton, Irving 212–15
Levi Yitschok of Berditchev, Rabbi 7,
    49, 93, 121
Levin, Harry 290
Levin, Shmarya (Shmaryahu) 243,
    284–5

Lewis, C. Day 172
Lewisohn, Ludwig 250, 251–5, 284–5
Li-Tai-Po 3
Lieberman, Chaim 48
Lindbergh, Charles 234
Lipshitz, Rabbi Israel 53
Literary criticism 174, 193–5, 216–21
Literary influences 34, 176, 217–18, 270–2
Literature, Canadian 203–21. See also poetry: European 238–40; Hebrew 32–5, 36.
Longfellow, Henry Wadsworth 184
Lopez, Rodrigo 229
Love 119–20, 190–1
Lovelace, Richard 185
Lowell, Amy 4, 126
Lowell, J.R. 237
Lowell, Robert 278, 281
Lowenthal, Marvin 24
Lowes, J.L. 14
Ludwig, Emil 38, 239, 243
Lullabies 94
Lunacharsky, V. 162
Luther, Martin 237
Lutzky, A. 82

Macaulay, Thomas Babington 193
MacLeish, Archibald 206
MacNeice, Louis 283
Magazines, literary 195–6, 212–13, 220
Maggid of Dubnow (Jacob Kranz) 275
Magic, white 10–13
Mahzor 137, 140
Maimonides, Moses 15, 29, 32, 43, 112, 131–2, 241, 276
Manasseh ben Israel 230
Manger, Itzik 28
Mani-Leib (Brahinsky) 50
Mann, Klaus 238–40
Mann, Thomas 38, 148

Mannerheim, Baron 245
Marlowe, Christopher 213, 228–9
Marriage 93, 96–9
Marx, Olga 66, 76
Marxism 9, 31, 161–2, 244, 256
Masefield, John 207
Mason, Ellsworth G. 320
Masorah 137, 139–40
Masoretes 139–40
Massinger, Philip 270
Maugham, Somerset 217
Mencken, H.L. 217, 235–8
Mendel of Rymanov, Rabbi 75
Mendele Moicher Sforim 122
Mendelssohn, Moses 31
Metempsychosis 71–2
Michelangelo 61
Mickey Mouse 166–9
Mikhailov, Sergei 164
Mikveh 58
Millay, Edna St Vincent 232
Milton, John 84, 170, 176, 188, 218, 229–30
Miracles 160–1
Mishna 52–4
Misnagdim 74–5, 106
Montreal Group, 209
Montreal Jewish Daily Eagle. See The Jewish Daily Eagle.
Morality plays 228
Mordecai (biblical) 102
More, Paul Elmer 22
Moscow Art Theatre 70
Moses 37, 61, 126–7, 132, 134–6, 139, 142, 176, 284–5
Moshe ben Asher 137, 140
Movies 40, 166–9, 243, 262–4
Murray, Gilbert 173
Music 19–22, 27, 109–12, 164–6, 181–2, 199–200
Mysticism 10–13, 60–1, 70–4, 282–3

Nachman, Rabbi of Bratzlav 7, 50, 63, 87, 90
Nadir, Moishe 106
Nahum-Ish-Gamsu 9
Nathan (biblical) 100
Nathan, Isaac 231
Nationalism 163–6, 257
Nazism 41–2; writers' attitudes towards: Ehrenburg 244–6; Eliot 274–5; Hamsun 258–9; Jeffers 232–5; Pound 278–81; Rilke 251–2
Nebuchadnezzar 245
Neumann, Ernst 205
Nietzsche, Friedrich 232–3
Niger, Shmuel 161
Nihilism 3–4, 157, 272–3
Nobel Prize 258, 268–75, 280
Norton, Mrs M.D.H. 253
Novels 255–6, 262

Objectivists 172
Oliver Twist 262–4
Optimism 154–5, 184
Ostropolyer, Hershel 122
Ovid 270, 278

Palestine 122–6, 256–7
Paine, Thomas 125
Papini, Giovanni 38
Paradox 153–5, 236, 283
Parody 155–7, 264–6, 276
Partisan Review, The 267, 276
Passover Haggada 23–6
PEN (International Association of Poets, Playwrights, Editors, Essayists and Novelists) 48
Peretz, Isaac Leib 78, 122
Pessimism 154–5, 184
Petrushka, Symcha 52–4
Philology, Jewish 30

Philosophy, eastern 3; existentialist 266–8
Photography 60–2
Pinchas, Rabbi of Koretz 90
Pius XI 238
Plato 31, 162, 190, 281
Poe, Edgar Allan 18, 178, 277
Poetry: and action 33–5, 205–9, 259; American – see also Frost, Jeffers, Pound, Shapiro; baby verse 188–91; Bible as 126–30, 131–3; Canadian 216–21 – see also Kennedy, Layton, Pratt, Smith; and creative process 182–92; criticism 283–4; definition 12, 14, 33, 87, 177–81; English 226–32 – see also Eliot; foreign sources 176; free verse 4, 151–3, 192; Hebrew 55 – see also Bialik, Tchernichovsky; and imagination 80, 144, 160–1, 166–9; influences of 34, 176, 270; Irish – see also Yeats; Japanese 187–8; and Nobel Prize 268–75; occasional 32; as prayer 14, 49; as propaganda 162; as prophecy 14, 15, 87; and the senses 185–7; techniques 169–77; and thought 12, 14, 174; translation – see also separate entry and Nobel Prize; Yiddish 79–81, 87–90 – see also Segal, Yehoash.
Poetry Magazine 221, 248, 250
Poets, role of 87, 143–8, 195–7
Pope, Alexander 151, 175, 230
Porter, Katherine Anne 278, 280
Pound, Ezra 151, 210, 264–6, 271–3, 278–81
Poverty 15, 47, 61–2, 94–5, 120
Pratt, E.J. 205–9

Prayer 42–6, 49, 63–6
Prayerbook 30, 42–6, 49, 63–6
Prokofieff, Sergei 181–2
Propaganda in art 9, 161–3, 181–2
Proverbs 112–22
Publishing 63, 77
Puns 5, 100, 129
Purim 59, 101, 122

Queen Mab 168–9

Rabbenu Tam 107
Rabelais, François 152
Rabinovitch, Israel 19–22, 181
Rabinovitch, Sholom. See Sholom
    Aleichem.
Racism 243, 249–50
Rachel (biblical) 142
Rambam. See Moses Maimonides.
Rank, J. Arthur 262–4
Rapaport, Solomon. See S. Anski.
Rashi 107, 125, 139, 249
Rationalism 10–11, 31
Ravitch, Melech 46–9
Ravnitsky, Yehoshua 15–16
Reconstructionist Movement 23, 42–6,
    267
Regelson, Abraham 25
Reise, Isaac. See Moishe Nadir.
Reinhardt, Max 70
Reincarnation 71–2
Renan, Ernest 38, 129, 131
Resh Lakish 102
Reuben (biblical) 145–6
Revere, Paul 250
Revision, textual 23–6, 42–6
Rhyme 109–10, 115, 126, 152, 175,
    184–5, 210, 239, 252–4. See also
    free verse.
Richard, King of England (the 'Lion-
    hearted') 227
Richards, I.A. 174

Riddle 28, 103
Rilke, Rainer Maria 90, 183, 210,
    251–5
Rimbaud, Arthur 172, 177, 191, 261
Robinson, E.A. 179–80
Rodman, Selden 206
Romanticism 159–61, 178
Roosevelt, Franklin D. 233–4
Rosenberg, Isaac 206
Rosner, Jacob 60–2
Rousseau, Jean-Jacques 125, 152
Russian revolution 259

Saadyah, Gaon 29–32, 43
Sadagoran, Rebbe 75–6
Salvemini, Gaetano 240
Saminsky, Lazure 20
Samson (biblical) 100, 102, 129
Samuel, Maurice 37, 267
Sandburg, Carl 151, 180
Sarah (biblical matriarch) 99–100
Sartre, Jean-Paul 266–8
Sassoon, Siegfried 206
Satire 151, 264–6
Schechter, Solomon 141
Schocken Books 59, 60, 63, 261, 266
Schwartz, Delmore 175, 247–8
Schwartz, Maurice 70
Scott, Evelyn 152
Scribes 135–9. See also calligraphy.
Segal, Jacob Isaac 6–10, 49–52, 79–81,
    87–90
Sentimentality 26–9, 260
Septuagint 31, 70, 84, 125, 142
Sforim, Mendele Moicher. See Mendele
    Moicher Sforim.
Shabbathai Zvi 230
Shakespeare, William 13, 29, 94, 156,
    162, 168–9, 178, 218, 228–9, 241,
    250, 270
Shapiro, Karl 169–77, 248–50
Shaw, George Bernard 163–6, 186

Schechina 76
Shelley, Percy Bysshe 178, 230–1
Shmulevitz, Shloime 26–9
Shnayur Zalman of Lyadi 22
Sholom Aleichem (Rabinovitch
        Sholom) 67–70, 77–9, 106, 122,
        243
Short stories 259–61; Kafka 275–8
Shostakovitch, Dmitri 181–2
Shoub, Mac 73
Shulchan Aruch 226
Siddur. *See* prayerbook.
Silberstein, Beinish 47
Silone, Ignazio 239–40
Sinclair, Upton 226
Singer, I.J. 26
Slavic culture 75-6
Sloan, J. 320
Slocum, John J. 320
Smart, Christopher 179
Smith, A.J.M. 209–12, 220
Smolenskin, Peretz 229
Socialism 268
Sokolow, Nahum 229–31
Solomon, King of Israel 3–6, 14, 100,
        143
Sombart, Werner 225, 237
Sorel, Georges 275
Souster, Raymond 216–21
Soviet Union 164–5, 181–2, 244–6
Spender, Stephen 173
Spengler, Oswald 192, 239
Spenser, Edmund 270
Spinoza 131
St John 161
Stalin, Joseph 162, 164, 181–2, 246,
        261
Stanislavsky, K.S. 70
Star Chamber 227
Stauffer, Donald 282–5
Steinbarg, Eliezer 82
Steinberg, Milton 42–6

Steinmann, Martin 282–5
Stern, Avraham 257
Stevenson, Burton 236
Stevenson, Robert Louis 188
Strauss, Richard 199–200
Streicher, Julius 267
Stutchkov, Nachum 114
Sutherland, John 177, 213
Svevo, Italo 240
Swinburne, Algernon Charles 185
Synaesthesia 191

Tagore, Rabindranath 43
Taine, Hippolyte 284
Talmud 11, 23, 31, 86, 100–2, 112,
        122, 142, 228
Tate, Allen 265
Taylor, Jeremy 44
Tchernichovsky, Saul 36
'Techsakna' 166
Ten Commandments. *See* Decalogue.
Ten Lost Tribes 226
Tennyson, Alfred Lord 159, 227,
        231
Tharaud brothers (Jerome and
        Jean) 225
Theatre 70–4
Thirty-six, the. *See* Lamed Vovnik.
Thomas, Dylan 188, 221
Tojo, Hideki 188
Tolstoy, Leo 47
Torah 42, 43, 94–6, 113, 122, 133–43
Toscanini, Arturo 200
Tradition 23, 45, 49, 52, 54, 87–8,
        139–40, 147–8, 157–9, 246–51
Translation 4–6, 31–2, 36, 52–4, 59,
        63–6, 69–70, 76–7, 79, 83–4,
        93–4, 109–12, 142, 161–3, 173,
        231, 246, 251–5, 265, 270, 273
Trotsky, Leon 181, 261
Truman, Harry 182
Typography, Hebrew 85–7

Unamuno, Miguel de 240
Untermeyer, Louis 179–80, 247
Usury 228

Valéry, Paul 239
Van Gogh, Vincent 60
Vansittart, Robert 243
Verlaine, Paul 154
Vers libre. See free verse.
Villon, François 7
Vishniac, Roman 60–2
Von Ossietzky, Karl 269

Wagner, Richard 173
War criminals 187–8
Waley, Arthur 4
Webster, John 270
Weiss, Ernst 240
Weizmann, Chaim 238
Werfel, Franz 240
Weston, Jessie 173
White Paper 61, 256
Whitman, Walt 125–6, 152, 221, 232
Williams, William Carlos 239
Wilson, Edmund 220
Winchell, Walter 279
Wit 102–3, 215
Witch of En-dor 100
Wordsworth, William 14, 20–1, 154,
    177–8, 231, 232

Wren, Sir Christopher 213

Yarmolinsky, Avram 261
Yeats, W.B. 14, 74, 174, 282–4
Yehoash (Bloomgarden, Yehoash
    Solomon) 69, 83–4
Yiddish 42; drama and dramatic
    reading 70–4, 81–3; folk
    songs 93–9, 109–12;
    language 42, 113–14;
    literature 26–9, 46–9. See also
    Chagall 57–9, Segal
    6–10, 49–52, 79–81, 87–90,
    Sholom Aleichem 67–70, 77–9,
    Yehoash 83–4; proverbs 112–22.
Yitschok, Levi, Rabbi of Berditchev. See
    Levi Yitschok.
Yoponchik, Mishka 261

Zangwill, Israel 44
Zaslavsky, David 261
Zebulun (biblical) 94, 101
Zeitlin, Hillel 43
Zim, Jacob 85–7
Zionism 165–6, 285
Zlotnik, Judah·L. 3–6, 25
Zohar 10–13
Zola, Emile 185
Zunz, Leopold 105, 237
Zweig, Stefan 240